ADDISON-WESLEY
UNITED STATES HISTORY to 1877

VOLUME 1

ANNOTATED TEACHER'S EDITION

Authors

DIANE HART
DAVID BAKER

Reading Consultant

RICHARD P. SANTEUSANIO

Program Directors

IRVING F. AHLQUIST
GEORGE O. ROBERTS

ADDISON-WESLEY PUBLISHING COMPANY
Menlo Park, California   Reading, Massachusetts
London   Amsterdam   Don Mills, Ontario   Sydney

ISBN 0-201-20907-1

BCDEFGHIJKL—VH—8987

CONTENTS

ANSWER KEY: STUDENT TEXT

ANSWER KEY: AMERICAN VOICES

INTRODUCTION TO THE STUDENT TEXT

HIGHLIGHTS

- Chronological presentation of American history

- 5 units, each covering a specific time period

- 16 chapters, each organized by short sections dealing with a manageable series of events

- 79 primary source readings, each expanding upon key concepts and events presented in the text

- Numerous maps, graphs, diagrams, and illustrations to enrich the text

- Carefully controlled readability level

- Skills program to build and develop the tools of history—including maps, graphs, diagrams, and timelines

- Comprehensive evaluation program

- Reference center to supplement text throughout the course of study

- Teacher's Resource Manual with lesson plans, worksheets, and tests to accompany text

UNIT OPENER

Colorful work of art characteristic of the era

Unit number

Unit title

Time period of unit

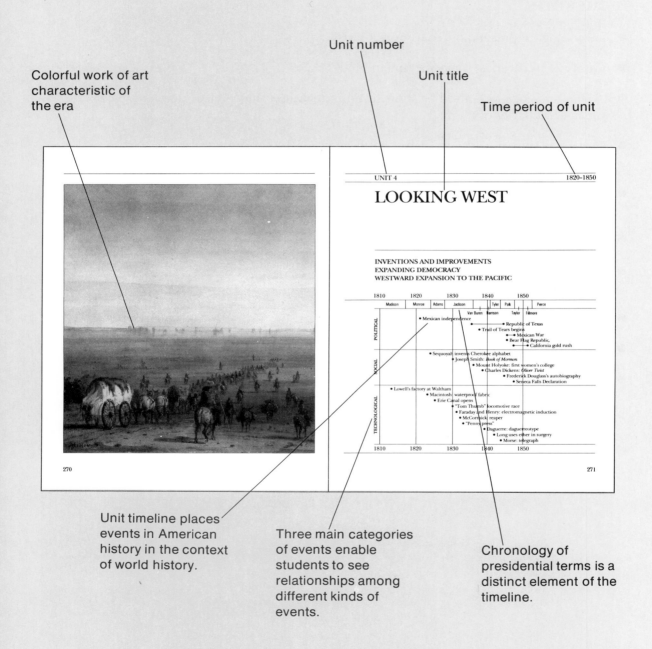

UNIT 4   1820–1850

LOOKING WEST

INVENTIONS AND IMPROVEMENTS
EXPANDING DEMOCRACY
WESTWARD EXPANSION TO THE PACIFIC

270   271

Unit timeline places events in American history in the context of world history.

Three main categories of events enable students to see relationships among different kinds of events.

Chronology of presidential terms is a distinct element of the timeline.

CHAPTER OPENER

Have students review what they have learned about the French and English in North America. Remind students that both nations were empire builders. Ask what might happen between two such ambitious peoples.

THE COLONIES MOVE TOWARD INDEPENDENCE

Time period of chapter

THE STRUGGLE FOR NORTH AMERICA
BRITAIN'S NEW POLICY
THE COLONIES UNITE IN PROTEST
FROM PROTEST TO REBELLION

Section titles outline chapter topics.

6-1 THE STRUGGLE FOR NORTH AMERICA

READ TO FIND OUT

—what the words *speculators, militia, delegates,* and *strategy* mean.

—why the French built forts in the Ohio Valley.

—why the colonies rejected the Albany Plan of Union.

—how the French and Indian War began.

—what Britain gained from the Treaty of Paris.

speculators: people who seek profits from a risky investment

militia: group of citizens trained to fight in an emergency

delegates: people chosen to speak and act for others

strategy: overall plan

These wars in the colonies were named after the reigning British monarchs. Reigns: William III, 1689–1702; Anne, 1702–1714; George II, 1727–1760.

By the late 1600s England and France were the most powerful nations in Europe. Each country tried to strengthen itself by building an empire abroad. Both had colonies in North America and the West Indies and trading stations in Africa and India. Between 1689 and 1748, the two nations went to war with each other three times. They fought not only in Europe but in their colonies as well.

King William's War, which began in 1689, set the pattern in the North American colonies for the conflicts that followed. The French

Introducing: Inform students that Andrew Jackson's slogan was "Let the people rule." Ask what they might expect from a President with such a slogan. Tell the class they will now study the Jackson era.

Chapter number

EXPANDING DEMOCRACY

Chapter title

THE ELECTIONS OF 1824 AND 1828
ANDREW JACKSON AS PRESIDENT
JACKSON'S SECOND TERM
THE REFORM MOVEMENT

12-1 THE ELECTIONS OF 1824 AND 1828

READ TO FIND OUT

—what the words *sectionalism, suffrage,* and *illiterate* mean.

—why John Q. Adams had troubles as President.

—how the Democrats built a national political party.

—why Andrew Jackson was a hero to the people of the West.

—why the election of 1828 was an important turning point.

sectionalism: loyalty to one's own section of the country

suffrage: right to vote

illiterate: unable to read

By the end of James Monroe's second term as President, there were no national political parties in the United States. The Federalist party had destroyed itself by failing to support the War of 1812. The Republicans then lacked a political enemy to unite against. That party had broken into rival groups.

THE ELECTION OF 1824

In the presidential election of 1824 all the candidates called themselves Republicans, but each looked to his own section of the country for support. Secretary of State John Quincy Adams was the candidate of the

INTRODUCTION TO THE STUDENT TEXT   T 3

SECTION ORGANIZATION

Ask students to consider this question: Now that Britain was in control of North America, what might be its attitude toward the colonists, especially since it no longer needed their aid against the French?

6-2 BRITAIN'S NEW POLICY

READ TO FIND OUT

—what the words *proclamation, revenue, customs duties,* and *repeal* mean.

—what the purpose of the Proclamation Line of 1763 was.

—how Britain tried to stop colonial smuggling.

—why the Sugar Act was passed.

—why colonists denied Parliament the right to tax them.

proclamation: official announcement

revenue: income to meet government expenses

customs duties: taxes on goods imported into the colonies

repeal: do away with

After the Treaty of Paris, Britain had to try to keep peace in its new territories. West of the Appalachian Mountains, most of the Indian tribes were hostile to the British. Some were still loyal to the French. Others sought revenge after being cheated by dishonest fur traders from the British colonies. All the tribes feared that the trickle of settlers coming across the mountains would soon become a flood. Many of Britain's leaders realized that a war between Indians and frontier settlers could break out at any moment.

THE PROCLAMATION OF 1763

Britain's new king, George III, tried to solve problems on the frontier. In October 1763 he issued a **proclamation,** or official announcement. The king proclaimed that the crest of the Appalachian Mountains was now a boundary line between the colonies and the Indian lands. To cross the Proclamation Line, as it was called, fur traders had to have a

Students can locate the Proclamation Line on the map on the facing page.

Erminnie A. Smith drew an Iroquois sun ceremony in the 1700s. The Iroquois danced to give thanks to the Great Spirit.

1750-1775   CHAPTER 6   137

"Read to Find Out" objectives guide students to key subjects in each section.

Subheadings display main topics.

This conference room was part of Virginia's House of Burgesses. The restored building is part of Colonial Williamsburg.

within its rights. But Grenville had said that the act was meant to raise revenue. If that was so, then Parliament was trying to tax the colonies.

In the British colonies, as in Great Britain itself, the power to tax was seen as the power to take away someone's property. Such a dangerous power could be given only to an assembly of representatives elected by the taxpayers themselves. But the colonists had no representatives in Parliament. Therefore, said the petitioners, Parliament had no right to tax them.

This argument made sense to the citizens of Boston. They held a town meeting to protest "taxation without representation." Boston merchants stopped wearing English lace and ruffles. The students at Yale College in New Haven, Connecticut, agreed that they could do without "foreign liquors" taxed by the Sugar Act.

•CT
Ask students to write in their own words a definition of "taxation without representation."

SECTION REVIEW   Answers will be found on page T 35.

1. Define these words: *proclamation, revenue, customs duties, repeal.*

2. Identify: Proclamation Line of 1763, Pontiac, George Grenville.

3. What event convinced Parliament that a large force of British troops was needed in America?

4. How did George Grenville try to stop colonial merchants from smuggling?

5. Why did Parliament pass the Sugar Act?

6. Why did colonists claim that Parliament had no right to tax them?

1750-1775   CHAPTER 6   141

Section Review tests objectives and reinforces student understanding.

Chapter numbers and time period appear along the bottom of the page for easy reference.

VOCABULARY AND HISTORICAL TERMS

"Read to Find Out" objectives include important terms introduced in the section.

Chapter Survey as well as Section Review includes items testing students' mastery of new terms.

Facsimile page 170:

Introducing: Ask the class what an army needs in addition to guns. (Possibilities: supplies of food and clothes, money, civilian support) Tell students they will now study these and other matters.

7-3 THE PATRIOTS AND THEIR ARMY

READ TO FIND OUT

—what the words *inflation* and *veterans* mean.

—why the Continental Army was often short of supplies.

—who helped the war effort.

—how strong leaders aided the Continental Army.

inflation: a general increase in the level of prices

veterans: former soldiers

The British failed to destroy the Continental Army in battle. Even so, the survival of the Army was threatened many times by hardships.

Late in 1777, after the fall of Philadelphia, the Continentals set up winter quarters at Valley Forge. Joseph Martin, a seventeen-year-old private, told their story in his diary. By December, he wrote, "the army was not only starved but naked. The greatest part were not only shirtless and barefoot, but lacked all other clothing, especially blankets." Soldiers with their feet wrapped in rags "might be tracked by their blood upon the rough frozen ground." More than 3,000 soldiers died that winter.

THE FAILURE TO PROVIDE

Congress tried to provide supp[...] power to tax. When Congress req[...] they were slow to respond. They [...]

John Trego painted the Patriots at Valley Forge as he imagined them more than 100 years after that terrible winter. George Washington reviewed his ragged troops from his white horse.

170   CHAPTER 7   1775-1783

Facsimile page 180:

Answers will be found on page T 38.

CHAPTER SURVEY

VOCABULARY REVIEW

From this list of vocabulary words, choose the one that best completes each sentence below.

(a) alliance
(b) campaign
(c) guerrillas
(d) inflation
(e) mercenaries
(f) moderates
(g) radicals
(h) tyranny
(i) veterans

1. A _____ is a planned series of connected military actions.

2. A general increase in the level of prices is called _____.

3. _____ are soldiers who set up bases in remote areas and launch hit-and-run attacks on the enemy.

4. The cruel use of power by an all-powerful ruler is _____.

5. _____ are people who favor extreme changes or reforms.

6. An _____ is an agreement between two or more nations to aid each other.

7. Former soldiers are _____.

8. _____ are people who favor gradual change.

9. Hired soldiers are called _____.

CHAPTER REVIEW

1. (a) What did the moderates in Congress hope to accomplish by sending the Olive Branch Petition? (b) How did Thomas Paine's pamphlet *Common Sense* help change the way the American colonists felt about their king?

2. Thomas Jefferson addressed the Declaration of Independence to the world,

but he also wrote it for the American people. Why did he think this was necessary?

3. (a) When the Revolutionary War began, what advantages did the British have? (b) What disadvantages did they face? (c) How did the British hope to win the war?

4. (a) What advantages did the American Patriots have? (b) What disadvantages did they face?

5. (a) What effect did the retreat of the Continental Army have on Loyalists and Patriots in New Jersey? (b) How did Loyalists in Georgia respond to the British capture of Savannah? (c) What effect did the Battle of King's Mountain have on Loyalists and Patriots in the Carolinas?

6. (a) How [...] American [...] Salomon [...] Smith ha[...] women h[...]

7. (a) In w[...] Lafayette [...] alike? (b[...]

Artist Char[...] Patriot mil[...] gun's barre[...] large screw[...]

180   CHAPTER SURVEY   1775-1783

Facsimile page 173:

ing a cannon. She was wounded and lost the use of one arm. Later Congress rewarded Corbin with a soldier's pension.

Black Americans, both slave and free, also played an important part in the war effort. Blacks tried to join the Patriot forces at the beginning of the war, but most were rejected. Then, as the need for soldiers grew, Congress and most of the states passed laws granting slaves their freedom in return for military service.

As many as 5,000 black Americans served in the armed forces. They fought in every major battle. After the war, their sacrifices were remembered by white **veterans,** or former soldiers. Some of these veterans joined the campaigns to end slavery.

LEADERSHIP

George Washington was, of course, an outstanding leader. Despite his lack of supplies and hardships like those at Valley Forge, Washington kept the Continental Army together. Some of his best officers were volunteers from Europe. The Marquis de Lafayette (LAH-fee-EHT), a brave nobleman from France, was made a major general before he was twenty. Americans were happy to serve under Lafayette. He used his own money to buy food and clothing for his soldiers.

Baron Friedrich von Steuben (fawn STYOO-ben), an officer from Prussia, came to Valley Forge in February 1778. From dawn until dusk, he worked to make Washington's troops "feel a confidence in their own skill." Von Steuben taught the Americans how to take orders and how to use bayonets. He taught them how to swing around from a marching column into a line of battle. By spring he was one of the most popular officers in the army.

Despite von Steuben's efforts, thousands gave up and went home. But the army did not fall apart. No matter how bad the situation was, the soldiers who stayed knew that their commander would not give up. Washington, in turn, drew strength from the soldiers who stayed with him. "We did not think of [going home]" wrote Private Joseph Martin. "We had engaged to fight in the defense of our injured country."

SECTION REVIEW   Answers will be found on page T 38.

1. Define these words: *inflation, veterans.*

2. Identify: Haym Salomon and Robert Morris, Margaret Cochran Corbin, Marquis de Lafayette, Baron von Steuben.

3. Why was Congress unable to provide supplies for the army?

4. How did women help the war effort?

5. What was granted to slaves who served in the armed forces?

This painting of a free black sailor was done in 1779. He was probably a member of the crew of the *General Washington,* the ship in the background.

Casimir Pulaski and Thaddeus Kosciusko, both Poles, were two other Europeans who distinguished themselves in the Revolutionary War. Pulaski led a corps of cavalry and infantry known as Pulaski's Legion. He was fatally wounded at the siege of Savannah. Kosciusko served as a colonel of engineers. For his services he was promoted to brigadier general.

1775-1783   CHAPTER 7   173

Important historical terms appear in boldface type and are explained in context and defined in the Glossary.

Hard-to-pronounce words are respelled to aid in correct pronunciation.

CHAPTER SUMMARY AND CHAPTER SURVEY

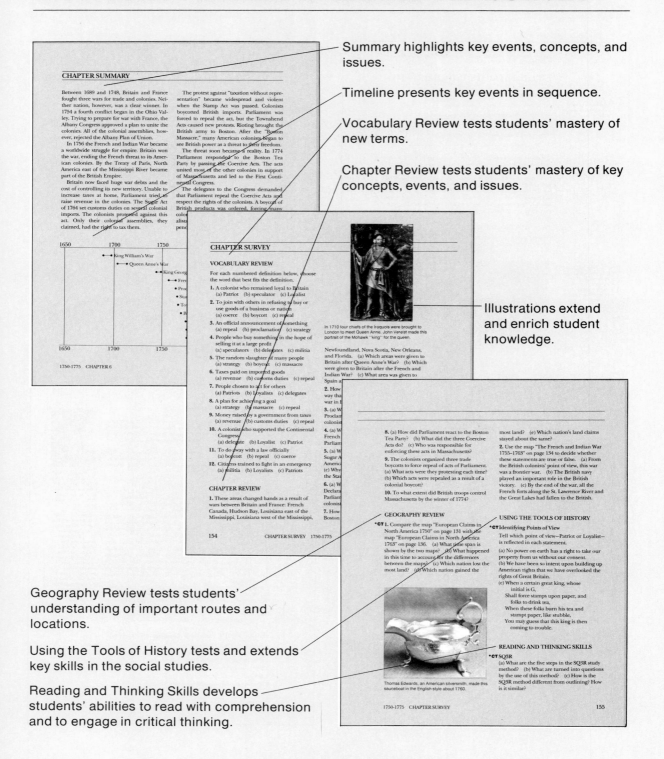

Summary highlights key events, concepts, and issues.

Timeline presents key events in sequence.

Vocabulary Review tests students' mastery of new terms.

Chapter Review tests students' mastery of key concepts, events, and issues.

Illustrations extend and enrich student knowledge.

Geography Review tests students' understanding of important routes and locations.

Using the Tools of History tests and extends key skills in the social studies.

Reading and Thinking Skills develops students' abilities to read with comprehension and to engage in critical thinking.

UNIT SURVEY

Unit Review tests students' mastery of key concepts, events, and issues.

Linking the Past and Present leads students to relate materials in the unit to contemporary American life.

Meeting the Builders of America reviews important individuals and groups, leads to further research, and offers a brief list of books for research.

Answers will be found on page T 39.

UNIT SURVEY

UNIT REVIEW

1. (a) What name did William Bradford give to the Separatists who founded Plymouth Colony? (b) What eventually happened to Plymouth Colony? (c) What two New England colonies were founded south of Massachusetts? (d) What two colonies located to the north of Massachusetts were taken over by it?

2. (a) What name did the Dutch give their colony stretching along the Hudson River? (b) How was this name changed when the English seized the colony? (c) Which two colonies were a haven to many Quakers? (d) Which colony had an assembly but no governor of its own?

3. (a) In what colony did Bacon's Rebellion take place? (b) What colony was a haven to many Catholics? (c) What two southern colonies were formed from a single land grant? (d) What colony was a haven to many debtors?

4. (a) In what places did most colonists live? (b) In what places were colonists best informed about current events? (c) What colonists relied most strongly on the mercantile system for their living? (d) How did these colonists differ from plantation owners?

5. (a) Who was responsible for local governments in the colonies? (b) Who was responsible for paying the salaries of royal governors?

6. (a) Why did Britain need to raise money after the French and Indian War? (b) Why did it seem fair to Parliament to tax the colonies in North America? (c) Why did this new taxation required by Parliament seem unfair to many colonists?

7. (a) What kind of taxes were called for by the Sugar Act of 1764 and the Townshend Acts of 1767? (b) What did colonists do to avoid paying these taxes?

8. (a) What colonial city was a scene of violence connected to the Townshend Acts? (b) What colony was the target of the Coercive Acts? (c) What event caused Parliament to pass the Coercive Acts?

9. (a) Why were Americans slow to declare their independence after the start of the Revolutionary War? (b) How did *Common Sense* help lead to the Declaration of Independence? (c) What people in the colonies opposed independence?

10. (a) What foreign nation gave most help to the Patriot war effort? (b) How did rivalries in Europe prompt that nation to help the Patriots? (c) In terms of the mercantile system, what did Britain lose by losing the Revolutionary War?

Mary Woodhull's needlepoint picture showed the new nation as a rich and beautiful New England farm. Here, two wheat reapers plan a picnic by a pond.

James Gillray's "American Rattle Snake" coils around the armies of Burgoyne and Cornwallis. In 1782 the snake was ready to crush the British.

LINKING THE PAST AND THE PRESENT

1. The occupations of blacksmith, cooper, and miller were popular in the 1700s. Look for these or similar occupations in the advertising pages of your telephone directory. Check under headings such as "blacksmith," "iron," "metal," "steel," "cooper," "barrels," "miller," and "flour." List the occupations you find.

*CT 2. Puritan ideas led to "blue laws" in New England. These laws banned selling, sports, and other activities on Sundays. (They were called blue laws because one list of the laws was printed on blue paper.) Find out whether businesses in your area stay closed or close early on Sundays. If so, try to discover whether local laws require them to close.

MEETING THE BUILDERS OF AMERICA

*CT 1. Review the descriptions of Eliza Lucas Pinckney (page 100), Andrew Hamilton (page 123), John Adams (page 146), and Deborah Sampson (page 172). In what ways did they contribute to America?

*CT 2. Prepare a report about the contributions to American life of some other person or group mentioned in Unit 2. For example, look for information about Roger Williams, Anne Hutchinson, William Penn, Benjamin Franklin, the Pennsylvania Dutch, Mercy Otis Warren, Crispus Attucks, Nathan Hale, Margaret Cochran Corbin, or others. You may be able to use one of the following books as a source of information.

Davis, Burke. *Black Heroes of the American Revolution.* New York: Harcourt Brace Jovanovich, 1976.
Latham, Frank B. *The Trial of John Peter Zenger, August 1735.* New York: Watts, 1970.
Phelan, Mary K. *Four Days in Philadelphia, 1776.* New York: Crowell, 1967.

SUGGESTIONS FOR FURTHER READING

Alderman, Clifford Lindsey. *The Story of the Thirteen Colonies.* New York: Random House, 1966.
Borden, Morton. *George Washington.* Englewood Cliffs, NJ: Prentice-Hall, 1969.
Chidsey, Donald Barr. *Valley Forge.* New York: Crown, 1962.
Lawson, Don. *The American Revolution.* New York: Abelard-Schuman, 1974.
Loeb, Robert H., Jr. *Meet the Real Pilgrims: Life on a Plimoth Plantation in 1627.* Garden City, NY: Doubleday, 1979.
Phelan, Mary K. *The Story of the Boston Massacre.* New York: Crowell, 1976.
Taylor, Theodore. *Rebellion Town, Williamsburg, 1776.* New York: Crowell, 1973.
Wibberley, Leonard. *A Dawn in the Trees, Thomas Jefferson, the Years 1776–1789.* New York: Farrar, Straus & Giroux, 1964.

182   UNIT SURVEY   1620–1783

1620–1783   UNIT SURVEY   183

Illustrations extend and enrich student knowledge.

Suggestions for Further Reading provides a list of stimulating books to increase students' knowledge.

SPECIAL FEATURES: USING THE TOOLS OF HISTORY AND APPROACHES TO READING

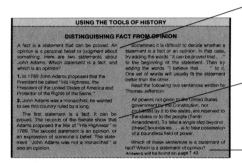

Develops social studies skills such as analyzing change and continuity, interpreting maps, graphs, and diagrams, and distinguishing fact from opinion.

Builds and develops skills in relation to chapter content.

Questions require students to apply what they have learned.

Develops critical thinking skills.

Builds and develops skills in relation to chapter content.

Develops reading skills such as previewing, outlining, sequencing events, and analyzing cause and effect.

Questions and exercises require students to apply what they have learned.

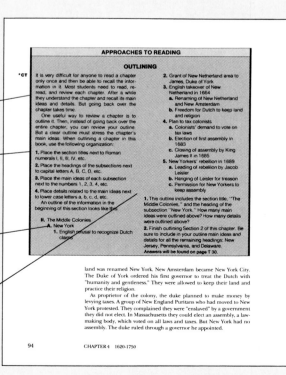

SPECIAL FEATURES: UNDERSTANDING GEOGRAPHY AND AMERICAN VALUES IN ACTION

Activity: Students can establish the meridian on (or near) which they live and the climate, vegetation, and elevation of their area.

UNDERSTANDING GEOGRAPHY

BEYOND THE 100TH MERIDIAN

The 100th meridian, 100° west longitude, slices through the center of the Interior Plains. It cuts through the heart of North Dakota, South Dakota, and Nebraska. Kansas, Oklahoma, and Texas are also split by this line 100° to the west of the prime meridian.

The 100th meridian, however, is much more than a line of longitude. It divides the Interior Plains into two distinct regions. The eastern region, the Central Plains, stretches from the 100th meridian to the Appalachians. The western region, the Great Plains, extends from this line to the Rockies. Each region presented settlers with dramatically different landscapes.

Climate, vegetation, and elevation above sea level are different in the Central Plains and the Great Plains. Of course, climate, vegetation, and elevation do not suddenly change at the 100th meridian. The change is gradual, but it is significant.

The most important difference is in rainfall patterns. The 20-inch (51-centimeter) rainfall line closely follows the 100th meridian. This line divides the plains region into two rainfall areas. East of this rainfall line, most places get more than 20 inches a year. West of the line, most places get less than 20 inches.

The rainfall line also marks changes in vegetation. Trees usually require more than 20 inches of rain a year. Grass can grow with as little as 10 inches. So forested land is found east of the line, and grassland to the west. On the Great Plains, trees are found only along river banks where more water is available or where people have planted and watered them.

Even today, travelers crossing the 100th meridian are struck by the change in landscape. The woodlands of the Central Plains seem closed-in and cozy. On the Great Plains travelers feel as if they can see forever.

Look at the "Physical Map of the United States" in the Resource Center. Find the line where the green and yellow-green areas of the Interior Plains meet. This is a contour line, which connects points that have the same elevation. All the points on this line are at 1,500 feet (500 meters).

The 1,500-foot contour line roughly parallels the 100th meridian. Places east of the line are below 1,500 feet. West of the 1,500-foot contour line, the land gradually rises until it reaches 7,000 feet (2,000 meters) at the base of the Rocky Mountains. Over approximately 400 miles (640 kilometers), the land rises more than a mile in elevation.

People who settled the Interior Plains formed different settlement patterns east and west of the 100th meridian. East of the line there was sufficient rainfall for settlers to grow corn and wheat. But when pioneers first traveled across the 100th meridian, they thought that the land was too dry for farming. Indeed, they called the region the "Great American Desert." Later settlers would learn special farming techniques to grow crops on the arid plains. And they would find that the grassland, where buffalo grazed, was ideal for other grazing animals—cattle.

The 100th meridian is a precise geographic line. It is also a boundary of sorts, which sets off distinctly western and eastern areas of the United States.

332   CHAPTER 13   1820-1850

Leads students to a clearer understanding of geography in relation to history.

Illustrations clarify geographical meanings.

Basic American values are explored through the thoughts and actions of individuals active in dealing with issues and events of the time.

Illustrations reinforce biographical data.

*CT Activity: Students can assume that they are Mariano Vallejo or one of his associates and write papers arguing (with good supporting reasons) that California's future lies with the United States.

★ ★ ★ ★ ★ ★ ★   AMERICAN VALUES IN ACTION   ★ ★ ★ ★ ★ ★ ★

MARIANO GUADALUPE VALLEJO

Mariano Vallejo (vah-YEH-hō) of California seemed to have everything. He was a handsome man, with thick black hair and lush sideburns. He had a beautiful wife and fine children. He was a respected leader in Mexican California. He owned vast lands and thousands of cattle and horses.

Yet Vallejo was not satisfied. As a child, he had seen French pirates attack his homeland. California was at that time a colony of faraway Spain, which provided little defense for the Californios.

When California became a Mexican colony, it fared no better. Californios who supported Mexican rule clashed with those who wanted local government. Californios and Indians fought. And by the 1840s, American settlers were streaming into California without permission from Mexico.

Vallejo yearned to bring order to his homeland. In 1833 he had been appointed military commander of northern California. Some people complained of his lordly ways and iron rule. Yet the haughty commander could unbend, embracing strangers with true warmth. He once invited Americans to celebrate the Fourth of July at a huge festival on his estate.

Vallejo warned the government of Mexico that California was slipping away from its control. But Mexico did nothing. Finally, Vallejo met with other leaders in California.

It was California's destiny, he argued, to become part of the United States. "We shall have a stable government and just laws," he said. "California will grow strong and flourish. Its people will be prosperous, happy, and free."

Vallejo's dream came true when the United States won California in the Mexican War. In 1849 he attended California's constitutional convention. Vallejo and other delegates decided that California should be a free state.

Vallejo welcomed statehood. At last his beloved homeland would be secure.

THE ELECTION OF 1848

As the election of 1848 approached, the Democrats chose Senator Cass, a veteran of the War of 1812, as their candidate. He supported popular sovereignty. Northern Democrats who supported the Wilmot Proviso were angered by Cass's nomination. A group led by Martin Van Buren left the party.

The Whigs chose General Zachary Taylor of Louisiana as their candidate. He was a slaveholder, a nationalist, and a hero of the war with Mexico. To Whig leaders he was the perfect candidate because his views on the Wilmot Proviso were unknown. But northern Whigs who opposed slavery refused to support Taylor. They took the name Conscience Whigs.

1850-1861   CHAPTER 14   363

AMERICAN VOICES

Primary sources give a sense of the everyday life of a period and promote historical skills development.

Content supplements issues, events, and concepts introduced in text.

Activity: Students can read to the class other selections from *The Lowell Offering*, edited by Benita Eisler.

pound was prepared at home with care. The meat scraps and bones were used and cooked with lye, drained in ash hoppers. It made perfect soap for domestic uses. For wounds and baby usage there could be bought Castile soap. Except salt, iron, sugar, and coffee, everything was raised by those early Georgia planters necessary for human comfort and sustenance.

Adapted from Henry Steele Commager and Allan Nevins, eds., *The Heritage of America* (Boston: Little, Brown and Company, 1939), pp. 377-380.

1. Rebecca Latimer Felton writes that on a Georgia plantation, nearly everything "necessary for human comfort and sustenance" was raised or made there. What food was raised? What things were made?

2. Felton admires her grandmother's "industry, her management, and her executive ability." What details show her grandmother's abilities?

A MILL WOMAN'S THOUGHTS

The women mill workers of Lowell, Massachusetts, were encouraged to submit stories and essays to the *Lowell Offering*, a magazine. Here, from the *Offering*, is Elizabeth E. Turner's essay, a "Factory Girl's Reverie." (A reverie is a daydream.)

This colored engraving of a "mill girl" was printed in 1841.

472   AMERICAN VOICES   CHAPTER

Evening is the time for thought and reflection. All is lovely outside, and why am I not happy? I cannot be, for a feeling of sadness comes stealing over me. I am far, far from that loved spot, where I spent the evenings of childhood's years. I am here, among strangers—a factory girl—yes, *factory girl;* a name that is thought so degrading by many....

But here I am. I toil day after day in the noisy mill. When the bell calls I must go. Must I always stay here, and spend my days within these walls, with this constant noise my only music?

I am sometimes asked, "When are you going home?" "*Home,* that name ever dear to me." But they would not often ask me, if they only knew what sadness it creates to say, "*I have no home.*"....

I will once more visit the home of my childhood. I will cast one long lingering look at the grave of my parents and brothers, and bid farewell to the spot. I have many friends who would not see me in want. I have uncles, aunts, and cousins, who have kindly urged me to share their homes. But I have a little pride yet. I will not be dependent upon friends while I have health and ability to earn bread for myself.

Discussion: Why might Frederick Douglass pretend not to be interested in the Irish dock workers' advice to run away?

him I was. He said to the other that it was a pity so fine a little fellow as myself should be a slave for life. They both advised me to run away to the North. I pretended not to be interested in what they said. Nevertheless, I remembered their advice. From that time I resolved to run away.

Adapted from Philip Butcher, ed., *The Minority Presence in American Literature, 1600-1900* Volume I (Washington, D.C.: Howard University Press, 1977), pp. 332-333.

1. How does Frederick Douglass learn the meanings of *abolition* and *abolitionist?*

2. What makes him resolve to run away?

American abolitionists wore medallions like this silk one, made in England about 1830, to show their antislavery sentiments.

FANNIE JACKSON COPPIN GOES TO COLLEGE

Fannie Jackson Coppin was born a slave. When she was a child, her aunt bought her freedom. Living in Massachusetts, she managed to get an elementary school education.

The African Methodist Episcopal Church helped her go to college in 1860, and afterwards she taught school. Eventually she became the head of the Female

478   AMERICAN VOICES   CHAPTER

Department of the Institute for Colored Youth in Philadelphia.

In 1913 Fannie Jackson Coppin wrote *Reminiscences of School Life.* Here, in a passage from her book, she tells of her education at Oberlin College in Ohio.

My aunt in Washington still helped me. I was able to pay my way to Oberlin. Oberlin was then the only college in the United States where colored students were permitted to study. The faculty did not forbid a woman to take the men's course. But they did not advise it. There was plenty of Latin and Greek in it. There was as much mathematics as one could shoulder.

It was the custom in Oberlin that forty students from the junior and senior classes should teach the preparatory classes. The faculty told me that they intended to give me a class. I was to understand that if the pupils rebelled against my teaching, the faculty did not intend to force it.

There was a little surprise on the faces of some when they came into class and saw the teacher. But fortunately for my own dear love of teaching, there were no signs of rebellion. The class went on increasing...

Activity: Students can research and write reports on heroes of the Alamo, such as William Barret Travis, Davy Crockett, Jim Bowie, and Juan Seguin.

CHAPTER 13
WESTWARD EXPANSION TO THE PACIFIC

THE ALAMO

The Alamo is an old Spanish mission in San Antonio, Texas. There, in 1836, a small band of Texans held out for eleven days against a much greater Mexican force. Finally, on March 6, the Alamo fell. Here, William Barret Travis, commander of the Alamo, appeals to Texans and "all Americans" for help.

February 24, 1836
To the People in Texas and
All Americans in the World

Fellow Citizens and Compatriots:

I am besieged by a thousand or more of the Mexicans under Santa Anna. I have sustained a continual bombardment and cannonade for twenty-four hours and have not lost a man. The enemy have demanded a surrender. Otherwise the garrison is to be put to the sword if the fort is taken. I have answered the summons with a cannon shot. Our flag still waves proudly from our walls. *I shall never surrender or retreat.*

I call on you, in the name of Liberty, of Patriotism, and of everything dear to the American character, to come to our aid. The enemy are receiving reinforcements daily. I am determined to sustain myself as long as possible and die like a soldier who never forgets what is due to his own honor and that of his country. *Victory or death!*

W. Barret Travis
Lieutenant Colonel, Commanding

Adapted and abridged from Paul M. Angle, *The American Reader: From Columbus to Today* (Skokie, IL: Rand McNally & Company, 1958), pp. 235-236.

1. What does William Barret Travis know will happen if the Alamo does not surrender?

2. What keeps him from surrendering to Santa Anna's superior force?

[engraving]

An engraving made in 1859 shows the ruins of the Alamo. The cannons of the Mexican army pounded away at the old mission for eleven days in 1836. Inside, the Texans vowed never to surrender.

SAM HOUSTON AT THE BATTLE OF SAN JACINTO

In 1836 the Texan army, led by General Sam Houston, crushed the Mexican army and gained independence for Texas. For weeks, Houston had retreated from the Mexicans, who were led by General Santa Anna. Then, when Santa Anna's troops were camped near the San Jacinto River, Houston attacked. Here, in a letter to Texas President David Burnet, Houston tells of the victory.

About nine o'clock on the morning of April 21, the enemy were reinforced by five hundred choice troops under the command of General Cós. This increased their force to upward of fifteen hundred men. Our force for the field numbered seven hundred and eighty-three.

480   AMERICAN VOICES   CHAPTER 13

Illustrations enhance content.

Questions reinforce students' grasp of material and lead them to explore issues raised by the readings.

ILLUSTRATIONS AND GRAPHICS

Diagrams and charts translate historical concepts into easy-to-read visuals.

Maps support and extend information provided in the text.

Graphs provide additional historical information.

Ideas That Made Exploration Possible

A.D. 200	Ptolemy, a Greek mathematician, devises a system of latitude and longitude.
1000	The magnetic compass comes into use.
1200	The development of the rudder allows a ship to be guided by one person.
1300	The compass card is added to the magnetic compass. The card allows navigators to determine direction more accurately. Cannons come into use on ships.
1400	The improved astrolabe allows sailors to determine their distance from the equator. The swift, easily handled caravel is developed. It combines the best features of Mediterranean triangular-sailed ships and square-rigged northern ships.
1500	Gerardus Mercator devises the first map projection that shows the middle latitudes with little distortion. The galleon, or carrack, comes into use. It is a heavy ship with many masts, and it carries more guns and cargo than did previous ships.

protection. With tax money, the king or queen built a strong government and a royal army.

Slowly the rulers brought the nobles under their control. As they unified the land under their rule, they created nations. By the end of the 1400s, there were four nations in western Europe—England, France, Spain, and Portugal.

The Christian monarchs of these nations searched for new ways to fill their royal treasuries. They soon saw that a water route to the trade of Asia could be a source of great wealth. Finding such a route might also make it possible for them to ... new direction.

PORTUGAL TAKES THE LEA...

Fearing competition from Spain, Portugal tried to keep its explorations and discoveries secret.

Prince Henry, son of the king of ... route to the East. In 1418 he bega... ship captains, and shipbuilders to ... about sea travel. He also began s... these expeditions sailed into the ... south along the west coast of A... through the land to Asia.

At first, Prince Henry's captains ... northwest Africa. They were cert... ters grew hot enough to boil. Th... horrible monsters. But with Princ... came their fear. Each time a ship ... ported everything that they had le...

Step by step, Henry and his ma... currents, winds, and the African ... maps were the best in Europe. A... West African kingdoms for spices, ...

28   CHAPTER 2   1000-1700

Agriculture in the South   1860

GULF OF MEXICO

- Corn, wheat, hogs
- Tobacco, hemp
- Cotton
- Rice, sugarcane

0   400 MILES
0 400 KILOMETERS

Cotton Production   1800–1860

(Thousands of bales: 4000, 3000, 2000, 1000, 0)
(years: 1800 1810 1820 1830 1840 1850 1860)

Between 1800 and 1860, the production of cotton almost doubled each decade.

By 1860 cotton was grown across the South wherever the climate and soil were suitable.

CORPORATIONS

Southern planters disapproved of one northern ... particular. People in the North were forming ... panies owned by stockholders. If a corporation ... while owing money, the stockholders were not li... sible, for its debts. The amount that stockholders ... to the money they had invested. This feature o... limited liability, seemed dishonorable to plante... they were honor-bound to pay their debts.

Corporations fueled the Industrial Revolution ... liability made investors less fearful about buyi... panies. Large amounts of investment capital ... rations to be invested in canals and railroads.

THE INDUSTRIAL NORTH GAINS POWER

The planters were proud of their way of life. Bu... ing economic power of the North. In 1860, while ... duced $245,000,000 worth of manufactured good... produced $1,213,900,000 worth. Most of the na... roads, like its factories, were in the North.

1850-1861   CHAPTER 14

Introducing: Ask students why southern planters might regard themselves as aristocrats who are superior to northern tradespeople. Tell the class they will now study the world of the southern planter.

14-2 THE ECONOMIES OF THE SOUTH AND THE NORTH

READ TO FIND OUT

—what the word *corporation* means.

—why southern farmers looked to the planters for leadership.

—how the northern and the southern economies differed.

—why the South feared the growing power of the North.

corporation: company owned by stockholders

Abolitionists pictured the South as a land of wealthy planters and huge plantations. Parts of the South fit that picture. Thousand-acre plantations were common in the rice lands along the coast of South Carolina and Georgia. The same was true in the band of fertile soil known as the Black Belt of Alabama. The Mississippi bottom lands were famous for large plantations.

Wealthy planters and their families gathered at places like the Oakland House Race Course for the popular sport of horse racing. Robert Brammer and Augustus A. Von Smith painted Oakland House in Louisville, Kentucky, in 1840.

1850-1861   CHAPTER 14   357

Contemporary art, photographs, and political cartoons enrich text as documents of the past.

Captions identify important artists and relate images to chapter content.

REFERENCE SECTION: RESOURCE CENTER

Separate contents page for easy reference.

Full-color maps present information on the American nation, people, and resources.

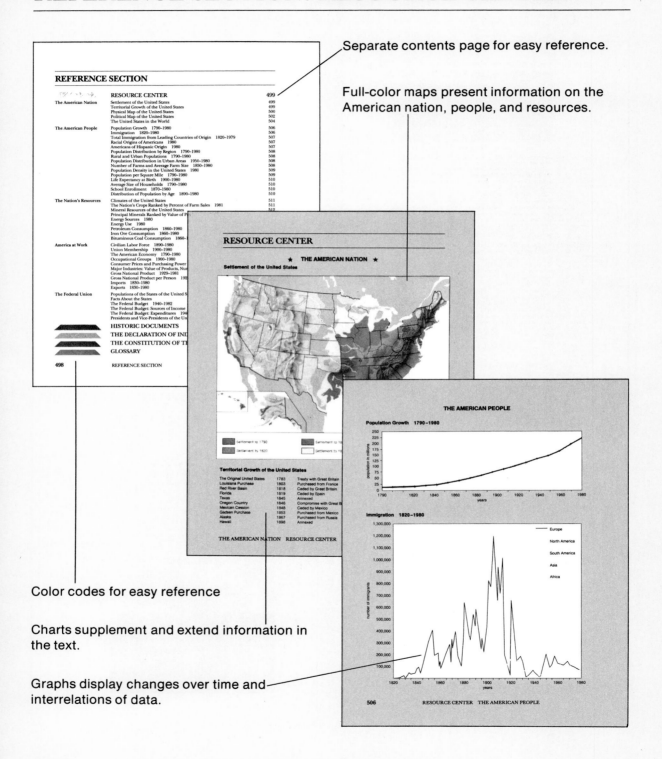

Color codes for easy reference

Charts supplement and extend information in the text.

Graphs display changes over time and interrelations of data.

REFERENCE SECTION: DOCUMENTS AND GLOSSARY

Mayflower Compact

Declaration and Resolves of the Continental Congress

Annotated Declaration of Independence and Constitution of the United States

---

HISTORIC DOCUMENTS

On arriving at Plymouth, the Pilgrims signed an agreement called the Mayflower Compact. It was the first document in the English colonies to describe the type of government that would be observed there. The Mayflower Compact was based on English laws and the consent of those to be governed.

THE MAYFLOWER COMPACT

This day, before we came to harbor, observing some not well affected to unity and concord, but gave some appearance of faction [disagreement], it was thought good there should be an association and agreement that we should combine together in one body, and to submit to such government and governors as we should by common consent agree to make and choose, and set our hands to this that follows word for word.

In the name of God, Amen. We whose names are underwritten, the loyal subjects of our dread sovereign lord, King James, by the grace of God, of Great Britain, France, and Ireland, King, Defender of the Faith, etc.

Having undertaken for the glory of God, and advancement of the Christian faith, and honor of our king and country, a voyage to plant the first colony in the northern parts of Virginia, do by these present, solemnly and mutually, in the presence of God and one another, covenant [agree] and combine ourselves together into a civil body politic, for our better ordering and preservation and furtherance of the ends aforesaid, and by virtue hereof to enact, constitute, and frame such just and equal laws, ordinances, acts, constitutions, and offices from time to time as shall be thought most meet [good] and convenient for the general good of the colony; unto which we promise all due submission and obedience. In witness whereof we have hereunder subscribed our names, Cape Cod, 11th of November, in the year of the reign of our sovereign lord . . . Ireland . . . 1620.

On October 14, 1774, the Continental Congress wrote a declaration of rights . . . mentioned in this document can be seen in the Declaration of Independence . . . colonists rejected British rule, but not traditions of English law and ideas about . . .

DECLARATION AND RESOL . . .
CONTINENTAL CONG . . .

The good people of the colonies, justly alarmed at the arbitrary proceedings of Parliament and administration, have [chosen] deputies to meet in the city of Philadelphia in order that their religion, laws, and liberties may not be subverted:

The deputies so appointed being now assembled, in a full and free representation of these colonies, do, as Englishmen, their ancestors, in like cases have usually done, declare,

That the inhabitants of the English colonies in North America, by the immutable [changeless]

laws of . . .
constituti . . .

1. Tha . . .
property, . . .
eign pow . . .
without t . . .

2. Tha . . .
onies, we . . .
mother c . . .
and imm . . .
within th . . .

522 HISTORIC DOCUMENTS

He has kept among us, in times of peace, standing armies, without the consent of our legislatures.

He has affected to render the military independent of and superior to the civil power.

He has combined with others to subject us to a jurisdiction foreign to our constitution, and unacknowledged by our laws; giving his assent to their acts of pretended legislation:

For quartering large bodies of armed troops among us;

For protecting them, by a mock trial, from punishment for any murders which they should commit on the inhabitants of these states;

For cutting off our trade with all parts of the world;

For imposing taxes on us without our consent;

For depriving us, in many cases, of the benefits of trial by jury;

For transporting us beyond seas to be tried for pretended offenses;

For abolishing the free system of English laws in a neighboring province, establishing therein an arbitrary government, and enlarging its boundaries, so as to render it at once an example and fit instrument for introducing the same absolute rule into these colonies;

For taking away our charters, abolishing our most valuable laws, and altering fundamentally the forms of our governments;

For suspending our own legislatures, and declaring themselves invested with power to legislate for us in all cases whatsoever.

He has abdicated government here, by declaring us out of his protection, and waging war against us.

He has plundered our seas, ravaged our coasts, burnt our towns, and destroyed the lives of our people.

He is at this time transporting large armies of foreign mercenaries to complete the works of death, desolation, and tyranny already begun with circumstances of cruelty and perfidy scarcely paralleled in the most barbarous ages, and totally unworthy the head of a civilized nation.

He has constrained our fellow citizens, taken captive on the high seas, to bear arms against their country, to become the executioners of their

The colonists wanted King George to send home the troops who had come to America during the French and Indian War.

In Massachusetts, the head of the British army in America was appointed governor.

Parliament had claimed the authority to make laws for the colonies. The colonists had never consented to this power, but the king had approved it.

The colonists resented having to provide lodging for British troops.

British soldiers accused of crimes in the colonies could be tried in England, where they were likely to escape punishment.

Parliament claimed the right to control trade in the colonies.

Colonists opposed all taxes since the Sugar Act of 1764 as "taxation without representation."

Colonists accused of smuggling could be tried in admiralty courts, which had no juries.

Colonists accused of treason could be taken to Britain for trial.

The Quebec Act of 1774 set up a royal government in Canada much like the former French government th . . . ada to the . . .

In 1774 . . . the counci . . . judges the . . .

In 1767 . . . Assembly . . . York.

After Le . . . declared t . . . claimed th . . . America b . . . attack the . . .

The Br . . . mercenari . . . naries we . . .

The co . . . American . . .

526 THE DECLARATION OF INDEPEND . . .

GLOSSARY

Certain words in the Glossary and in the text have been respelled as an aid to pronunciation. A key to pronouncing the respelled words appears below.

The words in the Glossary are defined to clarify their meaning in the text. The page numbers given after the definition refer to the places in the text where the words first appear. The words selected for definition in the Glossary are important in United States history.

PRONUNCIATION KEY

Like certain other words in this book, the word *Appalachian* has been respelled to indicate its pronunciation: AP-uh-LAY-chun. The small capital letters mean that the first syllable should be spoken with a minor stress. The large capital letters mean that the third syllable should be spoken with a major stress. The vowel sounds shown by the letters *uh*, *ay*, and *un* in the respelling correspond to the vowel sounds in the key below.

Pronounce	a	as in	hat
	ah		father
	ar		tar
	ay		say
	ayr		air
	e, eh		hen
	ee		bee
	eer		deer
	er		her
	ew		new
	g		go
	i, ih		him
	i		kite
	j		jet
	ng		ring
	o		frog
	ō		no
	oo		soon
	or		for
	ow		plow
	oy		boy
	sh		she
	th		thick
	u, uh		sun
	z		zebra
	zh		measure

556 GLOSSARY

Complete Glossary with pronunciation guide

INTRODUCTION TO THE TEACHER'S RESOURCE MANUAL

HIGHLIGHTS

- Designed to reduce teacher preparation time

- Lends itself to different teaching styles and classroom situations

- Offers teaching strategies on a unit-chapter-section basis

- Lesson plans and worksheets clearly referenced to student text

- Comprehensive evaluation program with chapter, unit, midterm, and final tests

- Blackline master worksheets and tests for easy duplication and distribution

- Answers printed on blackline masters in blue, which will not appear on duplicated copies

- Unit listings of audio-visual materials to supplement text

- Chart highlighting activities in Teacher's Resource Manual that foster critical thinking skills

- Chart suggesting when primary source readings in American Voices may be appropriately assigned

UNIT PREVIEW

UNIT 3

BUILDING
A NEW NATION

—— Unit number

—— Unit title

UNIT PREVIEW

SUMMARY

After winning independence from Britain, the United States proceeded to devise a workable form of government and steer a course of neutrality in foreign policy. Long-lasting precedents were set, including the establishment of political parties. The nation expanded westward with the lands claimed through the Louisiana Purchase. After the War of 1812, feelings of nationalism spread throughout the nation.

TIMELINE

The Unit 3 timeline notes events that will be covered in the unit—the establishment of California missions; the writing of the Articles of Confederation; the framing and ratification of the Constitution and the Bill of Rights; the Louisiana Purchase; the Latin American revolutions; and technological changes associated with the growth of industry and transportation. The timeline also notes events not extensively covered in the unit, for example, the French Revolution and the Battle of Waterloo, included because of their worldwide impact. The timeline identifies other events that had an effect on the world. These events—including Lavoisier's Table of the Elements, Beethoven's "Eroica" symphony, and Gibbon's history of the Roman Empire—may enrich student knowledge of science, art, literature, and music.

As students begin Unit 3, ask them to scan the timeline. Point out the names of American presidents, located at the top of the timeline. Also point out events that will be covered in the unit and determine which are familiar to students.

As students progress through the unit, you may want to have them use the timeline as a review of the material in each chapter. After students read Chapter 10, for example, ask them to explain why the Louisiana Purchase was chosen for the Unit 3 timeline.

You may also want students to compare the timeline at the end of each chapter with the unit timeline. After students read Chapter 8, for example, ask them to tell where an event such as "Shays' Rebellion" fits on the unit timeline. Ask students to explain how the rebellion relates to the drawing up and eventual ratification of the Constitution.

You may wish to have students consolidate the chapter and unit timelines into a large classroom chart. Ask students to suggest additions to the timeline of events that they might have discovered in their own reading.

In using the Unit 3 timeline, you may want to discuss the following information with students.

The French Revolution was important because of its significant impact on the times. Liberty, equality, and fraternity were the ideals of the French Revolution. French revolutionaries like the Marquis de Lafayette had been affected by—and some even helped in—the American Revolution. The French Revolution and Napoleon's rise to power were important causes of the hostilities between Britain and France that dominated the period.

The French Revolution began with the demands of the French populace for a reconvening of the Estates-General, a body similar to the British Parliament but without its traditions or authority. King Louis XVI convened the Estates-General, which subsequently became the National Assembly. Before the National Assembly could write a constitution for France, the king gathered his army in Paris with the purpose of dissolving the assembly. The people of Paris responded by attacking the Bastille—a prison—on July 14, 1789.

The National Assembly proceeded to pass laws to bring about social, economic, and political reforms in France. However, the revolution had sparked counterrevolutionary movements within France and attacks from Britain, Austria, and Prussia. In 1795 the

58   UNIT 3

—— Unit Summary gives overview of time period.

Timeline text offers background information on timeline events and suggested points for discussion.

Revolution went into the phase known as the Reign of Terror. Persons even suspected of being enemies of the Revolution were guillotined. Insurrections within France were put down, and an army was equipped to defend France against attacks.

In 1795 the Reign of Terror was replaced with the Directorate. The Directorate appointed a young Corsican soldier, Napoleon, to lead the armies of France. By 1799 he had become head of a new government that was in fact a dictatorship. In 1800, by treaty with Spain, France acquired Louisiana. Napoleon dreamed of reestablishing France's North American empire. But military setbacks caused him to sell Louisiana to the United States in 1803.

By 1807 Napoleon's authority extended to most of continental Europe. His downfall began when he invaded Russia in 1812. Although he occupied Moscow, the Russians refused to make peace. Napoleon retreated after five weeks, but cold, snow, and hunger crippled his army. Napoleon's downfall concluded with his defeat by the Duke of Wellington at the Battle of Waterloo, fought in Belgium in 1815.

The revolutions in America and France encouraged later revolutions in Latin America. Starting in 1810, Mexican mestizos and Indians fought Spanish rule for a decade. Finally, in 1821, Mexico won its freedom from Spain. In 1822 Portugal granted Brazil's demands for independence. In South America, Simon Bolívar, a Venezuelan soldier and revolutionary leader, freed Colombia, Venezuela, Ecuador, Peru, and Bolivia from Spanish rule between 1819 and 1825.

The decades after 1770 also were the time of transition between classicism and Romanticism in architecture and the arts. The classical style emphasized balance and order, as in works from ancient Greece and Rome. A good example of the classical style in the United States is the capitol.

At the end of the Classical Era, Charles Gibbon published the *Decline and Fall of the Roman Empire*, an outstanding historical work. Lucidly written, it connects the decline of the Roman Empire to Rome's lack of intellectual freedom.

Wolfgang Amadeus Mozart was one of the world's greatest composers. Before his death in 1791 at the age of thirty-five, he wrote more than six hundred works, including symphonies, church music, and operas. *The Magic Flute* was Mozart's last opera. Its theme—the triumph of enlightenment over superstition—was consonant with classical style.

If Mozart had lived longer, his style might have changed, as did that of Ludwig van Beethoven. The first compositions of Beethoven, who was fourteen years younger than Mozart, were classical in their proportions, but soon his compositions reflected the grandiose and passionate style of the Romantics. The

romantic style—in music, art, literature, and architecture—took as its themes nature, nationalism, and sometimes medieval events. Beethoven's "Eroica" symphony was originally dedicated to Napoleon but was later retitled by Beethoven because of Napoleon's decline into despotism.

The play *Faust* by Johann Wolfgang von Goethe is the story of a medieval scholar seeking ultimate wisdom. To find it, he makes a bargain with the devil. Faust, a representative of western civilization, unceasingly strives for knowledge, i.e. science, and yet searches for the simple faith of earlier times.

The Fairy Tales, by Jakob and Wilhelm Grimm, reflects the nineteenth-century interest in the past, particularly in those parts of the cultural experience that make a people or nation unique. Their fairy tales included such favorites as *Cinderella*, *Snow White*, and *Rumpelstiltskin*. Jakob Grimm was a philologist and linguist. Wilhelm was a literary scholar. It was Wilhelm who was most interested in collecting traditional folk tales and giving them a literary form.

Mary Shelley's novel *Frankenstein* expresses sympathy to a monster created by science. This theme reflected the romanticists' suspicion that science and technology were creating monsters rather than solving human problems.

While artists were rejecting much of the classical legacy of the eighteenth century, the scientists built on it. Lavoisier's Table of the Elements formed the basis of modern chemistry. Edward Jenner's introduction of smallpox vaccination was one of the major discoveries of western medical science. Jenner, having observed that milkmaids were immune to smallpox, used the cowpox virus to inoculate against smallpox. Alessandro Volta, an Italian physicist, perfected the battery in 1800 and thus was a pioneer in the field of electrochemistry.

UNIT ILLUSTRATION

Young women of the past spent hours learning ornamental needlework. To show their progress, they produced samplers like the one pictured, which is about 20 by 20 inches (50 by 50 centimeters). The background fabric is wool. The figures are made of silk thread in ten different types of stitches. Thus, the sampler exemplified the artist's skill in stitchery and functioned as a reference when planning the decoration on gowns, handbags, and so on.

The artist's name, Maria Bolen, appears in the upper left of the sampler, and the phrase "Her Work 1816" appears in the upper right. Because a feeling of nationalism had spread through the nation after the War of 1812, it was especially appropriate for Maria Bolen to include the American eagle—a patriotic motif.

UNIT 3   59

Illustration text offers helpful background information on the artist, work of art, and related historical events.

CHAPTER PREVIEW

CHAPTER 7

THE WAR FOR INDEPENDENCE

CHAPTER PREVIEW

PLANNING DATA

Text Features

Approaches to Reading: "Main Ideas and Topic Sentences" (text page 161). See the second "Text Reinforcement" activity for Section 1.

Using the Tools of History: "Using Scale on Maps" (text page 166). See the second "Text Reinforcement" activity for Section 2.

American Values in Action: "Deborah Sampson" (text page 172). See the first "Extension and Enrichment" activity for Section 3.

Chapter Summary: Chapter Timeline (text page 179). After students have completed the chapter, use the timeline to review events that occurred between the years 1775 and 1785.

Text Skills Focus

Section 1: Sequencing events, interpreting a document, writing memoirs

Worksheet 33: "The Outbreak of War: Recalling Information"

Worksheet 34: "*Common Sense:* Finding Main Ideas and Topic Sentences"

Section 2: Making predictions, researching details, making maps

Worksheet 35: "The War in the North: Organizing Information"

Worksheet 36: "The Revolutionary War 1775–1776: Using Scale on Maps"

Section 3: Analyzing information, writing epitaphs, analyzing primary sources, writing historical fiction

Worksheet 37: "People of the War for Independence: Recalling Information"

Section 4: Applying information, writing letters, analyzing character traits

Worksheet 38: "Ending the War: Synthesizing Information"

INTRODUCING THE CHAPTER

Read to the class this quotation from Thomas Paine's *The Crisis, Number 1.*

> These are the times that try men's souls. The summer soldier and the sunshine patriot will, in this crisis, shrink from the service of his country; but he that stands it now deserves the love and thanks of man and woman. Tyranny ... is not easily conquered; yet ... the harder the conflict, the more glorious the triumph. What we obtain too cheap, we esteem too lightly. ... Britain ... has declared that she has a right (not only to) tax but "to bind us in all cases whatsoever," and if being bound in that manner is not slavery; then is there not such a thing as slavery upon earth.

Discuss this passage with students, explaining any difficult words. Tell the class that Paine, an Englishman, had come to America in 1774. He believed in the Patriots' cause and wrote pamphlets to win colonists to it. One of Paine's main ideas was that the colonists were struggling not only for themselves but for the universal principle of freedom. How the Americans won their freedom is the subject of this chapter.

CHAPTER OUTLINE

I. Beginning of the War
  A. Battles of Lexington and Concord
  B. Battle of Bunker Hill
  C. Second Continental Congress
  D. Quebec and Dorchester Heights
  E. Move toward independence
  F. Declaration of Independence

II. War in the North
  A. British advantages and disadvantages
  B. Washington's struggle
  C. British capture of New York

CHAPTER 7 51

Chapter number

Chapter title

Introducing the Chapter provides a means of initiating study.

Chapter text features and skills are highlighted for ease in teacher planning.

Student text and worksheets are immediately correlated.

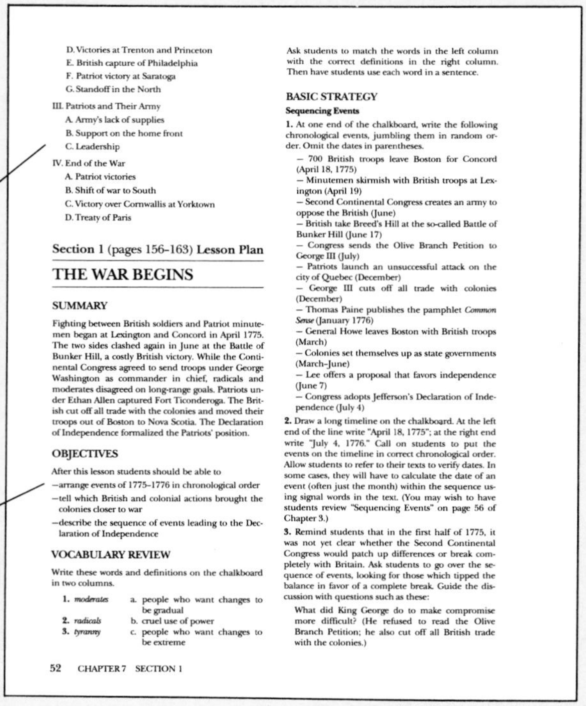

  D. Victories at Trenton and Princeton
  E. British capture of Philadelphia
  F. Patriot victory at Saratoga
  G. Standoff in the North

III. Patriots and Their Army
  A. Army's lack of supplies
  B. Support on the home front
  C. Leadership

IV. End of the War
  A. Patriot victories
  B. Shift of war to South
  C. Victory over Cornwallis at Yorktown
  D. Treaty of Paris

Section 1 (pages 156–163) Lesson Plan

THE WAR BEGINS

SUMMARY

Fighting between British soldiers and Patriot minutemen began at Lexington and Concord in April 1775. The two sides clashed again in June at the Battle of Bunker Hill, a costly British victory. While the Continental Congress agreed to send troops under George Washington as commander in chief, radicals and moderates disagreed on long-range goals. Patriots under Ethan Allen captured Fort Ticonderoga. The British cut off all trade with the colonies and moved their troops out of Boston to Nova Scotia. The Declaration of Independence formalized the Patriots' position.

OBJECTIVES

After this lesson students should be able to

—arrange events of 1775–1776 in chronological order

—tell which British and colonial actions brought the colonies closer to war

—describe the sequence of events leading to the Declaration of Independence

VOCABULARY REVIEW

Write these words and definitions on the chalkboard in two columns.

1. *moderates*	a. people who want changes to be gradual
2. *radicals*	b. cruel use of power
3. *tyranny*	c. people who want changes to be extreme

Ask students to match the words in the left column with the correct definitions in the right column. Then have students use each word in a sentence.

BASIC STRATEGY

Sequencing Events

1. At one end of the chalkboard, write the following chronological events, jumbling them in random order. Omit the dates in parentheses.

– 700 British troops leave Boston for Concord (April 18, 1775)
– Minutemen skirmish with British troops at Lexington (April 19)
– Second Continental Congress creates an army to oppose the British (June)
– British take Breed's Hill at the so-called Battle of Bunker Hill (June 17)
– Congress sends the Olive Branch Petition to George III (July)
– Patriots launch an unsuccessful attack on the city of Quebec (December)
– George III cuts off all trade with colonies (December)
– Thomas Paine publishes the pamphlet *Common Sense* (January 1776)
– General Howe leaves Boston with British troops (March)
– Colonies set themselves up as state governments (March–June)
– Lee offers a proposal that favors independence (June 7)
– Congress adopts Jefferson's Declaration of Independence (July 4)

2. Draw a long timeline on the chalkboard. At the left end of the line write "April 18, 1775"; at the right end write "July 4, 1776." Call on students to put the events on the timeline in correct chronological order. Allow students to refer to their texts to verify dates. In some cases, they will have to calculate the date of an event (often just the month) within the sequence using signal words in the text. (You may wish to have students review "Sequencing Events" on page 56 of Chapter 3.)

3. Remind students that in the first half of 1775, it was not yet clear whether the Second Continental Congress would patch up differences or break completely with Britain. Ask students to go over the sequence of events, looking for those which tipped the balance in favor of a complete break. Guide the discussion with questions such as these:

What did King George do to make compromise more difficult? (He refused to read the Olive Branch Petition; he also cut off all British trade with the colonies.)

52 CHAPTER 7 SECTION 1

Convenient chapter outline highlights events.

Lesson planning is outlined by skills.

LESSON PLANS

D. Victories at Trenton and Princeton
E. British capture of Philadelphia
F. Patriot victory at Saratoga
G. Standoff in the North

III. Patriots and Their Army
A. Army's lack of supplies
B. Support on the home front
C. Leadership

IV. End of the War
A. Patriot victories
B. Shift of war to South
C. Victory over Cornwallis at Yorktown
D. Treaty of Paris

Section 1 (pages 156–163) Lesson Plan

THE WAR BEGINS

SUMMARY

Fighting between British soldiers and Patriot minutemen began at Lexington and Concord in April 1775. The two sides clashed again in June at the Battle of Bunker Hill, a costly British victory. While the Continental Congress agreed to send troops under George Washington as commander in chief, radicals and moderates disagreed on long-range goals. Patriots under Ethan Allen captured Fort Ticonderoga. The British cut off all trade with the colonies and moved their troops out of Boston to Nova Scotia. The Declaration of Independence formalized the Patriots' position.

OBJECTIVES

After this lesson students should be able to
—arrange events of 1775–1776 in chronological order
—tell which British and colonial actions brought the colonies closer to war
—describe the sequence of events leading to the Declaration of Independence

VOCABULARY REVIEW

Write these words and definitions on the chalkboard in two columns.

1. *moderate*   a. people who want changes to be gradual
2. *radicals*   b. cruel use of power
3. *tyranny*   c. people who want changes to be extreme

Ask students to match the words in the left column with the correct definitions in the right column. Then have students use each word in a sentence.

BASIC STRATEGY

Sequencing Events

1. At one end of the chalkboard, write the following chronological events, jumbling them in random order. Omit the dates in parentheses.

— 700 British troops leave Boston for Concord (April 18, 1775)
— Minutemen skirmish with British troops at Lexington (April 19)
— Second Continental Congress creates an army to oppose the British (June)
— British take Breed's Hill at the so-called Battle of Bunker Hill (June 17)
— Congress sends the Olive Branch Petition to George III (July)
— Patriots launch an unsuccessful attack on the city of Quebec (December)
— George III cuts off all trade with colonies (December)
— Thomas Paine publishes the pamphlet *Common Sense* (January 1776)
— General Howe leaves Boston with British troops (March)
— Colonies set themselves up as state governments (March–June)
— Lee offers a proposal that favors independence (June 7)
— Congress adopts Jefferson's Declaration of Independence (July 4)

2. Draw a long timeline on the chalkboard. At the left end of the line write "April 18, 1775"; at the right end write "July 4, 1776." Call on students to put the events on the timeline in correct chronological order. Allow students to refer to their texts to verify dates. In some cases, they still have to calculate the date of an event (often just the month) within the sequence using signal words in the text. (You may wish to have students review "Sequencing Events" on page 56 of Chapter 3.)

3. Remind students that in the first half of 1775, it was not yet clear whether the Second Continental Congress would patch up differences or break completely with Britain. Ask students to go over the sequence of events, looking for those which tipped the balance in favor of a complete break. Guide the discussion with questions such as these:

What did King George do to make compromise more difficult? (He refused to read the Olive Branch Petition; he also cut off all British trade with the colonies.)

Each Lesson Plan corresponds to one section of student text.

Section title

Brief summary of section

Lesson objectives provide specific learning outcomes.

Teaching method offers an aid to students' mastery of vocabulary.

What actions did the Patriots take that made compromise more difficult? (They skirmished at Lexington, seized Fort Ticonderoga, set up new state governments, and declared their independence.)

4. Have students copy the timeline on their own paper. You may also wish to have several students copy it onto a long piece of paper for use in a classroom bulletin board display.

SUPPLEMENTARY STRATEGIES

Text Reinforcement

Recalling Information

Duplicate Worksheet 33, "The Outbreak of War," and distribute copies to students. Instruct students to do as much of the crossword puzzle as they can without referring to their texts. Review correct answers with students. Then discuss how each person, place, or document named in the puzzle contributed to the outbreak of the War for Independence.

Finding Main Ideas and Topic Sentences

Have students study the Approaches to Reading feature. Then review the topic sentences that students identified in the paragraphs under the heading "Moving Toward Independence." Also review topic sentences that students wrote for the paragraph at the end of the feature.

Duplicate Worksheet 34, *Common Sense*," and distribute copies to students. Go over the paragraph on the worksheet with students to be sure they understand the meaning, especially of the final three sentences. Then have students write answers to the questions. Review students' answers.

Extension and Enrichment

Interpreting a Document

In the Declaration of Independence, Thomas Jefferson lists almost thirty specific grievances against King George III (text pages 525–527). Assign one grievance to each student in the class. Students should read carefully and then rewrite the statements in their own words. Tell students to refer to the annotations. Also ask students to explain how the king's actions harmed the colonists. Instruct students to give specific examples from the text whenever possible.

Writing Memoirs

Ask students to choose one of the following figures and write that person's memoir of the event listed next to each figure.

— a minuteman: North Bridge in Concord
— General Howe: Breed's Hill
— John Dickinson: George III refused to read the Olive Branch Petition
— Benedict Arnold: left Canada in early 1776

Remind students that memoirs often contain opinions and interpretations of events. Students should include such opinions and interpretations wherever they are appropriate.

Section 2 (pages 164–169) Lesson Plan

THE WAR IN THE NORTH

SUMMARY

As the Revolution began, the Patriots seemed like David to the Goliath of Britain. With little training, ammunition, or supplies, the small Continental Army took on the large, well-trained, and well-supplied British forces. After losses on Long Island and Manhattan, Washington withdrew his troops through New Jersey to Pennsylvania. Crossing back over the Delaware River, he was victorious over the British at the Battles of Trenton and Princeton. Americans were not able to prevent British capture of Philadelphia, however. When the Patriots defeated the British at Saratoga, France decided to ally itself openly with the Americans. Washington led his troops to victory at Monmouth Court House in New Jersey, turning the war in the North into a standoff.

OBJECTIVES

After this lesson students should be able to
—tell the outcome of the Revolutionary War battles in the North between 1776 and 1778
—give reasons for American victories and defeats
—describe the impact of each battle on the war
—explain why the war in the North turned into a prolonged standoff

VOCABULARY REVIEW

Write these words on the chalkboard: *mercenaries, campaign, alliance.* Ask the class to look up the meaning of these words as they are defined in the text. Then call on students to give a modern example of each word.

BASIC STRATEGY

Organizing Information

1. Ask students to name advantages and disadvantages the British and American forces had at the beginning of the Revolutionary War. Write students' responses on the chalkboard. (The British had the

---

Supplementary teaching strategies reinforce and extend the text.

Strategies support the text's skills development program.

Basic teaching strategy covers main lesson topics.

WORKSHEETS

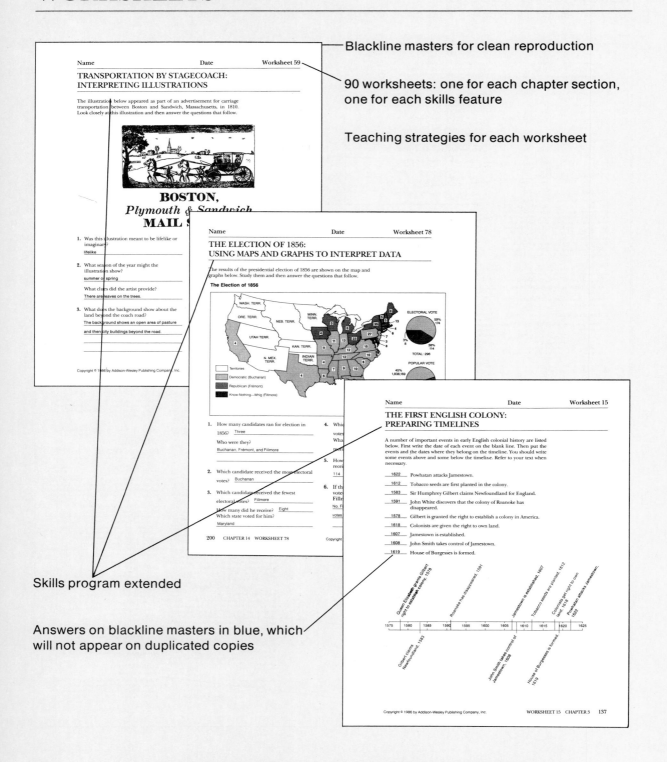

Blackline masters for clean reproduction

90 worksheets: one for each chapter section, one for each skills feature

Teaching strategies for each worksheet

Skills program extended

Answers on blackline masters in blue, which will not appear on duplicated copies

TESTS

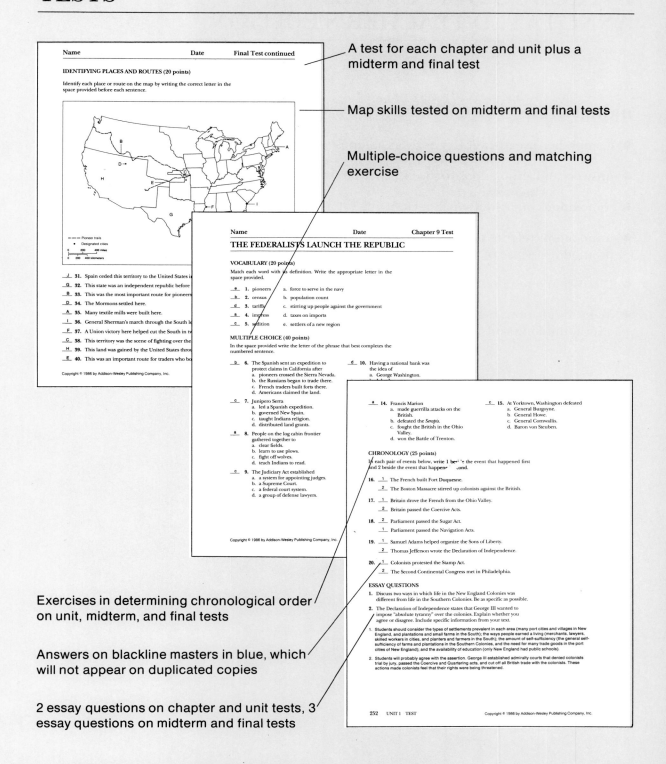

A test for each chapter and unit plus a midterm and final test

Map skills tested on midterm and final tests

Multiple-choice questions and matching exercise

Exercises in determining chronological order on unit, midterm, and final tests

Answers on blackline masters in blue, which will not appear on duplicated copies

2 essay questions on chapter and unit tests, 3 essay questions on midterm and final tests

---

Name   Date   Final Test continued

IDENTIFYING PLACES AND ROUTES (20 points)

Identify each place or route on the map by writing the correct letter in the space provided before each sentence.

  J   **31.** Spain ceded this territory to the United States in

  G   **32.** This state was an independent republic before

  B   **33.** This was the most important route for pioneers

  D   **34.** The Mormons settled here.

  A   **35.** Many textile mills were built here.

  I   **36.** General Sherman's march through the South le

  F   **37.** A Union victory here helped cut the South in tw

  C   **38.** This territory was the scene of fighting over the

  H   **39.** This land was gained by the United States throu

  E   **40.** This was an important route for traders who bo

Copyright © 1986 by Addison-Wesley Publishing Company, Inc.

Name   Date   Chapter 9 Test

THE FEDERALISTS LAUNCH THE REPUBLIC

VOCABULARY (20 points)

Match each word with its definition. Write the appropriate letter in the space provided.

  e   **1.** pioneers   a. force to serve in the navy

  b   **2.** census   b. population count

  d   **3.** tariffs   c. stirring up people against the government

  a   **4.** impress   d. taxes on imports

  c   **5.** sedition   e. settlers of a new region

MULTIPLE CHOICE (40 points)

In the space provided write the letter of the phrase that best completes the numbered sentence.

  b   **6.** The Spanish sent an expedition to protect claims in California after
    a. pioneers crossed the Sierra Nevada.
    b. the Russians began to trade there.
    c. French traders built forts there.
    d. Americans claimed the land.

  c   **7.** Junipero Serra
    a. led a Spanish expedition.
    b. governed New Spain.
    c. taught Indians religion.
    d. distributed land grants.

  a   **8.** People on the log cabin frontier gathered together to
    a. clear fields.
    b. learn to use plows.
    c. fight off wolves.
    d. teach Indians to read.

  c   **9.** The Judiciary Act established
    a. a system for appointing judges.
    b. a Supreme Court.
    c. a federal court system.
    d. a group of defense lawyers.

  d   **10.** Having a national bank was the idea of
    a. George Washington.

Copyright © 1986 by Addison-Wesley Publishing Company, Inc.

---

  a   **14.** Francis Marion
    a. made guerrilla attacks on the British.
    b. defeated the *Serapis.*
    c. fought the British in the Ohio Valley.
    d. won the Battle of Trenton.

  c   **15.** At Yorktown, Washington defeated
    a. General Burgoyne.
    b. General Howe.
    c. General Cornwallis.
    d. Baron von Steuben.

CHRONOLOGY (25 points)

In each pair of events below, write 1 beside the event that happened first and 2 beside the event that happened second.

16. 1 The French built Fort Duquesne.
    2 The Boston Massacre stirred up colonists against the British.

17. 1 Britain drove the French from the Ohio Valley.
    2 Britain passed the Coercive Acts.

18. 2 Parliament passed the Sugar Act.
    1 Parliament passed the Navigation Acts.

19. 1 Samuel Adams helped organize the Sons of Liberty.
    2 Thomas Jefferson wrote the Declaration of Independence.

20. 1 Colonists protested the Stamp Act.
    2 The Second Continental Congress met in Philadelphia.

ESSAY QUESTIONS

1. Discuss two ways in which life in the New England Colonies was different from life in the Southern Colonies. Be as specific as possible.

2. The Declaration of Independence states that George III wanted to impose "absolute tyranny" over the colonies. Explain whether you agree or disagree. Include specific information from your text.

1. Students should consider the types of settlements prevalent in each area (many port cities and villages in New England, and plantations and small farms in the South); the ways people earned a living (merchants, lawyers, skilled workers in cities, and planters and farmers in the South); the amount of self-sufficiency (the general self-sufficiency of farms and plantations in the Southern Colonies, and the need for many trade goods in the port cities of New England); and the availability of education (only New England had public schools).

2. Students will probably agree with the assertion. George III established admiralty courts that denied colonists trial by jury, passed the Coercive and Quartering acts, and cut off all British trade with the colonists. These actions made colonists feel that their rights were being threatened.

252   UNIT 1 TEST   Copyright © 1986 by Addison-Wesley Publishing Company, Inc.

INTRODUCTION TO THE TEACHER'S RESOURCE MANUAL   T 19

INTRODUCTION TO THE
ANNOTATED TEACHER'S EDITION

HIGHLIGHTS

- Comprehensive Answer Key answers all questions posed in the text.

- Answers and annotations reduce teacher preparation time.

- Annotations offer additional or clarifying information.

- Annotations refer to events and issues in other chapters and units, promoting a sense of the continuity of American history.

- Discussion questions facilitate teaching and learning.

- Many annotations highlight activities and questions that foster critical thinking skills.

ANNOTATIONS

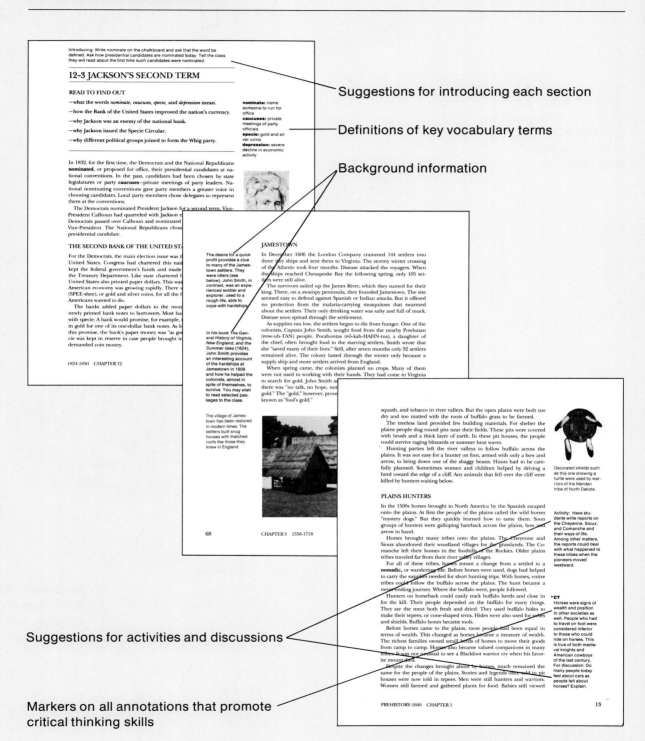

Suggestions for introducing each section

Definitions of key vocabulary terms

Background information

Suggestions for activities and discussions

Markers on all annotations that promote critical thinking skills

Introducing: Write *nominate* on the chalkboard and ask that the word be defined. Ask how presidential candidates are nominated today. Tell the class they will read about the first time such candidates were nominated.

12-3 JACKSON'S SECOND TERM

READ TO FIND OUT

—what the words *nominate, caucuses, specie,* and *depression* mean.

—how the Bank of the United States improved the nation's currency.

—why Jackson was an enemy of the national bank.

—why Jackson issued the Specie Circular.

—why different political groups joined to form the Whig party.

nominate: name someone to run for office
caucuses: private meetings of party officials
specie: gold and silver coins
depression: severe decline in economic activity

In 1832, for the first time, the Democrats and the National Republicans **nominated**, or proposed for office, their presidential candidates at national conventions. In the past, candidates had been chosen by state legislatures or party **caucuses**—private meetings of party leaders. National nominating conventions gave party members a greater voice in choosing candidates. Local party members chose delegates to represent them at the conventions.

The Democrats nominated President Jackson for a second term. Vice-President Calhoun had quarreled with Jackson e[...] Democrats passed over Calhoun and nominated [...] Vice-President. The National Republicans chose [...] presidential candidate.

THE SECOND BANK OF THE UNITED STA[...]

For the Democrats, the main election issue was t[...] United States. Congress had chartered this nati[...] kept the federal government's funds and made [...] the Treasury Department. Like state chartered b[...] United States also printed paper dollars. This was [...] American economy was growing rapidly. There w[...] (SPEE-shee), or gold and silver coins, for all the [...] Americans wanted to do.

The banks added paper dollars to the mon[...] newly printed bank notes to borrowers. Most ba[...] with specie. A bank would promise, for example, [...] in gold for one of its one-dollar bank notes. As lo[...] this promise, the bank's paper money was "as go[...] cie was kept in reserve in case people brought in [...] demanded coin money.

1824-1850   CHAPTER 12

JAMESTOWN

The desire for a quick profit provides a clue to many of the Jamestown settlers. They were idlers (see below). John Smith, in contrast, was an experienced soldier and explorer, used to a rough life, able to cope with hardships.

In his book *The General History of Virginia, New England, and the Summer Isles* (1624), John Smith provides an interesting account of the hardships at Jamestown in 1608 and how he helped the colonists, almost in spite of themselves, to survive. You may wish to read selected passages to the class.

The village of Jamestown has been restored in modern times. The settlers built snug houses with thatched roofs like those they knew in England.

In December 1606 the London Company crammed 144 settlers into three tiny ships and sent them to Virginia. The stormy winter crossing of the Atlantic took four months. Disease attacked the voyagers. When the ships reached Chesapeake Bay the following spring, only 105 settlers were still alive.

The survivors sailed up the James River, which they named for their king. There, on a swampy peninsula, they founded Jamestown. The site seemed easy to defend against Spanish or Indian attacks. But it offered no protection from the malaria-carrying mosquitoes that swarmed about the settlers. Their only drinking water was salty and full of muck. Disease soon spread through the settlement.

As supplies ran low, the settlers began to die from hunger. One of the colonists, Captain John Smith, sought food from the nearby Powhatan (pow-uh-TAN) people. Pocahontas (pō-kah-HAHN-tus), a daughter of the chief, often brought food to the starving settlers. Smith wrote that she "saved many of their lives." Still, after seven months only 32 settlers remained alive. The colony lasted through the winter only because a supply ship and more settlers arrived from England.

When spring came, the colonists planted no crops. Many of them were not used to working with their hands. They had come to Virginia to search for gold. John Smith s[...] there was "no talk, no hope, no[...] gold." The "gold," however, prove[...] known as "fool's gold."

68   CHAPTER 3   1556-1718

squash, and tobacco in river valleys. But the open plains were both too dry and too matted with the roots of buffalo grass to be farmed.

The treeless land provided few building materials. For shelter the plains people dug round pits near their fields. These pits were covered with brush and a thick layer of earth. In these pit houses, the people could survive raging blizzards or summer heat waves.

Hunting parties left the river valleys to follow buffalo across the plains. It was not easy for a hunter on foot, armed with only a bow and arrow, to bring down one of the shaggy beasts. Hunts had to be carefully planned. Sometimes women and children helped by driving a herd toward the edge of a cliff. Any animals that fell over the cliff were killed by hunters waiting below.

Decorated shields such as this one showing a turtle were used by warriors of the Mandan tribe of North Dakota.

PLAINS HUNTERS

In the 1500s horses brought to North America by the Spanish escaped onto the plains. At first the people of the plains called the wild horses "mystery dogs." But they quickly learned how to tame them. Soon groups of hunters were galloping bareback across the plains, bow and arrow in hand.

Horses brought many tribes onto the plains. The Cheyenne and Sioux abandoned their woodland villages for the grasslands. The Comanche left their homes in the foothills of the Rockies. Older plains tribes traveled far from their river valley villages.

For all of these tribes, horses meant a change from a settled to a **nomadic**, or wandering life. Before horses were used, dogs had helped to carry the supplies needed for short hunting trips. With horses, entire tribes could follow the buffalo across the plains. The hunt became a never-ending journey. Where the buffalo went, people followed.

Hunters on horseback could easily track buffalo herds and close in for the kill. Their people depended on the buffalo for many things. They ate the meat both fresh and dried. They used buffalo hides to make their tepees, or cone-shaped tents. Hides were also used for robes and shields. Buffalo bones became tools.

Before horses came to the plains, most people had been equal in terms of wealth. This changed as horses became a measure of wealth. The richest families owned small herds of horses to move their goods from camp to camp. Horses also became valued companions in many tribes. It was not unusual to see a Blackfoot warrior cry when his favorite mount died.

Despite the changes brought about by horses, much remained the same for the people of the plains. Stories and legends once told in pit houses were now told in tepees. Men were still hunters and warriors. Women still farmed and gathered plants for food. Babies still viewed

Activity: Have students write reports on the Cheyenne, Sioux, and Comanche and their ways of life. Among other matters, the reports could deal with what happened to these tribes when the pioneers moved westward.

*CT
Horses were signs of wealth and position in other societies as well. People who had to travel on foot were considered inferior to those who could ride on horses. This is true of both medieval knights and American cowboys of the last century. For discussion: Do many people today feel about cars as people felt about horses? Explain.

PREHISTORY-1600   CHAPTER 1   13

INTRODUCTION TO THE ANNOTATED TEACHER'S EDITION   T 21

ANSWER KEY

Complete sentences to give quick understanding of answers

Clear references to the text

Answers to all section reviews as well as all chapter reviews and unit reviews

Answers to all skills features

4. New Yorkers complained they were "enslaved" because they did not have an elected assembly.

5. West Jersey joined East Jersey in 1702.

6. William Penn founded Pennsylvania as a refuge for Quakers.

7. Before it became a separate colony, Delaware was originally a part of Pennsylvania.

Section 4-3 Review (text page 103)

1. See definitions on text page 98.

2. *Nathaniel Bacon:* leader of Bacon's Rebellion in Virginia in 1676. *George Calvert:* founder of Maryland as a place where Catholics could worship in freedom. *Cecilius Calvert:* son of George who carried out his father's plan. *Maryland Toleration Act:* act giving both Catholics and Protestants the right to religious freedom in Maryland. *James Edward Oglethorpe:* founder of Georgia.

3. Many colonists in Virginia paid for the voyages of new settlers in order to receive 50 acres of land for each settler.

4. Calvert wanted the Maryland Toleration Act to be passed because he feared that the Protestant majority in Maryland would take away the religious freedom of the colony's Catholics.

5. Many colonists left Georgia in the 1730s because James Oglethorpe did not allow people in Georgia to own more than 50 acres of land, and slavery was not allowed. Next door, South Carolina did not limit land or slave ownership.

Using the Tools of History: Using Circle and Line Graphs (text page 105)

1. The population in 1770 was about 2,150,000.

2. The population grew to more than 600,000 by the year 1730.

3. The most people were added to the colonial population during the period from 1760 to 1770.

4. Of the years shown, the percentage of blacks in the colonial population was smallest in 1640.

5. Of the years shown, the percentage of blacks in the colonial population was largest in 1760.

6. The graph should show a "slice" of about one eighth of the circle, labeled "12 percent black."

Section 4-4 Review (text page 108)

1. See definitions on text page 104.

2. *Pennsylvania Dutch:* Germans living in Pennsylvania. *Back country:* land stretching along the Appalachians from the southern border of Pennsylvania into Georgia. *Great Philadelphia Wagon Road:* narrow road extending through the back country. *Scotch-Irish:* Scots who had lived in Ireland.

3. There was a growing demand for slaves in North America because of the success of tobacco and rice plantations in the colonies.

4. Large plantations were located along rivers so that ships could bring slaves and other goods directly to the plantations and take out barrels of rice or tobacco.

5. The Pennsylvania Dutch usually settled in groups, the Scotch-Irish as separate families.

6. The main building on a plantation was the planter's house; in Albany, a fort; in a typical New England Village, the church.

CHAPTER SURVEY (text pages 110–111)

Vocabulary Review

1. (h)	**6.** (m)	**11.** (l)
2. (b)	**7.** (d)	**12.** (k)
3. (e)	**8.** (f)	**13.** (i)
4. (j)	**9.** (a)	
5. (g)	**10.** (c)	

Chapter Review

1. (a) Some English Separatists moved to the Netherlands to escape harsh treatment in England. (b) The Separatists who sailed to America were called Pilgrims because they were traveling for religious purposes.

2. (a) The mission of the leaders of Massachusetts was to build a community based on God's laws as an example to the rest of the world. (b) Self-government was important to their mission because they wanted to make rules to assure that everyone in their colony lived by God's laws.

3. Rhode Island's leaders, unlike Massachusetts's, paid the Indians for their land, welcomed people of all faiths, and did not try to force their religious beliefs on others.

CHAPTER 4   ANSWER KEY

T 31

ANSWER KEY

CHAPTER 1

Approaches to Reading: Previewing (text page 6)

1. Answers will vary. Many students will think of Indians or Ice-Age hunters.

Section 1–1 Review (text page 8)

1. See definitions on text page 2.

2. The Bering Strait lies between Asia and North America.

3. As glaciers grew, more water was trapped in them, and the sea level fell.

4. Accept any two of the following: Farming provided more food. It let many people live in one area. That change allowed people to build cities.

5. Accept any three of the following: The Maya built cities, including public plazas lined with pyramids, temples, ball courts, and palaces, and they developed arts, a system of government, a written language, and an accurate calendar.

6. The Aztec controlled the Valley of Mexico.

7. The Inca empire was linked by roads.

Using the Tools of History: Analyzing Change and Continuity (text page 14)

1. The middle part, where the circles overlap, shows continuity.

2. The right and left sides show change.

3. People changed from using dogs to using horses to carry goods.

4. No, plains people did not change their use of bows and arrows after the arrival of horses.

Section 1–2 Review (text page 14)

1. See definitions on text page 9.

2. The earliest woodland people obtained food by hunting and foraging. By A.D. 1000 woodland people had also learned to farm.

3. The Algonquian and Iroquois controlled areas in the northern woodlands.

4. The ancestors of the Muskogean people are called mound builders.

5. The Hopewell culture produced jewelry, pipes, and mounds.

6. Plains Indian women did the farming.

7. Horses brought a nomadic way of life to the plains, because on horseback entire tribes could follow the buffalo long distances.

Section 1–3 Review (text page 18)

1. See definitions on text page 15.

2. The southwestern people got water for farming by using dams and canals.

3. In the winter the Great Basin foragers ate food they had stored.

4. Oaks were important to California Indians because they yielded acorns, a food staple.

5. The goods at a potlatch were given away.

6. To survive, the Arctic people cooperated and shared food.

CHAPTER SURVEY (text pages 20–21)

Vocabulary Review

1. (b) **3.** (c) **5.** (b) **7.** (a)
2. (a) **4.** (b) **6.** (c)

Chapter Review

1. (a) During the Ice Age the sea level fell. (b) The Bering Strait area became dry land. (c) Animals could have walked between Asia and North America over the land bridge. (d) People would have traveled from Asia to North America to follow game.

2. (a) Hunting became more difficult about 10,000 years ago because many kinds of game animals disappeared. (b) People survived by foraging. (c) People in Mexico more than 8,000 years ago began developing farming. (d) Farming let many people live in one place, so they could work together to build cities.

3. (a) About A.D. 900 the Maya abandoned their cities. (b) The Aztec rose to power about 500 years later. (c) Their system of roads allowed the Inca to control a huge empire.

4. (a) Woodland people traveled on lakes and rivers because forests were hard to walk through. (b) The Huron kept the Iroquois from traveling anywhere they wished north of the Great Lakes.

5. (a) The Hopewell culture developed first. (b) The Hopewell culture spread farther north. (c) Cahokia represented the Mississippian culture.

6. (a) People stampeded the buffalo over cliffs, and hunters waiting below killed the buffalo. (b) Plains people before the 1500s lived mainly by farming because they had no easy way to hunt buffalo. (c) Plains tribes after the 1500s traveled most of the time to follow herds of buffalo.

7. (a) Plains farmers before the 1500s used pit houses for shelter. After the 1500s they often used tepees. (b) Tepees were smaller than longhouses, they were cone-shaped, and they were not built mainly of wood. (c) Tepees were smaller than pueblos, they were cone-shaped, and they were not built mainly of stone.

8. (a) The Anasazi developed pueblos. (b) The Zuñi and Hopi were living in pueblos in A.D. 1500. (c) Groups in the Southwest differed in language.

9. People in the Great Basin did not live in permanent shelters because they had to travel often to find food. (b) People in the Great Basin used more kinds of food plants because no single plant provided a lot of food.

10. (a) A chief in the Northwest who owned extra goods could give a potlatch in order to show off his wealth. (b) A hunter in the Arctic who had extra food would share it in order to help the group survive.

Geography Review

1. (a) Eight regions are shown on the map. (b) Florida is in the Gulf-Atlantic Coastal Plain. (c) The southern Great Lakes are in the Interior Plains. (d) The Appalachian Highlands region contains a long series of low and rounded mountains. The region containing the most rugged mountains is the Rocky Mountains. The Pacific Mountains and Valleys region contains the mountains that are farthest west.

2. (a) The words that show the location of the Iroquois are the names of the five tribes: Mohawk, Oneida, Onondaga, Cayuga, and Seneca. (b) The Cheyenne, Sioux, and Comanche are in the Plains region. (c) Three names of tribes appear in the Great Basin region. Nine names of tribes appear in the California region.

Using the Tools of History

1. The correct headings for each item are these:
(a) Both (c) Before (e) While
(b) While (d) Both (f) Before

2. "Before" matches the left part of the diagram, "While" matches the right part, and "Both" matches the middle.

Reading and Thinking Skills

1. (a) Two ways to find vocabulary words are to look at the first "Read to Find Out" statement and to look for the words in very heavy type in the text. (b) The quickest way is to look at the first "Read to Find Out" statement. (c) Phrases giving the meanings of the vocabulary words appear next to the words. (d) The Glossary also gives the meanings.

2. (a) All three landforms are flat. (b) A mesa is smaller than a plateau and has steep sides. (c) Answers will vary. Acceptable answers include: A plateau may have trees. It is raised above surrounding lands, unlike tundra. A plateau may be hot rather than frozen. It may be dry rather than wet.

CHAPTER 2

Section 2–1 Review (text page 29)

1. See definitions on text page 22.

2. *Leif Ericson:* leader of the Norse expedition to Vinland. *Marco Polo:* Italian who traveled in China in the late 1200s and dictated an account of his adventures. *Prince Henry the Navigator:* prince of Portugal who gathered information about sea travel and sent expeditions south along the African coast during the 1400s. *Vasco da Gama:* Portuguese sea captain who followed the route of Dias around Africa and went on to open a new trade route to Asia.

3. In the 800s and 900s, the Norse people built settlements in Iceland and Greenland.

4. The Norse abandoned Vinland because they were tired of warfare with the Indians.

5. The Crusaders brought Indian cotton goods, Chinese silks, and pepper, cloves, and cinnamon back to Europe.

6. Marco Polo told Europeans that spices came from the Spice Islands, south of the mainland of Asia.

7. Merchants wanted to pay lower prices for products by buying directly from Asians.

8. Accept any three of the following improvements: better maps, better navigational tools such as improvements in the compass and astrolabe, and the development of the caravel.

Using the Tools of History: Making Timelines (text page 36)

1–4. The completed timeline should look like the one at the bottom of this page.

5. Answers will vary. One possibility is "European Voyages of Exploration 1492–1635."

Section 2-2 Review (text page 38)

1. See definitions on text page 30.

2. *Queen Isabella:* Spanish queen who, in 1492, provided funds for Columbus's first voyage. *Pedro Álvarez Cabral:* Portuguese seaman who claimed Brazil for Portugal in 1500. *Amerigo Vespucci:* Italian merchant whose name was given to the lands he called a new world. *Vasco Núñez de Balboa:* Spanish explorer who, in 1513, became the first European to see the Pacific Ocean from the American shore.

3. In the Caribbean, Columbus discovered San Salvador, Cuba, and Jamaica.

4. Columbus's first voyage was important because it started the greatest migration in human history.

5. From Magellan's trip, Europeans learned that a great ocean lay between the Americas and Asia.

6. When they searched for the Northwest Passage, European explorers hoped to find a shorter sea route to Asia.

Section 2-3 Review (text page 43)

1. See definitions on text page 39.

2. *Juan Ponce de León:* conquistador who discovered Florida in 1513, while he was looking for the Fountain of Youth. *Hernando Cortés:* conquistador who conquered the Aztec empire. *Francisco Pizarro:* conquistador who conquered the Inca empire. *Bartolomé de Las Casas:* Spanish priest who tried to stop cruel treatment of South American Indians.

3. Malinche and local Indians hostile to the Aztec helped Cortés to defeat the Aztec.

4. The fact that the Inca were fighting among themselves helped Pizarro to defeat them.

5. Encomenderos had the right to use Indians as laborers and the duty to protect them.

6. African slaves were brought to Caribbean islands in the early 1500s because there were almost no Indians left to serve as laborers.

Section 2-4 Review (text page 48)

1. See definition on text page 44.

2. *Álvar Núñez Cabeza de Vaca:* survivor of the Narváez expedition who wrote an account of his eight-year journey from Florida to northern Mexico. *Estevanico:* African slave who traveled with Cabeza de Vaca, guided de Niza's expedition, and was killed on that expedition. *Juan de Oñate:* Spaniard who founded the province of New Mexico in 1598. *Eusebio Francisco Kino:* priest who explored Arizona and founded the first missions there.

3. The Spanish had trouble planting settlements in Florida because of Indian attacks.

4. Spanish settlers had to leave New Mexico because of the Pueblo Revolt.

5. The voyage of Juan Rodríguez Cabrillo in 1542 gave Spain a claim to California.

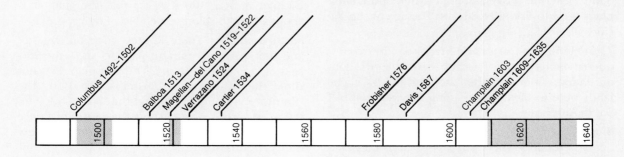

CHAPTER SURVEY (text pages 50–51)

Vocabulary Review

1. (e)	**6.** (i)	**11.** (c)
2. (b)	**7.** (f)	**12.** (a)
3. (k)	**8.** (l)	**13.** (d)
4. (g)	**9.** (h)	
5. (m)	**10.** (j)	

Chapter Review

1. (a) Norse artifacts discovered on Newfoundland and Norse sagas support the claim that the Norse reached America before Columbus. (b) News of Norse voyages did not reach most Europeans because news traveled slowly, if at all; news of Vinland had no practical importance to Europeans other than the Norse.

2. (a) Peasants were protected by the lord of the manor where they lived. (b) The lord of the manor served a more powerful lord, such as a duke or earl. (c) The system was feudalism.

3. (a) The purpose of the Crusades was to free Palestine from Muslim rule. (b) The Crusaders did not achieve their goal. (c) Trade goods from the Indies brought Christians and Muslims together.

4. (a) Marco Polo's account was about India, China, Japan, and the Spice Islands. (b) A water route would allow merchants to buy directly from Asians at lower prices than Muslim traders charged. (c) In the 1400s, Portugal led the search for a water route.

5. (a) Columbus's goal was to reach the Indies. (b) His voyages were a failure in that he did not reach the Indies. (c) His voyages were a success in that he reached lands then unknown to Europeans and started the largest migration in human history.

6. (a) Balboa found the Pacific Ocean in 1513. (b) Magellan reached the Pacific by sailing around South America. (c) Verrazano, Cartier, and Champlain tried to find a Northwest Passage to the Pacific.

7. (a) Hernando Cortés and Francisco Pizarro conquered lands of great wealth. (b) The two conquistadors conquered the Aztec and the Inca. The lands were in Mexico and along the west coast of South America.

8. (a) Conquistadors were conquerors. Encomenderos were landowners. (b) Missionaries educated Indians in the Catholic faith and in Spanish ways. Encomenderos treated the Indians as slaves.

9. (a) Indians told Spaniards about the Fountain of Youth and the Seven Cities of Cíbola. (b) Conquistadors reacted by searching for these places. (c) By encouraging Spanish exploration, the stories increased Spanish land claims.

10. (a) Coronado was looking for a rich kingdom. (b) He found only the plains. (c) Coronado's findings and similar lack of success by other explorers north of Mexico slowed settlement there.

Geography Review

1. The Norse found Iceland and Greenland before they found Vinland.

2. Italian merchants sailed across the Mediterranean to buy silks and spices from Muslim traders.

3. The Portuguese sent expeditions along the *western* coast of Africa.

4. Cartier and Champlain explored the St. Lawrence River.

5. Ponce de León explored the Florida peninsula.

6. Cabrillo's route was the only all-water route, and it was the farthest west.

Using the Tools of History

1. The events given have these dates:

(a) 1539	(c) 1542	(e) 1680
(b) 1540	(d) 1598	(f) 1692

2. Answers will vary. One possibility for a title is "The Pueblo People and Spanish Explorers and Settlers 1539–1672."

Reading and Thinking Skills

1. These words suggest that the chapter is about trade, sea routes, and exploration.

2. The map "New France 1720" on page 62 is in Chapter 3. The title suggests that the chapter is about a French colony called New France.

3. (a) Both the "Trade Routes" map on page 27 and the "Voyages" map on page 33 show the voyages of Dias and da Gama. The first map does not show the Americas or Australia. (b) Both the "Routes" map on page 40 and the "Spanish Exploration" map on page 45 show the routes of Ponce de León and Cortés. The second map shows very little of South America.

CHAPTER 3

Approaches to Reading: Sequencing Events
(text page 56)

1. The three signal words are *first, after,* and *meanwhile.* The calendar marker is 1588.

2. Event (b) occurred first. The word *after* in the sentence "After two years of preparation the Armada was ready" shows that Philip decided to conquer England before the Armada was ready. If students are puzzled by the phrase "the time had come to conquer England," point out that Philip was considering the rivalry between Spain and England in terms of years, not months or days.

3. The only calendar marker in the last paragraph is *1598.* The two signal words are *after* and *now.*

4. The three signal words are *then, soon,* and *next.* The two calendar markers are 1578 and 1579.

5. Event (b) occurred first.

Section 3-1 Review (text page 57)

1. See definitions on text page 52.

2. *Elizabeth I:* queen of England who led her nation against Philip II of Spain. *Francis Drake:* English sea raider who plundered Spanish ships, sailed around the world, and helped to defeat the Spanish Armada.

3. Colonies could improve a nation's balance of trade as a source of raw materials and as a market for the nation's manufactured goods.

4. England and the Netherlands became Protestant nations. Spain remained Catholic.

5. Sea raiders from England, the Netherlands, and France attacked Spain's empire in the Americas.

6. The Armada's defeat was important to the nations of northwestern Europe because they could more easily plant colonies across the Atlantic after Spain's defeat.

Using the Tools of History: Using Map Symbols (text page 63)

1. The symbol that represents forts is pictorial.

2. On this map a dot represents a settlement.

3. The route of Marquette and Joliet is different from the route of La Salle in color, as shown in the legend, and the two routes are labeled on the map.

4. The possessions of Spain, England, and France are shown by different colors in the legend and on the map.

5. Answers will vary. Pictorial symbols should look similar to the features they represent.

Section 3-2 Review (text page 64)

1. See definitions on text page 58.

2. *Samuel de Champlain:* geographer-explorer who founded Quebec, the beginning of New France. *Coureurs de bois:* French fur traders, or "forest runners," who traveled great distances. *Jean Nicolet:* French explorer who built a trading post at the present-day site of Green Bay, Wisconsin. *Sieur de La Salle:* French fur trader and explorer who claimed Louisiana for France.

3. The fur trade brought the French to Canada.

4. Marquette and Joliet hoped the Mississippi River would take them to the Pacific Ocean.

5. The Spanish built forts at Pensacola and San Antonio to keep the French out of Florida and Texas.

Section 3-3 Review (text page 72)

1. See definitions on text page 65.

2. *Sir Walter Raleigh:* Englishman who encouraged colonies in America and founded the "lost colony" of Roanoke. *Virginia Dare:* first English child born in America. *John Smith:* soldier who took charge of Jamestown and forced the colonists to plant crops. *Pocahontas:* daughter of a chief of the Powhatan who brought food to the starving settlers at Jamestown. *Lord De La Warr:* governor of Jamestown whose arrival prevented the colonists from abandoning the colony.

3. The colony founded on Roanoke Island in 1587 disappeared with scarcely a trace.

4. The Jamestown settlers faced the hardships of disease, bad water, hunger, and Indian attacks.

5. Rolfe helped Jamestown by introducing a tobacco that was popular in England.

6. The three events that helped Jamestown in 1618 and 1619 were the granting to the colonists of the right to own land, the arrival of women, and the establishment of a representative assembly, the House of Burgesses.

7. Poor English people could afford to come to Virginia as indentured servants.

8. The first representative assembly in the Americas was the House of Burgesses.

Section 3–4 Review (text page 76)

1. See definition on text page 73.

2. *Henry Hudson:* English explorer who claimed the Hudson River for the Dutch in 1609. *Peter Minuit:* governor of New Netherland who bought Manhattan and started the colony of New Sweden. *Peter Stuyvesant:* governor of New Netherland.

3. The Dutch came to the Hudson River valley to trade for furs.

4. The southern tip of Manhattan Island was the finest natural harbor on the Atlantic coast. It allowed control of the fur trade on the Hudson River.

5. Asher Levy won the right to serve as a soldier, buy land, and start a business.

6. New Sweden became a part of New Netherland when Peter Stuyvesant seized the Swedish settlements there.

CHAPTER SURVEY (text pages 78–79)

Vocabulary Review

1. (h)	**5.** (i)	**9.** (e)	**13.** (f)
2. (m)	**6.** (b)	**10.** (c)	**14.** (d)
3. (j)	**7.** (a)	**11.** (n)	
4. (l)	**8.** (g)	**12.** (k)	

Chapter Review

1. (a) Europe's rulers sought a favorable balance of trade so that more gold would flow into their treasuries, allowing them to strengthen their armies and navies. (b) Spain's empire in America was valuable because it was producing gold and silver as well as tobacco, cocoa, and sugar.

2. (a) Philip II used his army to force Protestants back into the Catholic religion. (b) French, English, and Dutch sea raiders attacked Spanish ships because they wanted Spanish gold. Spain was also the religious enemy of England and the Netherlands.

3. (a) The purpose of the Invincible Armada was to conquer England. (b) The defeat of the Armada made sea routes safer for the English, Dutch, and French, which made it easier for them to plant col-

onies in the Americas. (c) The English, Dutch, and French did not start North American colonies close to Florida because the Spanish were still strong enough to threaten new colonies there.

4. (a) Furs attracted the French to America. (b) The French offered trade goods, did not take Huron land, and helped the Huron against the Iroquois. (c) The Company of New France had trouble settling the St. Lawrence valley because newcomers could make more money in the fur trade than they could as settled farmers.

5. (a) La Salle wanted to establish a colony at the mouth of the Mississippi to expand the French fur trade and to have a base for attacking the Spanish in the Gulf of Mexico. (b) The French built forts along the Great Lakes and the Mississippi to guard the network of waterways that held their empire together. (c) The French empire in North America was weak because the French were spread too thinly over a vast area.

6. (a) The English government wanted to gain a favorable balance of trade from colonies in America. (b) English monarchs encouraged colonization by granting charters to individuals and companies, who set up colonies.

7. (a) The London Company financed its colony by selling shares in the company to investors. (b) The company planned to make a quick profit by having colonists look for gold and silver in Virginia. (c) This plan harmed the colony because the colonists spent their time searching for gold rather than planting the crops they needed for survival.

8. The London Company attracted more settlers to Jamestown by letting colonists own land, by sending women to the colony, and by letting the colonists have a voice in government through a representative assembly.

9. (a) Virginia's valuable crop was tobacco. (b) This crop led to war with the Indians because tobacco planters began to take Indian lands. (c) King James I made Virginia a royal colony after Indians had destroyed much of the colony, making it impossible for the London Company to earn a profit or pay its debts.

10. (a) Furs, especially beaver furs, attracted the Dutch to North America. (b) The Iroquois traded with the Dutch for weapons to use against the Huron and the French.

Geography Review

1. Drake sailed to the western coast of South America through the Straits of Magellan.

2. Many sea raiders went to the Caribbean Sea to capture Spanish treasure.

3. The homeland of the Huron was between Lake Huron and Quebec.

4. Marquette and Joliet followed the Fox, the Wisconsin, and the Mississippi Rivers to reach the mouth of the Arkansas River.

5. The St. Lawrence River was the most important in the founding of the first French settlement in North America, the James River was the most important in the founding of the first English settlement, and the Hudson River was the most important in the founding of the first Dutch settlement.

Using the Tools of History

1. The timeline should show the beginning of the Roanoke colony in 1587, the defeat of the Armada in 1588, the founding of Jamestown in 1607, the founding of Quebec in 1608, and the founding of New Amsterdam in 1626.

2. Answers will vary. One possibility is "Events in the Struggle for Power Among the Nations of Northwestern Europe."

3. (a) a pueblo; (b) a mission and presidio; (c) a mission.

Reading and Thinking Skills

(a) The signal words are *recently, as, then, when,* and *just as.* The calendar markers are *late 1608, the fall of 1609, the winter of 1609–1610, spring,* and *in June.*

(b) The order of events from the time John Smith took control to the time of Lord De La Warr's arrival is: Smith took control; he forced the colonists to plant crops; he was injured and returned to England; the colonists almost starved; they sailed down the James River to return to England; they met De La Warr and returned to Jamestown.

UNIT SURVEY (text pages 80–81)

Unit Review

1. (a) The first Americans probably came from Asia, or, more exactly, Siberia. (b) They probably reached Alaska first. (c) They could have walked there. (d) They could have walked across a land bridge between Asia and North America.

2. (a) The first Americans obtained food by hunting. (b) After many kinds of animals died out, people relied on foraging. (c) People slowly developed farming. (d) Farming allowed populations to grow more rapidly than in the past.

3. (a) Families lived in longhouses in the Eastern Woodland. (b) People lived in tepees on the plains. (c) People lived in pueblos in the Southwest. (d) Longhouses were made of logs, tepees were made of buffalo hides, and pueblos were made of stone.

4. (a) According to a Norse saga, Leif Ericson found Vinland, which is probably the land known today as Newfoundland. (b) According to Marco Polo's book, he knew about China, India, Japan, and the Spice Islands. (c) Marco Polo's story spread through Europe in the 1300s. (d) Merchants were interested in learning the source of spices and other trade goods from Asia.

5. (a) In the 1300s and 1400s, Muslim traders controlled routes east of the Mediterranean Sea. (b) By the end of the 1400s, the nations of England, France, Spain, and Portugal had developed in western Europe. (c) Portugal was the leader in sea travel along the coast of Africa. (d) Portugal wanted to send ships around Africa to open more profitable trade routes to Asia.

6. (a) When Columbus sailed west in 1492, he hoped to reach the Far East, or the Indies. (b) The islands he reached are in the Caribbean Sea. (c) Magellan first sailed from the Atlantic to the Pacific. (d) Explorers searched for a Northwest Passage because they hoped to find an easier route from the Atlantic to the Pacific. (e) Conquistadors hoped to find gold and other treasure.

7. (a) Spain's American colonies produced gold and silver, more valuable than tobacco, cocoa, and sugar. (b) The gold and silver were shipped to Spain. (c) The wealth helped Spain build its army and navy. (d) Mercantilism was the name of the theory that nations gained power through trade.

8. (a) The French called their lands in North America New France. (b) Furs were most valuable to the French. (c) The French used the St. Lawrence River in their early trade. (d) They used the Mississippi to extend their trade network.

9. (a) The Roanoke colony disappeared, and no one knows what happened to it. (b) The first settlers at Jamestown hoped to find gold. (c) Tobacco from the Jamestown area turned out to be a valuable product in trade. (d) In 1624 Virginia became a royal colony.

10. (a) The Hudson River was the most important to Dutch settlement in America. (b) The main Dutch city in America was New Amsterdam. (c) New Amsterdam was on Manhattan Island. (d) The Delaware River was the most important to the settlement of New Sweden.

Linking the Past and the Present

1. Answers will vary.

2. All of the state names have Indian sources except Indiana, a modern Latin term for "land of the Indians."

3. Answers will vary. Students who describe space exploration should be asked to compare it to old-fashioned exploration on earth.

Meeting the Builders of America

1. Answers will vary. Students may note the value of federation for the Iroquois, Sister Juana Inés de la Cruz's quest for education, and the compassion shown by Pocahontas.

2. Reports will vary.

CHAPTER 4

Section 4–1 Review (text page 92)

1. See definitions on text page 84.

2. *John Winthrop:* first governor of Massachusetts. *Thomas Hooker:* early leader in Connecticut. *Fundamental Orders of Connecticut:* the first written constitution in the colonies. *Roger Williams:* leader of Rhode Island after his banishment from Massachusetts. *Anne Hutchinson:* helped to found Portsmouth, Rhode Island, after her banishment from Massachusetts. *John Mason:* first proprietor of New Hampshire. *Ferdinando Gorges:* first proprietor of Maine.

3. The Pilgrims wrote the Mayflower Compact to give them a basis for self-government in New England, which was beyond the bounds of their permit to start a colony.

4. Winthrop meant that the Puritans in Massachusetts would set an example for the rest of the world.

5. People from Massachusetts settled in Connecticut and Rhode Island to find good farm land and to have religious freedom.

6. New Hampshire became independent of Massachusetts before Maine did.

Approaches to Reading: Outlining (text page 94)

1. Five main ideas are outlined, as shown by the numbers 1 through 5, and eight details are outlined, as shown by the letters a, b, c.

2. Answers will vary in details. Correct answers should be similar to the following:
B. New Jersey
    1. Duke of York grants area to John Berkeley and George Carteret in 1664
    2. Puritans and Quakers attracted to New Jersey
      a. Quakers followers of George Fox
      b. New Jersey a haven to them
    3. Colony divided in 1676, reunited in 1702
C. Pennsylvania
    1. Founded by William Penn
      a. King owed money to Penn's father
      b. King paid by giving land to Penn
    2. Penn wanted to try "Holy Experiment"
      a. He assured religious freedom
      b. He treated Indians fairly
    3. Philadelphia founded as main city
      a. It was a good port
      b. Ships brought settlers from many lands
D. Delaware
    1. Penn received title to land in 1682
    2. Delaware had own assembly but was ruled by governor of Pennsylvania

Section 4–2 Review (text page 97)

1. See definition on text page 93.

2. *Duke of York:* proprietor of New York. *Jacob Leisler:* leader of a rebellion in New York. *John Berkeley:* one of the first two proprietors of New Jersey. *George Carteret:* the other of the first two proprietors of New Jersey. *William Penn:* Quaker leader and proprietor of Pennsylvania.

3. Four English warships captured New Amsterdam; then English forces captured the rest of New Netherland, renaming it New York.

4. New Yorkers complained they were "enslaved" because they did not have an elected assembly.

5. West Jersey joined East Jersey in 1702.

6. William Penn founded Pennsylvania as a refuge for Quakers.

7. Before it became a separate colony, Delaware was originally a part of Pennsylvania.

Section 4-3 Review (text page 103)

1. See definitions on text page 98.

2. *Nathaniel Bacon:* leader of Bacon's Rebellion in Virginia in 1676. *George Calvert:* founder of Maryland as a place where Catholics could worship in freedom. *Cecilius Calvert:* son of George who carried out his father's plan. *Maryland Toleration Act:* act giving both Catholics and Protestants the right to religious freedom in Maryland. *James Edward Oglethorpe:* founder of Georgia.

3. Many colonists in Virginia paid for the voyages of new settlers in order to receive 50 acres of land for each settler.

4. Calvert wanted the Maryland Toleration Act to be passed because he feared that the Protestant majority in Maryland would take away the religious freedom of the colony's Catholics.

5. Many colonists left Georgia in the 1730s because James Oglethorpe did not allow people in Georgia to own more than 50 acres of land, and slavery was not allowed. Next door, South Carolina did not limit land or slave ownership.

Using the Tools of History: Using Circle and Line Graphs (text page 105)

1. The population in 1770 was about 2,150,000.

2. The population grew to more than 600,000 by the year 1730.

3. The most people were added to the colonial population during the period from 1760 to 1770.

4. Of the years shown, the percentage of blacks in the colonial population was smallest in 1640.

5. Of the years shown, the percentage of blacks in the colonial population was largest in 1760.

6. The graph should show a "slice" of about one eighth of the circle, labeled "12 percent black."

Section 4-4 Review (text page 108)

1. See definitions on text page 104.

2. *Pennsylvania Dutch:* Germans living in Pennsylvania. *Back country:* land stretching along the Appalachians from the southern border of Pennsylvania into Georgia. *Great Philadelphia Wagon Road:* narrow road extending through the back country. *Scotch-Irish:* Scots who had lived in Ireland.

3. There was a growing demand for slaves in North America because of the success of tobacco and rice plantations in the colonies.

4. Large plantations were located along rivers so that ships could bring slaves and other goods directly to the plantations and take out barrels of rice or tobacco.

5. The Pennsylvania Dutch usually settled in groups, the Scotch-Irish as separate families.

6. The main building on a plantation was the planter's house; in Albany, a fort; in a typical New England Village, the church.

CHAPTER SURVEY (text pages 110–111)

Vocabulary Review

1. (h)	**6.** (m)	**11.** (l)
2. (b)	**7.** (d)	**12.** (k)
3. (e)	**8.** (f)	**13.** (i)
4. (j)	**9.** (a)	
5. (g)	**10.** (c)	

Chapter Review

1. (a) Some English Separatists moved to the Netherlands to escape harsh treatment in England. (b) The Separatists who sailed to America were called Pilgrims because they were traveling for religious purposes.

2. (a) The mission of the leaders of Massachusetts was to build a community based on God's laws as an example to the rest of the world. (b) Self-government was important to their mission because they wanted to make rules to assure that everyone in their colony lived by God's laws.

3. Rhode Island's leaders, unlike Massachusetts's, paid the Indians for their land, welcomed people of all faiths, and did not try to force their religious beliefs on others.

4. (a) Colonists in New York were unhappy with their government under the Duke of York because they were not allowed to have an elected assembly. (b) After the rebellion of 1689, New Yorkers set up an assembly to make laws for their colony. (c) The rebellion shows that the colonists saw self-government as an important right.

5. (a) William Penn acquired Pennsylvania from the king as payment for a debt owed originally to Penn's father. (b) Penn kept peace with the local Indians by visiting with them and by paying them for their land. (c) To attract settlers, Penn offered toleration, an elected assembly, peaceful relations with the Indians, and a fine port city.

6. (a) The headright system encouraged rapid settlement by giving Virginians a reason to pay for the passage of more settlers. (b) Indentured servants did field work for Virginia tobacco planters in the early years of the colony. (c) Slaves were doing most field work for the planters by the late 1600s. (d) This change took place because indentured servants would work for a few years only, but slaves would work all their lives and so would the slaves' children.

7. (a) The Calverts' goals in founding Maryland were to provide a haven for Catholics and to make a profit. (b) When the goal of providing a haven for Catholics was threatened, the Maryland assembly passed the Toleration Act to protect the right of all Christians to worship in peace.

8. (a) James Oglethorpe's two goals in founding Georgia were to create a refuge for England's poor and to protect the Carolinas from Spanish attacks. (b) Oglethorpe ruled that settlers could have no more than 500 acres of land and no slaves. (c) The rules were changed by 1750 because many settlers left Georgia rather than submit to them.

9. (a) Families left Europe in the 1600s because of poverty, religious wars, and homelessness. (b) Many emigrants were attracted to the colonies by cheap land, religious freedom, and a chance to improve their lives.

10. (a) Plantations worked by slaves were most likely to be found in the Southern Colonies. (b) People from many nations lived in the Middle Colonies. (c) People were most likely to live in villages organized around a church in the New England Colonies.

Geography Review

1. (a) The map shows that England, France, Spain, the Netherlands, and Sweden had settlements on or near the east coast of North America by 1650. (b) France had settlements farthest to the north. (c) Spain had settlements farthest to the south. (d) England had the largest area of settlement.

2. The New England Colonies were Maine, New Hampshire, Massachusetts, Connecticut, and Rhode Island. The Middle Colonies were New York, Pennsylvania, New Jersey, and Delaware. The Southern Colonies were Maryland, Virginia, North Carolina, South Carolina, and Georgia.

3. (a) The map shows that more settlement of the Carolinas and Georgia took place between 1700 and 1760. (b) Settlers moved to large areas of the Piedmont between 1700 and 1760. (c) The Hudson, Potomac, James, and Savannah Rivers are within the British colonies.

Using the Tools of History

(a) According to the graph, one out of every two colonists in the late 1700s was English. (b) 19.3 percent of the population was African. (c) The Scottish, German, and Scotch-Irish groups were about the same size.

Reading and Thinking Skills

Answers will vary in statements of main ideas and details. Answers should be similar to the following:
III. The Southern Colonies
   A. Virginia
      1. Headright system helped growth
      2. Planters needed many workers
         a. Indentured servants did most field work at first
         b. Slaves replaced servants
         c. Fewer former servants, then, could get good land
      3. Bacon led a rebellion in 1676
   B. Maryland
      1. George Calvert and son Cecilius Calvert founded colony
         a. They wanted a haven for Catholics
         b. They wanted profit
      2. By 1649 most colonists were Protestants
      3. Assembly passed Toleration Act
   C. The Carolinas
      1. Founded by eight nobles in 1663

2. Northern part settled first
3. Southern part flourished after 1690
4. The two parts split
   a. North Carolina had small farms
   b. South Carolina had large plantations producing rice, indigo, pitch, tar, and turpentine
D. Georgia
   1. Founded by James Edward Oglethorpe in 1732
      a. He wanted a haven for debtors
      b. He wanted to protect the Carolinas
   2. Oglethorpe limited land ownership and prohibited slavery
   3. Settlers moved to South Carolina
   4. Restrictions lifted by 1750
   5. Georgia became a royal colony in 1752

CHAPTER 5

Section 5-1 Review (text page 115)

1. See definitions on text page 112.

2. A farm family could live on ten dollars a year by growing the food and making the clothes and most other items that the family members needed.

3. Cooking was a dangerous job because of the weight of cooking pots and the heat of the fire.

4. A young person could learn a trade from a parent or as an apprentice to a skilled worker.

5. Massachusetts and Connecticut provided publicly supported education for all children. Colonists believed that everyone should be able to read the Bible.

Using the Tools of History: Locating Places on Maps (text page 119)

1. Ships carrying rum, guns, and iron from North America to Africa traveled southeast.

2. Ships going from the West Indies to England traveled northeast.

3. The African continent is south of Europe.

4. The latitude of the West Indies is about 20° north.

5. The latitude of London is about 50° north.

6. Most of Europe is in the eastern longitudes.

7. Ships traveled through about 30 degrees of latitude from the West Indies to London. (Students should note that 30 degrees is the difference between the latitudes of the two places, as given in the answers to questions 4 and 5.)

Section 5-2 Review (text page 120)

1. See definitions on text page 116.

2. *Navigation Acts:* laws to let England control trade with the colonies. *Benjamin Franklin:* printer, publisher, and deputy postmaster of the colonies. *Poor Richard's Almanac:* almanac published annually by Franklin.

3. Colonial cities were centers of information because trading ships brought news from other ports.

4. Rum, guns, and iron were shipped from North America to western Africa, where they were traded for slaves, gold, and pepper destined for the West Indies.

5. The Navigation Acts helped Boston shipbuilders because they required trading ships to be built in the colonies or England. Colonial shipbuilders did not have to compete with shipbuilders from any nation but England.

6. The Navigation Acts helped fill the royal treasury by ensuring that England would not need to pay out gold for raw materials that were produced in its own colonies.

Section 5-3 Review (text page 126)

1. See definitions on text page 121.

2. *Magna Carta:* charter limiting the rights of the English monarch, signed in 1215. *Glorious Revolution:* overthrow of James II in 1688 and adoption of a Bill of Rights in 1689. *House of Lords:* the branch of Parliament made up of nobles. *House of Commons:* the branch of Parliament made up of elected representatives.

3. The Glorious Revolution increased the power of Parliament through the Bill of Rights, which gave Parliament alone the right to pass laws, set taxes, and control England's military forces.

4. The colonists viewed their assemblies as small Parliaments, with the right to vote on laws and taxes affecting them.

5. Local governments in the colonies were controlled by the colonists themselves.

CHAPTER SURVEY (text pages 128–129)

Vocabulary Review

1. (a)	**5.** (a)	**9.** (a)	**13.** (b)
2. (c)	**6.** (c)	**10.** (a)	**14.** (a)
3. (b)	**7.** (a)	**11.** (a)	
4. (a)	**8.** (c)	**12.** (b)	

Chapter Review

1. (a) Goods were usually sent between colonial cities by ship. (b) Colonial roads were narrow and rutted. (c) Colonial farmers were self-sufficient in part because it was difficult to obtain goods from cities over the roads and—in most rural places—impossible to obtain goods by ship.

2. (a) Education was important to Puritans because they wanted their children to be able to read the Bible. (b) To promote education, Massachusetts passed laws requiring towns to provide schooling for all children. (c) Children in the Southern and Middle Colonies could learn to read from their parents, from tutors, or from teachers at church schools.

3. (a) Raw materials were exported from the colonies. (b) Manufactured goods were brought into the colonies. (c) Colonists were satisfied with this pattern of trade because they had much raw material to trade and they produced few manufactured goods of their own.

4. (a) The purpose of the Navigation Acts was to control trade with the colonies. (b) The Navigation Acts protected English exports to the colonies by taxing most exports from other nations. (c) The acts made goods imported from other nations more expensive, and the acts did nothing to lower the cost of goods imported from England.

5. Franklin helped colonists become better informed by publishing a newspaper and improving mail service.

6. (a) In the Glorious Revolution, English people won the right to trial by jury and the right to petition the government; Parliament won the right to pass laws without fear of a royal veto. (b) Zenger fought for freedom of the press.

7. (a) Colonial assemblies were like Parliament in that their members were elected to vote on laws and taxes. (b) Colonial assemblies were different

because their acts could be vetoed by the English monarch or by royal governors.

8. From their town meetings the colonists learned how to solve their own problems without help from the monarch or royal officials.

9. (a) White male landowners voted in colonial elections. (b) They usually elected aristocrats.

Geography Review

(a) The colonies in the Humid Subtropical Zone were North Carolina, South Carolina, and Georgia. (b) Answers will vary. Any two of the following are colonies that were mainly or entirely in the Continental Warm Summer Zone: Rhode Island, Connecticut, Pennsylvania, Maryland, Delaware, and Virginia. (c) Answers will vary. Any two of the following are colonies that were mainly or entirely in the Continental Cool Summer Zone: Maine, Massachusetts, New Hampshire, and New York.

Using the Tools of History

(a) Europe is northwest of Australia. (b) Maine is northeast of Mexico. (c) The line of latitude that divides the United States through the middle is 40° north. (d) The line of longitude that passes through the Hawaiian Islands is 160° west.

Reading and Thinking Skills

(a–c) Statements of main ideas and details will vary. Correct answers should be similar to these:
III. Colonial Government
  A. The Rights of English People
    1. Magna Carta signed in 1215
    2. Parliament gained power
      a. House of Lords has nobles
      b. House of Commons has elected representatives
    3. English people and Parliament gained more rights in Glorious Revolution
    4. American colonists claimed rights
  B. Colonial Assemblies
    1. Colonists saw assemblies as small Parliaments
    2. British government saw assemblies as under royal veto
  C. Local Governments
    1. Governments run entirely by colonists

2. Town meetings gave practice in democracy
    a. People decided local questions
    b. People did not need royal help
D. Colonial Elections
    1. Most candidates were aristocrats
    2. Candidates met voters
    3. Candidates learned to trust voters

CHAPTER 6

Section 6-1 Review (text page 136)

1. See definitions on text page 130.

2. *George Washington:* colonel in the Virginia militia who took part in trying to drive the French out of the Ohio Valley in 1754. *Fort Duquesne:* French fort built at the fork of the Ohio River in 1754. *James Wolfe:* British general who captured Quebec.

3. The French built forts in the Ohio Valley in the 1750s because they were alarmed by the arrival of fur traders from Pennsylvania and land speculators from Virginia.

4. The colonial assemblies rejected the Albany Plan of Union because they wanted to keep the power to tax for themselves.

5. Pitt's strategy was to let Britain's German allies fight the French in Europe while most of Britain's forces fought against the French in North America.

6. In the Treaty of Paris, Britain gained French Canada, Louisiana east of the Mississippi except New Orleans, and Florida.

Using the Tools of History: Identifying Points of View (text page 140)

1. This statement means that Parliament ("the British legislature") has power over colonial assemblies (which are part of "the whole British Empire"), so it expresses the British point of view.

2. This statement denies the right of Parliament to pass laws for people outside Britain, so it expresses the American point of view.

3. "When they ask for protection" here refers to the colonists asking for protection from the French and their Indian allies in the French and Indian War. The statement asks why the colonists should consider themselves English when they need help, but not when they are asked to pay for the help, so

it expresses the British viewpoint.

4. This statement asserts the "right of Englishmen" not to be taxed except with "their own consent," so it expresses the American viewpoint.

Section 6-2 Review (text page 141)

1. See definitions on text page 137.

2. *Proclamation Line of 1763:* boundary line along the crest of the Appalachians, designed to separate the colonies from the Indian lands to the west. *Pontiac:* Ottawa chief who led Indians in war against the British in 1763. *George Grenville:* minister of finance in the British government who tried to increase the collection of customs duties in the colonies.

3. Pontiac's Rebellion convinced Parliament that a large force of British troops was needed in America.

4. Grenville tried to stop smuggling by giving British customs officers the power to search colonial warehouses and ships, by setting up an admiralty court in Nova Scotia to try colonists accused of smuggling, and by ordering the British navy to patrol the Atlantic coast in search of smugglers.

5. Parliament passed the Sugar Act to increase tax revenues from the colonies.

6. The colonists claimed that Parliament had no right to tax them because the colonies had no representation in Parliament.

Section 6-3 Review (text page 147)

1. See definitions on text page 142.

2. *Stamp Act:* British act passed in 1765 to raise revenue by requiring colonists to use special stamps or stamped paper. *Sons and Daughters of Liberty:* American colonists who protested the Stamp Act and the Townshend Acts. *Samuel Adams:* member of the Massachusetts assembly who helped to organize the Sons of Liberty in Boston. *John Hancock:* wealthy Boston merchant who supported the Sons of Liberty and whose ship *Liberty* was seized by customs officers. *Boston Massacre:* flare-up of violence in 1770, in which British troops fired into a Boston mob, killing five people. *John Adams:* Massachusetts lawyer who defended the British soldiers involved in the Boston Massacre.

3. To unite against the Stamp Act, nine of the colonies sent delegates to the Stamp Act Congress in 1765, many colonists joined the Sons and Daughters of Liberty, and large numbers of colonists boycotted British goods.

4. The Declaratory Act said that Parliament had the power to pass laws for the colonies in all cases whatsoever.

5. The colonists protested against the Townshend Acts because the acts taxed the colonies by placing duties on glass, lead, paint, paper, and tea; set up a new admiralty court; and sent more customs officers to colonial ports.

6. The Boston Massacre changed colonists' views by making Britain seem a danger to their freedom.

Approaches to Reading: SQ3R (text page 149)

The study guide questions for Section 6-4 will vary. They should be similar to the following:

What were committees of correspondence?
What happened at the Boston Tea Party?
What were the Coercive Acts?
Why was the First Continental Congress formed?
What was the difference between a Patriot and a Loyalist?

Answers to the study guide questions will vary depending on the questions asked.

Section 6-4 Review (text page 152)

1. See definitions on text page 148.

2. *Mercy Otis Warren:* playwright and poet who defended colonial rights. *Thomas Hutchinson:* royal governor of Massachusetts. *Committees of correspondence:* groups set up in the colonies to communicate news about British actions. *Boston Tea Party:* event in 1773 in which Bostonians dumped tea into the harbor to protest the Tea Act. *Minutemen:* special militia groups formed in Massachusetts to answer a call to arms quickly.

3. The committees united the colonies by spreading news of British actions and Patriot protests.

4. Colonists protested the Tea Act because they feared a British monopoly over tea.

5. Accept any three of the following: The acts closed Boston Harbor, gave the Crown power to appoint the governor's council, gave the governor power to control or forbid town meetings, and protected British officials and soldiers.

6. The colonies responded to the Intolerable Acts by calling for a continental congress.

7. The First Continental Congress backed up its demands by threatening to cut off trade with Britain and to boycott British products.

CHAPTER SURVEY (text pages 154–155)

Vocabulary Review

1. (c)	**5.** (c)	**9.** (a)
2. (b)	**6.** (b)	**10.** (c)
3. (b)	**7.** (c)	**11.** (b)
4. (a)	**8.** (a)	**12.** (a)

Chapter Review

1. (a) The areas Britain gained after Queen Anne's War were Newfoundland, Nova Scotia, and Hudson Bay. (b) The areas Britain gained after the French and Indian War were French Canada, Louisiana east of the Mississippi except New Orleans, and Florida. (c) After the French and Indian War Spain gained Louisiana west of the Mississippi plus New Orleans.

2. Braddock, who refused to accept George Washington's warnings, learned the difference between war in America and war in Europe in the surprise attack in which he and a thousand of his men were killed.

3. (a) The purpose of the Proclamation of 1763 was to keep peace with the Indians west of the Appalachian crest. (b) Colonists protested because they could not move west or keep or sell their land claims there.

4. (a) Parliament raised taxes because the French and Indian War had left Britain with a large debt. (b) Parliament looked to the colonies for revenue because English people were already heavily taxed.

5. (a) Customs duties were levied by the Sugar Act of 1764. (b) Few colonists were troubled by customs duties because importers paid them. (c) Colonists were troubled by the Stamp Act because they paid this tax directly.

6. (a) Parliament passed the Declaratory Act to

state its right to make laws for the colonies. (b) The repeal of the Stamp Act seemed more important at the time.

7. The Townshend Acts led to rioting in Boston, which led to the sending of British troops to Boston, which led colonists to taunt the troops, which led to the massacre.

8. (a) Parliament reacted to the Boston Tea Party by passing the Coercive Acts. (b) The acts closed the port of Boston, gave more power over Massachusetts to the king and the royal governor, and gave British officials and soldiers accused of crimes in the colonies the right to be tried in Britain. (c) The acts were to be enforced by General Thomas Gage and his force of British soldiers.

9. (a) The colonists organized boycotts to protest the Stamp Act, the Townshend Acts, and the Coercive Acts. (b) The Stamp Act and the Townshend Acts were repealed.

10. By the winter of 1774, British troops controlled Boston but not the rest of the colony.

Geography Review

1. (a) The time span shown by the two maps is 1750 to 1763. (b) The French and Indian War and the Treaty of Paris account for the differences in the maps. (c) France lost the most land. (d) Britain gained the most land. (e) Russia's land claims stayed about the same.

2. (a) True, from the British point of view the war was a frontier war. (b) True, the British navy played an important role in the British victory. (c) False, not all the French forts had fallen by the end of the war.

Using the Tools of History

(a) The statement gives the Patriot view. (b) The statement gives the Loyalist view. (c) The statement gives the Patriot view.

Reading and Thinking Skills

(a) The five steps are survey, question, read, recite, and review. (b) This method turns headings into questions. (c) SQ3R, unlike outlining, also gives steps for studying. Both methods stress finding main ideas.

CHAPTER 7

Approaches to Reading: Main Ideas and Topic Sentences (text page 161)

Answers will vary. The best will be similar to these: "The Declaration of Independence listed the many wrongs done to the colonists by the British monarch." "Thomas Jefferson pointed the finger of blame at King George III." Other topic sentences may state more simply, "The Crown had done many wrongs to the colonists" or "The colonists had much to complain about."

Section 7-1 Review (text page 163)

1. See definitions on text page 156.

2. *Paul Revere* and *William Dawes:* riders sent to warn the minutemen that the British were on their way to Lexington and Concord. *William Howe:* British general who won a costly victory over the Patriots at Bunker Hill. *John Dickinson:* Pennsylvanian who persuaded the Second Continental Congress to send the Olive Branch Petition. *Ethan Allen:* Patriot who led the Green Mountain Boys in capturing Fort Ticonderoga. *Benedict Arnold:* colonel who led one of two forces in an unsuccessful attack on Quebec. *Thomas Paine:* author of the pamphlet *Common Sense,* which called for American independence. *Thomas Jefferson:* author of the Declaration of Independence.

3. British troops were sent to Concord to seize Patriot military supplies.

4. The victory at Bunker Hill cost the British more than a thousand soldiers, many of whom were officers.

5. The Continental Army was formed by the Second Continental Congress, which took control of the Patriot forces outside Boston.

6. King George III rejected the Olive Branch Petition because in his view it was written by an illegal congress.

7. The British left Boston in 1776 because Washington placed cannons on the hills above the city.

8. The Declaration of Independence said that American colonists had the right to rebel because the British government had failed to protect their natural rights.

Using the Tools of History: Using Scale on Maps (text page 166)

1. St. Leger traveled southwest from Montreal to Lake Ontario. He traveled approximately 190 miles (300 kilometers) upriver.

2. The Continental Army won the battles of Fort Stanwix and Saratoga.

3. Montreal is approximately 125 miles (200 kilometers) from Fort Ticonderoga.

4. After the battle at Trenton, Washington crossed the Delaware River. He was traveling southwest.

Section 7-2 Review (text page 169)

1. See definitions on text page 164.

2. *Nathan Hale:* American captain executed by the British for spying. *John Burgoyne:* British general who surrendered his entire army at Saratoga, New York. *Henry Clinton:* British general who replaced General William Howe as commander of the British forces in America.

3. The British hoped to destroy the Patriots' will to resist by defeating the Continental Army.

4. Washington faced the problems of shortages, poorly trained troops, little discipline, and short terms of enlistment.

5. American victories at Trenton and Princeton helped New Jersey Patriots regain their confidence.

6. The American victory at Saratoga was a turning point because it prompted France to enter the war against Britain openly.

Section 7-3 Review (text page 173)

1. See definitions on text page 170.

2. *Haym Salomon* and *Robert Morris:* bankers who helped provide supplies for the Continental Army. *Margaret Cochran Corbin:* soldier's wife who took her husband's place loading a cannon, was wounded, and later received a soldier's pension from Congress. *Marquis de Lafayette:* French noble who served as a major general in the Continental Army. *Baron von Steuben:* Prussian officer who helped train Washington's soldiers.

3. Congress could not provide more supplies for the army because it lacked the power to tax, and most states kept their money to spend on their own military forces.

4. Women helped the war effort by managing farms and workshops, by doing work in army camps, by serving as nurses, by carrying ammunition to soldiers in battle, and sometimes by joining in the fighting.

5. Congress and most states granted freedom to slaves who served in the armed forces.

Section 7-4 Review (text page 178)

1. See definition on text page 174.

2. *George Rogers Clark:* leader of frontier militia who prevented the British from gaining control of the Ohio Valley. *John Paul Jones:* Continental Navy captain who defeated the British warship *Serapis*. *Francis Marion:* guerrilla leader, known as the "Swamp Fox," who prevented the British from gaining control of South Carolina. *Nathanael Greene:* general who led American forces in the South against Cornwallis.

3. After France entered the war, the British tried to gain a foothold in the South.

4. General Cornwallis failed to gain control of the Carolinas because guerrillas attacked Loyalist militias and kept the British troops busy guarding their supply lines.

5. Cornwallis was trapped at Yorktown by a French fleet in Chesapeake Bay and by American and French troops on land.

6. From the Treaty of Paris the United States gained independence, the land from the Great Lakes to Florida and from the Appalachians to the Mississippi, and the right to use the Mississippi.

CHAPTER SURVEY (text pages 180–181)

Vocabulary Review

1. (b)	**4.** (h)	**7.** (i)
2. (d)	**5.** (g)	**8.** (f)
3. (c)	**6.** (a)	**9.** (e)

Chapter Review

1. (a) The moderates hoped the Olive Branch Petition would settle the differences between the colonies and Parliament. (b) Thomas Paine's pamphlet *Common Sense* undermined the colonists' feelings of loyalty to the king.

2. Jefferson wrote the Declaration for Americans, too, because many were still trying to decide whether to support the new governments being set up in the former colonies.

3. (a) The British had the advantages of a large population, a large, well-trained army, many mercenaries, and a powerful navy. (b) They had the disadvantages of fighting at a great distance from Britain and of trying to conquer a huge territory. (c) The British hoped to destroy the colonists' will to fight.

4. (a) The Americans had the advantages of familiarity with the land, a spirit of patriotism among the soldiers, and an able commander. (b) They had the disadvantages of shortages, undisciplined troops, poorly trained troops, short terms of enlistment, and a weak central government.

5. (a) The retreat of the Continental Army caused Loyalists in New Jersey to seize control of local governments, and it caused many Patriots there to change to the Loyalist side. (b) Loyalists in Georgia responded to the British capture of Savannah by coming out to support the British. (c) The Battle of King's Mountain caused back-country Loyalists to desert the British, and it caused Patriots to gain strength.

6. (a) In trying to keep up with inflation, many Patriots ignored the needs of their army. (b) Haym Salomon, Christopher Ludwig, and Sarah Smith all put their country's needs above their personal welfare. (c) Women helped the war effort by running farms and workshops, by cooking and mending in army camps, by carrying supplies and ammunition, and sometimes by fighting.

7. (a) Both Lafayette and von Steuben were foreigners who served as officers in the Continental Army. (b) Lafayette was from France and von Steuben was from Prussia.

8. (a) The British changed their strategy in 1778 because the French navy threatened their sugar islands in the West Indies. (b) Clinton abandoned Philadelphia because he feared an attack by the French navy. (c) Cornwallis could not escape from Yorktown by sea because Admiral De Grasse blocked the entrance to Chesapeake Bay.

9. (a) Guerrillas kept Cornwallis from gaining control of South Carolina. (b) They used hit and run tactics against regular army troops.

10. In the Treaty of Paris, the United States gained independence and the territory between the Appalachian Mountains and the Mississippi River north of Florida.

Geography Review

1. (a) To cut off New England, the British needed to capture the Hudson River Valley. (b) The British wanted New York because it was the finest deep harbor on the east coast, and it would give them a base for attacking north and south.

2. (a) Britain, Spain, France and Russia held territory in North America after the Treaty of Paris. (b) Spain held the most territory. (c) France held the least (two islands off Newfoundland).

Using the Tools of History

1. (a) Because it assumes that the Patriots cannot succeed "by force of arms," this statement has a Loyalist viewpoint. (b) The mention of "our union" and the possible need for "foreign assistance" indicates that this statement has a Patriot viewpoint.

2. (a) British forces marched northwest from Savannah to Augusta. (b) The forces traveled about 100 miles (160 kilometers). (c) The Battle of Cowpens was fought in South Carolina. (d) The battle was an American victory.

Reading and Thinking Skills

(a) The topic sentence of the first paragraph is its first sentence. (b) The topic sentence of the second paragraph is its first sentence. (c) The details that support the topic sentence of the second paragraph are that profiteers charged high prices for food and supplies, that they sold spoiled meat, and that they sold the army shoes that fell apart. (d) The topic sentence of the last paragraph is its last sentence.

UNIT SURVEY (text pages 182–183)

Unit Review

1. (a) William Bradford called the Separatists who founded Plymouth Colony Pilgrims. (b) Plymouth Colony eventually became part of Massachusetts. (c) Rhode Island and Connecticut were founded south of Massachusetts. (d) New Hampshire and Maine were taken over by Massachusetts.

2. (a) The Dutch called their colony New Netherland. (b) When the English seized the colony, its name became New York. (c) New Jersey and Pennsylvania were a haven to many Quakers. (d) Delaware had an assembly but no governor of its own.

3. (a) Bacon's Rebellion took place in Virginia. (b) Maryland was a haven to many Catholics. (c) North Carolina and South Carolina were formed from a single land grant. (d) Georgia was a haven to many debtors.

4. (a) Most colonists lived in rural places. (b) Colonists in cities were best informed about current events. (c) Answers may vary. Merchants, traders, and shipbuilders all relied strongly on the mercantile system. (d) These people, unlike plantation owners, lived in cities, were found in the North as well as the South, did not usually own large areas of land, did not usually own many slaves, etc.

5. (a) The colonists themselves were responsible for local governments in the colonies. (b) Colonial assemblies were responsible for paying the salaries of the royal governors.

6. (a) Britain needed money after the French and Indian War to pay war debts. (b) It seemed fair to Parliament to tax the colonies because British soldiers were protecting them. (c) The new taxation seemed unfair to many colonists because they were used to having their elected assemblies approve tax laws, not Parliament, in which they had no representation.

7. (a) The Sugar Act of 1764 and the Townshend Acts of 1767 called for customs duties. (b) To avoid these duties, the colonists boycotted British goods and at times relied on smuggled goods.

8. (a) Boston was the scene of violence connected to the Townshend Acts. (b) Massachusetts was the target of the Coercive Acts. (c) The Boston Tea Party caused Parliament to pass the Coercive Acts.

9. (a) Americans were slow to declare their independence because no colony of a European country had become independent before, and Americans were not sure they could avoid being seized by a foreign country. (b) *Common Sense* helped lead to the Declaration of Independence by overcoming fears of independence. (c) Loyalists opposed independence.

10. (a) France gave the most help to the Patriot war effort. (b) France could hurt its old rival Britain by helping the Patriots. (c) Britain lost a source of raw materials and a market for manufactured goods, weakening its ability to benefit from trade.

Linking the Past and the Present

1. Answers will vary. This activity may be extended to interviews to discover how workers have learned the skills they need.

2. Answers will vary. Students may also try to discover whether their local and state laws governing businesses and public events on Sundays have changed in recent years.

Meeting the Builders of America

1. Answers will vary. Students may note the initiative and perseverance of Pinckney, the regard for truth and freedom of the press of Hamilton, the respect for law of Adams, and the heroism and courage of Sampson.

2. Reports will vary.

CHAPTER 8

Section 8–1 Review (text page 193)

1. See definitions on text page 186.

2. *Daniel Shays:* leader of Shays' Rebellion in Massachusetts in 1787.

3. The Articles of Confederation created a weak federation of states.

4. The low prices of imports hurt American manufacturers, who could not compete with the prices, and the banning of American-made goods in the British West Indies hurt American merchants, who lost their best customers for American exports.

5. The Articles of Confederation did not give Congress the power to tax imports or to stop the states from printing paper money.

6. Settlers in the Northwest Territory first had a territorial governor. After there were 5,000 free men in the territory, the settlers could elect their own legislature. Once there were 60,000 people in the territory, they could apply to Congress to become a state.

7. Shays' Rebellion shocked the nation because it showed how weak the national government was.

Section 8-2 Review (text page 200)

1. See definitions on text page 194.

2. *James Madison:* delegate from Virginia to the Constitutional Convention who helped draw up the Virginia Plan. *William Paterson:* delegate from New Jersey who presented the New Jersey Plan. *Three-fifths Compromise:* compromise that meant each slave would be counted as three fifths of a person in determining a state's representation in the House of Representatives. *Electoral college:* meeting of electors from each state to elect a President and Vice-President.

3. The original purpose of the convention of 1787 was to revise and improve the Articles of Confederation. The purpose changed to writing a new constitution.

4. The large states liked the Virginia Plan because it would have given them more representatives than small states, so that the large states would control the national government. The small states preferred the New Jersey Plan because it would have given each state the same number of representatives and votes, regardless of the state's population. The Great Compromise satisfied both groups of states because it gave the large states more votes in the House of Representatives and the small states equality of votes in the Senate.

5. The purpose of the electoral college was to elect the President and Vice-President.

Section 8-3 Review (text page 203)

1. See definition on text page 201.

2. *Federalists:* supporters of the Constitution, who wanted a strong federal government. *Federalist Papers:* articles written by Hamilton, Madison, and Jay to explain the Constitution. *Anti-Federalists:* opponents of the Constitution. *John Hancock:* governor of Massachusetts who persuaded that state's ratifying convention to approve the Constitution.

3. Nine states had to ratify the Constitution before it became the law of the land.

4. Singletary feared that only wealthy and educated people would control the government and that they would have no regard for ordinary folk.

5. Hancock convinced the Massachusetts Convention to ratify by suggesting that a bill of rights be added to the Constitution later.

Using the Tools of History: Interpreting Diagrams (text page 207)

1. The diagram shows the system of checks and balances.

2. The executive branch appoints judges, which is a check on the judicial branch.

3. The judicial branch can interpret laws and can declare laws unconstitutional, which are checks on the legislative branch.

4. Arrows show where the checks originate and to what branch they apply. Colors in the arrows relate to the branch where the checks originate. For example, the light green arrows originate in the legislative branch, represented by dark green in the diagram.

5.

Executive Branch · Legislative Branch · Judicial Branch

Section 8-4 Review (text page 210)

1. See definitions on text page 204.

2. *"Elastic clause":* a clause in the Constitution (Clause 18, Section 8, Article 1) giving Congress the power "to make all laws which shall be necessary and proper" to carry out its responsibilities.

3. The six purposes named in the Preamble are to form a more perfect union, to establish justice, to insure domestic tranquility, to provide for the common defense, to promote the general welfare, and to secure the blessings of liberty.

4. The framers divided power so that no one branch of government could become too powerful.

5. Answers will vary. See the diagram on text page 206 for possible answers.

6. Accept any two of the following: The Constitution is written in broad terms. It includes the "elastic clause." It can be amended.

7. Accept any six of the following: freedom of worship; of speech; of the press; to keep and bear arms; from unreasonable searches; from trial for a major crime without a written accusation by a grand jury; from losing life, liberty, or property without a fair trial; from a trial without jury; from large bail or cruel and unusual punishments (also see the annotated amendments to the Constitution in the Resource Center of the text).

CHAPTER SURVEY (text pages 212–213)

Vocabulary Review

1. (n)	**7.** (h)	**13.** (p)
2. (e)	**8.** (k)	**14.** (a)
3. (o)	**9.** (d)	**15.** (c)
4. (b)	**10.** (f)	**16.** (g)
5. (q)	**11.** (j)	**17.** (r)
6. (m)	**12.** (i)	**18.** (l)

Chapter Review

1. (a) After independence, each state adopted a republican form of government. (b) Each state government was based on the authority of the people. (c) The first national government got its authority from the states.

2. (a) Americans did not want a strong national government in 1776 because they feared it would be as bad as the British government. (b) Americans changed their minds because of problems in dealing with foreign governments, in controlling money and trade, and in keeping order.

3. Both the Virginia Plan and the New Jersey Plan called for three branches of government, including executive and legislative branches.

4. (a) The Great Compromise was called that because it kept the convention from breaking up over the question of representation. (b) The states are represented according to population in the House of Representatives; they are represented equally in the Senate.

5. (a) The Three-fifths Compromise, which required each slave to be counted as three fifths of a person in deciding a state's representation in the House, settled the issue of counting slaves. (b) The compromise on the slave trade said that Congress could not end it before 1808.

6. Congress was given the power to tax imports, protecting manufacturers in the North, but not exports, safeguarding the South's cash crops from export duties.

7. (a) Anti-Federalists worried that the President would be too much like a king. (b) They worried that Congress would be controlled by the rich and powerful. (c) They feared loss of liberty because the Constitution would give added power to a central government located far from most citizens.

8. (a) Representatives serve terms of two years, Presidents and Vice-Presidents serve terms of four years, and Senators serve terms of six years. (b) This staggering helps prevent tyranny by assuring that changes in government take place gradually.

9. The framers made general statements and left details up to Congress, they included the "elastic clause," and they provided methods for amending the Constitution.

10. (a) The first four amendments cover the rights of freedom of religion, speech, press, and petition; the right to bear arms to maintain a militia; the right to be free from having troops quartered in homes; the right not to be searched without good reason. (b) The second four amendments cover the rights of persons accused of crimes. (c) The last two amendments say that people may have other rights and that powers not given to the federal government belong to the states or to the people.

Geography Review

(a) Virginia ceded the largest area to Congress. Students may notice that several states had overlapping claims. (b) Vermont was an independent republic between 1777 and 1791. (c) The area claimed by both the United States and Britain was north of Maine. (d) The Mississippi River formed the boundary between the land cessions and Louisiana.

Using the Tools of History

(a) The 36 squares represent one township. (b) The square is a blowup of one section of a township. (c) A township is 36 square miles (92 square kilometers). (d) A section is one square mile (2.6 square kilometers, or 259 hectares).

Reading and Thinking Skills

1. The study guide questions for section 8–1 will vary. They should be similar to the following:

What happened in the new state governments?
What were the Articles of Confederation?
What problems faced the new government?

How was the Northwest Territory treated?
What conflicts arose with other countries?
Who was involved in Shays' Rebellion?

2. Answers will vary in statements of main ideas and details. Answers should be similar to these:

I. The New Nation
   A. New State Governments
      1. New constitutions
      2. New bills of rights
      3. Easier voting in most states
   B. Articles of Confederation
      1. Purpose
      2. Form—a weak federation
         a. Powers of Congress
         b. Limits—no taxes or courts
   C. The Northwest Territory
      1. Land Ordinance of 1785
         a. Division of land
         b. Sale of land
      2. Northwest Ordinance of 1787
         a. Rules of territorial government
         b. Rules for statehood
   D. Conflicts with Other Countries
      1. With British over troops in Northwest
      2. With Spain over blockage of American shipping to New Orleans
   E. Shays' Rebellion
      1. Conflict over taxes
         a. Taxes on Massachusetts back-country farmers
         b. Seizure of arsenal at Springfield by moneyless farmers
      2. Shock that national government could not stop rebellion

3. (a)–(c) Answers will vary. For many students, outlining will provide a better understanding of the text because it gives more details.

CHAPTER 9

Section 9–1 Review (text page 218)

1. See definition on text page 214.

2. *Gaspar de Portolá:* leader of the 1769 expedition to California. *Father Junipero Serra:* founder of the California missions.

3. Thousands of Indians died because they had no resistance to European diseases or because they were overworked.

4. Settlers helped one another clear fields, build houses, quilt, husk corn.

Using the Tools of History: Distinguishing Fact from Opinion (text page 221)

The first sentence is a fact; the second sentence is an opinion.

Section 9–2 Review (text page 225)

1. See definitions on text page 219.

2. *Judiciary Act of 1789:* act of Congress that set up the federal court system.

3. The court system had three levels. The bottom level, the district courts, heard cases involving the Constitution, laws passed by Congress, and treaties. The second level, circuit courts, ruled on appeals from district courts and heard cases involving citizens from different states. The top level, the Supreme Court, heard appeals from district courts and from the highest state courts whenever such cases involved federal laws or the Constitution.

4. Washington's precedent was the Cabinet.

5. Hamilton strengthened credit by exchanging full-value federal bonds for Confederation and state bonds, increasing public confidence.

6. The Bank of the United States held the funds of the federal Treasury. It accepted deposits, issued national paper money, and lent money to government, businesses, and individuals.

7. Congress built the capital on the Potomac.

8. (a) Federalists preferred a strong national government; (b) Republicans favored strict construction; (c) Federalists favored the growth of cities and manufacturing.

Approaches to Reading: The Cause-Effect Pattern (text page 229)

1. Effect: He sent Jay to England to discuss disagreements between the two countries.

2. Cause: Jay's Treaty was made public.

3. Effect: Spain worried that the United States and Britain were drawing closer together and decided to negotiate with the United States.

4. Cause: Spain and the United States signed the Treaty of San Lorenzo.

Section 9-3 Review (text page 230)

1. See definitions on text page 226.

2. *Anthony Wayne:* general who won the Battle of Fallen Timbers and helped open the Northwest Territory to American settlers. *Proclamation of Neutrality:* proclamation that the United States intended to remain neutral in the war between France and other European countries. *Jay's Treaty:* treaty with Great Britain giving United States ships the right to trade in the British West Indies, paying Americans for ships that had been seized by the British navy, and calling for Britain to abandon its forts in the Northwest Territory. *Treaty of San Lorenzo:* treaty with Spain fixing the northern boundary of Spanish Florida and giving the United States the right of deposit at New Orleans.

3. Hamilton wanted to teach citizens not to question the authority of the federal government.

4. Jay's Treaty and the Treaty of San Lorenzo helped the United States establish its authority over its western territories.

5. Washington warned against permanent alliances because he wanted to keep the United States out of European wars.

Section 9-4 Review (text page 234)

1. See definitions on text page 231.

2. *XYZ Affair:* scandal caused when French agents asked for bribes before France would negotiate with American envoys about an end to war. *Alien and Sedition Acts:* laws making it more difficult for immigrants to become citizens and for critics of the government to speak out. *Aaron Burr:* Republican candidate for Vice-President who challenged Jefferson for the presidency in 1800.

3. Adams chose to fight an undeclared "half war" with France.

4. Federalists thought the Alien and Sedition Acts would strengthen the war effort and weaken the Republican party.

5. Jefferson and Madison wrote the Virginia and Kentucky resolutions saying that the Sedition Act was unconstitutional and that the people did not have to obey it.

6. The election of 1800 proved that political power could change hands peacefully.

CHAPTER SURVEY (text page 236)

Vocabulary Review

1. (l)	**7.** (q)	**13.** (d)
2. (m)	**8.** (a)	**14.** (n)
3. (b)	**9.** (k)	**15.** (c)
4. (o)	**10.** (j)	**16.** (e)
5. (f)	**11.** (h)	**17.** (p)
6. (i)	**12.** (g)	

Chapter Review

1. (a) District courts heard cases involving the Constitution, laws passed by Congress, and treaties. (b) Circuit courts heard cases involving citizens from different states and ruled on appeals. (c) The Supreme Court was the court of last appeal for cases from lower courts.

2. Hamilton thought exchanging new federal bonds for old Confederation bonds would improve the credit of the federal government.

3. The Bank of the United States would help business by accepting deposits, issuing trustworthy paper money, and lending money to businesses.

4. (a) Strict construction means interpreting the Constitution strictly and narrowly, so that any power not listed in the Constitution belongs to the states. (b) Loose construction means interpreting the Constitution broadly, so that the federal government can do whatever is "necessary and proper" to fulfill its duties, provided that the Constitution does not forbid such action.

5. The Battle of Fallen Timbers opened the lands north of the Ohio River to settlers.

6. (a) Washington set the precedents of the Cabinet and the two-term presidency. (b) Washington warned Americans to avoid permanent alliances with European countries.

7. (a) Jay's Treaty avoided a war with Britain and established the nation's authority over the Northwest Territory. (b) The Treaty of San Lorenzo established the nation's southern boundary and gave Americans the right of deposit at New Orleans. (c) Adams avoided full-scale war by sending negotiators to France to make a peace treaty.

8. Jefferson and the Republicans were: (a) against a fancy title for the President; (b) against a national bank; (c) for strict construction; (d) for the French Revolution; (e) against a strong national government. (f) The Federalists agreed with none of these views.

9. Hamilton saw national greatness as the result of sea power and manufacturing. Jefferson saw it as the result of a strong landowning, farming class.

10. (a) The Constitution does not mention political parties. (b) By seeking a second term, Washington hoped to keep the conflict between the Republicans and the Federalists under control. (c) The Federalists feared that Jefferson threatened all they had done to put the Constitution into practice. (d) Jefferson's inauguration showed that power could change hands peacefully.

Geography Review

1. (a) The Spanish frontier extended from the plains of Texas to California. (b) The log cabin frontier lay between the Appalachians and the Mississippi.

2. Southwestern Pennsylvania was separated from its markets by the Allegheny Mountains, which made travel difficult.

3. The Treaty of San Lorenzo set Florida's northern boundary at 31° north latitude.

Using the Tools of History

1. (a) The circle graph should show 90 percent of Americans in 1790 as farmers. The graph might be titled "Farm Population 1790." (b) The second graph should show 6 percent of Americans in 1790 living in towns with more than 2,500 people. It might be titled "Population in Towns of More Than 2,500 People—1790."

2. (a) Fact (b) Opinion (c) Fact (d) Opinion

Reading and Thinking Skills

1. (a) The plains tribes got horses from the Spanish. (b) Spanish settlement in Texas and New Mexico was limited. (c) One effect—mounted warriors—is also a cause.

2. Answers will vary. Additional causes could include worry, loneliness, hard work, the deaths of loved ones, and Indian attacks.

CHAPTER 10

Using the Tools of History: Understanding Topography on Maps (text page 241)

1. Five mountain ranges are named.

2. Oregon is quite mountainous; Indiana appears to be level.

3. High mountains appear in the western part of the Louisiana Territory. They are called the Rocky Mountains. Pike's Peak is named.

4. Lewis and Clark followed the Yellowstone and Columbia rivers.

Section 10-1 Review (text page 243)

1. See definition on text page 238.

2. *John Marshall:* Chief Justice of the Supreme Court. *Toussaint L'Ouverture:* leader of a slave rebellion against the French colonists on Haiti. *Meriwether Lewis and William Clark:* leaders of the Lewis and Clark expedition through the Louisiana Territory to the Pacific Ocean. *Sacajawea:* Shoshone woman who helped Lewis and Clark as guide and translator. *Zebulon Pike:* explorer of the Mississippi and Louisiana Territory.

3. Jefferson wanted to create a wise and frugal government run by a natural aristocracy of able citizens. He believed that the purpose of government was to protect the rights of citizens, but otherwise to leave them alone.

4. *Marbury* v. *Madison* established the power of judicial review.

5. Napoleon decided to sell the Louisiana Territory because his troops had been defeated by rebel Haitian slaves. Without Haiti, he no longer wanted an empire in America.

6. The Louisiana Purchase raised the question whether the Constitution allowed the government to buy foreign land and make it part of the nation.

Section 10-2 Review (text page 247)

1. See definitions on text page 244.

2. *Barbary States:* countries on the north coast of Africa.

3. The United States paid tribute to protect American trade from pirate attacks.

4. Americans reacted to the *Chesapeake-Leopard* affair with calls for war.

5. Congress hoped that the Embargo Act and the Non-Intercourse Act would force Britain and France to respect the rights of neutral ships to trade in peace.

Approaches to Reading: Organizing Details
(text page 249)

1. The main idea is in the second sentence of the first paragraph. Students may paraphrase it as "In 1812, the United States invaded Canada." (a) A series of battles between the United States and the British. (b) 1812 and 1813. (c) At Detroit, near Montreal, on Lake Erie, at Queenston, and on the Thames River. (d) Madison thought that invading Canada would be an easy way to attack the British.

2. See the chart at the bottom of this page.

Section 10-3 Review (text page 254)

1. See definitions on text page 248.

2. *Tecumseh:* Shawnee warrior who organized an Indian confederacy. *War Hawks:* Congressmen from the South and West who wanted war with Britain. *Henry Clay:* Representative from Kentucky and a War Hawk. *Francis Scott Key:* author of "The Star-Spangled Banner." *Hartford Convention:* meeting of five New England states opposed to the War of 1812. *Treaty of Ghent:* treaty that ended the War of 1812.

3. The War Hawks wanted to end Indian attacks on the frontier, to add Canada and Florida to the United States, and to protect the rights of Americans on the high seas.

4. New Englanders thought the damage of war with Britain would be worse than the seizure of their ships and sailors.

5. Canadians took the invasion as an attack on their homeland, not as a liberation.

6. The Treaty of Ghent did not mention impressment.

Section 10-4 Review (text page 259)

1. See definitions on text page 255.

2. *National Road:* first interstate highway. It ran from Cumberland, Maryland, to the Ohio River. *James Monroe:* Madison's Secretary of State, elected President in 1816.

3. The three parts of the American System were tariffs on imports, a national bank, and internal improvements such as roads.

4. The Supreme Court ruled that a state cannot have the power to destroy an agency of the federal government.

5. The Supreme Court ruled that the Constitution gives Congress, not a state, the power to control interstate commerce.

6. Under the Missouri Compromise, Maine was admitted as a free state, Missouri as a slave state. The balance of slave and free states was maintained.

Section 10-5 Review (text page 264)

1. See definitions on text page 260.

2. *John Quincy Adams:* Monroe's Secretary of State. *Rush-Bagot Treaty:* treaty between Britain and the United States that disarmed their ships on the Great Lakes. *Convention of 1818:* treaty between Britain and the United States that permitted Americans to fish off Newfoundland, set the northern boundary of the Louisiana Territory, and allowed both countries to settle Oregon. *Adams-Onís Treaty:* treaty between Spain and the United States that gave Florida to the United States. The United States gave up its claim to Texas. Spain gave up its claim to Oregon.

3. "Control or cede" meant that Spain should con-

EVENT OR TOPIC	WHO OR WHAT	WHEN	WHERE	WHY
Hartford Convention	a meeting of delegates from five New England states	1814	Hartford, Connecticut	to discuss amendments to the Constitution
Treaty of Ghent	a peace treaty between Great Britain and the United States	1814	Ghent, Belgium	to end the war between Britain and the United States

trol the Indians of Florida and end their raids on Georgia settlements or cede the territory to the United States.

4. The Monroe Doctrine said that Europe should establish no new colonies in the Americas, that Europe should not interfere in American republics, and that the United States would stay out of European affairs.

CHAPTER SURVEY (text pages 266–267)

Vocabulary Review

1. (d)	**6.** (c)	**11.** (e)
2. (a)	**7.** (i)	**12.** (l)
3. (h)	**8.** (j)	
4. (f)	**9.** (k)	
5. (b)	**10.** (g)	

Chapter Review

1. Jefferson favored a government that protected the people's rights and that would tax and spend as little as possible.

2. (a) *Marbury* v. *Madison* declared the Judiciary Act of 1789 unconstitutional. (b) Congress had passed the law. (c) In *McCulloch* v. *Maryland* the Supreme Court struck down a state law. (d) The Court was using the power of judicial review. (e) Jefferson was unhappy with the decisions because he thought the Court was not following a strict construction of the Constitution.

3. (a) Monroe went to France to buy New Orleans and western Florida for $10 million. (b) Napoleon offered him all of Louisiana for $15 million. (c) Jefferson worried because he believed the federal government's powers should be limited to those listed in the Constitution.

4. (a) Jefferson imposed an embargo because France and Britain were seizing neutral ships and Britain was impressing American seamen. (b) The embargo caused unemployment and smuggling in New England. (c) The Non-Intercourse Act replaced the embargo. (d) "Peaceable coercion" was considered a failure because it had not ended the seizure of ships or impressment by 1812.

5. (a) New England most opposed the war. (b) Other sections were outraged by Britain's failure to observe the rights of neutral shipping; they hoped to take Florida and Canada from Britain. (c) New

England's economy gained the most because its textile industry could expand without competition when European textile imports were cut off.

6. The War of 1812 brought the United States respect from other nations, a safer frontier, an expanded textile industry, and strengthened American nationalism.

7. The Bank of the United States, the Tariff of 1816, and the National Road were all part of the American System, which was recommended to Congress by Madison after the War of 1812.

8. The debate over statehood for Missouri uncovered the deep divisions in the United States over slavery and was a warning that this issue would cause trouble in the future.

9. (a) The United States and Britain settled disputes by negotiation. (b) They agreed on the Rush-Bagot Treaty and the Convention of 1818.

10. (a) Monroe was afraid that Spain might be tempted to try to regain its American empire, and he worried about Russian activity along the Pacific coast. (b) European nations found the Monroe Doctrine arrogant.

Geography Review

1. (a) Battle blasts represent victories. (b) Most of the fighting took place in the Great Lakes region. (c) Jackson went from Nashville, Tennessee, to Horseshoe Bend in Mississippi Territory, to Pensacola, Florida, to New Orleans. (d) Jackson's forces marched about 525–600 miles (845–966 kilometers).

2. (a) Lakes Superior, Huron, Erie, and Ontario mark an international boundary. (b) The Arkansas, Red, and Sabine rivers help to mark an international boundary.

Using the Tools of History

(a) Different elevations are shown in different colors. (b) Swamps, glaciers, and mountain peaks are shown with symbols. (c) Most of the land is over 3,000 feet (1,000 meters) in the western half. (d) The Gulf-Atlantic Coastal Plain has the most swamps. (e) America's glaciers are in Alaska. The highest peak shown in the Appalachians is Mt. Mitchell; in the Rockies, Mt. Elbert; in the Sierra Nevada, Mt. Whitney; in Hawaii, Mauna Kea; and in Alaska, Mt. McKinley.

Reading and Thinking Skills

Charts will vary. Details should be similar to the chart at the bottom of this page.

UNIT SURVEY (text pages 268–269)

Unit Review

1. (a) By passing the Land Ordinance of 1785, Congress set up the Northwest survey system to divide and sell land. (b) Congress had no army or navy and no power to raise armed forces unless the states agreed. (c) Parliament was not able to tax the colonies successfully, just as Congress was not able to tax the states successfully.

2. (a) Small states feared that the large states would dominate the government if representation was based on population. (b) The Great Compromise won over the small states. All states have equal representation in the Senate. (c) Nine states had to approve. (d) Anti-Federalists opposed the new Constitution.

3. (a) It is the separate powers—the three branches of government—that check and balance each other. (b) Both have units—tribes or states—that give some but not all their independence to a central unit—a council or government.

4. (a) Father Junipero Serra caused the advance of Spanish missions in California. (b) Individual families crossing the Alleghenies caused the advance of the log cabin frontier.

5. (a) Hamilton favored a national bank because it could issue sound money and encourage manufacturing and trade. That would, he hoped, make the nation great. (b) Jefferson feared that bankers would become too powerful. (c) The Federalist party supported Hamilton. (d) The Republican party supported Jefferson.

6. (a) During the Revolutionary War, Patriots saw France as an ally. (b) At the time of the XYZ Affair, Americans saw France as an enemy. (c) Anti-French feeling led Congress to pass laws against immigrants and critics of the government. (d) The Virginia and Kentucky resolutions opposed the Sedition Act.

7. (a) Jefferson was interpreting his powers loosely. (b) Usually he made a strict interpretation. (c) Jefferson thought that Louisiana was too important to the future of the nation to be refused.

8. (a) All threatened to seize American ships and sailors. (b) In 1815 the pirate bases were destroyed. (c) Jefferson enforced a trade embargo in 1807. (d) The embargo was unpopular because it harmed Americans who made a living in shipping.

9. (a) The War of 1812 was called "Mr. Madison's War." (b) It was fought in the United States and Canada. (c) New England did not want the war because it would damage the region's trade more than British seizure of ships or impressment had done. (d) Tariffs on British goods appealed to manufacturers.

10. (a) The Federalist party fell apart after its backing of the Hartford Convention of 1814. Further, many of the party's ideas were taken over by the Republicans. (b) The Missouri Compromise was reached in 1820. (c) Missouri and Maine entered the Union in 1820 and 1821.

Linking the Past and the Present

Students' reports will vary.

EVENT OR TOPIC	WHO OR WHAT	WHEN	WHERE	WHY
Napoleon's army is defeated	Rebel slaves	1802	Haiti	To remain independent
Offer to buy Louisiana	Monroe, Jefferson, Republicans	1803	France and United States	Future of United States
Lewis and Clark Expedition	Eighty men	1804–1805	Louisiana Territory	To explore western lands

Meeting the Builders of America

1. Answers will vary. Students may mention Equiano's zeal for freedom, Rowson's patriotism, and Calhoun's love of liberty.

CHAPTER 11

Section 11–1 Review (text page 280)

1. See definitions on text page 272.

2. *Cyrus McCormick:* inventor of the mechanical reaper. *Eli Whitney:* inventor of the cotton gin. *Samuel Slater:* English textile worker who built the first spinning mill in the United States. *Francis Cabot Lowell:* American merchant who built the first factory in the United States to turn raw cotton into finished cloth.

3. Improved plows and McCormick's reaper made it possible for farmers to plant and harvest larger crops than before.

4. Cotton was "king" because it became the nation's most important export.

5. Mills were built in New England because it had water power to run machines and people willing to invest in new businesses.

6. Whitney's interchangeable system allowed lower labor costs, higher productivity, and products that were easy to repair.

7. Trade unions wanted limits on the number of apprentices in each workshop, higher wages, and a ten-hour day.

8. Lowell hired women because they were available and would work for lower wages than men.

Using the Tools of History: Interpreting Illustrations (text page 284)

1. The caption gives the title, approximate date, and location of the painting.

2. The title, "Geese in Flight," does not give much information about the painting. Students' titles will vary. Titles should suggest changes in methods of transportation.

3. This painting is imaginary. It is highly unlikely that all the forms of transportation would have appeared in the same scene.

4. The house, a road, and a railroad appear in the foreground.

5. The mountain and a body of water appear in the background.

6. Two types of land transportation shown are horse and buggy and train.

7. Three types of water transportation are shown (some students may say four types, distinguishing between the small sailboats and the large sailing vessel). They are sailboats, a steamboat, and a rowboat.

8. The train and steamboat have smokestacks. Both are powered by steam.

9. Red leaves and geese flying south are clues that the season is fall.

10. The large house suggests that the people living there are prosperous.

11. Answers will vary.

Section 11–2 Review (text page 286)

1. See definitions on text page 281.

2. *Robert Fulton:* inventor of the *Clermont,* the nation's first successful steamboat. *Erie Canal:* canal built by New York from Albany on the Hudson River to Buffalo on Lake Erie. *Tom Thumb:* steam locomotive, built by Peter Cooper, that raced a horse-drawn car in 1830. *Samuel Morse:* inventor of the telegraph.

3. After independence, America began trading with China and California.

4. Hides for leather factory belts and whale oil for lubricating machines were the products most useful to factory owners.

5. Before railroads, goods were moved by wagon on roads, by steamboat on rivers, and by flatboat on canals.

6. Accept any of the following: Railroads can be built where freight needs to go; unlike canals, railroads do not freeze; they are cheaper to build than canals; they are more durable than roads; they move freight faster than wagons or riverboats.

7. The telegraph and the penny press helped Americans become better informed.

Approaches to Reading: The Problem-Solution Pattern (text page 289)

1. Two solutions to the problem of unsafe drinking water are piping water from rivers and bringing it by tunnel from reservoirs.

2. Uncollected garbage and open sewage caused disease epidemics.

3. Problem: Britain prohibited export of textile machinery and blueprints.

4. Problem: Colonial hogs were thin and gave little meat.

5. Solution: Skilled workers formed trade associations (unions).

6. Problem: Newly settled areas needed ways to get their products to market; the government did not build roads.

7. Problem: Transporting goods upriver by flatboat was very slow and difficult.

8. Solution: New types of printing presses made newspapers inexpensive.

Section 11–3 Review (text page 290)

1. See definitions on text page 287.

2. *Elias Howe:* inventor of the sewing machine. *Charles Goodyear:* inventor of vulcanized rubber. *Know-Nothings:* members of the anti-immigrant American party.

3. Canals and railroads made Chicago the leading grain port by 1860.

4. Cities provided jobs, opportunities for learning, entertainment, window shopping in department stores, and access to new inventions that made life easier and more pleasant.

5. City problems included unsafe water, garbage and sewage disposal, disease epidemics, crime, fires, and slums.

6. Most of the Irish immigrants were too poor to travel west. Even those who could afford it chose not to farm.

7. Immigrants taught Americans improved farming methods, started new industries, and provided labor for canals, railroads, and factories.

CHAPTER SURVEY (text pages 292–293)

Vocabulary Review

1. (c)	**5.** (g)	**9.** (i)
2. (b)	**6.** (e)	**10.** (h)
3. (d)	**7.** (f)	**11.** (j)
4. (a)	**8.** (k)	

Chapter Review

1. All three improvements increased worker productivity.

2. As the factory system spread, the United States produced more and more of the products it had once imported.

3. Cotton was important to (a) the North because it was the raw material used in the New England textile industry; (b) the South because it was the main cash crop; (c) foreign trade because it was the nation's most important export.

4. (a) Steamboats increased river traffic, turning these towns into busy ports. (b) Railroads brought farm products from the prairies into Chicago to be shipped east by boat.

5. Mill girls became unhappy because factory work was sped up, the working day was lengthened, and pay was cut.

6. (a) Canal boats used horse power. (b) Clipper ships used wind power. (c) Reapers used horse power. (d) Locomotives used steam power. (e) Power looms used water power. (f) The telegraph used electricity. (g) Riverboats used steam power. (h) Brigs used wind power. (i) Plows used horse power. (j) Spinning machines used water power.

7. (a) The American (Know-Nothing) party wanted to ban immigrants and Catholics from holding public office. (b) The signs revealed open prejudice against immigrants.

8. Foreign trade produced the investment capital that was used to build factories.

9. The cost of shipping goods went down as a result of improvements in transportation.

10. (a) The largest groups of immigrants were the Germans and the Irish. (b) The Irish usually settled in eastern cities. Many Germans went west to farm the prairies.

Geography Review

1. (a) Dairy farming was important in New England. (b) By 1840 cotton farming had spread as far west as Texas. (c) Rice is primarily a coastal crop. (d) Boston was the center of the textile industry. (e) Baltimore's industries were forest products, flour milling, shipbuilding, and textiles. (f) Shipbuilding was important in Boston, Baltimore, and New Orleans.

2. (a) Most of the roads on this map run east-west. (b) The North had the most canals. (c) Factory owners could ship products by sea to New Orleans, then up the Mississippi River to St. Louis. (d) An alternate route was up the Hudson River to Albany; by the Erie Canal to Buffalo; across Lake Erie to Toledo, Cleveland, or Erie; by canal to the Ohio River; down the Ohio to the Mississippi River; up the Mississippi to St. Louis.

Using the Tools of History

1. (a) The caption says it is an illustration of the race between the locomotive *Tom Thumb* and a horse in 1830. (b) The illustration is lifelike. (c) Horse power and steam power are shown. (d) Both passenger cars are similar in size and in the number of passengers they carry. Both are covered and run on rails.

Reading and Thinking Skills

1. Solution: McCormick's reaper.

2. Problem: Answers may vary. Accept any of the following: Moving goods by land was expensive; east coast rivers were not navigable west of the Fall Line; rivers did not always go where freight needed to go.

3. Problem: Removing seeds from cotton by hand was very slow.

4. Solution: Hides were imported from California, where cattle were plentiful.

CHAPTER 12

Section 12-1 Review (text page 298)

1. See definitions on text page 294.

2. Jackson received the most electoral votes, but John Quincy Adams was elected when Henry Clay asked his supporters to vote for Adams. Jackson charged that Adams had promised to make Clay Secretary of State in return for his support.

3. Adams was unsuccessful because he was a nationalist at a time of growing sectionalism.

4. Van Buren planned to call for a weak national government and appeal to the common people, uniting interests of the South and the West.

5. White males had suffrage by 1828. Women, Indians, and blacks could not vote.

6. Jackson was a self-made man, an Indian fighter, and the hero of the Battle of New Orleans.

7. Jackson's victory showed the growing political power of the West and the voting strength of the common people.

Using the Tools of History: Making Generalizations (text page 300)

1. (c)

2. (a)

3. (a)

4. Creek, Seminole

Section 12-2 Review (text page 304)

1. See definitions on text page 299.

2. *Kitchen Cabinet:* a special group of friends who gave President Andrew Jackson advice. *Sequoyah:* inventor of a system for writing the Cherokee language. *Trail of Tears:* the forced westward migration of the Cherokee.

3. Jackson rewarded loyal party members with government jobs. This practice was called the spoils system.

4. The Indian Removal Act opened all the lands east of the Mississippi to white settlement.

5. Trickery, threats, and force were used to persuade the Indians to sign.

6. Calhoun's report proposed that a single state could declare an act of Congress unconstitutional. A state convention could then nullify the law.

7. Jackson warned that the officials of South Carolina might be charged with treason if the state seceded; at the same time he asked Congress to reduce the tariff.

Approaches to Reading: Literal and Inferential Reading (text page 306)

"The Panic of 1837": literal
"The Rise of the Whig Party": literal
"The Log-cabin Campaign": inferential
"His Accidency": inferential

Section 12-3 Review (text page 310)

1. See definitions on text page 305.

2. *"Wildcat banks":* western banks that kept no specie reserve. *"Pet banks":* state banks that received federal funds after Andrew Jackson stopped depositing funds in the Bank of the United States. *"His Accidency":* the Whigs' name for President John Tyler, who succeeded to the presidency when Harrison died.

3. Banks printed paper dollars because there was not enough specie to meet the needs of the rapidly growing economy.

4. Biddle kept a 50-percent specie reserve because he believed in sound currency.

5. Jackson felt that the bank had too much economic and political power.

6. Jackson ordered that all payment for federal land be made in specie in order to clamp down on reckless bankers and speculators.

7. The banking system was weakened when people demanded specie in return for their paper currency and the banks did not have enough reserves to pay them.

8. The groups that formed the Whig party were all opposed to Andrew Jackson.

Section 12–4 Review (text page 318)

1. See definitions on text page 311.

2. *Dorothea Dix:* reformer who advocated hospitals for the mentally ill. *Horace Mann:* educational reformer from Massachusetts. *Frederick Douglass:* escaped slave who lectured and wrote in favor of abolition. *Harriet Tubman:* escaped slave who led many slaves to freedom on the Underground Railroad. *Sarah and Angelina Grimké:* abolitionist and feminist sisters.

3. Traveling preachers made Americans aware of the religious movement to make the world perfect.

4. Temperance crusaders originally asked for moderation in the consumption of alcohol; later they asked for total abstention.

5. Radical abolitionists wanted an immediate end to slavery.

6. Northerners thought the "gag rule" preventing discussion of antislavery petitions in Congress was a violation of the right of petition.

7. The Declaration of Sentiments (1848) demanded the right for women to own property and to control their own earnings, equal opportunities for education and employment, and voting rights for women.

CHAPTER SURVEY (text pages 320–321)

Vocabulary Review

1. (n)	**6.** (f)	**11.** (i)
2. (k)	**7.** (a)	**12.** (c)
3. (d)	**8.** (g)	**13.** (m)
4. (h)	**9.** (l)	**14.** (j)
5. (e)	**10.** (b)	

Chapter Review

1. (a) Each candidate looked to his own section of the country for support. (b) Southerners opposed John Quincy Adams because they saw a strong, active national government as a threat to their section of the country.

2. (a) Van Buren created a new, nationwide political party. (b) Jackson was elected with support from every part of the nation. (c) The Whig party and the Democratic party had become national parties by 1840.

3. (a) Parades, rallies, and barbecues created interest in campaigns and brought out the voters. (b) Both parties gave government jobs to loyal party workers. (c) Accept any three of the following: Many new voters cast ballots for the first time in each election. Military heroes were nominated for President each time. Parties made personal attacks on their opponents. Party workers entertained many voters.

4. Accept any four of the following: The Cherokee grew cash crops and raised livestock, built towns, had courts with jury trials, wrote a constitution, developed a written language, published books and newspapers.

5. The South opposed high tariffs on products it had to buy; the North supported tariffs to protect its manufacturing industry.

6. Hayne argued that the states were sovereign. Webster insisted that the federal government was sovereign and that the doctrine of nullification was a threat to the Union.

7. (a) State banks did not want the national bank to tell them how much money they could print and lend. (b) Jackson stopped depositing federal funds in the national bank.

8. The idea that the world could become perfect in the sight of God encouraged reformers to work to improve American society.

9. Weld and the Tappans believed that abolitionists should seek political power.

10. Accept any three of the following: Feminists wanted women to have the right to own property, to control their own earnings, to vote, and to have equal opportunities in education and employment.

Geography Review

(a) Settlement extended along the Ohio and Mississippi rivers. (b) The main areas of new settlement were around Lake Michigan, west of the Mississippi, and south of the Appalachians. (c) The barrier that stopped settlement in the mid–1800s was the Great Plains. It was mostly overcome by 1890, although the blue areas were settled later.

Using the Tools of History

1. Statement (c) is the best generalization. Statement (a) is not true; statement (b) is true but is too narrow to cover most of the facts in the section.

Reading and Thinking Skills

1. Heading (a) is inferential, the rest are literal.

2. (a) In 1837 Britain stopped buying American cotton. (b) Cotton prices fell. (c) Land prices fell. (d) Cotton dealers and land speculators were unable to pay their debts. (e) Banks began to collapse. (f) People rushed to withdraw their savings from banks. (g) New York City banks stopped paying out gold and silver. (h) An economic depression resulted.

CHAPTER 13

Section 13-1 (text page 328)

1. See definitions on text page 322.

2. *Stephen F. Austin:* first American to start a colony in Texas. *Antonio López de Santa Anna:* dictator of Mexico, defeated by Texans at the Battle of San Jacinto. *William Barret Travis:* leader of the defenders of the Alamo. *Sam Houston:* commander in chief of the Texans in the Texas Revolution, later elected President of the Republic of Texas. *Lone Star Republic:* independent Republic of Texas.

3. Americans wanted cheap, fertile land in Texas.

4. Texans were unhappy with Mexico because they opposed the Mexican law banning further American immigration; they did not want to become Catholic; they feared Mexico would outlaw slavery.

5. Texans declared their independence after Santa Anna's army invaded Texas.

6. All the defenders of the Alamo were killed by the Mexicans. Susannah Dickerson was allowed to live to carry the message of the Alamo's defeat.

7. In 1836 the United States feared that admitting Texas would cause war with Mexico and would upset the balance of slave and free states.

Section 13-2 Review (text page 334)

1. See definition on text page 329.

2. *Mountain men:* traders and trappers who explored the Rocky Mountains. *Continental Divide:* the ridge that separates rivers that drain toward the Gulf of Mexico and the Atlantic Ocean from rivers flowing toward the Pacific Ocean. *South Pass:* a wide, low pass through the Rocky Mountains that made possible wagon travel to the Pacific Coast. *Narcissa Whitman and Eliza Spalding:* the first pioneer women to travel the Oregon Trail. *Joseph Smith:* founder of the Church of Jesus Christ of Latter Day Saints (Mormon Church). *Brigham Young:* Mormon leader who brought the Mormons to the Great Salt Lake valley to settle.

3. Missouri traders brought silver and furs back from Santa Fe.

4. Trappers and traders were the first to explore the Oregon Trail.

5. The first pioneers to Oregon were missionaries. Later settlers were farmers.

6. The Bidwell-Bartleson party opened the California Trail to settlers.

7. The Mormons left Illinois to escape prejudice and violence.

Using the Tools of History: Identifying Political Changes on Maps (text page 342)

1. The boundary symbols are the same on both maps, but the treaty dates are different. Other symbols differ.

2. In 1822 the states of Louisiana and Missouri, the Arkansas Territory, and Unorganized Territory were within the boundaries. In 1848 the new states of Iowa and Arkansas, part of Texas, Indian Territory, and part of Minnesota Territory appear.

3. Between 1822 and 1848, the boundary line was extended west to the Pacific Ocean, and the disputed boundaries were set by treaties.

4. Between 1822 and 1853, the southern boundary was established by the Gadsden Purchase and the Treaty of Guadalupe Hidalgo. Texas and Florida became part of the United States.

5. Six states were created between 1822 and 1848.

6. Oregon Territory was smaller in 1848. It lost the land above the Oregon Treaty line of 1846.

Section 13-3 Review (text page 344)

1. See definitions on text page 335.

2. *Webster-Ashburton Treaty:* agreement with Britain to settle the northern boundary of Maine and the United States-Canadian boundary between Lake Superior and Lake of the Woods. *Oregon Treaty:* agreement with Britain dividing Oregon along the 49th parallel. *Bear Flag Republic:* the independent Republic of California. *Gold rush:* the rush to California after gold was discovered in 1848. *Forty-niners:* gold seekers who came to California in 1849. *Gadsden Purchase:* the purchase from Mexico, in 1853, of a 45,000-square-mile strip of desert south of the Gila River.

3. Polk, an expansionist, won the presidential election of 1844. Expansionists favored adding Texas to the United States.

4. Polk sent Slidell to Mexico to offer to buy California and New Mexico.

5. Abolitionists opposed the Mexican War because they thought it was a plot to bring more slave states into the Union. Whigs questioned whether American troops had been attacked on American soil, because the attack was on disputed ground.

6. Zachary Taylor was the general of the northern army who defeated the Mexicans at Buena Vista. Stephen Watts Kearny led the western army; he marched his troops to California. Winfield Scott was the general in command of the army and leader of the American invasion of Mexico in 1847.

7. The United States gained one third of Mexico's territory, including the present states of California, Nevada, Utah, and Arizona and parts of Colorado, Wyoming, and New Mexico.

8. Law and order broke down during the gold rush in California.

9. Law and order improved after Californians organized a territorial government in 1849.

10. The United States made the Gadsden Purchase because it was the best site for a southern rail line to California.

CHAPTER SURVEY (text pages 346–347)

Vocabulary Review

1. (c) **4.** (a) **7.** (h)
2. (e) **5.** (f) **8.** (g)
3. (b) **6.** (d)

Chapter Review

1. (a) The Mexican Congress banned American immigration because it feared Texas was becoming an American state. (b) Austin went to Mexico City to ask that Texas become a separate Mexican state. (c) Austin failed.

2. (a) The Texans in San Antonio decided to defend the city to slow Santa Anna's advance. (b) Santa Anna agreed to an armistice and to recognize Texas as an independent nation with the Rio Grande as its western boundary. (c) The republic ended when Texas entered the Union in 1845.

3. Settlement jumped over the Great Plains because farmers thought the prairie was too dry.

4. (a) Yes, settlers followed traders and trappers to Oregon Territory and California. (b) No, Mormons settled in Utah despite the fact that traders were not active in that area.

5. (a) Expansionists believed that it was clearly the fate of the United States to spread across the entire North American continent. (b) Tyler's goal was to bring Texas into the Union.

6. (a) Expansionists meant that they wanted the United States to annex all of Oregon Territory. (b) Polk settled for half of Oregon.

7. (a) President Polk feared that Great Britain might try to take over California. (b) Polk hoped to buy California from Mexico. (c) Like the Texans, the American settlers in California revolted against the Mexican government and established an independent republic.

8. (a) The Whigs accepted that Mexico had shed American blood. (b) They denied that it was shed on American soil. The fighting took place on disputed land.

9. The Americans planned to attack Mexico from three directions. General Zachary Taylor was to march on the north of Mexico from Texas. Colonel Stephen Watts Kearny was to march his army west to take New Mexico and California. General Winfield Scott was to invade southern Mexico by sea and take the capital, Mexico City. Taylor commanded the northern army.

10. The four treaties that established the boundaries of the 48 states are the Webster-Ashburton Treaty, the Oregon Treaty, the Treaty of Guadalupe-Hidalgo, and the Gadsden Purchase Treaty.

Geography Review

(a) The Oregon Trail crosses the Rocky Mountains, the Wasatch Range, and the Cascade Range. (b) The Oregon Trail follows the Platte River and the Columbia River. (c) The California Trail separated from the Oregon Trail north of the Great Salt Lake. (d) The Old Spanish Trail crossed the Rio Grande and the Colorado River.

Using the Tools of History

1. (a) The symbols are the same, but in the 1835–1836 map a red arrow means a Texan route, and in the 1846–1848 map it means an American route. (b) In 1835–1836, fighting took place in Texas. In 1846–1848, fighting took place in Mexico and California. (c) The 1835–1836 map shows five battles, of which two were Mexican victories. The 1846–1848 map shows 12 battles, of which three were Mexican victories.

2. (a) Change. A new constitution would have to be written for the state. (b) Continuity. The Texas cattle industry continued to grow. (c) Continuity. Slavery continued. (d) Change. Texas would no longer be an independent nation receiving foreign diplomats. (e) Change. Texas would no longer be able to tax imports. The Constitution gives that power to Congress. (f) Continuity. The sale of cotton was not affected by statehood. (g) Continuity. Mexicans continued to believe that Texas had been stolen from Mexico. (h) Continuity. Relations with the Indians did not change because of statehood.

Reading and Thinking Skills

1. The third sentence expresses the main idea: "And even greater fortunes were made mining the miners."

2. Vigilante committees: Who or What?—Miners who took the law into their own hands. When?—in the early years of the gold rush. Where?—in California gold camps. Why?—To combat lawlessness and crime. Gadsden Purchase: Who or What?—A purchase of 45,000 square miles of land from Mexico. When?—1853. Where?—South of the Gila River. Why?—The United States wanted the land for a transcontinental railroad following a southern route to California.

UNIT SURVEY (text pages 348–349)

Unit Review

1. (a) The interchangeable system allowed the division of labor in New England mills. Many women left farms and began mill work for wages. (b) Cotton farming spread, and cotton became the "king" of crops in the South. (c) The great change was the Industrial Revolution.

2. (a) The problem of traveling upstream was solved by steamboats. The problem of shipping large quantities of goods between places not connected by water routes or roads was solved by canals. (b) Steamboats and canals increased trade through faster or cheaper shipping. (c) Steamboats and canals led to rapid growth in cities they served.

3. (a) Cities in the 1850s were located inland as well as on the coast. (b) Cities had many more people, including large numbers of Irish immigrants. (c) News about current events traveled quickly between cities by telegraph instead of slowly by ship or horse. Within cities, news spread through cheap newspapers.

4. (a) Women, Indians, and blacks could not vote in the colonies or in the new states. (b) In the new western states, white men could vote even if they did not own property or pay taxes. (c) Politicians reacted by appealing to the "common" people. Political parties sponsored entertainments. Campaigns relied on name-calling.

5. (a) The South opposed tariffs because they raised the cost of manufactured goods bought by southerners. (b) South Carolina nullified the tariffs. (c) South Carolina threatened to secede. (d) Jackson urged Congress to reduce the tariffs, and he made no threatening move with army troops.

6. (a) Hamilton wanted to strengthen the government and the economy. (b) Jackson believed the bank had too much economic and political power. (c) The supply of paper money increased rapidly, and people withdrew specie from circulation.

7. (a) Abolitionists wanted Congress to discuss ending slavery. (b) Southern members of Congress wanted to avoid the issue. (c) The "gag rule" was a rule banning all discussion in Congress of petitions against slavery. (d) The rule was defeated in 1844.

8. (a) Spanish explorers found no gold in Texas, and Indians attacked settlements. (b) After 1821 Mexico opened Texas to American immigration. (c) Mexico feared that Texas was turning into an American state. (d) In 1836 Texas became an independent nation.

9. (a) The Great Plains were a barrier because people of the time believed the plains were too dry for farming. (b) In colonial days, the barrier was the Appalachian Mountain chain. (c) Neither the plains nor the mountains could be easily farmed. The plains, unlike the mountains, could be easily crossed.

10. (a) Lewis and Clark traveled to explore on Jefferson's orders. (b) The mountain men traveled to trap fur animals and trade the furs. (c) The Whitmans and Spaldings traveled to bring the Christian faith to the Indians. (d) People in the 1840s traveled to settle in Oregon.

Linking the Past and the Present

Students' answers will vary.

Meeting the Builders of America

1. Answers will vary. Students may note Lukens's management ability or refusal to be discouraged, Swisshelm's courage and convictions, and Houston's leadership and patriotism.

CHAPTER 14

Section 14–1 Review (text page 356)

1. See definitions on text page 352.

2. *Denmark Vesey:* free black who attempted to start a slave rebellion in Charleston. *Nat Turner:* slave preacher who led slaves from plantation to plantation killing white people in Virginia.

3. Living conditions improved because rising slave prices made the slaves too valuable to mistreat; masters saw slaves as part of the plantation "family"; plantation owners wanted to prove abolitionist attacks were wrong.

4. Slave codes were intended to strengthen masters' control over their slaves.

5. Accept any three of the following: Slaves broke tools, put rocks in their cotton sacks, pretended not to understand orders, refused to accept punishment, ran away.

6. The uncertainty was that the family might be broken up by sale of some members.

Approaches to Reading: The Comparison-Contrast Pattern (text page 361)

1. *Yet* is the signal word that begins the first paragraph.

2. The first paragraph shows how the South contrasted with the abolitionists' picture of the region. Supporting facts include: three fifths of slaveholders owned fewer than ten slaves, seven white families out of ten had no slaves.

3. *Just as* are the signal words in the second paragraph of the subsection.

4. The words suggest similarity.

5. Planters thought that money earned from land was better than money earned in trade, whereas northern manufacturers felt that industry was a respectable occupation.

6. This subsection is about comparisons between planters and farmers. It also contrasts southerners with northerners, however.

Section 14–2 Review (text page 361)

1. See definition on text page 357.

2. Limited liability protected a corporation's stockholders from responsibility for paying the company's debts.

3. The southern economy was based on agriculture, primarily cotton. The northern economy was based on manufacturing and trade. The North had most of the nation's factories, canals, and railroads.

4. Trade on the Mississippi diminished as farmers began shipping produce to markets in the East on the railroads, rather than by boat to the Gulf of Mexico.

5. Southerners feared that northerners might increase the tariff, pass laws interfering with the interstate slave trade, and put an antislavery amendment into the Constitution.

Section 14–3 Review (text page 367)

1. See definitions on text page 362.

2. *Wilmot Proviso:* a legislative amendment that banned slavery in the territories acquired in the Mexican War. *Millard Fillmore:* Zachary Taylor's Vice-President, who became President when Taylor died. *Harriet Beecher Stowe:* abolitionist author of *Uncle Tom's Cabin. Franklin Pierce:* Democrat who was elected President in 1852. *Stephen A. Douglas:* the Senator from Illinois who backed popular sovereignty and introduced the Kansas-Nebraska bill.

3. The Free-Soil party stood for excluding slavery from the territories and for providing free homesteads to settlers.

4. The Compromise of 1850 preserved the Union.

5. The Fugitive Slave Act caused trouble in the North because northerners did not want to enforce its provisions.

6. Northerners opposed the Kansas-Nebraska Act because it repealed the Missouri Compromise and allowed slavery into territories that had formerly forbidden it.

7. The act split the Whig party, made the Democratic party more pro-southern, and caused the formation of the Republican party.

Section 14–4 Review (text page 370)

1. See definitions on text page 368.

2. *James Buchanan:* Democrat who was elected President in 1856.

3. "Bleeding Kansas and bleeding Sumner" convinced the North that the rule of law was being replaced by force.

4. The Democrats supported the Kansas-Nebraska Act in the election of 1856.

5. (a) The Democrats became more the party of

the South in 1856. (b) The Republican party represented only the North.

6. In the Dred Scott decision, the Supreme Court ruled that blacks were not citizens, that the Missouri Compromise was unconstitutional, and that Congress could not ban slavery in the territories.

7. Republicans charged that the Supreme Court had joined the "slaveholders' conspiracy."

Using the Tools of History: Using Maps and Graphs to Interpret Data (text page 375)

1. Seventeen states gave all their electoral votes to Lincoln.

2. New Jersey gave some of its electoral votes to Lincoln.

3. Lincoln received 180 electoral votes, or 59 percent of the total. He received only 40 percent of the popular vote.

4. Douglas received the second largest percentage of the popular vote, but he carried only one state, Missouri. He received only 4 percent of the electoral vote.

5. Douglas received nine votes from Missouri and three from New Jersey.

6. In 1860, 152 electoral votes were a majority.

7. If New York had voted for another candidate, the House would have had to decide the election.

Section 14–5 Review (text page 376)

1. *Freeport Doctrine:* Stephen Douglas's statement that people in a territory could exclude slavery by refusing to pass slave codes. *Jefferson Davis:* President of the Confederacy. *Alexander Stephens:* Vice-President of the Confederacy.

2. Lincoln believed that slavery was morally wrong and that it would die a natural death.

3. By heightening fears of abolitionists' stirring up slave rebellions, John Brown's raid at Harpers Ferry gained widespread support for southern radicals who favored secession.

4. The Democratic party split into northern and southern groups before the 1860 election. Douglas and the northern Democrats insisted on popular sovereignty. The southern Democrats insisted on protecting slavery in the territories.

5. Lincoln's election caused the South to secede.

6. When Confederate General P. G. T. Beauregard

ordered his artillery to fire on Fort Sumter, the ships sent by Lincoln stayed outside the harbor. Major Anderson surrendered his Union troops when their ammunition ran out. The Confederates let them leave on the supply ships.

CHAPTER SURVEY (text pages 378–379)

Vocabulary Review

1. (c)	**4.** (b)	**7.** (c)
2. (a)	**5.** (c)	
3. (a)	**6.** (b)	

Chapter Review

1. (a) Slaveholders believed that slaves could not take care of themselves, therefore it was the masters' duty and responsibility to take care of them. (b) The strongest tie between farmers and planters was their belief that freedom for the slaves would be a disaster for the South.

2. (a) Improving living conditions did not make it easier for masters to control their slaves. (b) Slaves tried to maintain self-respect by resisting control in many ways and by caring for each other in their families.

3. Yes, southerners had good reason to fear slave rebellions. There were several slave rebellions.

4. (a) The North was ahead of the South in factory production, railroads, canals, and population. (b) Plantation agriculture was still profitable, and planters were proud of their way of life as country gentlemen. They felt manufacturing was not an honorable profession.

5. (a) The Wilmot Proviso raised the question whether slavery should be allowed in the territories. (b) The doctrine of popular sovereignty let the people in each territory make the decision whether to allow slavery or forbid it. (c) The Dred Scott decision said the territories could not be closed to slaveholders.

6. (a) Southerners did not want to admit California as a free state. (b) Northerners did not want to enforce the Fugitive Slave Act. (c) The North passed "personal liberty laws" that made enforcement of the fugitive slave laws difficult.

7. (a) The Kansas-Nebraska Act repealed the Missouri Compromise and allowed slaveholders into territory the North thought should be free. (b) Popular sovereignty led to violence, bloodshed, and election fraud in Kansas.

8. The Whig party broke apart over the Kansas-Nebraska Act. The Democratic party divided into a northern and a southern party in 1860 and ran two different candidates for President.

9. (a) John Brown hoped to start a slave rebellion by raiding the arsenal at Harpers Ferry. (b) Abolitionists saw Brown as a martyr. (c) Brown's raid was used by radicals as evidence that the abolitionist North was plotting slave rebellions.

10. When Lincoln sent supply ships to Fort Sumter, he knew that the Confederacy would regard his action as an act of war and would respond in some way.

Geography Review

1. (a) Utah and New Mexico territories were opened to slavery by the Compromise of 1850. (b) Kansas and Nebraska territories were opened to slavery by the Kansas-Nebraska Act. (c) Oregon Territory and Minnesota Territory remained free.

2. (a) Rice and sugarcane grew along the coast and coastal waterways. (b) Rice, sugarcane, and cotton seldom grew north of North Carolina. (c) Cotton was most important in Florida.

3. (a) Most of the rail lines connect the East with the West. Atlanta and Chattanooga were linked by rail in 1850. Chattanooga and Memphis were linked by 1860.

Using the Tools of History

(a) Bell won the same percentage of popular and electoral votes. (b) Douglas received more than 25 percent of the popular vote but only 4 percent of the electoral vote. (c) Lincoln won less than half the popular vote. (d) He carried only northern and western states.

Reading and Thinking Skills

(a) *But, while,* and *like* are the signal words in the first paragraph. (b) The paragraph is about contrasts between the North and the South. *Like* signals a comparison between factories and transportation. (c) In the third paragraph, political power is compared to economic power; representation in the House of Representatives is contrasted with representation in the Senate. (d) The South dis-

liked tariffs because they raised the prices southerners paid for imported goods. The North liked
tariffs because they protected northern manufacturing.

CHAPTER 15

Section 15-1 Review (text page 383)

1. See definitions on text page 380.

2. *Robert E. Lee:* Confederate military leader.

3. Southerners were fighting to protect their
homes and way of life.

4. Northerners were fighting to preserve the
Union.

5. Accept any three of the following advantages of
the North: greater wealth, more factories, more
food production, more rail lines, a large number
of ships, a larger population.

6. Accept any three of the following advantages of
the South: cotton exports, defensive war, eager volunteers, the best officers.

7. (a) Lincoln set aside the right of habeas corpus
and had secessionists jailed during an incident of
violence in Maryland. (b) He stopped violence in
Missouri by putting the state under martial law.

Using the Tools of History: Interpreting
Political Cartoons (text page 389)

1. The subject is Abraham Lincoln and the Emancipation Proclamation.

2. The cartoonist thinks Lincoln is misusing his
power, acting more like a king than a President.

3. The devil's face replaces Lincoln's. It stands for
evil deeds.

4. Other symbols are a flag, a noose for hanging,
and a chain.

5. Students may describe Lincoln's expression as
mean, nasty, or ugly.

6. From the cartoon, it appears that the cartoonist
dislikes the President.

7. The message is that Lincoln has shown his true
face, that of an evil, power-hungry ruler, by issuing
the Emancipation Proclamation.

8. The cartoon appeared in a Confederate paper.
Confederates opposed the Emancipation Proclamation.

Section 15-2 Review (text page 389)

1. See definition on text page 384.

2. *Virginia* (also called *Merrimac*) and *Monitor:* first
ironclad ships to fight in the Civil War. *Thomas J.
"Stonewall" Jackson:* Confederate general who won
the first Battle of Bull Run (some students, especially in the South, may know the battle as First
Manassas). *David Farragut:* Union naval officer who
captured New Orleans and Baton Rouge. *Ulysses S.
Grant:* Union officer who won several battles in the
war for the Mississippi River. *Emancipation Proclamation:* statement from President Lincoln declaring all slaves in the Confederacy to be free as of
January 1, 1863.

3. The anaconda plan was supposed to choke off
supplies to the Confederacy with a naval blockade,
to divide the Confederacy along the Mississippi
River, and to capture Richmond.

4. The battle proved that wooden ships could not
stand up to ironclads.

5. The Union's four attempts to take Richmond all
ended in failure. They were: the first Battle of Bull
Run (First Manassas), the Battle of Seven Pines,
the Seven Days' Battles, and the second Battle of
Bull Run (also known as Second Manassas).

6. Lincoln wanted to keep France and Great Britain from recognizing the Confederacy. He wanted
the announcement to come after a Union victory
so that it would not appear to be an act of desperation. He wanted to make it clear that if the Union
won the war, arguments about slavery would no
longer divide the nation.

Section 15-3 Review (text page 394)

1. See definitions on text page 390.

2. *Copperheads:* northern Democrats who favored
an end to the war and negotiation with the Confederacy. *Elizabeth Blackwell:* first American woman
to graduate from a medical college. She directed
the training of Union nurses during the Civil War.
Clara Barton: Union nurse known as the "Angel of
the Battlefield," who later founded the American
Red Cross.

3. (a) Lincoln faced cabinet members who spoke
and acted against him and Copperheads who demanded an end to war and a negotiated peace. (b)
Davis faced cabinet members who opposed him,
state governments who favored states' rights, and

some citizens who openly opposed secession.

4. (a) The South tried to borrow money abroad and printed paper money. (b) The North raised taxes, sold bonds, taxed incomes, and printed paper money.

5. The South could not get cotton through the blockade to its foreign markets; the South could not import badly needed supplies.

6. Both North and South conscripted soldiers when the supply of volunteers ran low.

7. The black 54th Massachusetts Infantry refused to accept any pay at all until they received pay equal to that of white soldiers.

8. Accept any four of the following jobs done by women: soldier, spy, scout, nurse, factory worker, farmer, government worker.

Section 15-4 Review (text page 400)

1. *George C. Meade:* leader of the Army of the Potomac at Gettysburg. *George Pickett:* Confederate general who led Pickett's charge at Gettysburg. *George Thomas:* Union general called the Rock of Chickamauga for his brave stand in that battle. *Gettysburg Address:* Lincoln's speech at the dedication of Gettysburg Cemetery after the Battle of Gettysburg.

2. Lee's goals in invading the North were to convince Britain and France to recognize the Confederacy as an independent nation and to encourage the North to seek peace.

3. Grant's victories at Vicksburg and Port Hudson gave the Union control of the Mississippi River and divided the Confederacy.

4. Capturing Chattanooga was important because it was a major Confederate railroad center.

Section 15-5 Review (text page 404)

1. See definition on text page 401.

2. *William Tecumseh Sherman:* Union general who led the march through Georgia and the Carolinas. *Andrew Johnson:* Lincoln's running mate in 1864. *Appomattox Court House:* town where Lee surrendered to Grant.

3. Victories at Atlanta and the Shenandoah Valley helped Lincoln win reelection.

4. The North had a larger population and could replace Union casualties. By 1865 Lee could not replace the soldiers he lost.

5. Under the terms of the surrender, the Confederate troops were allowed to return home if they promised to fight no longer. They were allowed to take their horses and mules with them.

CHAPTER SURVEY (text pages 406–407)

Vocabulary Review

1. (f)	**3.** (e)	**5.** (b)
2. (a)	**4.** (d)	**6.** (c)

Chapter Review

1. At the beginning of the Civil War (the War Between the States), the North had three fourths of the nation's wealth, four fifths of its factories, more food production, and a better rail system. The South's white population was one third that of the North.

2. The South was running short of both troops and supplies by 1863, but the North was able to keep its armies supplied with troops and equipment. This made it possible for Grant and Sherman to destroy the South's will and ability to continue the struggle.

3. (a) Virginia, Arkansas, Tennessee, and North Carolina were the border states that seceded despite Lincoln's efforts to keep them in the Union. (b) Lincoln suspended the right of habeas corpus to keep Maryland from seceding.

4. (a) The Union strategies included the anaconda plan and capturing Richmond. (b) The anaconda plan involved steady pressure on the Confederacy by cutting off its trade and dividing it. The plan to take Richmond involved a quick attack. (c) The anaconda plan was more successful. The Confederacy foiled attempts to take Richmond.

5. (a) The Emancipation Proclamation did not free a single slave when it was issued. (b) It kept the nations of Europe from recognizing and aiding the Confederacy; it made the war into a struggle for freedom; and it led to the use of black troops in the Union armies.

6. (a) Both Presidents faced difficult cabinets, opposition to the war, lack of money, inflation, and the lack of enough volunteers. (b) Davis also had to deal with state governors who strongly supported states' rights.

7. Women moved into new jobs in factories, government, and nursing.

8. (a) Major Union victories in 1863 were the battles of Gettysburg, Vicksburg, and Chattanooga. (b) The Confederacy lost troops, a chance to cut off the Union capital from the rest of the Union, control of the Mississippi, and an important rail center. (c) The Union proved that Lee could be defeated, divided the Confederacy, beat back an invasion, and identified a general who could take charge of the war effort.

9. (a) Grant was met by Lee's forces. (b) He suffered very heavy casualties, like his predecessors. (c) Unlike the other generals, Grant did not retreat to Washington after his losses. Instead he followed Lee's army and fought more battles.

10. (a) Grant ordered Sherman to destroy the war-making resources of Georgia. (b) Sherman's troops destroyed cities, farms, houses, and railroads. (c) The orders meant total war, or complete destruction of their property.

Geography Review

(a) Eleven states joined the Confederacy. (b) Five slave states were part of the Union. (c) California and Oregon were separated from the rest of the Union.

Using the Tools of History

1. (a) Lincoln was very tall. (b) The cartoonist exaggerated his height. (c) Voters made Lincoln's presidency four years longer by reelecting him. (d) The cartoon is both humorous and political. It makes a joke and it also refers to Lincoln's political success in the election.

2. (a) The Confederacy controlled West Virginia and Kentucky in 1861–1862. (b) By 1863 the Confederacy controlled a smaller area, in West Virginia only. (c) By 1864–1865, it was a still smaller area of West Virginia. (d) The Confederacy was split along the Mississippi and then again by Sherman's march. (e) The legend of the 1863 map has a symbol for a Confederate victory. The later map does not. Instead, it has a new symbol representing an indecisive battle.

Reading and Thinking Skills

(a) Inferential. Sometimes war is the best solution to a conflict.

(b) Literal

(c) Inferential. The ironclad ship looked like a flimsy tin box on a floating platform.

(d) Literal

CHAPTER 16

Using the Tools of History: Analyzing Primary Sources (text page 410)

1. Yes, Lamon was an eyewitness to Lincoln's account.

2. Yes, he says he made notes "immediately after its recital."

3. Probably yes, because the President trusted him as an adviser for many years.

4. There were other witnesses—Lamon mentions "two or three others."

Section 16–1 Review (text page 411)

1. See definition on text page 408.

2. *Thirteenth Amendment:* amendment that ended slavery. *John Wilkes Booth:* actor who assassinated Lincoln. *Freedmen's Bureau:* agency set up to help freed slaves after the war.

3. Northern industries grew during the war.

4. The South suffered physical damage, financial ruin, and enormous human losses.

5. Freed slaves faced problems finding lost family members, finding work, and finding new ways to live with whites.

Approaches to Reading: The Persuasive Pattern (text page 414)

1. The two generalizations are: Four million slaves had been set free without homes or money. Slavery kept them from learning the skills needed by free people.

2. The two opinions are: Congress should care for ex-slaves until they can care for themselves. If Congress refuses to help the ex-slaves, it would have been better to leave them in slavery.

3. Stevens wanted Congress to pass laws giving ex-slaves land and protection.

4. The outcome is implied, but so strongly that some students may answer that it is clearly stated.

Section 16–2 Review (text page 415)

1. See definitions on text page 412.

2. *Ten percent plan:* Lincoln's Reconstruction plan, which allowed Confederate states to reorganize once 10 percent of the voters in 1860 had taken an oath of loyalty to the Union. *Radical Republicans:* Republicans who favored very strict requirements for readmission of the former Confederate states. *Wade-Davis bill:* bill passed by Congress in 1864 requiring a majority of the white men in a Confederate state to take a loyalty oath before a new government could be formed. *Homestead Act:* act promising a free farm to anyone who worked the land for five years.

3. Lincoln vetoed the Wade-Davis bill because he thought it was too harsh.

4. Johnson asked the Confederate states to repeal their acts of secession, to ratify the Thirteenth Amendment, and to cancel state war debts.

5. The black codes were intended to define the rights of blacks, to help economic recovery by providing labor for plantations, and to limit blacks to working on farms or as servants.

6. Republicans opposed Johnson's Reconstruction plan because they believed that justice demanded that rebels be punished and ex-slaves treated fairly. They also wanted to remain in control of Congress, as they would not if readmitted southern states elected Democrats.

Section 16-3 Review (text page 420)

1. See definitions on text page 416.

2. *Thaddeus Stevens:* Congressman from Pennsylvania and a leader of the Radical Republicans. *Charles Sumner:* Senator from Massachusetts and a leader of the Radical Republicans. *Civil Rights Bill of 1866:* bill to protect the civil rights of blacks. *Fourteenth Amendment:* constitutional amendment to protect the rights of blacks. *Reconstruction Acts of 1867:* Radical Republicans' plan for Reconstruction of the South.

3. The first two sections of the Fourteenth Amendment gave citizenship to all people born in the United States and encouraged states to give all black (and white) men the right to vote.

4. Radical Republicans gained control of Congress in the election of 1866.

5. The steps for readmission were: Hold a constitutional convention to write a new state constitution that guarantees black men the right to vote. Get approval of the constitution by the voters. Hold elections for a new state legislature. Have the legislature ratify the Fourteenth Amendment.

6. Andrew Johnson was charged with violating the Tenure of Office Act and harming the reputation of Congress.

7. Johnson escaped removal from office by only one vote.

Section 16-4 Review (text page 428)

1. See definitions on text page 421.

2. *Carpetbaggers:* northerners who came to live in the South after the Civil War. *Scalawags:* white southerners who supported the Republican party after the war. *Fifteenth Amendment:* constitutional amendment saying that the right to vote cannot be denied on the basis of race. *Hiram Revels:* first black to serve in the Senate. *Rutherford B. Hayes:* governor of Ohio, elected President in 1877.

3. Carpetbaggers, scalawags, and southern blacks gained political power in the South as Congressional Reconstruction began.

4. Most sharecroppers were unable to save enough money to buy land of their own because they were always in debt to landlords and storekeepers.

5. (a) Secret societies like the Ku Klux Klan wanted to put blacks "in their place" and return the South to white men's rule. (b) They used terrorism in the form of threats, burnings, beatings, and murder.

6. Democrats took control of state governments after 1872, when most former Confederates were allowed to vote and hold office again. Southern voters believed the Reconstruction Republicans spent too much tax money and were guilty of bribery and dishonesty in office.

7. In the Compromise of 1877, Democrats agreed to the election of Republican Rutherford Hayes as President in exchange for the Republicans' promise to remove the last troops from the South and to end Reconstruction.

CHAPTER SURVEY (text pages 430–431)

Vocabulary Review

1. (a)	**5.** (e)	**9.** (h)
2. (c)	**6.** (i)	**10.** (d)
3. (b)	**7.** (j)	**11.** (f)
4. (g)	**8.** (k)	

Chapter Review

1. (a) The difference that disappeared was slavery. (b) Economic differences increased during the war. Manufacturing in the North increased while the South was systematically ruined.

2. (a) Lincoln proposed the "ten percent plan," which allowed former Confederate states to reorganize their governments once 10 percent of the voters in the 1860 election had taken an oath of loyalty to the Union. (b) Congress thought Lincoln's plan was too generous and that Congress should control Reconstruction.

3. (a) Defeat meant financial ruin to southerners, because owners received no compensation for freed slaves and bonds were declared worthless by law. (b) Planters needed a dependable work force. (c) Sharecropping gave planters a way to attract workers to their land.

4. (a) Sharecropping offered former slaves a way to get their own land to farm. (b) No, because for most blacks, sharecropping led to a life of debt.

5. (a) Radicals thought Johnson's plan failed to punish former rebels enough and did not protect former slaves. (b) Johnson's plan would have given southern Democrats more seats in the House of Representatives.

6. (a) The Fourteenth Amendment declared all people born in the United States to be citizens, including blacks. (b) The amendment says that states cannot take away any citizen's life, liberty, or property without due process of law. (c) It guarantees equal treatment under law to all citizens.

7. (a) Northerners who moved south ("carpetbaggers"), southerners who supported the Union ("scalawags"), and southern blacks gained power under Congressional Reconstruction. (b) Secret societies like the Ku Klux Klan were formed to drive these groups out of power. (c) These organizations used terrorism against both black and white Republicans.

8. (a) The Fifteenth Amendment guaranteed the right to vote to adult males. (b) Northern states that denied the vote to blacks were most affected.

9. (a) The Amnesty Act of 1872 restored voting rights to former Confederates and allowed them to hold office. (b) The Amnesty Act helped the Democratic party because most of the disfranchised

southerners voted Democratic. (c) The act's passage showed that the Radicals were no longer as powerful as they had been.

10. (a) The Democrats gave up the presidency in the Compromise of 1877. (b) They gained removal of federal troops from the South and an end to Reconstruction. (c) Republicans gained Hayes's election as President. (d) Black voters in the South lost protection by federal troops.

Geography Review

(a) Three states west of the Mississippi voted for Tilden: Missouri, Arkansas, and Texas. (b) Five New England states voted for Hayes: Maine, New Hampshire, Vermont, Massachusetts, and Rhode Island. (c) There are six New England states. (d) South Carolina, Florida, and Louisiana voted for Hayes. All the rest voted for Tilden.

Using the Tools of History

(a) The writer was probably a white male.
(b) His "hands" were probably black males, who had gained the right to vote by 1868.
(c) The writer had economic power because he employed the workers and had the right to fire them.
(d) He used his power to discourage the "hands" from voting.
(e) Three of the workers refused to give in to the pressure; two agreed not to vote.
(f) The letter shows that economic power was used to disfranchise voters.

Reading and Thinking Skills

(a) The Republicans expected to win the election of 1868. (b) To win northern votes, the Republicans "waved the bloody shirt," that is, they kept the memory of the war alive. (c) Statement 2 would have been best. (d) In Philadelphia, a Republican parade featured wagonloads of wounded Union soldiers.

UNIT SURVEY (text pages 432–433)

Unit Review

1. (a) The slave population was still located in the south. (b) The slave population had spread south and southwest as tobacco, rice, indigo, and cotton plantations had spread.

2. (a) Southerners saw that people in the North seemed too concerned with making money and, if they failed, they escaped their debts through corporation laws. (b) The factory system was not common in the South.

3. (a) The Compromise of 1850 opened the Utah and New Mexico territories to slavery. (b) The Kansas-Nebraska Act opened the Kansas and Nebraska territories to slavery. (c) The Dred Scott decision opened all territories to slavery.

4. (a) In colonial times, northerners had no say in any government that made laws for the South. (b) Harriet Beecher Stowe increased antislavery feelings .with her novel *Uncle Tom's Cabin.* (c) Northerners were outraged by the Dred Scott decision and the Kansas-Nebraska Act.

5. (a) Lincoln's election triggered secession. (b) The Confederate firing on Fort Sumter, South Carolina, in April 1861 marked the start of the Civil War. (c) Northerners expected a quick war. (d) The war lasted four years.

6. (a) Lincoln opposed abolition just after his election. (b) On January 1, 1863, he issued the Emancipation Proclamation, abolishing slavery in Confederate states. (c) His stand helped convince Britain and France not to aid the Confederacy.

7. (a) Total war meant destruction of civilian property, including houses, farms, and food, as well as destruction of military targets. (b) After the surrender of Petersburg and Richmond, Lee had no choice but to surrender. (c) Appomattox was not an unconditional surrender, because Grant and Lee met to discuss the terms of surrender before the surrender was final.

8. (a) All three groups of states were sites of Revolutionary War battles. (b) The Middle and Southern states were sites of Civil War battles. (c) Gettysburg, Pennsylvania, was the northernmost battleground. (d) The locations of battles meant that devastation of property was almost entirely in the states of the South.

9. (a) Reconstruction was meant to reorganize southern states so that they could be readmitted to the Union. (b) Lincoln planned to readmit southern states when 10 percent of their voters in the 1860 election took loyalty oaths to the Union. (c) Radical Republicans prevented Johnson from completing Reconstruction quickly. (d) Reconstruction lasted 12 years.

10. (a) Sharecropping took the place of slavery. (b) Terrorism by the Ku Klux Klan and other groups kept many blacks from voting. (c) The election results in 1876 were disputed. In the Compromise of 1877, the Democrats in Congress agreed to accept Republican Rutherford B. Hayes as President if the Republicans would agree to withdraw all troops from the South.

Linking the Past and the Present

1. Answers will vary.

2. Answers will vary.

Meeting the Builders of America

1. Answers will vary. Students may mention Vallejo's desire for self-government in California, Forten's interest in education, and Revels's political leadership and fairness.

ANSWER KEY
AMERICAN VOICES

CHAPTER 1

The Law of the Great Peace (page 435)

1. The tree is planted to mark the alliance of the Five Nations. It stands for the "Great Peace," i.e., the alliance of the tribes. The roots stand for "Peace and Strength." The eagle stands for the Five Nations' concern with security.

2. When there is business to do, a message is sent to Atotarho, Hononwirehton, or Skanawate. Atotarho calls his cousin chiefs together to decide if the matter warrants assembling all the chiefs. If so, messengers are sent to notify them.

3. The Council Fire is lit to open a council meeting. Smoke from the fire also shows allies of the Five Nations that the council is in session.

A Papago Rain Song (page 436)

1. Students can cite the following word pictures: the "waves rolling . . . covered with many clouds" appealing to the eye; "the ocean—singing" and "the deep rumbling" appealing to the ear; and the "earth shaking—beneath me" appealing to the sense of touch.

2. The rain song shows the Papago's deep awareness of natural phenomena. They are very close to nature.

We Must Part (page 436)

1. Most students would agree that a poem about a parting is a sad one.

2. Answers will vary. One possible reason for parting is that the chief must go to war.

Zuñi Corn-Grinding Song (page 436)

1. The rhythm would probably be fairly fast. That way, the work would go quickly.

2. The song is about growing corn. Corn provides the raw material for the corn meal.

A Wasco Legend (page 437)

1. The snowstorm is unusual because it continued without stopping for seven months. It snowed only in one place.

2. The storm's cause is a girl striking a bird. The people learned this by asking a little bird "with a strawberry in its bill." They put the girl on ice and pushed the ice into the river.

3. The girl floated for five years until she returned to her starting place. She died, but later she came to life again.

4. Such phenomena as a snowstorm lasting seven months and a girl dying and coming to life again are part of a myth.

CHAPTER 2

Bjarni Herjulfson Searches for Greenland (page 438)

1. Bjarni has learned that Greenland has huge glaciers, and he can see none in this land. Also, the land has no mountains.

2. He decides not to stop at the third land because "it seems to be worthless."

3. The fourth land "agrees most with what I have been told about Greenland."

Queen Isabella and King Ferdinand Make an Agreement with Columbus (page 439)

1. The monarchs made Columbus an admiral and governor of "all the islands and mainlands" he would discover.

2. Columbus was allowed to keep a tenth of all the "pearls, precious stones, gold, silver, spices, and other things" he found.

Jacques Cartier Claims Gaspé Bay for France (page 440)

1. The ships were moved to escape the wind.

2. The Indians showed joy on seeing Cartier's sailors and came close to Cartier's ships. The male Indians sang and danced.

3. Cartier planted a cross inscribed "VIVE LE ROY DE FRANCE" at the harbor's entrance.

The Dream (page 440)

1. Sister Juana describes the sunrise as "rays of pure light," "darts of golden metal," and "sapphires gleaming bright."

2. Sister Juana was happy to be awake so early. Clues to her feelings are the words *pure, golden, gleaming, glowing, sparkling,* and *radiance.*

Hernando de Soto Discovers the Mississippi River (page 441)

1. Quizquiz was in western Tennessee. The soldiers moved to search for maize.

2. Answers will vary. Nothing in the selection indicates that the Indians had hostile intentions. It is possible, however, that de Soto was wary because of previous encounters with Indians.

3. The sentences are in the selection's second paragraph, beginning with, "The Governor moved to another town. . . ."

CHAPTER 3

Queen Elizabeth I Addresses Her Sailors (page 442)

1. Students may cite the third sentence of the first paragraph and the entire second paragraph.

2. Answers may differ. Many students will probably agree that Elizabeth's eloquence was an inspiration to her subjects.

Exploring with La Salle (page 442)

1. Father Membré is impressed by the beauty of the Indians' physiques.

2. He is impressed because the Indians are so polite that "none of them would take the liberty to enter our hut."

3. The last sentence suggests that the expedition suffered from thefts by other Indians.

John Smith Tells of His Rescue by Pocahontas (page 443)

1. Students can cite Powhatan's great robe of raccoon skins, the young girls at his sides, and the rows of men and women wearing finery.

2. The Indians decide to beat out Smith's brains with clubs. Pocahontas takes Smith's head in her arms and shields it with her own.

3. Smith is assigned to make hatchets for Powhatan and bells and beads for Pocahontas. That Powhatan is able to do this kind of work himself shows that he is not set apart from the people as are European monarchs.

Lady Margaret Wyatt Crosses the Atlantic (page 444)

1. The captain made amends for overcrowding by dying himself.

2. The Virginians need help from England because people and cattle have died, and the colonists are short of food.

A Colonist Criticizes Peter Stuyvesant (page 444)

1. Students can cite the sentences in the selection's first paragraph and the second sentence in the second paragraph.

2. Students can cite the two sentences in the second paragraph beginning, "For Stuyvesant's pride has ruled. . . ."

3. Van der Donck complains that taxes are so high no one wants to start a new enterprise (for fear of having to pay most of the profits in taxes).

CHAPTER 4

Margaret Winthrop to Her Husband (page 445)

1. Margaret Winthrop loves her husband because he loves God and because he loves her.

2. She ends her letter because she must go about her "household affairs" and the cold weather bids her make haste.

3. Students may cite the following sentences: "May those comforts we have in each other be daily increased, as far as they are pleasing to God." "Thou lovest God." "God will bring us together in His good time." "The Lord make us thankful for all His mercies."

William Penn Reports on Pennsylvania (page 446)

1. The various peoples live in one place and "under one allegiance" so that they are, in effect, "the people of one country."

2. Students may cite the following details: the large number (357) of houses built; the number of streets; the wharf; and the number of people working at useful trades.

3. Answers may differ. Most students will probably agree that Penn treated the Indians fairly, paying them for land and giving them equal treatment under Pennsylvania's laws.

Aulkey Hubertse Becomes an Indentured Servant (page 446)

1. Hubertse is forbidden by the contract to waste her master's goods; play cards or dice; buy or sell goods; go out without permission; and go to taverns, alehouses, or plays.

2. Delemont promises to provide meat and drink, washing, lodging, clothing, and other necessities.

3. Aulkey Hubertse can end her service by getting married.

Eliza Lucas Pinckney, Planter (page 447)

1. Eliza Pinckney reports that Charles Town is a polite and agreeable place, that the country abounds in game, and that there are six "agreeable" families nearby.

2. The running of three plantations occupied her time. For recreation she had her library, music, and garden, and her visits to Charles Town.

CHAPTER 5

A New England Alphabet (page 448)

1. The following words introduce the letters: *Adam* for *A; Glass* (hourglass) for *G; Job* for *J;* and *Lion* and *Lamb* for *L*.

2. "The idle Fool/Is whipt at school" teaches the importance of work. "In Adam's fall ..." and "Job feels the rod ..." show the importance of religion to the Puritans.

A Slave's Epitaph (page 449)

1. The first contrast is that God creates people free, but humanity enslaves them. The second contrast is that the slave was born a free man "in a land of slavery" but lived as a slave "in a land of liberty."

2. Death finally set the slave free. Because all are equal in the grave, the slave is now "on a footing with kings."

Anne Bradstreet to Her Husband (page 449)

1. Anne Bradstreet and her husband are so close that they are like one person.

2. The poet and her husband, if true to each other, will live forever in heaven as a couple. The line reflects the Puritan belief in an afterlife.

Canassateego's Speech (page 450)

1. William Penn was a good man because of his "kind regard" for the Indians. Considering the chief's complaints, we may assume that he does not think that these officials are as good as Penn.

2. The goods the Indians received for land, even if divided only among those present, would amount to "but a small portion for each." If the number of Indians "left behind" were included in the sharing, the portions would amount to practically nothing. The chief is concerned about the lands not sold because colonists are settling there.

3. The Indians' poverty is caused by colonists who settle on their land and spoil their hunting.

"What Then Is the American?" (page 450)

1. According to Crèvecoeur, in America the "rich and poor are not as far removed from each other as they are in Europe."

2. Americans work hard because "each person works for himself," not a superior.

3. Travelers will see log houses large and small, all of which are "dry and comfortable." In church travelers will see respectable farm families, clad in homespun, not "princes."

CHAPTER 6

Pontiac Calls for War (page 451)

1. Pontiac says that the goods the British sell the Indians do not last and cost twice as much as French goods. Also, the British refuse to extend credit to the Indians.

2. Students can cite sentences about the British commander laughing at the Indians, as well as the selection's last paragraph.

The Stamp Act: Benjamin Franklin Testifies (page 452)

1. According to Franklin, American colonists once "submitted willingly to the government of the

Crown." Now they have totally lost "respect and affection" for Great Britain. They are so angry they will not pay the stamp duty. Colonists will stop buying English manufactures, causing trade to decline.

2. Franklin says that a military force sent to America may create a rebellion.

3. Franklin tells the British that the colonists will go to any length to avoid buying British goods, so great is their displeasure.

The Daughters of Liberty Organize Boycotts
(page 453)

1. The Boston women agree to do completely without tea.

2. According to the planter's wife, the British are the enemies of America who would "enslave ourselves and future Americans."

3. The letters show that the colonists were outraged by British actions and felt that they should unite against a common enemy.

The Boston Massacre: Andrew's Testimony
(page 454)

1. Bostonians threw snowballs at the soldiers, jeered at them, and hit them with sticks. The soldiers attacked Bostonians with cutlasses.

2. The "stout man" (Attucks) attacked an officer with a cordwood stick and encouraged the Bostonians to make a rush at the soldiers.

3. Apparently Attucks was shot by one of the soldiers, perhaps Killroy.

CHAPTER 7

Letter to a British Army Officer (page 455)

1. Students may cite sentences relating to the writer's brother and to cutting unnecessary expenses and "I know this—that as free I can die but once. But as a slave I shall not be worthy of life."

2. The "plain truth" is that no one has the right to take the colonists' money without their consent. The truth refers to the Sugar Act, the Stamp Act, and the Townshend Acts.

Deborah Champion's Daring Ride (page 455)

1. The British were camped in Providence, Rhode Island. Washington was in Boston.

2. Champion avoided capture by persuading a British sentry that she was hurrying to see a friend in need.

3. Champion considered Washington grand, kind, and noble.

"And All the People Shall Say Amen"
(page 457)

1. Students may cite the troops assembled for the ceremony, the reading of the Declaration from the balcony of the State House, the three cheers, the ringing of the bells, the firing of the cannon, and the removal of the King's Arms.

2. The King's Arms were removed from the State House and "every trace of him was taken from every place in which it appeared" to show the end of "royal authority" in Massachusetts.

From the Diary of Margaret Hill Morris
(page 457)

1. Morris is first aware of the Battle of Trenton on January 3, 1777, when American soldiers coming into town tell her of it.

2. She learns that the Americans were victorious at Trenton and Princeton, and that 2,000 New Englanders were killed or wounded.

3. Students may cite Morris's compassion upon seeing the soldiers sleeping; her attention to the sick and wounded (implicit in the entry for January 4); and her efforts to give the leftover provisions to sick soldiers.

Valley Forge: Fire Cakes and Water (page 458)

1. The soldiers must eat "fire cakes and water" at all their meals. This fact suggests the near-starvation rations on which the soldiers had to subsist.

2. Waldo also tells of suffering from the cold and the smoke of the fires. A hut eventually makes his life more comfortable.

The Brave Volunteers (page 459)

1. The song mentions the merchant, the lawyer, and the farmer.

2. The lawyer may plead his country's cause by fighting bravely for it.

3. The farmer-soldier may win "bright fame" by heroism in battle.

CHAPTER 8

Saul's Petition (page 460)

1. Saul served America both as a soldier in the American army and as an American spy in the British army.

2. A black spy for the British disclosed that Saul was an American spy. "His heels saved his neck" indicates that Saul's swiftness in running away from the British saved him from being hanged.

Abigail Adams on Shays' Rebellion (page 461)

1. According to Adams, the rebels want paper currency, a division of property, the cancellation of all debts, and the abolition of the Senate and the Court of Common Pleas. Adams believes that the rebels want to destroy the government.

2. The causes of the rebellion, Adams reports, are vanity and extravagance.

3. Adams thinks that the rebellion was good in that it will lead to an investigation of its causes. One good effect already produced is the tax on some British imports and prohibition of others.

Delegates to the Constitutional Convention (page 462)

1. The "heavens obey" Franklin in the sense that his lightning rod prevents lightning from striking particular buildings.

2. Pierce thinks Franklin is a poor public speaker and lacks interest in politics.

3. Pierce values Washington's virtue, his willingness to be of service to the nation, and his retirement to his farm after the war. Pierce admires Madison for his learning and speaking ability, for blending "together the politician and the scholar," and for his agreeable nature.

On a Slave Ship (page 463)

1. Equiano's greatest fear was that he would be killed. The sentence means that working in "the white people's country" is not so desperate a fate as being put to death.

2. Two of the slaves drowned. The other was recaptured and whipped.

3. Students may cite the foul smells below deck, the "closeness of the place," the intolerable heat, chains and whippings, and "the groans of the dying."

CHAPTER 9

The Life of a *Llavera* (page 464)

1. Eulalia Perez passed out the daily rations at the mission and every eight days delivered rations to the troops and servants. She oversaw the distribution of supplies and managed the belt and shoe-making shop. She herself cut and fitted pieces for clothes, while her daughters sewed them. She worked the machine that pressed olive oil and made chocolate, candy, and lemonade.

2. In the morning, the Indian girls went to Mass, ate breakfast, and worked at assigned tasks. They stopped work at eleven, ate at twelve, and returned to work at one. At sundown, they stopped work and went to supper.

The Log Cabin (page 465)

1. The sides of the cabin are built with logs "placed upon one another" and held together by means of notches at the ends. The roof is made of similar logs "not quite so thick" and sloped on each side.

2. The cabins are cold because the space between the logs is "very carelessly" filled with clay, providing inefficient insulation.

3. The chimney is lined with clay to protect the wooden walls from the fire.

4. The beds are made of feathers.

The Whiskey Rebellion (page 465)

1. To Hamilton, the important question is whether the majority or a faction shall rule.

2. Hamilton tries to show that the situation is serious by stressing the legality of the excise tax: It stems from powers given Congress by the Constitution; it has been enacted and three times revised; and more than a million dollars has been collected under it. Sentences suggesting that the farmers want to overthrow the government can be found in the last paragraph: "They say, 'The Congress shall not have this power.'" "'We will punish the officers who shall attempt the collection. The control of the government shall not reside with you but with us.'"

The Life of a Young Southern Woman (page 466)

1. Lucinda Lee visits neighbors and dines and has tea with them; she takes walks and carriage rides and plays cards. Such amusements were an important part of the Virginia social life of the time.

2. Since the entry for October 5 reveals a keen interest in the races, it is unlikely that Lucinda Lee will keep her resolution.

Margaret Bayard Smith at Jefferson's Inauguration (page 467)

1. According to Smith, changes in government in other nations are often "times of confusion, villainy, and bloodshed." In America a change in administration takes place "without any disorder."

2. Students may cite such details as: The chamber was so crowded that "not another creature could enter"; "every inch of ground was occupied"; and "almost a thousand people were present."

CHAPTER 10

With Lewis and Clark (page 468)

1. Four of the six men fired at almost the same time. Then the other two fired, meaning to give the first four time to reload. But the bullets so little deflected the bear's charge that none of them had a chance to reload, and the men "took to flight."

2. Two men fled to a canoe. The others hid among the willows, reloaded, and fired again at the bear. The animal chased two men into the river. One man on shore finally killed the bear.

3. The men took the skin and got "several gallons of oil" from the fleece.

The British Invade Washington (page 469)

1. She is waiting for her husband.

2. She takes with her the silver and gold plates and other "most valuable articles that can be carried." At the last moment, she has the frame of George Washington's picture broken so that she can take the painting with her.

Margaret Bayard Smith: "The Poor Capitol!" (page 469)

1. According to Smith, the buildings most badly damaged are the House of Representatives and the White House. The pillars in the House are "cracked and broken" and the dome lies "in ashes." Of the White House, only the "cracked and blackened walls" remain. Inside, all is in ashes.

2. Smith reflects that the interior of so magnificent an edifice as the White House can in a few hours be reduced to ashes. Thus it is vain for humans to desire any kind of grandeur, since it can be brought low so quickly.

Jefferson's Epitaph (page 470)

1. The three achievements Jefferson valued most are drafting the Declaration of Independence and the Virginia statute for religious freedom and founding the University of Virginia.

2. Students may cite Jefferson's activities as diplomat, inventor, and statesman and his achievements as President. Most probably, Jefferson wished to be remembered for the achievements in his epitaph because all three promote freedom: political, religious, and intellectual.

CHAPTER 11

Life on a Georgia Plantation (page 471)

1. Plantation families raised grain, vegetables, cows, fowls of all kinds, and pigs. The families made most of their own clothing, quilts, leather for shoes, starch, and soap.

2. Students may cite the grandmother's hard work and management skills. She goes from house to garden to dairy to poultry house to loom house to meat house, making all her starch, and saving meat scraps and bones for soap. She organizes her own work and others'.

A Mill Woman's Thoughts (page 472)

1. Elizabeth Turner's parents and brothers are dead. Although uncles, aunts, and cousins offer her a home, she does not feel there is any place where she belongs.

2. She is sad because she lives "among strangers" and must work day after day in the mill.

3. She resolves not to complain, to save all she can, to "do all the good I can," to learn all she can, and as calmly as possible to await the day of judgment.

American Traders Visit the Californios (page 473)

1. A horseman tells the family that the ship is coming. The ship's captain seeks hides and tallow.

2. The Higueras render the tallow in iron kettles

and then pour the liquid fat into round pits to harden. Oak staffs, by which each cake of tallow can be carried, are put through the center. For their tallow and hides, the Higueras receive cloth, axes, shoes, fish-lines, grindstones, and jewelry.

3. The captain asks the father on board the ship to look over the goods that can be traded for the hides and tallow. The family is afraid that the father will be made a prisoner and carried off. The incident reveals the Californios' distrust of Americans.

Ellen Bigelow Sails on the *Illinois* (page 474)

1. The three chief perils of which Ellen Bigelow writes are the ship's striking a rock, being grounded on a rocky shoal, and being brought aground while trying to pass through a treacherous channel near Detroit.

2. The voyage's discomforts stemmed from the crowded state of the ship and the seasickness caused by the storm. Most students will probably agree that travel today is much more comfortable.

A Song of the Erie Canal (page 475)

1. The song mentions Albany, Buffalo, and Rome, New York.

2. Sal, the mule, was harnessed to the barge and pulled it along.

3. Everyone must get down to avoid being hit by a town's bridge. (All the towns along the Erie Canal would have bridges to enable pedestrians and riders to cross over it.)

CHAPTER 12

Margaret Bayard Smith: Andrew Jackson's Inauguration (page 476)

1. Jefferson's inauguration was orderly and dignified, but the rowdy, unruly crowd swarming into the White House deprived Jackson's inauguration of all dignity.

2. The administrations before Jackson had been essentially governments by upper-class persons. But Jackson, Smith notes, is "the people's President," and the crowd in the White House shows that "the people would rule." The new "era of the common people" stressed democracy.

Harriet Martineau in Washington (page 477)

1. Harriet Martineau thinks that southerners are the most civilized and polished of the Americans she meets. She contrasts their "ease" and "courtesy" to the "cautious and too respectful air" of New Englanders and to the odd appearance of westerners. English people of the time tended to look down on most Americans' free and easy ways.

2. Martineau thinks Clay and Webster are charming conversationalists and companions.

3. Martineau compares Calhoun to machinery because he seems to operate mechanically, either ignoring what people say or using it as a pretext for his lectures. He stops lecturing when he is with his family.

Frederick Douglass Learns About Abolition (page 477)

1. Douglass learns the meaning of the words by reading a newspaper article about northern petitions asking for the abolition of slavery in the District of Columbia and of the interstate slave trade.

2. Two Irishmen, whom Douglass helps unload stones, advise him to run away to the North.

Fannie Jackson Coppin Goes to College (page 478)

1. Coppin feared that the students would rebel against having her for a teacher. She might have feared this because she was both black and a woman. There was no rebellion in her class. In fact, the class increased until it was divided in two, and she was given both divisions.

2. Coppin felt under intense scrutiny when she recited in class. She felt that if she performed badly, it would reflect badly on all black people. This suggests her awareness that she was not simply gaining an education for her own sake but, by so doing, advancing the cause of blacks everywhere.

Angelina Grimké on Women's Rights (page 479)

1. The "stumbling block" is the limiting of women to their "appropriate sphere," which prevents them from advancing abolitionism.

2. It is inconsistent for abolitionists to work to free the slaves and yet favor limiting women's freedom.

A Female Seminary (page 479)

1. Dickinson studies ancient history at 10:30. She does calisthenics at 12:00. At 4:30 Miss Lyon gives advice in Seminary Hall.

2. "Section" is a period when students tell of their infractions of school rules.

3. Answers will differ.

CHAPTER 13

The Alamo (page 480)

1. Travis knows that if the Alamo does not surrender, "the garrison is to be put to the sword."

2. Travis's sense of honor and duty keep him from surrendering.

Sam Houston at the Battle of San Jacinto (page 480)

1. Houston estimates that the Mexican forces number "upward of fifteen hundred men," and the Texans number 783. This makes the odds slightly less than two-to-one.

2. The Texans used their rifles as clubs.

3. Students can cite the Texans' capture of a cannon as well as the enemy's equipment and baggage and the Texans' light losses as opposed to the Mexicans' heavy losses.

James Beckwourth Discovers Beckwourth's Pass (page 482)

1. While prospecting for gold in the Sierra Nevada, Beckwourth spots a place that seems "lower than any other."

2. After Beckwourth determines that the slope will afford the best road to the American Valley, he tells Mr. Turner of his discovery. Turner starts a subscription list so that money may be collected for building a road through Beckwourth's Pass.

Narcissa Prentiss Whitman Travels West (page 482)

1. The wagons—along with the tents and baggage—are arranged in a ring. All the animals except the cows are placed inside the ring. This makes them easier to guard.

2. When the supply of bread runs out, Whitman has to learn to bake outdoors.

3. The travelers eat breakfast and usually begin to travel at six in the morning. They stop at eleven, make camp, and feed (without pitching tents). They start again at two and travel until six in the evening.

San Francisco During the Gold Rush (page 483)

1. The first thing Pérez Rosales notices in San Francisco is all the new buildings. The village has become a boom town.

2. At high tide, the inflowing water can cause serious damage, "reducing the value of the highest quality merchandise," and thus ruining the unfortunate merchant.

3. Pérez Rosales tells of masters working as servants, lawyers as freight agents, doctors as stevedores, and sailors as diggers. He gives two specific examples: a gravedigger working as a doctor and an insurance agent passing himself off as an attorney.

4. Answers may differ. The excitement and opportunities of the gold rush days might appeal to some students.

The Life of a California Woman (page 484)

1. Mary Jane Megquier prepares meals for her boarders, makes "six beds every day," and does the washing and ironing. Since she must work hard all day, she needs a strong constitution. She plans to "give up" because she is "sick and tired of work."

2. Students' choice of words will differ.

CHAPTER 14

A Model Plantation (page 485)

1. Students can cite the following details of Dabney's kindness to his slaves: his requirement that slaves work only five and a half rather than six days a week; his distribution of prize money for work well done; and his generosity with corn, blankets, quilts, and clothes.

2. Dabney got his slaves to work hard by treating them kindly and rewarding them with prize money for great productivity.

3. Students may cite the two sentences in the last paragraph, which compare Dabney's slaves to children.

4. Answers may differ. Many students may agree that a life of freedom is preferable to even the most enlightened kind of slavery.

The Life of a Slave (page 486)

1. New field slaves were whipped and made to pick cotton as fast as they could. This enabled the master to determine how much cotton slaves could pick, and they were required to pick that weight each day thereafter.

2. Students may cite the following details: the slaves start work in the fields at daylight; they are not permitted a moment's idleness "until it is too dark to see"; they dare not stop working "even at dinner time"; and they sometimes have to work "till the middle of the night." The slaves must also do their chores and pack the cotton. After that, they must still light fires in their cabins, grind corn, and prepare that night's supper and the midday meal for the next day.

3. Students can contrast the five-and-a-half-day workweek of Dabney's slaves to the constant toil required by Northup's master; Dabney's kind treatment to the whippings on the other plantation; and Dabney's generosity with food to the scanty rations Northup received.

John C. Calhoun's Last Speech (page 486)

1. Students may cite the following sentences (in the third paragraph): "Yes, easily, but not by the weaker party." "The North can do justice by conceding to the South an equal right in the acquired territory." (This territory would eventually become slave or free states.)

2. According to Calhoun, the South can make no further concessions because she "has already surrendered so much that she has little left to surrender." It is for the North, the stronger party, to redress the balance, see that justice is done, and thus show that the South has good reason to remain in the Union.

Harriet Beecher Stowe: the Freed Slave (page 487)

1. Harriet Beecher Stowe cites slaves who have become a successful furniture maker, farmer, real estate dealer, coal dealer, and barber.

2. The story shows the daughter's industry, thrift, loyalty, "self-denial, energy, patience, and honesty."

From Charlotte Forten's Journal (page 488)

1. Forten has met schoolmates who, though "kind and cordial" in school, pretend not to know her when they encounter her on the street. She compares such trifles to the evils of slavery her people must endure.

2. Her conscience keeps her from despairing. It tells her that she must work to improve conditions so that, if not for her, then for future generations "slavery and prejudice shall vanish."

CHAPTER 15

Two Civil War Songs (page 489)

1. Students may cite the following inspiring words from "The Battle Cry of Freedom": "Shouting the battle cry of freedom," "We are springing to the call," and "we'll hurl the rebel crew from the land we love the best." From "The Bonnie Blue Flag": "First gallant South Carolina/Nobly made her stand" and "Like patriots of old we'll fight/Our heritage to save./And rather than submit to shame,/To die we would prefer."

2. The continual use of *freedom* implies that the North is fighting for the cause of freedom and the South opposes it.

3. The words imply that the South has a noble heritage to defend and its honor demands it fight. To give in would be shameful.

Elizabeth Keckley and the Contraband Relief Association (page 490)

1. Elizabeth Keckley says that the North "is not warm and impulsive" and did not welcome the freed slaves. Her words also imply that it was difficult for the ex-slaves to make a living.

2. She got the idea after coming upon a party given as a benefit for suffering soldiers. She proposed the idea in a black church, it caught on, and the Contraband Relief Association was founded.

Victory at Gettysburg (page 490)

1. Students may cite the following sentences: "The collapsed Confederacy has no place where it can hide its head." "Slavery has fallen."

2. Students may cite bells "ringing wildly all over the city"; citizens' grins; cannons firing; and boys "discharging pistols into empty barrels."

Sojourner Truth Meets President Lincoln
(page 491)

1. The "lions' den" may refer to those, both in the North and the South, who hate Lincoln, as well as the problems Lincoln faces as President.

2. Students may cite Lincoln's comment that other Presidents, especially Washington, "were just as good and would have done just as I have, if the time had come."

The View from Looking Glass Plantation
(page 492)

1. Edmonston thinks Lincoln is an ignorant, rough person and Lee a great noble man. Students may contrast "But it is hard to realize that he [Lincoln] is a dignity" with "Noble old man [Lee]."

2. Edmonston has lost faith in the army because it has been defeated at New Orleans and Vicksburg and is now, after the surrender, no more. The last sentence means that she has faith in the South's indomitable spirit.

CHAPTER 16

The Death of Lincoln (page 493)

1. For Eliot, the greatest horror is that Lincoln's death is "an assassination for political reasons." Eliot thinks that northern anger over the assassination will hinder a conciliation with the South.

2. Eliot estimates that Lincoln was not nearly as great as Washington. Lincoln's character was "rough and ungraceful," but he was nevertheless a "truly noble growth of republican institutions." For Eliot, Lincoln's policies will be carried out because these are the policies of the people.

Thomas Dabney After the Civil War
(page 493)

1. Students may cite Dabney doing all the washing, seeing to it that no light is used "but a fire in winter," and cultivating a garden to provide food.

2. Dabney's pride is revealed by his toiling to pay all his debts, sparing his daughters "all such labor as he could perform," and his meticulous care in gardening and doing the wash.

3. Answers may differ. Most students will probably agree that Dabney's industry and steadfastness in adversity are admirable.

Congressman Richard Cain Speaks (page 494)

1. Cain says that black people want "the right to enjoy precisely the same privileges accorded to every other class of citizens."

2. Cain cites his own experience of not being able to get a table in a restaurant and the experience of a fellow black Congressman who is told, "You cannot eat here."

Sarah Allen Testifies Before Congress
(page 495)

1. Allen was visited by terrorists, probably members of the Ku Klux Klan, between one and two in the morning. They wore "long white robes" and loose masks "trimmed with scarlet stripes."

2. Telling Allen about Colonel Huggins's beating is a way of warning her that the same might happen to her if she does not leave.

3. The visitors said they did not want "radicals" in the South and northerners teaching there, and they thought "the colored people could educate themselves if they needed any education." The visitors said they wanted Allen to leave because she was "a white person teaching in a colored school." The real reason was that she was helping to educate blacks.

"We Are a People Worthy to Be Free"
(page 496)

1. According to the writer, when black people "have rights that others respect, self-respect will greatly increase."

2. He thinks that the heroic deeds of blacks in the Civil War have earned respect for all blacks.

HOW TO HELP STUDENTS READ HISTORY

The techniques presented here have proved effective in increasing student comprehension. Several of the techniques are to be used *before* students read their assignments. Others are to be used *during* or *after* assignments. Each technique requires little teacher preparation and no specialized training in the teaching of reading.

Approaches to Reading features in the student text present previewing and reading skills and ask questions to check comprehension. The Teacher's Resource Manual contains a worksheet matched to each feature, giving another opportunity to practice the skill just introduced.

PRE-READING TECHNIQUES

Strategies that history teachers can easily use to prepare their students for their reading assignments are previewing the overall organization of the textbook, previewing a chapter, and developing prior knowledge.

Previewing the Book

To acquaint students with the organization of their text, conduct a text preview on the day books are distributed. You may ask students to read and analyze the title and copyright pages, the table of contents, "A Guide to Reading History," and "To the Student," and to skim the Index, Glossary, and other reference material at the back of the book. After the class has read the Table of Contents and skimmed the Index, ask students to predict some important topics to be studied.

Previewing the Chapter

Before reading an assignment, students will find it valuable to preview the chapter. The steps to follow are listed in the Approaches to Reading feature on page 6 (Worksheet 2). In general, students should be able to follow the steps with little or no teacher assistance.

Previewing visual material (illustrations, maps, charts, graphs) may require some guidance, however. Because many middle and junior high school students are reluctant to interrupt their flow of reading to look at the graphics, previewing ensures

that students will pay attention to them. Students will also be more likely to examine the visual materials again during their reading and to develop competence in interpreting graphics on their own. You may need to clarify the meaning and use of map legends, the numerical data on graphs, and so on. Using the Tools of History features that focus on interpreting graphics will help students gain analyzing skills.

Developing Prior Knowledge with PReP

The three-step procedure called PReP (prereading plan), devised by reading specialist Judith A. Langer, is an excellent way to develop students' prior knowledge. PReP develops a climate of questioning that allows students to draw upon what they already know about a subject, and group discussion encourages them to reflect on their ideas. PReP also allows the teacher to determine how much students already know about an assignment. Those who appear to have little prior knowledge may need extra instruction about central subjects of the assignment.

To use PReP, simply select a key word or phrase from the text students are about to read. For example, a key phrase from the first section of Chapter 4 might be its title, "The New England Colonies." To develop initial associations, you might say, "Tell me anything that comes to mind when you hear the phrase 'The New England Colonies.'" Write all students' responses on the chalkboard.

The next step helps students become aware of their thought processes. You might ask, "What made you think of those responses?" In answering, students become aware of their network of associations. They also listen to and interact with other students, and they evaluate, revise, and integrate their ideas.

In the final step of PReP, students think about what they know. You may ask, "From your responses and our discussion, what new ideas do you have about the New England Colonies?" At this point, responses are usually more refined than they were in step one, because students have now had an opportunity to review their prior knowledge and compare it with others'.

DURING AND AFTER READING

The skill of reading comprehension will help students in all their subjects. Particularly in history, the ability to grasp main ideas and to understand relationships is critical. You can help students develop better comprehension by presenting the reading skills of finding main ideas and recognizing patterns of organization. These skills are covered in the Approaches to Reading features in the text and the matching worksheets.

Main Ideas and Details

In identifying main ideas, students will benefit from reinforcement. You may from time to time ask, "What is this paragraph (or section, or sentence) all about?" When students have responded with the *topic* (usually a noun or brief phrase), you may then ask them to state the *main idea* of a paragraph, which is usually a single topic sentence, by asking, "What is the most important idea about the topic of this paragraph?"

Students can check the main idea by determining whether other sentences in the paragraph give details about it—items of information that support or explain the main idea. When students ask "W" questions (Who, What, When, Where, Why) about the main idea, they are seeking details.

If some students have difficulty in finding main ideas, you may ask them to follow these three steps: *find the topic of the paragraph, find the main idea (topic sentence), check to see whether other sentences give details about the main idea.*

Patterns of Organization

As they gain skill in comprehending history, students will identify dozens of main ideas and hundreds of details. At the same time, they should see that the main ideas and details are presented in a few patterns of organization that occur over and over again.

Main ideas and details are the subject matter of history. Patterns of organization are the forms in which the subject matter is expressed. Recognizing and understanding the patterns will help students improve their writing ability as well as their reading comprehension.

Approaches to Reading features point out the common patterns used in writing history: *sequencing, the cause-effect pattern, the problem-solution pattern, and the comparison-contrast pattern.* Worksheets act as reading guides by asking questions like those the students should learn to ask themselves. You may augment the worksheets by writing study guides about main ideas, sequencing, and so on. You may also model the process for students. For example, you may ask,

> "What is the main idea in this paragraph about the Articles of Confederation? What details support the main idea?"

> "Several events led to independence for Texas. In what sequence did these events take place?"

> "What caused the British to impress American sailors?"

> "It was difficult for flatboats to move upstream. How was this problem solved?"

> "Contrast the views of Hamilton and Jefferson about interpreting the Constitution. How did their views differ?"

INDEPENDENT LEARNING

A major goal of education is to teach students to become independent learners. One well-known technique for independent learning is *SQ3R:* survey, question, read, recite, review. Another technique that students can use on their own is *outlining.* Approaches to Reading features explain the steps for each technique, and Worksheets 32 and 19 offer practice.

One other technique deserves practice during or after reading. *Literal and inferential reading,* treated in the feature on text page 306 (Worksheet 66), helps students learn to make inferences. This ability leads to independence in reading.

—Richard P. Santeusanio

Reading Consultant

HOW TO HELP STUDENTS READ HISTORY

ADDISON-WESLEY
UNITED STATES HISTORY to 1877

VOLUME 1

ADDISON-WESLEY
UNITED STATES
HISTORY to 1877

VOLUME 1

In every age, the eagle has stood for freedom and power. Therefore it was a fitting symbol for the young United States. Here the popular design decorates a regimental drum from the mid-1800s. Marching in time to the steady drumbeat, soldiers defended the nation's liberties.

Authors

DIANE HART
DAVID BAKER

Program Directors

IRVING F. AHLQUIST
GEORGE O. ROBERTS

Reading Consultant

RICHARD P. SANTEUSANIO

ADDISON-WESLEY PUBLISHING COMPANY

Menlo Park, California   Reading, Massachusetts
Don Mills, Ontario   Wokingham, England   Amsterdam
Sydney   Singapore   Tokyo   Madrid   Bogotá
Santiago   San Juan

AUTHORS

Diane Hart, a Woodrow Wilson Fellow, received her Master of Arts degree in history from Stanford University and a teaching credential from San Jose State University. She then taught United States history. She has worked with teachers in curriculum development and with the GATE (Gifted and Talented Education) program in California. Diane Hart is coauthor of *Mind Movers: Creative Homework Assignments,* a book for social studies and language arts teachers.

David Baker received a Bachelor of Arts degree in history and social studies. He went on to receive a teaching certificate at Wayne State University and a Master of Arts degree, with honors, in United States history at San Francisco State University. He has taught social studies at the elementary, junior high, and high school levels.

Richard P. Santeusanio has taught social studies and language arts at the junior high school level and has served as a professor of education at the college level. He is currently administrator of a K-12 reading program for the public schools of Danvers, Massachusetts. He is the author of *A Practical Approach to Content Area Reading* and serves on the editorial board for the *Journal of Reading* and the *Journal of Educational Research.*

Toni Dwiggins, an author of the textbook *United States History,* contributed to the special features "American Values in Action" in the text.

PROGRAM DIRECTORS

Irving F. Ahlquist is Professor of History, California State University, Long Beach. A recipient of the California State Colleges Distinguished Teaching Award, he has taught courses in American colonial history, the early national period, the Civil War and Reconstruction, United States history since 1900, California history, immigration history, and the history of the South. Since 1965 he has contributed to the preparation of high school history teachers.

George O. Roberts was Professor of Comparative Culture and Director of the Master of Arts in Teaching program at the University of California, Irvine. He had served as a member of the California Curriculum Development Commission, as a program administrator of the United States Office of Education Teacher Corps, and as a consultant for the United States Agency for International Development. He had been among the authors of *Social Sciences Education Framework for California Public Schools.*

FIELD TEST & REVIEW

Daniel Bigelow, Miller Junior High School, Kingston, New York
Edward S. Folsom, Jr., Gardner Junior High School, Lansing, Michigan
Janice Hargrave, Crockett Junior High School, Amarillo, Texas
Joe Humphrey, former K-12 Social Studies Consultant for Abilene Independent School District,
   Principal, College Heights Elementary School, Abilene, Texas
Betty J. Ladd, Director of Social Sciences, Glastonbury Public Schools, Glastonbury, Connecticut
Josephine Lugo, Bret Harte Junior High School, San Jose, California
Rod Margherio, Trimpe Junior High School, Bethalto, Illinois
Richard F. Roath, Walker Junior High School, Orlando, Florida
John A. Waterhouse, Gideon Welles School, Glastonbury, Connecticut
Thermon O. Young, F. Ware Clary Junior High School, Syracuse, New York

CONTENTS

AMERICAN VOICES   434

MAPS

CONTENTS

CHARTS AND GRAPHS

AMERICAN VALUES IN ACTION

APPROACHES TO READING

UNDERSTANDING GEOGRAPHY

USING THE TOOLS OF HISTORY

TO THE STUDENT

The builders of America took great risks. In colonial days, people risked long and dangerous ocean voyages to reach North America. Once there, they faced the hazards of life in a strange land. The framers of the Declaration of Independence were willing to risk "our lives, our fortunes, and our sacred honor" to break away from Great Britain. The delegates to the Constitutional Convention also were risk-takers. They gave the United States a republican form of government at a time when other nations were ruled by royal families.

In this textbook you will meet many of the people who helped to build America. You also will learn about the risks they took and the hardships they faced.

Here is a guide to the book's organization.

TEXT ORGANIZATION

The text is divided into five units. Within each unit are three to four chapters. As you begin a unit, look at the full-page **Unit Illustration** to see what information this work of art can give you about the time period you are about to study. Look, too, at the **Unit Timeline,** showing different kinds of events and the term or terms of the President during which the events occurred.

When you begin to study a chapter, you will notice that the title of each section in that chapter is listed. After you skim over these titles, you may begin a section by reading the **Read to Find Out** topics (see page 2). These give you clues about the important information to be covered in that section. In the **Section Review** (page 8), you will be expected to answer questions about the topics listed in Read to Find Out.

As you study a chapter, you will see special features, in boxes. You will learn skills to help you understand history better in **Using the Tools of History** and **Approaches to Reading** (see pages 56 and

141). You will learn about important routes and places in **Understanding Geography** (see pages 4–5). You also will find out about important Americans in **American Values in Action** (see page 101).

After you have studied a chapter, the **Chapter Survey** (see pages 20–21) will help you to review what you have studied. You will be expected to answer questions about the vocabulary and important topics in the chapter. You also will have a chance to use maps, charts, and graphs and to show your understanding of history in **Geography Review, Using the Tools of History,** and **Approaches to Reading.**

After you have studied a unit, a **Unit Survey** (see pages 80–81) will help you to review what you have studied in the chapters. You also will have a chance to relate present to past events by using **Linking the Past to the Present** and to find out more about important Americans in **Builders of America.** The Unit Survey also gives you a list of **Suggested Readings,** books that you can read to find out more about the events and people of the time covered in the unit.

At the end of the book is **American Voices,** made up of readings. The readings are taken from actual speeches, books, letters, and diaries. These will give you valuable information about events in the text. Questions at the end of each reading test your understanding of the content.

At the back of the text, you will find a Reference Section for your use. There is a **Resource Center,** with charts of the Presidents and the states as well as other charts, graphs, and maps. There you also will find the **Mayflower Compact, Declaration and Resolves of the Continental Congress, Declaration of Independence,** and **Constitution of the United States,** with notes about their meaning. Finally, there is the **Glossary,** in which important historical words are defined.

A GUIDE TO READING HISTORY

The skill of reading is essential to mastery of almost all subjects in school. Instead of "learning to read," as you did in earlier years, you now are "reading to learn" history, science, literature, and other subjects.

When you read to learn, you really are using a number of different skills. The most important of these is comprehension, or understanding. An excellent way to develop your ability to read with understanding is to ask yourself questions about the textbooks you read.

The following questions apply directly to this textbook in history. A number of the questions, however, can be applied just as well to other books in other subjects.

HOW IS THE BOOK ORGANIZED?

To answer this question, you must preview the book. Start by looking at the title page and the information about the authors on the back of it. Skim the table of contents. It lists all the units, chapters, and sections of the text. Their titles will give you an idea of the important topics you will be studying.

Flip to the back of the book and skim the Glossary and the Index. These will alert you to important words and subjects.

Next, read the Introduction, titled "To the Student," carefully, if you have not already done so (it is on page xiii). In it the authors describe the parts of the book. Then skim these parts.

As the Introduction notes, there are special features about reading, called "Approaches to Reading," throughout the text. The features help you to develop skills that will increase your understanding of history.

After you preview the book, you are ready to work on individual chapters. To preview each chapter, ask yourself two more questions.

WHAT DO I ALREADY KNOW ABOUT THE TOPIC OF THE CHAPTER?

You probably can recall learning many facts and ideas about American history. Before you read a chapter, you may want to write down some of the items that come to mind when you think about the topic of the chapter.

You also may want to write down some questions you would like to be able to answer after reading the chapter. You may even want to predict the answers to your questions and then read to find out whether you made accurate predictions.

WHAT SHOULD I LEARN FROM READING THIS CHAPTER?

After you think about the topic of the chapter, you should take six more steps to complete your chapter preview. (These steps are summarized in "Approaches to Reading: Previewing," on page 6).

Read the major chapter topics. They are a guide to the main sections of the chapter.

Look over the Read to Find Out statements. They tell you what to look for as you read the section.

Read the headings within each section. These headings, in heavy type, tell you what topics are covered within the sections.

Examine the visual material in the chapter. Illustrations help to clarify points made in the chapter, and they usually add new information. So do maps, graphs, and charts.

Consider the questions in each Section Review. They, like the Read to Find Out statements, tell you the important information to look for as you read the section.

Read the Chapter Summary. It gives an overview of the entire chapter. Also note the Chapter Timeline. It shows key events from the chapter.

WHAT ARE THE MAIN IDEAS OF THIS CHAPTER?

As you read each chapter, your major concern is to understand its main ideas. The best way to do this is to study the section headings, which you have read quickly as part of your chapter preview.

As you reach each heading, ask yourself, "What, in general, do the authors tell me about the topic?" When you are able to answer that question, you have understood one of the section's *main ideas.* Be sure that your answer is a general statement, one that sums up the topic.

Specific statements telling who or what was involved and when, where, or why an event took place are *details.* They are important, too, but in reading for understanding you need to focus on main ideas.

In summary, your readings about the history of the United States will require you to concentrate and to think. Asking questions like the ones above will help you to become an active and a thinking reader. It can also make your reading more enjoyable.

—Richard P. Santeusanio
Reading Consultant

ABOUT THE COVER

A pair of steel-rimmed reading glasses rests on an account book from a Connecticut country store. A handmade candle in a brass candlestick lighted the room, and the storekeeper wrote with a goose quill pen. All the items date from the 1800s.

At right is an American gold coin, minted in 1795. It shows a woman representing Liberty wearing a ''liberty cap'' like those worn by freed Roman slaves. The stars represent the 15 states in the Union at that time.

Eli Whitney's 1794 cotton gin, below left, changed Southern agriculture by making cotton a practical crop. The hooks of the cotton gin removed the fibers from the cotton seeds fifty times faster than a worker could by hand.

Early postmasters issued their own stamps, good only at the post office where they were sold. In 1847 the first postage stamps good all over the United States were issued. The ten-cent stamp, below right, honored George Washington. The five-cent stamp honored Benjamin Franklin.

Map of the World by Juan Vespucci, 1526.

DISCOVERING THE AMERICAS

THE FIRST AMERICANS
THE ARRIVAL OF THE EUROPEANS
THE FRENCH, ENGLISH, AND DUTCH PLANT COLONIES

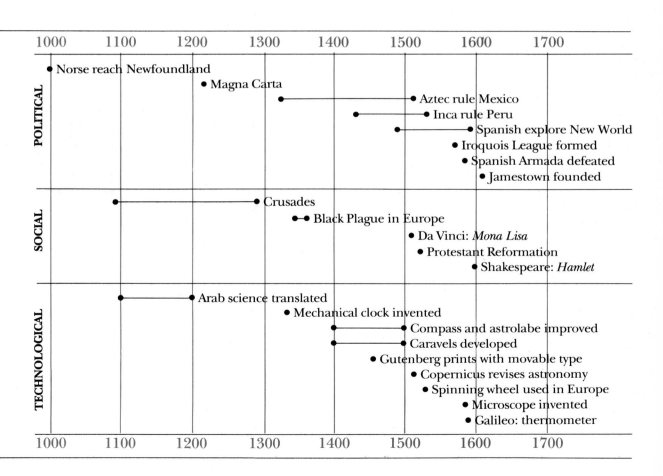

	1000	1100	1200	1300	1400	1500	1600	1700

POLITICAL
- Norse reach Newfoundland
- Magna Carta
- Aztec rule Mexico
- Inca rule Peru
- Spanish explore New World
- Iroquois League formed
- Spanish Armada defeated
- Jamestown founded

SOCIAL
- Crusades
- Black Plague in Europe
- Da Vinci: *Mona Lisa*
- Protestant Reformation
- Shakespeare: *Hamlet*

TECHNOLOGICAL
- Arab science translated
- Mechanical clock invented
- Compass and astrolabe improved
- Caravels developed
- Gutenberg prints with movable type
- Copernicus revises astronomy
- Spinning wheel used in Europe
- Microscope invented
- Galileo: thermometer

Introducing: Inform students that ice once covered about 5,200,000 square miles of North America, down to the valleys of the Ohio and Missouri rivers. Ask: How did nontechnological peoples manage to survive then?

THE FIRST AMERICANS

SETTLING A NEW WORLD
PEOPLES OF THE EAST AND THE PLAINS
PEOPLES OF THE WEST AND THE ARCTIC

1-1 SETTLING A NEW WORLD

READ TO FIND OUT

glaciers: sheets of ice

foragers: people who travel from place to place searching for wild plants and small game

—what the words *glaciers* and *foragers* mean.

—how Ice-Age hunters may have reached the Americas.

—how farming changed ways of life.

—what peoples built cities in Mexico and South America.

Scientists believe that people first came to North America because of a change in the world's climate. Fifty thousand years ago, small bands of hunters roamed across Europe, Asia, and Africa. The last Ice Age still gripped the world. Thick sheets of ice called **glaciers** covered much of North America and Europe.

Without fur, humans seemed poorly equipped to live near the ice. Yet they had something more important for their survival—the ability to reason and to remember. People understood how to control fire and to make tools. Huddled around their campfires at night, they escaped the cold. By day they hunted animals with stone-tipped spears. It may have been the search for game that led some of these hunters to become the first Americans.

Possible Routes of Ice-Age Hunters

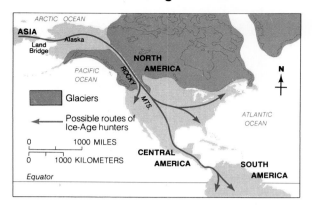

The first Americans probably crossed the land bridge that now lies under the Bering Strait.

Ice-age hunters chipped out stone spearheads like this one. It was found with the bones of an extinct bison near Folsom, New Mexico.

THE LAND BRIDGE

During the Ice Age, more and more water was trapped in glaciers. As the glaciers grew, the level of the oceans dropped. Areas that once were covered by shallow water became dry land. One of these areas stretched between Siberia and Alaska. It became a bridge of land many miles wide. And it connected two continents—Asia and North America. This area now lies under a narrow waterway called the Bering Strait.

A land bridge connecting North America and Asia would have served as a highway for Ice-Age animals. The animals could have wandered between the two continents. Hunters from Asia probably followed animals onto the land bridge. In time, they could have crossed it and entered the ice-free valleys of Alaska. From there, they found routes to the south through the glaciers. It may have taken thousands of years, but eventually the Ice-Age hunters spread across North and South America.

CHANGES IN THE LAND

The land bridge between Asia and North America may have appeared and disappeared several times. But scientists think that most of the people who crossed the land bridge did so 30,000 to 10,000 years ago.

About 20,000 years ago, the earth began to warm. The glaciers slowly melted, revealing a changed landscape. Narrow mountain canyons had been carved into broad river valleys. New valleys and river channels had been formed. Small pits and huge basins had been scooped out by the glaciers. These pits and basins filled with meltwater. The Great Lakes were the largest of the new glacial lakes.

The land itself looked different. Topsoil scraped from Canada had been pushed as far south as Ohio, Indiana, Illinois, and Iowa. As the glaciers melted, the sea level rose. The ocean once more washed over the land bridge—permanently. By then, Ice-Age hunters had reached many parts of the Americas.

UNDERSTANDING GEOGRAPHY

THE REGIONS OF NORTH AMERICA

The land that the Ice-Age hunters came to was the vast and beautiful continent that is called North America. The continent is made up of different **regions.** A region is an area, of any size, in which the shape of the land, the climate, and the plants are similar.

The following map shows one of the most important ways in which a continent can be di-

vided into regions. These are landform regions, which identify lowlands and highlands. The map shows the eight landform regions in North America.

The Arctic Coastal Plains region lies along the edge of the Arctic Ocean. Much of this flat land is only a few feet above sea level. The ground is permanently frozen. But in summer,

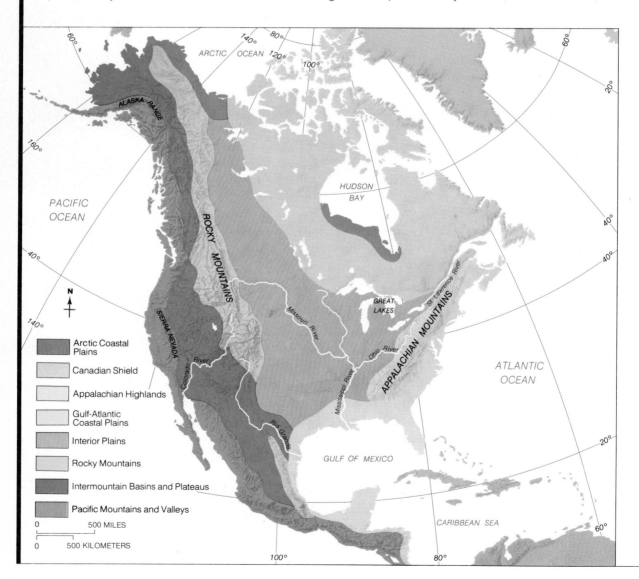

Arctic Coastal Plains

Canadian Shield

Appalachian Highlands

Gulf-Atlantic Coastal Plains

Interior Plains

Rocky Mountains

Intermountain Basins and Plateaus

Pacific Mountains and Valleys

0   500 MILES

0   500 KILOMETERS

the top layer of soil thaws and is carpeted with grasses and moss. Low bushes grow there. This landscape is called the tundra.

The Canadian Shield is a low-lying region that covers nearly one fourth of the continent. It rests on a layer of ancient rock called a shield. The thin, sandy soil has rich deposits of iron, nickel, copper, gold, and uranium. The northern part of this region is permanently frozen and covered by tundra. The area from Hudson Bay south contains North America's largest forests.

The Appalachian Highlands region extends from Newfoundland to Alabama. This is mountainous country, broken by broad valleys. The Appalachians are old mountains, low and rounded. They are covered with hardwood forests in the South and spruce and fir forests in the North.

The Gulf-Atlantic Coastal Plains region snakes from Cape Cod southward, following the coast into Central America. This coastal plain is an elevated sea floor. In fact, half of the region is still below sea level. The undersea area is the continental shelf, which extends out into the Atlantic Ocean and Gulf of Mexico. Most of the land above the sea is low and flat, with many marshy areas.

The Interior Plains region is the great central lowland of North America. It is flat land, broken by gently rolling hills. The eastern portion of the region has some of the finest agricultural soil in the world. This area is also the home of the Great Lakes, hardwood forests, and some

of North America's mightiest rivers. The western part of the plains is higher and drier. Tallgrass prairies sweep north into Canada, and desert grasslands stretch south into Texas.

The Rocky Mountain region rises from the western edge of the Interior Plains. This is the backbone of the North American continent, running from Alaska to Mexico. The Rockies are young mountains compared to the old, rounded Appalachians. Some of the most spectacular scenery in North America—rugged snowy peaks, colorful canyons, and dense forests—is found in the Rockies.

The Intermountain Basins and Plateaus region lies on the western side of the Rocky Mountains. This is a land of deserts and steep, flat-topped plateaus. In places, wild rivers have carved canyons through the plateaus. This region contains the lowest place in North America—Death Valley. Death Valley is 282 feet (86 meters) below sea level.

The Pacific Mountains and Valleys region extends along the entire western edge of North America. It consists of two parallel mountain chains separated by valleys. The western Coast Range rises steeply out of the Pacific Ocean. The eastern chain—made up of the Sierra Nevada, the Cascade Range, and the Alaska Range—is almost as rugged as the Rockies. Here is Mt. McKinley, the highest point in North America at 20,320 feet (6,194 meters). Some of the eastern mountains are active volcanoes.

APPROACHES TO READING

PREVIEWING

One way to help you understand a chapter is to *preview* it. Previewing was discussed in "A Guide to Reading History" on pages xiv–xv. Here is a summary of how to preview chapters in this book.

1. Read the title of the chapter and think about what you already know about the topic. For example, what comes to mind when you think about the topic "The First Americans"?

2. Read the major chapter topics at the beginning of each chapter.

3. Look over the Read to Find Out statements at the beginning of each chapter.

4. Glance at all of the headings in very dark type in each chapter section.

5. Study the visual material in the chapter—maps, charts, graphs, photographs, etc.

6. Consider the questions in each Section Review.

7. Read all of the Chapter Summary.

If you previewed this chapter, what would you have discovered about Section 1–1, "Settling a New World"? The Read to Find Out statements clearly indicate that Ice-Age hunters will be discussed. Farming and peoples in Mexico and South America will be covered. The meanings of certain words will also be discovered.

The first heading in very dark type tells that there will be a discussion of the land bridge. The second tells that changes in the land will be described.

The Section Review asks specific questions about vocabulary words, the Bering Strait, the Maya, the Aztec, and the Inca. It focuses on specific information that you should look for as you read through the chapter.

Previewing helps you to focus on important ideas in each chapter. It gives a purpose to reading. When you complete a chapter preview, you have a clear idea of what you should learn from reading the chapter.

Answers will be found on page T 23.

CHANGING WAYS OF LIFE

For a long time, early Americans could fill most of their needs by hunting. Game animals provided food, furs for clothing, and bones for tools. Then, around 10,000 years ago, many of the Ice-Age animals began to disappear. More than one hundred kinds of animals in North America died out. Hunters could no longer find the mammoths and giant bison they had tracked.

With much of their game disappearing, hunters had to change their ways of life. In many places, hunters became wandering **foragers.** They traveled from place to place, searching for wild plants and small game. The foragers invented new stone tools for chopping tough plant fibers and grinding hard seeds.

More than 8,000 years ago, foragers in Mexico began growing food plants, including squash and lima beans. Farming brought changes in the way people lived. Families no longer had to wander in search of food. With a more dependable food supply, the population grew more rapidly than in the past.

This pattern of change was repeated in many places. Foragers became farmers. They grew a wide variety of plants, including potatoes, pineapples, tomatoes, and sunflowers. Their most important crop, however, was corn.

THE MAYA

As farming improved, there was enough food to support many people in one area. Working together, the people could build cities. Between A.D. 300 and A.D. 900, the Maya of Mexico and Central America built cities of stone. These splendid cities contained large public plazas lined with pyramids, temples, ball courts, and palaces.

The Maya did more, however. They developed arts, a system of government, and a written language. They also observed the stars. From their study of the heavens, they created the most accurate calendar known until modern times. The Maya carved stories of their past and their gods into the stones of their buildings.

For over 600 years, the stone cities of the Maya bustled with activity. About A.D. 900, however, the people abandoned their cities. Why the Maya left is a great mystery that has never been solved.

Activity: Students can form committees to make oral reports on aspects of Mayan civilization: government, cities, language, art, astronomy. Some of these reports could be enhanced by artwork showing Mayan pyramids, art, etc.

THE AZTEC

After the Maya, other centers of activity flowered and faded to the north and south of their empty cities. From time to time, small tribes grew into conquering armies. One such tribe was the Aztec, who lived in the Valley of Mexico.

The Codex Mendoza, drawn by Aztec artists in 1541, shows scenes of daily life. Here an Aztec mother teaches her daughter weaving skills. Two tortillas are at the top.

During the 1400s, Aztec armies brought half of modern Mexico under their control. Conquered tribes sent treasure and prisoners to the Aztec capital city, Tenochtitlán (tay-NOCH-tee-TLAHN). The Aztec were skilled builders as well as fierce warriors. They constructed cities, roads, and aqueducts to carry water. They also developed schools in which Aztec children learned about their history, government, religion, music, and dance.

Later, when Spanish conquerors first reached Tenochtitlán, they found 100,000 people living there. No Spanish city was so large. The Spaniards saw buildings "whose size and magnificence no human tongue could describe."

THE INCA

At the time that the Aztec ruled the Valley of Mexico, the Inca were conquering parts of South America. By 1500 the Inca empire stretched over 2,000 miles (3,200 kilometers) along the Pacific Coast. The empire extended inland from the ocean to the Andes Mountains. At the center of the empire was the Inca capital, Cuzco (KOOS-koh).

Cuzco was linked to other cities and towns by a great network of roads. A Spaniard who later traveled the main Inca highway described it as "the finest road to be seen in the world, and the longest." Runners were stationed along the road. When a message arrived, a runner carried it to the next station. In this way a message could travel as far as 150 miles (240 kilometers) in a single day. When Inca armies marched, they stopped in shelters along the road. Storehouses nearby held food for the soldiers.

The Inca constructed buildings of huge stones carefully shaped to fit together. Their engineers built walls to hold soil in their fields, canals to carry water, and bridges over deep canyons. The Inca produced fine weaving and metalwork. Inca rulers wore gold and silver jewelry, and their palaces contained plates of gold.

This gold cup was made by an Inca goldsmith sometime between A.D. 1000 and 1400.

SECTION REVIEW   Answers will be found on page T 23.

1. Define these words: *glaciers, foragers.*

2. The Bering Strait lies between two continents. Which two?

3. What caused the Bering Strait to become an area of dry land?

4. Name two changes brought about in people's lives by farming.

5. List three achievements of the Maya.

6. What area did the Aztec control?

7. What linked parts of the Inca empire together?

1–2 PEOPLES OF THE EAST AND THE PLAINS

READ TO FIND OUT

—what the words *culture* and *nomadic* mean.

—what two groups controlled the northern woodlands.

—what the mound builders achieved.

—how horses changed the way of life on the plains.

culture: a people's way of life, including customs, skills, tools, and ideas

nomadic: wandering

This picture of an Indian woman and her baby was drawn by the Dutch explorer David De Vries.

Hundreds of years ago, most of the eastern half of the United States was woodland. Dark stands of towering spruce and fir covered the Interior Plains around the northern Great Lakes. Over the Appalachian (AP-uh-LAY-chuhn) Highlands grew a mixed forest of maples, birches, and beeches. Farther south, in the Ozarks, maples gave way to hickory and oak. Pine forests cloaked the Gulf-Atlantic Coastal Plains except in lowland swamps. There bald cypress and tupelo stood draped with moss. Along the coasts of Florida and the Gulf of Mexico, dense mangrove thickets kept soil from being washed out to sea.

The earliest woodland people lived by hunting and foraging. The forests were filled with deer and beaver. There were also nuts and berries to gather. Because travel through the tangled forests was difficult, the woodland people made canoes out of logs and bark. Lakes and rivers became watery highways. These waterways and nearby streams offered many kinds of fish. People who lived on the coast gathered shellfish from shallow tide pools.

By A.D. 1000 a number of woodland people had taken up farming. From the Gulf Coast to Canada, people cleared patches of forest to plant "the three life-giving sisters"—corn, beans, and squash. Most woodland people continued to rely on hunting and foraging, as well.

THE EASTERN WOODLAND

Dozens of tribes lived in the northern part of the woodlands. But two groups controlled the area. One group spoke Algonquian (al-GAHN-kee-uhn). The Algonquian were scattered through southern Canada, in the Great Lakes area, and along the Atlantic Coast to Virginia. The other group, speaking Iroquois (IHR-uh-KWOY), lived in what is now the New York area.

Both the Algonquian and the Iroquois lived in longhouses. These were sturdy, wood-framed structures that housed several families.

For many years, the Algonquian and the Iroquois warred with each other. Iroquois war parties were said to "approach like foxes, fight like lions, and disappear like birds." Young warriors were supposed to prove themselves in battle by bringing back prisoners. The prisoners were often adopted by Iroquois families who had lost sons in earlier fighting.

THE SOUTHEAST

In the southern part of the woodlands lived tribes speaking Muskogean (muhs-KŌ-gee-uhn). These were the Creek, Choctaw, Seminole, and Chickasaw. They were descendants of mound builders, people who had lived in the Ohio Valley and the Mississippi Valley long before.

Among the mound builders were the Hopewell people. No one knows their real name. They are called Hopewell now because clues to their past were first studied at Hopewell farm, near Cincinnati, Ohio. The Hopewell people made copper and silver jewelry, and they carved elegant smoking pipes of stone. In some places they constructed great mounds of earth. The mounds were burial sites or locations for special buildings.

Jewelry, pipes, and mounds were part of the Hopewell **culture.** A culture is a people's way of life, including their customs, skills, tools, and ideas. The Hopewell culture reached its height about A.D. 400. It spread widely, across parts of present-day New York, Pennsylvania, Tennessee, Indiana, Illinois, Iowa, Kansas, Wisconsin, and Michigan.

Around A.D. 1000 another culture of mound builders developed along rivers in the Mississippi Valley. Today it is known as the Mississippian culture. It extended to places that are now parts of Georgia, Alabama, Mississippi, Arkansas, Missouri, Kentucky, Illinois, Indiana, and Ohio. The Mississippian people built many flat-topped mounds. The largest, covering more than a dozen acres, is at Cahokia (kah-HŌ-kee-ah), Illinois, across the river from St. Louis. To build it, people carried earth to the site in baskets.

Cahokia was once a woodland city surrounded by a wall of logs. Skilled workers in Cahokia made jewelry, leather goods, and many other items. These products were traded for goods as far south as the Gulf coast and as far west as the Rocky Mountains.

PLAINS FARMERS

West of the woodlands, flat open plains stretch from the Missouri River to the Rocky Mountains. The people of the plains, like their woodland neighbors, lived mainly by farming. Women planted corn, beans,

This charming stone bird is actually a pipe carved by a Hopewell artist.

For discussion: A thousand years from now, what artifacts of our culture might people find? What would the artifacts tell them about the way we live? What name might the people of the future give our culture?

★ ★ ★ ★ ★ ★ ★ **AMERICAN VALUES IN ACTION** ★ ★ ★ ★ ★ ★ ★

THE LEAGUE OF THE IROQUOIS

Five Iroquois tribes lived in the area of present-day New York. Although they all spoke the same language, they were separate nations: Mohawk, Oneida (o-NĪ-dah), Onondaga (AHN-uhn-DAH-guh), Cayuga (kay-YOO-guh), and Seneca. The Iroquois often warred with neighboring tribes. They also fought each other.

About 1570, legend says, an Iroquois named Deganawidah (dee-gan-ah-WEE-dah) had a dream. He saw a huge tree soaring to the sky. It was supported by five thick roots. The roots were the Five Nations, and the tree was their union.

Deganawidah traveled from tribe to tribe to describe his dream. His handsome face showed the dream's power. But he stammered so much that he could hardly speak. Then Deganawidah met a Mohawk leader named Hiawatha, who shared his vision. Together, they convinced the Five Nations to form a union called the League of the Iroquois.

The league, like Deganawidah's great tree, grew from tribal roots. The league ended the fighting among the Five Nations. It established a council, or ruling group. The council made laws to keep the peace and rules to run the league. Each tribe was still free to deal with its own affairs.

The tribes were organized around clans—groups of related women and their families.

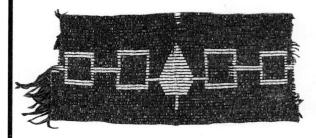

This wampum belt shows the linked tribes of the Iroquois League joined together by a tall tree. The belt was made of polished shells.

The women appointed men to represent their clans in tribal meetings. Clan women also named sachems, or chiefs, to represent the tribes in the ruling council of the league.

Every summer, the council met at an Onondaga village. The sachems sat beneath the Tree of Peace, planted as a symbol of Deganawidah's vision. Summer after summer, generation after generation, the roots of unity sank deeper into the earth.

The league grew more powerful. The Five Nations had stopped fighting each other, but they still fought their old enemies to protect the league. By the early 1700s the Five Nations controlled an area stretching from the Hudson River to the Great Lakes. Some of the defeated tribes joined the League of the Iroquois.

The league was not the only power in eastern America. Two European nations—France and Great Britain—had planted colonies there and clashed over land claims. Each tried to win the support of the Iroquois. The Iroquois formed ties with the British, but they clung to their independence. "We are a free people," they declared, "uniting ourselves to what sachem we please."

In 1754, at a meeting in Albany, New York, the Iroquois urged the British colonies to unite. Benjamin Franklin drew up a plan of union for the colonies based on the League of the Iroquois. "It would be a strange thing," said Franklin, if the Iroquois could form such a union and the colonies could not.

But the colonies did not unite until 1776. They fought for their independence from England, and the Iroquois League was dragged into the war. Some tribes sided with the English, others with the colonists. When the war ended, a new union—the United States of America—had taken root.

The Iroquois tribes, divided against each other in war, did not reunite. After two hundred years, the League of the Iroquois had ended.

This map of American Indian tribes should reinforce your introduction to the section (see page 9).

North American Indian Tribes and Culture Regions

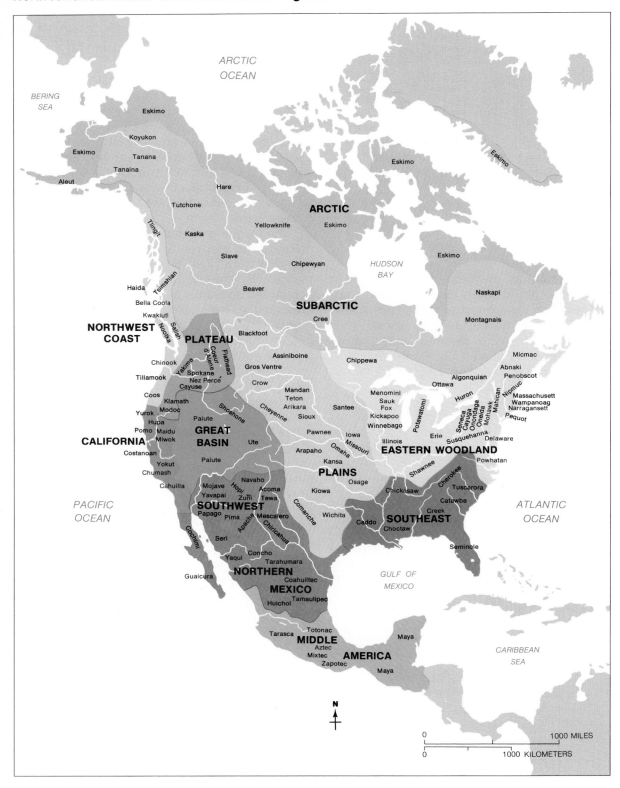

squash, and tobacco in river valleys. But the open plains were both too dry and too matted with the roots of buffalo grass to be farmed.

The treeless land provided few building materials. For shelter the plains people dug round pits near their fields. These pits were covered with brush and a thick layer of earth. In these pit houses, the people could survive raging blizzards or summer heat waves.

Hunting parties left the river valleys to follow buffalo across the plains. It was not easy for a hunter on foot, armed with only a bow and arrow, to bring down one of the shaggy beasts. Hunts had to be carefully planned. Sometimes women and children helped by driving a herd toward the edge of a cliff. Any animals that fell over the cliff were killed by hunters waiting below.

Decorated shields such as this one showing a turtle were used by warriors of the Mandan tribe of North Dakota.

PLAINS HUNTERS

In the 1500s horses brought to North America by the Spanish escaped onto the plains. At first the people of the plains called the wild horses "mystery dogs." But they quickly learned how to tame them. Soon groups of hunters were galloping bareback across the plains, bow and arrow in hand.

Horses brought many tribes onto the plains. The Cheyenne and Sioux abandoned their woodland villages for the grasslands. The Comanche left their homes in the foothills of the Rockies. Older plains tribes traveled far from their river valley villages.

For all of these tribes, horses meant a change from a settled to a **nomadic,** or wandering, life. Before horses were used, dogs had helped to carry the supplies needed for short hunting trips. With horses, entire tribes could follow the buffalo across the plains. The hunt became a never-ending journey. Where the buffalo went, people followed.

Hunters on horseback could easily track buffalo herds and close in for the kill. Their people depended on the buffalo for many things. They ate the meat both fresh and dried. They used buffalo hides to make their tepees, or cone-shaped tents. Hides were also used for robes and shields. Buffalo bones became tools.

Before horses came to the plains, most people had been equal in terms of wealth. This changed as horses became a measure of wealth. The richest families owned small herds of horses to move their goods from camp to camp. Horses also became valued companions in many tribes. It was not unusual to see a Blackfoot warrior cry when his favorite mount died.

Despite the changes brought about by horses, much remained the same for the people of the plains. Stories and legends once told in pit houses were now told in tepees. Men were still hunters and warriors. Women still farmed and gathered plants for food. Babies still viewed

Activity: Have students write reports on the Cheyenne, Sioux, and Comanche and their ways of life. Among other matters, the reports could deal with what happened to these tribes when the pioneers moved westward.

*CT
Horses were signs of wealth and position in other societies as well. People who had to travel on foot were considered inferior to those who could ride on horses. This is true of both medieval knights and American cowboys of the last century. For discussion: Do many people today feel about cars as people felt about horses? Explain.

USING THE TOOLS OF HISTORY

ANALYZING CHANGE AND CONTINUITY

History can be thought of as a study of change and continuity. Continuity is lack of change, or connectedness. All cultures undergo both change and continuity. This section on the Plains Indians describes the changes brought about by the introduction of horses to the plains. But it also points out the areas in which there was continuity, or lack of change.

A Venn diagram can be helpful in analyzing continuity and change. Such a diagram is made up of two overlapping circles. In the diagram at right, the left circle contains facts about the lives of plains tribes before they had horses. The right circle contains facts about their lives after they came to depend on horses. The facts listed in the area where the circles overlap describe plains life both before and after horses.

Use the Venn diagram at right to answer the questions that follow.

1. What part of this diagram shows areas of continuity?

2. What parts of this diagram illustrate changes in the life of the plains people?

3. How did the way that people carried heavy goods change, according to this diagram?

4. Did the arrival of horses cause change in the weapons used by plains people?

Life on the Plains

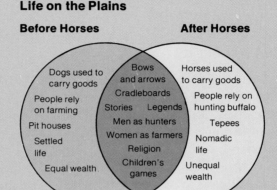

Before Horses   **After Horses**

Dogs used to carry goods
People rely on farming
Pit houses
Settled life
Equal wealth

Bows and arrows
Cradleboards
Stories Legends
Men as hunters
Women as farmers
Religion
Children's games

Horses used to carry goods
People rely on hunting buffalo
Tepees
Nomadic life
Unequal wealth

Answers will be found on page T 23.

---

the world from cradleboards. Children still sang the same songs and played the same games. And tribal priests still helped their people feel closer to the spirit world.

SECTION REVIEW   Answers will be found on page T 23.

1. Define these words: *culture, nomadic.*

2. How did the earliest woodland people obtain food? How did this change by A.D. 1000?

3. What two groups of people controlled areas in the northern part of the woodlands?

4. What were the ancestors of the Muskogean people called?

5. List three items produced in the Hopewell culture.

6. Among plains peoples, who did the farming?

7. Why did the coming of horses to the plains bring about a nomadic way of life?

1-3 PEOPLES OF THE WEST AND THE ARCTIC

READ TO FIND OUT

—what the words *plateaus, mesas,* and *tundra* mean.

—how people farmed the dry lands of the Southwest.

—how people foraged for food in the Great Basin.

—what kinds of foods were found along the Pacific Coast.

—how people survived in the Arctic.

plateaus: land that is raised and level

mesas: small plateaus with steep sides

tundra: a vast treeless plain

West of the Rocky Mountains lies a wide, dry region called the Southwest. This is a land of **plateaus,** or tablelands. Like the surface of a table, a plateau is raised and level. On the Colorado Plateau, wind and water have carved deep canyons and left tall **mesas.** Mesas are small plateaus with steep sides.

PEOPLE OF THE SOUTHWEST

The Colorado Plateau is dry most of the year. But in late July and August, thunderstorms drench the desert. Farming peoples had to learn to save the rain for the dry times.

Among the early peoples to farm in the Southwest were the Anasazi (ahn-eh-SAH-zee), who lived in present-day New Mexico. They learned to capture the summer rain and hold it in dams. The Anasazi planted corn, pumpkins, beans, and cotton. Besides becoming expert farmers, they learned to be master builders. Using stone, the Anasazi constructed houses up to six stories high. One of these buildings had 800 rooms, including storerooms for food. In time, the Anasazi culture spread to places in Arizona, Colorado, and Utah.

By A.D. 1300, however, the Anasazi had moved away from their settlements. What happened to the Anasazi is unclear. But their culture lived on among other groups, who were also farmers and town builders. These groups were called the Pueblo (PWEB-lō) by Spanish explorers, who named them after their apartment-like villages. Pueblo is the word for "village" in Spanish.

By 1500 the Zuñi (ZOON-yee), Hopi (HŌ-pee), and other Pueblo groups were living in some eighty pueblos in the Southwest. Although each group had its own language, they all shared similar cultures.

An Anasazi potter made this clay figure between A.D. 1100 and 1300. It may have been used in a religious or magic ceremony.

Activity: Students can
research the cultures
of the western Indian
tribes, especially in
anthologies present-
ing Indian myths, sto-
ries, poems, and
songs. They can then
read some of these to
the class.

The men of the pueblos spent about half of their time in religious ceremonies. The ceremonies took place in underground rooms called kivas (KEE-vahs). For the Pueblo peoples, religion was at the heart of everyday life. Children were expected to be gentle and polite. Adults were expected to solve problems without fighting. If everyone lived in harmony, the Pueblo believed, then rains would come each summer to make the desert bloom.

THE GREAT BASIN FORAGERS

North of the plateau country is a region called the Great Basin. This forms a huge bowl between the Rockies and the Sierra Nevada range. It is a dry, harsh land. The little rain that does fall is lost in the expanse of rocks and sand.

The Great Basin was too dry for farming. The people living there—the Paiute (PĪ-yoot), Shoshone (sho-SHŌ-nee), and Ute—survived by foraging. They hunted lizards, gophers, rabbits, and antelope. They gathered seeds, roots, leaves, or other parts of almost a hundred kinds of plants.

Life in the Great Basin centered around the search for food. Each season brought different possibilities. In spring, people followed streams created by melting snow. They caught fish and set traps for ducks. By summer, when the streams dried up, the people searched out seeds, roots, nuts, and berries. They stored some of what they gathered for wintertime, when food would be scarce.

In autumn, small bands of foragers hunted rabbits. When winter approached, the foragers traveled to their winter camps in the hills along the edge of the Great Basin.

PEOPLE OF CALIFORNIA

Unlike the Great Basin, the lands along the Pacific Coast offer great variety. Covered by evergreen forests, the Sierra Nevada range lines the eastern edge of the oak-studded Central Valley of California. Winters in the valley are rainy. Summers are hot and dry. To the west of the valley are low mountains that drop down to the cold waters of the Pacific.

California provided many kinds of foods for foragers' baskets. Among the most important were acorns. Where oaks grew, people harvested large quantities of acorns. After removing the shells, they pounded the acorns into flour. Then they carefully soaked and rinsed the flour to wash away the bitter taste of tannic acid. When the flour was ready, they mixed it with water and put the mix into a basket woven so tightly that it could hold water. To cook the mix, they added fire-heated stones to the basket.

The basketry cap was made by Great Basin people about A.D. 1000.

Northwest peoples painted their lodges with animal figures and recorded the history of their clans in the carvings of their totem poles.

PEOPLE OF THE NORTHWEST

From northern California to Alaska, the Northwest Coast is covered by dense forests. The forest was rich in game, berries, and nuts, and the sea provided fish. The Northwest Coast tribes—the Tillamook, Haida (HĪ-dah), and others—lived in settled villages. They were skilled woodworkers. With tools made of stone and shell, they built large wooden houses and ocean-going canoes.

Wealth was important to many of these tribes. The chief of a village could show off his wealth in a ceremony called a potlatch. To prepare for a potlatch, the chief's family worked long hours making blankets, wood carvings, baskets, and even canoes. Then the chief announced that a time of feasting and games would begin. He invited his rivals from nearby villages.

On the last day of the potlatch, the host displayed his wealth by giving away all of the things that his family had made. Each guest was called forward to receive a gift. When all of the gifts had been presented, the chief folded his own blanket and asked, "Who wishes to take it?" The chief who came forward would be the next one to give a potlatch. He would compete with his host by trying to give away even more lavish gifts.

For discussion: Is the potlatch similar to any customs in other cultures with which students are familiar? If so, what are the similarities?

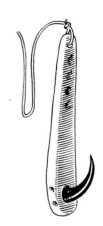

Tattannaeuk, an Eskimo hunter, served as interpreter to a British Arctic expedition in the 1830s. Eskimos still hunted then in the ways they had used for centuries.

This Eskimo fishhook is made of bone and the claw of a hawk.

PEOPLE OF THE ARCTIC

Along the northern shores of Alaska, the climate is too cold for trees. Here the Arctic Ocean is bordered by vast, treeless plains called **tundra.** In winter the Arctic tundra is a huge expanse of snow and ice. In summer the top layer of the tundra thaws, allowing some plants to grow. The plants provide food for grazing deer called caribou.

To survive in this cold land, the Aleut (AL-ee-oot) and the Eskimo people relied on hunting. Besides caribou, they hunted ocean mammals such as seals, walruses, and whales. These animals did not provide only food. Oil from the sea mammals was used as fuel for cooking and lighting. Seal and walrus skins were used for clothing, tents, ropes, and skin-covered boats called kayaks. Whale ribs became runners for sleds that dog teams pulled over ice and snow.

Cooperation was as important to the people of the Arctic as competition was to the people of the Northwest. The Eskimo lived in small groups. They had no chiefs, though people might look to the best hunters for advice. The Eskimo needed teamwork to survive the cold and the hunger. Even the best hunters were happy to share food. They knew that when they had bad luck in hunting, other families would share with them.

Eskimo works of art, especially carved sculptures, are highly prized by collectors. You may wish to have students find and show photographs of such art to the class.

SECTION REVIEW   Answers will be found on page T 23.

1. Define these words: *plateaus, mesas, tundra.*

2. How did the southwestern people get water to use for farming?

3. What did the Great Basin foragers eat in the winter?

4. Why were oak trees important to the people who lived in California?

5. What happened to goods at a potlatch?

6. How did the Arctic people treat each other in order to survive?

CHAPTER SUMMARY

The first Americans may have been Ice-Age hunters who traveled to the Americas more than 10,000 years ago. They may have crossed from Asia to North America on a land bridge. As the glaciers melted, the sea once more covered the land bridge.

After that, groups of hunters probably moved south through ice-free valleys. Then they spread across the land.

As many Ice-Age animals died out, hunters spent more of their time in foraging. In time, some groups of foragers turned to farming. Settled farmers built America's first cities. The Maya built stone cities in Central America, but they abandoned the cities about A.D. 900.

By A.D. 1500, there were two great empires in the Americas. The Aztec empire spread over half of Mexico, and the Inca empire controlled Peru.

North of Mexico, people developed many different cultures. Woodland tribes used trees for building houses, hunted forest game, and traveled by canoe on woodland waterways. Woodland farmers constructed large mounds in many places.

When horses came to the plains, foragers and farmers took up new ways of life. Traveling on horseback, entire tribes followed herds of buffalo across the grasslands.

In the dry lands of the Great Basin, people could not count on finding large game. Foragers there spent most of the year on foot, searching out plants and small animals to eat.

Acorns were a main part of the diet of many groups of people in central and southern California. The Northwest Coast offered a wide variety of foods. Village chiefs there showed off their wealth by giving it away in ceremonies called potlatches.

Far to the north, Arctic people relied on hunting for food and shelter. The people cooperated to survive in the icy land.

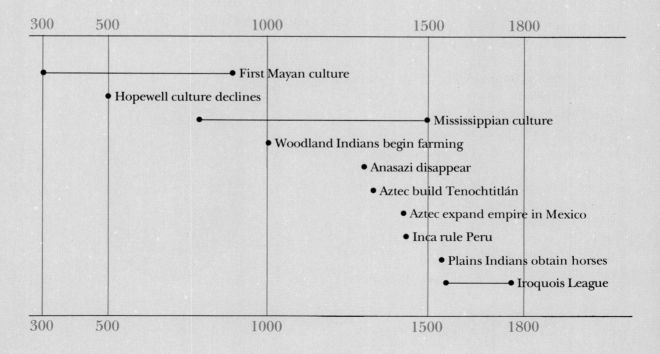

Answers will be found on page T 23.

CHAPTER SURVEY

VOCABULARY REVIEW

For each numbered word below, choose the word or phrase closest in meaning.

1. glacier
   (a) Arctic plain   (b) ice sheet   (c) snow
2. forager
   (a) gatherer   (b) hunter   (c) builder
3. culture
   (a) customs   (b) land   (c) ways of life
4. nomadic
   (a) lost   (b) wandering   (c) proud
5. plateau
   (a) slope   (b) tableland   (c) mountain
6. mesa
   (a) island   (b) cone-shaped volcano
   (c) flat land with steep sides
7. tundra
   (a) Arctic plain   (b) slope   (c) route

CHAPTER REVIEW

1. (a) What happened to the sea level during the Ice Age?   (b) What happened to the area now called the Bering Strait?   (c) How could animals have moved between Asia and North America during the Ice Age?   (d) At that time, why would people have traveled from Asia to North America?

2. (a) Why did hunting become more difficult in North America about 10,000 years ago? (b) When hunting became more difficult, how did people survive?   (c) What other way of obtaining food did people in Mexico begin developing more than 8,000 years ago? (d) How did this way of obtaining food allow people to build cities?

3. (a) What great change did the Maya make about A.D. 900?   (b) About how many years later did the Aztec rise to power?   (c) What allowed the Inca to control a huge empire?

4. (a) Why did woodland people travel on lakes and rivers instead of by land?   (b) What kept the Iroquois from traveling anywhere they wished north of the Great Lakes?

5. (a) Which culture developed first, the Hopewell or the Mississippian?   (b) Which spread farther north?   (c) Which was represented by the woodland city of Cahokia?

6. (a) How did plains tribes use cliffs in hunting buffalo?   (b) Why did plains people live mainly by farming instead of hunting before the 1500s?   (c) Why did plains tribes travel most of the time after the 1500s?

7. (a) What shelters were often used by plains tribes before the 1500s? After the 1500s? (b) How did these shelters differ from those built by the Iroquois?   (c) How did the plains shelters differ from the pueblos of the Southwest?

8. (a) Who developed the buildings called pueblos?   (b) Name two groups living in pueblos in A.D. 1500.   (c) What important part of culture differed from group to group in the Southwest?

Northwest Coast people carved masks for their religious ceremonies. A Kwakiutl artist made this raven mask of wood, brass, nails, and fiber.

The Maya made wheeled toys like this dog, but they did not use wheeled vehicles for transportation.

9. (a) People in the Great Basin did not live all year in permanent shelters. Why not? (b) Why did people in the Great Basin need to use more kinds of food plants than did the people of California?

10. (a) When a chief in the Northwest owned extra goods, what ceremony could he take part in? Why? (b) When a hunter in the Arctic had extra food, what would he do with it? Why?

GEOGRAPHY REVIEW

1. Look at the text and the map "The Regions of North America" on pages 4 and 5. (a) How many regions are shown on the map? (b) In what region is Florida? (c) In what region are the southern Great Lakes? (d) What region contains a long series of low and rounded mountains? The most rugged mountains? The mountains that are the farthest west?

2. Now look at the map "North American Indian Tribes and Culture Regions" on page 12. (a) What words on the map show the location of the Iroquois? (b) In what culture region are the Cheyenne, Sioux, and Comanche? (c) How many different names of tribes appear in the Great Basin region? In the California region?

USING THE TOOLS OF HISTORY

Analyzing Change and Continuity

*CT **1.** Make a chart with three headings: "Before the Land Bridge Appeared," "While the Land Bridge Was Open," and "Both Before and During the Time of the Land Bridge." Place each of the following items under the correct heading.

(a) Hunters used stone-tipped spears.
(b) Animals crossed between Asia and North America.
(c) There probably were no people in the Americas.
(d) Hunters made campfires.
(e) The sea level was at its lowest.
(f) Fish swam in the Bering Strait.

*CT **2.** Look at the Venn diagram on page 14. How do the three headings in your chart match the three parts of the diagram?

READING AND THINKING SKILLS

Previewing Vocabulary Words

1. Look at the beginning of Section 1–3, "Peoples of the West and the Arctic," page 15. (a) What are two ways to find vocabulary words in the section? (b) What is the quickest way to find all the words? (c) Where in the section can you find the meanings of the vocabulary words? (d) Where else in this book can you find the meanings?

Analyzing Meanings

*CT **2.** The vocabulary words in Section 1–3 are *plateaus, mesas,* and *tundra.* (a) How do these three landforms look alike? (b) How does a mesa differ from a plateau? (c) Name at least one way in which a plateau and tundra look different.

CHAPTER 2   1000-1700

THE ARRIVAL
OF THE EUROPEANS

EUROPE LOOKS OUTWARD
CROSSING THE ATLANTIC
SPAIN'S EMPIRE IN THE AMERICAS
NEW SPAIN'S NORTHERN FRONTIER

2-1 EUROPE LOOKS OUTWARD

READ TO FIND OUT

feudalism: system of land ownership based on military and other kinds of service

communication: exchange of information and ideas

geography: an area's lands, climate, plants, animals, and people

navigation: the science of finding a ship's location and direction

technology: application of knowledge to practical problems

—what the words *feudalism, communication, geography, navigation,* and *technology* mean.

—how the Norse explored the North Atlantic and found Vinland.

—what the Crusaders brought home to Europe.

—what Europeans learned from Marco Polo.

—why Europeans wanted to find a water route to Asia.

—how ocean travel improved in the 1400s.

Ice-Age hunters from Asia probably were the first discoverers of America. Where the next discoverers came from is still a question. Perhaps they sailed east from China and reached the Americas by crossing the Pacific Ocean. Or they may have come westward across the Atlantic from Africa or the Middle East. Central and South American Indian legends tell of visitors from beyond the sea. But there is no solid proof that such visitors came.

A Swedish tapestry from the 1100s shows a Viking riding to war in a suit of chain mail. Norse helmets extended downward to protect the nose.

NORSE VOYAGES

There is good evidence that Europeans came to Newfoundland about 1,000 years ago. Norwegian archeologists found there the remains of eight houses, two outdoor cooking pits, a smithy for producing iron, and boat sheds. A spinning tool and a pin for fastening a cape were also found. These objects had been made by the Norse people.

The Norse, or Vikings, were a Scandinavian people who burst out of their homeland during the 700s to seek new lands and wealth. They explored and established trade routes and settlements. They also raided villages on the coasts of northern Europe. For nearly six centuries they were Europe's boldest sailors. Other Europeans feared to sail beyond the sight of land. But the Norse steered their sturdy wooden ships across the storm-tossed waters of the North Atlantic. In about 870 Norse explorers discovered Iceland. Greenland was found in about 982. Norse settlers soon followed the explorers to these lands.

Norse sagas, or stories that are part history and part legend, tell of voyages to a land west of Greenland. One saga tells of a group of Greenlanders, led by Leif Ericson, who sailed west about the year 1000. They found a beautiful land of grassy meadows and salmon-filled streams. Because they saw grape or berry vines, they named the place "Vineland," or Vinland. Vinland was probably Newfoundland.

The sagas say that several years after Leif's expedition, some Greenlanders sailed back to Vinland. They built houses and traded milk and cloth to the Indians for furs. Later, fighting broke out between the Indians and the Greenlanders. Seeing no end to the warfare, the Greenlanders gave up and sailed for home.

The Irish also have some claim to discovering Iceland and Greenland. There are accounts, real or imagined, of Irish monks sailing to these lands in the eighth century.

Paintings in a prayer book made for the Duke of Berry show detailed scenes of life on a feudal manor in the 1400s. Peasants here are harvesting the grapes in the vineyards outside the castle wall.

FEUDAL LORDS

Norse stories about lands across the Atlantic did not reach other Europeans. In the time of the Vikings, Europe was a patchwork of small territories divided into landholdings called manors. The smaller manors belonged to men known as lords. The lord of a manor gave protection to the peasants, the people who lived in his villages and tilled his fields. He, in turn, served a more powerful lord—a noble with a title like duke or earl.

In return for service in the noble's army, the lord was granted ownership of his manor. This system of land ownership based on military and other kinds of service is called **feudalism.** In some parts of feudal Europe, nobles served kings or queens.

Often, deep forests separated one manor from the next. There was little trade because products of the manor supplied the needs of the people. **Communication,** the exchange of information and ideas, was difficult. News traveled slowly, if at all.

THE CRUSADES

Despite poor communication, most of the people of Europe had one thing in common. They were part of the Christian world, which at the time meant the Roman Catholic Church. In 1095 Pope Urban II was the head of the Church. That year he called on Europeans to free Palestine (PAL-ehs-tīn), the Christian Holy Land in the Middle East, from Muslim rule. Muslims are people who believe in the teachings of Islam, a religion founded by the Arab prophet Muhammad.

Thousands of Europeans answered the pope's call. They joined expeditions and sewed the symbol of the Christian religion—the cross of Christ—on their clothes. They were called Crusaders, from a Latin word meaning "cross." Their expeditions became known as the Crusades.

For the next two centuries, armies of Crusaders swept into the Middle East. In the end, they failed to take Palestine from the Muslims. But the Crusaders returned home with treasures unknown to most Europeans. They brought Indian cotton goods, Chinese silks, and, most precious of all, pepper, cloves, and cinnamon. Spices such as these helped cover the taste of spoiled meat and made eating more interesting. Demand for the products of the "fabulous Indies"—India, China, and the islands off the coast of Asia—began to grow.

Trade between Europe and Asia soon developed, but Europeans were uncertain about where the Indies were. They knew only that Italian merchants bought silks and spices from Muslim traders at the eastern end of the Mediterranean (MED-uh-teh-RAY-nee-uhn) Sea. The Muslims brought the goods overland from the lands far to the east.

For discussion: The spice trade was very important to Europeans. Today students may take spices for granted. Ask students what spices they like. Have them consider what food would taste like without spices, particularly if it spoiled quickly. Then ask why spices were so important in the Middle Ages.

A hand-painted book in the 1200s showed Crusader knights sailing across the Mediterranean to the Holy Land. A priest steers the boat.

This picture of the emperor of China sending out messengers is from Marco Polo's book, *The Description of the World.*

Activity: Marco Polo's *Description of the World* is one of the most famous of all travel books. Have students read excerpts, especially about Kublai Khan's court, and report on them. Other students can report on Marco Polo's life and how he came to write the book.

MARCO POLO

Marco Polo, the son of a merchant in the Italian city of Venice, knew more about these eastern lands than most Europeans. His father and uncle had traveled to China to trade. Marco Polo had listened to their tales and was eager to see this land for himself. In 1271, at the age of seventeen, he joined his father and uncle on a second journey to China. When he returned, at the age of forty-one, he wrote an account of his adventures.

As the years passed, Marco Polo's account was copied and recopied. Europeans who read it learned something about Asian **geography,** the area's lands, climate, plants, animals, and people. They found out that China and India bordered oceans. They read about an island kingdom called Cipangu (Japan). There, temples and palaces were said to be roofed with gold. Marco Polo's story also showed that the highly prized spices came from the Spice Islands, south of the Asian mainland. The wealth of the Indies could be reached by sea.

TRADE AND NATIONS

This information was of great interest to merchants who lived on Europe's Atlantic coast. They were unhappy with the prices they had to pay for the products of Asia. On the long land route controlled by the

Trade Routes Between Europe and Asia   1271-1498

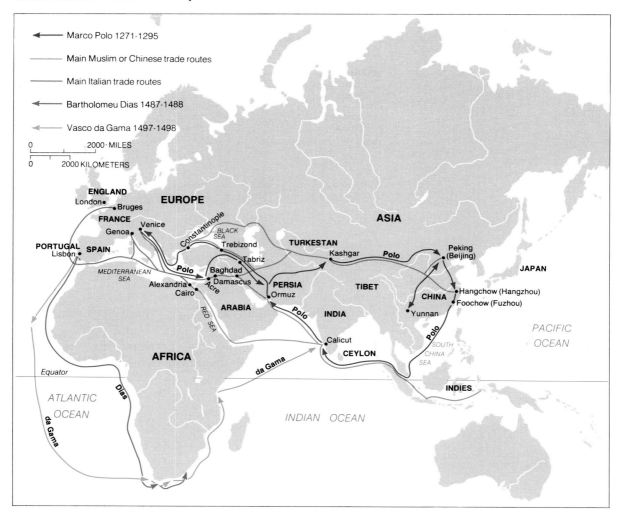

Muslims, goods changed hands many times. Each time, the price went up. Then the Italian traders raised the price again. How much less expensive it would be to bypass the Muslims and Italians and to buy directly from Asians.

Without help, the merchants could not afford to build expensive ships and to send explorers in search of a water route to the East. In time, help came from powerful European rulers who shared the merchants' interest in Asia.

Under the feudal system, most European monarchs had been little stronger than nobles. Then the rulers found a way to expand their power. By the 1400s the pace of trade and communication had quickened. Where merchants gathered, towns and then cities had sprung up. When the great nobles of the countryside tried to control the towns, the townspeople turned to the ruler. They paid taxes willingly in return for

*CT
Be sure students understand the connection between the decline of feudalism, the growth of powerful nations, the rise of wealthy merchants, and the consequent interest in exploration and money available for it. Without the first three conditions, the last two might not have existed.

Ideas That Made Exploration Possible

A.D. 200	Ptolemy, a Greek mathematician, devises a system of *latitude* and *longitude*.
1000	The *magnetic compass* comes into use.
1200	The development of the *rudder* allows a ship to be guided by one person.
1300	The *compass card* is added to the magnetic compass. The card allows navigators to determine direction more accurately.
	Cannons come into use on ships.
1400	The *improved astrolabe* allows sailors to determine their distance from the equator.
	The swift, easily handled *caravel* is developed. It combines the best features of Mediterranean triangular-sailed ships and square-rigged northern ships.
1500	Gerhardus Mercator devises the first *map projection* that shows the middle latitudes with little distortion.
	The *galleon,* or carrack, comes into use. It is a heavy ship with many masts, and it carries more guns and cargo than did previous ships.

protection. With tax money, the king or queen built a strong government and a royal army.

Slowly the rulers brought the nobles under their control. As they unified the land under their rule, they created nations. By the end of the 1400s, there were four nations in western Europe—England, France, Spain, and Portugal.

The Christian monarchs of these nations searched for new ways to fill their royal treasuries. They soon saw that a water route to the trade of Asia could be a source of great wealth. Finding such a route might also make it possible for them to attack their Muslim enemies from a new direction.

PORTUGAL TAKES THE LEAD

Prince Henry, son of the king of Portugal, was determined to find a sea route to the East. In 1418 he began bringing Europe's best mapmakers, ship captains, and shipbuilders together in order to collect information about sea travel. He also began sending ships out to explore. Some of these expeditions sailed into the mid-Atlantic Ocean. Others moved south along the west coast of Africa, looking for a way around or through the land to Asia.

At first, Prince Henry's captains and crews were afraid to sail beyond northwest Africa. They were certain that farther south the ocean's waters grew hot enough to boil. The unknown seas might be filled with horrible monsters. But with Prince Henry's help, the sailors slowly overcame their fear. Each time a ship returned, the captain and the crew reported everything that they had learned.

Step by step, Henry and his mapmakers expanded their knowledge of currents, winds, and the African coastline. Before long, Portuguese maps were the best in Europe. And the Portuguese began trading with West African kingdoms for spices, gold, and African slaves.

Fearing competition from Spain, Portugal tried to keep its explorations and discoveries secret.

Prince Henry and his co-workers also studied **navigation,** the science of finding a ship's location and direction at sea. They improved Muslim inventions such as the magnetic compass to show direction and the astrolabe (AS-truh-LAYB). The astrolabe was an instrument for sighting the stars in order to find a ship's location. Because of his tireless efforts, Henry became known as Prince Henry the Navigator.

The Portuguese made many improvements in the **technology** of ocean travel. Technology is the application of knowledge to practical problems. The Portuguese not only improved maps and navigational tools, they invented a new kind of ship, the caravel (KAR-uh-VEL).

The caravel was small and light and carried triangular sails like those on Muslim trading ships. It could sail into the wind instead of just sailing with it. Sailors no longer needed to depend on the wind to blow them directly home. The Portuguese could now sail beyond the sight of land and still be sure of returning home safely. The unknown became less frightening.

Before the fifteenth century ended, the courage and skill of the Portuguese brought them to their goal of finding a sea route to the east. In 1487 Bartholomeu Dias (DEE-ahs), a Portuguese sea captain, rounded the southern tip of Africa and sailed into the Indian Ocean. Certain that a sea route to the East would now be found, the king of Portugal named the southern tip of Africa the Cape of Good Hope.

Ten years later, in 1497, Portuguese sea captain Vasco da Gama (duh GAM-uh) followed the route of Dias around Africa. He then crossed the Indian Ocean, reached India, and returned home with Indian goods. With his voyage, Portugal opened a new route to the trade of Asia. Soon the Portuguese had a string of forts and trading stations stretching from the west coast of Africa to India and the Spice Islands.

Activity: Students can make sketches of the Portuguese caravel, report on the ship, and show their sketches to the class.

Dias wanted to press on, but his crew feared going further. On the return voyage Dias explored the coast for the great cape, which had been obscured by a storm. Later, Dias wanted to call the African cape the Cape of Storms. However, the Portuguese king said it should be named the Cape of Good Hope.

SECTION REVIEW   Answers will be found on page T 24.

1. Define these words: *feudalism, communication, geography, navigation, technology.*

2. Identify: Leif Ericson, Marco Polo, Prince Henry the Navigator, Vasco da Gama.

3. Where did the Norse people build settlements in the 800s and 900s?

4. Why did the Norse abandon Vinland?

5. List three new items that the Crusaders brought back to Europe.

6. What did Marco Polo tell Europeans about spices?

7. Why were merchants eager to find a water route to Asia?

8. What three improvements were made in the technology of ocean travel in the 1400s?

2-2 CROSSING THE ATLANTIC

READ TO FIND OUT

—what the words *colony, migration,* and *treaty* mean.

—what Columbus discovered.

—how Europeans discovered the size of the earth.

—why explorers searched for a Northwest Passage.

colony: settlement of people leaving their land for another but remaining citizens of the home country

migration: movement from one land to another

treaty: written agreement between nations

The Portuguese worked their way southward along the African coast, looking for a way to Asia. Meanwhile, an Italian sea captain thought he had a better idea. Christopher Columbus of Genoa had gone to sea at an early age. When he was twenty-five years old, he was shipwrecked off the coast of Portugal. Aided by the Portuguese, he improved his knowledge of shiphandling, navigation, and mapmaking.

Christopher Columbus bids farewell to Queen Isabella and King Ferdinand before setting out on his voyage.

Like the geographers, Columbus knew that the earth was round. He thought that it was possible to sail from Europe westward to Asia. But he estimated that this distance was smaller than it is. He became convinced that the shortest route to Asia lay west, across the Atlantic.

Columbus was not the first person to hold this belief. He was the first who was willing to risk his life for it. In 1484 Columbus asked King John II of Portugal for money to pay for a western voyage. The king rejected the plan. His advisers correctly guessed that the distance from Europe west to Asia was much greater than Columbus believed.

The following year Columbus presented his plan to King Ferdinand and Queen Isabella of Spain. Their advisers also questioned the plan. Besides, the Spanish were waging war against North African Muslims who held part of Spain. Columbus was told to wait.

For six years Columbus waited. Finally, early in 1492, the Spanish defeated their Muslim enemies. At the same time, Queen Isabella decided that Spain should not lose this chance for exploration. She promised to provide Columbus with ships even if she had to pledge her royal jewels to pay for them.

Activity: Ask students to imagine themselves Columbus or a member of his crew. Have them write a diary entry for one day during the first voyage. The entry might deal with Columbus placating his crew's fears or with the day when land was first sighted.

THE VOYAGES OF COLUMBUS

Queen Isabella kept her promise, and Columbus got three ships. On August 3, 1492, the *Niña*, the *Pinta*, and the *Santa María* set sail due west from Spain. Days grew into weeks with no sight of land. Columbus's crew began to mutter about turning back. To quiet their fears, Columbus kept two records of the journey. The first contained his best guess of how far they had traveled. The second, which he shared with the crew, showed a much shorter distance.

At last, on October 10, Columbus promised to turn back if land were not found in three days. A day passed and then another. Early in the morning of the third day, a lookout on the *Pinta* sighted land in the moonlight. The three ships dropped anchor off a small island in the Caribbean (KAR-uh-BEE-uhn) Sea. Columbus went ashore and claimed the land for Spain. Grateful for his success, he named the island San Salvador, Spanish for "Blessed Savior."

The next day Columbus met the people of the island. "Of anything they possess," he later wrote, "they invite you to share it and show as much love as if their hearts went with it." He added, "How easy it would be to convert these people and to make them work for us." Because Columbus thought that he had reached the Indies, he named these people Indians.

For the next three months, Columbus sailed in the Caribbean, searching for the treasures of the Indies. He explored present-day Cuba and another island that he named Hispaniola (HIS-puhn-YOH-luh), or

This 1493 engraving shows Columbus's ship, the *Santa María*. The engraving was included in the official report of his discoveries.

UNDERSTANDING GEOGRAPHY

CROSSING THE ATLANTIC

When Columbus and the explorers that followed him sailed across the Atlantic, they began a new age of navigation. They had to learn how to navigate beyond the sight of land.

The magnetic compass had a needle that pointed to the magnetic North Pole. With this tool, sailors could tell if they were heading north, south, or in any other direction.

Navigators could also find how far north or south of the **equator** they were. The equator is an imaginary line that circles the earth halfway between the North and the South Pole.

Using an astrolabe, sailors measured the angle between the horizon and the sun at noon. They then turned to a table that showed the sun's position above the equator each day. By checking their measurement against the table, they figured their distance from the equator.

Accuracy, however, was a problem. On the rolling deck of a ship, it was difficult to measure the angle accurately. Also, in cloudy weather, measurements could not be taken.

To find their exact position, navigators also had to determine how far east or west they had sailed from their home port. Unfortunately, they did not have a reliable method of determining this distance. At best, they could attempt to figure out how fast they were traveling. From that, they could try to estimate the distance that they had traveled.

To determine speed, navigators made a speedometer of sorts. They tied knots in a rope at certain intervals and tied the rope to a log.

Then they threw the log overboard. Using a sandglass as a timer, they could see how much rope was let out in an hour. This gave a rough estimate of speed and distance traveled.

Prevailing winds were another factor in navigating the Atlantic. These are winds caused by the circulation, or movement, of air around the earth. They almost always blow from the same direction and travel long distances.

Look at the map on page 33. Notice that in sailing to America, Columbus traveled from northeast to southwest. In this region north of the equator, prevailing winds flow from the northeast to the southwest. These winds are called the "northeast trade winds" because they come from a northeasterly direction. The northeast trade winds literally blew Columbus's ships to the Caribbean islands.

Getting back across the Atlantic to Europe, however, was not so easy. Sailing into the northeast trade winds made for slow traveling. In time, navigators found prevailing winds farther north, along the Atlantic coast of North America, that flowed from the west to the east. These winds are called the "prevailing westerlies" because they come from a westerly direction. The prevailing westerlies carried ships from America to Europe.

Ocean currents also became a factor in sailing back across the Atlantic to Europe. An ocean current is a flow of water in a definite direction within the larger body of water.

The Gulf Stream is a strong ocean current in which water moves northward along the east coast of North America. Notice on the map how the North American continent juts eastward into the Atlantic. This eastward thrust turns the Gulf Stream, steering it toward Europe.

Once the Gulf Stream and the prevailing winds were discovered, explorers had a natural set of navigational aids. The northeast trade winds carried them to America. They rode the Gulf Stream and the westerly winds back home.

Voyages of Discovery   1487-1522

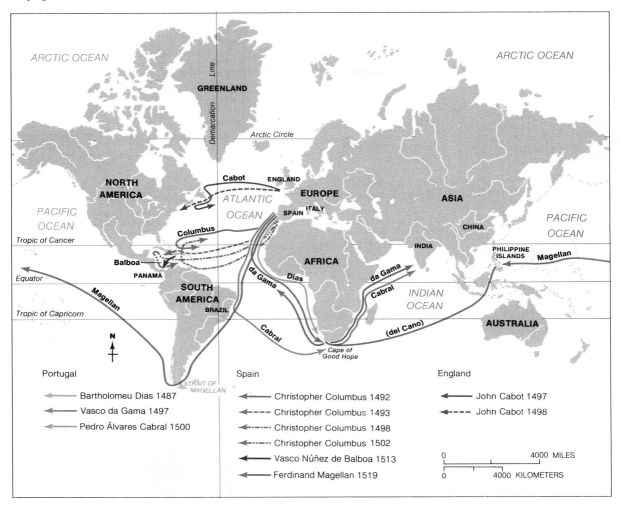

Portugal
- ←— Bartholomeu Dias 1487
- ←— Vasco da Gama 1497
- ←— Pedro Álvares Cabral 1500

Spain
- ←— Christopher Columbus 1492
- ←--- Christopher Columbus 1493
- ←-·- Christopher Columbus 1498
- ←-··- Christopher Columbus 1502
- ←— Vasco Núñez de Balboa 1513
- ←— Ferdinand Magellan 1519

England
- ←— John Cabot 1497
- ←--- John Cabot 1498

0   4000 MILES

0   4000 KILOMETERS

"Little Spain." A few of the island people wore gold jewelry, but the golden temples of Cipangu were nowhere to be seen. Instead, Columbus discovered new foods like corn and sweet potatoes. Also, one of the crew saw islanders set rolled leaves on fire and "drink" the smoke. This was Europe's introduction to tobacco.

While they were exploring, the *Santa María* caught on a reef and sank. Early in 1493, the *Niña* and *Pinta* made the return voyage to Spain. There Columbus and his crew were welcomed as heroes.

Over the next ten years, Columbus made three more voyages to the Caribbean. He explored Puerto Rico (PWER-tō REE-kō), Jamaica (juh-MAY-kuh), the northern coast of South America, and the Isthmus of Panama. On Hispaniola he started the city of Santo Domingo. It was the first permanent European **colony** in the Americas. A colony is a settlement made by a group of people in a faraway region that is under

Columbus fell out of favor with the Spanish court because he did not bring back the wealth of the Indies. On his last voyage, he was shipwrecked. Rescued, he returned to Spain. There, considered a failure, he lived out the remaining years of his life.

This African saltcellar, carved from ivory, includes Portuguese soldiers as part of its design. The carving was made after the Portuguese had begun to sail to Africa.

Students can find the imaginary line drawn by the Treaty of Tordesillas—called the Demarcation Line—on the map on page 33.

For discussion: In what way did Cabot's voyages provide a basis for the later English colonization of North America? (Point out that this is discussed in Chapters 3, 4, and 5.)

the control of their home country. When Columbus died in 1506, however, he still believed that the lands he had found were part of Asia.

Unlike Leif Ericson's discovery of Vinland, the voyages of Columbus had important results. The printing press had recently been invented. As a result, news of his first voyage spread rapidly throughout Europe. When other explorers learned that Columbus had crossed the western ocean and returned safely, they decided to attempt voyages of their own. In doing so, they began the largest **migration,** or movement of people from one land to another, in human history.

EUROPEAN CLAIMS IN THE NEW WORLD

The first voyage of Columbus had another result—a **treaty,** or written agreement, between the nations of Portugal and Spain. Both nations were exploring the Atlantic Ocean, searching for the Indies. Portugal claimed parts of the west coast of Africa and islands in the Atlantic. The rulers of Spain wanted Portugal to respect their claim to the lands that Columbus had discovered.

The pope stepped in to prevent conflict between the two Catholic nations. In 1494 Spain and Portugal signed the Treaty of Tordesillas (TOR-day-SEE-yahs). Under the treaty, an imaginary line was drawn from north to south through the Atlantic Ocean. All lands discovered east of the line belonged to Portugal. Lands to the west of the line belonged to Spain.

Later, it was discovered that the line passed over an eastward bulge in the South American continent. In 1500 a Portuguese sailor named Pedro Álvares Cabral (kuh-BRAHL) sailed for India along Vasco da Gama's route. Cabral drifted too far west. He landed on the coast of what is now Brazil and claimed it for Portugal.

Meanwhile, other explorers began to cross the Atlantic. The English sent John Cabot (KAB-uht), an Italian navigator, to North America. Cabot hoped to find a route to the Indies that was shorter than the one Columbus claimed he had found. In 1497 Cabot probably landed at Newfoundland. A year later, he made another voyage and explored southward along the eastern coast of North America. Like Columbus, Cabot believed that he had reached Asia. He found no riches, but he claimed the lands that he saw for England.

The Portuguese sent ships to explore the South American coast. On one voyage was an Italian merchant and navigator named Amerigo Vespucci (ves-POO-chee). He wrote a colorful account of his adventures in "a new world." Martin Waldseemüller (VAHLT-zay-MYOOL-ur), a German geographer, drew a new map of the world soon afterward. On it he named the new world "America" after Amerigo Vespucci. Soon this name was used throughout Europe.

THE DISCOVERY OF THE PACIFIC

Vasco Núñez de Balboa (bal-BŌ-ah), a Spanish explorer, proved that Christopher Columbus had discovered a new continent. In 1513 Balboa followed Indian guides through the jungles on the Isthmus of Panama. He became the first European to see the Pacific Ocean from the American shore. His discovery made it clear that America was not part of the Asian continent. The wealth of the Indies lay farther west.

In 1519 a Portuguese sea captain named Ferdinand Magellan (muh-JEHL-uhn) led a Spanish expedition south along the Atlantic coast of South America. He was looking for a passage through the continent to the Pacific Ocean. After a year of searching, he found a narrow channel among the islands at the southern tip of South America. For more than five weeks, Magellan threaded his way through the stormy strait that bears his name.

When the expedition finally reached the Pacific, Magellan set a course for the Indies. His crew did not see land again until they reached the island of Guam (gwahm). A crew member wrote:

> We were three months and twenty days without refreshment from any kind of food. We ate biscuit which was no longer biscuit but powder, swarming with worms, the rats having eaten all the good. . . . Often we ate sawdust.

This 1535 painting shows Portuguese carracks entering Lisbon Harbor. Better suited for ocean voyages than the caravel, the carrack was rounder, heavier, and more able to cope with ocean winds.

Magellan first appealed to the king of Portugal to send an expedition, but his request was denied. He then turned to Charles I, king of Spain, who gave him a fleet of five ships.

MAKING TIMELINES

Timelines are valuable tools for studying history. Timelines show the key events that took place during a period of time. They also show chronology, or the order in which events took place in time. Finally, timelines show the interval, or amount of time between events.

Timelines can cover any number of years. The timeline below represents a period of 160 years. For practice, copy it on a sheet of paper. Using a ruler, make a timeline 8 inches (20.3 centimeters) long. This timeline can easily be divided into 16 equal sections. Because the timeline covers a period of 160 years, each half-inch (1.3-centimeter) section represents 10 years.

The timeline below can show events that took place during a single year, such as Balboa's discovery of the Pacific Ocean. The timeline can also show events that occurred over a span of years, like the voyages of Columbus or Magellan's voyage around the world. To show events that took place over a span greater than one year, a shaded area can be used.

The timeline that you copied is incomplete. Look at the map on the opposite page and add the following events to your timeline:

1. The voyage of Giovanni da Verrazano

2. The first voyage of Jacques Cartier

3. The first voyage of Martin Frobisher

4. The voyage of John Davis

5. Samuel de Champlain's voyages beginning in 1609

Now, put a title on your timeline.

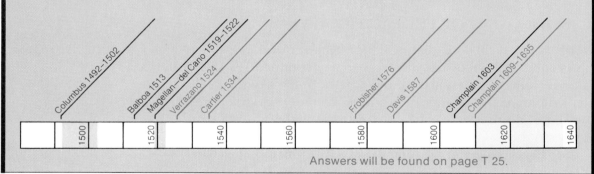

Answers will be found on page T 25.

At Guam Magellan's crew found food and water. Then they sailed to the Philippine (FIHL-uh-peen) Islands. There Magellan was killed when he took part in a battle between two warring groups of Filipinos. The responsibility for the expedition fell to Magellan's first officer, Juan Sebastián del Cano (dehl KAH-nō).

Del Cano, born in the Basque region between Spain and France, took command. He sailed south to the Indies where he traded for spices. Then, following the route of da Gama, he crossed the Indian Ocean and rounded Africa. After three years at sea, del Cano and the surviving crew members reached Spain. They were the first to sail around the world. Their voyage proved to Europeans that the Indies were separated from the Americas by a vast ocean.

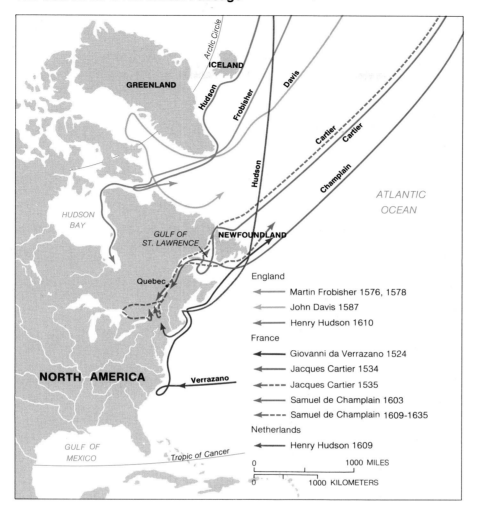

Map legend:

England
- ← Martin Frobisher 1576, 1578
- ← John Davis 1587
- ← Henry Hudson 1610

France
- ← Giovanni da Verrazano 1524
- ← Jacques Cartier 1534
- ←--- Jacques Cartier 1535
- ← Samuel de Champlain 1603
- ←--- Samuel de Champlain 1609–1635

Netherlands
- ← Henry Hudson 1609

0   1000 MILES
0   1000 KILOMETERS

THE SEARCH FOR THE NORTHWEST PASSAGE

Magellan's voyage was long and dangerous. Many Europeans thought that a passage through North America might be a better route to the Indies. Soon after Magellan's voyage, King Francis I of France began a search for this "Northwest Passage." His rivals, the monarchs of Portugal and Spain, had found water routes to Asia, and he did not want to be left behind. Francis sent out a ship guided by an Italian navigator named Giovanni da Verrazano (VEHR-rah-TSAH-noh).

In 1524 Verrazano sailed up the American coast from the Carolinas to Newfoundland. He saw the mouth of the Hudson River, near present-day New York City. He decided, though, that it was not an opening to the Northwest Passage. Still, his voyage gave Francis I his first claim to lands in North America.

This ceramic figurine of Giovanni da Verrazano was made during his lifetime. Verrazano wrote the first description of the North American coast from Maine to Georgia.

Point out that the French settlements in North America will be discussed in Chapter 3 and the struggle between England and France for dominance in North America in Chapter 6.

Activity: A bridge in New York City, connecting Manhattan and Staten Island, is named after Verrazano. Students can consult an atlas or a geographical dictionary to discover what places are named after Champlain (a lake between Vermont and New York, a county in Quebec); Frobisher (a bay in Canada); and Hudson (a river in New York, a city in New York, a county in New Jersey).

Francis I also sent Jacques Cartier (KAR-TYAY) on three voyages to the Gulf of St. Lawrence between 1534 and 1541. On his second voyage, Cartier sailed up the St. Lawrence River as far as present-day Quebec (kwee-BEK). Then he and some of his crew traveled upstream in small boats to an Indian village where Montreal (MAHN-tree-AWL) stands today. Cartier did not find the Northwest Passage, but Indians told him about a great inland kingdom called Saguenay. There, they said, he would find gold and silver.

Cartier searched for this kingdom, but he did not find it. Even so, he had explored one of North America's greatest waterways. He had also given France a claim to the land the Indians called Canada.

That claim was made stronger by French explorer Samuel de Champlain (sham-PLAYN). In 1603 he sailed to the St. Lawrence River to search for the Northwest Passage. Champlain made many other trips to North America for France.

Cartier proved that the St. Lawrence River did not lead to the Indies. Still, Europeans went on looking for the Northwest Passage. Two were English. Martin Frobisher (FRŌ-bish-ur) and then John Davis explored the icy waters off Greenland and northeastern Canada between 1576 and 1587. Each made three trips to North America. Their search for a water route to Asia, however, met with no success.

Another English explorer, Henry Hudson, sought the Northwest Passage for the Dutch. In 1609 he found the harbor of New York and a broad river flowing into it. In his ship *Half Moon*, Hudson sailed up the river that bears his name as far as present-day Albany. But the river was not the Northwest Passage.

Hudson made a second voyage a year later, this time for the English. He reached the waters west of Greenland and then sailed into Canada's Hudson Bay. There he and his crew spent a winter trapped in the ice. By the time spring arrived, his sailors had had enough of exploring. They set their captain adrift in a small boat, leaving him to die. Then they sailed for home.

SECTION REVIEW   Answers will be found on page T 25.

1. Define these words: *colony, migration, treaty.*

2. Identify: Queen Isabella, Pedro Álvarez Cabral, Amerigo Vespucci, Vasco Núñez de Balboa.

3. What Caribbean islands did Columbus discover?

4. Why was the first voyage of Columbus important?

5. What did Europeans learn from Magellan's voyage?

6. What were explorers hoping to find when they searched for the Northwest Passage?

2-3 SPAIN'S EMPIRE IN THE AMERICAS

READ TO FIND OUT

—what the words *conquistadors, peninsula, missions,* and *missionaries* mean.

—how the Spanish discovered Florida.

—how the Spanish conquered the Aztec and the Inca.

—how Spain governed its new empire.

conquistadors: Spanish conquerors

peninsula: piece of land connected to a continent but mostly surrounded by water

mission: settlement where missionaries teach their religion to people of other faiths

missionaries: people who go to another land to spread the teachings of a religion

Years before other European nations had settlements in the Americas, Hispaniola was providing an income for the ruler of Spain. Soon after the last voyage of Columbus, the Spanish on the island were sending home almost $1 million in gold every year. Hispaniola also provided a base for Spanish expansion in the Caribbean Sea. Between 1508 and 1511, the Spanish conquered Puerto Rico, Jamaica, and Cuba. Then they looked to the mainland.

THE CONQUISTADORS

The Spanish conquerors of the Caribbean islands were hard men, shaped by years of service to their country. Many had fought in the recent fierce battles with North African Muslims. These hard-fighting Spaniards were eager to expand Spain's empire and to spread its Catholic religion. They also sought adventure and wealth. Ready to die for

An Aztec in the 1500s drew this picture of Cortés, a conquistador, with his army in Mexico. Leading the way is Malinche, an Aztec woman.

The Spanish came to the Americas seeking gold like this beautiful pendant from Oaxaca, Mexico. Most of it was then melted into bars.

Routes of Early Spanish Conquistadors 1513-1533

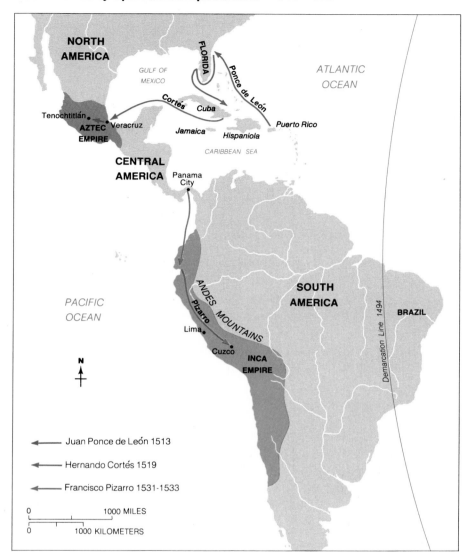

gold, God, and the glory of Spain, they took the name **conquistadors** (kohn-KEES-tah-DORZ), or conquerors.

From their island bases, the conquistadors explored the lands around the Caribbean. Juan Ponce de León (POHN-say day lay-OHN) was one of the first. While governor of Puerto Rico, he had heard Indian tales about a magical fountain on an island. One drink of its waters was supposed to make old people young again.

In 1513 Ponce de León sailed north, searching for this "Fountain of Youth." He found what he thought was a large island. He named it Florida and claimed it for Spain. Then he explored much of its coastline. Voyages by other Spaniards soon showed that Ponce de León's

Juan Ponce de León was governor of Puerto Rico when he heard of an island called Bimini with a wonderful fountain. When he reached Florida, he thought he had found Bimini.

island was really a **peninsula.** A peninsula is a piece of land that is connected to the mainland but is mostly surrounded by water. Florida was Spain's first claim to land on the mainland of North America.

CONQUEST OF THE AZTEC AND INCA

Conquistadors in Cuba also heard Indian tales. They heard about a city of gold somewhere in Mexico. Hernando Cortés (kor-TEHZ), a soldier who had taken part in the conquest of Cuba, was eager to search for the city. He had his chance when the governor of Cuba chose him to lead an expedition to Mexico. The governor told him to explore and to trade with the Indians. Cortés, however, had other plans.

In 1519 Cortés and about 600 soldiers landed on the east coast of Mexico. He soon learned that the city he sought was Tenochtitlán. It was the capital of the mighty Aztec empire. While making plans to conquer the city, Cortés met Malinche (mah-LEEN-chay), the daughter of an Aztec chief. She became his translator and most important adviser. Cortés also gained the support of Indians who were ready to rebel against their harsh Aztec rulers.

Cortés and his army marched inland, toward Tenochtitlán. When they arrived, they were greeted warmly by the Aztec king, Montezuma II (MAHN-tuh-ZOO-muh). Because of an old Aztec legend about bearded gods from the east, Montezuma believed that Cortés was an Aztec god who was returning to his home. He welcomed Cortés and gave him gifts of gold.

Cortés repaid Montezuma by putting him in prison and taking control of his empire. Spanish soldiers seized the Aztec's gold and destroyed their temples. But the Aztec rebelled, and the Spanish had to flee the city.

The Aztec victory was short-lived. In May 1521 Cortés and his army returned. Aided by their Indian allies, they forced the Aztec to surrender after three months of bitter fighting. Tenochtitlán was destroyed. Near the ruins, Cortés started building a new capital, Mexico City.

Francisco Pizarro (pih-ZAHR-ō) followed the example set by Cortés. While living in Panama, Pizarro had heard rumors of treasure-filled cities to the south. In 1532, with fewer than 200 soldiers, he invaded the empire of the Inca in Peru.

The Inca were fighting among themselves. Pizarro took advantage of the warfare to capture the Inca ruler, Atahualpa (AHT-ah-WAHL-pah). He promised to spare Atahualpa's life in return for riches. Pizarro waited until the Inca had given him a fortune in gold and silver. Then he killed their ruler. After a three-year struggle, Pizarro overcame the Inca and took control of their empire. In 1535 he founded Lima (LEE-muh), which became a center of Spanish rule in South America.

*CT
For discussion: Students should consider more closely the question posed at the beginning of the section: Why were the conquistadors so successful? (Aside from the general reasons suggested on page 39, Cortés was aided by the Aztec's thinking he was a god, Pizarro by the civil war in Peru.)

★ ★ ★ ★ ★ ★ ★ **AMERICAN VALUES IN ACTION** ★ ★ ★ ★ ★ ★ ★ ★

SISTER JUANA INÉS DE LA CRUZ

New Spain was an empire of riches, glory, and adventure. It was settled in European traditions of church and family. In this vast empire the place of a young girl was small. She could embroider, play music, and perhaps learn to read at a church school.

Juana Inés de Asbaje (WAH-nah ee-NAYS day ahs-BAH-hay) was full of mischief. At three years of age, she sneaked off to a church school and learned to read. By the time she was seven, she had mastered all of the learning girls were allowed. Then she heard about high schools and a college in Mexico City, where boys could study. She begged her mother to disguise her as a boy and send her to school.

Juana's plan failed, but soon her family moved to the capital. There she plunged into her grandfather's library. Many of his books were written in Latin, so Juana set out to learn Latin. Unhappy with her progress, she cut off her hair. "I did not think then that it was right that a head so slow in learning Latin should be covered with pretty hair. When I could read Latin well, I let my hair grow again."

When Juana was thirteen years old, in 1664, her grandfather sent her to live in the viceroy's court. He hoped that she would marry a rich nobleman. But Juana's head was filled with ideas. She began to write poems so fine that they amazed the viceroy. Proud of her learning, he invited professors from the university to quiz her. Juana solved every problem—in her head and not on paper.

In time, Juana grew bored with the court. She found a new life in a convent, or religious house. She trained the nuns to teach in the church schools. Juana, too, became a nun. She took the name Sor Juana Inés de la Cruz (day lah KROOZ), or Sister Juana of the Cross.

Sister Juana collected a library of 4,000 books. She wrote many poems and plays. She also experimented in the sciences. Her works were published in Europe, and her fame as a poet spread.

Then the bishop insisted that she concentrate on religious matters. Juana defended her work, but in time decided to devote herself to the poor. She sold her books and gave the money to a home for orphan girls. Two years later, in 1695, she died in a smallpox epidemic while nursing sick Indian children.

Sister Juana was a scholar, poet, scientist, and finally sister of mercy. She had the courage of a conquistador and the mind of an explorer. She more than filled her place in the empire of New Spain.

ORGANIZING THE SPANISH EMPIRE

By the 1540s the Spanish had conquered much of Central and South America and part of North America for the king of Spain. The king appointed two officials, called viceroys, to rule this new empire. The Viceroyalty of New Spain included Mexico and the Caribbean islands.

Mexico City was its capital. Lima was the capital of the Viceroyalty of Peru. The two viceroyalties were divided into provinces, each with a governor appointed by the viceroy.

Watching over a government thousands of miles away was difficult for Spanish rulers. But an even larger problem was what to do with the people they had conquered. Spanish rulers wanted to use Indian labor. As Christian monarchs, they also wanted to persuade Indians to accept Christianity in order to save their souls.

Spanish monarchs gave large land grants to Spaniards. These land-owners were called encomenderos (en-kō-mehn-DEH-rōz). They had the right to make the Indians who lived on their land work for them. By law, the encomenderos were supposed to allow the Indians to keep part of their crops. They were also supposed to protect the Indians. But the farther an encomendero was from the center of government, the harder the laws were to enforce. Most Indian laborers were treated like slaves.

Saving Indian souls was the duty of Catholic priests who arrived soon after the conquistadors. Priests established settlements called **missions,** where Indians were brought to live. The priests were **missionaries,** people who go to another country to spread the teachings of a religion. They educated the mission Indians in the Catholic faith and in the ways of Spain.

Like the encomenderos, the priests used Indian labor. The mission Indians built churches, houses, and workshops. They also cared for live-stock, cleared land, and raised crops. Some priests, like Bartolomé de Las Casas (lahs KAH-sahs), spoke out against the cruelty of the enco-menderos. But they had little success.

Indians not only were overworked, but also died in huge numbers from European diseases, such as smallpox. These diseases had been unknown in the Americas, and the Indians had no resistance to them. It was not long before almost all of the Indians on the Caribbean islands had died. Early in the 1500s, the Spanish began to bring in Africans to work as slaves.

*CT
For discussion: Once every three years inspectors appointed by the viceroys were sent out to check on local conditions. One of the inspectors' jobs was to make sure the Indians were praying in churches. Ask why students think the Spanish were so interested in the Indians' souls. Why might they have been less interested in their working conditions?

SECTION REVIEW   Answers will be found on page T 25.

1. Define these words: *conquistadors, peninsula, missions, missionaries.*

2. Identify: Juan Ponce de León, Hernando Cortés, Francisco Pizarro, Bartolomé de Las Casas.

3. Who helped Cortés and his soldiers to defeat the Aztec?

4. What helped Pizarro to defeat the Inca?

5. What were the rights and duties of encomenderos?

6. Why were African slaves brought to the Caribbean islands in the early 1500s?

2–4 NEW SPAIN'S NORTHERN FRONTIER

READ TO FIND OUT

frontier: edge of a settled area, where the wilderness begins

—what the word *frontier* means.

—why conquistadors explored Florida.

—why the Spanish sought the Seven Cities of Cíbola.

—how the Province of New Mexico was established.

Spain gained great wealth from the Aztec and the Inca. Conquistadors soon turned their attention to unexplored lands to the north. There they hoped to find other rich empires.

EXPLORING THE SOUTHEAST

Florida was the first of the northern lands to be explored. In 1521 Juan Ponce de León returned to the peninsula he had discovered and tried to build a settlement. But Indians drove him away.

You may wish to find Cabeza de Vaca's account (some of it appears in anthologies) and read passages to the class.

The Spanish king named another conquistador, Pánfilo de Narváez (nahr-VAH-ayz), governor of Florida and of much of the land along the Gulf coast. In 1528 Narváez landed on the west coast of Florida with about 400 settlers. Searching for gold, they raided the villages of the Apalachee (AP-uh-LATCH-ee). But the Apalachee were skilled warriors. Drawing their large oaken bows, they shot arrows through joints in the conquistadors' armor.

Narváez gave up his search and tried to leave Florida, but he lost contact with his supply ships. He and most of his party drowned as they made their way along the Gulf coast in small boats and rafts. Four survivors were held captive by Indians for six years. When they finally escaped, the four walked all the way across Texas to Mexico. One of them, Álvar Núñez Cabeza de Vaca (kah-BAY-sah day VAH-kuh), wrote an account of their journey.

The African slave Estevanico survived the Narváez expedition. Cabeza de Vaca later wrote the story of the terrible hardships that the survivors suffered.

The next conquistador who hoped to be governor of Florida was Hernando de Soto (day SOH-toh). De Soto had brought home a fortune from Peru. Now he planned to find the Seven Cities of Cíbola (SEE-boh-lah). Indians had told Cabeza de Vaca that these were cities of gold somewhere in North America.

In 1539 de Soto sailed from Cuba to Florida with about 600 soldiers. For the next three years, he searched for gold in the Southeast. Like Narváez, de Soto soon learned to respect the fighting skills of the

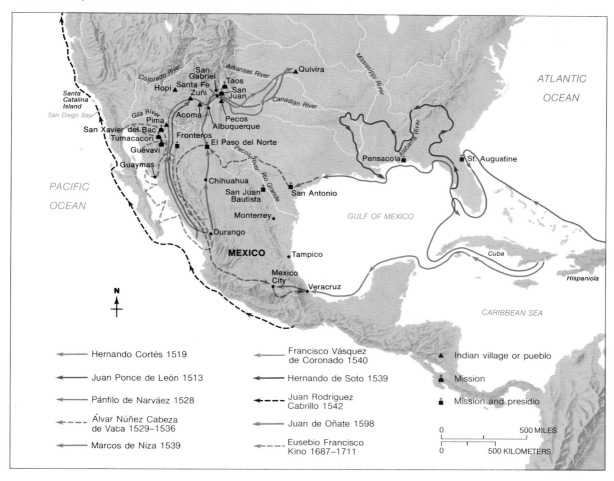

Map legend:

——— Hernando Cortés 1519

——— Juan Ponce de León 1513

——— Pánfilo de Narváez 1528

– – – Álvar Núñez Cabeza de Vaca 1529–1536

——— Marcos de Niza 1539

——— Francisco Vásquez de Coronado 1540

——— Hernando de Soto 1539

– – – Juan Rodríguez Cabrillo 1542

——— Juan de Oñate 1598

– – – Eusebio Francisco Kino 1687–1711

▲ Indian village or pueblo

✝ Mission

■ Mission and presidio

0   500 MILES

0   500 KILOMETERS

Indians. De Soto traveled into Georgia and Alabama and as far west as Oklahoma. He discovered a great river, the Mississippi, but he never found gold. In 1542 de Soto died of fever. His remaining soldiers went on into Texas. Then they built boats and sailed to Mexico.

EXPLORING THE SOUTHWEST

At the same time that de Soto's expedition took place, another effort to find the Seven Cities of Cíbola was under way. In 1539 the Viceroy of New Spain sent a priest named Marcos de Niza (NEE-sah) north to the land of the Zuñi, in present-day New Mexico. De Niza's expedition was guided by Estevanico (es-tay-vah-NEE-kō), an African slave who was one of the four survivors of the Narváez expedition. Riding ahead, Estevanico reached the Zuñi pueblos and sent a report to Father Marcos. Then he was killed, probably by the Zuñi. Father Marcos returned to Mexico and reported Estevanico's discovery.

Most of the Spanish explorers started from settlements in Mexico and the Caribbean. They thought North America contained riches like those they had found in South and Central American cities.

Activity: Have students consult books and encyclopedia articles about Ponce de León, Pánfilo de Narváez, Hernando de Soto, Father Marcos de Niza, Francisco de Coronado, and Juan Cabrillo, and report on them to the class. As part of their reports, students can draw maps showing these explorers' routes.

From a distance, pueblos in sunlight look a little like cities of gold. Spanish explorers were disappointed, however, when they found no great riches in the Southwest.

The viceroy was convinced that the Zuñi pueblos were the Seven Cities of Cíbola. In 1540 he sent another expedition north to conquer them. It was led by a young conquistador named Francisco Vásquez de Coronado (KOR-uh-NAH-dō). After weeks of traveling under a burning sun, Coronado and his soldiers found a pueblo. Instead of golden palaces, they saw a little village with walls of rock.

The Zuñi refused to share their food and water, so the conquistadors rode in to take the pueblo. For an hour, arrows flew and swords flashed. Coronado's shining helmet made him a good target for the Zuñi. They showered him with rocks and knocked him unconscious. But the village fell to the attackers.

In the months that followed, Coronado sent out exploring parties. One patrol came upon the Grand Canyon. Another found more villages near a great river, the Rio Grande. There the Spanish heard stories about a rich kingdom farther east. Eager to find it, Coronado led his soldiers across the Texas plains, as far as present-day Kansas. He found nothing but buffalo, grass, and sky. In 1542 Coronado and his soldiers returned to Mexico empty-handed.

Farther west, another conquistador was searching for the Seven Cities of Gold—by sea. From the west coast of Mexico, Juan Rodríguez Cabrillo (kah-BREE-yō) sailed along the coast of California in 1542. He did not find gold, but he claimed the land for Spain. Over two centuries would pass, however, before Spain made use of that claim.

NORTHERN SETTLEMENTS

Cabeza de Vaca, de Soto, and Coronado had gone beyond New Spain's northern **frontier** to search for treasure. A frontier is the edge of a settled area, where the wilderness begins. When the conquistadors failed to find treasure, the Spanish viceroys in America lost interest in their northern borderlands. As a result, the northern frontier of new Spain advanced very slowly.

In Florida there were a few attempts to start settlements and to build missions. Because of Indian attacks, these efforts ended in failure. Finally, in 1565, St. Augustine was founded. Its most important building was a presidio, or fort. The fort was intended to prevent Spain's rivals from starting colonies on the eastern coast of North America. The presidio at St. Augustine also encouraged priests to start missions among the Indians. By 1655 there were 38 missions along the Florida Gulf coast and in present-day Georgia.

Settlement of the lands visited by Coronado did not begin until 1598. In that year the Viceroy of New Spain sent Juan de Oñate (oh-NYAH-tay) north to create the Province of New Mexico. With him went soldiers, priests, and settlers. When Governor Oñate arrived among the pueblos on the Rio Grande, he gave land grants to many of his friends. They used the Pueblo Indians as laborers. By 1610 the town of Santa Fe was started, and several churches had been built.

*CT
For discussion: Students should reconsider the question posed on page 44: What was the chief motive of the Spanish explorers? (the quest for gold) Why then did Spain not colonize the northern part of the continent?

St. Augustine, Florida, is the oldest city in the United States.

In the 1500s, the Navaho painted Spanish soldiers on horseback on the walls of Canyon de Chelly, Arizona. Other rock paintings in the canyon were made by the Anasazi more than a thousand years earlier.

Pueblo religious leaders made sacred paintings for healing ceremonies. Popé told his people that the gods had killed their crops because the Pueblo were following Spanish ways. Driving out the Spanish would bring rain back to the land.

Some of the Pueblo people accepted the new faith. But most continued to follow the religion of their ancestors in secret. When the priests learned of this, they had the Pueblo religious leaders whipped.

In 1680, after years of planning, the Pueblo rose in revolt. Led by a religious leader named Popé (PŌ-peh), they killed more than 400 of the Spaniards and drove the rest out of their homeland. Twelve years passed before the Spanish could return to rebuild their settlements in the Province of New Mexico.

As the Spanish returned, they expanded into other areas. During the Pueblo Revolt, a priest named Eusebio Francisco Kino (KEE-noh) had arrived in present-day Arizona. He spent the last twenty years of his life exploring the lands south of the Gila (HEE-lah) River. And in 1700 he began work on Arizona's first missions.

In time, the language, religion, and culture of Spain spread across much of the American Southwest. The people of the pueblos learned from the Spanish how to use plows and hoes, make bricks, and raise sheep for wool. In turn, they introduced the Spanish to new foods and taught them new ways to grow crops in desert soil.

Students should be aware that much of what we think of as Mexican cooking, particularly the use of corn and spices, came from the Indians.

SECTION REVIEW Answers will be found on page T 25.

1. Define this word: *frontier.*

2. Identify: Álvar Núñez Cabeza de Vaca, Estevanico, Juan de Oñate, Eusebio Francisco Kino.

3. Why did the Spanish have trouble planting settlements in Florida?

4. Why did Spanish settlers have to leave the Province of New Mexico?

5. What voyage gave Spain a claim to California?

CHAPTER SUMMARY

The Norse probably were the second discoverers of America. But sagas about Leif Ericson and Vinland did not travel from Scandinavia to the rest of Europe.

In the centuries following the Norse discoveries, Europe was changing in important ways. From the Crusaders and Marco Polo, Europeans learned about the wealth of the Indies, and trade developed between Europe and Asia. Trading centers grew into cities. Rulers began to bring the nobles under their control and to create nations.

By the 1400s the nation-building rulers of western Europe were ready to help merchants find a water route to Asia. Improvements in shipbuilding, navigation, and mapmaking made such voyages possible.

Europe's knowledge of the globe grew with the voyages of Vasco da Gama, Christopher Columbus, Ferdinand Magellan, and other bold explorers. It became clear that America was a new continent, separated from Asia by a great ocean. European explorers soon began to search for a Northwest Passage, a water route through America to Asia.

Meanwhile, Spanish conquistadors took control of islands in the Caribbean Sea and then looked to the mainland. The Aztec and Inca empires were conquered. Spanish priests arrived to teach the Indians Christianity. The Spanish king granted Spanish settlers the right to use Indian labor. Overwork and European diseases killed many Indians.

While the king was organizing his empire, the conquistadors went north into the area that is now the United States. No treasures were found, and Indians fought hard to keep their homelands. Settlement went forward slowly. By the 1600s there were Spanish outposts in Florida and New Mexico. The language, religion, and culture of Spain began to spread across the Southwest.

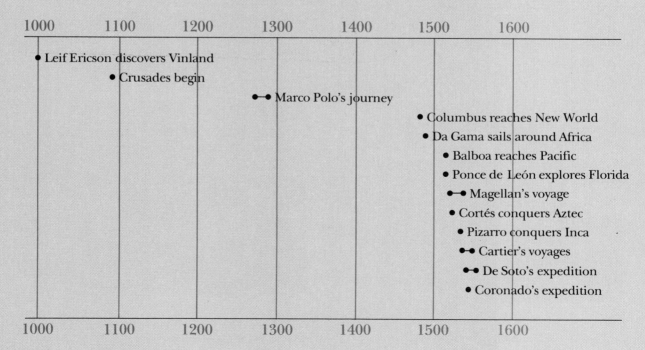

| 1000 | 1100 | 1200 | 1300 | 1400 | 1500 | 1600 |

- Leif Ericson discovers Vinland
- Crusades begin
- Marco Polo's journey
- Columbus reaches New World
- Da Gama sails around Africa
- Balboa reaches Pacific
- Ponce de León explores Florida
- Magellan's voyage
- Cortés conquers Aztec
- Pizarro conquers Inca
- Cartier's voyages
- De Soto's expedition
- Coronado's expedition

| 1000 | 1100 | 1200 | 1300 | 1400 | 1500 | 1600 |

CHAPTER SURVEY

VOCABULARY REVIEW

From this list of vocabulary words, choose the one that best completes each sentence below.

(a) colony
(b) communication
(c) conquistadors
(d) feudalism
(e) frontier
(f) geography
(g) migration

(h) missions
(i) missionaries
(j) navigation
(k) peninsula
(l) technology
(m) treaty

1. A _____ is the edge of a settled area, where the wilderness begins.

2. _____ takes place when people exchange ideas and information.

3. A _____ is a long, narrow piece of land jutting into a lake or an ocean.

4. The discovery of America led to the largest _____ of people in history.

5. A _____ is a written agreement between two or more nations.

6. People who travel to spread religious teachings are _____.

7. A person studying _____ learns about lands and their people, climates, etc.

8. _____ is the application of knowledge to practical problems.

9. _____ are places where missionaries live and work.

10. The science of _____ can help keep a ship on course.

11. _____ were warriors who conquered new lands for Spain.

12. A _____ is a settlement controlled by the settlers' homeland.

13. _____ is a system of land ownership based on service to a lord.

CHAPTER REVIEW

1. (a) What evidence supports the claim that the Norse reached America before Columbus did? (b) News of Norse voyages to Vinland did not reach most Europeans. Why not?

2. (a) In Viking times, whom did the lord of a manor protect? (b) Whom did the lord serve? (c) Under what system did the lord have rights and duties?

3. (a) What was the purpose of the Crusades? (b) Did the Crusaders achieve their goal? (c) What brought Christians and Muslims together despite their differences?

4. (a) What lands did Marco Polo write about? (b) Why were European merchants interested in a water route to them? (c) In the 1400s, what nation led the search for that route?

5. (a) What was Columbus's goal in sailing west? (b) In what way were his voyages a failure? (c) In what way were they a success?

6. (a) What body of water did Balboa find in 1513? (b) How did Magellan reach this body of water? (c) How did Verrazano, Cartier, and Champlain try to reach it?

A Flemish prayer book showed peasants mowing hay on a manor about 1515.

Artists decorated navigational instruments with beautiful designs. Sailors found their position by sighting stars with this Italian astrolabe.

7. (a) Which two conquistadors conquered lands of great wealth? (b) What peoples did they conquer? Where?

8. (a) How did conquistadors differ from encomenderos? (b) How did missionaries and encomenderos treat the Indians?

9. (a) Who told Spaniards about the Fountain of Youth and the Seven Cities of Cíbola? (b) How did conquistadors react to the stories? (c) How did the stories affect Spanish land claims?

10. (a) When Coronado crossed the plains, what was he looking for? (b) What did he find? (c) How did his findings affect settlement in the borderlands north of Mexico?

GEOGRAPHY REVIEW

1. What two lands west of Scandinavia did the Norse find before they found Vinland?

2. Across what sea did Italian merchants sail to buy silks and spices from Muslim traders?

3. Correct this statement: In their search for a water route to Asia, the Portuguese sent expeditions along the eastern coast of Africa.

4. What waterway did Cartier and Champlain explore?

5. What peninsula did Ponce de León explore?

*CT 6. The map on page 45 shows that Cabrillo's route was different from the routes of other explorers. How was it different?

USING THE TOOLS OF HISTORY

Making Timelines

*CT 1. Make a timeline showing these events:
(a) Estevanico is killed.
(b) Coronado conquers the Zuñi.
(c) Coronado returns to Mexico.
(d) Spanish settlers first travel to the pueblos of the Southwest.
(e) Pueblo people revolt.
(f) Spanish settlers return to the land of the Pueblo people.

2. Write a title for the timeline.

READING AND THINKING

Previewing Maps

*CT 1. Find the list of maps in the Table of Contents at the front of this book. Five of the maps appear in Chapter 2 (pages 22 through 51). The map titles include the words *routes, voyages, search,* and *exploration.* What do these words suggest about the chapter?

2. Chapter 3 runs from page 52 through page 79. What map in the Table of Contents appears in Chapter 3? What does the title of the map tell you about the chapter?

Comparing Maps

*CT 3. Look at the five maps in Chapter 2.
(a) Which two of the maps show the voyages of Dias and da Gama? How do these maps differ in the area they show? (b) Which two of the maps show the routes of Ponce de León and Cortés? How do these maps differ in the area they show?

CHAPTER 3   1556–1718

THE FRENCH, ENGLISH, AND DUTCH PLANT COLONIES

THE CHALLENGE TO SPAIN
NEW FRANCE
THE FIRST ENGLISH COLONY
THE DUTCH AND SWEDISH START COLONIES

3-1 THE CHALLENGE TO SPAIN

READ TO FIND OUT

mercantilism: the theory that a nation can increase its wealth and power by controlling trade with other nations

balance of trade: the difference between the value of goods sold abroad by a nation and the value of goods it buys from other nations

refuge: a safe place

privateers: privately owned warships sailing with government permission

—what the words *mercantilism, balance of trade, refuge,* and *privateers* mean.

—how colonies could help European nations.

—how religion caused conflict in Europe.

—which nations sent sea raiders to attack the Spanish empire.

—how the Armada's defeat helped Spain's rivals.

When Philip II became king of Spain in 1556, he had every reason to be proud. In the years since the Treaty of Tordesillas was signed, his country had become a great empire. Spain ruled Mexico, much of South America, and the islands of the Caribbean, now called the West Indies. Spain also claimed parts of North America and, because of Magellan's voyage, the Philippine Islands.

Other European countries saw the riches of Spain's colonies. England, under its new queen, Elizabeth I, especially wanted a share of the American treasure. So did France and the Netherlands.

King Philip's portrait painter showed him as the firm and powerful ruler of the world's richest empire in the 1500s.

By 1593, when this portrait was probably painted, Queen Elizabeth I ruled a strong nation. The unknown artist shows her standing on a map of England.

THE VALUE OF COLONIES

Philip believed that the purpose of an empire was to enrich the parent country. Other rulers shared this belief, which was called **mercantilism** (MUR-kuhn-tih-LIHZ-uhm). According to this theory, a nation could increase its wealth and power by controlling trade with other nations.

The main goal of a mercantilist nation was to improve its **balance of trade.** A nation's balance of trade is the difference between the value of goods sold abroad and the value of goods bought from other nations. If a nation could sell more goods to other nations than it bought from them, it would have a favorable balance of trade. More gold would flow into the treasury than would flow out. With gold, a nation could build up its army and navy and become stronger.

Colonies, mercantilists believed, could improve a nation's balance of trade. Colonies could produce many of the materials that a nation would otherwise have to buy from foreign nations. In this way, gold would not flow out of the treasury. Overseas settlements would also provide a market for a nation's goods.

Have students write a definition of *mercantilism* in their own words and then explain why this theory led Spain and other nations to colonize the American continent.

Viewed in this way, the rich Spanish empire in America was a prize that other European nations envied. Spain's Caribbean colonies produced tobacco, cocoa, and sugar—products that were becoming popular in Europe. Even more important were the precious metals from the mines of Mexico and Peru. Year after year, tons of gold and silver were loaded into large ships called galleons for the voyage home. By law, one fifth of all treasure taken from Spanish colonies in America belonged to the Spanish monarch.

THE CRUSADE OF PHILIP II

Philip II was married to England's Queen Mary I. The marriage was unpopular because many of the English believed that Spain was England's worst enemy. When the Catholic Mary died in 1558, she was succeeded by her half-sister, the Protestant Elizabeth I.

Philip II used the wealth from his colonies to strengthen his army, already the most powerful in Europe. The soldiers of Spain, he believed, were more than just conquerors. They were Crusaders, fighting for their faith. The Spanish had defeated the Muslims a century before. But Philip believed his armies were at war with a new and even more dangerous enemy of the Christian world.

In the late 1500s, Europeans were no longer united in the same faith. Many had followed Martin Luther, John Calvin, and other religious leaders out of the Roman Catholic Church. The reformers called themselves Protestants. Some monarchs, including Elizabeth I of England, supported the new Protestant religion. Philip II saw himself as a defender of the Catholic faith. He used his army to force Protestants back into the Catholic Church.

SPAIN'S EMPIRE UNDER ATTACK

Activity: Have students research and write reports on the Dutch rebellion against the Spanish. (This is the subject of a classic work, *The Rise of the Dutch Republic,* by an American historian, John Lothrop Motley. This work, however, is too advanced for students.)

Philip II's empire in the Americas was a tempting target for his Protestant enemies—and for those who wanted a share of Spain's new wealth. In 1564 French Protestants, known as Huguenots (HYOO-guh-NAHTZ), settled at Fort Caroline on the east coast of Florida. They were seeking a **refuge,** or safe place, where they could practice their religion in peace. They also wanted a base for attacking Spain's galleons. The Spanish responded the following year by destroying the French settlement and founding St. Augustine.

Among Philip II's enemies were the Dutch. For years they had lived under Spanish rule. Then they rebelled, creating a new Protestant country called Holland, or the Netherlands. Dutch **privateers**—privately owned warships sailing with government permission—were sent to raid Spain's Caribbean ports and to capture treasure ships.

English sea raiders were also in the Caribbean. Their queen, Elizabeth I, knew that England was not strong enough to face Spain in a full-scale war. Instead, she aided the Dutch rebels and looked the other way while her sea captains stole Philip's gold.

Caca Fogo.   Caca Plata.

This 1579 engraving shows Sir Francis Drake's ship *Golden Hind* in combat with a Spanish treasure ship. Drake's ship is at right.

SIR FRANCIS DRAKE

Queen Elizabeth's favorite raider was Francis Drake. In 1578 he sailed through the Strait of Magellan. He then sailed along the Pacific coast of South America, plundering Spanish galleons and settlements. Soon his ship, the *Golden Hind,* bulged with treasure.

Drake next sailed north along the Pacific coast of North America. Landing near San Francisco Bay in 1579, his crew repaired the ship and took on supplies. Drake claimed the California coast for his queen.

Fearing attacks by Spanish warships if he sailed south, Drake made a bold move. To return home he sailed west, like Magellan, across the Pacific. The *Golden Hind* finally returned to England in 1580. It was the second ship to sail around the world.

When news reached Spain that "the pirate Drake" was still alive, Philip II demanded that he be hanged. Instead, Elizabeth made him a knight. The "pirate" was now *Sir* Francis Drake.

*CT

For discussion: What does the knighting of Francis Drake reveal about England's relations with Spain and Elizabeth's attitude toward Philip? Why might Philip wish to remove England as an enemy once and for all?

SEQUENCING EVENTS

*CT

Often a chapter in a history book will cover many events. To understand these events, it is helpful to place them in their correct time order, or *sequence.*

Writers of history provide clues to the sequence of events. They do this by using *signal words.* Here are some examples:

first, second, third, last
beginning, ending
earlier, later, now
next, soon, then, while
when, until, as soon as
during, meanwhile
at the same time as
before, after, following

Some other clues to ordering events are *calendar markers,* such as days, months, years, and centuries.

1. Read the first paragraph under the heading "The Spanish Armada." Find three signal words and one calendar marker and write them on a piece of paper.

2. Read the two statements below. Which event occurred first?

(a) The Armada was ready.

(b) Philip decided that the time had come to conquer England.

What signal word in the text helped you to choose your answer?

3. Read the last paragraph on page 57, under the heading "The Spanish Armada." Can you find any calendar markers? If so, what are they? Can you find any signal words in the last paragraph? If so, what are they?

4. Now turn back to the first two paragraphs under "Sir Francis Drake." Find three signal words and two calendar markers and jot them down on your paper.

5. Read the two statements below. Which event occurred first?

(a) Drake and his crew landed near San Francisco Bay.

(b) Drake plundered Spanish galleons.

The rest of this chapter contains many more calendar markers and signal words. Take note of them as you learn the order in which the events took place.

Answers will be found on page T 27.

THE SPANISH ARMADA

The sea raiders and English aid to the Dutch angered the king of Spain. Philip decided that the time had come to conquer England. First he built up an invasion force. He proudly named it the Invincible Armada (ar-MAH-duh), or unconquerable fleet of warships. After two years of preparation the Armada was ready. In 1588 its 130 ships, carrying 30,000 sailors and soldiers, set out to cross the English Channel. Meanwhile the English had assembled their own fleet of fighting ships. One of the fleet's commanders was Sir Francis Drake.

In the channel the small English ships sailed swiftly among the heavy Spanish galleons, first dividing them and then attacking one at a time. The Spanish anchored off the French coast to regroup. But the English filled eight ships with gunpowder, set them on fire, and sent them toward the wooden Armada. When the Spanish saw the dreaded

Activity: Have students write an account of one day in the English battle with the Armada. The account can be written from the point of view of an English or a Spanish seaman or Sir Francis Drake himself.

The Spanish Armada entering the English Channel might have looked like this. A later artist made this colored engraving of the scene.

fire ships, they panicked and fled in disorder. The English once more attacked, sinking two ships and damaging the others.

The weakened Armada fled to the North Sea. There a fierce storm destroyed many of the remaining ships. Only 76 returned home to Spain. The ten-day battle had ended in a crushing defeat for Spain.

After much of Philip's navy had been destroyed, the sea routes to America were safer for his rivals. The English, Dutch, and French planned more voyages of exploration. And the idea of planting colonies became increasingly attractive now that colonies could be more easily supplied and defended. When Philip II died in 1598, the first successful American settlements by England, the Netherlands, and France were only a few years in the future.

*CT
You may wish to direct particular attention to the connection between the Armada's destruction and England, Holland, and France's establishment of colonies in America. Ask students to consider whether the latter nations might have been such active colonizers if Spain had remained the major naval power.

SECTION REVIEW Answers will be found on page T 27.

1. Define these words: *mercantilism, balance of trade, refuge, privateers.*

2. Identify: Elizabeth I, Francis Drake.

3. According to mercantilists, colonies could improve a nation's balance of trade. Describe how.

4. How did religion cause conflict in Europe?

5. Sea raiders from which three nations attacked Spain's empire in North and South America?

6. Why was the Armada's defeat important to the nations of northwestern Europe?

3-2 NEW FRANCE

READ TO FIND OUT

monopoly: complete control of the sale of a product

allies: people or nations who agree to help one another in time of trouble

A French mapmaker in 1547 showed the arrival of Jacques Cartier and French colonists in Canada five years earlier. The Indians they met were Iroquois.

—what the words *monopoly* and *allies* mean.

—what brought the French to Canada.

—why the French got along well with the Huron.

—how New France expanded in North America.

The defeat of the Armada weakened Spain. Still, the Spanish were strong enough to hold on to their empire in America. The nations of northwestern Europe had to start their first colonies along the Atlantic coast north of Spanish Florida.

Indian fishers and French trappers lived peacefully together in France's North American colonies.

THE FUR TRADE

The French chose to settle the region explored by Jacques Cartier. It was not gold that drew them to the lands along the St. Lawrence River, but something almost as valuable—beaver fur.

By the 1600s beaver hats were very popular in Europe, and hatmakers were willing to pay a high price for pelts. Several wealthy French merchants wanted a **monopoly** of the fur trade. Monopoly means complete control, by a person or a group, of the sale of a product. Each of these merchants wanted to be the only one to have the right to buy and sell shipments of beaver pelts. With no one else bidding, furs could be bought at a low price in America. With no one else selling furs in France, the merchant's price could be kept high.

The king of France was willing to grant a fur-trade monopoly to anyone who would plant a colony in Canada. Early colonizing attempts, however, all ended in failure.

THE FATHER OF NEW FRANCE

The first permanent French settlement in America was the work of Samuel de Champlain. He was a geographer who preferred the deck of a ship to a desk in a library. Working for a number of different monopoly holders, Champlain made 11 voyages to North America. On his

Activity: Students can research Champlain's voyages to North America and on a map trace the route of one of the voyages. (For a simplified route, see map on page 37.)

The Wyandot were a tribe of the Huron Confederacy. This Wyandot mother and baby were painted in the 1700s.

Have students review what they have learned about the League of the Iroquois in Chapter 1 (page 11).

third voyage, in 1608, he sailed up the St. Lawrence River and built a fort at Quebec. This was the beginning of New France, the French empire in America.

In the years that followed, Champlain used Quebec as a base for exploring. His companions were often *coureurs de bois* (koo-RUR deh BWAH), French for "forest runners." These were French traders who traveled great distances over Indian trails and waterways in search of furs. Champlain and the forest runners set up a trading post at present-day Montreal. They also traveled up the Ottawa (AHT-uh-wuh) River and made their way to Lake Huron.

There, Champlain hoped, was an entrance to the Northwest Passage. By 1634 Champlain's friend Jean Nicolet (nick-oh-LAY) had explored as far as the Wisconsin shore of Lake Michigan. He was, however, unable to find the long-sought route to Asia. He built a trading post at the mouth of the Fox River, where Green Bay, Wisconsin, stands today.

THE FRENCH AND THE HURON

The main trading partners of the French were the Huron. Their homeland was the region between Lake Huron and Quebec. Soon after Champlain founded Quebec, he joined Huron warriors in an attack on their enemies to the south, the Iroquois. In the attack Champlain shot and killed two Iroquois chiefs. From then on, the Iroquois were the bitter enemies of the French. The Huron and the French became **allies,** people who agree to help one another in time of trouble.

The Huron and the French got along well together because the French did not take Huron land. They were traders, not farmers. Instead of building towns, the coureurs de bois lived in Huron villages. Many married Huron women. From the Huron, the forest runners learned how to build canoes and to travel by water for hundreds of miles. The Huron also taught the French how to make snowshoes and how to trap and hunt.

Soon French missionaries arrived in Canada. Although they taught the Huron the Catholic religion, the priests did not try to make them live like French people. Instead, the missionaries lived in Huron villages and learned the Huron language.

SETTLEMENT PROCEEDS SLOWLY

Tell students they will learn more about French and Indian alliances when they study the struggles between the French and the English in Chapter 6 (pages 130–136).

As missionaries and forest runners pushed the boundary of French Canada westward, the territory claimed by the king of France grew larger. There were a few tiny settlements in Acadia, or French Nova Scotia, and Quebec was a busy trading center. But there were not enough French settlers to hold a territory the size of New France.

CHAPTER 3   1556-1718

To attract more settlers, a group called the Company of New France was formed in 1627. It was given control of the St. Lawrence River valley and a monopoly of the fur trade. In return, the company granted land along the St. Lawrence River to French nobles. The nobles could have the title of *seigneur* (seen-YUR), or lord, if they would bring in settlers to farm. These settlers, called *habitants* (ah-bee-TAHNZ), would pay rent to the seigneurs and would provide some free labor. The seigneurs were very much like feudal lords of manors.

The company's plan attracted few settlers. Many who did make the journey refused to play their parts. Soon after arriving, the habitants disappeared into the forest to join the coureurs de bois in their profitable search for furs.

Scattered over a wide area, the French were unable to defend themselves when the Iroquois sent their warriors north in 1642. The fighting lasted 11 years. During that time Montreal was raided, and France's allies, the Huron, were driven from their homeland.

In 1663 King Louis XIV took steps to strengthen his empire in America. He took control of New France and appointed officials to govern it. Louis also sent 1,000 soldiers to Canada. Forts were built at key points north of the Iroquois country to defend New France.

By 1640, when this painting was made, the city of Quebec was the center of New France's trade along the St. Lawrence River.

For discussion: Other than profit, why might some of the French prefer the life of a coureur de bois to the life of an habitant? (Possibilities: more adventure, not tied down to one place, not immediately under the thumb of a seigneur)

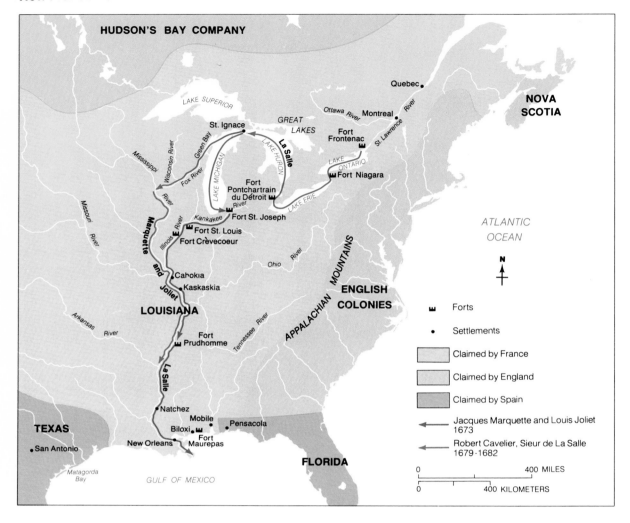

EXPLORING THE MISSISSIPPI

For discussion: Why might a missionary, such as Father Marquette, wish to explore the Mississippi?

Meanwhile, the French explored farther inland. In present-day Michigan, a French missionary named Jacques Marquette (mahr-KEHT) heard from Indians about a great river to the west. He thought it might be the Northwest Passage.

In 1673 Father Marquette and the explorer Louis Joliet (JŌ-lee-et) set out to find this river with five other men. Leaving St. Ignace, they paddled south along the western shore of Lake Michigan to Green Bay. From there, they traveled up the Fox River. Then they carried their canoes overland to the Wisconsin River.

Following the river southward, they reached the Mississippi River. Here at last, they thought, was the Northwest Passage. But the mighty river stubbornly flowed southward. By the time the explorers reached

USING MAP SYMBOLS

A map tells a story with pictures and a few words. The title introduces the subject of the map. The legend explains what the map symbols mean.

Symbols are small pictures that represent information. Mapmakers use them as a shorthand system to place a large amount of information on a single map.

Map symbols come in two forms: pictorial and abstract. Pictorial symbols look something like the features they represent. A tree-shaped symbol, for example, could show that an area is forested. An airplane symbol tells the map reader, "This is the location of an airport."

Abstract symbols do not look like the features they represent. What, for example, does a black dot on a map mean? It could represent such totally different items as a city, 100,000 people, or the location of steel mills. The map reader must check the legend to find out what the dot represents. Other abstract symbols are lines, squares, triangles, letters, and colors.

Map readers can never assume that they know what a symbol means. Even pictorial symbols may be confusing. A tree symbol might represent a forest—or an orchard. Map readers should always check the meaning on the legend.

Look at the map on page 62. In the legend, both pictorial symbols and abstract symbols are used. Use the map legend to answer the following questions.

1. Is the symbol that represents forts pictorial or abstract?

2. What does a dot represent on this map?

3. How can you tell which was the route of Joliet and Marquette and which was the route of La Salle?

4. How can you tell the possessions of Spain and England from those of France?

5. If you could create new pictorial symbols for each of the things shown on this map, what would you draw?

Answers will be found on page T 27.

*CT

the mouth of the Arkansas River, it was clear that they were on their way to the Gulf of Mexico, not the Pacific Ocean. Disappointed, Marquette and Joliet returned to New France.

Robert Cavelier, Sieur de La Salle (SYUR duh lah SAHL), a fur trader, completed the journey down the Mississippi. From 1679 to 1681 La Salle had explored the Great Lakes region. Early in 1682 he led an expedition of French and Indians in canoes down the Illinois River to the Mississippi. La Salle reached the Gulf of Mexico in April. He claimed for France all of the land touched by all of the rivers flowing into the Mississippi. To this vast region, stretching from the Great Lakes to the Gulf of Mexico, he gave the name Louisiana in honor of the king of France, Louis XIV.

La Salle was eager to set up a colony at the mouth of the Mississippi to expand the French fur trade. The colony would also be a good base for attacking the Spanish in the Gulf of Mexico. In 1684 La Salle sailed from France to the Gulf coast with settlers. By accident, they landed on the coast of present-day Texas at Matagorda Bay. While trying to find the Mississippi, some of the settlers rebelled and murdered La Salle.

You may wish to point out (or have students point out) places named after Marquette, Joliet, and La Salle on a map of present-day America.

SETTLING LOUISIANA

La Salle's exploration of the Mississippi opened the heartland of North America to France. French fur traders and missionaries established a network of trading posts and missions along the shores of the Great Lakes and the banks of the Mississippi as far north as present-day Minnesota. They started settlements in the Illinois country to link Canada with Louisiana. The land there was so fertile that French farming villages were soon sending food to other settlements.

A chain of forts was built to protect the waterways that tied France's inland empire together. One of the most important was Fort Pontchartrain, located between Lake Huron and Lake Erie in what is now southeastern Michigan. It guarded the water route to the St. Lawrence River valley. The fort was built in 1701 by Antoine de la Mothe Cadillac (KAD-ihl-ak). Around it grew the village of Detroit.

The French also built a chain of trading posts, missions, and forts along the lower Mississippi. A fort near Biloxi, in present-day Mississippi, was founded in 1699. Several years later, the French started a settlement at the site of Mobile, in what is now Alabama. Other settlers followed rivers into present-day Arkansas and Tennessee.

In 1718 New Orleans was founded. Its location made it a perfect trading center and seaport. From the waterways to the north came the riches of the fur trade. Soon New Orleans began to rival Quebec as the leading town in New France.

Even before New Orleans was founded, the Spanish had begun to worry about the arrival of the French on the Gulf coast. In 1698 they had founded Pensacola to keep the French from expanding into Florida. In 1718 Spanish soldiers built a presidio at San Antonio to keep the French out of Texas, which was also claimed by Spain.

France's American empire seemed impressive. The French controlled a huge area, tied together by the St. Lawrence, the Great Lakes, and the Mississippi. But the French were spread too thinly over their vast territory. In time, this weakness would cause the downfall of New France.

SECTION REVIEW   Answers will be found on page T 27.

1. Define these words: *monopoly, allies.*

2. Identify: Samuel de Champlain, coureurs de bois, Jean Nicolet, Sieur de La Salle.

3. What brought the French to Canada?

4. Where did Jacques Marquette and Louis Joliet hope the Mississippi River would take them?

5. Why did the Spanish build forts at Pensacola and San Antonio?

Louis XIV, the ''Sun King,'' ruled a vast empire. Artist H. Rigaud painted him at his palace at Versailles (vayr-SĪ).

Activity: Students can form committees to research the achievements of Cartier, Champlain, Marquette and Joliet, La Salle, and Cadillac. Each committee can elect one member to report its findings to the class. Maps and other art work will make the reports more interesting.

3-3 THE FIRST ENGLISH COLONY

READ TO FIND OUT

—what the words *invest, joint-stock company, charter, indentured servants, representatives, legislature,* and *royal colony* mean.

—why the English wanted colonies.

—what hardships the first English settlers faced.

—how Jamestown grew.

—how self-government first came to America.

invest: use money to make a profit

joint-stock company: business organization raising money by selling stock to investors

charter: government document giving permission to do something

indentured servants: people who signed contracts to work for a certain term of years

representatives: people with the power to speak and act for others

legislature: group given power to make laws

royal colony: one controlled by a monarch, who chooses the governor and the council of advisers

By the 1570s the English had learned a great deal about the eastern coast of North America. They began to think about planting colonies there. In 1578 Queen Elizabeth gave explorer Sir Humphrey Gilbert the right to set up a colony in America. English explorers searching for a Northwest Passage could use the colony as a base. It would also be a refuge for English privateers attacking Spanish seaports and galleons.

Gilbert made two unsuccessful attempts to plant a colony. In his second attempt, in 1583, he claimed Newfoundland for England. On the return voyage, his ship, the *Squirrel,* was lost at sea in a wild September storm. Others, however, took up the challenge.

SIR WALTER RALEIGH

One of the members of Gilbert's second expedition was his half brother Sir Walter Raleigh (RAW-lee). Raleigh wanted English bases in America in order to attack Spain's empire and to search for gold.

Raleigh also thought colonies could improve England's balance of trade. Colonies could produce goods that England had to buy from foreign nations, such as lumber, silk, and wine. In this way England could hold on to its gold. Also, English merchants could sell tools, dishes, furniture, and woolen cloth to the settlers. This would create more jobs for workers in England.

THE LOST COLONY OF ROANOKE

Queen Elizabeth liked Raleigh's ideas. In 1584 she granted him the right to found a colony on the Atlantic coast north of Spanish Florida. He named the region Virginia.

The following year 108 Englishmen, many of them soldiers, landed on Roanoke (RŌ-ah-nŌK) Island, off the coast of present-day North Carolina. Indians welcomed the settlers and provided them with fish traps. But the settlers were more interested in searching for gold than in fishing. As supplies ran low, they began taking food from the Indians, and fighting broke out. In 1586 Sir Francis Drake's fleet stopped by, after a raid on Spain's West Indies. The discouraged settlers returned to England with him.

In 1587 Raleigh sent another expedition to Roanoke Island, led by John White. White had been a member of the earlier expedition, too. This time the settlers included 89 men, 17 women, and 11 children. White's granddaughter, Virginia Dare, was the first English child born in America.

The colonists built a fort on the ruins of the earlier camp. Each family had been given 500 acres (200 hectares) to farm, but they lacked tools and seed. They sent White back to England for supplies.

The next year, Spain sent its armada against England. White was unable to return immediately to Roanoke Island. When he finally returned in 1590, the settlers had disappeared. In a tree someone had cut the letters *CRO*. Carved on a doorpost was the word *CROATOAN*—the name of another island off the Carolina coast and of the Indian tribe living there. What became of the "lost colony" still remains a mystery.

*CT

For discussion: What might have happened to the "lost colony"? What evidence, if any, can students cite to support their theories?

The Roanoke colonists visited the Indian village of Pomeiooc soon after arriving. John White made this drawing, probably in July 1585. It shows eighteen thatched houses surrounded by a fence of wooden stakes.

King James VI of Scotland became King James I of England in 1603. He was a distant cousin of Queen Elizabeth I. Jamestown colony was named for him.

THE VIRGINIA COMPANY

The next effort to plant a colony in America was led by merchants. By the 1600s many of England's merchants had grown wealthy selling woolen goods in Europe. They were looking for new ways to **invest** their money. To invest means to use money to make a profit.

Some merchants risked their money in a new kind of investment, a **joint-stock company.** A joint-stock company was a business organization. It raised money by selling shares in the company, or stock, to investors. With many people investing, the company obtained the large amounts of money that it needed for goods, warehouses, or ships. The investors, or shareholders, hoped that the company would make a profit. All profits would be divided among the investors according to the number of shares that each person held.

Early in the 1600s two groups of merchants asked England's new ruler, King James I, for the right to plant colonies in Virginia. One group was from London and the other from Plymouth. King James agreed. In 1606 he granted the groups a **charter.** A charter is a written document from a government giving a person or a group permission to do something.

Two joint-stock companies were formed. The London Company was granted the right to settle land in present-day North Carolina and Virginia. The Plymouth Company had the right to start settlements farther north, around present-day New England. Together, the two companies were known as the Virginia Company. The companies were to send settlers to America to search for the Northwest Passage. Settlers were also expected to find precious metals, as the Spanish had done. In this way, the companies hoped to make a quick profit for their shareholders.

A number of operations in North America were financed by companies. The Dutch colony New Netherland was financed by the Dutch West India Company (page 73). Massachusetts Bay Colony was initiated by the Massachusetts Bay Company (page 88). Fur trading in Canada was sponsored by the Hudson's Bay Company.

JAMESTOWN

The desire for a quick profit provides a clue to many of the Jamestown settlers. They were idlers (see below). John Smith, in contrast, was an experienced soldier and explorer, used to a rough life, able to cope with hardships.

In December 1606 the London Company crammed 144 settlers into three tiny ships and sent them to Virginia. The stormy winter crossing of the Atlantic took four months. Disease attacked the voyagers. When the ships reached Chesapeake Bay the following spring, only 105 settlers were still alive.

The survivors sailed up the James River, which they named for their king. There, on a swampy peninsula, they founded Jamestown. The site seemed easy to defend against Spanish or Indian attacks. But it offered no protection from the malaria-carrying mosquitoes that swarmed about the settlers. Their only drinking water was salty and full of muck. Disease soon spread through the settlement.

In his book *The General History of Virginia, New England, and the Summer Isles* (1624), John Smith provides an interesting account of the hardships at Jamestown in 1608 and how he helped the colonists, almost in spite of themselves, to survive. You may wish to read selected passages to the class.

As supplies ran low, the settlers began to die from hunger. One of the colonists, Captain John Smith, sought food from the nearby Powhatan (POW-uh-TAN) people. Pocahontas (PŌ-kah-HAHN-tus), a daughter of the chief, often brought food to the starving settlers. Smith wrote that she "saved many of their lives." Still, after seven months only 32 settlers remained alive. The colony lasted through the winter only because a supply ship and more settlers arrived from England.

When spring came, the colonists planted no crops. Many of them were not used to working with their hands. They had come to Virginia to search for gold. John Smith said of that first year at Jamestown that there was "no talk, no hope, nor work, but dig gold, wash gold, refine gold." The "gold," however, proved to be iron pyrite, a common mineral known as "fool's gold."

The village of Jamestown has been restored in modern times. The settlers built snug houses with thatched roofs like those they knew in England.

In 1616 John Rolfe took his bride, Pocahontas, to England. There she was treated as the princess she was. John Smith wrote that she had become "very formal and civil after our English manner." In 1617 she was presented to the king.

★ ★ ★ ★ ★ ★ ★ **AMERICAN VALUES IN ACTION** ★ ★ ★ ★ ★ ★ ★ ★

POCAHONTAS

The longhouse of Powhatan, chief of the Powhatan tribe, was crowded with warriors, elders, and priests. Great bonfires heated the room. Smoke from long-stemmed clay pipes clouded the air.

All eyes were on the captive Englishman, Captain John Smith. The council argued over whether Smith and the English had come to America as traders or invaders. Finally, the bold stranger was sentenced to death. Warriors forced Smith's head down on a stone and raised their heavy war clubs. Suddenly, a young girl ran forward and placed her head on top of Smith's. Smith was saved.

Pocahontas, daughter of the chief, had claimed the right of adoption. Among the Powhatan, women could adopt a captive into the tribe. Many elders opposed any show of mercy to Smith. But they could not overrule the claim of Pocahontas.

Pocahontas was Powhatan's favorite, his "dearest jewel." As a princess, she was spared household chores. Instead, Pocahontas explored the pine-carpeted forests and dove for mussels in the rivers. For her lively curiosity, she was called Pocahontas, which meant "playful one."

In sponsoring Smith, the twelve-year-old girl had acted as an adult. She may have admired his courage. She may have acted out of curiosity. But adopting Smith as her brother was a serious commitment.

When John Smith returned to Jamestown in early 1608, he found the English colony near starvation. The discouraged colonists talked bleakly of abandoning the settlement. Then, out of the forest, help arrived from Captain Smith's adopted family.

A long line of Indians approached the fort. They carried baskets of corn bread, strings of fish, and deer and turkeys lashed to long poles. Pocahontas led the procession.

Throughout the fierce winter, the princess brought food to the starving colonists. In taking responsibility for Smith, she had also shouldered the burden of caring for his people. Pocahontas, Smith wrote gratefully, "preserved this colony from death, famine, and utter confusion."

In late 1608 Smith took control of the struggling colony. He ended the hunt for gold and forced the colonists to plant crops. He told them that those who did not work in the fields would not eat.

In the fall of 1609, Smith was burned in a gunpowder explosion and returned to England for treatment. Without his leadership, the colony fell into disorder. Four hundred new settlers had recently arrived. They

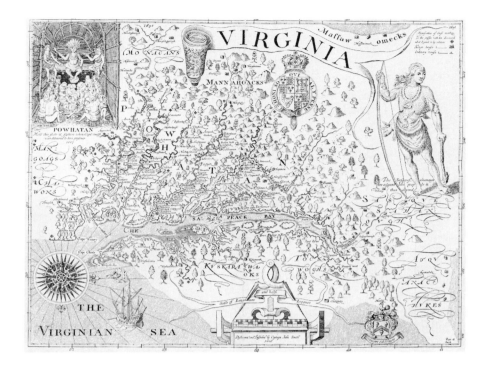

Captain John Smith's map of Virginia was the first to show the Chesapeake Bay and its rivers correctly. William Hole made this engraving in 1612 from Smith's chart and description.

brought little food and were too weak from their voyage to work. As supplies ran out, a grim search for food began. The colonists ate their horses and dogs, then tried to catch rats and snakes to stay alive. The winter of 1609-1610 became known as the "starving time." When spring came, only 60 colonists were still alive.

In June the survivors abandoned Jamestown and sailed down the James River for England. Just as they were about to reach the open sea, ships carrying 300 settlers and the colony's new governor arrived. Governor Thomas West, Lord De La Warr, ordered the colonists to return and join in the work of rebuilding the settlement.

A NEW BEGINNING FOR JAMESTOWN

Under Lord De La Warr and the governors who came after him, the colony grew stronger. Strict new laws forced the colonists to work. They were marched by drumbeat into the fields to tend crops or into the forest to cut wood. Cargoes of timber and furs were sent to England.

About 1612 a settler named John Rolfe planted tobacco seeds from the West Indies in Virginia's soil. The result was a mild tobacco pleasing to English smokers. At last the colony had a valuable product. Colonists began to grow tobacco everywhere, even in the streets.

The London Company was pleased by the colonists' success at growing tobacco. But life in Jamestown was no easier than before, and few

Tobacco became the "gold" of the Jamestown colony. Its flowers have a sweet scent.

English people wanted to live there. To attract more settlers, the company made three important changes in the colony.

First, in 1618 colonists were given the right to own land. Until then, the London Company had owned all land in Virginia. Now, colonists who paid their own way to Virginia were granted 50 acres (20 hectares) of land. They could receive another 50 acres (20 hectares) for each new settler that they brought to Virginia.

Many settlers were unable to pay their own way to the colony and came as **indentured** (in-DEN-churd) **servants.** They signed an indenture, or contract, agreeing to work for four to seven years for the colonist who paid for their passage. At the end of this period, they were free and received some money or land.

The company also sent women to Virginia in 1619. It was hoped that if settlers married and started families, they might make Virginia their permanent home. Many of the women who arrived that year married at once. Others became indentured servants.

Finally, the London Company changed its government in Virginia. Previously, a company-chosen governor and council of advisers had run the colony. Now the company decided to give the settlers a voice in the government of Virginia.

The settlement was divided into 11 districts. In each district, all adult males elected two **representatives,** or people with the power to speak and act for them. The representatives, called burgesses (BUR-jis-ez), were to meet as an assembly known as the House of Burgesses. The assembly, together with the governor's council, became the **legislature,** or group of people responsible for making laws, for the colony. When the Virginia House of Burgesses first met in 1619, it was the first representative assembly in the Americas.

VIRGINIA BECOMES A ROYAL COLONY

While making these changes, the London Company spent the last of its money sending over more settlers. Among them were workers skilled in the making of wine, silk, glass, ships, iron, and many other products needed by England. When the workers landed, however, most of them began doing what everyone else was doing—growing tobacco.

As new settlements spread along the James River, the Powhatan made war plans. Too often they had seen their villages burned and their fields taken by tobacco planters. In 1622 the Powhatan attacked the colony. All outlying settlements were destroyed, and 347 colonists—about one third of the colony—were killed.

Much of the London Company's American colony lay in ruins. There was little hope of making a profit for investors or even paying the colony's debts. In 1624 King James I took away the company's charter and

This drawing of "Virginia potatoes" was published in 1629.

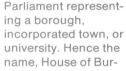

In England, a *burgess* was once a member of Parliament representing a borough, incorporated town, or university. Hence the name, House of Burgesses, as adapted in Virginia.

By 1622 Jamestown was a small city surrounded by walls of logs. Indian raids were a constant problem. Here, a cannon fires at a war party in canoes.

For discussion: Ask students how Virginia's House of Burgesses differs from our present national legislature. Tell students they will learn why we have two legislative houses, rather than one, when they study Chapter 8.

made Virginia a **royal colony.** Now the monarch appointed the governor and the governor's council of advisers. James tried to do away with Virginia's representative assembly, but the Virginians insisted on taking part in their government. Soon the House of Burgesses was meeting again and making laws.

Despite the company's failure, the settlers had found a valuable crop that grew well in Virginia's soil and climate. With their House of Burgesses, they had also taken the first step toward self-government.

SECTION REVIEW   Answers will be found on page T 27.

1. Define these words: *invest, joint-stock company, charter, indentured servants, representatives, legislature, royal colony.*

2. Identify: Sir Walter Raleigh, Virginia Dare, John Smith, Pocahontas, Lord De La Warr.

3. What happened to the colony founded on Roanoke Island in 1587?

4. What hardships did the Jamestown settlers face?

5. How did John Rolfe help Jamestown?

6. What three important events in 1618 and 1619 helped the Jamestown colony to grow?

7. How could poor English people afford to come to Virginia?

8. What was the first representative assembly in the Americas?

3-4 THE DUTCH AND SWEDISH START COLONIES

READ TO FIND OUT

—what the term *minority groups* means.

—why the Dutch came to America.

—how New Amsterdam Jews struggled for their rights.

—how New Sweden became a part of New Netherland.

minority groups: groups of people differing in language, race, religion, or some other way from most of the population

Like the French and the English, the Dutch first sailed to North America in search of a water route to Asia. In 1609 they sent English explorer Henry Hudson across the Atlantic to find this Northwest Passage. He discovered the river that bears his name and claimed the Hudson River valley for the Netherlands. His crew found that the Indians along the Hudson River were willing to trade beaver pelts for metal goods. Soon the Dutch returned to America for furs.

NEW NETHERLAND

In 1610 Dutch traders arrived in the Hudson River valley. There they met the Iroquois, who were eager for weapons to use against the Huron and the French. The Dutch supplied guns, powder, and shot in exchange for beaver pelts, and the two groups became allies.

In 1621 merchants formed the Dutch West India Company to start a colony in America. The Dutch government gave the company a charter allowing it to trade and colonize there. Three years later, the company sent thirty families to the valleys of the Hudson and Delaware rivers. Most of the families settled along the upper Hudson. There they built Fort Orange, near present-day Albany.

A picture on a map made in 1655 shows the port of New Amsterdam on Manhattan Island. Traders sailed down the Hudson River with furs for shipment to Europe.

NIEUW AMSTERDAM
of t Eylant Manhattans

Joost Hartgers drew the earliest known view of New Amsterdam in about 1626. This print of his sketch was published in 1651.

By sending settlers, the company hoped to keep the French out of the region, now called New Netherland. The company offered large estates along the Hudson River to anyone who brought fifty settlers to the colony. These landowners, known as patroons (pah-TROONZ), would have the rights of feudal lords of manors. Settlers would work the land and pay rent to the patroon.

Few Dutch, however, wanted to leave their homeland, where life was peaceful and prosperous. And nearby, the English were selling farm land at low prices. As one Englishman wrote, "Who will be such a fool as to become a bare tenant, when for crossing Hudson's River that person can for a song buy a good freehold?" By 1630, only five patroons had settled their estates.

NEW AMSTERDAM

In 1626 the Dutch bought Manhattan Island from the Indians living there. Peter Minuit, the governor appointed by the Dutch West India Company, traded 24 gold dollars' worth of tools and jewelry for Manhattan. On the southern tip of the island, the Dutch founded the town of New Amsterdam. From this location, at the mouth of the Hudson River, they could control the fur trade coming downriver from the Iroquois country. They could also control the finest natural harbor on America's Atlantic coast.

Tell the class that many minority groups, particularly English, colonized America. They will study several of these groups (e.g., Pilgrims, Catholics, Quakers) in Chapter 4.

Soon the island was dotted with rich farms. To protect themselves from Indian attacks, the Dutch built a wall across Manhattan. It gave its name to Wall Street in present-day New York City. Behind the wall, a tidy Dutch village of steep-roofed brick houses grew up.

By 1640 New Netherland had been opened to settlers from other countries. Soon New Amsterdam was home for several **minority groups.** A minority group is a group of people who differ in language, race, religion, or some other way from most of the population. By 1646 a Catholic missionary who visited the town reported that "there may well be 400 or 500 people of different religions and nations. The director general told me that there were people of 18 different languages."

At first, only Dutch Calvinists, followers of John Calvin's teachings, were allowed to practice their religion in public. In 1654 a small group of Jews arrived. They asked permission to live and worship in New Amsterdam. The governor, Peter Stuyvesant (STĪ-vuh-suhnt), warned that if the Jews were given liberty, Catholics and other religious groups "would also have to be given liberty." The Jews were allowed to stay, but like the Baptists and the Quakers, they could not worship openly. The Jews continued to demand the freedom to follow their religion.

The Jews of New Amsterdam also wanted the same rights that other citizens enjoyed. Asher Levy, for example, asked to serve as a soldier. Dutch leaders said he could not. He asked for the right to buy land and to start a business. He was refused again. Levy kept demanding these rights and finally won them all.

Governor Stuyvesant was stubborn about giving rights to minority groups. But in other ways, New Amsterdam needed Stuyvesant's leadership. When Stuyvesant arrived, one building out of every four was a tavern. Brawling sailors made the streets unsafe for everyone. Stuyvesant did his best to bring law and order to the town. The stern hero of battles in the West Indies was not a popular governor, but most of his policies made New Amsterdam safer.

Peter Stuyvesant was not a popular administrator. Ask students to research this belligerent ex-soldier and write reports on his life and rule of New Netherland. Points to consider: How did he get the nickname "Old Silver Leg"? What were some of the disagreements between him and the citizens? On the whole, was he a good or bad governor?

Merchants like the ones in this counting house prospered in New Amsterdam.

The Dutch colony allowed some religious freedom. Here, a Jewish family celebrates the harvest festival.

NEW SWEDEN

Stuyvesant also protected Dutch claims to land in North America. The Swedish government had granted a charter to start a colony to the New Sweden Company in 1637. Peter Minuit, the former governor of New Netherland, was one of the directors of the company. In 1638 Minuit led about fifty Swedes and Finns to begin a colony called New Sweden in America.

The new settlers built Fort Christina, named in honor of the young Swedish queen, at present-day Wilmington, Delaware. From Wilmington, Swedish settlements spread north along the Delaware River.

Although Governor Minuit died at sea in 1639, the Swedish settlers did well. They made friends with the Indians and traded with them. They were able to grow or make almost everything they needed to live. The crops and orchards of the Swedish settlers thrived in the fertile soil of the Delaware valley. In hard times, the Swedes could buy supplies from English colonists.

The expanding colonies of New Netherland and New Sweden began to come into conflict with each other. Both colonies claimed some of the same land. The Dutch West India Company and the New Sweden Company did not want to share the profits from American trade. In 1655 Peter Stuyvesant sailed into Delaware Bay with three ships and an army. He seized the Swedish settlements and forced the settlers to accept the government of New Netherland or leave the colony. Most chose to stay.

New Sweden disappeared, but not the woodland skills of its settlers. They introduced the log cabin to America. It became the kind of home most often built by colonists on the frontier. Easy to build from available materials, the log cabin gave good protection from the weather.

The Dutch settlers continued to build their colony. Farms spread north along the banks of the Hudson and onto Long Island. The village of New Amsterdam became a busy seaport.

SECTION REVIEW   Answers will be found on page T 28.

1. Define this term: *minority groups.*

2. Identify: Henry Hudson, Peter Minuit, Peter Stuyvesant.

3. Why did the Dutch come to the Hudson River valley?

4. Why was the southern tip of Manhattan Island a good location for a European settlement?

5. What rights did Asher Levy win in New Amsterdam?

6. How did New Sweden become a part of New Netherland?

CHAPTER SUMMARY

By the mid-1500s, the nations of northwestern Europe were interested in colonies and ready to challenge Spain's empire in America. Sea raiders from France, the Netherlands, and England attacked Spanish treasure ships and Spain's American seaports. When Philip II's Invincible Armada was defeated by the English, it became easier for his rivals to start colonies across the Atlantic.

New France began when Samuel de Champlain built a fur-trading post at Quebec in 1608. From Quebec the French explored the lands along the St. Lawrence River and around the Great Lakes. The Huron became their trading partners and their allies against the Iroquois.

French coureurs de bois and missionaries lived among the Huron and learned their language. They also traveled to unknown regions and expanded the boundaries of New France into the Mississippi River valley. In 1718 New Orleans was founded. By then, French settlers were scattered throughout a vast North American empire tied together by a network of waterways.

England's first successful American colony was started at Jamestown in 1607 by a joint-stock company. After suffering terrible hardships, the Jamestown settlers found a product, tobacco, that was valuable in England. New colonists were attracted when the London Company allowed settlers to own land and to elect representatives to the House of Burgesses. In 1624, however, the company lost its charter, and Virginia became a royal colony.

The main settlement of the Dutch in North America was started on the southern tip of Manhattan Island in 1626. New Amsterdam controlled the Hudson River fur trade and the best harbor on the Atlantic coast. It soon became a busy seaport, whose people came from many different lands.

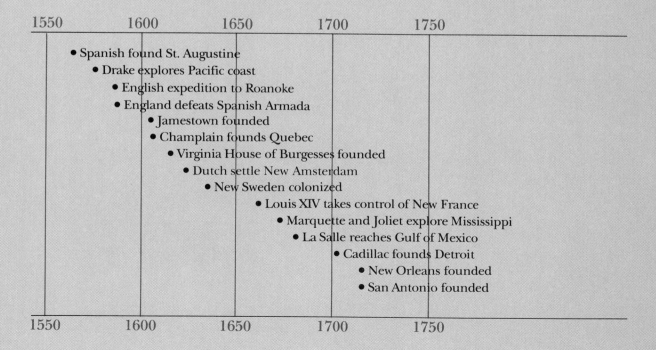

1550	1600	1650	1700	1750

- Spanish found St. Augustine
- Drake explores Pacific coast
- English expedition to Roanoke
- England defeats Spanish Armada
- Jamestown founded
- Champlain founds Quebec
- Virginia House of Burgesses founded
- Dutch settle New Amsterdam
- New Sweden colonized
- Louis XIV takes control of New France
- Marquette and Joliet explore Mississippi
- La Salle reaches Gulf of Mexico
- Cadillac founds Detroit
- New Orleans founded
- San Antonio founded

1550	1600	1650	1700	1750

CHAPTER SURVEY

VOCABULARY REVIEW

Choose the word or phrase that best completes each sentence below.

(a) allies
(b) balance of trade
(c) charter
(d) indentured servants
(e) invest
(f) joint-stock company
(g) legislature
(h) mercantilism
(i) minority groups
(j) monopoly
(k) privateers
(l) refuge
(m) representatives
(n) royal colony

1. _____ is the theory that nations can increase their wealth and power by controlling trade.

2. _____ are people who can speak for others.

3. _____ is complete control over the sale of a product.

4. A _____ is a safe place.

5. _____ differ in some way from most of the population.

6. A nation's _____ is the difference between the value of goods sold to other nations and the value of goods bought from them.

7. _____ agree to give help in time of trouble.

8. A _____ is responsible for making laws.

9. To _____ means to use money to try to make a profit.

10. A _____ is a written document giving a person or a group permission to do something.

11. In a _____, the monarch appointed the governor and council of advisers.

12. _____ are warships sailing with government permission.

13. A _____ was a business organization that sold shares to investors in order to raise money.

14. _____ agreed to work for a certain number of years in exchange for passage to America.

CHAPTER REVIEW

1. (a) Why did Europe's rulers seek a favorable balance of trade? (b) From a mercantilist point of view, what made Spain's empire in America valuable?

2. (a) How did Philip II combat the Protestant movement? (b) Why did French, English, and Dutch sea raiders attack Spanish ships?

3. (a) What was the purpose of the Invincible Armada? (b) How did its defeat affect the English, Dutch, and French? (c) What kept the English, Dutch, and French from starting North American colonies close to Florida?

4. (a) What trade goods attracted the French to America? (b) Why did the Huron get along well with the French? (c) Why did the Company of New France have trouble settling the St. Lawrence valley?

5. (a) Why did La Salle want to establish a colony at the mouth of the Mississippi? (b) Why did the French build forts along the Great Lakes and the Mississippi?

Some North American animals were similar to European ones. John White drew this box tortoise in 1585.

NOVA BRITANNIA.

OFFERING MOST

Excellent fruites by Planting in VIRGINIA.

Exciting all such as be well affected to further the same.

Pamphlets like this one printed in 1609 attracted settlers to the English colonies, or "New Britain."

(c) What made the French empire in North America weak?

6. (a) What did the English government want from colonies in America? (b) How did its monarchs encourage colonization?

7. (a) How did the London Company finance its Virginia colony? (b) How did the company plan to make a quick profit? (c) What harmful effect did this plan have on the Jamestown settlement?

8. What three things did the London Company do in order to attract more settlers to Jamestown?

9. (a) What valuable crop did Virginia produce? (b) How did producing this crop lead to war with the Indians? (c) Why was Virginia made a royal colony?

10. (a) What trade goods attracted the Dutch to North America? (b) Why did the Iroquois trade with the Dutch?

GEOGRAPHY REVIEW

1. Through what passage did Drake sail to reach the western coast of South America?

2. To what sea did many sea raiders go to capture Spanish treasure?

3. Where was the homeland of the Huron?

4. Name three rivers followed by Marquette and Joliet's expedition.

5. What river was most important in the founding of the first French settlement in North America? The first English settlement? The first Dutch settlement?

USING THE TOOLS OF HISTORY

Making Timelines

*CT **1.** Make a timeline showing these events.
(a) Jamestown is founded.
(b) The Spanish Armada is defeated.
(c) Quebec is founded.
(d) Roanoke settlement is founded.
(e) New Amsterdam is founded.

2. Write a title for the timeline. Include the words "The Nations of Northwestern Europe" in the title.

Using Map Symbols

3. Look at the map "Spanish Exploration and Settlement 1519–1720" on page 45. Use the symbols to tell what kind of settlement was at each of the following places: (a) Acoma (b) San Antonio (c) Tumacacori

READING AND THINKING SKILLS

*CT **Sequencing Events**

In Section 3, reread the *last* three paragraphs under the heading "Jamestown." These paragraphs start on page 69. (a) List all signal words and calendar markers you find in the three paragraphs. (b) List in chronological order the events that took place from the time Captain John Smith took control to the time Lord De La Warr arrived.

UNIT SURVEY

UNIT REVIEW

1. (a) Where did the first Americans probably come from? (b) What part of the Americas did they probably reach first? (c) How could the first Americans have traveled there? (d) What probably allowed the first Americans to travel in that way?

2. (a) How did the first Americans obtain food? (b) In time, many kinds of animals died out in the Americas. What different way of obtaining food did people rely on then? (c) What other way of obtaining food did people slowly develop? (d) How did that way of obtaining food affect populations?

3. (a) In what culture area of North America did families live together in longhouses? (b) In what culture area did people live in tepees? (c) In what culture area did people live in pueblos? (d) What were these three kinds of dwellings made of?

4. (a) According to a Norse saga, what place did Leif Ericson find? (b) What Asian places did Marco Polo know about according to his book? (c) Which of the two stories spread through Europe in the 1300s, Leif Ericson's or Marco Polo's? (d) Why were European merchants interested in this story?

5. (a) In the 1300s and 1400s, who controlled trade routes east of the Mediterranean Sea? (b) What four nations had developed in western Europe by the end of the 1400s? (c) Which one was the leader in sea travel along the coast of Africa? (d) Why did this nation want to send ships around Africa?

6. (a) What land did Columbus hope to reach in 1492? (b) Where are the islands that he did reach? (c) What explorer first sailed from the Atlantic to the Pacific? (d) Why did explorers search for the Northwest Passage?

(e) What did conquistadors hope to find in Mexico and South America?

7. (a) What did Spain's American colonies produce that was more valuable than tobacco, cocoa, and sugar? (b) Where were these valuable products sent? (c) How did Spain's wealth help it compete with other European nations? (d) What was the name of the theory that nations could become powerful through trade?

8. (a) What did the French call their lands in North America? (b) What trade good from these lands was most valuable to the French? (c) What was the main river used by the French in their early trade in North America? (d) What was the main river used by the French to extend their trade network?

9. (a) What happened to the English colony on Roanoke Island? (b) When the first settlers arrived at Jamestown, what valuable product did they hope to find? (c) What product from the Jamestown area turned out to be valuable in trade? (d) What kind of colony was Virginia after 1624?

10. (a) What river was most important to Dutch settlement in America? (b) Name the main Dutch city in America. (c) Where was it? (d) What river was most important to Swedish settlement?

LINKING THE PAST AND THE PRESENT

1. Many place names in the United States have Indian origins. List the names of some of the rivers, lakes, and mountains or other landforms in your state. Use a dictionary or another reference book to find which names come from Indian words. Add those name origins to the list.

European merchants were strange sights in the Middle East. Persian rugmakers in the 1500s used boatloads of traders as part of their designs.

2. Choose any five of the following state names, and then find and list their origins: Alabama, Alaska, Arizona, Arkansas, Connecticut, Hawaii, Idaho, Illinois, Indiana, Iowa, Kansas, Kentucky, Massachusetts, Michigan, Minnesota, Mississippi, Missouri, Nebraska, North Dakota, Ohio, Oklahoma, South Dakota, Tennessee, Texas, Utah, Wisconsin, Wyoming.

*CT **3.** Young people a hundred years ago could still become explorers. One of them, Alexandra David-Neel, grew up to be an explorer of Tibet. Is it still possible for young people to become explorers? Why or why not?

MEETING THE BUILDERS OF AMERICA

CT **1.** Review the descriptions of the League of the Iroquois (page 11), Sister Juana Inés de la Cruz (page 42) and Pocahontas (page 69). In what ways did they contribute to America?

CT **2.** Prepare a report about the contribution to American life of some other person or group mentioned in Unit 1. For example, look for information about Bartolomé de Las Casas, John Smith, John Rolfe, or the Pueblo people. You may be able to use one of the following books as a source of information.

Baker, Betty. *Settlers and Strangers: Native Americans of the Desert Southwest and History as They Saw It.* New York: Macmillan, 1977.

Campbell, Elizabeth A. *Jamestown: The Beginning.* Boston: Little, Brown, 1974.

Erdos, Richard. *The Rain Dance People.* New York: Knopf, 1976.

Marriott, Alice. *The First Comers.* New York: Longman, Green, 1960.

SUGGESTIONS FOR FURTHER READING

DeWitt, Dorothy, ed. *The Talking Stone: An Anthology of Native American Tales and Legends.* New York: Greenwillow, 1979.

Ensign, Georgianne. *The Hunt for the Mastodon.* New York: Watts, 1971.

Herbert, Wally. *Eskimos.* New York: Watts, 1977.

Irwin, Constance. *Strange Footprints on the Land: Vikings in America.* New York: Harper & Row, 1980.

Jensen, Malcolm C. *Francisco Coronado: A Visual Biography.* New York: Watts, 1974.

Nee, Kay Bonner. *Powhatan: The Story of an American Indian.* Minneapolis: Dillon, 1971.

Detail from *The Plantation* by an unknown artist, about 1825.

FROM COLONIES TO INDEPENDENT STATES

THE THIRTEEN ENGLISH COLONIES
LIFE IN THE COLONIES
THE COLONIES MOVE TOWARD INDEPENDENCE
THE WAR FOR INDEPENDENCE

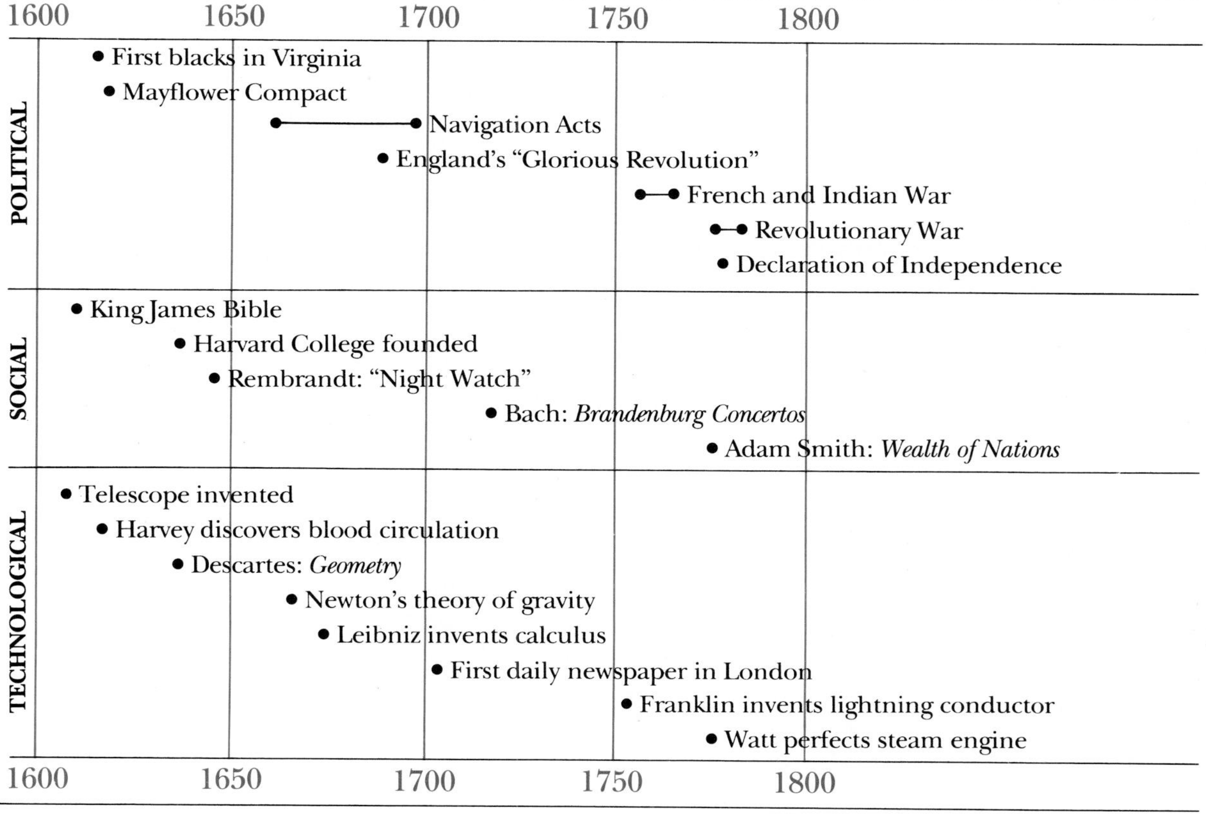

1600	1650	1700	1750	1800

POLITICAL

- First blacks in Virginia
- Mayflower Compact
- ●——● Navigation Acts
- England's "Glorious Revolution"
- ●——● French and Indian War
- ●——● Revolutionary War
- Declaration of Independence

SOCIAL

- King James Bible
- Harvard College founded
- Rembrandt: "Night Watch"
- Bach: *Brandenburg Concertos*
- Adam Smith: *Wealth of Nations*

TECHNOLOGICAL

- Telescope invented
- Harvey discovers blood circulation
- Descartes: *Geometry*
- Newton's theory of gravity
- Leibniz invents calculus
- First daily newspaper in London
- Franklin invents lightning conductor
- Watt perfects steam engine

1600	1650	1700	1750	1800

CHAPTER 4   1620-1750

THE THIRTEEN ENGLISH COLONIES

THE NEW ENGLAND COLONIES
THE MIDDLE COLONIES
THE SOUTHERN COLONIES
PATTERNS OF SETTLEMENT

4-1 THE NEW ENGLAND COLONIES

READ TO FIND OUT

—what the words *Puritans, Pilgrims, compact, self-governing colony, toleration,* and *proprietary colony* mean.

—why voyagers on the *Mayflower* settled in New England.

—why the Massachusetts Bay Colony was started.

—how the colonies of Connecticut and Rhode Island were settled.

—what happened to early settlements in New Hampshire and Maine.

Puritans: Protestants who wanted a simpler form of worship in the Church of England

Pilgrims: people who made the journey to America for religious reasons

compact: written agreement

self-governing colony: one in which voters chose governor, council, and assembly

toleration: freedom for people of different beliefs

proprietary colony: one for which the proprietor, or owner, chose the governor

Hundreds of bays and inlets dot the jagged coast of New England. They offer safe harbor to small ships. Away from the sea, the hills and ridges of New England border narrow valleys. The valleys, running mainly north and south, once were scoured by Ice-Age glaciers. The great sheets of ice left behind only a thin layer of rocky soil. Farther west, beyond the hills, the land rises to the crest of the Appalachian Mountains.

English settlers first set up a colony in this rugged land in 1620. They called it Plymouth Colony. Unlike Jamestown, Virginia, the first New England colony was started by people seeking religious freedom.

The Bible was a treasured possession in early settlers' homes. It was often kept in a large carved wooden box like this one.

This portrait of David, Joanna, and Abigail Mason is one of the earliest paintings of American children. The Masons were Boston Puritans.

THE PILGRIMS

Like some other nations in Europe, England had broken away from the Roman Catholic Church. In 1534 King Henry VIII established the new, Protestant, Church of England. All English people were expected to worship in the new church. But not all of them did. Some remained Catholics. Others felt that the new Church of England was too much like the Roman Catholic Church. These people were called **Puritans** because they believed in simpler, "purer" forms of worship.

Most Puritans stayed within the Church of England and tried to change it. Some English Puritans, however, set up a separate church. They were called Separatists. As rivals of the official church, the Separatists were treated harshly. William Bradford, one of their leaders, complained that "some were taken and clapt up in prison."

Fears of harsh treatment drove many of the Separatists out of England. Some went to the Netherlands, but they never felt at home there. Their children were growing up more Dutch than English. After a dozen years in the Netherlands, a number of the English Separatists decided to set out for America.

In England, the Separatists joined a group planning to sail to Virginia. They were given permission by the London Company to settle north of Jamestown. On September 16, 1620, about one hundred voyagers set out for America in a small ship, the *Mayflower*. One third of

Plymouth Colony was named after an English seaport southwest of London. Plymouth was the last European city touched by the *Mayflower*.

Pilgrim women spun wool to weave into cloth to make clothing for their families.

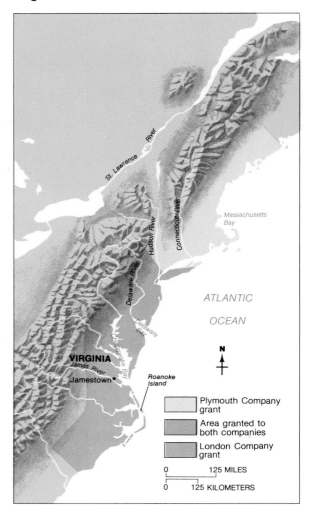

them were Separatists from the Netherlands. Years later, William Bradford referred to these Separatists as **Pilgrims**—people who made the journey for religious reasons.

For two months the Pilgrims were battered by heavy seas. Then they sighted land. But it was not Virginia. Instead, they had arrived at Cape Cod, in the region English sailors called New England. The Pilgrims did not want to risk a longer voyage on the rough Atlantic. Yet they had permission only to settle in Virginia. Also, the laws and rules set forth in their charter applied only to Virginia.

Before deciding to settle in New England, Pilgrim leaders on the *Mayflower* drew up a **compact,** or written agreement. Forty-one voyagers signed it on November 21, 1620. They agreed to make "just and equal laws" and to abide by them. The Mayflower Compact gave the Pilgrims a basis for self-government.

The text of the Mayflower Compact appears on page 522.

CHAPTER 4   1620-1750

PLYMOUTH COLONY

The Pilgrims began their settlement at Plymouth Harbor in December. Soon the "starving time" began. By April 1621, when the *Mayflower* sailed back to England, hunger and disease had claimed half of the colonists. Yet none of the survivors chose to return with the ship.

Spring brought the settlers help from an Indian named Squanto. He taught them how to plant corn, where to fish, and how to hunt. Squanto also helped the Pilgrims stay on good terms with the local tribe, the Wampanoag (WAHM-puh-NŌ-ahg), and their leader, Massasoit (MAS-eh-SOYT). In the fall, after their first harvest, the Pilgrims held a feast of Thanksgiving. They invited Massasoit, who came with ninety men and five freshly killed deer. The settlers cooked wild turkeys, geese, and ducks. For three days they celebrated and gave thanks to God.

Life for the Pilgrims was by no means easy in later years. Farming was difficult in the rocky soil of New England. Yet the Pilgrims continued to be thankful for the freedom they had found.

William Bradford, who became governor of Plymouth, wrote *Of Plymouth Plantation*, a history of the colony. You may wish to read to the class selected passages from the chapter dealing with the rough voyage: "Of Their Voyage and How They Passed the Sea...."

During the winter of 1621, the Pilgrims of Plymouth Colony suffered from cold and starvation. Half of them died before spring.

Activity: Students can write papers about the Pilgrims' dealings with the Indians, either from the Indians' or Pilgrims' point of view. To get students started, ask: What might the Indians have thought on seeing the Pilgrims? What might the Pilgrims have thought?

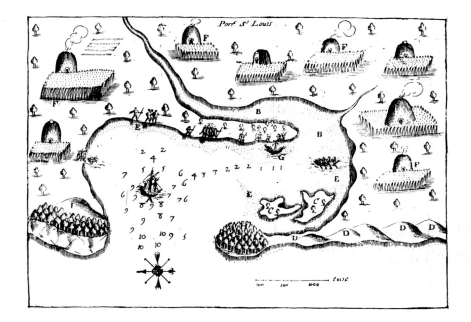

Samuel de Champlain drew this map of Plymouth harbor, which he called St. Louis, about 1605. Early mapmakers often drew pictures of the landscape on their maps. The Indian village shown here was probably the home of Squanto.

MASSACHUSETTS

While Plymouth Colony struggled, other Puritans in England received a charter for a colony of their own. The charter gave them the right to settle north of Plymouth, between the Merrimack and Charles rivers. In 1629 these Puritans, organized as the Massachusetts Bay Company, began sending settlers to New England. In the next year, more than 2,000 settlers made the voyage. The Puritan migration, the greatest outflow of people from England in history, had begun.

The Massachusetts Bay Company had a mission, or a special purpose. Its leaders planned to create a community where Puritans would live together under God's laws. They called the colony a "holy experiment." John Winthrop was elected the first governor of Massachusetts. He hoped the community would set an example for the rest of the world. "We shall be as a city upon a hill," he said. "The eyes of all people are upon us."

The colonists were expected to live godly lives. On Sunday, they were supposed to attend church. After the long service ended, the colonists were expected to spend the rest of the day in prayer or Bible reading. They were not supposed to play games, drink in taverns, dance, or even argue on Sunday. Many of these ideas about what people should and should not do were written into law.

You may wish to point out that, despite restrictions, the Puritans were not a joyless people. They did have their pleasures, and they took joy in living godly lives.

The Puritans were able to make such laws because they had set up their own government. Laws were passed by the General Court, made up of elected representatives. In the first years of the colony, only

The meeting house at Plymouth was built in 1683. Church services were held there. The townsfolk also gathered there to make laws and vote.

church members could choose the members of the General Court. Yet all colonists, Puritan or not, were bound by law to live by Puritan rules.

The Massachusetts Bay Company prospered. Some 20,000 settlers from England reached Boston Harbor or nearby ports in the 1630s. Eventually, in 1691, Plymouth Colony was joined to Massachusetts.

CONNECTICUT

The leaders of Massachusetts hoped to keep the Puritan settlers together in one colony. But before long, people were moving southwest to the broad valley of the Connecticut River. There they found the best farm land in New England.

In 1633, some settlers from Plymouth moved into an area of Dutch settlement to the west. In 1634 a group of Puritans settled along the river at Windsor. In 1635 others settled farther downstream at Wethersfield. The next year a Puritan minister, Thomas Hooker, led his congregation out of Massachusetts to found Hartford along the Connecticut River.

As settlers moved onto Indian lands, the local tribe, the Pequot (PEE-kwaht), struck back. Fighting between the Pequot and the Puritans ended in 1637 when Puritan soldiers killed most of the Pequot tribe. The Pequot War helped unite the towns of Windsor, Wethersfield, and Hartford under a new plan of government. The plan was called the Fundamental Orders. Adopted in 1639, it was the first written constitution in the colonies.

The Fundamental Orders reflected the views of Thomas Hooker. He believed that a government's power to act should come from the free consent of the people. The governor and other officials in Connecticut

You may wish to have students take special note of the Fundamental Orders as a *written* constitution. This is an important departure from British practice. The British Constitution, consisting of customs and traditions, is unwritten.

were chosen by vote. Voting, though, was limited to "freemen," men who owned land and were accepted members of their towns. Church membership was not required for voting, as it was in Massachusetts.

Connecticut received a royal charter in 1662. But it remained a **self-governing colony,** one in which the governor, the council, and the assembly were chosen by voters.

RHODE ISLAND

*CT
For discussion: Do students see any contradiction between the Puritans' seeking religious freedom for themselves but denying it to others? How might the Puritans justify this?

Activity: Students can write reports on Roger Williams and Anne Hutchinson.

Anne Hutchinson held weekly meetings to discuss sermons. Her ideas led to her banishment from Massachusetts.

Roger Williams was another minister who led settlers out of Massachusetts. Williams, though, did not leave by choice. He fled after being banished, or ordered to leave.

Williams had quarreled with the leaders of Massachusetts. He said that the colonists there did not own the land because it had never been bought from the Indians. He also said that the government should not force all people to go to church or enforce religious laws. In 1635 he was found guilty of holding "new and dangerous opinions" and was told to leave the colony.

Early in 1636 Williams found refuge with the Narragansett (NAYR-uh-GAN-sit) tribe, whose homeland was south of Massachusetts. In the spring he bought land from the tribe. His followers joined him in a new settlement he called Providence.

Two years later an intelligent, strong-willed woman named Anne Hutchinson helped to found Portsmouth, Rhode Island. She, too, had been banished from Massachusetts. Hutchinson had questioned the need to pray and do good works in order to win God's favor. She believed that faith alone was enough. Her ideas seemed dangerous to some Puritan leaders. In 1638 they forced her to leave Massachusetts with her husband and children.

In 1643 Williams sailed to England to get a charter for the colony of Rhode Island. The charter was granted in 1644. It established Rhode Island as a self-governing colony and promised religious **toleration**—freedom for people of different beliefs. In Rhode Island, Catholics and Jews as well as Protestants could follow their faiths in peace.

Puritan ministers in Massachusetts called the new colony "that sewer." Williams, though, was proud of Rhode Island. He wrote that settlers there had "as great liberty as any people we can hear of under the whole heaven."

NEW HAMPSHIRE AND MAINE

To the north, between Massachusetts and New France, lay a region rich in timber, furs, and fish. Both the English and the French tried to start settlements there in the early 1600s. Both attempts failed.

The Colonies in 1650

Pilgrim children learned to read from the rhymes of the New England Primer. The pictures are woodcuts.

Early settlements in North America spread inland along rivers. Most of the early towns were along the Atlantic coast.

James I gave most of this area to two wealthy Englishmen in 1622. They became its proprietors, that is, its owners or managers. As owners of this **proprietary colony,** they controlled the colony and appointed its governor. The proprietors hoped to make money from their colony, but they failed to do so. Only a few small settlements were started.

The two proprietors divided the area in 1629. One, John Mason, claimed the southern part. He named it New Hampshire after his

In 1641 Gorges founded the community of Gorgeana (now called York). Students may be interested to know that this is the first chartered English city within what are now the boundaries of the United States.

A lithograph printed in Cologne, Germany, in 1618 showed New England women cleaning freshly caught fish.

The Massachusetts pine tree shilling of 1652 was the first colonial coin minted in America.

home in Hampshire, England. Mason died in 1635. A few years later, Massachusetts took over the area. The Massachusetts Bay Company claimed the land under its charter. But in 1680 King Charles II declared that New Hampshire was a royal colony, separate from Massachusetts.

To the west of New Hampshire lay the land that is now Vermont. In colonial times, this region was claimed by New Hampshire, Massachusetts, and New York. It was not a separate colony.

The other proprietor, Sir Ferdinando Gorges (GOR-jehz), kept the area called Maine. After his death, Massachusetts bought Maine from his heirs. Maine remained part of Massachusetts until it became a state in 1820.

SECTION REVIEW   Answers will be found on page T 30.

1. Define these words: *Puritans, Pilgrims, compact, self-governing colony, toleration, proprietary colony.*

2. Identify: John Winthrop, Thomas Hooker, Fundamental Orders of Connecticut, Roger Williams, Anne Hutchinson, John Mason, Ferdinando Gorges.

3. Why did the Pilgrims write the Mayflower Compact?

4. What did John Winthrop mean when he said, "We shall be as a city upon a hill"?

5. Give two reasons why people from Massachusetts settled in Connecticut and Rhode Island.

6. Both New Hampshire and Maine were claimed by Massachusetts. Which one first became independent of Massachusetts?

4-2 THE MIDDLE COLONIES

READ TO FIND OUT

—what the word *treason* means.

—how New Netherland became New York.

—why a rebellion took place in New York.

—how New Jersey was governed.

—why William Penn founded Pennsylvania.

—how Delaware was governed.

treason: actions taken to overthrow the government

While the English were settling New England and Virginia, the land between these colonies was controlled by the Dutch. The Dutch colony, New Netherland, stretched north from New Amsterdam along the Hudson River. In 1655 the Dutch extended their rule. Led by Peter Stuyvesant, they took control of New Sweden on the Delaware River.

The Dutch felt at home in their part of North America. The winter snows and summer heat were much like the climate in the Netherlands. Dutch settlers could wear the same kind of clothing and build the same kind of houses that they had known in their homeland. They could also grow the same crops and raise the same animals. Unlike New England, most of the area had not been scoured by glaciers. It offered deep, rich soil to Dutch farmers.

This etching shows Peter Stuyvesant at the surrender of New Amsterdam in 1664.

NEW YORK

To the English, New Netherland was a barrier. It kept English settlers from moving westward out of New England. King Charles II refused to recognize Dutch claims to the area. In 1664 he granted the territory claimed by the Dutch to his brother, James, the Duke of York. James then sent four warships to capture New Netherland.

When the English arrived at New Amsterdam, they sent Peter Stuyvesant a note demanding surrender. New Amsterdam's chief gunner reported to Stuyvesant that the city's supply of gunpowder was damp and useless. The Dutch colonists were ready to give up, but Stuyvesant tore up the English note in anger. He surrendered only when the townspeople refused to fight.

By the end of 1664, the English had taken over Dutch holdings along both the Hudson and the Delaware rivers. The colony of New Nether-

*CT

For discussion: What does Stuyvesant's refusal to give up suggest about his character? Why, other than the damp gunpowder, might the colonists have been unwilling to support him?

OUTLINING

*CT

It is very difficult for anyone to read a chapter only once and then be able to recall the information in it. Most students need to read, re-read, and review each chapter. After a while they understand the chapter and recall its main ideas and details. But going back over the chapter takes time.

One useful way to review a chapter is to outline it. Then, instead of going back over the entire chapter, you can review your outline. But a clear outline must stress the chapter's main ideas. When outlining a chapter in this book, use the following organization:

1. Place the section titles next to Roman numerals I, II, III, IV, etc.

2. Place the headings of the subsections next to capital letters A, B, C, D, etc.

3. Place the main ideas of each subsection next to the numbers 1, 2, 3, 4, etc.

4. Place details related to the main ideas next to lower case letters a, b, c, d, etc.

An outline of the information in the beginning of this section looks like this:

II. The Middle Colonies
   A. New York
      1. English refusal to recognize Dutch claims

      2. Grant of New Netherland area to James, Duke of York
      3. English takeover of New Netherland in 1664
         a. Renaming of New Netherland and New Amsterdam
         b. Freedom for Dutch to keep land and religion
      4. Plan to tax colonists
         a. Colonists' demand to vote on tax laws
         b. Election of first assembly in 1683
         c. Closing of assembly by King James II in 1685
      5. New Yorkers' rebellion in 1689
         a. Leading of rebellion by Jacob Leisler
         b. Hanging of Leisler for treason
         c. Permission for New Yorkers to keep assembly

1. This outline includes the section title, "The Middle Colonies," and the heading of the subsection "New York." How many main ideas were outlined above? How many details were outlined above?

2. Finish outlining Section 2 of this chapter. Be sure to include in your outline main ideas and details for all the remaining headings: New Jersey, Pennsylvania, and Delaware.

Answers will be found on page T 30.

land was renamed New York. New Amsterdam became New York City. The Duke of York ordered his first governor to treat the Dutch with "humanity and gentleness." They were allowed to keep their land and practice their religion.

As proprietor of the colony, the duke planned to make money by levying taxes. A group of New England Puritans who had moved to New York protested. They complained they were "enslaved" by a government they did not elect. In Massachusetts they could elect an assembly, a law-making body, which voted on all laws and taxes. But New York had no assembly. The duke ruled through a governor he appointed.

Many colonists felt that they ought to be able to approve or disapprove the duke's tax laws. In 1683 the duke gave in to their demands. New York elected its first assembly. Then, in 1685, the duke became James II, king of England, and New York became a royal colony. As king, James gave orders to close down the assembly.

In 1689 New Yorkers rebelled. Led by a German colonist named Jacob Leisler (LĪCE-lur), they set up their own assembly to govern the colony. After almost two years, English troops and a new royal governor arrived. Leisler and one of his followers were arrested and convicted of **treason**—trying to overthrow the government. They were hanged. After the rebellion, however, the colonists of New York were allowed to keep their assembly.

NEW JERSEY

In 1664, soon after New Netherland became New York, the Duke of York gave much of it away. To his friends Lord John Berkeley and Sir George Carteret, he granted the land from the mouth of the Hudson River west to the Delaware River. They became the "true and absolute lords proprietors" of New Jersey.

Both Berkeley and Carteret were eager to bring in colonists. They offered land at good prices and promised an elected assembly. Some of the Puritans from New England were attracted to New Jersey. So were members of another religious group, the Society of Friends. They were better known as Quakers.

The Quakers were followers of an English preacher named George Fox. Beginning in 1647, he urged people to trust their "inner light" and

James II was an unpopular English king, partly because he was a Catholic. In the "Glorious Revolution" of 1688, he was overthrown and went into exile. His Protestant daughter, Mary, and her husband, William of Orange, succeeded him. (Tell students they will read about this in Chapter 5, page 122.)

A group of Quakers led by Edward Byllynge bought Lord John Berkeley's grant. They made West Jersey the first Quaker colony in America.

Tidy farms like the one in this early drawing dotted the countryside of the Middle Colonies.

to live by their beliefs. To avoid the sin of pride, Quakers wore plain clothes. To show that all people are equal before God, they refused to bow to anyone, even the king. Many people scorned the Quakers, in both England and the colonies. But the Quakers found a haven in New Jersey. Many of them moved in quickly.

In 1676 New Jersey was divided into two parts, West Jersey and East Jersey. Each part was sold to new proprietors, including some Quakers. In 1702 the two parts were joined as a royal colony with an elected assembly. The proprietors, however, kept their rights to the land.

PENNSYLVANIA

Activity: Students can form committees, research the life of William Penn, and present dramatic scenes based on their research. Possible scenes: Penn and his father; Penn's dealings with the Leni-Lenape; Penn's discussing colonial affairs with Pennsylvanians.

Pennsylvania also became a haven for Quakers. Its founder was William Penn. As a young man, Penn was locked up in an English prison for preaching Quaker beliefs. After eight months passed, his wealthy father, Admiral William Penn, gained his release. The admiral did not like the Quaker religion. He hoped his son would give it up.

When Admiral Penn died in 1670, the king owed him a large sum of money. Ten years later, William Penn offered to forget the debt in exchange for land in America. The king agreed, and in 1681 William Penn received a charter for land west of the Delaware River. The land was named Pennsylvania, or Penn's Woods, in honor of his father.

William Penn viewed his colony as a "Holy Experiment" where Quakers and others "would be allowed to shape their own laws." Before sailing to the colony in 1682, he issued a Frame of Government. This document called for an elected assembly in Pennsylvania. In addition, it gave religious freedom to Quakers and others. Unlike the Puritan leaders of Massachusetts, Penn believed in toleration.

In the tribe's language, Leni-Lenape means "genuine people." The English called them the Delaware tribe.

Penn also believed in fair dealings with the local Indians. When visiting the Leni-Lenape, according to one account, "he sat with them on the ground, and ate with them of their roasted acorns and hominy." Penn paid the Leni-Lenape for their land.

German settlers decorated special family documents with painted figures and fancy script called *fraktur*.

Poor Richard's Almanac showed carpenters and blacksmiths hard at work. Benjamin Franklin published it in Philadelphia each year for 26 years.

For the main city of his colony, Penn wanted a place that was "high, dry, and healthy." He chose the land where the Schuylkill (SKOOL-kill) River meets the Delaware. There he founded Philadelphia, meaning "Brotherly Love."

The city was well placed to be a port. Ships brought in settlers from all over Europe. The Quakers in Pennsylvania were joined by German Protestants, French Huguenots, Irish Catholics, and others. Pennsylvania grew so rapidly that Penn could write in 1684, "I have led the greatest colony into America that ever anyone did upon private credit."

Have students review what they learned in Chapter 3 (page 76) about New Sweden and its conquest by New Netherland. When the English in turn conquered New Netherland (page 93), they acquired the Delaware region.

DELAWARE

Delaware was settled by Swedes in 1638. William Penn received title to the land on the west side of the Delaware River in 1682. People living there were allowed to have their own assembly. It met for the first time in 1704. But Delaware was ruled by the governor of Pennsylvania. Delaware did not become a fully separate colony until 1776.

SECTION REVIEW   Answers will be found on page T 30.

1. Define this word: *treason.*

2. Identify: Duke of York, Jacob Leisler, John Berkeley, George Carteret, William Penn.

3. Briefly tell how New Netherland became New York.

4. Why did some people in New York complain about being "enslaved"?

5. When were West Jersey and East Jersey joined together?

6. Why did William Penn found the colony of Pennsylvania?

7. What colony was Delaware originally a part of?

4-3 THE SOUTHERN COLONIES

READ TO FIND OUT

—what the words *Piedmont, cash crop,* and *sound* mean.

—how offers of land attracted settlers to Virginia.

—how slaves replaced servants on Virginia plantations.

—how religious toleration came to Maryland.

—what products helped the Carolinas prosper.

—why Georgia did not, at first, attract many colonists.

Piedmont: rolling upland plateau between the Fall Line and the Appalachians

cash crop: crop that could be sold for profit

sound: long, broad inlet from the sea

From New England to the Gulf of Mexico, a low coastal plain stretches inland from the sea. The plain is narrow in New England, but it widens to the south. In Georgia it extends 300 miles (480 kilometers) inland.

To the first colonists at Jamestown, the coastal plain brought misery. Winters were wet and cold. Summers seemed far too long and hot. Only later, when colonists planted tobacco, were they grateful for Virginia's long growing season.

Inland, the plain slopes gently upward for many miles. Then the land rises sharply at the Fall Line. Here, rivers tumble down in rapids and waterfalls. Above the Fall Line is the **Piedmont** (PEED-mahnt). It is a rolling, upland plateau between the Fall Line and the Appalachians.

Tobacco was Virginia's most profitable crop. An English magazine showed its readers how tobacco was cured and prepared for use. The plant in the background is shown much larger than its actual size.

VIRGINIA

Within fifty years of the founding of Jamestown, much of Virginia's coastal plain had been settled. To attract new settlers, the Virginia Company had begun giving away land. Colonists who paid their way to Virginia received a headright, the right to a certain amount of land. Usually a headright was worth 50 acres (20 hectares) per head. Settlers in Virginia could receive additional headrights by paying for the passage of other colonists to Virginia. The headright system continued after Virginia became a royal colony in 1624.

Many Virginians acquired large landholdings under this system. The headright system helped Virginia's population grow from 1,100 in 1624 to 40,000 by 1671. The system was used in other southern colonies too.

*CT
For discussion: Why was the headright system an effective way to foster colonial growth? Why might it not have been adopted by Plymouth Colony?

SERVANTS AND SLAVES

Most Virginians raised tobacco as their **cash crop,** or crop that could be sold for profit. Planting, tending, and harvesting tobacco took endless hours of work. At first, Virginia tobacco planters used indentured servants as farm workers. The servants worked for a few years and then were free.

In 1619 a Dutch ship brought the first Africans to Virginia. It is not clear whether they were brought as slaves or as indentured servants. By 1650 there were about 300 blacks in Virginia. Some were slaves. Others were indentured servants, working side by side with white servants in the fields. Other blacks were free. Some started farms and had servants of their own, both black and white.

In time, planters came to prefer slaves to servants. Slaves cost more, but they did not leave after a few years. In the 1660s the House of Burgesses began to pass laws taking away the rights of black people. After 1670 all blacks who were brought into Virginia by sea had to be slaves. By law, their children were slaves for life.

Life changed for white servants, too. By the 1670s Virginia had little good farm land left to give to indentured servants when their terms of service ended. More and more of these landless former servants began wandering about the countryside. They survived by doing odd jobs and hunting or stealing. In 1676 some of them joined in a rebellion against Virginia's government.

BACON'S REBELLION

The rebellion was led by a university-educated planter named Nathaniel Bacon. He had come to Virginia in 1673. Bacon's farm was near the frontier, the edge of the settled area. Indians had attacked his farm

In 1677, a year after Bacon's Rebellion, Sir William Berkeley was recalled to England. He was the author of a history of the colony, *A Discourse and View of Virginia.*

and others on the frontier. The settlers asked Virginia's royal governor, William Berkeley, for help in fighting the Indians. The governor, who considered himself the Indians' protector, refused.

Bacon led a force of frontier farmers and landless young men against the Indians. He killed any Indians he could find, including those who had been friendly to the white settlers. Next, Bacon's army marched on Jamestown. They seized the government and held power in Virginia for a few months. Bacon's Rebellion ended when its leader died suddenly of an illness. After the uprising, more of Virginia's planters replaced their troublesome indentured servants with slaves.

MARYLAND

You might wish to have students note that, like Plymouth Colony and Pennsylvania, Maryland was founded to enable a minority to escape religious persecution. And like Rhode Island's charter (page 90), the Toleration Act helped establish a tradition of religious freedom.

John Moale sketched the harbor of Baltimore in 1752. The town had only 100 residents, but it was a busy port.

The success of the tobacco plantations in Virginia stirred interest in starting other proprietary colonies nearby. In 1632 King Charles I granted land north of the Potomac River to George Calvert, who was the first Lord Baltimore. The new colony was named Maryland after Charles's wife, Queen Mary.

Calvert, who was a Catholic, wanted more than profit from Maryland. He wanted to start a colony where Catholics would have religious freedom. Calvert died before receiving his charter. The charter was granted to his son Cecilius, the second Lord Baltimore, who carried out his father's plans.

Colonists began arriving in Maryland in 1634. Many were wealthy Catholics. Most, though, were Protestants. By 1649 the Protestant majority seemed likely to turn against the Catholics. Lord Baltimore asked the Maryland assembly to approve a law guaranteeing freedom of worship to both groups. The assembly passed the Toleration Act of 1649. It gave religious freedom to Catholics and Protestants alike.

You may wish to point out to students the eighteenth-century drawing below. It shows skilled slaves harvesting, pressing, and drying indigo on a plantation in South Carolina. Until the development of synthetic dyes in the mid-1800s, indigo was in great demand as the major source of blue dye.

★ ★ ★ ★ ★ ★ ★ AMERICAN VALUES IN ACTION ★ ★ ★ ★ ★ ★ ★

ELIZA LUCAS PINCKNEY

"We are 17 mile by land and 6 mile by water from Charles Town," Eliza Lucas wrote to one of her friends in 1740. And, she continued cheerfully, "I have the business of three plantations to transact."

Eliza's father was stationed in the West Indies with the military. Her mother was in poor health. The seventeen-year-old was left to run the family plantations on her own.

A husband, Colonel Lucas felt, would make his daughter's life easier. Politely—and firmly—Eliza refused the suitor proposed by her father. If the suitor had all "the riches of Peru and Chile," she wrote, she would not make him her husband. Several years later, she would marry Charles Pinckney—a husband not selected by her father.

Having failed at matchmaking, her father settled for business. He urged Eliza to experiment with different crops in order to find an alternative cash crop for rice. In his letter he enclosed one possibility—indigo seeds.

This was more to Eliza's taste. "I love the vegetable world extremely," she admitted. Indeed, Eliza had the initiative to do the job. And, as a friend put it, she had a "fertile brain."

Eliza soon reported to her father that indigo was the most promising crop she had tried. But the process of producing dye from indigo plants was complex. Others in South Carolina had tried it and failed.

The troublesome plant nearly defeated Eliza, too. Frost ruined the first year's crop. The second crop was far too small. Then the first dyes lacked the right color.

Despite the setbacks, Eliza kept experimenting. In 1744 she sent 6 pounds (2.7 kilograms) of that year's crop to England. Then she waited, anxious to hear "how 'tis approved of there." A few months later she got an answer. "The sample of indigo sent here," wrote the London agent, "has been tried and found better than the French indigo."

Delighted, Eliza gave seeds to neighboring planters. Soon, millions of pounds of blue indigo dye-cakes were being sold in England. Eliza's "fertile brain" had created a valuable new product for South Carolina.

The Thirteen British Colonies 1740

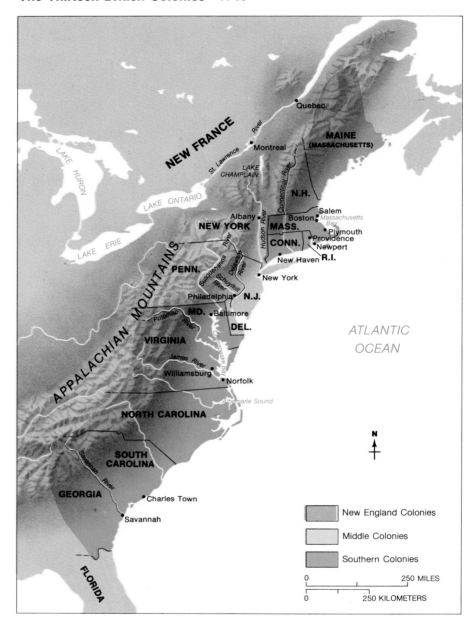

The Thirteen British Colonies 1740

Quebec

NEW FRANCE

St. Lawrence River

Montreal

LAKE CHAMPLAIN

MAINE (MASSACHUSETTS)

LAKE HURON

LAKE ONTARIO

N.H.

Connecticut River

LAKE ERIE

Albany

Hudson River

Salem
Boston
Massachusetts Bay
Plymouth
Providence
Newport

NEW YORK

MASS.

CONN.

New Haven

R.I.

APPALACHIAN MOUNTAINS

PENN.

Susquehanna River

Delaware River

Schuylkill River

New York

Philadelphia

N.J.

Potomac River

MD.

Baltimore

DEL.

VIRGINIA

James River

Williamsburg

Chesapeake Bay

ATLANTIC OCEAN

Norfolk

Albemarle Sound

NORTH CAROLINA

N

SOUTH CAROLINA

Savannah River

GEORGIA

Charles Town

Savannah

FLORIDA

New England Colonies

Middle Colonies

Southern Colonies

| 0 | | 250 MILES |
| 0 | | 250 KILOMETERS |

THE CAROLINAS

In 1663 Charles II gave a huge area of land south of Virginia to eight English nobles. The proprietors named their colony Carolina in honor of the king. Carolina comes from the Latin name *Carolus,* or "Charles."

The northern part of Carolina was settled first. Former servants from Virginia started small tobacco farms near Albemarle Sound. A **sound** is a long, broad inlet from the sea. Settlers came from the West Indies to the southern part of the colony. In 1670 they founded Charles Town, today called Charleston. It flourished after 1690, when planters began growing rice. Rice became the colony's most valuable cash crop.

The proprietors could not prevent Spanish attacks south of Charles Town. Nor could they unify their colony. After 1691 the area around Albemarle Sound was called North Carolina. Charles Town was the center of South Carolina. In 1729 North and South Carolina became separate royal colonies.

North Carolina continued to be a colony of small farms. Large plantations were common in South Carolina. In the 1740s Eliza Lucas Pinckney introduced indigo as a cash crop. The colony also sold pitch, tar, and turpentine, which were products made from pine sap.

By the middle of the eighteenth century, Charles Town was the largest city in the Southern Colonies.

GEORGIA

In 1732 King George II granted the land between the Savannah River and Spanish Florida to a group of wealthy people led by James Edward Oglethorpe. The new colony was named Georgia in honor of the king.

As a young man, Oglethorpe had watched a good friend die in debtors' prison. His friend's only crime was being too poor to pay his debts. Oglethorpe wanted to save other debtors from jail. He hoped that in Georgia debtors could become independent farmers.

A second purpose for founding Georgia was to protect the Carolinas. Oglethorpe arrived in Georgia with the first group of settlers in 1733. After founding the town of Savannah, he had forts built on islands along the Georgia coast.

Oglethorpe limited the size of farms in Georgia. At first, no settler there could own more than 500 acres (200 hectares). No settler could own any slaves. The colonists grew more and more unhappy with these rules. Many of them moved to South Carolina, where there was no limit on the amount of land or the number of slaves they could buy.

By 1750 these limits had vanished. Families in Georgia were allowed to own 2,000 acres (800 hectares) and slaves as well. Two years later Georgia became a royal colony.

*CT
For discussion: Like Plymouth Colony and Pennsylvania, Georgia was established as a haven. In what way was it different?

SECTION REVIEW   Answers will be found on page T 31.

1. Define these words: *Piedmont, cash crop, sound.*

2. Identify: Nathaniel Bacon, George Calvert, Cecilius Calvert, the Maryland Toleration Act, James Edward Oglethorpe.

3. Why did Virginia colonists pay for the voyages of new settlers?

4. Why did Calvert want the Maryland Toleration Act to be passed?

5. Give two reasons why many colonists left Georgia in the 1730s.

4-4 PATTERNS OF SETTLEMENT

READ TO FIND OUT

—what the words *emigration, plantations,* and *rural* mean.

—what caused people to leave their homelands.

—how the slave trade grew.

—where large plantations were located.

—what colonial cities and villages were like.

emigration: leaving one country to settle in another

plantations: large farms including housing for their workers

rural: in the country

Until 1680, most people settling in the English colonies in North America were from England. In the early 1600s English landowners had found that they could make more money by raising sheep than by renting their land to farmers. Large numbers of farmers were forced off the land. Farm families, reduced to begging for food, were willing to begin new lives in America.

After 1680, England was no longer the main source of **emigration** to the colonies. Emigration means leaving one country to settle in another. Throughout Europe religious wars and poverty drove millions of people from their homes and villages. For many, the lure of cheap land and religious freedom in America was too powerful to resist. Thousands of emigrants willingly left France, Germany, Ireland, Scotland, Switzerland, and the Netherlands for the English colonies. Only in Africa was emigration forced.

THE SLAVE TRADE

*CT
For discussion: What might be the future consequences of the growing demand for slaves?

In the mid-1500s, Portuguese traders began to carry slaves from West Africa to Brazil. There the African slaves were put to work on sugar **plantations.** Plantations were large farms that included housing for the farms' workers.

During the 1600s, traders from many lands shipped large numbers of Africans to South America and the West Indies. The success of tobacco and rice plantations in the English colonies led to a growing demand for slaves in North America as well. By the late 1600s, slave ships were a common sight in colonial port cities. Tightly packed into the ships, many of the slaves died of disease before reaching America. Through the slave trade, the black population in English North America grew rapidly. By 1760 blacks made up one fifth of the total population.

USING THE TOOLS OF HISTORY

USING CIRCLE AND LINE GRAPHS

A graph is one of the best ways to show numerical information. Two kinds of graphs are shown here—a line graph and a circle graph.

A line graph can show how the total amount of something has changed. The span of time is usually shown on the horizontal scale, or bottom of the graph. The amount is shown on the vertical scale, or left-hand side of the graph.

Before you read a graph, look at its title. It should describe the information that is shown on the graph. Then read the labels on the different parts of the graph. They will help you to interpret the graph correctly.

Use the line graph below to answer the following questions:

1. In 1620 the colonial population was about 2,300. What was the population in 1770?

2. By what year did the population grow to more than 600,000 people?

3. During which 10-year period were the most people added to the colonial population? (Hint: The longer the line is between two dots on the graph, the greater is the number of people added to the population between those years.)

A circle graph is used to show percentages, or parts of a whole. The entire circle represents 100 percent. The "pie slices" in the circle must always add up to exactly 100 percent.

Use the circle graphs below to answer the following questions:

4. In which year was the percentage of blacks in the colonial population the smallest?

5. In which year was it the largest? Use both graphs to answer this question.

6. Today the percentage of blacks in the American population is about 12 percent. Show this information on a circle graph. (Hint: 12 percent is close to one eighth of a circle.)

Population of the Thirteen Colonies

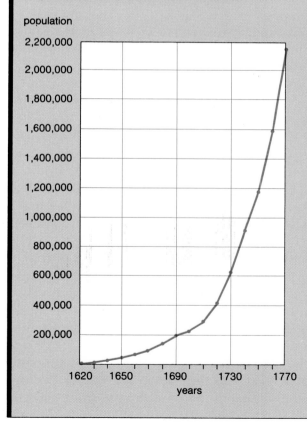

Black Percent of the Total Population

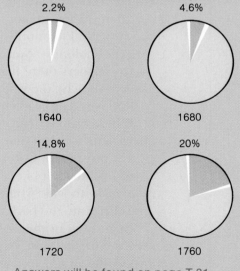

Answers will be found on page T 31.

LARGE PLANTATIONS

Southern plantation owners tended to see themselves as akin to the English nobility. Indeed, some of them were related to important English families. Thus there developed a southern tradition of aristocracy that other colonists, particularly New Englanders, resented. You may wish to point out to students that this tradition later aggravated the friction between the North and the South.

Many slaves were bought by plantation owners in the Southern Colonies. Most plantations were located on rivers. Slaves could be delivered by ship directly to the plantation's own wharf. The same wharf was used for shipping out barrels of rice or tobacco.

Sometimes a ship arrived carrying fine china or silk dresses. Planters ordered these products from England. Most other goods the planter wanted were made on the plantation by slaves who were artisans, or skilled workers. Slave artisans made nails, barrels, shoes, cloth, and many other items.

The main building on a large plantation was the house where the planter lived. Gunston Hall was one of the grandest of Virginia's plantations. The main house overlooked the Potomac River. The view toward the river included a wide lawn bordered by an orchard.

Looking away from the river, one saw a garden, a park filled with tame deer, and then fields of tobacco. On one side of the house were stables and woods that hid the cabins of slaves from view. A kitchen, a well, poultry houses, and cattle pens were located on the other side of the planter's house.

Few planters owned property as grand as Gunston Hall. Away from the large rivers there were small farms with few slaves or none. But most settlers in the Southern Colonies dreamed of someday having a plantation like Gunston Hall.

THE BACK COUNTRY

In the early years of the colonies, most colonists settled near the coast or along a few major rivers. By 1700 settlement was moving inland toward the Piedmont or the back country. This happened first in the Middle Colonies. Small farms dotted the land west of Philadelphia. Many farmers there had emigrated from Germany. Because they spoke *Deutsch* (doich), the word for German in their language, they were called the Pennsylvania Dutch.

When the German settlers started farms, they usually built large barns and small houses. They did not put up larger houses until their farms prospered. Germans in the Conestoga (KAHN-eh-STŌ-gah) Valley west of Philadelphia built the famed Conestoga wagons. These sturdy wagons with wide wheels and canvas-covered tops were used by families traveling into the back country.

Beginning in the 1740s, large numbers of settlers were following the Great Philadelphia Wagon Road into the back country. This twisting woodland track followed old Indian trails southwest from western Pennsylvania to Georgia. It wound for more than 730 miles (1,170 kilo-

Settlement of the British Colonies

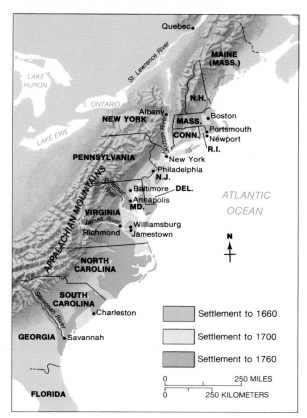

Settlement to 1660
Settlement to 1700
Settlement to 1760

0   250 MILES
0   250 KILOMETERS

Colonial Population by Nationality

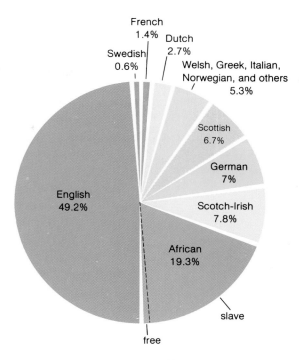

Nearly half the colonists in the 1790 census had English surnames. Because many non-English colonists changed their names in America, this graph shows only an estimate of the nationality of the population in America.

meters). Pioneers on foot, on horseback, or in Conestoga wagons traveled the rutted, narrow road to start new lives on the frontier.

Many back-country pioneers were Scotch-Irish. Their ancestors were Scots who had settled in northern Ireland. Used to fighting the Irish, they were willing to take their chances against Indians in the wilderness. Unlike the Germans, the Scotch-Irish did not often settle in groups. Each family cleared a few acres, built a cabin, and planted crops.

Emigrants from other countries joined the Scotch-Irish on the frontier. So did colonists moving west from the coastal plains. One man called these settlers "a mixed medley from all countries."

CITIES AND VILLAGES

From the early years of New Amsterdam on, the Middle Colonies continued to attract "a mixed medley" of people. In 1769 a Frenchman, Jean de Crèvecoeur (krev-KOOR), settled on a farm in New York. There he met "a man whose grandfather was an Englishman, whose wife was Dutch, whose son married a Frenchwoman, and whose present four sons have now four wives of different nations."

*CT
For discussion: Later the United States was compared to a "melting pot." What does the comparison suggest about the different nationalities coming together? How might it be related to the famous question Crèvecoeur asked in *Letters from an American Farmer:* "What then is the American, this new man?"

The "Broad Way" is, of course, Broadway, a diagonal thoroughfare that is the longest in Manhattan. You may wish to have the class speculate why a number of cities have a main or business street called Broadway. (Other common business street names to consider: Main, State.)

In the port cities of New York and Philadelphia a mixture of languages was heard on the docks and streets. An English traveler, Andrew Burnaby, visited New York City in 1760. "More than half of the people here are Dutch," he wrote. Other people in the city "are of different nations, languages, and religions." The city had between 2,000 and 3,000 houses, Burnaby estimated. Most of the streets were very narrow. "There are two or three which are wide," he reported, "especially the Broad Way."

The largest colonial cities were close to the ocean. They grew up around harbors, because ships were the fastest means of transportation. Inland, near the frontier, the largest settlements were forts. Settlers banded together for protection against Indian attacks. One fort, Albany, "consists of three pretty compact streets," wrote a traveler in the mid-1700s. "The greatest length of the streets is half a mile" (0.8 kilometer). The main buildings of the log-built fort overlooked the Hudson River. The entire settlement was enclosed by a wall of pine logs pounded into the ground.

In New England and the Middle Colonies, small villages dotted the land between the coast and the frontier. A typical New England village was centered on the village church, or meetinghouse. It was used for town meetings as well as worship. Nearby was an open area called the village green. People met there for games or military training. The villagers' houses were clustered around the green. Their fields and pastures were within easy walking distance.

Southern farms and plantations were isolated from each other. Because transportation was slow and difficult, southern families treasured their few chances to meet for social occasions.

Most colonists lived in **rural** areas, or out in the country. Whether they lived on plantations, in villages, on small farms, or in frontier clearings, their lives were guided by the rising and the setting of the sun and the changing of the seasons.

SECTION REVIEW Answers will be found on page T 31.

1. Define these words: *emigration, plantations, rural.*

2. Identify: Pennsylvania Dutch, back country, Great Philadelphia Wagon Road, Scotch-Irish.

3. Why was there a growing demand for slaves in North America?

4. Why were large plantations located along rivers?

5. How were the settlements of the Pennsylvania Dutch different from the settlements of the Scotch-Irish?

6. Name the main building on a plantation, in Albany, and in a typical New England village.

New England was settled by English Puritans seeking religious freedom. The Pilgrims started Plymouth Colony in 1620. In 1629 other Puritans started the Massachusetts Bay Colony. Their mission was to create a community based on God's laws. Some colonists left Massachusetts and founded Connecticut and Rhode Island in the 1630s. Rhode Island was the first colony to practice toleration, welcoming settlers of all faiths.

In 1622 two proprietors were given the region that was later divided into New Hampshire and Maine. New Hampshire became a royal colony in 1680. Maine, claimed by Massachusetts in 1652, did not become a separate state until 1820.

The Dutch colony of New Netherland became the English colony of New York in 1664. Many New Yorkers were unhappy with their colonial government. Two years after their rebellion in 1689, New Yorkers were allowed to have an elected assembly.

New Jersey, given to two proprietors in 1664, attracted many Quakers. Quakers also settled in Pennsylvania, founded by William Penn in 1681. Pennsylvania attracted settlers from many parts of Europe. Delaware was part of Pennsylvania from 1682 to 1776, but had its own assembly.

The headright system encouraged the settlement of Virginia and other southern colonies. The growth of tobacco and rice plantations increased the demand for farm workers. At first, planters used both servants and slaves to work their fields. By 1700, however, slaves had replaced indentured servants on most plantations.

Maryland, first settled in 1634, became a haven for Catholics. The Carolinas, given to eight proprietors in 1663, became two royal colonies in 1729. Georgia was first settled in 1733 as a refuge for debtors. In 1752, it too became a royal colony.

By the 1700s, the colonies had become a "mixed medley" of English, African, Scotch-Irish, German, Scottish, and other emigrants. Most colonists lived in rural settlements ranging from large plantations to frontier clearings. Some clustered in villages. Colonial seaports grew into thriving cities.

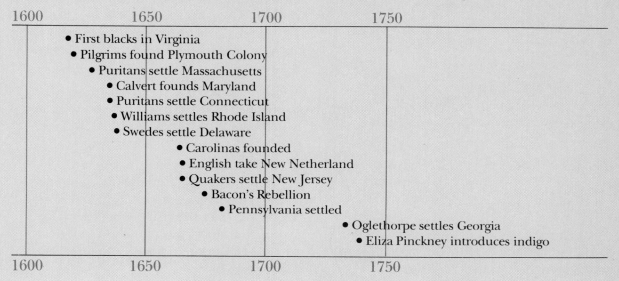

Timeline (1600–1750):
- First blacks in Virginia
- Pilgrims found Plymouth Colony
- Puritans settle Massachusetts
- Calvert founds Maryland
- Puritans settle Connecticut
- Williams settles Rhode Island
- Swedes settle Delaware
- Carolinas founded
- English take New Netherland
- Quakers settle New Jersey
- Bacon's Rebellion
- Pennsylvania settled
- Oglethorpe settles Georgia
- Eliza Pinckney introduces indigo

CHAPTER SURVEY

VOCABULARY REVIEW

From this list of vocabulary words, choose the one that best completes each sentence below.

(a) cash crop
(b) compact
(c) emigration
(d) Piedmont
(e) Pilgrims
(f) plantations
(g) proprietary colony
(h) Puritans
(i) rural
(j) self-governing colony
(k) sound
(l) toleration
(m) treason

Elizabeth Blackwell published *A Curious Herbal,* a book of drawings, in 1739. The tomato, called the "love apple," was one of many plants in the colonies that were new to Europeans.

1. Protestants wanting a simpler form of worship in the Church of England were _____.

2. A _____ is an agreement among people.

3. _____ travel for religious reasons.

4. In a _____, the colonists chose their own assembly and governor.

5. The owners chose the governor in a _____.

6. Trying to overthrow a government is _____.

7. The _____ is an upland plateau between the Fall Line and the Appalachians.

8. _____ are large farms that include housing for the farm's workers.

9. Tobacco was Virginia's first _____.

10. _____ means leaving one country to settle in another country.

11. The New England Puritans did not believe in _____ of other religious beliefs.

12. A long, broad inlet of the ocean is a _____.

13. Most colonists lived in _____ areas.

CHAPTER REVIEW

1. (a) Why did some English Separatists move to the Netherlands? (b) Why were those who sailed to America called Pilgrims?

2. (a) What was the mission of the leaders of Massachusetts? (b) Why was self-government important to their mission?

3. In what important ways was Rhode Island different from Massachusetts?

4. (a) Why were colonists in New York unhappy with their government under the Duke of York? (b) How did New Yorkers govern the colony after rebelling in 1689? (c) What does the rebellion show about the colonists' attitude toward self-government?

5. (a) How did William Penn acquire Pennsylvania? (b) How did he keep peace with the local Indians? (c) What did Penn offer to attract settlers from many lands?

6. (a) How did the headright system encourage the rapid settlement of Virginia? (b) Who did field work for Virginia tobacco planters in the early years of the colony? (c) Who was doing most field work for the planters by the late 1600s? (d) Why did this change take place?

7. (a) What were the Calverts' goals in founding Maryland? (b) What did the Maryland assembly do when one of those goals was threatened?

8. (a) What were James Oglethorpe's two goals in founding Georgia? (b) What rules did he make about land and slaves? (c) Why were these rules changed by 1750?

9. (a) What problems caused families to leave Europe in the 1600s? (b) What attractions drew many of the emigrants to the colonies?

10. (a) In which group of colonies were plantations worked by slaves most likely to be found? (b) Which group of colonies contained people from many nations? (c) In which group of colonies were people most likely to live in villages organized around a church?

GEOGRAPHY REVIEW

*CT **1.** Refer to the map "The Colonies in 1650" on page 91. (a) Which countries had settlements on or near the east coast of North America by 1650? (b) Which country had settled farthest north? (c) Which had settled farthest south? (d) Which had the largest area of settlement?

2. Refer to the map "The Thirteen British Colonies 1740" on page 102. List the New England Colonies, the Middle Colonies, and the Southern Colonies.

*CT **3.** Refer to the map "Settlement of the British Colonies" on page 107. (a) Did more settlement of the Carolinas and Georgia take place between 1660 and 1700 or between 1700 and 1760? (b) In what years did settlers move to large areas of the Piedmont? (c) Settlement in the North American

colonies often followed rivers. What rivers within British colonies are shown on this map?

USING THE TOOLS OF HISTORY

*CT **Interpreting Circle Graphs**

Study the circle graph "Colonial Population by Nationality" on page 107. (a) According to this graph, one out of every two colonists in the late 1700s belonged to which group? (b) What percentage of the population was African? (c) Which three groups of colonists from Europe were about the same size?

READING AND THINKING SKILLS

*CT **Outlining**

Review the method of outlining described on page 94. Outline Section 4–3, adding main ideas and including some important details. Use these main entries in the outline:

   III. The Southern Colonies
      A. Virginia
      B. Maryland
      C. The Carolinas
      D. Georgia

''Two Women and the Bear'' illustrated a textbook that schoolmaster Thomas Perry made for his students in Georgia. Few printed books were available in the back country in the 1700s.

CHAPTER 5   1620–1763

LIFE IN THE COLONIES

RURAL LIFE
CITIES AND TRADE
COLONIAL GOVERNMENT

5-1 RURAL LIFE

READ TO FIND OUT

self-sufficient: able to take care of one's own needs

crop rotation: practice of growing different crops on the same land in different years to preserve the soil's fertility

apprentices: persons agreeing to work for a skilled worker for some period to learn a skill

—what the words *self-sufficient, crop rotation,* and *apprentices* mean.

—why farm families relied on homemade goods.

—what work was done by rural families.

—how rural people learned important skills.

—what schooling was available in the colonies.

During colonial times, farm families relied on themselves to take care of their own needs. In other words, they were largely **self-sufficient.** As one farmer wrote: "I never laid out (besides my taxes) more than ten dollars a year, which was for salt, nails, and the like. Nothing to wear, eat, or drink was purchased, as my farm provided all."

COLONIAL FARMS

Everyone in a farm family worked to produce what they needed. Farmers and their sons plowed, planted, and harvested. They also built houses and barns, butchered hogs, sheared sheep, made furniture, and tanned leather for harnesses and boots.

The women of the family spent countless hours making clothing. They began by spinning flax or wool into thread and then weaving the thread into cloth. The cloth was hand sewn into shirts or dresses. More hours were spent washing, ironing, and mending clothes.

Farm women also tended the garden and orchard. They milked the cows, gathered the eggs, and plucked the geese to make feather pillows. From tallow, or animal fat, they made soap and candles. At harvest time they often worked beside the men in the fields.

Cooking was one of the most dangerous jobs on colonial farms. Food was cooked in iron pots in a large fireplace. When the pots were empty, they weighed as much as 40 pounds (18 kilograms). And they were seldom empty. While lifting pots off their hooks above the fire, a woman could hurt her back, get smoke in her eyes, burn her hands, or scorch her clothes.

The hardest work done by farm families was clearing the land. As farmers in New England moved westward, they had to carve farms and villages out of hilly, forested country. Colonial farmers also had to clear new fields often because their farming methods wore out the soil. Only the Pennsylvania Dutch knew how to renew soil by adding natural fertilizers. Farmers in colonial times did not know about **crop rotation.** This is the practice of growing different crops on the same land in different years in order to preserve the soil's fertility.

Despite their lack of knowledge about good farming methods, many colonial farmers were able to grow more grain than they needed for their own use. In the Middle Colonies, for example, farmers grew wheat, rye, barley, oats, and corn. These grains were their main crops. Any grain the family did not need was sent to New York, Baltimore, or Philadelphia for sale.

Activity: Students can give oral reports on foods colonists ate and dishes they prepared (along with recipes). Several students can report on the use of plants the colonists found growing wild, such as sassafras, nettle leaves, shadblow, papaws, and persimmons.

LEARNING A TRADE

In the American colonies, as in the rest of the eighteenth-century world, childhood ended early. By the age of seven, children put aside their baby clothes and dressed like their parents. By this age, too, most youngsters began working alongside their parents. Boys joined their fathers in the fields or in family workshops. Girls learned from their mothers how to spin, weave, sew, and cook.

If a rural family ran a mill, a tannery, or a blacksmith shop, the children learned how the business operated. Women who outlived their husbands often carried on the family mill or shop.

When they were ten or twelve, boys and girls might be sent to live in other households. There they would work as servants or **apprentices** until they reached the age of 21. An apprentice agrees to work for a skilled worker for some period in order to learn a trade.

A skilled worker made this Boston weather vane. It is made of copper in the shape of a grasshopper. Its eyes are green glass.

UNDERSTANDING GEOGRAPHY

TOWNS THAT WENT DOWNHILL

When New England colonists began building towns away from the coast, they found themselves in a hilly, stony area. Dense forests covered the land. Streams cut through narrow V-shaped valleys.

The colonists had two immediate decisions to make. First, where was the best place for their village? Second, where was the best place to clear land to grow their crops and raise their livestock?

The sketch below shows the possible locations for the village and for the farmland. If you were a colonist, would you choose area A, B, or C for the village? Why? Which area would you choose for your farmland? Why?

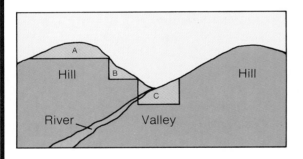

Most colonists chose area A for the village. The reason is quite simple. They wanted to guard against surprise Indian attacks. Area A gave them a good view of the surrounding land and was easier to defend than the other areas.

The farmland that most villagers selected might surprise you. Almost all chose area B. You might think that the land along the river, in the valley, would be the best. In many regions, bottom land is the best—fertile, level, and easy to plow. In much of New England, however, river valleys are quite narrow. There is little level land. And in the springtime when winter snows melt, the rivers can flood the valleys.

The colonists also had another reason for choosing area B. They strongly believed that the best soil would be found near certain species of trees, such as chestnut and black walnut. In fact, these trees usually grow on hillsides, where the soil is well drained and suited for farming.

In addition, the colonists wanted to plant their crops where they would not be damaged by frosts. They looked for the warmest area. Area A, at the highest elevation, would get cold before areas B and C. This is because temperatures drop about 3.5° Fahrenheit (1.9° Celsius) for every 1,000 feet (304.8 meters) above sea level.

Cold air is heavier than warm air. Therefore, as the air got cold at A, it would slide down into the valley (C). Thanks to this ''good air drainage,'' as farmers call it, area B would be the warmest location.

These settlement choices worked well during most of the seventeenth century. In time, however, living patterns changed. New England began to develop manufacturing, and many villagers stopped farming and, instead, worked in the mills.

But the mills were built in the valleys, near the rivers. Mills needed power. In colonial America, the sources of power that we use today—coal, natural gas, oil—were not considered. Water provided the power. The swift-flowing rivers and waterfalls drove waterwheels, which powered the mill machinery.

Each day, workers had to hike down from their hilltop villages to go to work. Even harder, after 12 hours in the mill, they had to climb back up the steep hills to their homes. Gradually, family after family moved downslope to the valley. The towns literally went downhill.

Today there are few traces of the seventeenth-century New England settlements. Forests cover fields where corn, wheat, and hay were once harvested. Stone walls and lonely chimneys stand in silence to mark the outlines of the past.

The eighteenth-century embroidery on the left put parts of two buildings together to make one picture. Both buildings were part of Harvard College.

The hornbook at the right has the alphabet and the Lord's Prayer on it. Children learned to read from hornbooks.

COLONIAL SCHOOLING

Most colonial children received little education. The Middle Colonies and the Southern Colonies had no system of public schools. Instead, wealthy families hired tutors or sent their sons to church schools. Farm families taught their children at home as best they could. There were no schools for slaves, and very few slave owners allowed any sort of schooling for slave children.

New England took the first steps toward a system of public education. It was important to the Puritans that each child learn to read the Bible. After 1647, a town with more than 50 families was required by Massachusetts law to build a school. Connecticut followed with its own public school laws.

Older boys in New England could go from village schools to grammar schools, where they learned Latin, geography, and mathematics. A few young men went on to study at a colonial college such as Harvard, Dartmouth, or Yale. Girls and women were not allowed to attend grammar schools or colleges.

*CT
For discussion: How have Americans' ideas about the importance of education and the place of education in American life changed since colonial times?

SECTION REVIEW Answers will be found on page T 33.

1. Define these words: *self-sufficient, crop rotation, apprentices.*

2. How could a farm family live without spending any more than ten dollars a year?

3. Why was cooking a dangerous job in colonial times?

4. How could a young person learn a trade?

5. Which colonies provided publicly supported education for all children? Why was it important for people to learn how to read?

5-2 CITIES AND TRADE

READ TO FIND OUT

—what the words *exports, triangular trade, raw materials, manufactured goods,* and *imports* mean.

—how cities served as centers of news as well as trade.

—what products were shipped from colonial seaports.

—what products were brought into the colonies.

—how the Navigation Acts improved England's balance of trade.

exports: products sent to another country to sell

triangular trade: colonial pattern of trade between North America, West Indies, and Africa

raw materials: products still in their natural state

manufactured goods: products made by people working with tools or machines

imports: products brought in from another country to sell

In 1750 one out of twenty colonists lived in a city. City dwellers worked as merchants, lawyers, doctors, skilled workers, servants, and laborers. Most blacks living in cities were slaves, but there were also free blacks working in skilled trades and as laborers.

The largest colonial cities—Boston, New York City, Philadelphia, and Charleston—were located on natural harbors or along major rivers, close to the sea. Most roads linking cities and towns were little better than narrow and rutted tracks through the forest. The rivers and sea were the main highways of trade.

CITIES AS CENTERS OF TRADE

Visitors to colonial cities were struck by the noise and the rapid pace of city life. Carriages and freight wagons clattered down the cobblestone streets, chased by packs of barking dogs. Pigs were everywhere, rooting around in the garbage that lined the streets.

The streets were lined with shops displaying an abundance of goods. There were shops selling English silks, laces, telescopes, mousetraps, books, and dozens of other products. Workshops produced American-made copies of the latest English fashions in clothes, hats, and furniture. There were barbers to cut hair and wig makers to make it look long again. Among the shops were inns and taverns. Taverns were good places to hear news from Europe or the other colonies.

NEWSPAPERS AND LETTERS

The same ships that brought trade goods also carried information from distant places. Returning from the docks with the latest news, printers published it in their weekly newspapers. These newspapers kept both

This eighteenth-century engraving shows a tinware shop. The owner, at the left, is showing her wares to a customer.

city and country readers informed about recent events. Benjamin Franklin was the best known publisher of a colonial newspaper. By the age of twenty-four, he owned his own print shop and was publishing the weekly *Pennsylvania Gazette.*

Benjamin Franklin also published a yearly collection of advice, information, and wise sayings. Called *Poor Richard's Almanac*, it was published yearly from 1732 through 1757. In many homes, *Poor Richard's Almanac* was the only book aside from the Bible.

Franklin also improved the colonial postal service. In the 1600s and early 1700s, letters took a long time to reach their destination. Post riders were paid by the postage due on the letters they carried. They usually waited until they had enough letters to pay the expenses of the delivery trip.

Most mail was delivered to an inn or a tavern. A letter might sit there for days or weeks until the person it was intended for claimed it and paid the postage. As late as 1760, mail was carried south from Philadelphia to the Potomac River only eight times a year. Trade goods traveled faster than the mail between many places.

Franklin became deputy postmaster for the colonies in 1753. He shortened routes and introduced road marking and day-and-night riding. He also lowered postage rates. Under Franklin, mail service became swifter and more reliable.

Poor Richard's Almanac was published under Franklin's pen name, Richard Saunders. You may wish to read to the class some of the sayings Franklin included in the almanac, as well as the essay "The Way to Wealth." The essay and many sayings express the spirit of industrious, up-and-coming colonials. (Example: "God helps those who help themselves.") You may wish to concentrate on these.

Colonial Overseas Trade Routes

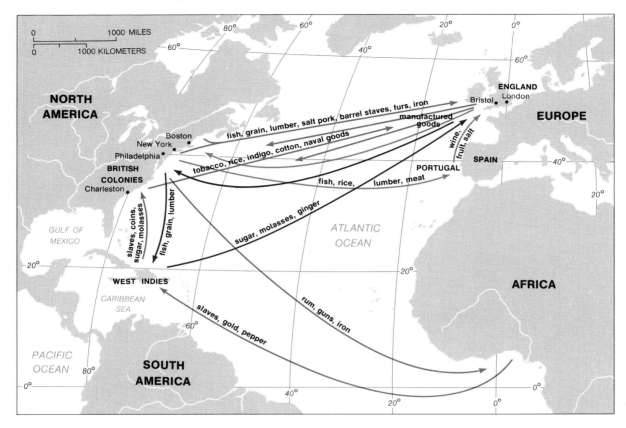

Colonists traded primarily with Europe. One important trade route made a triangle from the American colonies to Africa to the West Indies. Another triangle led from the colonies to the West Indies to England.

For discussion: Have students cite materials and products America exports today. (Two of the most important are wheat and steel.) Why are such exports important to the nation's economy?

MERCHANTS AND TRADE

The leading citizens in colonial cities were the merchants. Boston merchants bought salted cod from New England fishing villages and furs and lumber from settlers in Maine. In New York and Philadelphia, merchants filled their ships with corn, wheat, cattle, and horses from the Middle Colonies. Charleston merchants bought the rice and indigo grown on Carolina plantations.

These goods were valuable **exports.** An export is a product sent to another country to sell. Ships carrying these goods sailed for Spanish, French, and British colonies in the West Indies. Sugar planters there needed food for their slaves and for the horses that turned their sugar mills. The ships returned from the West Indies with slaves, sugar, and molasses, a product left over from sugar making.

Colonial distillers made the molasses into rum, the common drink in taverns. Rum that was not sold in the colonies was shipped to Africa, where it was traded for slaves. The slaves were then taken to the West Indies. Ships carrying West Indian products to North America, American rum to Africa, and African slaves to the West Indies followed a

Activity: On a local map, ask students to trace the routes they take to school every day. Ask them also to determine the longitude and latitude of their homes and school. (They may need to consult a large map or an atlas.)

USING THE TOOLS OF HISTORY

LOCATING PLACES ON A MAP

"Where is it?" is one of the most basic questions geographers ask. To find the answer on a map, they must know where north, south, east, and west are.

Some maps have a compass rose, a diagram that shows these directions. On maps that do not, such as the map on the opposite page, there is a simple way to determine direction. North is *always* at the top of the map. South is at the bottom, east is at the right, and west is at the left. Northeast is between north and east, southwest is between south and west, and so on.

Use the map on the opposite page to answer the following questions.

1. In what direction did ships travel carrying rum, guns, and iron from North America to Africa?

2. In what direction did they travel from the West Indies to England?

3. In what direction is the African continent from Europe?

Many maps contain another guide to finding location: the grid. Grid lines that run north and south are called meridians. Those that run east and west are parallels. The lines are parts of circles, as can be seen on a map of the world or a globe. Because circles are divided into degrees, grid lines are marked in degrees.

The parallel marked 0° is the equator, halfway between the North and South Poles. Distance in degrees north or south of the equator is called **latitude.** The first parallel, in moving north from the equator, is at 20° north latitude. The first parallel south of the equator (not shown) would be 20° south latitude.

The meridian marked 0° is known as the prime meridian. Distance in degrees east or west of this line is called **longitude.** The first meridian west of the prime meridian is 20° west longitude. The first meridian to the east is 20° east longitude.

Using the map again, answer the following questions.

4. What is the latitude of the West Indies?

5. What is the approximate latitude of London?

6. Is most of Europe in the eastern or western longitudes?

7. Through how many degrees of latitude did ships travel from the West Indies to London?

*CT

Answers will be found on page T 33.

triangular route. This pattern is sometimes called the **triangular trade.** In another kind of triangular trade, ships sailed from North America to the West Indies with fish, grain, and lumber. They carried sugar, molasses, and ginger to England, and then sailed back to ports in North America with English goods.

Colonial merchants also shipped goods directly to English ports. Their ships carried lumber, indigo, tobacco, and other **raw materials**—products still in their natural state. In England these raw materials were processed to become **manufactured goods,** or products made by people working with tools or machines. Tobacco leaves were shredded into snuff. Tree trunks were made into masts for ships. Indigo became blue dye. The ships returned to the colonies with manufactured goods such as woolen cloth, dishes, cooking pots, and farm tools.

Remind students that it was John Rolfe, the husband of Pocahontas, who first planted tobacco and thus began the tobacco trade. (See Chapter 3, page 70.)

Fashionable men in the colonies wore powdered wigs made of real hair.

This exchange of colonial raw material for manufactured goods worked well for England's mercantile system. The more manufactured goods the colonists bought, the more jobs there were for English workers. The exchange also worked well for the colonies during the years when very few goods were manufactured in America. The colonists were eager to trade their raw materials for English **imports,** products brought into America to sell.

THE NAVIGATION ACTS

Between 1660 and 1696, Parliament passed a series of laws called the Navigation Acts. They were intended to control trade with the colonies. The acts said that all colonial imports or exports had to be carried in English or colonial ships. Colonial merchants were not allowed to buy and sell goods brought to the colonies by ships from Spain, France, or other nations. Boston shipbuilders kept busy meeting the demand for more colonial cargo ships.

The Navigation Acts also said that certain colonial exports could be shipped only to England or to another English colony. These exports included tobacco, sugar, and indigo. In addition, most colonial imports from the European mainland or from Asia had to pass first through England. There the goods were taxed before they were shipped on to America. The taxes raised money for the English government and also increased the price of foreign-made goods imported into the colonies. As a result, English manufacturers could sell their untaxed goods at lower prices in America.

From the viewpoint of British mercantilists, the Navigation Acts were a success. England did not have to use its precious gold to buy tobacco, sugar, indigo, or other raw materials from foreign nations. It obtained these things from its own colonies in exchange for manufactured goods. The result was an improvement in England's balance of trade and more money in the royal treasury.

Have students review what they learned about mercantilism. (See Chapter 3, page 53.)

SECTION REVIEW   Answers will be found on page T 33.

1. Define these words: *exports, triangular trade, raw materials, manufactured goods, imports.*

2. Identify: Navigation Acts, Benjamin Franklin, *Poor Richard's Almanac.*

3. Why were colonial cities the centers of information as well as trade?

4. Describe the trade between North America and Africa.

5. Explain how the Navigation Acts helped shipbuilders in Boston.

6. Explain how the Navigation Acts helped fill the royal treasury.

5-3 COLONIAL GOVERNMENT

READ TO FIND OUT

—what the words *Parliament, petition, veto, democracy, aristocrats,* and *candidate* mean.

—what rights were important to the colonists.

—who controlled local government in the colonies.

—whom the colonists elected to their assemblies.

Parliament: The English legislature

petition: make a formal request to someone in authority

veto: refuse to approve

democracy: government by the people

aristocrats: people above most of the community in wealth, power, or social standing

candidate: person running for office

In 1707 the Kingdom of England and Wales united with the Kingdom of Scotland under one government, called Great Britain. Colonies were then officially ruled by the British government. By 1750, eight of the thirteen American colonies had become royal colonies. They were New Hampshire, Massachusetts, New York, New Jersey, Virginia, North Carolina, South Carolina, and Georgia. Their governors and other officials were appointed by the British monarch, who had direct control over these officials.

Pennsylvania, Delaware, and Maryland were still proprietary colonies. Their governors were appointed by their proprietors. Connecticut and Rhode Island were self-governing colonies. Under their charters, voters had the right to elect their own governors.

THE RIGHTS OF ENGLISH PEOPLE

In all the colonies, English Americans could trace their political rights back to 1215 and the signing of the *Magna Carta.* The Magna Carta, which is Latin for "Great Charter," was drawn up by nobles and Church leaders unhappy with the rule of King John. It placed limits on the king's power. The Magna Carta listed several rights that the king had to respect. These included the right to be judged by their peers, or equals, for those accused of crimes. By signing the Magna Carta, John was agreeing that even a king's power had limits under law.

In 1265 English people won additional rights when they set up **Parliament,** the English legislature. Gradually, Parliament won the right to pass laws and approve taxes. Parliament had (and still has) two branches, or houses. The House of Lords drew its members from the nobles. The House of Commons was made up of representatives who were not nobles. They were elected by landowners. As the years passed, the House of Commons became the more powerful branch.

Much of the thinking about rights and the limits of rulers was formulated by the English philosopher John Locke, whose *Two Treatises of Government* had a great influence on Thomas Jefferson.

In the late 1600s, Parliament further strengthened its power. King James II had refused to accept some of Parliament's laws. In 1688 many English people rose against him, and in 1689 he was removed from the throne. James was replaced by his daughter Mary and her husband William, ruler of the Netherlands. Parliament agreed to accept William as the new king of England. In return, William agreed to accept a Bill of Rights passed by Parliament. The overthrow of James II and the acceptance of the Bill of Rights are known as the Glorious Revolution.

The Bill of Rights adopted in 1689 gave English people the right to trial by jury. It also gave them the right to **petition,** or make a formal request to, the government. In addition, the Bill of Rights ended the power of the king to **veto,** or refuse to approve, an act of Parliament. After the Glorious Revolution, Parliament alone had the right to pass laws, set taxes, and control England's military forces.

English colonists in America thought of themselves as English citizens. They believed that all the rights gained during the Glorious Revolution belonged to them. Some colonists went even further and began demanding rights not yet recognized in England.

In 1734 a newspaper publisher named John Peter Zenger was jailed for criticizing the royal governor of New York. For eight months Zenger remained in jail while his case became the talk of New York City. His newspaper, however, continued to appear. His wife, Anna, and his children continued to print the weekly paper.

When the case finally came to trial, Zenger's lawyer, Andrew Hamilton, argued that freedom of the press should be a basic right. The jury agreed, finding Zenger not guilty. The Zenger case became a landmark in the history of freedom of the press in America.

Andrew Hamilton addresses the judges at John Peter Zenger's trial. Hamilton's face and posture suggest "a confidence which no terrors could awe."

★ ★ ★ ★ ★ ★ ★ **AMERICAN VALUES IN ACTION** ★ ★ ★ ★ ★ ★ ★ ★

ANDREW HAMILTON

On the morning of August 4, 1735, the attention of all New York centered on a city hall courtroom. John Peter Zenger, a poor printer, was on trial for publishing criticisms of the royal governor.

Zenger had little hope. The governor had handpicked the judges to hear the case. The judges appointed an inexperienced young lawyer to defend Zenger. Now, as morning sunlight slanted through the courtroom windows, the lawyer began a halfhearted defense.

Then a white-haired gentleman rose from his seat at the back of the room. He walked slowly down the aisle, limping from a touch of joint disease. Yet he had, as a friend put it, "a confidence which no terrors could awe."

The courtroom buzzed. The gentleman was Andrew Hamilton, said to be the best lawyer in America. He had come from Philadelphia to try to save the printer.

Hamilton had handled cases for the Penn family of Pennsylvania. He had served as attorney general for the colony and as speaker of the Pennsylvania assembly. The lawyer had even designed Pennsylvania's statehouse—Independence Hall.

Hamilton was born into a noble Scottish clan, and in his twenties fled a Scotland torn by political and religious feuds. Once in the colonies, he favored no religious or political group. Only justice, liberty, and law claimed his loyalty.

The Zenger case rested on questions of justice, liberty, and law. The royal governor had taken bribes and interfered with elections. New York's only newspaper, controlled by the governor, dared not criticize him. Then Zenger started the rival *Weekly Journal,* the first American newspaper to be independent of government control. The little four-page paper boldly attacked the governor's behavior.

For this, Zenger was charged with seditious (seh-DISH-us) libel—making statements to stir up opposition to the government. Under English law, it did not matter whether the statements were true or false.

Hamilton admitted that Zenger had printed the statements. If they were false, Zenger would be guilty of libel. But, he argued, Zenger had printed the truth, and the truth could not be called libel.

Irritated, the judges warned Hamilton that his argument was against English libel law. But Hamilton simply turned to the jurors. He asked them to ignore the opinions of the judges. He urged them "to see with their own eyes, to hear with their own ears, and to make use of their own consciences."

What they heard was a moving defense of freedom of the press. Hamilton insisted that people had the right to know what the government was doing. They must have the freedom to protest the abuses of government. A free press could report government actions and publish the people's opinions. Of course, he said, the press must print only the truth.

This case, Hamilton concluded, "is not the cause of the poor printer, nor of New York alone. . . . It is the best cause. It is the cause of liberty." He placed the fate of Zenger—and of a free press—in the jurors' hands.

Within ten minutes the jurors reached their verdict: "Not guilty." The spectators cheered Zenger, Hamilton, and the jury. The printer was set free to pursue the truth with his ink pots and type.

The Zenger case did not end government attempts to control the press. But, in time, freedom of the press became a basic American right. When Americans created their own government many years later, they wrote that right into the law.

Hamilton did not live to see that final success. He died on August 4, 1741—six years to the day after he rose in that courtroom to defend freedom to print the truth.

COLONIAL ASSEMBLIES

By the 1750s each colony had an elected assembly. The colonists viewed each assembly as a small Parliament. It had the right, they believed, to vote on laws and taxes and to control the colony's military affairs. If a royal governor refused to approve an assembly's laws, the assembly could punish him by refusing to vote funds for his salary. One stubborn governor of North Carolina went 11 years without being paid.

The British government had a different view of colonial assemblies. Both kings and proprietors saw that assemblies were useful for attracting settlers and handling everyday problems. But the British did not see the assemblies as small Parliaments. British monarchs could not veto an act of Parliament, but they had the power to strike down any colonial law. Colonial governors appointed by the Crown, or the ruling monarch, had the same power.

By striking down colonial laws, Britain's rulers were telling the colonists that their rights were limited. Colonial assemblies were supposed to obey the Crown.

LOCAL GOVERNMENTS

Local governments in the colonies were run entirely by the colonists themselves. In New England each town had its own government. In the Southern Colonies local government was organized by county. Both patterns of government were found in the Middle Colonies.

Even today, some New England towns are governed by town hall meetings called by the First Selectman (the chief of the town's board of elected officials).

Drawn swords at a town meeting suggest how heated such discussions sometimes became.

In New England towns, people gathered at the meetinghouse each month to decide local questions. How much should each family pay in local taxes? Where should a new road go? Should pigs be allowed to run loose on the village green or be kept in pens? Each person could speak out on a question before the men of the village voted.

In these meetings, New England villagers were practicing **democracy,** or government by the people. At times, town meetings were filled with heated arguments. Yet the villagers found that they could run their everyday affairs quite well without the help of a king or his officials.

COLONIAL ELECTIONS

In talking with Europeans about America, Benjamin Franklin said that no one should go there if all he or she had to offer was a noble name and title. Americans, Franklin said, "do not inquire concerning a stranger, What is the person?, but, What can the person do?" The leading citizens of the British colonies were hardworking people who gained respect for what they did. They were successful merchants, farmers, planters, and businesspeople.

These leading citizens were the people usually elected to colonial assemblies. They were **aristocrats,** or people who had risen above the rest of the community in terms of wealth, power, or social standing. When

In 1774, when Franklin was in London, he became acquainted with an Englishman named Thomas Paine. On Franklin's advice, Paine went to America and quickly became involved in the American struggle for freedom.

George Washington entertains a visitor. When aristocrats like Washington ran for public office, they also received voters on their estates.

Joshua Johnston was probably the first black portrait painter in America. His portrait of "the McCormick Family" shows one of Baltimore's prosperous merchant families.

In 1758 George Washington was elected to Virginia's House of Burgesses. In his later years as a Burgess, he was a leader in Virginia's opposition to British policies.

running for the assembly, they did not campaign by giving speeches or asking for votes. Yet they did meet the voters. A Virginia planter named George Washington entertained voters by treating the men of his county to an outdoor feast of barbecued beef, ginger cakes, and punch.

Elections took place at the county courthouse or on the village green. Each **candidate,** or person running for office, sat at a table along with the clerk who recorded the votes. One by one, the voters came forward and stated their choice. The candidate receiving a vote would then rise, bow to the voter, and thank him personally.

The right to vote was limited to property owners. By 1750 more than half of all white males owned land and could vote. Year after year the voters chose men of wealth and talent like Washington and Franklin to represent them in colonial affairs. As these leaders worked in the assemblies, they gained valuable experience. They also learned that the people they represented were able to govern themselves.

SECTION REVIEW   Answers will be found on page T33.

1. Define these words: *Parliament, petition, veto, democracy, aristocrats, candidate.*

2. Identify: Magna Carta, Glorious Revolution, House of Lords, House of Commons.

3. How did the Glorious Revolution increase the power of Parliament?

4. How did the colonists view their assemblies?

5. Who controlled local governments in the colonies?

Families on colonial farms relied on themselves for most of the goods they needed. They built their own buildings and furniture, raised their own food, and made their own clothes. They worked to clear new land when the soil in their fields would no longer produce large crops.

Children learned how to do farm work from their parents. Some young people went to live as apprentices in the homes of skilled workers. In New England, young children went to public schools to learn to read and write. The other colonies did not have systems of public schooling.

Port cities along the Atlantic coast were centers of trade and of information as well. Merchants shipped goods to and from ports in the West Indies, Africa, and Europe. Some of the shipping followed a triangular route.

In trade between the colonies and England, the colonies exported raw material and imported manufactured goods. This exchange was part of England's mercantile system.

Trade with the colonies was controlled by the Navigation Acts passed between 1660 and 1696. These acts required that trade goods going to and from the colonies be carried in English or colonial ships. The acts also required that certain exports could be shipped only to England.

By 1750 most of the colonies were royal colonies. The American colonists expected to have the same political and legal rights enjoyed by the people of England. They saw their assemblies as small Parliaments with the right to vote on laws and taxes. But British leaders did not share this view. The British monarch had the power to strike down any colonial law.

The colonists' belief in self-government was strengthened by the experience they had gained in governing their own towns and counties. The belief was felt most strongly by the leading citizens who were elected to the assemblies and by the property owners who voted for these leaders.

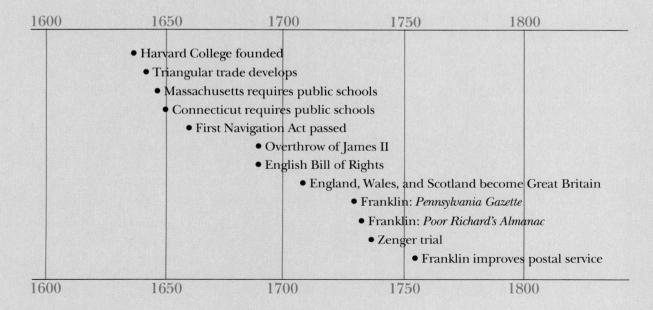

Timeline 1600–1800:
- Harvard College founded
- Triangular trade develops
- Massachusetts requires public schools
- Connecticut requires public schools
- First Navigation Act passed
- Overthrow of James II
- English Bill of Rights
- England, Wales, and Scotland become Great Britain
- Franklin: *Pennsylvania Gazette*
- Franklin: *Poor Richard's Almanac*
- Zenger trial
- Franklin improves postal service

CHAPTER SURVEY

VOCABULARY REVIEW

Choose the phrase that best completes each sentence below.

1. Apprentices
   (a) serve a skilled worker to learn a trade.
   (b) study with a tutor.   (c) work as servants.

2. Aristocrats
   (a) own plantations.   (b) run for elective office.   (c) are above others in wealth or social standing.

3. A candidate
   (a) is a political adviser.   (b) runs for elective office.   (c) is appointed to office.

4. Crop rotation prevents damage to
   (a) soil from loss of fertility.   (b) crops from frost.   (c) crops from drought.

5. Democracy is government by
   (a) the people.   (b) a colonial assembly.
   (c) a king and Parliament.

6. Imports are products
   (a) sent to another country for sale.
   (b) sold in the country where they are made.   (c) brought in from another country for sale.

7. Manufactured goods are products made
   (a) by people working with tools.   (b) for sale abroad.   (c) for shipment to factories.

8. Parliament is
   (a) the House of Lords.   (b) a colonial assembly.   (c) England's law-making body.

9. To petition means to
   (a) make a formal request.   (b) divide something.   (c) vote for someone.

10. Raw materials are
    (a) products still in their natural state.
    (b) the last stages in manufacturing.
    (c) heat used in processing.

11. Self-sufficient means
    (a) able to meet one's own needs.
    (b) self-centered.   (c) able to make up one's own mind.

12. To veto means to
    (a) refuse to do a favor.   (b) refuse to approve.   (c) refuse to pay.

13. Triangular trade involved the
    (a) exchange of rum for slaves.   (b) trade between American colonies, Africa, and the West Indies.   (c) sale of three-cornered hats.

14. Exports are products
    (a) sent to another country for sale.
    (b) smuggled into the country.   (c) used to make other products.

CHAPTER REVIEW

1. (a) How were goods usually sent between colonial cities?   (b) What were the roads like?
(c) How do these facts help to explain why colonial farmers were self-sufficient?

2. (a) Why was education important to Puritans in New England?   (b) What did Massachusetts do to promote education?
(c) How could children learn to read in the Southern and Middle Colonies?

3. (a) What kinds of goods were exported from the colonies?   (b) What kinds of goods were brought into the colonies?   (c) Why were colonists satisfied with this pattern of trade for many years?

4. (a) What was the purpose of the Navigation Acts?   (b) How did the acts protect English exports from foreign competition in the colonies?   (c) Did the acts make imports cheaper or more expensive for colonists?

5. In what two ways did Benjamin Franklin help colonists to become better informed about events in the colonies?

6. (a) What important rights were won during the Glorious Revolution? (b) What right did John Peter Zenger fight for?

7. (a) How were colonial assemblies like Parliament? (b) How were they different?

8. What important lesson did the colonists learn from their town meetings?

9. (a) Who voted in colonial elections? (b) What kind of people did they usually elect to public office?

GEOGRAPHY REVIEW

The crops raised by colonial farmers depended on the soil conditions and the climate where they lived. Use the map "Climates of the United States" in the Resource Center to answer these questions. (a) Rice and indigo grew well in the Humid

A Boston woman embroidered this picture of daily life in the colonies in the 1700s. The "Fishing lady" was a popular needlework pattern.

Subtropical Zone. Which colonies were in that climate zone? (b) Wheat grew best in the Continental Warm Summer Zone. Name at least two colonies that were mainly or entirely in that zone. (c) Farmers in the Continental Cool Summer Zone found corn to be their most dependable crop. Name at least two colonies that were mainly or entirely in that zone.

USING THE TOOLS OF HISTORY

*CT Locating Places on Maps

Study the map "The United States in the World" in the Resource Center to answer these questions. (a) In what direction is Europe from Australia? (b) In what direction is Maine from Mexico? (c) Which latitude line divides the United States through the middle? (d) Which longitude line passes through the Hawaiian Islands?

READING AND THINKING SKILLS

*CT Outlining

(a) Begin an outline of Section 5-3 by using these headings.
    III. Colonial Government
        A. The Rights of English People
        B. Colonial Assemblies
        C. Local Governments
        D. Colonial Elections
(b) Add main ideas to the outline. Place the main ideas next to numbers 1, 2, 3, etc., as shown on page 94. The main ideas for Section 5-3 should cover topics such as New England town meetings, the British view of assemblies, the Magna Carta, the colonial view of assemblies, and the Glorious Revolution.
(c) Add details under some main ideas.

CHAPTER 6   1750-1775

THE COLONIES MOVE TOWARD INDEPENDENCE

THE STRUGGLE FOR NORTH AMERICA
BRITAIN'S NEW POLICY
THE COLONIES UNITE IN PROTEST
FROM PROTEST TO REBELLION

6-1 THE STRUGGLE FOR NORTH AMERICA

READ TO FIND OUT

—what the words *speculators, militia, delegates,* and *strategy* mean.

—why the French built forts in the Ohio Valley.

—why the colonies rejected the Albany Plan of Union.

—how the French and Indian War began.

—what Britain gained from the Treaty of Paris.

speculators: people who seek profits from risky investments

militia: group of citizens trained to fight in an emergency

delegates: people chosen to speak and act for others

strategy: overall plan

These wars in the colonies were named after the reigning British monarchs. Reigns: William III, 1689–1702; Anne, 1702–1714; George II, 1727–1760.

By the late 1600s England and France were the most powerful nations in Europe. Each country tried to strengthen itself by building an empire abroad. Both had colonies in North America and the West Indies and trading stations in Africa and India. Between 1689 and 1748, the two nations went to war with each other three times. They fought not only in Europe but in their colonies as well.

King William's War, which began in 1689, set the pattern in the North American colonies for the conflicts that followed. The French

European Claims in North America 1750

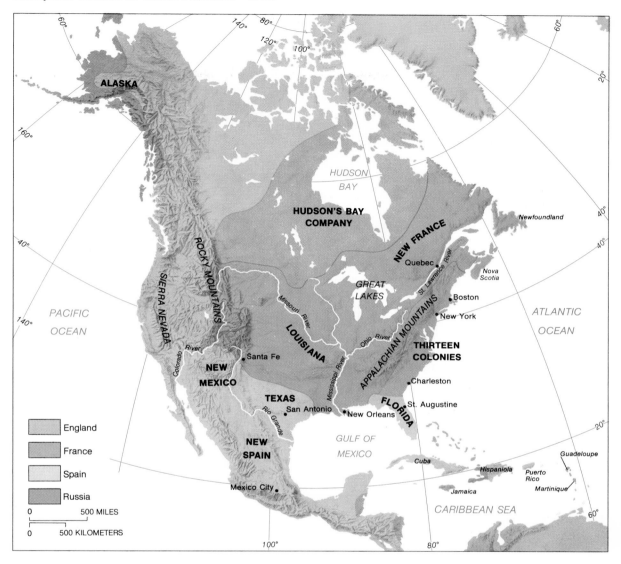

and their Indian allies attacked frontier settlements in New England and New York. At the same time, New England troops, British forces, and Iroquois warriors attacked New France.

King William's War ended in 1697 without a clear winner. Both sides returned captured territory to the previous owner. Queen Anne's War, however, which lasted from 1702 to 1713, was a victory for Great Britain. The treaty that ended the war gave Newfoundland, Nova Scotia, and Hudson Bay to Great Britain. The third war, King George's War, lasted from 1744 to 1748. Neither side gained any territory. Although France and Great Britain were no longer at war, they continued to compete for colonies and trade.

Queen Anne outlived her six children. Her cousin George ruled after her.

CONFLICT OVER THE OHIO VALLEY

During King George's War, the seeds of a new conflict were planted in the Ohio Valley. French coureurs de bois had been the first Europeans to reach the valley, and France claimed the region as part of New France. Pennsylvania and Virginia, however, insisted that it belonged to them. Pennsylvanians began crossing the Appalachian Mountains to set up fur-trading stations.

The traders were soon joined by land **speculators** from Virginia. A speculator is a person who seeks large profits from a risky investment. A group of speculators persuaded the Iroquois and the Delaware to sign a treaty giving Virginia the land south of the Ohio River. The speculators hoped to sell some of the land to settlers at a profit.

The leaders of New France were alarmed. They sent troops to take control of the northern Ohio Valley. By 1753 the French had built a string of forts in what is now western Pennsylvania.

Washington had applied to the governor of Virginia for a military commission. In 1753 he was appointed a major. Without previous military experience, he read books on tactics and strategy. In 1754 he was promoted to lieutenant colonel. In May 1754 he had a skirmish with the French and captured 21 prisoners. He wrote, ''I heard the bullets whistle, and believe me there is something charming in the sound.''

Governor Robert Dinwiddie of Virginia realized that the French would not leave the Ohio Valley unless they were driven out by force. In 1754 he ordered a twenty-two-year-old colonel in the Virginia **militia** (muh-LISH-uh) to challenge the French. A militia is a group of citizens who are trained to fight in an emergency. Colonel George Washington was told to build a fort at the point where the Allegheny (AL-uh-GAY-nee) and the Monongahela (muh-NAHN-guh-HEE-luh) rivers join to form the Ohio River.

Washington led 150 troops across the Appalachian Mountains into southwestern Pennsylvania. There he found that the French had reached the fork of the Ohio River first and were building Fort Duquesne (doo-KAYN). Washington and his troops quickly built a stockade called Fort Necessity. A large French and Indian force attacked Washington's fort. After a nine-hour battle, the Virginians were forced to surrender. Washington and his surviving troops were allowed to return home, leaving the Ohio Valley to the French.

THE ALBANY PLAN OF UNION

Before the fall of Fort Necessity, seven colonies sent **delegates**—people chosen to speak and act for them—to a meeting, or congress, in Albany, New York. The delegates were concerned about renewed war with France. They knew that the colonies were not prepared for a conflict and needed a plan of defense.

Tell the class they will learn more about Franklin in Chapters 7 and 8.

Benjamin Franklin, a Pennsylvania delegate, offered a plan of union for the defense of the colonies. He suggested that the colonial assemblies send representatives to a "grand council." It would make treaties with the Indians and tax the colonies to pay for soldiers and forts. The

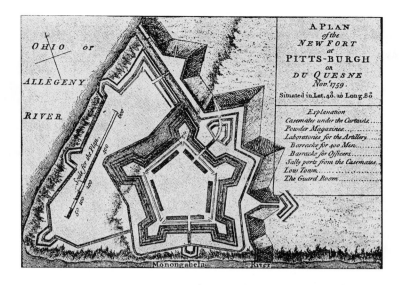

General Braddock was killed near France's Fort Duquesne. This drawing is a plan of Fort Pitt, built by the British in 1759 on the site of Fort Duquesne.

delegates approved Franklin's Albany Plan of Union, but not a single colonial assembly accepted it. The assemblies wanted to keep the power to tax for themselves.

THE FRENCH AND INDIAN WAR

In 1755 British General Edward Braddock arrived in Virginia to drive the French out of the Ohio Valley. He marched on Fort Duquesne with about 1,400 British troops. There were an additional 450 colonial soldiers led by Washington.

Braddock was used to fighting on the open battlefields of Europe, where he could keep the enemy in view. War in America was different. Washington warned Braddock that the French and their Indian allies would use the forest for cover and would launch surprise attacks. The general, however, had no time for the opinions of a colonial officer. The result was a disaster for the British. Near Fort Duquesne, Braddock and 1,000 soldiers were killed or wounded in a French ambush.

The conflict, which the colonists called the French and Indian War, now spread beyond North America. In 1756 Britain and France officially declared war on each other. Battles were fought in Europe, Africa, India, and the West Indies and on the high seas.

The British continued to lose ground in North America. In 1756 the Marquis de Montcalm (mar-KEE duh mahnt-KAHM), commander of the French forces, destroyed Britain's Fort Oswego on Lake Ontario. The next year Montcalm advanced southward. He built Fort Ticonderoga (tī-kahn-dur-Ō-guh) and destroyed Britain's Fort William Henry. Western New England and central New York were now open to attacks.

*CT
For discussion: What might Washington have learned about military tactics and strategy from the French victory over Braddock?

The French and Indian War   1755-1763

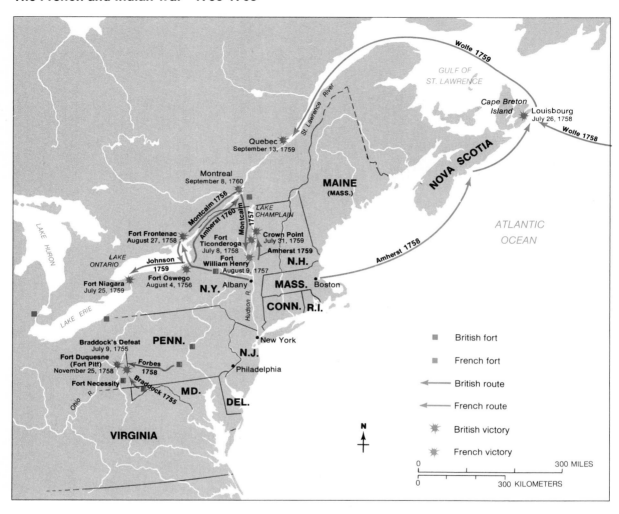

Early in the war, France seemed likely to win. The year 1759 brought glory to the British and disaster to the French.

Activity: Have students write reports on Pitt, one of England's great prime ministers. Points to consider: What was Pitt's attitude toward the colonists? To the Patriots during the Revolutionary War?

FROM DEFEAT TO VICTORY

Faced with defeat, King George II and Parliament gave one of Britain's most capable leaders, William Pitt, complete control of the war effort. Pitt had a **strategy,** or overall plan, for seizing France's North American empire and winning the war. First, he left the fighting in Europe to Britain's German allies. He sent them money but no troops. Second, he hurled most of Britain's forces against the French in North America.

To lead these forces, Pitt chose two young commanders, Jeffrey Amherst and James Wolfe. In 1758 they took the French fortress of Louisbourg, opening the Gulf of St. Lawrence to British warships. In the West, British and New England troops captured Fort Frontenac (FROHNT-NAHK). General John Forbes, aided by Washington and the Virginia militia, advanced to the fork of the Ohio River. The out-

General Wolfe's troops climbed the cliffs below Quebec in the dark. An English artist showed the landing, the climb, and the battle all taking place at once.

numbered French blew up Fort Duquesne rather than turn it over to the British. In its place the British built Fort Pitt.

In 1759 Fort Niagara fell to the British. Then Crown Point was captured. Meanwhile, General Wolfe and his 9,000 troops sailed up the St. Lawrence River toward Quebec, the heart of New France.

Quebec was located on high, jagged cliffs above the river. It was protected by Montcalm's battle-tested troops. The city seemed secure. But Wolfe found a narrow path up the cliffs. When September 13 dawned, the astonished French found the Plains of Abraham outside the city swarming with British troops. In the battle that followed, both generals were killed, but the British won a decisive victory.

In 1760 General Amherst captured Montreal. New France then surrendered. Fighting continued in other parts of the world through 1762, but the French were defeated on all battlefields.

THE TREATY OF PARIS

The French and Indian War ended in February 1763, when a peace treaty was signed in Paris. From France, Britain gained French Canada and Louisiana east of the Mississippi, except for the city of New Orleans. From France's ally, Spain, Britain received Florida. France kept its Caribbean islands and two islands near Newfoundland. To repay Spain for its aid, France gave its ally New Orleans and Louisiana west of the Mississippi.

Britain was now the most powerful nation in the world. The British navy ruled the seas. The French army had been defeated in Europe. North America east of the Mississippi was part of the British Empire.

The American colonists joined in the victory celebrations. They were glad to be rid of the French threat to their frontiers. They were also proud to be part of a mighty empire.

After Braddock's defeat, Washington returned to Mount Vernon. But several months later—in August 1755—he accepted a new commission. As a colonel he commanded Virginia's troops. By the end of the war, he was the best–known colonial soldier.

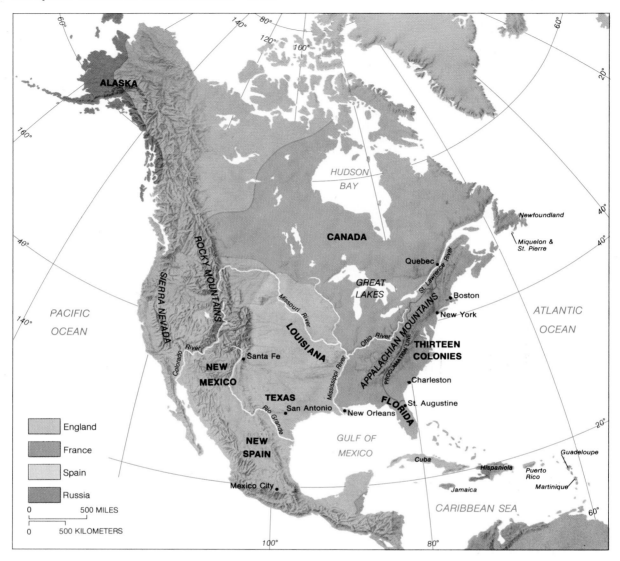

After the Treaty of Paris, France held only two small islands off Newfoundland and part of Hispaniola. France had been driven from North America, and British territory now extended west to the Mississippi River.

SECTION REVIEW   Answers will be found on page T 35.

1. Define these words: *speculators, militia, delegates, strategy.*

2. Identify: George Washington, Fort Duquesne, James Wolfe.

3. Why did the French build forts in the Ohio Valley in the 1750s?

4. Why did the colonial assemblies reject the Albany Plan of Union even though their delegates had approved it?

5. What was William Pitt's strategy for winning the war?

6. What territory in North America did Great Britain gain in the Treaty of Paris?

6-2 BRITAIN'S NEW POLICY

READ TO FIND OUT

—what the words *proclamation, revenue, customs duties,* and *repeal* mean.

—what the purpose of the Proclamation Line of 1763 was.

—how Britain tried to stop colonial smuggling.

—why the Sugar Act was passed.

—why colonists denied Parliament the right to tax them.

proclamation: official announcement

revenue: income to meet government expenses

customs duties: taxes on goods imported into the colonies

repeal: do away with

After the Treaty of Paris, Britain had to try to keep peace in its new territories. West of the Appalachian Mountains, most of the Indian tribes were hostile to the British. Some were still loyal to the French. Others sought revenge after being cheated by dishonest fur traders from the British colonies. All the tribes feared that the trickle of settlers coming across the mountains would soon become a flood. Many of Britain's leaders realized that a war between Indians and frontier settlers could break out at any moment.

THE PROCLAMATION OF 1763

Britain's new king, George III, tried to solve problems on the frontier. In October 1763 he issued a **proclamation,** or official announcement. The king proclaimed that the crest of the Appalachian Mountains was now a boundary line between the colonies and the Indian lands. To cross the Proclamation Line, as it was called, fur traders had to have a

Students can locate the Proclamation Line on the map on the facing page.

Erminnie A. Smith drew an Iroquois sun ceremony in the 1700s. The Iroquois danced to give thanks to the Great Spirit.

Chief Pontiac had fought on the side of the French in the French and Indian War. He and the 18 tribes that he led traveled more than 1,000 miles (1,600 kilometers) during the rebellion.

royal license. Colonists could not settle on lands west of the line until treaties were signed with the Indians. Colonists who had already settled on these lands were ordered to leave.

The Proclamation of 1763 was greeted by a storm of protest in the colonies. Colonists who wanted to move westward resented the new rules. Colonies claiming land west of the Appalachians were afraid that their claims would no longer be respected by Britain. Investors who had received western land grants from colonial governments feared that their grants were now worthless.

PONTIAC'S REBELLION

While the leaders of Parliament were still debating the proclamation, they received distressing news from America. Pontiac, an Ottawa chief, had united several tribes and declared war on the English. The Indians destroyed every British fort west of the Appalachians except Detroit, Pitt, and Niagara. Then they attacked the back-country settlements in Pennsylvania, Maryland, and Virginia. The Indians killed 2,000 settlers. It took two years of hard fighting to defeat Pontiac's warriors. Most of that fighting was done by British army troops.

The British called this war Pontiac's Rebellion. It convinced Parliament that a large force of British soldiers, perhaps 10,000, was needed in America to keep order on the frontier. Supplying such a force would cost a great deal of money.

WAR DEBTS AND NEW TAXES

Parliament did not suggest that the money come from taxpayers in England. Britain was staggering under a heavy debt left over from the French and Indian War. To pay the war debt, Parliament had already increased taxes in Britain. A new tax on cider had so angered taxpayers in one part of Britain that they rioted.

Taxpayers in Britain were unwilling to pay more taxes. So Parliament looked for a new source of **revenue**—income to meet the expenses of government. Parliament was guided in its search for revenue by George Grenville. He was the minister of finance in the British government. Like most members of Parliament, Grenville believed that the colonies should help to pay for their own defense.

Many American colonists saw things differently. The Navigation Acts, they said, gave British merchants a monopoly of valuable colonial products. Britain's control of colonial trade added greatly to Britain's wealth. The colonies felt they were already helping enough. Besides, Britain had not kept an army in America in peacetime before. Colonists did not want a permanent force of British soldiers in the colonies now.

Colonists paid import duties with money like this 16-shilling note from Pennsylvania.

Richard Brunton painted Mrs. Reuben Humphreys of Connecticut wearing fashionable clothes imported from England.

REVENUE FROM THE COLONIES

These arguments did not impress George Grenville. He set out to make the colonies a source of revenue. One way to do this was to change the way of collecting **customs duties**—charges paid on goods imported into the colonies.

In the past, the king's customs officers had done a poor job of collecting duties on imports. Colonial merchants often smuggled goods into the colonies without paying the necessary duties. Grenville gave customs officers the power to search colonial warehouses and ships for smuggled goods. Shipowners were ordered to fill out detailed forms every time one of their ships entered or left a harbor. The British navy was commanded to patrol the Atlantic coast for smugglers.

In addition, colonists accused of smuggling were to be tried in a new admiralty court set up in Nova Scotia. British admiralty courts, which dealt with laws covering shipping, did not have juries. An accused person was treated as guilty until proven innocent. The new court was needed, Grenville felt, because colonial juries seldom found local smugglers guilty. To colonial merchants, however, the admiralty court was a threat to their rights as British citizens. It was especially a threat to the right to trial by jury.

Grenville's efforts to raise revenue also included changes in customs duties on goods entering the colonies. In 1764 Parliament passed the Sugar Act. The act put new duties on imports, including sugar, coffee, cloth, and wines. Duty was reduced on imported molasses.

In the past, colonial merchants had avoided the molasses duty by smuggling molasses into the colonies from the French West Indies.

*CT

Students are now beginning their study of the events that drove Britain and America apart. Ask students to consider two very different points of view. Americans felt they were being treated unjustly. The British thought they were doing what was right and necessary. What arguments can students find to support each side?

IDENTIFYING POINTS OF VIEW

*CT

Two people viewing the same fact, event, or situation may describe it in very different ways. A parent, for example, may say that 11:00 P.M. is too late to go to bed on a week night. A teenager may insist that 11:00 P.M. is too early for bedtime on a week night. The time is the same, but the viewpoints of the people describing it are different.

A person's point of view is the way that he or she looks at life. A viewpoint is the result of the person's age, experiences, and beliefs.

Sometimes a large group of people—or even a whole nation—shares a point of view. The British saw the thirteen American colonies as a part of their worldwide empire. They expected the colonists to share the costs of defending the empire. The British also expected the colonists to obey the empire's laws—the acts of Parliament.

The American colonists also saw themselves as citizens of the British Empire. The colonists, however, had grown accustomed to governing themselves and deciding what taxes they should pay.

The following statements express different points of view about Parliament and taxation. Decide which of the statements express the British viewpoint and which express the American viewpoint.

1. "The British legislature, as to the power of making laws, represents the whole British Empire."

2. "The Parliament of Great Britain has no right to legislate for us."

3. "Are they only English when they ask for protection, but not English when taxes are required to enable this country to protect them?"

4. "It is . . . essential to the freedom of a people, and the undoubted right of Englishmen, that no taxes be imposed on them but with their own consent."

Answers will be found on page T 35.

Customs officials had looked the other way. Grenville believed that the merchants could afford to pay the new duty. He made sure that it would be collected.

PROTESTING THE SUGAR ACT

Merchants were outraged by the Sugar Act. They were not used to paying duties on molasses at all. Because rum made from molasses was a highly profitable product, New England would be hard hit by a tax that would really be collected. "Men of war [warships] are sent here not to protect our trade, but to distress it," said a merchant.

Seven of the thirteen colonial assemblies sent petitions to the British government. Most of the petitions claimed that the new duties would ruin colonial trade. The petitioners asked that the duties be **repealed,** or done away with.

A few petitions, however, raised a different issue: Did Parliament have the right to pass the Sugar Act in the first place? If the act was just another effort to control trade, like the Navigation Acts, Parliament was

*CT
Activity: Students can stage a debate over the Sugar Act. Several students can represent Lord Grenville and his aides. Others can represent the American merchants. Each side can have seven minutes for presentation and five minutes for rebuttal. Remind students they must find good reasons and arguments to support their sides. Later, other students can tell which side they would support and why.

This conference room was part of Virginia's House of Burgesses. The restored building is part of Colonial Williamsburg.

within its rights. But Grenville had said that the act was meant to raise revenue. If that was so, then Parliament was trying to tax the colonies.

In the British colonies, as in Great Britain itself, the power to tax was seen as the power to take away someone's property. Such a dangerous power could be given only to an assembly of representatives elected by the taxpayers themselves. But the colonists had no representatives in Parliament. Therefore, said the petitioners, Parliament had no right to tax them.

This argument made sense to the citizens of Boston. They held a town meeting to protest "taxation without representation." Boston merchants stopped wearing English lace and ruffles. The students at Yale College in New Haven, Connecticut, agreed that they could do without "foreign liquors" taxed by the Sugar Act.

*CT

Ask students to write in their own words a definition of "taxation without representation."

SECTION REVIEW Answers will be found on page T 35.

1. Define these words: *proclamation, revenue, customs duties, repeal.*

2. Identify: Proclamation Line of 1763, Pontiac, George Grenville.

3. What event convinced Parliament that a large force of British troops was needed in America?

4. How did George Grenville try to stop colonial merchants from smuggling?

5. Why did Parliament pass the Sugar Act?

6. Why did colonists claim that Parliament had no right to tax them?

6-3 THE COLONIES UNITE IN PROTEST

READ TO FIND OUT

boycott: refuse to buy or use

massacre: random killing of many people

—what the words *boycott* and *massacre* mean.

—how the colonists united against the Stamp Act.

—what the Declaratory Act said.

—why the colonists protested against the Townshend Acts.

—how the Boston Massacre changed colonists' thinking.

The protest against the Sugar Act did not spread beyond the northern colonial cities. Most American colonists did not feel as though they had been taxed. The new duties were simply included in the price of the imported products they bought. But George Grenville, Britain's minister of finance, had another idea for raising revenue in America. Soon colonists from New Hampshire to Georgia would be protesting "taxation without representation."

THE STAMP ACT

Stamps like this one caused an uproar in the colonies. All printed documents were required to bear stamps.

In 1765 Parliament passed the Stamp Act. Under this act, every legal document, almanac, diploma, and newspaper in British America had to use special stamped paper or had to have a stamp on it. Even dice and playing cards were to be stamped.

Colonists were to buy the special paper or stamps from stamp agents appointed in the colonies. Colonists who refused to obey the Stamp Act would be tried in admiralty court. Again, the right of British citizens to trial by jury was in danger. Unlike the Sugar Act duties, the Stamp Act would be felt by almost everyone in the colonies. For the first time, Parliament was directly taxing the colonists in order to raise revenue.

PROTESTING THE STAMP ACT

When news of the Stamp Act's passage reached America, a storm of protest arose. The Virginia House of Burgesses, led by a fiery new member named Patrick Henry, declared that only Virginians could tax Virginians. The Rhode Island General Assembly ordered the colony's officials to ignore the Stamp Act. Then the Massachusetts assembly called for a meeting of all the colonies to protest the new act.

In October 1765 delegates from nine colonies met at New York City in the Stamp Act Congress. At first there was a confusing clamor as people from different regions tried to make themselves heard. Then Christopher Gadsden of South Carolina spoke the words that brought order to the meeting. "There ought to be no more New Englanders, no New Yorkers," he said, "but all of us Americans."

The delegates drew up petitions addressed to Parliament. They insisted that Parliament had no right to tax the colonies and called for the repeal of the Stamp Act. Their statements were bold, but their language was respectful. One petition said that American colonists "glory in being subjects of the best of kings, having been born under the most perfect form of government."

For discussion: What was important about Gadsden's words? What relatively new idea did they suggest? (You may wish to point out that even many years after the Revolution, some Americans thought their primary allegiance was to their states.)

SONS AND DAUGHTERS OF LIBERTY

Less respectful forms of protest were also used to fight the Stamp Act. First in Boston and then in other cities, there were riots. Throughout the colonies, local groups were organized to resist the Stamp Act. These groups, which took the name Sons of Liberty, were often led by business people or local politicians.

Samuel Adams, a member of the Massachusetts assembly, helped to organize the Boston Sons of Liberty. People listened to Adams because he spoke plainly and directly. More than any other leader, he knew how to put arguments about the rights of the colonists into words that everyone could understand.

Some Bostonians thought Samuel Adams was a dangerous radical. He was a constant critic of British rule. Point out that students will learn more about him in connection with the Boston Massacre and the Boston Tea Party.

The Sons of Liberty stirred up crowds against the stamp agents. Before the act took effect in November, all the agents had resigned. The Sons of Liberty warned court officers, shipowners, newspaper publishers, and everyone else not to use the hated stamps. The threats of violence angered some of the colonists. Most, however, supported their local Sons of Liberty, electing many of the leaders to the town government or the colonial assembly.

Colonists also took other action against the Stamp Act. They made banners reading, "Liberty, property, and no stamps." In town meetings, they agreed to **boycott** British products, refusing to buy or to use them. To support the boycott, women organized Daughters of Liberty groups. Trade came to a standstill.

THE DECLARATORY ACT

Soon the stamps were not being sold or used anywhere in the colonies. In addition, the colonial boycott was hurting British trade. Exports to America fell sharply. Angry English merchants petitioned Parliament, demanding the act's repeal.

The *Pennsylvania Journal* stopped publishing rather than pay for stamps. It showed a stamp as the cause of the paper's "death."

Colonial Trade with Britain

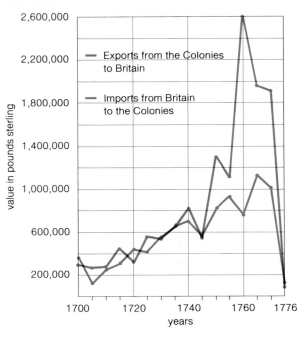

Colonial boycotts caused a steep drop in trade with Britain.

News of protests in the colonies spread to Europe. A German book showed Bostonians burning stamped papers.

Activity: Students can write editorials for colonial newspapers about Parliament's enactment of the Declaratory Act. Each student can decide whether the editorial should represent the views of a loyal supporter of the Crown or a Patriot.

In March 1766 Parliament voted to repeal the Stamp Act. Yet the members of Parliament did not accept the colonists' claim that Parliament had no right to tax them. To be sure that the American colonists understood this, they passed the Declaratory Act. The act stated that Parliament had the right to pass laws for the colonies "in all cases whatsoever." Most of the colonists were too busy celebrating their victory to notice Parliament's challenge.

Perhaps they were also too busy to notice a change in their own thinking. After the struggle against the Stamp Act, the colonists began to wonder about many other acts of Parliament. More and more, they were unhappy with the laws that controlled trade and limited what the colonies could manufacture.

THE TOWNSHEND ACTS

The Declaratory Act made the members of Parliament feel better, but it raised no revenue. In 1767 a new minister of finance, Charles Townshend, tried again to tax the colonies through customs duties. He persuaded Parliament to pass laws placing new duties on glass, lead, paint, paper, and tea. These laws, called the Townshend Acts, also set up new admiralty courts. More customs officers were sent to colonial ports.

The Sons of Liberty sprang into action. Samuel Adams and his friends in Boston wrote letters to groups in other towns. They flooded the newspapers with articles warning that Britain was trying to destroy the rights of the colonists. Marching in torchlight parades, the Sons of Liberty protested against the Townshend Acts and sang "liberty songs."

Again, colonists boycotted British products. In New England and Virginia, Daughters of Liberty asked their fellow colonists to stop drinking tea. They also held spinning bees with their neighbors. They would, they said, make clothes out of homespun instead of English cloth.

There was new violence in Boston. In June 1768 customs officers accused John Hancock of smuggling and seized his ship *Liberty*. Hancock was one of Boston's wealthiest merchants and a strong supporter of the Sons of Liberty. The rioting that followed the seizure of the *Liberty* frightened customs officials so much that they called for protection from British troops.

John Hancock was a leading figure in the colonies' struggle against Great Britain. He was president of the Continental Congress and first to sign the Declaration of Independence. His bold signature is responsible for all signatures being known as "John Hancocks."

THE BRITISH ARMY IN BOSTON

In October 1768 two regiments of red-coated British soldiers arrived in Boston. Three years earlier Parliament had passed the Quartering Act. The act required colonial governments to provide quarters, or lodging, for British troops. The Boston city government declared that there were no quarters available. The British commander then took the buildings that he needed. Included was the town's favorite meeting place, Faneuil (FAN-el) Hall.

Each morning the people of Boston woke to the beating of drums and the tramp of marching feet. To Samuel Adams, the troops were proof that Great Britain would stop at nothing to control the colonies. His cousin John Adams, a widely respected lawyer, agreed with him. The two cousins began to think about a complete break between the colonies and Great Britain. Samuel Adams and other Sons of Liberty set out to show the people of Boston that Britain was their enemy.

Colonists met in taverns such as Boston's Red Lyon Inn to discuss the events of the day.

THE BOSTON MASSACRE

In Boston tension grew between citizens and soldiers. Then, on March 5, 1770, an angry crowd jeered at a group of nine soldiers. They threw whatever came to hand—sticks, snowballs, oyster shells, ice chunks. One soldier fell to the ground.

Without orders, the troops began firing into the crowd. Five people, including a black sailor named Crispus Attucks, were killed. Rioting was prevented only when the Massachusetts governor promised citizens that the troops would be removed from Boston. He also promised that the soldiers involved in the shooting would be brought to trial.

Tell students they will learn more about John Adams as a member of the Continental Congress (Chapter 7) and as the United States' second President (Chapter 9).

★ ★ ★ ★ ★ ★ ★ **AMERICAN VALUES IN ACTION** ★ ★ ★ ★ ★ ★ ★

JOHN ADAMS

When John Adams was a child, his father hoped that he would go to college and study for the ministry. But the boy preferred to escape the classroom and roam the countryside.

At wits' end, his father finally asked, "What would you be, child?"

"Be a farmer," John stubbornly replied.

The stubborn boy was also fiercely competitive. He wanted to fly his kite higher than other boys did, to be better. When he decided that lack of schooling would make him a "fool," he plunged into his studies. John did well enough to enter Harvard College. But he took up law instead of the ministry.

Adams yearned for glory and success as a lawyer. Yet he also wanted to serve the people with "noble achievements."

When the conflict with Parliament began, Adams was swept up in the colonists' cause. He used his legal training to protest British policies. Then, on March 5, 1770, British soldiers fired on a mob in the "Boston Massacre."

That night, Adams stayed up late worrying. Justice and the law, he believed, were more important than political passions. And the law said that every accused person had the right to a fair trial. Who, he wondered, would defend the hated British in Boston?

As a supporter of colonial rights, Adams would be expected to condemn the soldiers. Adams, however, was as independent as ever. He decided to defend the British.

Adams's decision outraged many Bostonians. Rocks were flung through his windows. He was jeered on the streets. He lost nearly half of his clients. But he marched firmly into court and, with his colleague Josiah Quincy, argued that the British soldiers had fired in self-defense.

Thanks to Adams, the British soldiers received a fair trial in Boston. This was the first of the many "noble achievements" for which he would long be remembered.

Colonial artist John Singleton Copley sketched John Adams in wig and knee breeches. Copley painted Adams's portrait from this study.

A special issue of the Boston *Gazette* screamed "BOSTON MASSACRE" in a headline. A **massacre** is the random killing of many people. By using this word, the *Gazette* blamed the violence on the soldiers.

John Adams and Josiah Quincy agreed to defend the soldiers at their trial. They based their case on law, not feelings. Adams carefully explained to the jury that it was not murder under English law to fight back when attacked. The jury found seven of the soldiers innocent. Two others received mild punishments.

Josiah Quincy later served as a member of Congress and as president of Harvard College.

Crispus Attucks, a runaway slave who became a sailor, was one of five colonists killed in the Boston Massacre. The artist did not see the scene himself. The engraving was made in the 1800s.

Samuel Adams hoped that the Boston Massacre would convince colonists that Britain was their enemy. Americans' anger did not last, however, because their boycott of British products had cut imports by half. In 1770 Parliament repealed all of the Townshend duties except the one on tea. The colonists could avoid the tea duty by buying smuggled tea. They ended their protests, and life returned to normal.

Yet an important change had taken place. British soldiers had fired on British subjects in Boston. The might of Great Britain no longer gave American colonists a feeling of security. Many now saw British power as a threat to their freedom.

*CT
Activity: Students can research the Boston Massacre and write papers presenting what they think might be the closing arguments of the prosecuting or defense attorneys.

SECTION REVIEW   Answers will be found on page T 35.

1. Define these words: *boycott, massacre.*

2. Identify: Stamp Act, Sons and Daughters of Liberty, Samuel Adams, John Hancock, Boston Massacre, John Adams.

3. How did colonists unite to protest the Stamp Act?

4. What power did the Declaratory Act say Parliament had?

5. Why did the colonists protest against the Townshend Acts?

6. How did the Boston Massacre change colonists' views of Britain?

6-4 FROM PROTEST TO REBELLION

READ TO FIND OUT

—what the words *Patriots* and *Loyalists* mean.

—how committees of correspondence united the colonies.

—why colonists protested against the Tea Act.

—how Parliament reacted to the Boston Tea Party.

—how the First Continental Congress backed up its demands.

Patriots: colonists supporting the Continental Congress (and finally independence for the colonies)

Loyalists: colonists remaining loyal to Britain

A period of calm followed the repeal of the Townshend Acts. Still, a few American colonists tried to keep the spirit of protest alive. Mercy Otis Warren of Massachusetts wrote a play about a greedy tyrant, a ruler who misused power. Everyone who read the play knew immediately that the tyrant was really Thomas Hutchinson. Hutchinson was the royal governor of Massachusetts. In the years that followed, Warren continued to write plays and poetry in defense of the rights of the colonists.

John Singleton Copley painted many wealthy Bostonians. At right is Patriot, playwright, and poet Mercy Otis Warren.

Mrs. Hallam was the most popular actress in the colonies.

COMMITTEES OF CORRESPONDENCE

In 1772 Governor Hutchinson announced that he and the colony's judges would now be paid by the king. The governor and judges no longer had to worry that the Massachusetts assembly might refuse to pay their salaries. It would now be easier for them to carry out unpopular acts of Parliament.

Alarmed by the governor's announcement, the people of Boston came together in a town meeting. At Samuel Adams's suggestion, they set up a committee of correspondence. The committee was to correspond, or exchange information by letter, with other towns about British actions. Soon riders were carrying news, protests, and ideas to committees of correspondence throughout the colonies.

THE BOSTON TEA PARTY

In the summer of 1773, the committees spread the news that Parliament had passed the Tea Act. The law was designed to help the British East India Company. Its warehouses overflowed with unsold tea.

The Tea Act gave the East India Company the right to bypass British and colonial merchants and to sell tea directly to colonial shopkeepers.

Activity: Students can write letters as they might have been written by members of the committee of correspondence. The letters can inform other members of the committee living some way from the city about the Boston Tea Party.

The Sons of Liberty made "salt water tea" at the Boston Tea Party. This British engraving of the scene was published in 1789.

*CT

For discussion: What events other than the Boston Tea Party might have made Parliament think the Coercive Acts were necessary? Why might Parliament think the Tea Party was the most extreme and dangerous act yet?

The act did not remove the Townshend duty on British tea brought to the colonies. But the price was made so low that it was cheaper for colonists to buy taxed English tea than smuggled Dutch tea.

Merchants in America feared that they would be driven out of the tea business by the East India Company. Once the company had a monopoly, they warned their fellow colonists, the price of tea would be raised and the tea tax along with it. Also, they asked, what would keep the British from trying to control other businesses? By now, many American colonists were ready to believe the worst about any act of Parliament.

Bostonians held town meetings to protest the arrival of three East India Company tea ships. Citizens demanded that the tea be sent back to England. Governor Hutchinson refused and ordered the ships to unload their cargoes. Samuel Adams had prepared for this moment. On December 16, 1773, he sent Bostonians disguised as Mohawk Indians to dump the 342 chests of tea into Boston Harbor. This event, called the Boston Tea Party, was a direct challenge to British authority.

THE COERCIVE ACTS

Angry members of Parliament accepted the challenge. The destruction of property, they insisted, should not go without punishment. In the spring of 1774 Parliament passed the Coercive Acts. To coerce means to force someone to obey.

The first of these laws closed the port of Boston to all trade until the destroyed tea was paid for. The second changed the Massachusetts government, giving the king and his governor more power. A third law gave Crown officials and soldiers accused of serious crimes in the colonies the right to be tried in Britain. Soldiers who used violence against colonists would no longer have to face local juries.

To carry out the Coercive Acts, General Thomas Gage was appointed governor of Massachusetts. Gage was commander of the British forces in North America. British troops returned to Boston. To insure that lodging would be provided, Parliament passed a new quartering act. If there were not empty buildings available, the troops could be quartered in homes.

Parliament also passed the Quebec Act. The act took away Canada's representative assembly and returned the province to a royal form of government. This reminded Americans of the kind of government Canada had had under French rule. Canadians would not be allowed to have jury trials. The Quebec Act also extended the province of Quebec to the Ohio River. Colonial claims to this region were once again threatened. American colonists called the Coercive Acts and the Quebec Act the "Intolerable Acts."

*CT
For discussion: What is the difference in meaning between *coercive* and *intolerable*? How does "Coercive Acts" suggest the view of a ruler and "Intolerable Acts" the view of dissatisfied subjects?

THE FIRST CONTINENTAL CONGRESS

The Intolerable Acts led a number of colonial assemblies to call for a continental, or all-colony, congress. Their first concern was to help Massachusetts. "An attack on any one colony should be considered as an attack on the whole," said the Virginia assembly.

The First Continental Congress met on September 5, 1774, in Philadelphia. Every colony except Georgia sent delegates. The delegates drew up a declaration, stating the rights of the colonists. It included the right of colonial assemblies alone to make laws and to levy taxes. The delegates demanded that Parliament repeal the Intolerable Acts. They called, too, for repeal of all laws passed since 1763 to raise revenue in the colonies.

To back up these demands, the delegates pledged that their colonies would cut off trade with Britain and boycott British products. The delegates planned to meet again the following May.

PATRIOTS AND LOYALISTS

Colonists had to choose sides. Those who supported the Continental Congress called themselves **Patriots.** Colonists who remained loyal to Britain were known as **Loyalists.** About a fifth of the colonists were Loyalists. Many felt that the Patriots' actions amounted to treason.

Patriot silversmith Paul Revere made a punchbowl engraved with the names of 92 Massachusetts legislators who protested the Townshend Acts.

For discussion: Why is *minutemen* an appropriate term for the volunteers?

You may wish to read all of Patrick Henry's famous speech to the class.

By the winter of 1774, the Patriots had almost succeeded in making Massachusetts an independent province. Most of the king's officials had been replaced by local committees. Only Boston remained under British rule. Against General Gage's orders, the Massachusetts assembly continued to meet. It organized special militia groups of "minutemen," volunteers who were ready to answer a call to arms at any time.

In the other colonies, militia groups began to train harder. In spite of all this, most colonists still hoped that the conflict with Britain could be settled peacefully. Yet Patrick Henry, a leader in the Virginia House of Burgesses, faced the issue squarely.

Gentlemen may cry peace, peace; but there is no peace. The war is actually begun! The next gale that sweeps from the North will bring to our ears the clash of resounding arms! Our brethren are already in the field! Why stand we here idle? What is it that gentlemen wish? What would they have? Is life so dear or peace so sweet as to be purchased at the price of chains and slavery? Forbid it, Almighty God. I know not what course others may take; but as for me, give me liberty or give me death.

SECTION REVIEW   Answers will be found on page T 36.

1. Define these words: *Patriots, Loyalists.*

2. Identify: Mercy Otis Warren, Thomas Hutchinson, committees of correspondence, Boston Tea Party, minutemen.

3. How did committees of correspondence unite the colonies?

4. Why did colonists protest against the Tea Act?

5. Name three ways that the Coercive Acts punished Massachusetts.

6. How did the colonies respond to the Intolerable Acts?

7. How did the First Continental Congress back up its demands?

CHAPTER SUMMARY

Between 1689 and 1748, Britain and France fought three wars for trade and colonies. Neither nation, however, was a clear winner. In 1754 a fourth conflict began in the Ohio Valley. Trying to prepare for war with France, the Albany Congress approved a plan to unite the colonies. All of the colonial assemblies, however, rejected the Albany Plan of Union.

In 1756 the French and Indian War became a worldwide struggle for empire. Britain won the war, ending the French threat to its American colonies. By the Treaty of Paris, North America east of the Mississippi River became part of the British Empire.

Britain now faced huge war debts and the cost of controlling its new territory. Unable to increase taxes at home, Parliament tried to raise revenue in the colonies. The Sugar Act of 1764 set customs duties on several colonial imports. The colonists protested against this act. Only their colonial assemblies, they claimed, had the right to tax them.

The protest against "taxation without representation" became widespread and violent when the Stamp Act was passed. Colonists boycotted British imports. Parliament was forced to repeal the act, but the Townshend Acts caused new protests. Rioting brought the British army to Boston. After the "Boston Massacre," many American colonists began to see British power as a threat to their freedom.

The threat soon became a reality. In 1774 Parliament responded to the Boston Tea Party by passing the Coercive Acts. The acts united most of the other colonies in support of Massachusetts and led to the First Continental Congress.

The delegates to the Congress demanded that Parliament repeal the Coercive Acts and respect the rights of the colonists. A boycott of British products was ordered, forcing many colonists to choose between Patriots and Loyalists. Massachusetts Patriots set up an independent government and prepared for war.

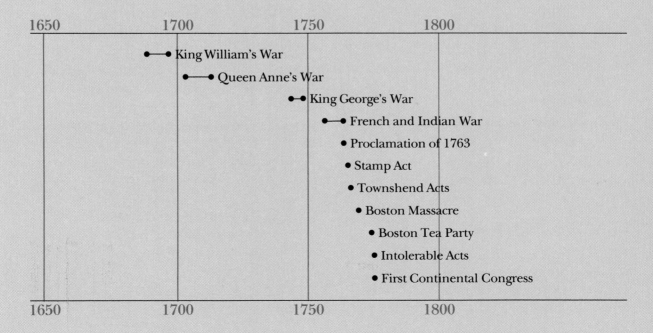

Timeline 1650–1800:
- King William's War
- Queen Anne's War
- King George's War
- French and Indian War
- Proclamation of 1763
- Stamp Act
- Townshend Acts
- Boston Massacre
- Boston Tea Party
- Intolerable Acts
- First Continental Congress

CHAPTER SURVEY

VOCABULARY REVIEW

For each numbered definition below, choose the word that best fits the definition.

1. A colonist who remained loyal to Britain
 (a) Patriot   (b) speculator   (c) Loyalist

2. To join with others in refusing to buy or use goods of a business or nation
 (a) coerce   (b) boycott   (c) repeal

3. An official announcement of something
 (a) repeal   (b) proclamation   (c) strategy

4. People who buy something in the hope of selling it at a large profit
 (a) speculators   (b) delegates   (c) militia

5. The random slaughter of many people
 (a) strategy   (b) boycott   (c) massacre

6. Taxes paid on imported goods
 (a) revenue   (b) customs duties   (c) repeal

7. People chosen to act for others
 (a) Patriots   (b) Loyalists   (c) delegates

8. A plan for achieving a goal
 (a) strategy   (b) massacre   (c) repeal

9. Money raised by a government from taxes
 (a) revenue   (b) customs duties   (c) repeal

10. A colonist who supported the Continental Congress
 (a) delegate   (b) Loyalist   (c) Patriot

11. To do away with a law officially
 (a) boycott   (b) repeal   (c) coerce

12. Citizens trained to fight in an emergency
 (a) militia   (b) Loyalists   (c) Patriots

CHAPTER REVIEW

1. These areas changed hands as a result of wars between Britain and France: French Canada, Hudson Bay, Louisiana east of the Mississippi, Louisiana west of the Mississippi,

In 1710 four chiefs of the Iroquois were brought to London to meet Queen Anne. John Verelst made this portrait of the Mohawk "king" for the queen.

Newfoundland, Nova Scotia, New Orleans, and Florida.   (a) Which areas were given to Britain after Queen Anne's War?   (b) Which were given to Britain after the French and Indian War?   (c) What area was given to Spain after the French and Indian War?

2. How did General Braddock learn the hard way that war in America was different from war in Europe?

3. (a) What was the purpose of the Proclamation of 1763?   (b) What reasons did colonists have for protesting it?

4. (a) Why did Parliament raise taxes after the French and Indian War?   (b) Why did Parliament look to the colonies for revenue?

5. (a) What taxes were imposed by the Sugar Act of 1764?   (b) Why were so few American colonists troubled by these taxes?   (c) Why were so many colonists troubled by the Stamp Act?

6. (a) Why did Parliament pass the Declaratory Act?   (b) What other action of Parliament seemed more important to colonists at the time?

7. How did the Townshend Acts lead to the Boston Massacre?

8. (a) How did Parliament react to the Boston Tea Party? (b) What did the three Coercive Acts do? (c) Who was responsible for enforcing these acts in Massachusetts?

9. The colonists organized three trade boycotts to force repeal of acts of Parliament. (a) What acts were they protesting each time? (b) Which acts were repealed as a result of a colonial boycott?

10. To what extent did British troops control Massachusetts by the winter of 1774?

GEOGRAPHY REVIEW

*CT **1.** Compare the map "European Claims in North America 1750" on page 131 with the map "European Claims in North America 1763" on page 136. (a) What time span is shown by the two maps? (b) What happened in this time to account for the differences between the maps? (c) Which nation lost the most land? (d) Which nation gained the

most land? (e) Which nation's land claims stayed about the same?

2. Use the map "The French and Indian War 1755–1763" on page 134 to decide whether these statements are true or false. (a) From the British colonists' point of view, this war was a frontier war. (b) The British navy played an important role in the British victory. (c) By the end of the war, all the French forts along the St. Lawrence River and the Great Lakes had fallen to the British.

USING THE TOOLS OF HISTORY

*CT **Identifying Points of View**

Tell which point of view—Patriot or Loyalist— is reflected in each statement.

(a) No power on earth has a right to take our property from us without our consent.
(b) We have been so intent upon building up American rights that we have overlooked the rights of Great Britain.
(c) When a certain great king, whose
    initial is G,
  Shall force stamps upon paper, and
    folks to drink tea,
  When these folks burn his tea and
    stampt paper, like stubble,
  You may guess that this king is then
    coming to trouble.

Thomas Edwards, an American silversmith, made this sauceboat in the English style about 1760.

READING AND THINKING SKILLS

*CT **SQ3R**
(a) What are the five steps in the SQ3R study method? (b) What are turned into questions by the use of this method? (c) How is the SQ3R method different from outlining? How is it similar?

CHAPTER 7   1775-1783

THE WAR FOR INDEPENDENCE

THE WAR BEGINS
THE WAR IN THE NORTH
THE PATRIOTS AND THEIR ARMY
ENDING THE WAR

7-1 THE WAR BEGINS

READ TO FIND OUT

radicals: people who favor extreme change

moderates: people who prefer gradual change

tyranny: cruel and unjust use of power

—what the words *radicals, moderates,* and *tyranny* mean.

—why British troops marched on Lexington and Concord.

—why the British victory at Bunker Hill was costly.

—how the Continental Army was formed.

—why George III rejected the Olive Branch Petition.

—why the American colonies declared their independence.

On the night of April 18, 1775, General Thomas Gage ordered 700 of his best troops out of Boston. They marched through the darkness toward Concord, 21 miles (34 kilometers) away. Their mission was to seize Patriot war supplies. They may also have had orders to capture Samuel Adams and John Hancock, who were in Lexington.

Boston Patriots learned of Gage's plans. Paul Revere and William Dawes rode to alert the minutemen of Lexington and other towns on the road to Concord. Soon more riders were spreading the alarm, "To arms! To arms! The war has begun!"

Lexington and Concord 1775

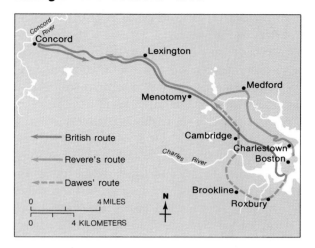

- — British route
- — Revere's route
- ---- Dawes' route

0 ————— 4 MILES
0 ————— 4 KILOMETERS

Concord River · Concord
· Lexington
· Medford
Menotomy ·
Cambridge ·
Charlestown ·
Boston ·
Charles River
Brookline ·
Roxbury ·

At Concord's North Bridge, "the embattled farmers stood, / and fired the shot heard round the world." The British lost 247 troops on the retreat to Boston.

LEXINGTON AND CONCORD

At dawn the red-coated British troops reached Lexington. They saw a group of minutemen standing on the village green in two uneven lines, with muskets at the ready. With a shout, the redcoats began running toward the outnumbered minutemen. Then a shot rang out, and the British troops opened fire. Before their officers could stop them, they killed eight minutemen and wounded ten more.

The British troops marched on to Concord. There they destroyed Patriot war supplies. The hastily gathered Patriots charged Concord's North Bridge, guarded by a hundred redcoats. The British retreated toward Boston.

Word of the deaths at Lexington had spread quickly. Farmers left their fields and picked up their muskets. A British lieutenant later wrote that the hills, woods, and stone walls on both sides of the road to Boston were "all lined with people," who kept up a steady "fire upon us." British casualties, or losses in war due to deaths, wounds, or capture, numbered almost three hundred.

By the following morning, thousands of minutemen were camped in the hills around Boston. Soon militia groups arrived from towns throughout New England. The British, too, were strengthening their forces. Generals William Howe, Henry Clinton, and John Burgoyne (bur-GOYN), arrived to help the surrounded General Gage.

THE BATTLE OF BUNKER HILL

On the night of June 16, Massachusetts Patriots sent 1,200 soldiers to put cannons on Bunker Hill, overlooking Boston. Once the cannons were set, the Patriots could do great damage to the British forces below. The Americans bypassed Bunker Hill in favor of Breed's Hill, which

Paul Revere placed this lantern in the steeple of Boston's North Church to warn the Patriots of the British approach.

Point out to the class that America has long had a tradition of citizen-soldiers, those who leave their civilian occupations to spring to the defense of the nation.

was a little closer to Boston. Working through the night, they dug trenches and put up walls of dirt and timber.

The next day General Howe ordered his troops to drive the Patriots from the hill. As thousands watched from Boston rooftops, three long lines of redcoats formed. Shoulder to shoulder, the British soldiers in the first line began to advance up the hill. The other two lines followed. Fancy uniforms made it easy for American sharpshooters to tell who the British officers were.

In the hilltop fort, the Patriots watched as rows of gleaming bayonets came closer and closer. At last, the Americans fired. Huge gaps appeared in the scarlet lines. The king's troops broke ranks and retreated. From the foot of the hill, they advanced again. Patriot fire once more forced the British to turn back. Joined by fresh troops, the redcoats re-formed their ranks and attacked a third time. The defenders, who were running out of powder and shot, failed to stop them. By the end of the day, both Breed's Hill and Bunker Hill were in British hands.

The Battle of Bunker Hill was a costly victory for the British. American casualties numbered about 400. But the British lost 1,054 soldiers, many of them officers. General Howe later admitted that "our success was too dearly bought."

For discussion: Although the British took Breed's Hill and Bunker Hill, did they (considering their casualties) really win the battle? Why or why not?

THE SECOND CONTINENTAL CONGRESS

While the Battle of Bunker Hill was being fought, the Second Continental Congress was meeting in Philadelphia. Delegates from 12 colonies had begun their work on May 10, soon after the first reports of the fighting at Lexington and Concord. Delegates from Georgia arrived later, in September.

Because Massachusetts was already at war, the delegates felt a new spirit of unity. In June Congress took control of the forces outside Boston, creating the Continental Army. George Washington was appointed commander in chief. John Adams felt that the "gentleman from Virginia" could unite the colonies "better than any other person." Pennsylvania, Maryland, and Virginia sent troops north to join the new army.

Shortly after Washington left for Massachusetts, news of the Battle of Bunker Hill reached Philadelphia. Members of the Continental Congress reacted in different ways.

Radicals—people who favored extreme change—wanted a complete break with Britain. They included the Adams cousins, Benjamin Franklin of Pennsylvania, and Patrick Henry of Virginia. **Moderates**—people who preferred gradual change—wanted to avoid a break with Britain, especially a violent one. They felt that the colonies and Britain could solve problems without bloodshed. The moderates were led by lawyer John Dickinson of Pennsylvania and included George Washington.

The Revolutionary War 1775–1776

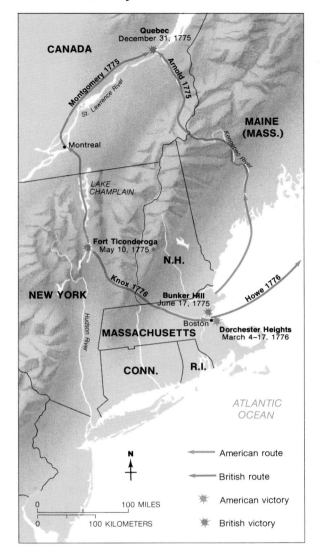

A British cartoon in 1776 made fun of the enormous wigs then in fashion. It shows the Battle of Bunker Hill being fought on a lady's head. The main part of the battle was actually fought at Breed's Hill.

General Henry Knox and his troops dragged Fort Ticonderoga's cannons 300 miles (480 kilometers) to Boston.

In July 1775 Dickinson persuaded the Congress to send George III a petition. In the petition, the delegates asked the king to stop using military force against the colonists so that they could settle their differences with Parliament peacefully.

This appeal, known as the Olive Branch Petition, began, "We, your Majesty's faithful subjects." The petitioners still considered themselves to be loyal British citizens. George III, however, refused to read anything written by an "illegal congress." Instead, he declared the American colonies to be in open rebellion. This meant that the members of the Continental Congress were now guilty of treason, or disloyalty to the king. The punishment for treason was death.

Tell the class that Benjamin Franklin reminded the Second Continental Congress: "We must all hang together, or assuredly we shall all hang separately" (i.e., for treason).

Thomas Davies, a British soldier, painted this watercolor of Fort Ticonderoga in 1759.

General John Burgoyne was known as "Gentleman Johnny" because of his elegance. He was a dramatist and a member of Parliament as well as a soldier.

DEFEAT IN CANADA, VICTORY IN MASSACHUSETTS

Even before the Olive Branch Petition was sent, the British were gathering Canadian forces for an invasion of New York. In response, Congress launched an invasion of Canada from Fort Ticonderoga. Fort Ticonderoga had already been captured by Patriot Ethan Allen and his force of "Green Mountain Boys" from the future state of Vermont.

From Ticonderoga a force of 1,200 Americans set out for the St. Lawrence River valley. Led by General Richard Montgomery, they captured Montreal. A second invasion force under Colonel Benedict Arnold marched into Canada from what is now Maine. In December 1775 Arnold and Montgomery joined forces for an unsuccessful attack on Quebec. Montgomery was killed. Arnold was driven from Canada in the spring of 1776.

Fort Ticonderoga was important in another way. Within the captured fort were cannons that Washington needed to drive the British out of Boston. During the winter of 1775–1776, a small band of militia hauled 59 cannons from Ticonderoga overland to the army outside Boston. Washington then moved the cannons to Dorchester Heights, the hills above the city.

In Boston General Howe had replaced Gage as the British commander. He realized that the city and most of the harbor were now within range of American guns. In March 1776 Howe and his soldiers sailed for Nova Scotia. With them went about 1,000 Loyalists. They were the first of almost 100,000 Americans who fled their homes rather than rebel against England.

MAIN IDEAS AND TOPIC SENTENCES

A *main idea* is a general statement about a subject or topic. Specific facts about the topic are called *details*. Nearly all paragraphs contain both a main idea and some details.

Most paragraphs contain a *topic sentence* that states the main idea. When you look for the topic sentence of a paragraph, try to find the sentence that makes a general statement about the subject of that paragraph.

The topic sentence is often the first sentence in a paragraph. But not all paragraphs follow that pattern. Sometimes the topic sentence will appear in the middle or at the end of a paragraph.

Look under the heading "Moving Toward Independence." What is the topic sentence of the first paragraph? The last two sentences include details telling how Britain and the colonies became more divided. Therefore, the first sentence is the topic sentence.

Now examine the second paragraph. There are a lot of details here about how the American colonists thought. But only one sentence summarizes these details in a general statement that tells how the American colonists felt about independence. In this case, the last sentence is the topic sentence.

Look at the next paragraph and write its topic sentence on a piece of paper.

The fourth paragraph is tricky. It has two topic sentences—one for the first two sentences and another for the second three. Write down both of these topic sentences.

The fifth and final paragraph in this section also has two topic sentences. Write them on your paper.

The following paragraph about one part of the Declaration of Independence is missing a topic sentence. Read it carefully and then write a good topic sentence for this paragraph.

The "present King of Great Britain" had, for example, kept armies in the colonies "without the consent of our legislatures." He had cut off "our trade with all parts of the world." He had imposed "taxes on us without our consent." And finally, he had waged war against the colonists and "destroyed the lives of our people."

Answers will be found on page T 37.

*CT

MOVING TOWARD INDEPENDENCE

Four months before the British left Boston, King George III took a step that further divided the colonies and Britain. Hoping to force an end to the rebellion, the king cut off all trade with the colonies. Now that Americans were on their own, argued the radicals in the Continental Congress, why not declare independence?

No European colony had ever separated from its parent country before. Without Britain's protection, Americans worried that the colonies might be seized by some other nation. Independence also troubled Americans because it meant cutting all ties with the king. Loyalty to the king gave people in the 1700s a feeling of safety, a feeling that they were part of a nation. For these reasons, independence was a frightening idea to most Americans.

Thomas Paine helped many Americans overcome their fears with a pamphlet called *Common Sense*. Paine was an Englishman who had only

Edward Savage and Edward Pine painted "Congress Voting Independence." Thomas Jefferson is presenting the Declaration to Benjamin Harrison, president of the Congress. Benjamin Franklin sits at the center, chin in hand.

So popular was *Common Sense*, it sold 120,000 copies in three months. You may wish to read passages from *Common Sense* to the class.

recently arrived in America. He published his ideas about independence in January 1776. In plain language, he told Americans that a continent could not be "governed by an island." Concerning kings, he said that one honest person was worth "all the crowned ruffians that ever lived." The colonists, he argued, had nothing to fear and much to gain from independence.

Paine's arguments made sense to Americans. As his ideas spread from colony to colony, Washington noticed "a powerful change" in the colonists' thinking. By spring public opinion had turned to favor those who wanted to leave the British Empire. One after another, the colonies threw out their royal governors, set up new governments, and became states. First North Carolina, then Virginia, then other states told their delegates in Congress to vote for independence.

On June 7, 1776, Richard Henry Lee of Virginia asked the Second Continental Congress to call for independence. "These united colonies," he declared, "are, and of right ought to be, free and independent states." Congress debated Lee's proposal and then appointed a committee to draw up a Declaration of Independence. Its members included Benjamin Franklin of Pennsylvania, John Adams of Massachusetts, Thomas Jefferson of Virginia, Robert Livingston of New York, and Roger Sherman of Connecticut. Jefferson was asked to write the first draft.

THE DECLARATION OF INDEPENDENCE

On July 2, 1776, Congress approved Lee's call for independence. The delegates then debated Jefferson's declaration. They made a number of changes and, on the fourth of July, adopted it.

The Declaration of Independence was addressed to the world, but it was also written for the American people. Jefferson wanted to convince Americans that rebelling against the king was right. He began by stating that all human beings are born with certain natural, or God-given, rights. People set up governments to protect these rights. When a government fails to protect natural rights, the people have the right to put an end to it and to set up a new government.

Jefferson admitted that people should not change their system of government without good reason. But George III, he insisted, was guilty of **tyranny**—cruel and unjust use of power. Jefferson then set out a long list of the king's actions to prove his charge.

Most Americans have forgotten the details of Jefferson's list. But the idea that the people establish governments in order to protect their natural rights has grown more powerful with the passing of time.

When Jefferson and other leaders of the American Revolution talked about "the people," they meant white male Americans. Abigail Adams felt this deeply. When her husband, John, was helping the new state governments decide who should vote, she asked him to "remember the ladies." The states were not yet ready to follow her advice. Yet, as the years passed, the meaning of "the people" expanded to include women, black Americans, and other groups who were once left out. Today Jefferson's words belong to all Americans.

As the class studies this account of the Declaration of Independence, have them refer to the annotated Declaration on pages 524–527 and cite Jefferson's actual words for each point summarized here. One question to consider: How does Jefferson support his charge that George III is a tyrant?

SECTION REVIEW   Answers will be found on page T 37.

1. Define these words: *radicals, moderates, tyranny.*

2. Identify: Paul Revere and William Dawes, William Howe, John Dickinson, Ethan Allen, Benedict Arnold, Thomas Paine, and Thomas Jefferson.

3. Why were British troops sent to Concord?

4. Why did General Howe say that his victory at Bunker Hill was "too dearly bought"?

5. How was the Continental Army formed?

6. Why did George III reject the Olive Branch Petition?

7. Why did the British leave Boston in 1776?

8. According to the Declaration of Independence, why did the American colonists have the right to rebel?

7-2 THE WAR IN THE NORTH

READ TO FIND OUT

mercenaries: hired soldiers

campaign: series of connected military actions

alliance: agreement between two or more nations to aid each other

—what the words *mercenaries, campaign,* and *alliance* mean.

—how the British hoped to defeat the Patriots.

—what difficulties Washington faced.

—what helped New Jersey Patriots regain their confidence.

—why the battle at Saratoga was a turning point in the war.

In the weeks after July 4, 1776, the Declaration of Independence was read in the streets of towns and villages throughout the colonies. But before the "united colonies" could be truly "free and independent states," they had to defeat Great Britain.

BRITISH STRENGTHS AND WEAKNESSES

In 1776 Britain was the most powerful nation in the world. Its army was large, well trained, and well supplied. To British troops were added thousands of German **mercenaries,** or hired soldiers. Called Hessians (HESH-uhnz), most came from the German state of Hesse-Cassel. In addition, the Royal Navy controlled the waters off the American coast and could land British forces wherever they were needed.

Still, the British had two major problems. The first was the distance they had to travel to fight in America. All army supplies and troops had to be shipped from England. Many British soldiers died of illness during the long voyage across the Atlantic. The second disadvantage was the vast size of the territory that Britain had to conquer. Just capturing the cities would not crush the colonists.

To defeat the Patriots, the British had to break their will to fight. They hoped to do this by drawing the Continental Army into battle and destroying it.

WASHINGTON'S DIFFICULTIES

Washington had to build an army strong enough to withstand heavy British attacks. It seemed impossible. There were shortages of ammunition, food, clothing, and medical supplies. Most of his soldiers were militiamen with little training.

Sir James Wallace sketched the British warships *Phoenix* and *Rose* attacking New York August 16, 1776. This engraving shows an American fire ship trying to set fire to the British ships.

Discipline was terrible. Militia companies usually elected their own officers and treated them as equals. Instead of giving orders, the officers made requests. Why should the regular army be any different, Americans wondered.

Washington's troops were mostly farmers eager to get back to their fields. They enlisted only for short periods of time. Just when they were learning to be soldiers, they took their muskets and went home to plant or harvest their crops.

THE BRITISH CAPTURE NEW YORK

After General Howe withdrew from Boston, Washington correctly guessed that he would next appear at New York. The city was a good starting place for a British attack on either Boston or Philadelphia. Also, the Royal Navy would want to use New York's fine harbor. Washington moved his entire army of 20,000 soldiers to New York. To defend the city, he divided his forces between Manhattan Island and Long Island.

In August 1776 the British landed 20,000 troops on Long Island. Washington's soldiers there were badly beaten. The Americans were saved from disaster only because General Howe paused in his attack. Washington pulled his panic-stricken troops together and slipped across the East River to Manhattan.

In mid-September British troops landed on Manhattan and forced the Americans back. Once again, Howe stopped his attack. For three weeks he considered his next move. During that time, he ordered the execution of a Patriot spy, Captain Nathan Hale. Hale had disguised

Activity: Students can form committees to research the espionage activities and death of Nathan Hale. The committees can then present short plays based on these events.

USING SCALE ON MAPS

*CT

The map on page 167 shows the movement of American troops and British troops during the Revolutionary War. The map's title explains that the map covers only the first two years of the war.

The cartographer, or mapmaker, used colored arrows to show what routes American and British troops traveled. Find the red arrows that show Howe's routes. They show that he traveled west across the Atlantic Ocean in 1776, then headed south. Symbols called battle blasts show American and British victories. Find the symbol showing Howe's victory at Brandywine Creek.

Because distances are important in a map like this, the cartographer has included a **scale.** A scale shows what distance on the earth is represented by a given measurement on the map. Scales vary according to how much area a map shows.

The scale on this map uses a measurement of just under 1 inch (2.5 centimeters) to represent 100 miles (160.9 kilometers). To find out how far troops traveled, you can make a mileage indicator. Take a strip of paper and mark off 300 miles in 50-mile segments, using the scale as a guide. (If you wish, you may work with metric measurements.)

Place the mileage indicator along the arrows showing Howe's route south. You will find that he traveled about 300 miles from New York to the mouth of Chesapeake Bay. Of course, a route marked on a map can only come close to the route actually traveled. Howe's ships probably zigzagged in ways not shown by the arrows.

Use the map and the mileage indicator to answer the following questions. Use either miles or kilometers.

1. In what direction did St. Leger travel as he headed from Montreal to Lake Ontario? Approximately how far did he travel up the St. Lawrence River?

2. What battle(s) did the Continental Army win in New York?

3. Approximately how far is Montreal from Fort Ticonderoga?

4. What river did Washington cross after the battle at Trenton? In what direction was he traveling?

Answers will be found on page T 38.

himself as a Dutch teacher. Then he had crossed British lines to gain information on Howe's position for Washington. By mid-October Howe was attacking again, and Washington's troops were forced to abandon Manhattan.

About the next two months, Thomas Paine wrote, "These are the times that try men's souls." Washington's army was driven out of New York and forced to retreat southward through New Jersey. Sick, hungry, and discouraged, many soldiers headed for home. In December Washington took what was left of his army across the Delaware River into Pennsylvania. Howe returned to New York for the winter, leaving a string of posts in New Jersey.

The Continental Army's retreat encouraged the Loyalists of New Jersey and New York. Their militia troops seized control of local governments. Many former Patriots swore loyalty to the king.

Paine's famous words begin the first of his *Crisis* papers written when he was with Washington's army. Washington ordered that the paper be read aloud to his troops. You may wish to read *The Crisis*, Number 1, to the class.

The Revolutionary War 1776–1778

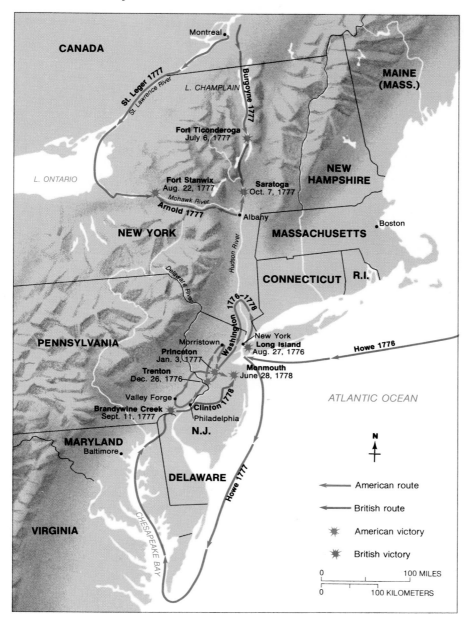

Have students find New York City, Trenton, Princeton, and Valley Forge on the map.

In the North, the British had been pinned down in New York City and Newport, Rhode Island, by mid-1778. Washington's army spent the next three years camped around New York while fighting continued in the South.

TRENTON AND PRINCETON

Washington desperately needed a victory because he was about to lose his army. On the first of January, most of his soldiers would complete their one-year terms of enlistment.

With time running out, Washington made a bold move. On Christmas night the American army rowed back across the ice-choked Delaware River and marched on Trenton, New Jersey. They surprised a large

William Mercer painted the colorful ''Battle of Princeton.'' Mercer was the deaf-mute son of American General Hugh Mercer, who was killed in the battle. The Patriot victory caused the British to abandon New Jersey.

force of German mercenaries and forced them to surrender. Washington begged his troops to stay with the army a little longer, and many of them agreed.

Early in January 1777 Washington struck again, defeating British troops near Princeton. Then he led his tired army into the hills near Morristown, New Jersey, for the winter. Because of the American victories, the British abandoned most of New Jersey. Local Patriots regained their confidence and forced the Loyalists into hiding.

THE PATRIOTS LOSE THEIR CAPITAL

Tell students that later they will read of Benedict Arnold's betrayal of the American cause. (See page 176.)

In February 1777 General John Burgoyne told the British government that he planned to win the war in America with a single **campaign.** A campaign is a series of connected military actions.

From Canada, Burgoyne would lead 8,000 soldiers south by way of Lake Champlain and the Hudson River. A smaller force led by Colonel Barry St. Leger (saint LEHJ-ur) would take Fort Stanwix in central New York and advance eastward. Near Albany the two forces would meet General Howe's army, which would move north along the Hudson from New York City. With the Hudson River valley in British hands, New England would be cut off from the other states.

Howe did not hear of his part in the plan until August. By then, he and his army were on ships in Chesapeake Bay, on their way to take the Patriot capital of Philadelphia.

When Howe landed, Washington tried to stop him at Brandywine Creek. But the Continentals were defeated, and Philadelphia fell. Congress fled to York, Pennsylvania. Washington attacked the main British camp outside Philadelphia, but was defeated again. He withdrew to Valley Forge for the winter. Howe stayed in the capital.

THE PATRIOT VICTORY AT SARATOGA

At first it seemed that Burgoyne's campaign would be as successful as Howe's. In July Burgoyne easily captured Fort Ticonderoga. Then he chose a route to the Hudson River that took his army and 600 supply wagons through 20 miles (32 kilometers) of wilderness. It took his soldiers more than three weeks to cut a road through the forest.

This delay gave the Patriots time to prepare. As Burgoyne moved south, local militia attacked his forces again and again. Burgoyne's troubles were only beginning. Colonel St. Leger failed to take Fort Stanwix and was driven from central New York by Generals Nicholas Herkimer and Benedict Arnold. Then Washington sent a force of Continental soldiers north to help the Patriot militia. Soon Burgoyne was surrounded and outnumbered three to one. In October he surrendered an entire army of 5,700 British and German troops at Saratoga.

The Patriot victory at Saratoga was a major turning point in the war. It showed France, England's bitter enemy, that the Americans had a chance to win. The French had secretly been sending money and war supplies to the Americans. Now they came out into the open.

In February 1778 France and the United States signed a treaty of **alliance**—an agreement to aid each other. France agreed to enter the war against Britain. Spain and the Netherlands later joined the conflict.

STANDOFF IN THE NORTH

General Henry Clinton, who had replaced Howe as commander of British forces, feared that the French navy might trap him in Philadelphia. In June 1778 he abandoned the city and set out for New York. Washington pursued Clinton to Monmouth Court House, New Jersey. A day-long battle ended in an American victory.

Clinton went on to New York. Washington followed and camped north of the city. The British could not trap Washington and defeat him. Yet the Americans were too weak to drive the British from New York City. The war in the North had become a standoff.

Military drummers sent signals to troops. This Revolutionary War drum bears the flags of France and the North Carolina militia.

You may wish to have students take special note of Saratoga as a turning point in the war. To consider: Might the colonies have won without France's help?

For discussion: Have students review Washington's experiences in the French and Indian War, especially as a witness of Braddock's defeat (page 133). What did Washington learn about unorthodox military tactics that became useful to him in the Revolutionary War?

SECTION REVIEW   Answers will be found on page T 38.

1. Define these words: *mercenaries, campaign, alliance.*

2. Identify: Nathan Hale, John Burgoyne, Henry Clinton.

3. How did the British hope to defeat the Patriots?

4. List four problems Washington faced with the Continental Army.

5. What helped New Jersey Patriots regain their confidence?

6. Why was the American victory at Saratoga a turning point in the war?

7-3 THE PATRIOTS AND THEIR ARMY

READ TO FIND OUT

inflation: a general increase in the level of prices

veterans: former soldiers

—what the words *inflation* and *veterans* mean.

—why the Continental Army was often short of supplies.

—who helped the war effort.

—how strong leaders aided the Continental Army.

The British failed to destroy the Continental Army in battle. Even so, the survival of the Army was threatened many times by hardships.

Late in 1777, after the fall of Philadelphia, the Continentals set up winter quarters at Valley Forge. Joseph Martin, a seventeen-year-old private, told their story in his diary. By December, he wrote, "the army was not only starved but naked. The greatest part were not only shirtless and barefoot, but lacked all other clothing, especially blankets." Soldiers with their feet wrapped in rags "might be tracked by their blood upon the rough frozen ground." More than 2,000 soldiers died that winter.

THE FAILURE TO PROVIDE SUPPLIES

Congress tried to provide supplies for the soldiers, but it lacked the power to tax. When Congress requested aid from the state governments, they were slow to respond. They needed their funds for their own militia.

John Trego painted the Patriots at Valley Forge as he imagined them more than 100 years after that terrible winter. George Washington reviewed his ragged troops from his white horse.

Women of all ages helped the war effort. A colored engraving from the 1800s shows sixteen-year-old Sybil Ludington riding through the night to rally her father's militia regiment. The Patriots met British troops near Danbury, Connecticut.

Another problem was profiteering—making a profit in a way that harms others. Dishonest people charged the army high prices for scarce food and supplies. Often they sold spoiled meat and shoes that fell apart. "No punishment," wrote Washington, "is too great for the person who can build greatness upon the country's ruin."

Partly to blame for profiteering was runaway **inflation**—a general increase in the level of prices. Because Congress and the states lacked gold or silver, they had printed paper money to pay for war supplies. Americans did not trust the paper money because it was not backed by gold or silver. A person selling an item for one dollar in gold demanded several paper dollars for the same item. Prices began to rise. Congress and the states tried to keep up by printing even more paper money. The more they printed, the less the money would buy.

As prices rose, people became desperate to get as much money as possible. For many, profiteering seemed the only way. In the scramble to keep up with inflation, it was difficult to be patriotic.

SUPPORT ON THE HOME FRONT

Though some Americans did nothing to support the army, others did more than their share. Haym Salomon, a Jewish settler from Poland, used his banking skills to raise money for Congress. He and Robert Morris, a wealthy banker, bought supplies for Washington's troops using loans from France. As Congress slid deeper into debt, Salomon gave his own fortune. When he died in 1785, he was penniless.

Haym Salomon was twice arrested by the British as a spy, in 1776 and in 1778. The second time he was sentenced to death. Salomon escaped by bribing a jailer and fleeing behind American lines.

DEBORAH SAMPSON

In May 1782 the war was almost over. But in New York, British troops fought on. The Continental Army desperately needed recruits.

One of the few volunteers was Robert Shurtleff. Shurtleff was tall and strong, but had the beardless face of a young boy. Still, the recruiting agent was glad to sign him up. He never guessed that Shurtleff was a woman. The new soldier's real name was Deborah Sampson.

Sampson had spent most of her life as an indentured servant, doing farm chores. When the war broke out, she pored over newspaper accounts of the Patriot cause.

By the time she completed her servitude, Sampson could think of nothing but "freedom

and independence." She made a suit of men's clothing and tied back her hair in the male fashion. She became Robert Shurtleff.

Shurtleff-Sampson began her military life at West Point. She marched, drilled, and learned how to load a musket. Soon, the raw soldier learned the hardships of war. In a skirmish with the Loyalists, she was shot in the leg.

Sampson was taken to a field hospital. Fearing discovery of her identity, she hid the wound from the doctors. Then she took out the musket ball herself. Before the wound was half-healed, Sampson went back to the army.

Sampson's identity was revealed when she was hospitalized with a fever. The doctor informed her commander. Amazed, he refused to believe that a woman was in his regiment.

Sampson received an honorable discharge in late 1783. She returned to a woman's life, married, and had children. But her "soldier's duty" was not forgotten. Several years later, Congress voted to give Deborah Sampson a soldier's pension. "The whole of the American Revolution records no case like this," wrote the pension committee. It was, the committee said, a striking example of "heroism, fidelity, and courage."

In Philadelphia, women bought up linen and made shirts for soldiers. Christopher Ludwig, a German baker, told Philadelphians that he would bake any flour they gave him into bread for the troops. In New York, an elderly widow named Sarah Smith brought food and clothing to American prisoners of the British. "While I have anything to give," she said, "you are welcome to share it with me."

Among the strongest supporters of the army were women married to soldiers. While men were in the army, women managed farms and workshops. Some women joined their husbands in camp. They cooked and washed for the soldiers. They nursed the wounded. When the army fought, they took ammunition to the soldiers in the front lines.

Some women fought. When Margaret Cochran Corbin's husband was killed during the battle for Manhattan Island, she took his place load-

Activity: Students can research the achievements of other women during the Revolutionary War and make oral or written reports. You may wish to tell students that women who carried water to troops on the front lines were nicknamed "Molly Pitchers."

ing a cannon. She was wounded and lost the use of one arm. Later Congress rewarded Corbin with a soldier's pension.

Black Americans, both slave and free, also played an important part in the war effort. Blacks tried to join the Patriot forces at the beginning of the war, but most were rejected. Then, as the need for soldiers grew, Congress and most of the states passed laws granting slaves their freedom in return for military service.

As many as 5,000 black Americans served in the armed forces. They fought in every major battle. After the war, their sacrifices were remembered by white **veterans,** or former soldiers. Some of these veterans joined the campaigns to end slavery.

LEADERSHIP

George Washington was, of course, an outstanding leader. Despite his lack of supplies and hardships like those at Valley Forge, Washington kept the Continental Army together. Some of his best officers were volunteers from Europe. The Marquis de Lafayette (LAH-fee-EHT), a brave nobleman from France, was made a major general before he was twenty. Americans were happy to serve under Lafayette. He used his own money to buy food and clothing for his soldiers.

Baron Friedrich von Steuben (fawn STYOO-ben), an officer from Prussia, came to Valley Forge in February 1778. From dawn until dusk, he worked to make Washington's troops "feel a confidence in their own skill." Von Steuben taught the Americans how to take orders and how to use bayonets. He taught them how to swing around from a marching column into a line of battle. By spring he was one of the most popular officers in the army.

Despite von Steuben's efforts, thousands gave up and went home. But the army did not fall apart. No matter how bad the situation was, the soldiers who stayed knew that their commander would not give up. Washington, in turn, drew strength from the soldiers who stayed with him. "We did not think of [going home]" wrote Private Joseph Martin. "We had engaged to fight in the defense of our injured country."

This painting of a free black sailor was done in 1779. He was probably a member of the crew of the *General Washington,* the ship in the background.

Casimir Pulaski and Thaddeus Kosciusko, both Poles, were two other Europeans who distinguished themselves in the Revolutionary War. Pulaski led a corps of cavalry and infantry known as Pulaski's Legion. He was fatally wounded at the siege of Savannah. Kosciusko served as a colonel of engineers. For his services he was promoted to brigadier general.

SECTION REVIEW   Answers will be found on page T 38.

1. Define these words: *inflation, veterans.*

2. Identify: Haym Salomon and Robert Morris, Margaret Cochran Corbin, Marquis de Lafayette, Baron von Steuben.

3. Why was Congress unable to provide supplies for the army?

4. How did women help the war effort?

5. What was granted to slaves who served in the armed forces?

7-4 ENDING THE WAR

READ TO FIND OUT

guerrillas: soldiers who set up bases in remote areas and launch hit-and-run attacks on the enemy

—what the word *guerrillas* means.

—how British strategy changed after France entered the war.

—why the British failed to gain control of the Carolinas.

—how the British were defeated at Yorktown.

—what the United States gained from the Treaty of Paris.

In summer 1778 Washington camped north of New York City to keep watch on the British under Clinton. Washington placed his troops so that he could attack if the British moved toward Philadelphia or up the Hudson. But Clinton did not move that summer. Instead, fighting raged in the West, in the South, and on the high seas.

GEORGE ROGERS CLARK AND JOHN PAUL JONES

While Washington watched Clinton, a frontier militia leader attacked the British in the West. George Rogers Clark and 175 soldiers from the region known as Kentucky sailed down the Ohio River in flatboats. They captured three British forts, which had been supplying Indian raiding parties. Clark and his soldiers prevented the British from gaining control of the Ohio Valley. Meanwhile, a Spanish force led by Bernardo de Gálvez drove the British from the Mississippi River.

Activity: Students can research the sea battle between the *Bonhomme Richard* and the *Serapis*. They can then assume they served on one of these ships and write letters to friends telling about the battle.

While Clark and Gálvez fought in the wilderness, John Paul Jones fought on the high seas. Jones was a captain in the tiny Continental Navy. In September 1779 his ship, the *Bonhomme Richard,* met the British warship *Serapis* off the coast of England. A furious three-hour battle turned both ships into blazing wrecks, but it was the British captain who surrendered. Jones's victory lifted the spirits of Patriots, but it did little to weaken Britain's control of the sea.

THE WAR MOVES SOUTH

Unlike the Continental Navy, the French navy was a serious threat to the British. When France entered the war in 1778, Britain's strategy changed. Britain needed a foothold in the South. From a southern base, the British could shift troops to the West Indies to keep France

John Paul Jones named his ship after Poor Richard of Franklin's *Almanac*. This etching of the battle between *Bonhomme Richard* and *Serapis* was copied from an engraving published in 1781. The original drawing was by Richard Paton.

from seizing British islands. At the same time, British troops could move north, crushing the Americans one state at a time.

In December 1778 the British took Savannah. Loyalists came out to support them. The royal governor returned, and Georgia rejoined the British Empire.

Encouraged by British success in Georgia, General Clinton invaded South Carolina by sea. In May 1780 he handed the Americans their worst defeat of the war. Clinton captured Charleston, forcing the surrender of 5,400 American troops. He then returned to New York, leaving General Charles Cornwallis to conquer the Carolinas.

As Cornwallis moved inland, Patriot **guerrillas** resisted him. Guerrillas are soldiers who set up bases in remote areas and launch hit-and-run attacks on the enemy. Guerrilla leaders like Francis Marion, "the Swamp Fox," attacked Loyalist militia forces and kept large numbers of British troops busy protecting their own supply lines. The guerrillas could not defeat Cornwallis. But they kept him from gaining control of South Carolina.

For discussion: The word *guerrilla* means "little war" in Spanish. Why is the word an appropriate name for guerrilla tactics?

VICTORY AT YORKTOWN

At the same time, units of the Continental Army marched south to help local militia forces build a southern army. In August 1780 the Americans attacked a British supply base at Camden, South Carolina, but they were driven off with heavy losses.

The Americans retreated from Camden. Cornwallis took advantage of their retreat by marching on North Carolina. At King's Mountain, near

The Revolutionary War 1778–1781

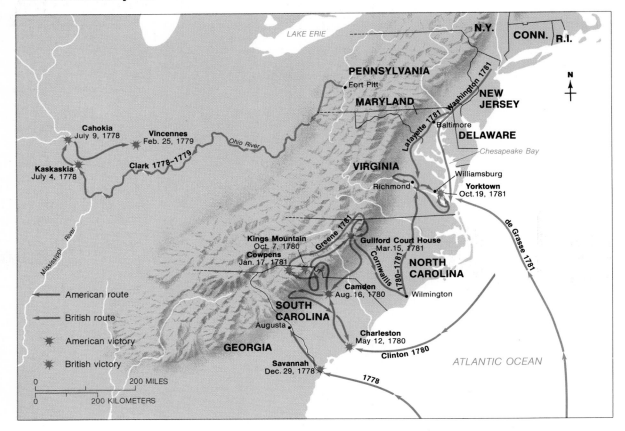

The last years of the War for Independence saw action on three fronts. Clark attacked British forts in the West, Greene and guerrilla bands fought in the South, and Washington and Lafayette pushed through the Middle Colonies.

Activity: Remind students of Arnold's previous loyal service. (See pages 160 and 169.) Ask them to research and report on what happened to turn Arnold against the Revolutionary cause.

the border between North and South Carolina, he suffered his first setback. A force of Loyalists with him was crushed by Patriot militia in a bloody battle. Loyalists now began to desert the British side, while Patriot strength grew.

Washington sent his best general, Nathanael Greene, to command the southern army. Early in 1781 Greene's soldiers routed Loyalist troops near Cowpens, South Carolina. By spring Greene felt strong enough to hit Cornwallis's main force at Guilford Court House in North Carolina. Cornwallis won, but lost almost one fourth of his army. He gave up the struggle and retreated to the coast.

British ships off the Carolina coast brought Cornwallis more troops. They marched to Virginia to join the traitor Benedict Arnold, who was fighting Lafayette. Arnold had gone over to the British the year before. Together, Cornwallis and Arnold attacked American forces. Lafayette was defeated but saved his army by retreating. In late summer Cornwallis led his troops to Yorktown, on Virginia's coast. There he expected to make contact with a British fleet.

His plans were ruined by the French navy and the Continental Army. Admiral de Grasse (grahs) brought his fleet north from the West Indies.

The fleet blocked the entrance to Chesapeake Bay. Then de Grasse put 4,000 soldiers ashore to help Lafayette. The forces kept Cornwallis from leaving Yorktown by land.

To complete the trap, Washington joined forces with a second French army, 5,000 troops under the command of the Comte de Rochambeau (RŌ-shahm-BŌ). Together, they marched south from New York toward Virginia. The allied forces were joined by Lafayette at Williamsburg, just outside Yorktown. Cornwallis was now surrounded and outnumbered. On October 19, 1781, his army of nearly 8,000 soldiers laid down their arms. When Lord North, the head of the British government, heard the news, he cried out, "It is all over!"

THE TREATY OF PARIS

The British had lost the will to continue. But it took more than a year and a half to make peace with the United States, France, Spain, and the Netherlands. At the peace talks in Paris, the United States was represented by Benjamin Franklin, John Adams, John Jay, and Henry Laurens. Jay, from New York, and Laurens, from South Carolina, had both been presidents of the Second Continental Congress.

The British agreed to recognize the colonies as independent states. But the Americans had other demands as well. They insisted that all territory from the Great Lakes south to Florida and from the Appalachian Mountains to the Mississippi River become part of the United States. West Florida had been won by the Spanish when Bernardo de Gálvez took Mobile in 1780 and Pensacola in 1781. Therefore, Florida, in British hands since 1763, was returned to Spain.

The Americans also wanted the right to use the Mississippi and to fish off the coast of Newfoundland. And they asked that British forces leave the territory of the United States "with all convenient speed."

After much hard bargaining, the British gave in to the demands. In return, the Americans made two promises. Congress, they pledged, would recommend that the states return Loyalist property that had been taken during the war. Congress would also ask the states not to prevent British merchants from collecting prewar debts from Americans.

On September 3, 1783, the Treaty of Paris was signed. Benjamin Franklin represented the United States at the signing of the agreement. The colonies were free to govern themselves. About the infant nation, George Washington said, "With our fate will the destiny of unborn millions be involved."

The Treaty of Paris marked the beginning of "the Great Experiment"—a representative government based on law and ideals. Many other countries watched the newly independent colonies. Would the Great Experiment work?

North America After the Treaty of Paris 1783

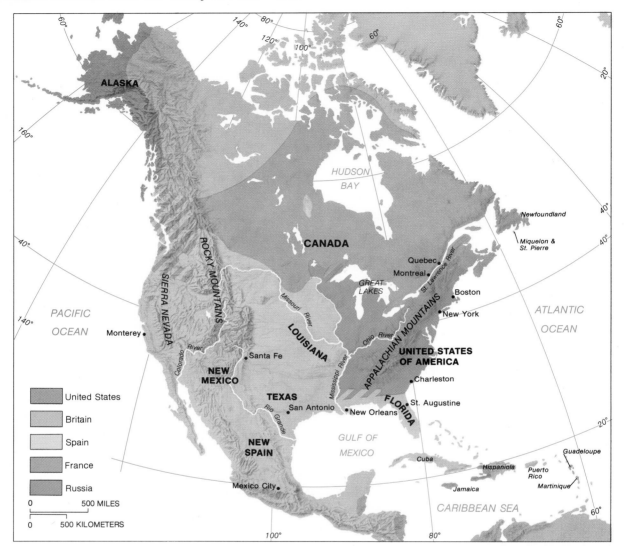

The first Treaty of Paris, in 1763, had divided North America between Britain and Spain. The second, twenty years later, greatly changed the balance of power.

SECTION REVIEW Answers will be found on page T 38.

1. Define this word: *guerrillas.*

2. Identify: George Rogers Clark, John Paul Jones, Francis Marion, Nathanael Greene.

3. How did British strategy change after France entered the war?

4. Why did General Cornwallis fail to gain control of North and South Carolina?

5. How was Cornwallis trapped at Yorktown?

6. What did the United States gain from the Treaty of Paris?

CHAPTER SUMMARY

The Revolutionary War began at Lexington and Concord, Massachusetts, in the spring of 1775. The Second Continental Congress asked George Washington to make an army out of the militia troops surrounding Boston. Although George III declared that the colonies were in rebellion, Americans had a hard time deciding to separate from the British Empire. Finally, in July 1776, Congress declared that the "United Colonies" were free and independent states.

Britain hoped to crush the American Revolution quickly by destroying the Continental Army. Washington was defeated and driven out of New York and south through New Jersey. But he struck back boldly at Trenton and Princeton, raising the spirits of the Patriots. Although the British took Philadelphia in 1777, Burgoyne surrendered a large army at Saratoga. France then came into the war on the side of the United States.

Because of hardships suffered by Washington's soldiers, it was difficult to keep the Continental Army in the war. The weak Congress, uncooperative states, and profiteering caused supply shortages. The army was saved by Americans who did more than their share, the leadership of Washington, and the patriotism of the soldiers.

After France came into the war, the British changed their strategy and tried to conquer the southern states. They were successful in Georgia. But Patriot guerrillas pinned down General Cornwallis in the Carolinas. Then a new southern army led by General Nathanael Greene stopped the British.

In 1781 combined French and American forces trapped Cornwallis at Yorktown. He surrendered, and the British government lost the will to continue the war. At peace talks in Paris, the United States gained independence and territory for future settlement.

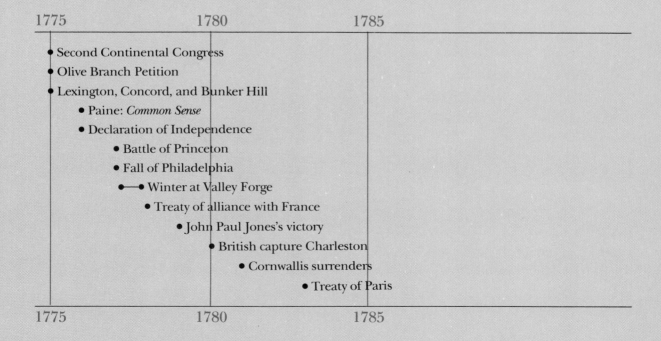

1775   1780   1785

- Second Continental Congress
- Olive Branch Petition
- Lexington, Concord, and Bunker Hill
- Paine: *Common Sense*
- Declaration of Independence
- Battle of Princeton
- Fall of Philadelphia
- Winter at Valley Forge
- Treaty of alliance with France
- John Paul Jones's victory
- British capture Charleston
- Cornwallis surrenders
- Treaty of Paris

1775   1780   1785

CHAPTER SURVEY

VOCABULARY REVIEW

From this list of vocabulary words, choose the one that best completes each sentence below.

(a) alliance   (f) moderates
(b) campaign   (g) radicals
(c) guerrillas   (h) tyranny
(d) inflation   (i) veterans
(e) mercenaries

1. A ___ is a planned series of connected military actions.

2. A general increase in the level of prices is called ___.

3. ___ are soldiers who set up bases in remote areas and launch hit-and-run attacks on the enemy.

4. The cruel use of power by an all-powerful ruler is ___.

5. ___ are people who favor extreme changes or reforms.

6. An ___ is an agreement between two or more nations to aid each other.

7. Former soldiers are ___.

8. ___ are people who favor gradual change.

9. Hired soldiers are called ___.

CHAPTER REVIEW

1. (a) What did the moderates in Congress hope to accomplish by sending the Olive Branch Petition? (b) How did Thomas Paine's pamphlet *Common Sense* help change the way the American colonists felt about their king?

2. Thomas Jefferson addressed the Declaration of Independence to the world, but he also wrote it for the American people. Why did he think this was necessary?

3. (a) When the Revolutionary War began, what advantages did the British have? (b) What disadvantages did they face? (c) How did the British hope to win the war?

4. (a) What advantages did the American Patriots have? (b) What disadvantages did they face?

5. (a) What effect did the retreat of the Continental Army have on Loyalists and Patriots in New Jersey? (b) How did Loyalists in Georgia respond to the British capture of Savannah? (c) What effect did the Battle of King's Mountain have on Loyalists and Patriots in the Carolinas?

Artist Charles Willson Peale was a captain in the Patriot militia. In his diary, he sketched a cannon. The gun's barrel was raised and lowered by means of a large screw at the back.

6. (a) How did wartime inflation affect American patriotism? (b) What did Haym Salomon, Christopher Ludwig, and Sarah Smith have in common? (c) How did women help the war effort?

7. (a) In what ways were the Marquis de Lafayette and Baron Friedrich von Steuben alike? (b) In what way were they different?

8. (a) Why did the British change their strategy in 1778? (b) Why did General Clinton abandon Philadelphia? (c) Why was General Cornwallis unable to escape from Yorktown by sea?

9. The Continental Army fought the British at Monmouth Court House and at Yorktown. (a) What kind of American soldiers kept Cornwallis's army from gaining control of South Carolina? (b) How did they achieve their goal?

10. What were the main features of the Treaty of Paris?

Abigail Smith Adams kept her husband informed of British troop movements in her letters during the Revolutionary War. She was an early supporter of rights for women. Gilbert Stuart made this sketch of her for a portrait he painted in 1812.

GEOGRAPHY REVIEW

1. (a) What valley did the British need to capture in order to cut the New England colonies off from the other American colonies? (b) Why did the British want to take New York City?

*CT **2.** Look at the map "North America After the Treaty of Paris 1783" on page 178. (a) What four foreign countries held territory in North America after the treaty? (b) Which of the four held the most territory? (c) Which held the least?

Using Scale on Maps

2. Look at the map "The Revolutionary War 1778–1781" on page 176. (a) In which direction did British forces go when they marched from Savannah to Augusta? (b) Approximately how far did they travel? (c) In what state was the Battle of Cowpens fought? (d) Was the Battle of Cowpens a British or an American victory?

USING THE TOOLS OF HISTORY

Recognizing Points of View

*CT **1.** What point of view, Loyalist or Patriot, is reflected in each of the following statements? (a) "To think of succeeding by force of arms . . . is proof of shameful ignorance, pride, and stupidity." (b) "Our cause is just. Our union is perfect. Our internal resources are great, and, if necessary, foreign assistance is undoubtedly available. . . . "

READING AND THINKING SKILLS

*CT **Main Ideas and Topic Sentences**

Find the heading "The Failure to Provide Supplies" on page 170. (a) What is the topic sentence of the first paragraph under the heading? (b) What is the topic sentence of the second paragraph? (c) In the second paragraph, what details or examples are given to support the topic sentence? (d) What is the topic sentence of the last paragraph?

Answers will be found on page T 39.

UNIT SURVEY

UNIT REVIEW

1. (a) What name did William Bradford give to the Separatists who founded Plymouth Colony? (b) What eventually happened to Plymouth Colony? (c) What two New England colonies were founded south of Massachusetts? (d) What two colonies located to the north of Massachusetts were taken over by it?

2. (a) What name did the Dutch give their colony stretching along the Hudson River? (b) How was this name changed when the English seized the colony? (c) Which two colonies were a haven to many Quakers? (d) Which colony had an assembly but no governor of its own?

3. (a) In what colony did Bacon's Rebellion take place? (b) What colony was a haven to many Catholics? (c) What two southern colonies were formed from a single land grant? (d) What colony was a haven to many debtors?

4. (a) In what places did most colonists live? (b) In what places were colonists best informed about current events? (c) What colonists relied most strongly on the mercantile system for their living? (d) How did these colonists differ from plantation owners?

5. (a) Who was responsible for local governments in the colonies? (b) Who was responsible for paying the salaries of royal governors?

6. (a) Why did Britain need to raise money after the French and Indian War? (b) Why did it seem fair to Parliament to tax the colonies in North America? (c) Why did this new taxation required by Parliament seem unfair to many colonists?

7. (a) What kind of taxes were called for by the Sugar Act of 1764 and the Townshend Acts of 1767? (b) What did colonists do to avoid paying these taxes?

8. (a) What colonial city was a scene of violence connected to the Townshend Acts? (b) What colony was the target of the Coercive Acts? (c) What event caused Parliament to pass the Coercive Acts?

9. (a) Why were Americans slow to declare their independence after the start of the Revolutionary War? (b) How did *Common Sense* help lead to the Declaration of Independence? (c) What people in the colonies opposed independence?

10. (a) What foreign nation gave most help to the Patriot war effort? (b) How did rivalries in Europe prompt that nation to help the Patriots? (c) In terms of the mercantile system, what did Britain lose by losing the Revolutionary War?

Mary Woodhull's needlepoint picture showed the new nation as a rich and beautiful New England farm. Here, two wheat reapers plan a picnic by a pond.

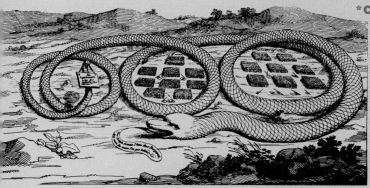

James Gillray's "American Rattle Snake" coils around the armies of Burgoyne and Cornwallis. In 1782 the snake was ready to crush the British.

LINKING THE PAST AND THE PRESENT

1. The occupations of blacksmith, cooper, and miller were popular in the 1700s. Look for these or similar occupations in the advertising pages of your telephone directory. Check under headings such as "blacksmith," "iron," "metal," "steel," "cooper," "barrels," "miller," and "flour." List the occupations you find.

*CT 2. Puritan ideas led to "blue laws" in New England. These laws banned selling, sports, and other activities on Sundays. (They were called blue laws because one list of the laws was printed on blue paper.) Find out whether businesses in your area stay closed or close early on Sundays. If so, try to discover whether local laws require them to close.

MEETING THE BUILDERS OF AMERICA

*CT 1. Review the descriptions of Eliza Lucas Pinckney (page 101), Andrew Hamilton (page 123), John Adams (page 146), and Deborah Sampson (page 172). In what ways did they contribute to America?

*CT 2. Prepare a report about the contributions to American life of some other person or group mentioned in Unit 2. For example, look for information about Roger Williams, Anne Hutchinson, William Penn, Benjamin Franklin, the Pennsylvania Dutch, Mercy Otis Warren, Crispus Attucks, Nathan Hale, Margaret Cochran Corbin, or others. You may be able to use one of the following books as a source of information.

Davis, Burke. *Black Heroes of the American Revolution.* New York: Harcourt Brace Jovanovich, 1976.

Latham, Frank B. *The Trial of John Peter Zenger, August 1735.* New York: Watts, 1970.

Phelan, Mary K. *Four Days in Philadelphia, 1776.* New York: Crowell, 1967.

SUGGESTIONS FOR FURTHER READING

Alderman, Clifford Lindsey. *The Story of the Thirteen Colonies.* New York: Random House, 1966.

Borden, Morton. *George Washington.* Englewood Cliffs, NJ: Prentice-Hall, 1969.

Chidsey, Donald Barr. *Valley Forge.* New York: Crown, 1962.

Lawson, Don. *The American Revolution.* New York: Abelard-Schuman, 1974.

Loeb, Robert H., Jr. *Meet the Real Pilgrims: Life on a Plimoth Plantation in 1627.* Garden City, NY: Doubleday, 1979.

Phelan, Mary K. *The Story of the Boston Massacre.* New York: Crowell, 1976.

Taylor, Theodore. *Rebellion Town, Williamsburg, 1776.* New York: Crowell, 1973.

Wibberley, Leonard. *A Dawn in the Trees, Thomas Jefferson, the Years 1776–1789.* New York: Farrar, Straus & Giroux, 1964.

Detail from a sampler by Maria Bolen, 1816.

BUILDING A NEW NATION

FORMING A UNION
THE FEDERALISTS LAUNCH THE REPUBLIC
THE REPUBLICANS IN CHARGE

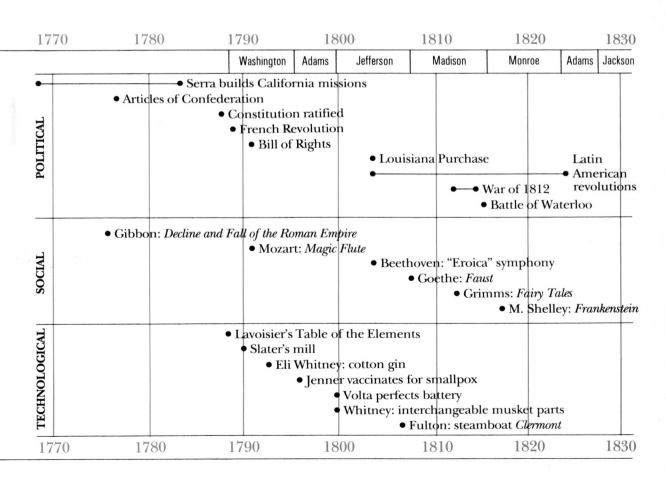

1770	1780	1790	1800	1810	1820	1830

| | Washington | Adams | Jefferson | Madison | Monroe | Adams | Jackson |

POLITICAL
- Serra builds California missions
- Articles of Confederation
- Constitution ratified
- French Revolution
- Bill of Rights
- Louisiana Purchase
- Latin American revolutions
- War of 1812
- Battle of Waterloo

SOCIAL
- Gibbon: *Decline and Fall of the Roman Empire*
- Mozart: *Magic Flute*
- Beethoven: "Eroica" symphony
- Goethe: *Faust*
- Grimms: *Fairy Tales*
- M. Shelley: *Frankenstein*

TECHNOLOGICAL
- Lavoisier's Table of the Elements
- Slater's mill
- Eli Whitney: cotton gin
- Jenner vaccinates for smallpox
- Volta perfects battery
- Whitney: interchangeable musket parts
- Fulton: steamboat *Clermont*

1770	1780	1790	1800	1810	1820	1830

Introducing: Direct students' attention to Mercy Otis Warren's comparison below. Ask in what ways a new nation might be like a child. What skills might it have to master?

CHAPTER 8 1777-1788

FORMING A UNION

THE FIRST NATIONAL GOVERNMENT
THE CONSTITUTIONAL CONVENTION
THE STRUGGLE FOR RATIFICATION
THE CONSTITUTION

8-1 THE FIRST NATIONAL GOVERNMENT

republic: government based on the will of the people, in which elected representatives act for them
federation: union formed by agreement among states, nations, or groups
currencies: money
cede: transfer
ordinance: law

READ TO FIND OUT

—what the words *republic, federation, currencies, cede,* and *ordinance* mean.

—what kind of government the Articles of Confederation created.

—what problems the new national government faced.

—how the Northwest Ordinance set the pattern for the settlement of new territories.

With the signing of the Treaty of Paris in 1783, the War for Independence was over. Yet the future seemed unsure. Writer Mercy Otis Warren said that America was "as a child just learning to walk."

NEW STATE GOVERNMENTS

During the war the states had written new constitutions. The constitutions replaced the colonial governments. These constitutions gave the states a republican form of government. In a **republic,** the power, or authority, of the government is based on the will of the people. The

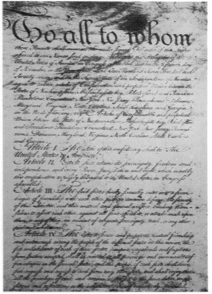

New Jersey women were allowed to vote by their new state constitution. This right was taken away in 1807.

The Articles of Confederation and Perpetual Union Between the States went into effect after all the states had approved them in 1781.

people give their elected representatives the power to act for them. The representatives meet and make laws for the people.

State constitutions included bills, or lists, of rights. The Virginia Declaration of Rights listed rights such as trial by jury, freedom of the press, and freedom of religion. The Massachusetts Declaration of Rights included a statement from the Declaration of Independence that "all men are born free and equal." A state court ruled that this statement ended slavery in Massachusetts. In the other northern states, laws were passed ending slavery.

Voting became easier in most states after the war. In every state but Massachusetts, the amount of property a person had to own in order to vote was reduced. In Georgia and Pennsylvania any man who paid taxes could vote. New Jersey briefly allowed women who met the property requirement to vote.

THE ARTICLES OF CONFEDERATION

Creating a workable national government was more difficult than setting up state governments. During the war with Britain, delegates from the states met in Congress. As they wrote the Declaration of Independence, they also debated the need for a national government.

Most delegates believed that a strong central government would not work in America. Voters would not be able to control a national government located hundreds of miles away. The delegates also worried that a strong national government might threaten the same rights they were

For discussion: How might the states' experience in governing themselves (and before the Revolution in governing themselves as colonies) aid them in governing the nation as a whole? (You may wish students to take special note of the fact that states had constitutions with bills of rights.)

Point out that during the Revolution and the early years of the United States, many Americans were inclined to think of themselves more as citizens of particular states than as citizens of one nation.

fighting to preserve. But Americans wanted a national government strong enough to represent them in dealings with powerful nations like Britain and France.

The first national government was designed to be a weak **federation** of states. A federation is a union formed by an agreement among states, nations, or groups. The delegates in Congress put the agreement in writing and called it the Articles of Confederation.

The Articles created a Congress in which each state had one vote. The representatives to Congress were chosen by state legislatures. The powers of Congress were limited to matters that concerned all the states. Congress could make war and peace and direct affairs with other nations and with Indian nations. It could coin money, set up post offices, and raise an army or a navy.

Yet Congress had been given no power to carry out its decisions. There was no head of government to put laws into effect. There were no national courts to enforce the laws that Congress made. Congress could not even set taxes to pay its own expenses and the nation's war debts. Instead, it had to ask the state legislatures for funds. Often the states ignored such requests.

PROBLEMS FACING THE NEW GOVERNMENT

Have students review what they have learned about balance of trade (Chapter 3, page 53).

The new government faced difficult economic problems. With the war over, merchants went on a buying spree, filling their shops with manufactured goods from Britain. Many of these imports were priced so low that American manufacturers could not compete.

Even more serious, the nation was not earning enough to pay for these imports. After the war Britain closed the British West Indies to American exports. Farmers, fishers, and merchants lost their best customers. The United States was buying more from Britain than it was selling to that country. As a result, the new nation suffered from an unfavorable balance of trade. Its tiny supply of gold and silver shrank rapidly as Americans paid for the imported goods.

If Congress could tax imports, it could raise the price of British-made goods and make them less attractive to Americans. But Congress did not have that power.

Because gold and silver were in short supply, Congress did not have enough to coin money. States began printing their own paper money, which was not backed by gold or silver. The result was a confusion of **currencies,** or money. Congress did not have the power to stop the states from printing money.

Congress even lacked the power to control trade between the states. Some states began to tax imports from other states. Merchants complained, but Congress could not help them.

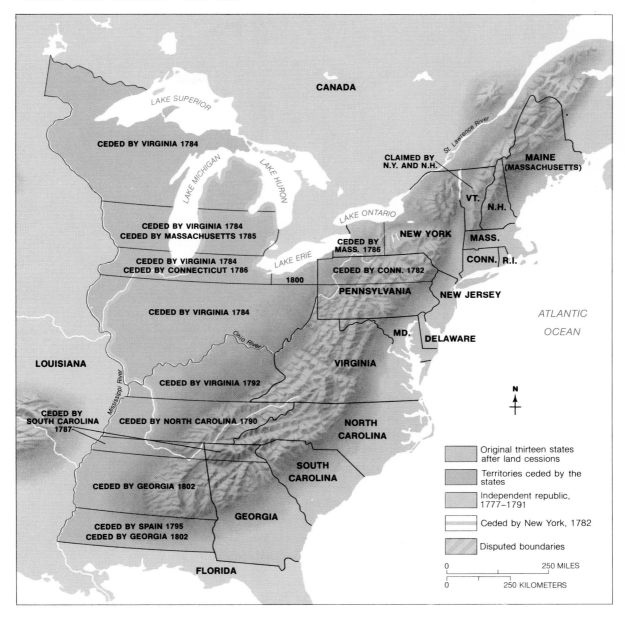

THE NORTHWEST TERRITORY

Congress had more success in planning for the settlement of the Northwest Territory. Several colonies claimed the vast area northwest of the Ohio River, east of the Mississippi, and south of the Great Lakes. After the war, the new states **ceded,** or transferred, their western lands to Congress. In 1785 Congress passed an **ordinance,** or law. The Land Ordinance of 1785 created a system for settling the Northwest Territory.

Have students compare this map with a present-day map of the United States to determine what states were created from the original thirteen states' land cessions.

The Northwest Territory 1787

The Northwest Territory offered settlers rich forest lands. After the Northwest Ordinance was adopted, frontier villages sprouted in the wilderness. Often they were located on the many rivers that drain this region.

You may wish to point out that, as the United States acquired more territory (such as the Louisiana Purchase), the question of which territories and new states should be free and which should allow slavery became a burning issue dividing the North and South. Students will discover the consequences of this issue when they study Chapters 13, 14, and 15.

Congress was eager to sell land in order to raise money. When a land company called the Ohio Company offered to buy 1,500,000 acres (607,050 hectares), Congress agreed. At the same time, it passed the Northwest Ordinance of 1787. The ordinance said that the Northwest Territory should be divided into three, four, or five territories. In time, these territories could become states. New settlers there would have the same rights as other Americans. Slavery was forbidden.

Once settlers arrived in a territory, Congress would appoint a territorial governor. When there were 5,000 free men in the territory, they could elect their own legislature. Once there were 60,000 people there, they could apply to Congress to become a state. New states were equal to the existing states in every way.

This system of settling new lands worked well. The same pattern was followed as the nation expanded westward.

CONFLICTS WITH OTHER COUNTRIES

While Congress planned for the settlement of the West, British soldiers refused to leave their forts in the Northwest Territory. Americans protested that they were breaking the Treaty of Paris. The British replied that the Americans had already broken the treaty by not paying the debts that they owed to Britain.

In the Mediterranean, American ships were not safe. While the ships sailed under the British flag, they were protected. But after the war when they sailed under the Stars and Stripes, they were in danger. Pirates attacked many of them. The captains and crews of the captured

UNDERSTANDING GEOGRAPHY

THE NORTHWEST SURVEY SYSTEM

At the end of the Revolutionary War, the new nation was deeply in debt. The war debts had to be repaid, but where was the money going to come from?

The best source of money seemed to be the Northwest Territory. Selling this land could raise the money needed to pay off the war debts. But there was no procedure for the orderly division of new lands.

At the time, settlers simply went into the wilderness and chose the land they wanted. Their claims often had odd shapes because they drew boundary lines to exclude swamps, steep slopes, and other unusable land.

The descriptions of such land were confusing. A typical description was, "Start at the granite boulder. Run a line southeast to the old chestnut stump. Turn at an angle of 45° and run a line to the old barn," and so on.

This description was fine as long as everyone knew what it meant. After several generations, however, the boulder might have been moved or the barn might have burned down. Not surprisingly, people often argued about boundary claims.

To avoid such problems, Congress passed the Land Ordinance of 1785. It created a system for the sale and settlement of the Northwest Territory.

The new land was broken up into areas called *townships,* each 6 miles square (9.6 kilometers square). Each township was then divided into 36 *sections* of 640 acres (259 hectares). The sections could be further subdivided into half-sections, quarter-sections, and so on.

Four sections of each township were set aside for use by the national government. One was to be used for public schools. The rest of the land could then be sold to settlers.

To lay out boundaries, geographers had to survey, or measure, the land. They used lines of latitude and longitude, like those on a map, to divide the townships. The parallels (latitude lines) and meridians (longitude lines) made a checkerboard pattern of sections. The diagram below shows how the survey worked.

This survey system was followed in territories and states across the country. It has produced a landscape in the American heartland that looks like a checkerboard. Roads and fences often follow township lines and thus run directly north, south, east, or west. Farms are often a section or a subsection in size. Even many state boundaries are drawn along parallels and meridians. This compass-based landscape is distinctly American.

Land Ordinance Survey System

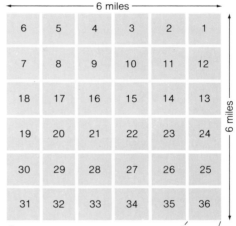

One township

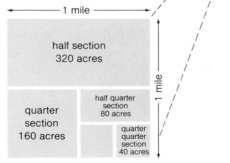

One section

ships were sold as slaves. The United States was powerless to stop the raids and had to buy protection from Morocco.

Spain did not accept American claims to land south of the Ohio River. The Spanish refused to let settlers west of the Appalachians ship their crops down the Mississippi River to New Orleans. New Orleans was the only place where these farmers could load their goods onto ocean-going ships for export.

Congress had no army or navy to back up its protests with force. Meanwhile, Spain and Britain waited, expecting the new nation to fall apart. When it did, they could pick up the pieces.

SHAYS' REBELLION

The new nation did not fall apart, but in the summer of 1786, a rebellion flared in Massachusetts. In Boston, the legislature had voted for high taxes in order to pay off the state's war debts. Back-country farmers had no money to pay their taxes. They faced the loss of their farms. Resentment grew. In one county after another, farmers began to break up court sessions. Such action prevented judges from ordering farms sold to pay tax bills.

Violence broke out in January 1787. A farmer and veteran named Daniel Shays led 1,200 followers into Springfield to seize weapons from a national government arsenal, or place for storing weapons. State militia troops quickly put down the rebellion.

Shays' Rebellion had many sympathizers. When Massachusetts governor James Bowdoin, who had called out the state militia, ran for reelection, he was defeated.

When Daniel Shays led his band of angry farmers into Springfield, Massachusetts, they were met by state militia troops. The troops fired to protect the federal arsenal. The retreating rebels left four of their band lying dead in the January snow.

The ending of slavery in the northern states helped to create new opportunities for blacks living there. Lemuel Haynes became the first black minister of the Congregational Church in America during the 1780s. On this metal tray, Haynes is in the pulpit.

Shays' Rebellion shocked the nation. Law and order were breaking down. The national government could not even protect its own arsenal. More and more Americans came to believe that only a strong national government could enforce law, keep order, and solve the problems facing the federation. Throughout the country there was a desire to bring the thirteen states into agreement and form a workable government.

SECTION REVIEW   Answers will be found on page T 40.

1. Define these words: *republic, federation, currencies, cede, ordinance.*

2. Identify: Daniel Shays.

3. What kind of national government was created by the Articles of Confederation?

4. Britain sold its manufactured goods to Americans at low prices. It also banned American-made goods in the British West Indies. How did this hurt American merchants and manufacturers?

5. Why was Congress unable to tax imports or stop the states from printing paper money?

6. Once settlers arrived in the Northwest Territory, what steps did they need to go through to make their territory into a state?

7. Why did Shays' Rebellion shock the nation?

8-2 THE CONSTITUTIONAL CONVENTION

READ TO FIND OUT

legislative branch:
branch of government
that makes laws
executive branch:
branch that carries out
laws
judicial branch:
branch that judges
laws' meaning in court
cases
bicameral: having
two chambers or
houses
unicameral: having
one chamber or house
compromise: agree-
ment in which each
side gives up part of
what it wants

—what the words *legislative branch, executive branch, judicial branch, bicameral, unicameral,* and *compromise* mean.

—why a constitutional convention was called in 1787.

—why states with large populations favored the Virginia Plan.

—why states with small populations favored the New Jersey Plan.

—what compromises saved the convention from failure.

—what method the delegates chose for electing a President.

In September 1786 delegates from five states—New York, New Jersey, Delaware, Pennsylvania, and Virginia—held a convention at Annapolis, Maryland. They met to talk about trade problems but soon decided that little could be done by only a few states. The Annapolis Convention ended with a call for a meeting of all thirteen states to discuss the problems facing the nation.

Shays' Rebellion shocked Congress into acting on this suggestion. On February 21, 1787, Congress invited the states to send representatives to Philadelphia in May. The purpose of this convention was to revise and improve the Articles of Confederation. Many people felt that the government, unable to tax, regulate trade, or enforce laws, was not working.

THE DELEGATES TO THE CONVENTION

Fifty-five delegates, from every state except Rhode Island, came to Philadelphia. They were a remarkable group. More than half had served in the Continental Congress. Many had helped write their state constitutions, and most had served in their state legislatures. Seven had been state governors. Twenty-one had fought in the Revolutionary War. Two of the young nation's most important leaders were absent. Thomas Jefferson was representing the United States in France. John Adams was serving as ambassador to England.

For a group with so much experience in government, the delegates were surprisingly young. Five of them were under 30. George Washington, at 55, was one of the older members. Benjamin Franklin, at 81, was

the honored elder of the convention. The delegates were among the best-educated citizens of the nation. And they had learned to think nationally. They could see beyond the interests of their own states to the interests of the nation as a whole.

THE CONVENTION BEGINS

The delegates met in the Philadelphia statehouse on May 25. Their first action was to elect Washington president of the convention. The former general took the president's chair, which had a sun painted on its back. He said very little from that chair. Yet his presence helped hold the convention together in the stormy days ahead.

James Madison of Virginia came to the convention better prepared than anyone else. He had spent months studying other governments, both ancient and modern. He helped the representatives from Virginia draw up a plan of government for the convention to consider.

THE VIRGINIA PLAN

The convention delegates had come to revise the Articles of Confederation. But the Virginia Plan went far beyond the Articles. It was a proposal for a new constitution. The Virginia Plan called for a government with three branches. The **legislative branch** would make laws. The **executive branch** would carry out laws. The **judicial branch** would judge the meaning of laws.

When Washington took his place as president of the Constitutional Convention, he had no idea that he would be sitting in that chair for the next four months.

Only thirty-six, James Madison came to the Constitutional Convention with considerable political experience. He had served on the committee drafting Virginia's constitution and Declaration of Rights. He had been a member of the Virginia state assembly and a Congressman. Tell students they will learn more about Madison as an author of the *Federalist Papers* (page 201) and as our fourth President (Chapter 10).

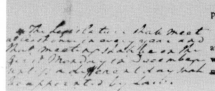

WE the People of the States of New-Hampfhire, Maffachufetts, Rhode-Ifland and Providence Plantations, Connecticut, New-York, New-Jerfey, Pennfylvania, Delaware, Maryland, Virginia, North-Carolina, South-Carolina, and Georgia, do ordain, declare and eftablifh the following Conftitution for the Government of Ourfelves and our Pofterity.

A R T I C L E I.

The ftile of this Government fhall be, " The United States of America."

II.

The Government fhall confift of fupreme legiflative, executive and judicial powers.

III.

The legiflative power fhall be vefted in a Congrefs, to confift of two feparate and diftinct bodies of men, a Houfe of Reprefentatives, and a Senate; each of which fhall, in all cafes, have a negative on the other. The Legiflature fhall meet on the firft Monday in December in every year.

IV.

During the convention, delegates worked from printed copies of the latest draft of the Constitution. Changes were written in by hand. This draft shows changes in the delegates' thinking about the Congress.

The inkstand used during the convention had one container for ink and another for sand. Sand was used to help blot wet ink.

William Paterson served as governor of New Jersey, Senator, and Supreme Court Justice. The city of Paterson, New Jersey, was named after him.

For discussion: Why might the larger states be against the New Jersey Plan?

The plan suggested a **bicameral** legislature. *Bicameral* means "having two chambers." Under the plan, Congress would be made up of two chambers, or houses. The number of representatives sent by a state to each house depended on its population. States with large populations would have more representatives. States with smaller populations would have fewer. Laws would be made by a majority vote of the members of both houses. Congress would also choose a chief officer for the executive branch and judges for the judicial branch.

The large states found much to like in the Virginia Plan. They would control the new government. The smaller states, however, were fearful of the Virginia Plan and suggested a plan of their own.

THE NEW JERSEY PLAN

The New Jersey Plan, put forward by William Paterson, also called for a government with three branches. The legislature, however, would be **unicameral,** having one house. Each state would have an equal number of representatives and votes. The legislature would choose the people who made up the executive and judicial branches.

Paterson and other delegates from the smaller states wanted a federation of equal and independent states. Otherwise, Paterson argued, a small state like New Jersey would be "swallowed up" by larger states.

After a hot debate, the New Jersey Plan was voted down on June 19. That night Washington wrote home that he would not be back for the spring harvest. "God knows how long it may be after that," he said.

OLAUDAH EQUIANO

In 1756 an African boy named Olaudah Equiano was thrown into the hold of a slave ship. The hold was dark, hot, and cramped. Africans in chains were jammed so closely together that they could scarcely breathe.

Terrified, the boy asked what was to be done with them. He was told that they would be taken to the "white people's country" to work. Equiano was relieved. "If it were no worse than working," he thought, "my situation was not so desperate."

The boy survived the nightmarish journey to the West Indies. There, the Africans were marched to a merchant's yard and penned "like so many sheep." Finally Equiano understood. He was to be sold into slavery.

Equiano was sold to a Virginia planter, who then sold him to an English sea captain. Once more, the boy went to sea. But this time there was no one who spoke his language.

Born in the African kingdom of Benin, Equiano was proud of his native land. He described it as "a nation of musicians and poets."

Aboard ship, he began to watch his master reading books. Once, Equiano took a book and "talked to it and then put my ears to it . . . in hopes it would answer me." He was dismayed when it remained silent. Slowly, the boy learned to speak and read English.

In 1763 Equiano was sold again. Now he served an American merchant in the West Indies. Equiano's sailing skills were put to use on the merchant's trading ships. The ships carried rum and sugar between the West Indies and America. They also carried, as Equiano sadly put it, "a live cargo, as we call a cargo of slaves." Equiano was above decks, but still an unwilling part of the slave trade.

Equiano decided to escape the "sound of the cruel whip." Eventually, he earned enough money to buy his freedom. Just twenty-one years old, with the proud new title of "freeman," he set out to see the world.

Years later, Equiano described his life in a book. He wrote of the slave trade, and how it violated the fundamental human right of freedom. The book, published in 1789, became a best seller in England and America.

Americans had compromised on the slave trade in their new Constitution. But many still opposed the slave trade. Their opposition was strengthened by the moving story of Equiano. Equiano's book, unlike the books of his one-time master, would not remain silent.

The compromise on slavery is discussed on page 198.

THE GREAT COMPROMISE

In Philadelphia the summer of 1787 was hot and humid. In the state-house, tempers often rose with the temperature. The delegates could not agree on how the states should be represented in the legislative branch. Delegates of large states favored the Virginia Plan. Gunning Bedford of tiny Delaware threatened that the small states might pull out of the convention and look for "some foreign ally."

Later Bedford blamed the "warmth" of his language on the "habits of his profession" (lawyer). Still, he did not retreat far from his original

You may wish to call special attention to the disagreement about runaway slaves, which became a burning issue in the years before the Civil War.

For discussion: Why is the ability to compromise important to the democratic process?

position. The search for representation that would be acceptable to all delegates had turned into a bitter battle. Alexander Hamilton of New York called it a "contest for power, not for liberty" that had divided otherwise sensible people into foes. Control of the new government for years to come was at stake.

Roger Sherman of Connecticut saved the convention by proposing a **compromise.** A compromise is an agreement in which each side gives up part of what it wants. Sherman's proposal combined ideas borrowed from both the Virginia Plan and the New Jersey Plan.

The compromise called for a bicameral legislature. One house, the House of Representatives, would represent the people directly. The number of Representatives from each state would depend on the state's population. Voters in each state would elect members of the House.

The second house, the Senate, would represent the states. Each state would have the same number of Senators, who would be elected by state legislatures. In the Senate all states would be equal regardless of size of population. This plan was accepted after a few days of debate. It came to be known as the Great Compromise because it kept the convention from falling apart.

COMPROMISES ON SLAVERY

Poet Phillis Wheatley was born in Africa and sold into slavery in Boston. She became the first black American to have her work published. A slave named Scipio Moorhead drew this portrait for the title page of her book.

Other compromises followed. Some of them touched on slavery, which was disappearing in the northern states. Northern delegates argued that slaves should not be counted as part of each state's population in determining its number of seats in the House of Representatives. Slaves, they said, were looked upon as property. Slaves should be counted, then, when property taxes were set.

Southern states, though, wanted as many Representatives as possible. Their delegates believed slaves should be counted for representation in the House but not for property taxes. The argument between the North and the South was settled by the Three-fifths Compromise. Each slave would be counted as three fifths of a person both for representation in the House and for taxation.

The delegates also clashed over the slave trade. Northerners wanted an end to slavery and the slave trade. Southerners argued that they needed more slaves to work their farms and plantations. They would not give up the right to bring slaves into the country.

Then there was the problem of runaway slaves. Many slaves had been escaping to free states, where they became free citizens. Slave states wanted slaves returned to their owners. Finally, both sides agreed that Congress could make no law ending the slave trade until after 1808. They also agreed that all states would be required to return runaway slaves to their owners.

COMPROMISES ON TRADE

Northerners and southerners also argued over issues of trade. In the North, trade and manufacturing were growing in importance. Because of this, northern delegates thought Congress should have the power to control trade between states and with foreign countries. They wanted Congress to be able to levy customs duties on foreign imports. These taxes would raise the price of imports. American businesses would then be protected from foreign competition.

Southern states depended on exporting cash crops. Southerners were afraid that Congress would use the power to control trade to tax their exports. That would make their crops more expensive to foreign buyers and less likely to be sold. General Charles Cotesworth Pinckney, a delegate from South Carolina, summed up the fears of many southerners. He warned the other delegates not to leave out "some security to the southern states against . . . taxes on exports." In yet another compromise, Congress was given the power to tax imports but not exports.

Trade was the lifeblood of northern port cities like New York. The corner of Water Street and Wall Street was often clogged with goods and people.

THE ELECTORAL COLLEGE

For discussion: Students should remember that many of the delegates to the Constitutional Convention were leading citizens and officials of their states. How then does this final agreement on the Constitution suggest that the states were now going to make an important commitment to becoming a nation rather than simply a confederation?

It was hard to decide how to choose the nation's chief executive officer, the President. Many delegates did not want the people to elect the President directly. They thought that people could not vote wisely for candidates from distant states. Some delegates believed that Congress should choose the President. Yet others felt that a President could not be independent if he depended on Congress for his office.

At first a committee recommended that the national legislature elect the executive for one seven-year term. After that was voted down, many other proposals were suggested. Confusion and tension reigned. One delegate, Elbridge Gerry of Massachusetts, said, "We seem to be entirely at a loss on this head." Whatever method of presidential election was decided upon, it had to be politically workable—it had to balance between small and large states.

After long argument, the delegates decided to have each state choose electors. The electors would then meet as the electoral college to elect a President and a Vice-President. Since the electors were expected to be people experienced in government, it was believed that they would make good choices.

THE RISING SUN

Finally the convention had finished its work. Franklin said that he approved the Constitution "because I expect no better, and because I am not sure that it is not the best." On September 17 the delegates met for the last time to sign the Constitution. Thirty-nine of the 55 delegates signed it. Franklin remarked to Madison that he had often looked at the sun painted on Washington's chair "without being able to tell whether it was rising or setting. But now, at length, I have the happiness to know that it is a rising and not a setting sun."

The "rising sun" chair was used by Washington as president of the convention.

SECTION REVIEW   Answers will be found on page T 41.

1. Define these words: *legislative branch, executive branch, judicial branch, bicameral, unicameral, compromise.*

2. Identify: James Madison, William Paterson, Three-fifths Compromise, electoral college.

3. What was the original purpose of the convention in 1787? How did that purpose change?

4. What group of states liked the Virginia Plan? The New Jersey Plan? How did the Great Compromise satisfy both groups?

5. What was the purpose of the electoral college?

ratify: approve

Alexander Hamilton

8-3 THE STRUGGLE FOR RATIFICATION

READ TO FIND OUT

—what the word *ratify* means.

—who the Federalists and Anti-Federalists were.

—how the Constitution became the law of the land.

Washington described the new Constitution as "much to be wondered at." That it had, at last, come together so well seemed "little short of a miracle." Soon he worried that another miracle would be needed to get it **ratified,** or approved.

Special conventions were called in each of the thirteen states to consider the Constitution. Delegates to the conventions were elected by the people of each state. These delegates then had to decide whether to ratify or reject the Constitution. Nine of the states had to ratify the Constitution before it could become the law of the land.

THE FEDERALISTS

The supporters of the Constitution were called Federalists. They supported a strong federal, or national, government. James Madison, Alexander Hamilton, and John Jay wrote a series of newspaper articles explaining how the new government would work. These articles were later collected and called *The Federalist Papers.*

In their articles the Federalists recalled the weaknesses of the national government under the Articles of Confederation. They showed how the Constitution would create a more powerful government. This government would not threaten the liberties of Americans because the powers given to it were limited. They also explained how power was divided among the three branches. Any one branch could keep the other two from misusing its power.

THE ANTI-FEDERALISTS

The Anti-Federalists opposed ratification of the Constitution. In Massachusetts, Mercy Otis Warren wrote a pamphlet objecting to the new plan. The Constitution, she pointed out, had no bill of rights. The powers given the President made the executive too much like a monarch.

James Madison

You may wish to read passages from *The Federalist Papers* to the class.

John Jay

Other parts of the Constitution, such as the taxation clause, frightened the Anti-Federalists. Many of them felt that no matter how perfect in design the new government might be, it could not govern fairly over so vast a territory as the United States.

A delegate to the South Carolina convention put his arguments more simply. He asked, "What have you been fighting for these ten years past? Liberty? What is liberty? The power of governing yourselves. If you adopt this constitution, have you this power?" He answered this question by saying, "No: you give it into the hands of a set of men who live one thousand miles distant from you."

THE MASSACHUSETTS CONVENTION

By early January 1788 the Constitution had been ratified by Delaware, New Jersey, Georgia, Connecticut, and Pennsylvania. Then the Massachusetts Convention met. At first, 192 delegates were against ratification and 144 in favor.

A farmer named Amos Singletary worried that "the lawyers, and men of learning, and moneyed men . . . expect to get into Congress." Once in power "they will swallow up all us little folks." Another farmer, Jonathan Smith, replied, "I have known the worth of good government by the want of it. When I saw this Constitution, I found that it was a cure for these disorders."

The one person who might convince delegates to ratify the Constitution was Governor John Hancock. A group of Federalists pointed out to him that Virginia did not seem likely to ratify the Constitution. In that case Washington could not be the first President. But if Massachusetts approved the Constitution, who would be a better candidate for President than Governor Hancock?

The governor urged the delegates to approve the Constitution and to suggest that a bill of rights be added later. The vote was close, but Massachusetts became the sixth state to ratify.

Massachusetts ratified the Constitution by a majority of only 19 votes out of 355.

THE LAW OF THE LAND

Maryland ratified in April and South Carolina in May. In June New Hampshire became the important ninth state to ratify. After a long and bitter debate, Virginia also voted to ratify. New York followed in July, but Rhode Island and North Carolina held back.

The Fourth of July celebrations in 1788 were especially grand. Philadelphia was awakened early by cannon fire from the ship *Rising Sun*. A grand parade followed. The ships *Federal Constitution* and *Union* were put on wagons and pulled through the streets. The grandest float was drawn by ten white horses, one for each state that had ratified by that

Remind students that Rhode Island refused to attend the Constitutional Convention. It finally joined the Union in May 1790.

CHAPTER 8   1777-1788

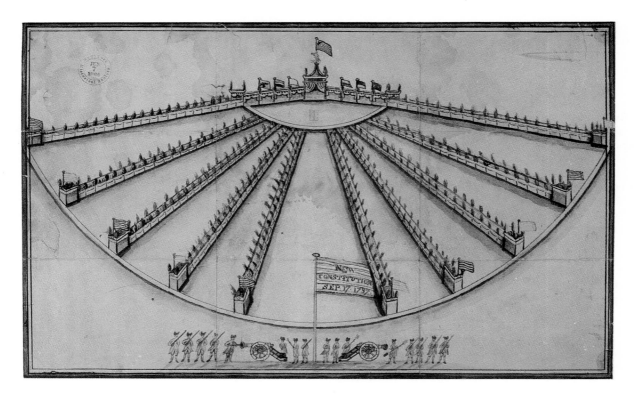

date. The float showed thirteen columns, three of them not yet complete. The ten complete columns were holding up a dome, a "New Roof" as the Constitution was called.

Dr. Benjamin Rush of Philadelphia, a signer of the Declaration of Independence, described the celebration in a letter to a friend. "Never upon any occasion during the late war," he wrote, "did I see such deep-seated joy in every face." He closed his letter saying, "Tis done. We have become a nation."

New York City celebrated the ratification of the Constitution with a huge banquet.

SECTION REVIEW   Answers will be found on page T 41.

1. Define this word: *ratify.*

2. Identify: Federalists, *The Federalist Papers,* Anti-Federalists, John Hancock.

3. How many states had to ratify the Constitution before it became the law of the land?

4. At the Massachusetts Convention, a farmer named Amos Singletary voiced the fear of many people about a strong national government. What was that fear?

5. How did John Hancock convince the Massachusetts Convention to ratify the Constitution?

Activity: After the Constitution's ratification, Dr. Benjamin Rush wrote to John Adams, ambassador to England, that it "makes us a nation. It rescues us from anarchy and slavery. It revives agriculture and commerce. It checks moral and political iniquity." Ask students to imagine they are citizens of the new nation. Have them write letters to friends abroad about what the newly-ratified Constitution means to them.

8-4 THE CONSTITUTION

READ TO FIND OUT

—what the words *separation of powers, constitutional, judicial review, checks and balances, impeach, federalism,* and *amend* mean.

—what the Preamble says about the purposes of the Constitution.

—why powers were divided among the three branches of government.

—how the system of checks and balances works.

—how and why the Constitution is flexible.

—what important rights are included in the Bill of Rights.

separation of powers: division of powers among three branches of government

constitutional: allowed under the Constitution

judicial review: power to decide whether a law is constitutional

checks and balances: system that allows each branch of government to limit powers of other two

impeach: bring charges against an official

federalism: division of powers between states and federal government

amend: change

This 1795 gold coin was decorated with the national bird, the bald eagle. The eagle holds an olive branch as a symbol of the nation's desire for peace. It also holds a cluster of arrows to show the nation's ability to defend itself.

When the Constitutional Convention was over, a friend asked Benjamin Franklin, "What kind of government have you given us, Dr. Franklin?" He answered, "A Republic, Madame, if you can keep it." Like most Americans in 1787, Franklin worried that a strong national government might end in tyranny if Americans were not watchful.

The framers, or designers, of the Constitution gave the new government the powers it needed. At the same time, they built in protections against tyranny. It was a remarkable balancing act.

THE PREAMBLE

The Constitution begins with a preamble, or a short introduction. "We the People of the United States" are the first words. These words were carefully chosen to show that the government created under the Constitution is based on the consent, or agreement, of the people.

The Preamble lists the purposes of the Constitution. The first is "to form a more perfect Union." The framers hoped that this new Constitution would hold the states together better than the Articles of Confederation had done. The second purpose is "to establish justice." The third is "to insure domestic tranquility." This means to keep peace within the country.

The fourth purpose is to "provide for the common defense," or protect the nation from foreign enemies. A fifth purpose is to "promote the general welfare." The framers intended for the government to do what was in its limited power to do to improve life in America.

The final purpose stated in the Preamble is to "secure the blessings of liberty to ourselves and our posterity." This means preserving and protecting our freedoms not just for ourselves, but for all Americans who come after us. These purposes are as important today as they were in 1787. They state what a good government should do for the people who live under it.

THREE BRANCHES OF GOVERNMENT

The Constitution is divided into seven articles, or sections. The first three articles set up three branches of government, each with its own powers. By this **separation of powers,** the framers believed they could keep any one branch from becoming too powerful.

Article 1 describes the Congress with its two houses, the House of Representatives and the Senate. Congress has two main tasks. One is to levy, or set, taxes. The second is to pass laws needed to carry out the purposes stated in the Preamble. Congress also has the power to declare war, approve treaties, coin money, and approve officials appointed by the President.

Article 2 states that the executive branch of the government is to be headed by a President and a Vice-President. The President's job is to carry out the laws passed by the Congress. As head of the government, the President chooses people to fill important government positions. The President serves as head of the armed forces and oversees the nation's foreign affairs. The President may also suggest laws to Congress and veto a law passed by Congress.

The third article creates a Supreme Court. This court is given power to make the final decision in court cases involving the Constitution. It also has power over laws passed by Congress. In the years since the Constitution was adopted, the Supreme Court has often been asked to decide whether a law is **constitutional,** or allowed by the Constitution. This power to decide if a law is constitutional is called **judicial review.** Judicial review is not mentioned in the Constitution, but it has become an important part of our system of government.

For discussion: How does the separation of powers safeguard American freedom?

Activity: Students can write papers on how the separation of powers and the system of checks and balances provided a compromise between those who sought and those who feared a strong central government.

The words on the eagle's banner are the Latin motto of the United States. They mean, "Out of many, one." Under the Constitution, one enduring nation was created out of many states.

Checks and Balances

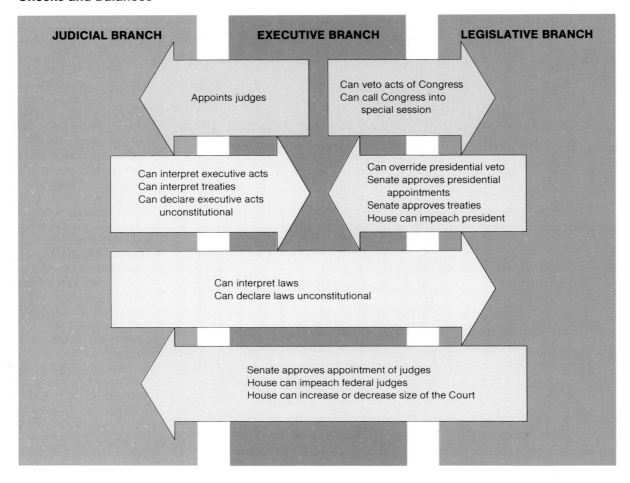

JUDICIAL BRANCH   EXECUTIVE BRANCH   LEGISLATIVE BRANCH

Appoints judges

Can veto acts of Congress
Can call Congress into
special session

Can interpret executive acts
Can interpret treaties
Can declare executive acts
unconstitutional

Can override presidential veto
Senate approves presidential
appointments
Senate approves treaties
House can impeach president

Can interpret laws
Can declare laws unconstitutional

Senate approves appointment of judges
House can impeach federal judges
House can increase or decrease size of the Court

The framers of the Constitution wanted to be sure that no one group could take over the government and destroy the rights of other Americans. They guarded against this by staggering the terms of officeholders. Members of the House serve for two years, Presidents and Vice-Presidents for four years, and Senators for six. Justices of the Supreme Court hold office for as long as they carry out their duties properly. In any one year it would be almost impossible for a group to gain complete control of the House, the Senate, the presidency, and the Supreme Court.

Activity: Have students compare the chart above with Articles 1, 2, and 3 of the Constitution (pages 528–539). Which sections and clauses of these articles grant the powers shown on each arrow?

CHECKS AND BALANCES

Another protection is the system of **checks and balances.** The purpose of this system is to give each branch a way to check, or limit, the powers of the other two. The President, for example, has the power to veto, or to refuse to approve, a proposed law passed by Congress. In that way, the President can limit the lawmaking power of Congress.

Congress can check the President's veto power. If two thirds of the members of both the House and Senate agree, they can override, or refuse to accept, the President's veto. The bill then becomes a law. The Supreme Court's power of judicial review is a check on Congress and the President. The review allows the court to strike down a law not allowed by the Constitution, even though the law was approved by Congress and the President.

Congress has an important check on both the President and the Supreme Court. If an official misuses power, the House can **impeach,** or bring charges against, that person. The Senate acts as a jury in the case. If found guilty, that person is removed from office.

A FEDERAL SYSTEM OF GOVERNMENT

Power is not only balanced between the three branches of the national government. It is also balanced between the national and state governments. This division of power between the states and the national government is called **federalism.** Because the national government shares power with the states, it is often called the federal government.

Under this federal system of government, the states delegated, or gave, certain powers to the national government. Such delegated powers include the power to coin money, to set up post offices, to raise and maintain armies, to declare war, to conclude peace, and to control trade with foreign countries and between states. These powers are all listed in the Constitution.

*CT
Activity: Students can hold a debate on which is more important to our nation's well-being, a strong central government or states' rights. After the debate, other students can decide which side they found more persuasive and why.

Federalism

National Government		State Government
DELEGATED POWERS	**CONCURRENT POWERS**	**RESERVED POWERS**
Maintain an army and a navy	Maintain law and order	Conduct elections
Admit new states	Establish courts	Establish schools
Establish post offices	Charter banks	Establish local governments
Coin money	Borrow money	Charter and regulate corporations
Declare war	Levy taxes	Regulate business within the state
Conduct foreign relations	Build roads	Regulate marriages
Regulate foreign and interstate commerce	Protect the health and safety of the people	Assume other powers not given to the national government or prohibited to the states
Makes all laws necessary and proper for carrying out the delegated powers		

Powers not listed there are reserved, or kept, by the states. States, for example, reserved the powers to create public schools and to conduct state and local elections.

Some powers are shared by both the state and national governments. These are called concurrent powers. Examples of concurrent powers include the power to tax, to borrow money, to build roads, and to maintain law and order.

A FLEXIBLE PLAN OF GOVERNMENT

The framers of the Constitution knew that their plan of government would have to be flexible to serve a growing, changing nation. To be flexible means to be able to adapt to fit new situations.

They provided flexibility by stating the purposes and powers of the government in broad terms. The Constitution states, for example, that the government should "establish justice." But it does not spell out the details of a national court system. Instead, it gives Congress the power to set up courts as they are needed.

Congress is also given the power "to make all laws which shall be necessary and proper" to carry out the purposes of the government. This statement is sometimes called the "elastic clause." It gives Congress the flexibility to adjust to changes over time.

The Constitution is flexible in another way. It can be **amended,** or changed. The framers purposely made the process for amending difficult. They wanted people to think very carefully about making changes. An amendment must be proposed by at least a two-thirds vote of each house of Congress or by a convention called by two thirds of the state legislatures. To become part of the Constitution, the amendment must be ratified by three fourths of all of the states. In all of American history the Constitution has been amended only 26 times.

For discussion: Students can compare our Constitution, an explicit written document, with the British Constitution, an implicit collection of customs and precedents. Why is it important for our written Constitution to contain an explicit "elastic clause"?

THE BILL OF RIGHTS

The first ten amendments, called the Bill of Rights, were proposed by the first Congress elected under the Constitution. During the ratification debates, Federalists had agreed to add a list of rights to the Constitution. The Bill of Rights was passed by two thirds of the Congress, as required by the Constitution. Three fourths of the states also had to approve the Bill of Rights. In 1791 these ten amendments became part of the Constitution. These amendments clearly define the rights of individuals. Almost all restrict the actions of the federal government.

The first four amendments list the general rights of Americans. The First Amendment says that the government cannot set up an official religion. Nor can it interfere with the freedoms of worship, speech, or the press. The government also cannot break up peaceful gatherings of citizens. In the Second Amendment, citizens are given the right to "keep and bear arms" in order to insure that "a well-regulated militia" can be maintained. The Third Amendment says that the government cannot house soldiers in private homes without permission of the owners. The Fourth Amendment says that the government cannot search people or their property without good reason. Nor can it take property without reason. A search or arrest warrant must be obtained.

The next four amendments protect the rights of people who are arrested. The Fifth Amendment says that people cannot be put on trial for a major crime without a written accusation by a grand jury. Nor can they be "deprived of life, liberty, or property" unless the proper legal steps are followed. The Sixth Amendment gives an accused person the right to a "speedy and public trial by an impartial jury." It also gives that person the right to have a lawyer. The Seventh Amendment extends the right to trial by jury to some noncriminal cases. In the Eighth Amendment, large bails and fines and "cruel and unusual punishments" are forbidden.

The last two amendments cover rights not listed in the other eight. The Ninth Amendment says that the Constitution and its amendments do not list all the rights of the people. Other important rights also exist. These rights will be protected, too. The Tenth Amendment says that the powers not given to the federal government by the Constitution belong to the states or to the people.

As the class studies the Bill of Rights, you may wish to have students read each of these ten amendments aloud to the class. (See pages 543–545.)

AN ENDURING PLAN OF GOVERNMENT

The "New Roof" created in Philadelphia and ratified by the states in 1788 has proved to be remarkably strong. It has provided a framework for the government as the United States has grown from 13 states to 50. It has kept the nation together through numerous wars, including two

Preserving and applying the "supreme law of the land" is the job of the Supreme Court. The first home of the Supreme Court was the Exchange Building in New York City.

Activity: James Madison said, "In framing a system which we wish for all ages, we should not lose sight of the changes which the ages will produce." Students can write papers considering both parts of Madison's statement. Does the Constitution provide "a system . . . for all ages"? Does it take account of "the changes which the ages will produce"?

world wars, and through many crises in peacetime. It held the nation together through the Great Depression and many lesser ones. And it has put to rest the fears of many Americans that a republic the size of the United States could not succeed.

The American Constitution is the oldest written plan of government still in use. It has served as a model for new nations setting up governments around the world. In the United States it remains today what it became in 1788, "the supreme law of the land."

SECTION REVIEW Answers will be found on page T 41.

1. Define these words: *separation of powers, constitutional, judicial review, checks and balances, impeach, federalism, amend.*

2. Identify: "elastic clause."

3. List the six purposes of the Constitution named in the Preamble.

4. Why did the framers of the Constitution divide power among three branches of government?

5. Give one example showing how the system of checks and balances works under the Constitution.

6. Name two ways in which the Constitution is flexible.

7. List six rights or freedoms included in the Bill of Rights.

Once they had won their independence, Americans set about the task of building a nation. Former colonies became states under new constitutions.

These states were loosely joined in a federation by the Articles of Confederation. The government created under the Articles was not strong enough to deal with many problems facing the new nation. Its most important action was passage of the Northwest Ordinance in 1787. This law set the pattern for settling territories and admitting new states.

In 1787 a Constitutional Convention was held in Philadelphia. The delegates included many of the nation's political leaders. Rivalry between large and small states almost ended the convention. Both groups were able to agree to the Great Compromise. Other compromises prevented a split between northern and southern states.

The Constitution written in Philadelphia could not go into effect until it was ratified by nine states. The country was quickly divided between Federalists, who supported the new plan, and Anti-Federalists, who opposed it. The vote was close in several states. By the summer of 1788, however, the Constitution was the law of the land.

The government created under the Constitution has three branches. A system of checks and balances keeps any one branch from misusing its power. The government is also a federal government that shares power with the states. The first Congress added a Bill of Rights to the Constitution. It protects important rights and freedoms of individuals.

1770	1780	1790	1800
		Washington	Adams	Jefferson

- Mercy Otis Warren: *The Group*
- Revolutionary War
- Articles of Confederation
- Land Ordinance of 1785
- Annapolis Convention
- Northwest Ordinance
- Shays' Rebellion
- Constitutional Convention
- Constitution ratified
- Olaudah Equiano's autobiography
- Bill of Rights

1770   1780   1790   1800

Answers will be found on page T 42.

CHAPTER SURVEY

VOCABULARY REVIEW

From this list of vocabulary words, choose the one that best matches the meaning of each word or phrase in heavy type.

(a) amend
(b) bicameral
(c) ceded
(d) checks and balances
(e) compromises
(f) constitutional
(g) currencies
(h) executive branch
(i) federalism
(j) impeach
(k) judicial branch
(l) judicial review
(m) legislative branch
(n) ordinance
(o) ratify
(p) republic
(q) separation of powers
(r) unicameral

1. In 1785 Congress passed a **law** creating a system for surveying new territories.

2. The writing of the Constitution required **agreements in which both sides gave up something.**

3. The states had to **approve** the Constitution.

4. The Constitution created a **two-house** legislature.

5. The Constitution called for a **division of authority** among three branches.

6. The **House and Senate** make laws.

7. The **President and his officers** are responsible for carrying out laws.

8. The **Supreme Court** decides cases that involve the Constitution.

9. A system of **limitations by one branch on the powers of another** keeps any one branch from becoming too powerful.

10. The Supreme Court decides if an act of Congress is **allowed by the Constitution.**

11. The House has the power to **bring charges against** a President.

12. Division of powers between the national and state governments is another important feature of the Constitution.

13. The Constitution created a **representative government based on the will of the people.**

14. Americans can **change** the Constitution.

15. After the Revolutionary War, the states **transferred** their western lands to Congress.

16. The states had several kinds of **money** in circulation.

17. The New Jersey Plan called for a **one-house** legislature.

18. The Supreme Court has **the power to decide whether laws are constitutional.**

CHAPTER REVIEW

1. (a) What form of government did each state adopt after declaring independence? (b) On what authority was each state government based? (c) Where did the first national government get its authority to govern?

2. (a) Why did Americans *not* want a strong national government in 1776? (b) What led them to change their minds by 1787?

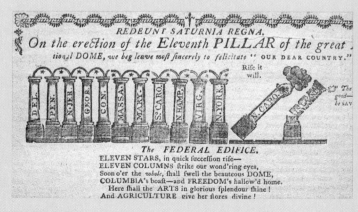

This print celebrated the ratification of the Constitution by the eleventh state, New York, in 1788.

Rhode Islander John Brown, one of the first Americans to trade in China, brought back this bowl showing the harbor and city of Canton.

3. Two plans for a new government, the Virginia Plan and the New Jersey Plan, were presented to the Constitutional Convention. How were they similar?

4. (a) Why was the compromise on the states' representation in Congress called the Great Compromise? (b) How are the states represented under this compromise?

5. (a) What compromise was reached on counting slaves? (b) What compromise was reached about the slave trade?

6. How did the compromise on exports and imports satisfy both the North and the South?

7. (a) What worried Anti-Federalists about the office of President? (b) What worried Anti-Federalists about the Congress? (c) Why did they fear they would lose their liberty under the Constitution?

8. (a) How are terms of office staggered under the Constitution? (b) How does this staggering help prevent tyranny?

9. In what ways did the framers of the Constitution try to make their plan flexible enough to meet changing needs?

10. (a) What basic American rights are listed in the first four amendments of the Bill of Rights? (b) What kinds of rights are covered by the second four amendments? (c) What do the last two amendments say about powers and rights not listed in the Constitution?

GEOGRAPHY REVIEW

*CT Look at the map "Western Land Cessions 1782–1802" on page 189. (a) Which state ceded the largest area to Congress? (b) What future state was an independent republic between 1777 and 1791? (c) Where was the area claimed by both the United States and Britain? (d) What formed the boundary between the land cessions and Louisiana?

USING THE TOOLS OF HISTORY

Interpreting Diagrams

Look at the diagram of the Northwest Survey System on page 191. (a) What do the 36 squares at the top of the diagram represent? (b) How does the square titled "One section" relate to the rest of the diagram? (c) How many square miles are in a township? (d) How many square miles are in a section?

READING AND THINKING SKILLS

SQ3R

*CT **1.** Review the SQ3R method of creating study guides as described on page 149. Use this approach to create a study guide for the first section of this chapter.

Outlining

*CT **2.** Review outlining as described on page 94. Then create an outline for the same section.

Comparing Study Methods

*CT **3.** When you have finished both the study guide and outline, answer these questions. (a) Which method seemed easier to use? (b) Which method gave you a better understanding of the text? (c) Which method would be most helpful to you in reviewing this chapter in a month?

CHAPTER 9   1789-1801

THE FEDERALISTS LAUNCH THE REPUBLIC

THE TWO FRONTIERS
THE FEDERALISTS SET UP A GOVERNMENT
WASHINGTON'S SECOND ADMINISTRATION
THE PRESIDENCY OF JOHN ADAMS

9-1 THE TWO FRONTIERS

READ TO FIND OUT

pioneers: first settlers of a new region

—what the word *pioneers* means.

—why few settlers went to the Spanish frontier.

—how the settlement of California began.

—what life was like along the log cabin frontier.

When the United States became an independent nation, there were two frontiers in North America. One was being pushed westward by **pioneers,** or first settlers, of the new lands across the Appalachians. The other was the Spanish frontier. It stretched across the plains of Texas and the mountains and deserts of New Mexico and Arizona into California.

THE SPANISH BORDERLANDS

The strongest Spanish settlements were in New Mexico, among the Pueblo Indians. The Pueblo people, who were used to a settled farming life, came to accept Spanish rule. But the nomadic tribes of the plains and desert accepted only one thing from the Spanish—their horses.

Spanish California

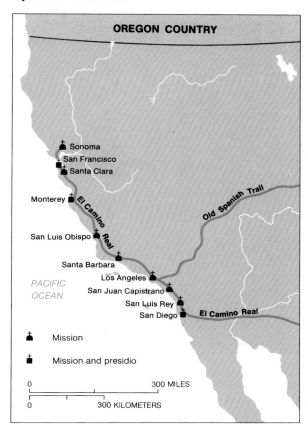

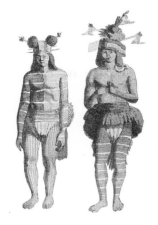

Native Californians at San Francisco Bay used body paint for ceremonies.

Students can refer to the map on page 45 (Spanish Exploration and Settlement 1519–1720) for the location of the Pueblo settlements of the Zuñi, Hopi, and Acoma.

Spanish missions were built a day's journey apart along El Camino Real—the King's Highway. The Old Spanish Trail linked California and New Mexico.

Mounted on Spanish steeds and armed with French rifles, these tribes became dangerous enemies of the frontier settlers. The Comanche blocked Spanish settlement in Texas except for a handful of mission-forts. In New Mexico and Arizona, the raids of Apache warriors held the Spanish to a few protected settlements.

CALIFORNIA

Spain had claimed California ever since Juan Cabrillo explored its coastline in 1542. Yet for more than 200 years, California remained isolated from the rest of New Spain. Then Russia began building fur-trading posts in Alaska. Russian traders and explorers moved down the coast into northern California. The rulers of New Spain saw this as a threat to California. In 1769 an expedition led by Gaspar de Portolá (POR-toh-LAH) arrived in California to protect Spanish claims. Portolá founded settlements at San Diego and Monterey.

Portolá was accompanied by a priest named Junipero Serra (SEHR-rah). Father Serra spent the rest of his life teaching the California Indians the Catholic faith. He began by building a chain of missions,

each one a day's journey from the next. In time, 21 missions were built from San Diego north to San Francisco Bay.

Serra planned to bring the Californians into the missions. There they would hear the word of God. They would also learn how to use European tools, tend livestock, and grow crops. Most of the Indians resisted. They preferred hunting small game and gathering plant foods to laboring in mission fields. Soldiers sometimes rounded up Indians and forced them to live and work in the missions. There the California Indians died by the thousands from overwork and new diseases brought by the Europeans.

Settlers from Mexico began to trickle into California in the 1780s. New Spain rewarded these settlers, called *Californios*, with huge grants of land. The newcomers enjoyed a life of abundance. Cattle and horses thrived in the sun-drenched grasslands. Orchards and gardens produced an amazing variety of fruits and vegetables. No wonder the Californios boasted, "We live here like princes."

THE LOG CABIN FRONTIER

The other American frontier, the log cabin frontier, was advancing across the Appalachian Highlands. Frontier farmers settled in forested valleys. There they cut down trees and pulled stumps to prepare their land for planting. They sawed the tree trunks into logs to build cabins.

Cooking over an open fire was hard on a woman's back and a frequent cause of serious burns. The trees behind the cabin have been killed by girdling, or removing a ring of bark from the trunk.

Most of the first cabins had only one main room and perhaps a sleeping loft. Cracks between the logs were stuffed with moss or straw and plastered with mud. A stone fireplace provided heat, light, and a place for cooking. Furniture was simple—a table and a few stools.

Most cabins were gloomy inside. Greased paper covered the small window openings. After sunset, the only light came from the smoky fireplace and smelly, grease-burning lamps. Frontier families went to bed early, sleeping on mattresses of oak leaves or lice-infested bear skins.

For many families, life was as gloomy as their cabins. Often they did not have enough to eat. Wolves attacked their sheep and hogs. Wandering cattle trampled gardens, and squirrels and raccoons robbed cornfields. Frost and drought often destroyed crops.

Disease could strike at any time. Many women lost their lives in childbirth, and many babies died before their first birthday. Families also lived in fear of Indian attacks. The hardened faces of frontier people showed the effects of worry, hard work, disease, and loneliness. They looked old at thirty-five.

There was another side to frontier life. As soon as there were a number of settlers in an area, they got together to clear fields and raise

Activity: Students can imagine they are members of families who have moved westward to the log cabin frontier. They can write letters about their new life to friends and relatives back east.

This picture of a flax scutching party suggests that frontier get-togethers were more play than work. The paddles, or scutches, were used to beat woody flax stalks in order to free the flax fibers. Flax is spun to make linen.

For discussion: That Americans attached great importance to a postal service is shown by the fact that the Postmaster General was one of the first four executive department heads appointed by President Washington. (The others were the Secretaries of War, State, and the Treasury.) Why would a postal service become increasingly important as America continued to expand westward?

houses. Women and girls gathered at quilting bees to share news and precious scraps of fabric. Men and boys turned the tiresome task of corn husking into wild contests.

When the shared work was done, the settlers ate a hearty meal. Then out came the fiddle. For a few hours the pioneers forgot their cares. Songs, laughter, and the thump of dancing feet echoed through the forest. Young people used these events for courting.

Gatherings were important to frontier people because they often felt cut off from one another. They also felt cut off from "Atlantic America," on the other side of the mountains. In 1788 post riders began to carry letters and newspapers. Their route was the rough road between Philadelphia and Pittsburgh, the new town growing up around Fort Pitt. Frontier people followed with great interest the news about the federal government being set up in New York City.

SECTION REVIEW   Answers will be found on page T 43.

1. Define the following word: *pioneers.*

2. Identify: Gaspar de Portolá, Father Junipero Serra.

3. What happened to many California Indians as a result of Spanish settlement in California?

4. Settlers on the log cabin frontier often helped one another. Give three examples.

9-2 THE FEDERALISTS SET UP A GOVERNMENT

READE TO FIND OUT

—what the words *inaugurate, precedents, census, credit, interest, tariffs,* and *negotiate* mean.

—how the three branches of the federal government were organized.

—how Hamilton strengthened the nation's credit.

—what differences separated Federalists from Republicans.

inaugurate: bring into office with formal ceremony
precedents: examples to be followed
census: population count
credit: ability to borrow money
interest: fee paid for use of borrowed money
tariffs: taxes on imports
negotiate: hold discussions in order to reach agreement

On April 30, 1789, George Washington dressed in a suit of brown American-made broadcloth and had his graying hair powdered. He was escorted to Federal Hall in New York City, where he stood on a balcony overlooking Wall Street. While a large crowd watched, he was **inaugurated,** or formally brought into office, as the first President of the United States. The onlookers cheered so loudly they could not hear Washington speak.

Together, the President and the new Congress shared a grand opportunity and a heavy burden. It was their duty to put the Constitution into practice. The choices they made would set important **precedents,** or examples to be followed in the future.

THE TITLE FIGHT

Vice-President John Adams was thinking about precedents when he suggested that Washington have a title with more dignity than "President." The President needed a title that would make him seem equal to the rulers of European countries. Many senators agreed, suggesting titles like "His Highness" or "His Elective Majesty."

James Madison, a leader in the House of Representatives, felt that such titles were not proper in a republic. Most representatives agreed. After three weeks of debate, Adams's allies in the Senate gave up. Washington would be addressed simply as "Mr. President."

The two sides in this argument had very different ideas about leadership. Those who sided with Adams believed that the nation's leaders would not be respected unless they stood far above ordinary citizens. Those who agreed with Madison thought that in a republic, leaders and voters should be seen as equals.

A decorated barge carried George Washington across New York harbor for his inauguration as President. He was welcomed by cheering crowds and booming cannons. This painting probably celebrated the hundredth anniversary of his first inauguration.

ORGANIZING THE GOVERNMENT

Putting aside their differences, the members of Congress began to organize the federal government. The Constitution described, in a broad way, the responsibilities of the three branches of government. But it gave only a framework. The lawmakers began to fill in the details.

To strengthen the executive branch, three departments were created. The Department of State was established to help the President represent the United States in dealings with foreign countries. Congress also created the War Department and the Treasury Department. Next, it set up the office of Postmaster General. To run the new executive departments, President Washington chose people he trusted. He named Thomas Jefferson Secretary of State and Alexander Hamilton Secretary of the Treasury. His old friend Henry Knox became Secretary of War.

Next, Congress set up the judicial branch of government. The Constitution said that the judicial branch was to be made up of a Supreme Court and whatever other courts Congress found necessary. In 1789 Congress passed the Judiciary Act. It called for a three-level federal court system.

At the lowest level were 13 district courts, one for each state. These courts were to hear cases involving the Constitution, laws passed by Congress, and treaties. District court decisions could be appealed, or taken to a higher court for reexamination. Above the district courts

Remind students that Alexander Hamilton had been one of the authors of *The Federalist Papers* (page 201). He had also served as Washington's aide during the Revolutionary War.

DISTINGUISHING FACT FROM OPINION

A fact is a statement that can be proved. An opinion is a personal belief or judgment about something. Here are two statements about John Adams. Which statement is a fact, and which is an opinion?

1. In 1789 John Adams proposed that the President be called "His Highness, the President of the United States of America and Protector of the Rights of the Same."

2. John Adams was a monarchist; he wanted to see this country ruled by a king.

The first statement is a fact. It can be proved. The records of the Senate show that Adams proposed the title of "His Highness" in 1789. The second statement is an opinion, or an expression of someone's belief. The statement "John Adams was not a monarchist" is also an opinion.

Sometimes it is difficult to decide whether a statement is a fact or an opinion. In that case, try adding the words "It can be proved that . . ." to the beginning of the statement. Then try adding the words "I believe that . . . " to it. One set of words will usually fit the statement better than the other.

Read the following two sentences written by Thomas Jefferson:

All powers not given to the United States government by the Constitution, nor prohibited by it to the states, are reserved to the states or to the people (Tenth Amendment). To take a single step beyond [these] boundaries . . . is to take possession of a boundless field of power.

Which of these sentences is a statement of fact? Which is a statement of opinion?

Answers will be found on page T 43.

*CT

were three circuit courts. The circuit courts were to rule on appeals from district courts and to hear cases involving citizens from different states.

The court of last appeal was the Supreme Court. It heard appeals from the lower federal courts. It also heard appeals from the highest state courts when the cases involved federal laws or the Constitution. To put the Supreme Court into operation, the Judiciary Act called for the appointment of a Chief Justice and five associate judges. The act also set up the office of Attorney General. This official was to act as a lawyer for the federal government in cases heard by the Supreme Court. The Attorney General was also to give legal advice to the executive branch.

During his first administration, or term in office, President Washington regularly met with his department heads. These top officers of the executive branch gradually came to be known as the President's Cabinet. The Constitution said nothing about a cabinet, but future Presidents followed the precedent set by Washington.

THE CENSUS OF 1790

In 1790, after the three branches of the federal government were organized, the first **census,** or population count, was taken. The Constitution says that the American people must be counted every ten years. The

Activity: Have students compare figures from the most recent census to those of the first census. You may wish to call attention to the Resource Center graphs on pages 506, 508, and 509.

number of Representatives allowed a state can then be changed if the state's population has changed.

According to the first census, there were almost 4 million Americans, including 700,000 slaves. Nine out of ten were farmers. Less than 6 percent of the population lived in towns of more than 2,500 people. Only six cities—Philadelphia, New York, Boston, Charleston, Baltimore, and Salem—had more than 8,000 people.

HAMILTON'S ECONOMIC PROGRAM

*CT
For discussion: Why is it important for a nation to have good credit? What might happen if people and other nations lost trust in a nation's ability to pay its bills?

Treasury Secretary Hamilton believed that the federal government should be strong enough to do "great things." His first challenge was to improve the government's **credit,** or ability to borrow money. The new government had almost no credit. People with money to lend feared that they would not be paid back. To calm their fears, the government had to prove that it could pay off its huge war debt.

During the war, the Confederation government and the state governments had paid soldiers and suppliers with bonds. Bonds are written promises to pay amounts owed within a certain time. Bonds also include **interest,** a payment for the use of borrowed money. The value of these bonds fell rapidly when the Confederation and state governments could not pay even the interest on them.

Hamilton offered a two-part plan to Congress. First, he suggested that new, federal bonds be exchanged for the old Confederation bonds. The new bonds would be backed by the promise of the federal government to repay bondholders the original value of the bonds. The federal government also promised to make regular interest payments. These payments could be made because money was flowing into the federal treasury. It came from the sale of federal land and from **tariffs,** or import taxes, on many foreign goods.

If bondholders received regular interest payments, wealthy people in America and Europe would learn to trust the federal government. People would then be willing to buy more bonds when the government needed to borrow money in the future.

Second, Hamilton wanted to exchange new, federal bonds for old state bonds. The federal government would take over the war debts of the states. With federal bonds in their hands, Hamilton hoped, the "rich and well born" of every state would be more likely to support a strong national government.

For discussion: In the case of the war debt, Jefferson and Madison put the interest of their state ahead of the interest of country as a whole. Do students think they were justified? Why or why not?

Thomas Jefferson and James Madison opposed the second part of Hamilton's plan. Their state, Virginia, had already paid most of its war debt. Now Virginians would be taxed, along with all other Americans, to pay the debts of other states. Jefferson and Madison persuaded their supporters in the House to oppose Hamilton's plan.

222   CHAPTER 9   1789-1801

Benjamin Banneker, a mathematician and author of yearly almanacs, helped survey the site chosen for the new nation's capital. The south wing of the Capitol building was sketched by architect Benjamin Latrobe.

The argument went on for six months. Then Hamilton and the two Virginians sat down to **negotiate**—to discuss whether they could reach an agreement. At the time, Congress was debating where to locate the nation's capital. The Virginians wanted the capital on the Potomac River bordering Virginia. Hamilton promised Jefferson and Madison that his friends in Congress would vote to build the capital by the Potomac. In return, Madison and his supporters helped Hamilton's plan become law. Each side got part of what it wanted.

THE BANK OF THE UNITED STATES

A few months later, Hamilton asked Congress to set up a national bank with branches in major American cities. Owned mainly by wealthy citizens, it would hold the funds of the federal treasury. The government, businesses, and individuals could all put funds in the bank and borrow money from it. The bank would issue paper money that people could trust. This paper currency would have the same value throughout the country and could be exchanged for gold and silver.

For Hamilton, the most important activity of the bank would be lending money to business people who wanted to build ships and factories. Sea power and manufacturing, he believed, would make the United States a great nation like Britain.

Thomas Jefferson measured national greatness differently from Hamilton. Jefferson believed that the well-being of the United States depended on farmers who owned their own land and voted to protect their liberty. He preferred state banks. These could be controlled by farmers through their state governments. Both Jefferson and Madison

For discussion: Students should note that Hamilton's plan for a national bank was like his plan for federal bonds in that both were calculated to appeal to the "rich and well born" (page 222). Why might Hamilton think it beneficial to the nation to appeal to such people?

The first Bank of the United States was built in Philadelphia in 1795. American architects in this period wanted Americans to feel that their public buildings were both important and impressive.

feared that a national bank would give a small group of city people, the bank's owners, too much power.

When Congress passed Hamilton's bank bill, Jefferson tried to persuade Washington to veto it. He pointed out that the Constitution did not give Congress the power to set up a bank. Any power not listed in the Constitution belonged to the states, argued Jefferson. His point of view came to be called a "strict construction," or word-for-word interpretation, of the Constitution.

Hamilton argued in favor of a "loose construction" of the Constitution. He insisted that Congress could make any law that helped the federal government use its listed powers as long as the Constitution did not forbid such a law. The Constitution gave the federal government the power to pay the debts of the United States. A national bank would be very useful for paying the nation's debts. Therefore, said Hamilton, the bank was constitutional.

Jefferson was horrified. Hamilton, he believed, was trying to make the Constitution so flexible that the federal government would have unlimited power. If Congress could set up a bank, what would it do next? Despite Jefferson's opposition, Washington signed the bank bill. The Bank of the United States opened in December 1791.

POLITICAL PARTIES APPEAR

During the fight over the bank, two opposing groups grew in strength. One group was led by Jefferson and James Madison. Its members called themselves "Republicans." Hamilton and supporters of his policies, such as Vice-President John Adams, called themselves "Federalists." The

To avoid possible confusion, you may wish to inform the class that Jefferson's Republicans eventually became the Democratic party. The present Republican party was founded in 1854.

In this Federalist cartoon, Washington has a firm grip on the reins of government. Jefferson is shown clinging to a wheel of the cart, trying to stop the government's progress.

two groups began to harden into political parties, which had very different ideas about government. Republicans favored a weak central government, while Federalists argued for a strong central government.

The Constitution said nothing about political parties. Washington feared that the "demon of party spirit" would tear the new government apart. Hoping to keep the "demon" under control, he ran for a second term as President. Washington, the only candidate, won the election of 1792 easily. Political parties, however, did not disappear. In fact, the Republicans and Federalists drew further apart.

SECTION REVIEW Answers will be found on page T 43.

1. Define the following words: *inaugurate, precedents, census, credit, interest, tariffs, negotiate.*

2. Identify: Judiciary Act of 1789.

3. Describe the court system set up by the Judiciary Act of 1789.

4. What precedent did Washington create by meeting regularly with his department heads?

5. How did Hamilton strengthen the nation's credit?

6. What services did the Bank of the United States provide?

7. Where did Congress decide to build the nation's capital?

8. Tell whether the Federalists or the Republicans preferred (a) a strong national government, (b) strict construction of the Constitution, (c) the growth of cities and manufacturing.

*CT

For discussion: In his Farewell Address (see page 230), Washington warned against the "alternate domination of one faction over another, sharpened by the spirit of revenge natural to party dissension. . . ." He said that "the common and continued mischiefs of the spirit of party are sufficient to make it the interest and duty of a wise people to discourage and restrain it." Do students think Washington's warning is valid today? Why or why not?

9-3 WASHINGTON'S SECOND ADMINISTRATION

READ TO FIND OUT

—what the words *neutral, impress,* and *diplomacy* mean.

—why Hamilton wanted to use troops in the Whiskey Rebellion.

—how America's neutrality was challenged.

—how the government gained control of the Northwest Territory.

—what gains the new nation made through diplomacy.

neutral: to be unwilling to take sides in a conflict
impress: force to serve in the British navy
diplomacy: art of conducting negotiations between nations

Washington's hopes for bringing the rival parties together were dashed by the French Revolution. The revolution had begun in 1789, and Americans had followed its progress with great interest. In 1792 they cheered when France became a republic. Then, as Washington began his second term, the news from France turned grim. Mobs were rioting in Paris. While angry crowds shouted encouragement, the new French government beheaded King Louis XVI and many nobles.

Federalists warned that the same thing could happen in America. The Republicans were saddened by the bloodshed. But they continued to admire the French republic. Federalists accused them of being "democrats," a word they used to describe supporters of mob rule. Many Americans began to see themselves as Federalists or Republicans depending on how they felt about the French Revolution.

THE WHISKEY REBELLION

In 1794 Alexander Hamilton thought he saw the beginning of mob rule in southwestern Pennsylvania. Farmers west of the Alleghenies had difficulty hauling their surplus grain to market over narrow mountain roads. They made the extra grain into whiskey, a product that pack horses could carry easily. At Hamilton's urging, Congress had placed a high tax on whiskey. When the government tried to collect it, backcountry farmers rebelled. They tarred and feathered tax collectors. A few farmers even boasted that they would overthrow the government.

Hamilton urged Washington to respond strongly. Then no citizen would ever again dare to question the authority of the federal government. The President called up the militia of four states. A force of 13,000 troops was sent across the Allegheny Mountains.

This unfortunate tax collector was first smeared with hot tar and then covered with feathers as a protest against the whiskey tax.

Instead of armed rebels, the army found only signs reading "Liberty and No Tax. O, Whiskey." After arresting a few of the leaders of the Whiskey Rebellion, the army withdrew. Jefferson, who felt that the tax was wrong, hoped that Hamilton had made a fool of himself. But the Treasury Secretary was certain that the federal government had gained "reputation and strength."

THE BATTLE OF FALLEN TIMBERS

West of the whiskey rebels, hostile Indians presented a more serious challenge to the authority of the government. Several tribes in the Northwest Territory were waging a bitter struggle to keep American settlers south of the Ohio River.

In August 1794 General "Mad" Anthony Wayne defeated a large Indian force at Fallen Timbers, in the northwestern part of present-day Ohio. A year later Wayne signed a treaty with all the Indian tribes of the Northwest. The Indians moved farther west, and the lands north of the Ohio River were opened to settlement.

"Mad" Anthony Wayne, a hero of the Revolutionary War, earned his nickname because of his reckless courage. His attack to recapture Stony Point, N.Y., from the British was one of the war's most daring actions.

CHALLENGES FROM EUROPE

War in Europe brought another challenge to the United States during Washington's second administration. King George III of England and other European monarchs feared the spread of revolution to their own countries. As a result, they formed an alliance against France. By 1793 France was at war against the British alliance.

After the Battle of Fallen Timbers, General Anthony Wayne and his staff met with Indian leaders to discuss a treaty. Twelve tribes signed the Treaty of Greenville in 1795.

The Federalists favored Britain. They argued that the French Revolution should be crushed. They also pointed out that Britain was the nation's best trading partner. Most of the funds in the federal treasury came from import taxes, and most American imports came from the British Empire. If the United States supported France, said the Federalists, Britain would cut off trade. The federal government would lose its main source of revenue. The Republicans disagreed. They wanted closer ties and increased trade with France.

Although the Federalists favored Britain and the Republicans France, both wanted the United States to remain **neutral**—to refuse to take sides. On April 22, 1793, Washington issued a Proclamation of Neutrality. The United States would "pursue a conduct friendly and impartial" toward the warring nations. The Proclamation also urged Americans not to aid any of the countries.

Remaining neutral proved difficult. Britain declared that it would seize all neutral ships carrying weapons or food to France. British warships also stopped American merchant ships to search for deserters from the Royal Navy. Any sailor who talked like an English subject might be **impressed,** or forced to serve in the British navy. His protests and papers showing he was American made no difference. Americans were deeply angered by impressment.

The failure of British troops to withdraw from forts in the Northwest Territory also angered Americans. They accused the British there of aiding Indians who were attacking American settlers on the frontier. Republicans wanted to cut off all trade with Great Britain. But Washington was afraid Britain would declare war on the United States.

Life on a British naval ship was extremely hard. A captain had the power of life and death over his crew. A common form of punishment was whipping—thirty or forty lashes for an infraction. Another was keelhauling—dragging a sailor under the ship's keel from one side to the other so that he nearly drowned.

THE CAUSE-EFFECT PATTERN

When we read history, it is important to understand that one event often causes another. That is, the event makes something else happen. In this kind of relationship, the event is called the *cause*. The result of the event is called the *effect*.

For example, reread the first paragraph under the heading "The Whiskey Rebellion." A cause-effect relationship is discussed there. The cause is the federal government's attempt to collect a tax on whiskey. The effect is the rebellion of back-country farmers in Pennsylvania. The rest of the paragraph gives examples of how the farmers rebelled.

Cause-effect events can also form a *chain reaction*. In a chain reaction, the effect of one event becomes the cause of another. Read the next paragraph to find the chain reaction. The farmers' rebellion was an effect of the government's attempts to collect taxes. It, in turn, became the cause of another event—the President's action to stop the rebellion.

Read the section titled "Strengthening the Nation Through Diplomacy." Then complete on a piece of paper the cause-effect statements below.

1. Cause: President Washington decided that the American quarrel with Britain should be settled through diplomacy.
   Effect: _____

2. Cause: _____
   Effect: Americans were outraged at how little they had gained from Jay's Treaty.

3. Cause: The United States signed Jay's Treaty with Britain.
   Effect: _____

4. Cause: _____
   Effect: Americans were guaranteed the right to deposit goods at New Orleans docks.

Answers will be found on page T43.

STRENGTHENING THE NATION THROUGH DIPLOMACY

Washington decided that the nation should not try to settle its quarrel with Britain by using military force. It should, instead, use **diplomacy**—conduct talks—to solve the problems. In the summer of 1794, the President sent John Jay to England to discuss the major disagreements between the two countries. After five months of talks, Jay signed a treaty with Great Britain.

When Jay's Treaty was made public, many Americans were outraged at how little they had gained. The treaty did reopen the British West Indies to American ships. On the other hand, it limited the number of ships. Britain agreed to pay for the American ships it had seized, but it did not give up its right to seize ships or sailors in the future. Britain would withdraw from the Northwest Territory, but the treaty did not mention stopping aid to the Indians.

Although Jay's Treaty was protested throughout the country, it was ratified by the Senate. Despite its flaws, the treaty kept the peace at a time when America was not prepared to go to war.

Activity: John Jay served as delegate to the Continental Congress, minister to Spain, secretary for foreign affairs under the Articles of Confederation, and the first Chief Justice of the Supreme Court. He resigned from the Court to become governor of New York. Students can present written reports about this outstanding American.

Martha Washington retired with her husband to Mount Vernon in 1797. This miniature portrait of her was painted by Charles Willson Peale.

Washington's diplomacy helped bring about a second treaty, this time with Spain. For years the Spanish had refused to accept American control over the lands bordering Spanish Florida. They had ignored American attempts to reach an agreement about Florida's northern boundary. They also refused to give Americans the right to deposit goods on New Orleans docks to be picked up by ocean-going ships. Without the "right of deposit," western farmers could not use the Mississippi River to send their grain to market.

Jay's Treaty caused the Spanish to worry that the United States and Britain were drawing closer together. Britain, they feared, might back an American attempt to seize Spanish Florida and Louisiana. The Spanish decided to negotiate.

Washington sent Thomas Pinckney to Spain. There, in 1795, Spain and the United States signed the Treaty of San Lorenzo. Pinckney's treaty fixed the Florida boundary at 31° north latitude. It also guaranteed Americans the right of deposit at New Orleans. The Treaty of San Lorenzo, like Jay's Treaty, helped the United States strengthen its hold over its western territories.

WASHINGTON SAYS FAREWELL

You may wish to read to the class passages from George Washington's famous Farewell Address.

As the election of 1796 drew near, Washington decided not to seek re-election. In his Farewell Address to the nation, Washington warned Americans to avoid "permanent alliances" with European countries. He did not want to see the United States drawn into European wars.

Looking back over his years as President, Washington had reason to be satisfied. Under his leadership the federal government had been organized. The nation's credit had been established. The authority of the government had been strengthened. Furthermore, the United States had gained control over its western territory. Most satisfying of all, the young nation had not stumbled into a war.

SECTION REVIEW Answers will be found on page T44.

1. Define the following words: *neutral, impress, diplomacy.*

2. Identify: Anthony Wayne, Proclamation of Neutrality, Jay's Treaty, Treaty of San Lorenzo.

3. Why did Alexander Hamilton want to put down the Whiskey Rebellion with force?

4. Which two treaties helped the United States establish its authority over its western territories?

5. Why did Washington warn Americans to avoid permanent alliances with European nations?

9-4 THE PRESIDENCY OF JOHN ADAMS

READE TO FIND OUT

—what the words *bribe, tribute, immigrants, alien, sedition,* and *states' rights* mean.

—how John Adams responded to the XYZ Affair.

—what the purposes of the Alien and Sedition Acts were.

—how Jefferson and Madison protested the Sedition Act.

In the election of 1796, Federalists and Republicans each put forward candidates for President and Vice-President. The vote in the electoral college was very close—71 for John Adams and 68 for Thomas Jefferson. Adams, the Federalist candidate for President, became President. Jefferson, the Republican candidate for President, became Vice-President. Adams and Jefferson, once close friends, had become political enemies.

THE "HALF WAR"

President Adams's first challenge was to keep his country out of the war between Britain and France. After Jay's Treaty was ratified, France accused the United States of taking Britain's side. The French navy began to seize American merchant ships trading with Britain. Adams hoped to avoid war. He sent Charles Cotesworth Pinckney, John Marshall, and Elbridge Gerry to negotiate with the French.

The three Americans arrived in France in the fall of 1797. There they met with three agents of the French foreign minister. In reports to Adams, the Americans called them Mr. X, Mr. Y, and Mr. Z. The agents said that negotiations could not begin until the United States agreed to certain terms. France was to receive a $10 million loan. America must also pay a **bribe** of $240,000 to the foreign minister. A bribe is money given to persuade someone to do something wrong or illegal. Pinckney's angry reply was "No, no, not a sixpence!"

When Americans at home learned about the "XYZ Affair," they were outraged. "Millions for defense, but not one cent for **tribute**!" became a popular rallying cry. Tribute is money paid by a weak nation to a strong one as the price for peace or protection. Some Federalists wanted Congress to declare war immediately.

Adams felt the nation was too weak to fight a full-scale war. Instead, he fought an undeclared "half war" with France. The United States

bribe: money given to persuade someone to do something wrong or illegal
tribute: money paid by a weak nation to a strong one as the price for peace or protection
immigrants: foreigners entering a country to settle there
alien: foreigner
sedition: speech or action stirring up people against the government
states' rights: doctrine that the states have the right to refuse to enforce any unconstitutional acts of Congress

The letters of John and Abigail Adams to each other are among the most informative and endearing in U.S. history. You may wish to read passages from these letters to the class. (Remind students that it was Abigail who admonished her husband, when he was a delegate to the Continental Congress to "remember the ladies," i.e., that women deserved to have the vote.)

In this painting an American ship, the *Planter*, on the right, is chasing a French privateer. Many privateers were captured by American ships during the "half war."

Navy was ordered to attack French warships. But the Republicans were not eager to support even a half war against the French republic. President Adams called them "the French party."

THE ALIEN AND SEDITION ACTS

In 1798 the Federalists in Congress took advantage of anti-French feelings resulting from the half war and the XYZ Affair. They hoped to strengthen the war effort and weaken the Republicans. To do this, they passed laws restricting foreigners and critics of the government.

Three of these laws, known as the Alien Acts, were aimed at recent **immigrants**—people who had come to the United States to settle. One law gave the President the power to order out of the country any **alien,** or foreigner, who was thought to be a threat to the government. Another law made it more difficult for immigrants to become citizens with voting rights. The Federalists favored this change because the new immigrants usually voted Republican.

Congress also passed the Sedition Act. **Sedition** (sih-DISH-uhn) is speech or action that stirs up people against their government. The act

SUSANNA HASWELL ROWSON

Susanna Haswell's first experience in America was a shipwreck. The ship bringing the Haswells from England in 1762 sank in Boston Harbor. Rescued, the six-year-old girl reached the American shore.

The Haswells settled near Boston. In the following years, they found themselves in the midst of the American Revolution. Patriot James Otis befriended the bright girl, calling her "my little scholar." But Susanna had to keep her budding patriotism to herself when her Loyalist father took her back to England.

There, Susanna grew up and married William Rowson. Both began careers on the stage. In 1793 they toured the United States and decided to settle in Boston.

Susanna became known as "the celebrated Mrs. Rowson." Besides acting, she wrote plays, poems, songs, and novels. She also opened a school and wrote books for her classes.

In Rowson's songs and plays, the patriotism kindled so long ago blazed brightly. Her great hero was George Washington. When the Whiskey Rebellion troubled his presidency, Rowson wrote a play making fun of the rebels.

The half war with France also stirred Rowson's patriotism. She wrote plays and songs calling for a stronger American navy to protect merchant shipping. In 1799 the nation was thrilled when an American named Thomas Truxton captured a French warship. Rowson celebrated this event in her popular song "Truxton's Victory."

> The sons of France our seas invade,
> Destroy our commerce and our trade,
> 'Tis time the reckoning should be paid,
> To brave Yankee boys.

Susanna Rowson, daughter of a Loyalist, would forever be an heir of the Revolution.

---

said that Americans could be jailed for making statements harmful to the good name of government leaders. Under this law, several Republican newspaper editors were thrown into jail.

THE VIRGINIA AND KENTUCKY RESOLUTIONS

Jefferson and Madison secretly wrote resolutions that were passed by the state legislatures of Virginia and Kentucky. The resolutions said the Sedition Act was unconstitutional, or not allowed by the Constitution, because it violated the First Amendment guarantee of freedom of speech.

In Kentucky's resolution, Jefferson went even further. He argued that the individual states had the right to refuse to enforce any unconstitutional acts of Congress. This idea came to be called the doctrine of **states' rights.**

Over the years arguments over what constitutes states' rights have varied. However, states' rights doctrines are generally based on the idea that the states gave up many powers to the national government when they accepted the Constitution and that the powers not given to the national government in the Constitution remain with the states.

THE ELECTION OF 1800

If the United States and France had been at war, criticism of the government would have seemed unpatriotic. Americans might then have accepted the Sedition Act. But in 1800 Adams again sent negotiators across the Atlantic. They brought back a peace treaty with France. In peacetime, most Americans saw the Sedition Act as unnecessary and unfair. The Federalists' support of the act cost them many votes in the next presidential election.

In the election of 1800, Jefferson and the Republicans defeated Adams and the Federalists. But the Republican victory was nearly spoiled by a flaw in the rules guiding presidential electors. According to the Constitution, each elector had to cast two ballots without showing which was for President and which was for Vice-President. (This rule was changed by the Twelfth Amendment to the Constitution, in 1804.)

Both Jefferson and Aaron Burr, the Republican candidate for Vice-President, had 73 electoral votes. In case of a tie, the Constitution says that the House of Representatives shall choose the President.

Republican Representatives backed Jefferson, but the Federalists, who controlled the House, gave most of their votes to Burr. Again the vote was tied. The deadlock lasted through 30 votes. Finally Hamilton gave his support to Jefferson. Jefferson was elected.

For 12 years the Federalists had labored to put the Constitution into practice. Now they felt that all their work was threatened. Looking into the future, one Federalist saw only "blood and ashes."

On March 4, 1801, Thomas Jefferson became the third President of the United States. In his inauguration speech he did his best to calm Federalist fears. "We are all Republicans, we are all Federalists," he said.

A woman who saw the inauguration wrote that in most countries there was confusion and bloodshed when one group took control of the government away from another. "In this our happy country," however, power had changed hands peacefully.

SECTION REVIEW Answers will be found on page T 44.

1. Define these words: *bribe, tribute, immigrants, alien, sedition, states' rights.*

2. Identify: XYZ Affair, Alien and Sedition Acts, Aaron Burr.

3. How did John Adams respond to the XYZ Affair?

4. Why did the Federalists pass the Alien and Sedition Acts?

5. How did Jefferson and Madison protest the Sedition Act?

6. Which election showed that political power could change hands peacefully in the United States?

Activity: Students can compose election slogans and songs—either for Adams or for Jefferson—for the presidential campaign of 1800.

*CT
Activity: Each student can write two letters—the first by a Federalist and the second by a Republican—telling about Jefferson's victory over Adams. The letters should point up differences between members of the two political parties.

When the United States became an independent nation, there were two frontiers in North America. One was the Spanish frontier, stretching across Texas, New Mexico, Arizona, and California. The other was the log cabin frontier, pushed westward by settlers crossing the Appalachians. In 1789 post riders from "Atlantic America" brought news of George Washington's inauguration as the first President of the United States.

Under Washington's leadership, Americans put the Constitution into practice. The executive branch of the federal government and the federal court system were organized. Treasury Secretary Alexander Hamilton established the credit of the United States. Disagreements between Hamilton and Thomas Jefferson over Hamilton's economic program led to the formation of two political parties. These were the Republicans and the Federalists.

During Washington's second term, the authority of the federal government was strengthened. Military force was used to frighten the "Whiskey Boys" and defeat the Indians living north of the Ohio River. Through diplomacy the United States gained control of its territory west of the Appalachians. The outbreak of war between Great Britain and revolutionary France widened the gap between the Federalists and the Republicans. Republicans supported the revolution, but Federalists saw in it mob rule.

The presidency of John Adams was marked by a struggle for power between the two political parties. When the Republicans failed to support the "half war" against France, the Federalists passed the Alien and Sedition Acts.

The unpopularity of the Sedition Act helped the Republicans win the election of 1800. Despite the hostility between the rival parties, political power changed hands peacefully in 1801. Jefferson's inauguration proved that the American system of government could work.

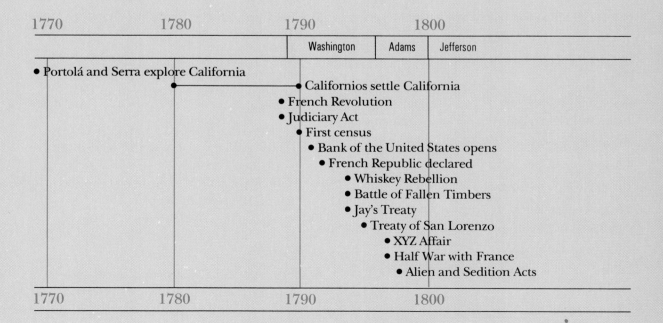

1770	1780	1790	1800
		Washington	Adams	Jefferson

- Portolá and Serra explore California
- Californios settle California
- French Revolution
- Judiciary Act
- First census
- Bank of the United States opens
- French Republic declared
- Whiskey Rebellion
- Battle of Fallen Timbers
- Jay's Treaty
- Treaty of San Lorenzo
- XYZ Affair
- Half War with France
- Alien and Sedition Acts

1770   1780   1790   1800

CHAPTER SURVEY

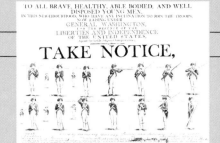

This 1798 army poster urged young men to defend their country. Their pay was $60 a year.

VOCABULARY REVIEW

From this list of vocabulary words, choose the one that best matches each definition below.

(a) alien   (j) negotiate
(b) bribe   (k) neutral
(c) census   (l) pioneers
(d) credit   (m) precedents
(e) diplomacy   (n) sedition
(f) immigrant   (o) states' rights
(g) impress   (p) tariff
(h) inaugurate   (q) tribute
(i) interest

1. settlers of a new region

2. examples for the future

3. money given to persuade someone to do something wrong or illegal

4. the doctrine that states may refuse to enforce unconstitutional acts of Congress

5. a person who enters a country in order to live there

6. a fee paid for the use of borrowed money

7. money paid by a weak nation to a strong one for protection

8. a foreigner

9. not taking sides

10. to hold discussions to reach an agreement

11. to bring into office formally

12. to force someone to serve in the military

13. the ability to borrow

14. speech or action that stirs up people against their government

15. a population count

16. the art of conducting talks to solve problems

17. an import tax

CHAPTER REVIEW

1. (a) In the federal court system set up during Washington's first administration, what kinds of cases were heard by district courts? (b) What kinds by circuit courts? (c) What kinds by the Supreme Court?

2. Why did Hamilton want to exchange new federal bonds for old Confederation bonds?

3. How was the Bank of the United States supposed to help business people?

4. (a) In relation to the Constitution, what does "strict construction" mean? (b) What does "loose construction" mean?

5. What important result did the Battle of Fallen Timbers have?

6. (a) What two precedents for the executive branch did Washington set? (b) What warning did he give to Americans in his Farewell Address?

7. (a) What treaty avoided a war with Britain and established the nation's authority over the Northwest Territory? (b) What treaty established the nation's southern boundary and gave it the right of deposit at New Orleans? (c) How did Adams prevent the "half war" with France from becoming a full-scale war?

8. Were Jefferson and the Republicans for or against (a) a fancy title for the President? (b) a national bank? (c) strict construction?

(d) the French Revolution? (e) a strong national government? (f) Which of these views did the Federalists agree with?

9. How did Hamilton's view of the basis for national greatness differ from Jefferson's?

10. (a) What does the Constitution say about political parties? (b) What did Washington hope to accomplish by seeking a second term? (c) How did Federalists feel about the election of Jefferson in 1800? (d) What did the inauguration of Jefferson show about the American system of government?

GEOGRAPHY REVIEW

1. (a) In 1800 where was the Spanish frontier in North America? (b) Where was the log cabin frontier?

2. Why did farmers in southwestern Pennsylvania have trouble bringing their crops to market?

3. What was Florida's northern boundary, according to the Treaty of San Lorenzo?

After 1808, no more slaves could be imported into the United States. Packed into slave ships like the *Albatross,* painted by Godfrey Meynall, Africans had suffered terribly.

USING THE TOOLS OF HISTORY

Making Circle Graphs

*CT **1.** Find the heading "The Census of 1790" on page 221. (a) Use the information under the heading to make a circle graph showing the percentage of Americans working as farmers in 1790. Add a title to the graph. (b) Make a second circle graph showing the percentage of Americans living in towns of more than 2,500 people. Add a title to this graph, too.

Distinguishing Fact from Opinion

*CT **2.** Decide whether each statement is a fact or an opinion. (a) In 1794, 13,000 militia troops crossed the Alleghenies to put down the Whiskey Rebellion. (b) Hamilton looked foolish in using a large army to arrest a few tax dodgers. (c) On March 4, 1801, control of the executive branch of the government passed from the Federalists to the Republicans. (d) The inauguration of Thomas Jefferson was one of the most interesting scenes a free people could witness.

READING AND THINKING SKILLS

Recognizing the Cause-Effect Pattern

*CT **1.** (a) How did the Spanish cause Indians to become warriors on horseback? (b) What effect did Indian warriors on horseback have on Spanish settlements? (c) How are these effects part of a chain reaction? (Refer to the information about causes and effects on page 229 if necessary.)

*CT **2.** Many causes may contribute to one effect. For example, both disease and hunger might cause frontier people to look old at thirty-five. Review the paragraphs under the heading "The Log Cabin Frontier" on page 216. Then list four other possible causes for this effect.

Introducing: Remind students that Jefferson wrote the Declaration of Independence. Have them review the paragraph beginning, "We hold these truths. . . ." Ask: What policies might such a President institute?

CHAPTER 10 1801-1824

THE REPUBLICANS IN CHARGE

JEFFERSON AS PRESIDENT
TROUBLES AT SEA
THE WAR OF 1812
AN ERA OF NATIONALIST FEELINGS
MONROE'S FOREIGN POLICY

10-1 JEFFERSON AS PRESIDENT

elite: powerful group of wealthy aristocrats

*CT
For discussion: Jefferson wrote, "To preserve the freedom of the human mind . . . and the freedom of the press, every spirit should be ready to devote itself to martyrdom; for as long as we may think as we will and speak as we think, the condition of humanity will proceed in improvement." What does this statement reveal about Jefferson's ideas about the perfectibility of humanity?

READ TO FIND OUT

—what the word *elite* means.

—what kind of government Jefferson wanted to create.

—how the case *Marbury* v. *Madison* expanded the power of the Supreme Court.

—how the United States acquired Louisiana.

—what Lewis and Clark and Pike discovered west of the Mississippi.

President Thomas Jefferson believed that he and his fellow Republicans were part of an experiment. They intended "to show whether [people] can be trusted with self-government." For Jefferson, self-government included not only the right to vote, but also the right of the people to take part in their government.

Jefferson rejected the Federalist idea that the government should be run by a political **elite,** or a powerful group of wealthy aristocrats. He believed in government by a "natural aristocracy." By this he meant people who were born with intelligence and ability rather than people born to wealth.

A WISE AND FRUGAL GOVERNMENT

As President, Jefferson planned to head "a wise and frugal government." A wise government would protect the people's rights. It would "leave them otherwise free" to improve their lives. A frugal, or nonwasteful, government would tax and spend as little as possible.

Jefferson and the Republicans did not try to undo the main Federalist programs. They left the Bank of the United States and the tariff alone. But the whiskey tax was repealed. When the Alien and Sedition Acts ran out in 1801, they were not renewed.

THE FEDERALIST JUDICIARY

Republicans controlled the presidency and Congress, but Federalists remained in control of the judicial branch. The Supreme Court, led by Chief Justice John Marshall, strengthened the power of the federal government in a series of important decisions. The first was the 1803 case of *Marbury* v. *Madison.* (The *v* stands for "versus," or against.)

MARBURY V. MADISON

During his last days in office, John Adams appointed Federalists to several judgeships. The Federalist-controlled Senate quickly gave its approval. When Jefferson took office, some of the appointment papers had not yet been delivered to the people chosen. Jefferson told his new Secretary of State, James Madison, not to deliver them. Without the papers, the judges could not take office.

One of the appointees was William Marbury. He asked the Supreme Court to order Madison to deliver his appointment papers. He argued that the Judiciary Act of 1789 gave the Court the power to require federal officials to perform their duties.

Chief Justice Marshall wrote out the Supreme Court's decision. The Court agreed that Marbury had a right to his appointment, but ruled that they could not order Marbury's official papers to be delivered. The section of the Judiciary Act giving the Court that power was unconstitutional. It gave the Court powers not listed in the Constitution.

For the first time, a law of Congress had been found to be unconstitutional. The Supreme Court had been strengthened by taking on the power of judicial review. In the decision Marshall wrote that the Court has the duty "to say what the law is."

George Washington died December 14, 1799. In 1801 Paul Revere made this gold urn in the classical style to hold a lock of Washington's hair.

Appointed by John Adams, John Marshall took office as Chief Justice of the Supreme Court on February 4, 1801. Marshall had previously served as an officer in the Revolutionary War, a delegate to the Virginia state convention adopting the Constitution, a Congressman, and Secretary of State. Washington had offered him the post of Attorney General, which he declined.

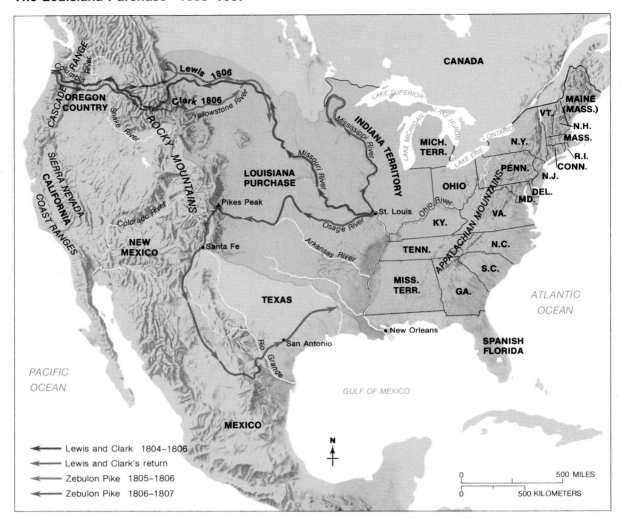

Lewis and Clark 1804–1806
Lewis and Clark's return
Zebulon Pike 1805–1806
Zebulon Pike 1806–1807

THE LOUISIANA PURCHASE

In 1800 Spain returned Louisiana to France. Farmers living west of the Appalachians feared that Napoleon (nah-PŌ-lee-uhn), the ruler of France, might close the port of New Orleans to Americans. To prevent this, Jefferson sent James Monroe to France. Monroe offered to buy New Orleans and western Florida for $10 million.

Napoleon had planned to rebuild France's empire in North America. Most of that empire's profits came from the sugarcane plantations on France's Caribbean islands. But the islands did not produce enough food for slaves who worked on the plantations. Napoleon planned to send French farmers to Louisiana to raise food for the "sugar islands."

A few years earlier, however, a slave named Toussaint L'Ouverture (too-SAN loo-vehr-TYOOR) had led a successful slave rebellion on

Activity: Students can research the life of the remarkable Toussaint L'Ouverture and give oral reports on him, as well as on his associate, Henri Christophe, who eventually became king of northern Haiti.

USING THE TOOLS OF HISTORY

UNDERSTANDING TOPOGRAPHY ON MAPS

Cartographers often want to show physical features of the land, such as mountains and valleys, on a map. Early mapmakers simply drew tiny pictures of the landscape on maps. But that did not leave much room for symbols and lettering. Also, changes in elevation could not be shown with much accuracy.

Today mapmakers use techniques such as coloring and shading to show landscape, or **topography,** on a map. Topography includes lakes, rivers, and *relief.* Relief is the difference in elevation between high and low lands.

To show changes in elevation, cartographers often use different colors. All areas from sea level to 1,000 feet (305 meters) might be colored green. The mapmaker might then choose yellow to show the areas from 1,000 to 3,000 feet, orange for areas from 3,000 to 7,000 feet, and brown for above 7,000 feet.

Shading gives a more realistic impression of the landscape than does coloring. It represents the land as it would look from an airplane. The unshaded areas are flat lands. The most darkly shaded areas are the steepest mountains. But shading does not show elevation in number of feet above or below sea level.

The map on page 240 is a good example of how shading is used to show relief. It shows quite clearly which areas of North America are mountainous.

1. How many mountain ranges are named on this map?

2. How would you describe the landscapes of the Oregon Country and the Indiana Territory?

3. The Louisiana Territory includes some high mountains. In what part of the territory are these mountains? What are they called? What peak is named?

4. What rivers did Lewis and Clark follow through rugged mountain areas?

Answers will be found on page T 45.

Haiti. Haiti was France's most productive sugar island. In 1802 Napoleon sent 20,000 troops to Haiti to crush the revolt. The rebels, aided by yellow fever, destroyed Napoleon's army.

Napoleon's dream of an American empire died with his troops in Haiti. When the Americans offered to buy New Orleans, the French leader surprised them. He offered to sell all of Louisiana for $15 million.

Jefferson and the Republicans favored the purchase. They also believed in a strict construction of the Constitution. The Constitution does not give Congress the power to buy land from other nations. But there was no time to amend the Constitution, giving Congress that power. Napoleon was showing signs of changing his mind.

Many Federalists opposed the purchase. They adopted the strict constructionist view and questioned the government's right to buy Louisiana. One complained, "We are asked to give money of which we have too little for land of which we already have too much."

Finally Jefferson decided that removing France from Louisiana was of great importance to the nation's future. He ignored his strict constructionist views. He accepted France's offer, and Congress approved.

Toussaint L'Ouverture

Meriwether Lewis stands while William Clark sits near his servant, York. Inside the tent is Sacajawea. Both Lewis and Clark praised Sacajawea's skill and bravery.

*CT
Activity: Some historians have claimed that Jefferson's purchase of the Louisiana Territory was inconsistent with his principles. Students can debate this claim. (In order to debate it intelligently, each side must first establish exactly what Jefferson's principles were.)

Activity: Students can find passages from the journals of Lewis and Clark and of Zebulon Pike and read them to the class.

The United States acquired a vast, but unknown, territory between the Mississippi and the Rocky Mountains. Even before the purchase was final, Jefferson had made plans to find out more about it.

THE LEWIS AND CLARK EXPEDITION

In 1804 Jefferson sent an expedition to explore Louisiana and blaze a trail to the Pacific Ocean. Captain Meriwether Lewis and Captain William Clark led about eighty men, including Clark's slave, York, northwest from St. Louis. Slowly they worked their way up the Missouri River.

Beyond the wooded plains of the Mississippi Valley, the explorers found endless stretches of tall grass. Lewis and Clark observed the Great Plains, which cover most of the Louisiana Territory. They saw that this area received too little rain for trees. Like most people at the time, they believed that land without trees was too dry to farm.

The explorers spent their first winter in North Dakota. There a young Shoshone woman, Sacajawea (SAK-uh-juh-WEE-uh), and her husband Toussaint Charbonneau (SHAR-bohn-ō), a French-Canadian fur trapper, joined them. With her baby strapped to her back, Sacajawea helped guide the expedition across the Rocky Mountains. West of the Rockies, the expedition followed the Columbia River to the Pacific Ocean. After a damp Oregon winter, the explorers made their way back to St. Louis in 1806. The expedition returned with priceless information.

UNDER MY WINGS EVERY THING PROSPERS

While Lewis and Clark were crossing the Rockies, Jefferson sent a young army officer named Zebulon Pike to explore the Upper Mississippi River. Then, in 1806, Pike followed the Osage and Arkansas rivers to Santa Fe and the Spanish Borderlands. Lewis and Clark's and Pike's journals gave most Americans their first glimpse of the West.

The United States acquired New Orleans as part of the Louisiana Purchase. This painting shows the American eagle hovering over the new acquisition.

SECTION REVIEW   Answers will be found on page T 45.

1. Define the following: *elite*.

2. Identify: John Marshall, Toussaint L'Ouverture, Meriwether Lewis and William Clark, Sacajawea, Zebulon Pike.

3. Describe the kind of government Jefferson wanted to create.

4. What Supreme Court power was established in *Marbury* v. *Madison*?

5. What caused Napoleon to decide to sell the Louisiana Territory?

6. What constitutional question was raised by the Louisiana Purchase?

10–2 TROUBLES AT SEA

READ TO FIND OUT

—what the words *blockade* and *embargo* mean.

—why the United States paid tribute to the Barbary States.

—how Americans reacted to the attack on the *Chesapeake.*

—how Presidents Jefferson and Madison tried to protect the rights of neutral ships.

blockade: forced closure of an area
embargo: government order to end trade with another country

American ships attacked Tripoli harbor on August 3, 1804. Captain Edward Preble led the attack. His ship, the *Constitution,* is the largest of the vessels in this 1805 engraving.

Jefferson won reelection in 1804 with a huge majority of the vote. His Vice-President was George Clinton of New York. The Republicans had refused to support Aaron Burr, Vice-President during Jefferson's first term, for reelection. Earlier that year, Burr had quarreled bitterly with his Federalist rival Alexander Hamilton. The quarrel ended in a duel that left Hamilton dead.

In his second term, Jefferson was forced to increase the power of the federal government in order to deal with threats to American shipping. The first threats came from the Barbary States—Algiers, Tunis, Tripoli, and Morocco—on the north coast of Africa.

The Barbary States

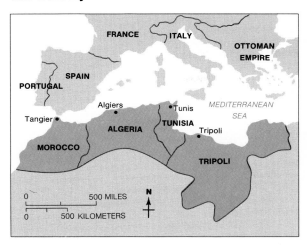

"The Impressment of an American Sailor Boy" was written to protest British actions at sea. The song was first sung on July 4, 1814.

THE BARBARY PIRATES

Since the 1780s, American merchant ships sailing in the Mediterranean Sea had risked capture by pirates from the Barbary States. Presidents Washington and Adams had paid tribute to their rulers who, in return, stopped the pirate attacks. The yearly bribes had cost the new nation $10 million by 1801.

Jefferson found paying bribes intolerable. He wrote to the Barbary States' rulers, "We mean to rest the safety of our commerce on the resources of our own strength and bravery in every sea." He sent several warships to the Mediterranean to back up his words.

In 1803 the warship *Philadelphia* ran aground on the shores of Tripoli while chasing pirates. The crew was captured and held for $3 million in ransom. In response, American ships set up a **blockade** of Tripoli Harbor. A blockade is the forced closure of an area to keep people and supplies from going in or out.

In 1805 the ruler of Tripoli agreed to a peace treaty with the United States. He released the American sailors for the bargain price of $60,000. Still, pirate attacks from the other states continued. Finally, in 1815, an American force led by Stephen Decatur (dih-KAY-ter) joined with European warships to destroy the pirate bases.

Activity: Stephen Decatur is one of America's great naval heroes. Students can research and write reports about Decatur's career and achievements.

THE *CHESAPEAKE-LEOPARD* AFFAIR

After selling Louisiana, France again went to war with Britain. In 1806 Britain declared that neutral ships could not trade in French-controlled ports unless they first stopped in Britain. There they would have to pay fees and get permission to continue their voyage. Napoleon then ordered French warships to seize any ship sailing to British ports.

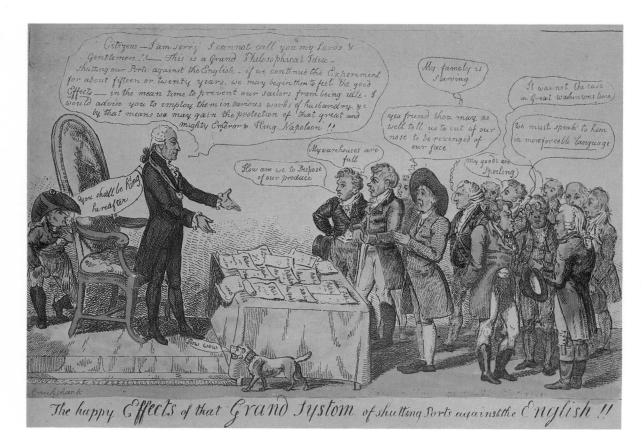

The happy Effects of that Grand System of shutting Ports against the English !!

This cartoon shows merchants protesting the Embargo Act.

American shippers were caught between the two warring nations. Their only choice was to stop trade with Europe or risk having their ships captured by England or France. By 1807 Britain had seized 1,000 American ships. The French had taken half that many. British warships also began to stop American merchant ships again to search for deserters from the Royal Navy. Some 6,000 American sailors were impressed into service on British warships.

In 1807 the British frigate *Leopard* stopped the American warship *Chesapeake* off the coast of Virginia. The British commander asked for permission to search the *Chesapeake* for deserters. The Americans refused. Such searches were allowed only on merchant ships. The *Leopard* answered with a surprise attack, killing three sailors and wounding eighteen. British officers then boarded the American ship and took away four sailors. One was an English deserter, but two black sailors and one white seaman were American citizens.

The crippled *Chesapeake* limped back to port. Americans were outraged. "Never since the battle of Lexington," wrote Jefferson, "have I seen this country in such a state of exasperation." All about him he heard calls for war to protect American rights at sea.

PEACEABLE COERCION

Instead, Jefferson tried a policy he called "peaceable coercion" to force France and Britain to leave American ships alone. His main weapon was an **embargo,** a government order to end trade with another country. Late in 1807 Congress passed the Embargo Act. It stopped American ships bound for Europe from leaving their home ports. Jefferson hoped that France and Britain would become desperate for American food and raw materials. They might then stop seizing neutral ships.

The first people to become desperate were Americans who depended on shipping for their living. Soup kitchens were set up to feed unemployed sailors and dock workers. In a letter to the President, an angry New Englander wrote, "How much longer are you going to keep this embargo on to starve us poor people?" Many merchants began smuggling to survive.

Despite the unpopular embargo, the Republicans won the election of 1808. Jefferson, following Washington's precedent, refused to run for a third term. James Madison was elected President with George Clinton as his Vice-President. Jefferson was free to return to his beloved home, Monticello. One of Jefferson's last acts as President was to sign the Non-Intercourse Act and the repeal of the embargo.

The Non-Intercourse Act allowed Americans to trade with all countries except France and Britain. As with the embargo, the purpose of this act was to force France and Britain to agree to leave neutral shipping alone. But both countries continued to seize American ships.

In 1810 Madison tried a different approach. Trade with both warring nations was allowed. If either one of the nations agreed to respect the rights of neutral ships, however, Madison would cut off trade with the other. Napoleon announced an end to the seizure of American ships. Madison then halted trade with Britain. Yet letters from Europe told of continued attacks on American ships by the French navy. No matter how many different ways it was carried out, the policy of peaceable coercion seemed to have failed.

The embargo was called the terrapin (turtle) policy because it backed the United States into a shell. "The Death of the Embargo" shows President Madison as the dying terrapin's last victim.

*CT

For discussion: Under what circumstances might an embargo be an effective nonmilitary weapon against another nation? Under what circumstances might it be ineffective?

SECTION REVIEW   Answers will be found on page T 45.

1. Define the following words: *blockade, embargo.*

2. Identify: Barbary States.

3. Why was the United States paying tribute to the rulers of the Barbary States?

4. How did most Americans react to the *Chesapeake-Leopard* affair?

5. What did Congress hope the result of the Embargo Act and the Non-Intercourse Act would be?

10-3 THE WAR OF 1812

READ TO FIND OUT

liberators: people who set other people free

offensive: advance into enemy territory

secession: withdrawal from the Union

—what the words *liberators, offensive,* and *secession* mean.

—why the War Hawks wanted war.

—what sections of the country opposed war.

—where the major battles of the war took place.

—what the main results of the war were.

President Madison worried about the rights of American merchant ships. Western farmers, however, were more concerned about the Indians. A Shawnee warrior named Tecumseh (tih-KUM-suh) and his brother, who was called the Prophet, were uniting the tribes along the frontier. Tecumseh asked the Indians to unite to defend their lands against American settlers. The Prophet, who was nearly blind, called on Indians to follow the religion of their ancestors.

Tecumseh's brother, the Prophet, was known by the Shawnee name of Tenskwatawa. He encouraged Indians to reject anything that came from whites.

ORGANIZING DETAILS

To support a main idea, an author gives further information through details or examples. The details may be organized in different ways.

One way is to consider each subheading in a chapter as a major event or topic. You have practiced finding major topics and topic sentences in Chapter 7. The topic sentence usually gives the main idea of a paragraph.

Often, the details will answer one of the "W" questions: Who or what, When, Where, and Why.

Look at the first subheading in this section, "The War Hawks." The third sentence of the second paragraph gives the main idea. Now answer the "W" questions to fill in the details.

Who or what were the War Hawks? (members of Congress who were eager for war with Britain)
When did they call for war? (about 1812)
Where were the War Hawks from? (the South and the West)

Why were they eager for war? (They thought war would end Indian troubles and win new territory for the United States.)

In the subsection titled "The War Hawks," you can see that all the "W" questions are answered. Sometimes you will find that not all of the questions are answered.

1. Find the main idea in the first paragraph under the subheading "The Invasion of Canada" on page 250. Now apply the "W" questions to the entire subsection. Write the answers on a piece of paper.
   (a) What was the invasion of Canada?
   (b) When did the invasion take place?
   (c) Where did the invasion take place?
   (d) Why did the invasion take place?

2. Copy the chart below on your paper. Refer to pages 253–254 to complete it.

EVENT OR TOPIC	WHO OR WHAT	WHEN	WHERE	WHY
Hartford Convention	a meeting of delegates from five New England states			
Treaty of Ghent				

Answers will be found on page T 46.

In 1811 William Henry Harrison led 1,000 troops to Prophetstown, Tecumseh's headquarters on Tippecanoe Creek. Tecumseh was not there, but the Prophet led Tecumseh's warriors into battle. In the Battle of Tippecanoe, many were killed on both sides.

THE WAR HAWKS

Westerners claimed that Britain was arming the Indians and encouraging them to attack frontier settlers. There would be no peace on the frontier, they said, until the British were driven from Canada.

Inform the class that in 1841 Harrison became the nation's ninth President. His election slogan was "Tippecanoe and Tyler too." (His running mate was John Tyler.) Students will learn more about him in Chapter 12.

Members of Congress from the South and West were eager for war with Britain. Because of this, Federalists called them "War Hawks." The War Hawks wanted not only an end to Indian troubles. They wanted new territory for the United States as well.

Representative Henry Clay of Kentucky told Congress that "the conquest of Canada is in your power." Southern War Hawks hoped to take Florida away from Britain's ally, Spain. The War Hawks added their voices to the more widespread call for action to protect "Free Trade and Sailors' Rights."

In June 1812 Madison sent a war message to Congress. He wrote of the need to protect Americans at sea and along the frontier. On June 18 Congress officially declared war on Great Britain. South Carolina Representative John C. Calhoun called the coming conflict "the second struggle for our liberty."

MR. MADISON'S WAR

In the War of 1812, events often had a very different outcome from what was expected. The war even began strangely. Just two days before the United States declared war, the policy of peaceable coercion finally worked. Feeling the effects of the trade embargo, the British government ordered the navy to stop seizing American ships. By the time the news reached the United States, however, the war had started.

The unexpected happened in New England, too. That section of the country had suffered most from Britain's attacks on trade. Yet New Englanders thought the war would damage their trade far more than the seizure of ships or impressment had done. When Madison ran for re-election in 1812, he was supported by western and southern states. New York and the New England states backed the Federalist, DeWitt Clinton. They wanted no part of "Mr. Madison's War."

THE INVASION OF CANADA

There were times in 1812 when Mr. Madison himself may have wanted no part of "his" war. Madison's strategy was to attack the British by invading Canada from several points. Like most Americans, he believed that an invasion would be easy. But when General William Hull marched 1,500 soldiers to Detroit, he found himself facing Tecumseh's army. Fearing defeat, he surrendered without firing a shot. Two more armies were sent to Canada. The first was defeated at Queenston. The second headed toward Montreal but turned back when state militia troops refused to leave American soil.

Later assaults on Canada were also unsuccessful. Americans had expected the Canadians to welcome them as **liberators,** people who would

Tell students that they will learn more about War Hawk Henry Clay when they study the Missouri Compromise. (See page 258.)

*CT

For discussion: Was the War of 1812 fortunate or unfortunate for the United States? What (if any) were the good and bad consequences of the war?

The War of 1812

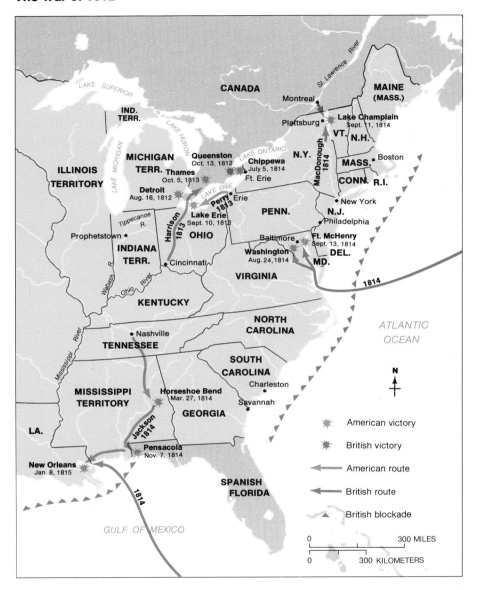

Have students find the sites of important events of the war on this map.

Map labels:
LAKE SUPERIOR
CANADA
St. Lawrence River
MAINE (MASS.)
Montreal
IND. TERR.
Plattsburg
Lake Champlain Sept. 11, 1814
VT.
N.H.
LAKE HURON
LAKE MICHIGAN
MICHIGAN TERR.
Queenston Oct. 13, 1812
LAKE ONTARIO
Chippewa July 5, 1814
N.Y.
MacDonough 1814
MASS.
Boston
ILLINOIS TERRITORY
Thames Oct. 5, 1813
Ft. Erie
CONN. R.I.
Detroit Aug. 16, 1812
LAKE ERIE
Perry 1813
Erie
Harrison 1813
Lake Erie Sept. 10, 1813
PENN.
N.J.
New York
Tippecanoe R.
Prophetstown
INDIANA TERR.
OHIO
Baltimore
Washington Aug. 24, 1814
Ft. McHenry Sept. 13, 1814
DEL.
MD.
Philadelphia
Wabash R.
Ohio River
Cincinnati
VIRGINIA
1814
KENTUCKY
Mississippi River
NORTH CAROLINA
ATLANTIC OCEAN
Nashville
TENNESSEE
SOUTH CAROLINA
N
Charleston
MISSISSIPPI TERRITORY
Horseshoe Bend Mar. 27, 1814
GEORGIA
Savannah
LA.
Jackson 1814
Pensacola Nov. 7, 1814
New Orleans Jan. 8, 1815
SPANISH FLORIDA
1814
GULF OF MEXICO

Legend:
✳ American victory
✴ British victory
← American route
← British route
▲ British blockade

0   300 MILES
0   300 KILOMETERS

The War of 1812 was mainly a series of small battles on land and sea. American victories at sea did not win the war, but they did fill Americans with pride.

set them free. Most Canadians, however, saw the invasion attempts as attacks on their homeland. For them, the conflict with the United States was "the War of Defense."

In the fall of 1813, Americans won two badly needed victories. The first, on Lake Erie, was won by a hastily built fleet of ships commanded by Captain Oliver Perry. With a sturdy group of militia troops, black sailors, and frontier scouts, Perry went after the British Lake Squadron. On September 10 the two forces met. They pounded at each other until the British ships went down. Perry reported to General Harrison, "We have met the enemy, and they are ours."

Activity: Students can research and give reports on Oliver Hazard Perry and his equally distinguished brother, Matthew Calbraith Perry, who opened Japan to world trade.

Perry's victory made it possible for General Harrison to move 4,500 troops across Lake Erie. The Americans then chased the British and Indian forces from Detroit to the Thames (temz) River in Canada. During the Battle of the Thames, Tecumseh was killed. With him died the dream of unifying the frontier tribes.

Indians suffered another setback six months later. At Horseshoe Bend in Mississippi Territory, Creek warriors were defeated by Tennessee militia troops under Andrew Jackson. The Creek were forced to cede much of their land to the United States.

THE BRITISH OFFENSIVE

In 1814 the war between Britain and France finally ended. Britain was able to send more troops to Canada. The British also sent more ships to complete a blockade of the Atlantic coast. British commanders planned an **offensive,** or advance into enemy territory, from three points. They also planned raids on coastal towns.

The offensive began when British troops moved toward Niagara Falls early in July. The British were stopped when American General Jacob Brown crossed the Niagara River and defeated British forces at the Battle of Chippewa. In a second battle, at Lundy's Lane, both sides suffered heavy losses. But Americans took control of Fort Erie and held it against the British.

At the same time, a British force entered Chesapeake Bay. The force had orders "to destroy and lay waste such towns and districts" as they might find. On August 24 they captured Washington, D.C. British officers arrived at the White House in time to eat a dinner set out for the President and his wife, Dolley Madison.

The first lady refused to flee the White House until the last moment. She wanted to save "the most valuable portable articles belonging to the house" and "the large picture of General Washington." She acted just in time. British troops piled up the remaining White House furniture and set it afire. Other public buildings were burned, too.

From Washington the British sailed to Baltimore, Maryland. For two nights they bombarded Fort McHenry, which protected the city. Francis Scott Key watched "the bombs bursting in air." When dawn broke on the second morning, he was thrilled to see a tattered American flag still waving above the fort. It inspired him to write "The Star-Spangled Banner." In time, Key's song would become the national anthem.

While Fort McHenry was under attack, the second stage of the British offensive began. A force of 10,000 troops sailed south on Lake Champlain to invade New York. The much weaker American fleet, led by Thomas Macdonough, stopped the invasion. New York was saved. New England would not be cut off from the rest of the nation.

Dolley Madison

THE HARTFORD CONVENTION

Some New Englanders were not upset by the idea of being cut off from the rest of the nation. A small minority began talking about **secession,** or leaving the Union. There were ugly rumors about "Blue Light Federalists." These New Englanders were opponents of the war who reportedly flashed lantern signals to the Royal Navy when an American ship tried to run the blockade.

Late in 1814 delegates from five New England states met in Hartford, Connecticut. The few who spoke for secession were quickly voted down. But the delegates did call for several amendments to the Constitution. They hoped these changes would protect New England's interests.

Three representatives carried these demands to the capital. They arrived just in time to hear that the Americans had stopped a third British invasion at New Orleans. General Jackson had put together an army of militia troops made up of free blacks from Louisiana, Indian fighters, and pirates. They stopped the invasion on January 8, 1815. The British lost 2,000 soldiers compared to a dozen American dead.

The British bombard Fort McHenry. The flag flies above the fort in the center. This flag inspired Francis Scott Key to write "The Star–Spangled Banner."

You may wish to have students note that at this period in our history, it was New Englanders, rather than Southerners, who wished to secede from the Union.

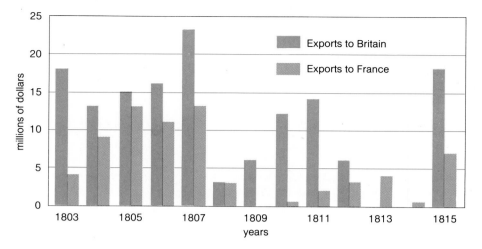

American Exports 1803–1815

millions of dollars / years

Exports to Britain
Exports to France

American trade with Britain was usually greater than with France. At times, trade with both nations was hurt by political events.

THE TREATY OF GHENT

A war that had begun strangely ended strangely. The Battle of New Orleans had no military value. Two weeks earlier a peace treaty had been signed in Ghent, Belgium. While the nation rejoiced, the representatives from Hartford left the capital in disgrace. The Federalists never recovered from the belief that they had been disloyal during the war.

The Treaty of Ghent gave no clear advantage to either side. The treaty did not even mention impressment or other problems that had led to war. But the United States had made some gains since 1812. It had won the respect of other nations. The region east of the Mississippi had become safer for frontier settlers.

There was one final unexpected outcome of the war. New England, the section opposed to the war, gained the most from it. With trade from Britain cut off, New England had greatly expanded its cloth-making industry. New England came out of the war with thousands of new spindles whirling in spinning mills.

For discussion: How did the development of New England's textile industry promote the United States' independence from other nations?

SECTION REVIEW   Answers will be found on page T 46.

1. Define the following words: *liberators, offensive, secession.*

2. Identify: Tecumseh, War Hawks, Henry Clay, Francis Scott Key, Hartford Convention, Treaty of Ghent.

3. Why did the War Hawks want war with Great Britain?

4. Why did New Englanders oppose war with Great Britain?

5. How did Canadians view the invasion of Canada?

6. What did the Treaty of Ghent say about impressment?

10-4 AN ERA OF NATIONALIST FEELINGS

READ TO FIND OUT

—what the words *nationalism, economy, interstate,* and *commerce* mean.

—what the "American System" was.

—how the Supreme Court placed federal power over state power in *McCulloch* v. *Maryland* and *Gibbons* v. *Ogden.*

—what happened to the Federalist party after the War of 1812.

—what the Missouri Compromise accomplished.

nationalism: feeling of loyalty to one's nation
economy: way a country produces, uses, and divides goods, services, and money
interstate: from one state to another
commerce: business

The War of 1812 left Americans with a strong sense of **nationalism,** or a feeling of loyalty to their nation. Treasury Secretary Albert Gallatin noted that "the war has renewed and reinstated the national feeling and character which the Revolution had given." Americans, he wrote, "feel and act more as a nation."

MADISON'S PROGRAM

Jefferson had said in 1801 that "we are all Republicans, we are all Federalists." At that point he was stating a hope. But by 1815 his statement was almost a fact. In his message to Congress that year, Republican Madison called for a series of measures that could well have been written by Federalist Alexander Hamilton.

Have students review Alexander Hamilton's views and achievements, especially his establishment of a national bank. (See pages 222–225.)

Madison asked Congress to create a new national bank. Five years earlier, the charter of the Bank of the United States had run out. The government no longer had a central bank to handle its funds. It turned to state banks. Each state bank issued its own paper money. The result was a confusing variety of currencies. Merchants found it difficult to do business outside their own states. Madison hoped a new national bank would create a standard currency for the whole country.

The President also called for a tariff on imported goods. With the war over, British manufactured goods were flooding the country. The "infant industries" of America could not produce goods as cheaply as the British could. Many American factory owners were going out of business. Madison hoped that a tariff would raise the price of foreign goods, thus protecting these factory owners until they could compete with the European manufacturers.

★ ★ ★ ★ ★ ★ ★ **AMERICAN VALUES IN ACTION** ★ ★ ★ ★ ★ ★ ★

JOHN C. CALHOUN

John C. Calhoun was born in March 1782 on the South Carolina frontier. Only a year before, the gunfire of the Revolutionary War had echoed through the mountains. As a young child, John was thrilled by stories of Camden and Cowpens and Carolina Patriots.

The stories told around the Calhoun fireside were also of politics. John's father told him how he had led back-country settlers in their struggle for representation in the South Carolina legislature.

Young John grew up with a frontier pioneer's fierce love of liberty. He was a shy man, solitary as a mountain hawk. But his blazing eyes revealed a keen intelligence.

With his fiery zeal and coolly logical mind, Calhoun was drawn to politics. He took his father's old seat in the state legislature. Then, in 1811, South Carolinians sent him to the United States House of Representatives.

Aroused by British "hostilities," Calhoun became a War Hawk. A towering man, with a mane of black hair, he was a commanding presence on the House floor. The British, he vowed, would not trample American liberty again. Calhoun called ringingly for a "second American Revolution."

The War of 1812 left Americans with a warm feeling of nationalism. Calhoun supported President Madison's American System after the war. But by the 1820s the issue of slavery was dividing the North and the South. Calhoun began to speak for southern rights.

The Union, Calhoun felt, had been formed in order to preserve liberty. Liberty was the right of a state to do as it wished, as long as it did not hurt the common good. To preserve liberty, the Union must protect the rights of all of the states.

Throughout his life, Calhoun loved both the Union and the South. But disagreement between the North and the South grew, tearing at the Union. The conflict would leave John Calhoun a brokenhearted patriot.

Madison also asked Congress to set aside funds for "internal improvements" such as roads. He saw such improvements as necessary for "binding more closely together" the regions of the expanding nation. Improvements were especially important to the western states, which needed better ways to get their products to market in the East.

THE AMERICAN SYSTEM

Congressman Henry Clay called Madison's program the "American System." He and South Carolina Congressman John C. Calhoun worked hard to get it written into law. The first step was the Tariff of 1816. By

Power–driven looms made it possible for workers to produce cotton cloth cheaply. Such looms helped New England's textile mills compete with Britain's.

For discussion: How might an interstate highway promote a sense of national unity?

taxing foreign imports, Congress hoped to make the American **economy** less dependent on trade with Europe. A nation's economy is the way it produces, uses, and divides up goods, services, and money.

Congress created the second Bank of the United States in 1816 and gave it a 20-year charter. The new bank encouraged business activity by providing paper money people could trust. Congress also funded the National Road, which was begun under Jefferson. This road was the first **interstate** highway—the first that crossed from one state to another. The road ran from Cumberland, Maryland, to the Ohio River.

The passage of these acts pleased Madison as his second term came to an end in 1816. He noted that "the American people have reached in safety and success their fortieth year as an independent nation."

THE MARSHALL COURT

After the War of 1812, the Supreme Court strengthened the power of the federal government in several important cases. One was *McCulloch v. Maryland.* A Maryland law placed a tax on a branch of the Bank of the United States. The questions in the case were: Did Maryland have the power to tax a federal bank? Did Congress have the power to charter such a bank in the first place?

Chief Justice Marshall wrote that the bank was constitutional. Congress, he said, has broad powers to act, as long as it followed the "letter and the spirit of the Constitution." Maryland's law was unconstitutional because "the power to tax involves the power to destroy." No state had the power to destroy an agency of the federal government.

In the case of *Gibbons* v. *Ogden*, the Court declared a New York contract, or agreement, unconstitutional. In this contract, New York had given a steamship company a monopoly on passenger service across the Hudson River between New York and New Jersey. Marshall wrote that a state could control **commerce,** or business, within its own borders. But the Constitution gives control of interstate commerce, including transportation, to Congress.

Such decisions led Jefferson to complain that "the Constitution is a mere thing of wax in the hands of the judiciary which they may twist and shape as they please." But John Adams, who had appointed the Chief Justice, wrote, "My gift of John Marshall to the people of the United States was the proudest act of my life."

MONROE BECOMES PRESIDENT

In 1816 Madison's Secretary of State, James Monroe, easily won the presidency. The Federalist party was in ruins. Federalist backing of the Hartford Convention during the war had lost the party many supporters. After the war many Federalist ideals and programs had been taken over by the Republicans. When Monroe ran for reelection in 1820, the Federalists did not even put forward a candidate.

In 1817 Monroe visited New England. His warm welcome in Boston led a Federalist newspaper to write that an "era of good feelings" had begun. The good feelings, however, would not last long.

THE MISSOURI COMPROMISE

Before the War of 1812, five new states had entered the Union—Vermont, Kentucky, Tennessee, Ohio, and Louisiana. Between the end of the war and 1819, four more new states were admitted—Indiana, Mississippi, Illinois, and Alabama. The total number of states became 22. Eleven were slave states, and eleven were free. The free states had larger populations and thus more Representatives in the House. But in the Senate, slave and free states had the same number of votes.

Then Missouri applied for admission as a slave state. Many northerners in Congress supported statehood only if Missouri abolished slavery. Congressman Arthur Livermore of New Hampshire attacked slavery as "a sin which sits heavy on the soul of every one of us." If slavery were allowed to spread westward, he argued, Congress should "declare that our Constitution was made to impose slavery, and not to establish liberty."

The Missouri Compromise 1820

OREGON COUNTRY

CANADA

MAINE 1820

MICHIGAN TERRITORY

UNORGANIZED TERRITORY

MISSOURI 1821

36°30' MISSOURI COMPROMISE LINE

ARKANSAS TERR.

MEXICO

FLORIDA TERRITORY

☐ Free state or territory

☐ Territory closed to slavery

☐ Slave state or territory

Southerners, however, felt that the Constitution did not give Congress the power to decide whether a state should be slave or free. Also, if Missouri were admitted as a free state, there would no longer be a balance of power in the Senate. The free states would have a majority.

Under the guidance of Henry Clay, a compromise was reached in 1820. Maine, which had recently applied for statehood, was admitted to the Union as a free state. Missouri was admitted as a slave state. A line was then drawn across the Louisiana Territory at latitude 36°30′. South of that line slavery would be permitted. North of that line there would be no slavery except in the state of Missouri. The compromise ended the conflict over slavery for a time. Jefferson, however, warned that "sooner or later," the conflict would again "burst on us as a tornado."

This portrait of a black skilled worker was painted by John Singleton Copley. This man was free, but he lived in New England at a time when slavery was still common there.

Henry Clay was known as the "Great Pacificator" because of his repeated efforts to reconcile differences between slave and free states and so preserve the Union. He is the source of the famous saying, "I had rather be right than be President." (He ran unsuccessfully for President in 1824, 1832, and 1844.) Students will learn more about him in Chapter 12.

SECTION REVIEW   Answers will be found on page T 46.

1. Define the following words: *nationalism, economy, interstate,* and *commerce.*

2. Identify: National Road, James Monroe.

3. What were the three parts of the American System?

4. Why did the Supreme Court declare a Maryland tax on a branch of the Bank of the United States unconstitutional?

5. Why was a New York contract giving a steamship line a monopoly on passenger service between New York and New Jersey found to be unconstitutional?

6. How did the Missouri Compromise keep the balance between slave and free states?

10-5 MONROE'S FOREIGN POLICY

READ TO FIND OUT

—what the words *disarm* and *czar* mean.

—what agreements Britain and the United States reached after the War of 1812.

—how the United States acquired Florida.

—what the Monroe Doctrine was.

In foreign affairs, President Monroe was ably assisted by his Secretary of State, John Quincy Adams. The son of the second President, Adams had been foreign minister to four European countries. He had also helped to negotiate the Treaty of Ghent ending the War of 1812.

AGREEMENTS WITH BRITAIN

The war did not settle the conflicts between the United States and Britain. But it won the United States new respect from Britain's leaders. After 1815 the two nations settled their differences through diplomacy rather than by force of arms.

In 1817 Charles Bagot, Britain's minister to the United States, and Richard Rush, representing Monroe, negotiated a treaty. They agreed that both countries would **disarm,** or remove weapons from, their naval forces on the Great Lakes. In time the Rush-Bagot Treaty became the basis for disarming the whole Canadian-American border.

The following year, the Convention of 1818 gave Americans the right to fish in Canadian waters off Newfoundland. It also set the northern boundary of the Louisiana Territory at 49° north latitude from Lake of the Woods to the crest of the Rocky Mountains.

West of the Rockies, between Spanish California and Russian Alaska, lay the Oregon Country. It was claimed by the United States, Britain, and Spain. Ignoring the Spanish claim, Britain and the United States agreed to leave Oregon open to settlers from both countries.

FLORIDA BECOMES UNITED STATES TERRITORY

One of the War Hawks' goals in the War of 1812 was to make Florida part of the United States. Earlier Presidents, including Thomas Jefferson, had tried to acquire Florida but had not succeeded. In 1810 James

The United States in 1822

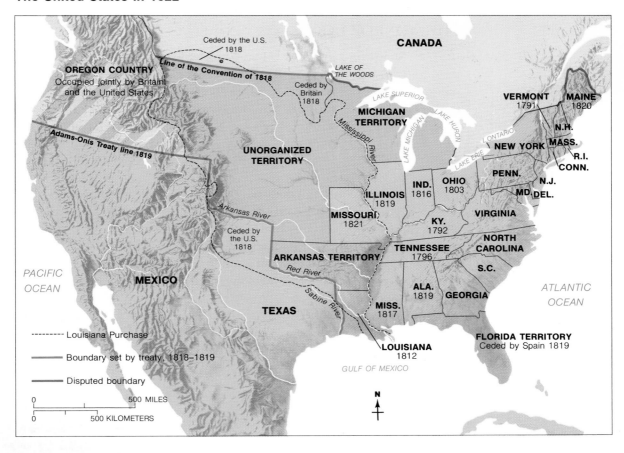

Madison took advantage of a revolt of American settlers in western Florida to add part of the area to the United States. Spain, however, continued to hold the Florida peninsula.

Hoping to acquire all of Florida, Secretary of State Adams began negotiations with Luis de Onís (ō-NEES), Spain's minister to the United States. Meanwhile, Monroe ordered Andrew Jackson, the hero of New Orleans, to end Indian raids on frontier settlements in Georgia. Jackson chased Seminole and Creek raiders into Florida. Then he seized the Spanish forts at St. Marks and Pensacola.

Most Americans cheered Jackson on. One newspaper wrote of the general that "his popularity is unbounded—old and young speak of him with rapture." The Spanish, however, viewed Jackson's attacks as acts of war. Monroe returned the forts to Spain. But Adams told Onís that Spain would either have to govern Florida properly and end Indian raids or cede it to the United States.

In the Adams-Onís Treaty of 1819, Spain ceded Florida to the United States. Spain also gave up its claim to Oregon. In return, the United States gave up its claim that Texas was part of the Louisiana Purchase.

THE MONROE DOCTRINE

By 1819 Spain had lost more than Florida. From Mexico to Argentina, its American colonies were in revolt. Only Cuba and Puerto Rico remained in the Spanish empire. The rebellion was led by Simon Bolívar (boh-LEE-var) in South America and Agustín de Iturbide (EE-toor-BEE-thay) in Mexico. New republics were established in South and Central America as Latin Americans won their wars of independence from Spain. In 1822 the United States officially recognized these republics as free and independent nations.

Monroe and Adams worried that Spain might try to regain its former colonies. They were also concerned by Russian activities along the Pacific coast. In 1812 Russians had built Fort Ross, north of San Francisco Bay. Then, in 1821, the Russian **czar,** or monarch, claimed the Pacific coast as far south as the Oregon Country. Adams warned the czar that "the American continents are no longer subjects for any new European colonial establishments."

Britain approved of this attitude. British trade with the new Latin American nations was growing. In 1823 Britain suggested that the United States and Britain issue a joint message to the nations of Europe. The message would warn those powers not to help Spain regain its empire in Latin America. Adams, however, convinced Monroe that it would be "more dignified" for the United States to issue the message on its own.

On December 2, 1823, Monroe gave a speech to Congress. The President repeated what Adams had told the Russians. The Americas, he

*CT
For discussion: In what sense can the Monroe Doctrine be considered an extension of America's nationalism?

To many, Simon Bolívar is *El Libertador* (the Liberator). He won independence for Colombia, Peru, Ecuador, Venezuela, and Bolivia. Bolivia is named after him. Bolívar has been called "the George Washington of South America."

Revolution in Latin America 1804-1825

The United States was the first nation to recognize the new Latin American nations that had won their freedom from Spain. Many United States citizens looked forward to an expanding trade with Latin America.

said, were no longer open "for future colonization by any European powers." He warned those powers not to interfere with the newly independent republics of Latin America. He warned the Europeans that any attempt to control the Latin American republics or to change their governments would be seen "as dangerous to our peace and safety." For its part, the United States would stay out of the affairs of European nations. These principles became known as the Monroe Doctrine.

The French artist Théodore Géricault painted the Battle of Chacabuco, February 12, 1817. The Mexican patriot army defeated the Spanish in Mexico's war for independence.

*CT

Activity: Students can assume they are diplomats representing the U.S. in countries hostile to the Monroe Doctrine. As ministers or ambassadors, they must write papers addressed to the rulers of these countries explaining and defending the Doctrine. (Remind students that diplomats always phrase their arguments as tactfully as possible.)

In the courts of the European monarchs, Monroe's message was called "arrogant," "haughty," and "blustering." That a young, weak nation would tell European powers what to do seemed overly bold. Most Americans were pleased by the speech, but they soon forgot it. Thirty years would pass before the term Monroe Doctrine became part of the American vocabulary. By then the "blustering" young nation was powerful enough to back the doctrine with force.

SECTION REVIEW   Answers will be found on page T 46.

1. Define the following words: *disarm, czar.*

2. Identify: John Quincy Adams, Rush-Bagot Treaty, Convention of 1818, Adams-Onís Treaty.

3. Adams's message to Spain after Jackson invaded Florida has been summarized as "control or cede." Explain what this meant.

4. In as few words as possible, state the three main principles of the Monroe Doctrine.

After Thomas Jefferson became President in 1801, he worked to reshape the federal government to fit Republican ideals. The Supreme Court, however, remained under the control of Federalists. Led by Chief Justice John Marshall, the court established its power of judicial review in *Marbury* v. *Madison*. Jefferson's most important action was the purchase of Louisiana from France.

During the administrations of Jefferson and James Madison, the United States faced troubles at sea. Both France and Britain began seizing American ships in 1806. Britain was also impressing American sailors into its navy. The embargo and the Non-Intercourse Act were efforts to force Britain and France to respect the rights of neutral ships.

When peaceful means failed, the United States declared war on Britain in 1812. War Hawks blamed Britain for Indian raids on the frontier. They saw war as a way to bring Florida and Canada into the United States.

The war ended in 1814 with no territory gained by either side and no agreement about the rights of neutral ships. After the war, however, Britain showed more respect for the United States. Conflicts over boundaries and fishing rights were settled by treaties.

The War of 1812 left Americans with a strong feeling of nationalism. By the time James Monroe became President in 1817, the nation seemed united in "an era of good feelings." Good feelings disappeared in a battle over the admission of Missouri as a slave state in 1820. In a compromise, Maine was admitted as a free state, and the Louisiana Purchase was divided into slave and free territory.

During Monroe's first administration, Florida was added to the United States. By 1819 Spain had lost most of its colonies in the Americas. Many Latin American republics were formed. In 1823 Monroe warned the European powers that the American continents were closed to future colonization.

1800	1810	1820	1830	
Jefferson	Madison	Monroe	Adams	Jackson

- *Marbury* v. *Madison*
- Louisiana Purchase
- Lewis and Clark expedition
- Embargo Act
- Battle of Tippecanoe
- War of 1812 begins
- Hartford Convention
- Treaty of Ghent
- Second Bank of the United States
- Spain cedes Florida to the United States
- Missouri Compromise
- United States recognizes Latin American republics
- Monroe Doctrine

1800   1810   1820   1830

CHAPTER SURVEY

VOCABULARY REVIEW

From this list of vocabulary words, choose the one that best completes each sentence below.

(a) blockade
(b) commerce
(c) czar
(d) disarm
(e) economy
(f) elite

(g) embargo
(h) interstate
(i) liberators
(j) nationalism
(k) offensive
(l) secession

1. To remove weapons is to ____.

2. A ____ is the forced closure of an area to keep people and supplies from going in or out.

3. ____ means between two or more states.

4. The most powerful and successful people in a country make up the nation's ____.

5. ____ means business and trade.

6. A ____ is a Russian king.

7. People who free others are ____.

8. ____ means feelings of loyalty to one's country.

9. An advance into enemy territory is called an ____.

10. An order cutting off trade with another nation is an ____.

11. A nation's ____ is the way that country produces, uses, and divides up goods and services.

12. ____ means withdrawing from a nation.

CHAPTER REVIEW

1. What was Thomas Jefferson's idea for a "wise and frugal government"?

2. (a) What law was declared unconstitutional in the case of *Marbury* v. *Madison*? (b) Which legislature had passed that law? (c) In *McCulloch* v. *Maryland* did the Supreme Court strike down a federal or a state law? (d) What power was the Supreme Court using in these cases? (e) Why was President Jefferson unhappy with these court decisions?

3. (a) Why did James Monroe go to France in 1803? (b) What did Napoleon offer him? (c) What belief made Jefferson worry before he accepted Napoleon's offer?

4. (a) What led Jefferson to impose an embargo on trade with France and Britain? (b) What were the effects of the embargo in New England? (c) What replaced the embargo in 1809? (d) Why was the policy of "peaceable coercion" considered a failure by 1812?

5. (a) Which section of the United States most opposed the War of 1812? (b) Why did the other sections support the war? (c) Which section's economy gained the most from the war? Why?

"Red Mill at Yellow Springs, Ohio," painted by a folk artist, represents growing industry in the nation.

6. What were the major gains made by the United States as a result of the War of 1812?

7. What did the second Bank of the United States, the Tariff of 1816, and the National Road have in common?

8. Why did Jefferson say that the debate over statehood for Missouri was "like a fire bell in the night"?

9. After the War of 1812, how did the United States and Britain settle disputes between them? (b) What two settlements did the two nations reach soon after the war?

10. (a) What led Monroe to issue his warnings to the nations of Europe? (b) How did the nations of Europe react to Monroe's message?

GEOGRAPHY REVIEW

*CT **1.** Look at the map "The War of 1812" on page 251. (a) What symbol is used for victories? (b) According to the map, where did most of the fighting take place? (c) What route did Jackson follow from his home in Tennessee to New Orleans? (d) About how many miles did Jackson's forces have to march to reach New Orleans?

2. Look at the map "The United States in 1822" on page 261. (a) What four lakes help to mark an international boundary? (b) What three rivers help to mark an international boundary?

USING THE TOOLS OF HISTORY

Understanding Topography on Maps

Look at the "Physical Map of the United States" in the Resource Center. (a) How does the map show differences in elevations? (b) How does the map show swamps, glaciers, and mountain peaks? (c) In which half of the country is most of the land at an elevation of 3,000 feet or higher? (d) Which region has the most swamps? (e) Where are America's glaciers located? (f) Which is the highest mountain peak shown in the Appalachians? In the Rockies? In the Sierra Nevada? In Hawaii? In Alaska?

READING AND THINKING SKILLS

*CT **Details**

Copy this "W" questions chart and fill in the missing details from the first section of the chapter.

EVENT OR TOPIC	WHO OR WHAT	WHEN	WHERE	WHY
Napoleon's army is defeated		1802		To remain independent
Offer to buy Louisiana	Monroe, Jefferson, Republicans	1803		
		1804–1805		To explore western lands

A printed cotton kerchief made soon after the War of 1812 celebrated the American victory. Even though there were 18 states at that time, the flag showed 15 stars until 1818.

Answers will be found on page T 48.

UNIT SURVEY

UNIT REVIEW

1. (a) How did Congress under the Articles of Confederation arrange to sell western land? (b) What kept Congress under the Articles of Confederation from backing its words with force? (c) How did Congress then have tax problems similar to Parliament's tax problems in the 1760s and 1770s?

2. (a) Why did small states fear the Virginia Plan for a new Constitution? (b) What change in the plan of government won over the small states? (c) How many states needed to approve the new plan before it could go into effect? (d) What group of people were against approving the plan?

3. (a) Why does the Constitution need to have a separation of powers in order to have a system of checks and balances? (b) In what way is the federalism of the Constitution like the organization of the League of the Iroquois?

4. (a) Who caused the advance of Spanish missions in California? (b) Who caused the advance of the log cabin frontier?

5. (a) Why did Alexander Hamilton favor a national bank? (b) Why did Thomas Jefferson oppose it? (c) What party supported Hamilton's views? (d) What party supported Jefferson's views?

6. (a) During the Revolutionary War, how did Patriots view France? (b) At the time of the XYZ Affair, how did many Americans view France? (c) How did the XYZ Affair lead to the Alien and Sedition Acts? (d) What state actions opposed the Sedition Act?

7. (a) When Jefferson approved the Louisiana Purchase, was he interpreting his powers strictly or loosely? (b) What kind of interpretation did he usually make? (c) What convinced Jefferson to approve the Louisiana Purchase?

8. (a) In what way were threats from the Barbary pirates, British warships, and French warships all alike? (b) How did the threat from the Barbary pirates end in 1815? (c) In 1807 how did Jefferson try to end the threat from British and French warships? (d) Was his approach popular? Why or why not?

9. (a) What war was called "Mr. Madison's War"? (b) In what two nations was the war fought? (c) Did New England want the war? Why or why not? (d) What part of the American System appealed to American manufacturers who competed with Britain?

10. (a) Why did the Federalist party not have a candidate in the election of 1820? (b) What compromise about slavery was reached in 1820? (c) What two states entered the Union in 1820 and 1821?

In 1796, Benjamin Latrobe sketched Martha Washington's granddaughter Nelly Parke Custis at teatime at Mount Vernon. Latrobe shows her gowned in a classical Greek costume.

LINKING THE PAST AND THE PRESENT

*CT **1.** The Supreme Court of the United States decides cases by interpreting the Constitution. Look for news stories about recent decisions of the Supreme Court. Find out how the court ruled and what part of the Constitution was involved.

2. The Sixth Amendment and the Seventh Amendment of the Constitution give an accused person the right to a trial by jury. Look for news stories about recent jury trials, or talk to someone who has served as a juror to find out how the trial proceeded.

3. While the United States was setting up a new government, Noah Webster called for an American language. "Let us then seize the present moment and establish a *national language,* as well as a national government," he wrote in 1789. He later produced his famous *American Dictionary of the English Language.* Refer to an encyclopedia to find out more about him and why many dictionaries today are named for him.

MEETING THE BUILDERS OF AMERICA

*CT **1.** Review the descriptions of Olaudah Equiano (page 197), Susanna Rowson (page 233), and John C. Calhoun (page 256). In what ways did they contribute to America?

*CT **2.** Prepare a report about the contribution to American life of some other person or group mentioned in Unit 3. For example, look for information about John Hancock, Father Junípero Serra, John Marshall, Sacajawea, or Francis Scott Key. You may be able to use one of the following books as a source of information.

Electricity was a game to these Philadelphians. Its practical uses had not yet been discovered.

Akers, Charles W. *Abigail Adams, an American Woman.* Boston: Little, Brown, 1980.

Chidsey, Donald Barr. *Lewis and Clark: The Great Adventure.* New York: Crown, 1970.

Chidsey, Donald Barr. *Mr. Hamilton and Mr. Jefferson.* Nashville: Thomas Nelson, 1975.

Wibberley, Leonard. *Time of Harvest: Thomas Jefferson, the Years 1801–1826.* New York: Farrar, Straus & Giroux, 1966.

SUGGESTIONS FOR FURTHER READING

Commager, Henry Steele. *The Great Constitution.* New York: Bobbs-Merrill, 1961.

Falkner, Leonard. *For Jefferson and Liberty: The United States in War and Peace, 1800–1815.* New York: Knopf, 1972.

Latham, Frank. *Jacob Brown and the War of 1812.* New York: Cowles, 1971.

Leckie, Robert. *The War Nobody Won: 1812.* New York: Putnam, 1974.

Tunis, Edwin. *The Young United States: 1783–1830.* New York: World, 1970.

Detail from *Prairie Scene: Mirage* by A. J. Miller, 1858–1860.

LOOKING WEST

INVENTIONS AND IMPROVEMENTS
EXPANDING DEMOCRACY
WESTWARD EXPANSION TO THE PACIFIC

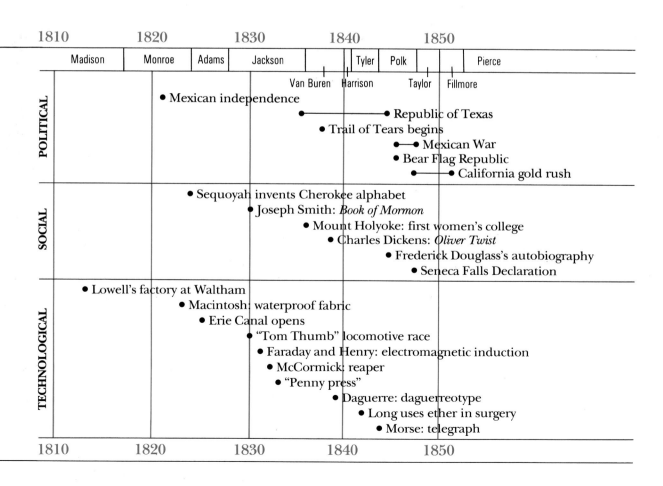

CHAPTER 11   1820–1850

INVENTIONS AND IMPROVEMENTS

CHANGES IN FARMING AND INDUSTRY
TRADE, TRANSPORTATION, AND
    COMMUNICATION
CITY GROWTH AND IMMIGRATION

11–1 CHANGES IN FARMING AND INDUSTRY

Industrial Revolution: shift of manufacturing from homes and workshops to factories
factory system: use of factories for making goods
interchangeable parts: parts so nearly alike any could be changed for another
division of labor: division of work so that each worker does only one or two tasks
trade unions: associations of skilled workers to improve work conditions
strike: refusal of workers to work until employers agree to meet their demands
mass production: manufacture of goods in large quantities

READ TO FIND OUT

—what the words *Industrial Revolution, factory system, interchangeable parts, division of labor, trade unions, strike,* and *mass production* mean.

—how improved tools and livestock made farmers more productive.

—why southerners saw cotton as the "king" of crops.

—why the factory system first took root in New England.

—what the advantages of the interchangeable system were.

—what goals the early trade unions had.

—why women were hired to work in textile factories.

In the first half of the 1800s, the American wilderness was rapidly settled. Americans were constantly pushing westward, looking for good farm land and new business opportunities. By mid-century the original 13 states had multiplied to 31.

272   CHAPTER 11   1820-1850

Agriculture and Industry 1840

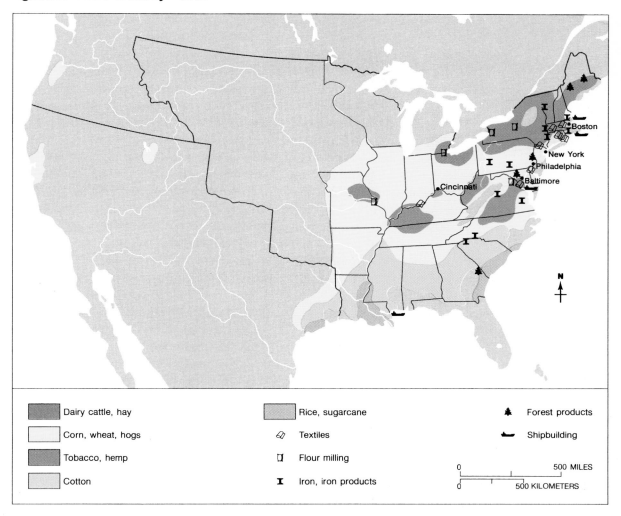

Dairy cattle, hay		Rice, sugarcane		Forest products		
Corn, wheat, hogs		Textiles		Shipbuilding		
Tobacco, hemp		Flour milling				
Cotton		Iron, iron products				

0 ——— 500 MILES
0 ——— 500 KILOMETERS

During this same period, a revolution in industry was beginning in New England. Most goods were still produced at home or in small workshops where a few employees used simple hand tools. But manufacturers were beginning to use large machines driven by water power or steam power in factories. This shift of manufacturing from homes and workshops into factories with machines has been called the **Industrial Revolution.**

THE FARMING FRONTIER

Between 1780 and 1850, the farming frontier moved westward at the average rate of 30 miles (48 kilometers) a year. The early pioneers followed the Wilderness Road, first cut through the Appalachians by the explorer Daniel Boone. The road took them through the Cumberland

Using new machines, American workers made industrial goods and produced farm crops. More than half of the industrial goods came from factories, not home workshops, by 1840. Most workers then—seven of every ten—labored on farms.

Gap, a break in the Appalachian ridges, and onto the Allegheny Plateau. This was hilly land with dense forests. But farmers found good soil in river valleys for growing corn and tobacco.

As the best land on the plateau was claimed, frontier farmers moved down onto the Central Plains. Here forests thinned and often gave way to prairies, or flat grasslands, with some of the richest soil in the world. By the late 1830s, pioneers on the Central Plains had crossed the Mississippi and reached the Missouri River.

West of the Central Plains lie the Great Plains. This is a treeless region where less than 20 inches (51 centimeters) of rain fall each year. Most pioneers believed that the Great Plains were too arid, or dry, for successful farming.

As American farmers moved west and cleared forests, they greatly increased the nation's arable land, or land ready for the plow. At the same time, they experimented with crops, livestock, and tools. Their success made Americans the most productive farmers in the world.

IMPROVED TOOLS AND LIVESTOCK

The farm tools that the colonists brought from Europe had not changed much for a thousand years. In the 1800s American farmers began to redesign the most basic farm tool, the plow. Wooden parts were replaced with iron. By hitching four strong horses to a two-bladed plow,

The horse-drawn reaper introduced by Cyrus McCormick could do in a day the harvesting that took a week of work with hand tools.

Students can research and report on inventor Cyrus McCormick (see page 275) and his horse-drawn reaper.

CHAPTER 11   1820-1850

farmers could plow and plant twice as much land as before. In time, teams of ten horses drew eight-bladed plows across the prairie.

Farms stayed small as long as a farmer could harvest only about 1 acre (0.4 hectare) of grain a day using hand tools. Then, in 1831, Cyrus McCormick introduced a mechanical reaper. Now a farmer could reap, or harvest, 5 to 6 acres (2 to 2.4 hectares) of grain a day. The result was an increase in farm productivity, or the amount produced per worker.

*CT

For discussion: How did the invention of the mechanized reaper stimulate the development of what is now the American Middle West?

Farmers also bred stronger workhorses, woolier sheep, and plumper chickens. No animal, however, showed more improvement than the humble hog. The colonial hog was said to be thin like a fish and "not worth slaughtering." Some of these hogs got loose and ran wild. They feasted on acorns and corn. The animals that returned from the forest a few years later were huge beasts, weighing 200 to 300 pounds (90 to 135 kilograms). Farmers learned that by feeding their pigs corn, they doubled the animals' weight. Ham, bacon, salt pork, and lard became important farm products.

Dairy farming, which was brought to the Middle Colonies by German and Dutch settlers, spread into New England in the 1800s. In 1794 a farmer said of a typical cow that it "gives little milk and looks like a slatted fence." Then farmers tried feeding corn to cows. The result was fatter cows with richer milk.

Horses and mules helped to plow cotton fields in the South. After plowing, most of the season's work—planting, weeding, and picking—was done by hand. Cleaning seeds from the cotton fibers was done by a machine, the cotton gin.

KING COTTON

Southern farmers experimented with new crops such as sugarcane, hemp, and cotton. These grew well in the South's warm climate. Cotton plants produce bolls, or pods of cotton fiber mixed with seeds. A worker

picking out the seeds could clean only about a pound of cotton a day. In 1793 a young man named Eli Whitney invented a machine called a cotton gin. (*Gin* was short for "engine.") Whitney's machine cleaned 50 pounds (23 kilograms) of cotton a day. Within a few years, cotton was the South's leading cash crop.

Year after year, the cotton frontier shifted westward. From the Carolina Piedmont it moved over the southern Appalachians and into the Mississippi Valley. From there it spread across the Ozark Plateau, an area of rolling hills rising out of the Central Plains. Where the climate was too damp for cotton, rice and sugarcane were planted. Across the South anyone with money invested it in land and slaves.

Textile, or cloth making, factories in Britain and New England were eager customers for southern cotton. Cotton production went from about 3,000 bales a year in 1790 to more than 2,000,000 bales by 1850. During this time, cotton became the nation's most valuable export product. Southerners called it the "king" of crops.

THE FACTORY SYSTEM COMES TO AMERICA

The **factory system,** or the use of factories for making goods, was first used in the British textile industry. Machines were developed for spinning cotton fibers into thread and then weaving thread into cloth. To protect its textile industry, Parliament forbade export of these machines or drawings of them.

The first spinning mill in America was built in Pawtucket, Rhode Island, by Samuel Slater. Earlier, in Britain, he had memorized the details of the machines he built in America.

A young English textile worker named Samuel Slater memorized the details of Britain's best spinning machines. Then he sailed for New England. There merchants were willing to invest in new businesses. In 1790 Slater built America's first spinning mill, or factory, in Pawtucket, Rhode Island.

During the War of 1812, the United States turned from imported European cloth to American-made cloth. Merchants built spinning mills throughout southern New England. Along the Appalachian Fall Line, rapid rivers provided the power to make gears turn and spindles whirl.

A waterfall on the Charles River attracted a merchant named Francis Cabot Lowell to Waltham, Massachusetts, in 1813. There he built the first factory to combine spinning with the weaving of cloth on power looms. Raw cotton was carried into Lowell's factory, and finished cloth was carried out.

After Francis Cabot Lowell's death, his associates put into effect his plans for factories and living quarters for workers in Lowell, Massachusetts, a city named after him.

THE INTERCHANGEABLE SYSTEM

Spinning thread by machine was simple compared to producing such complicated items as guns. Firearms have many parts that must fit together precisely. They were produced by skilled gunsmiths who carefully filed and shaped one part to fit the next. Guns were expensive, one-of-a-kind weapons that took a long time to make.

In 1798 Eli Whitney found a better way to produce muskets. He divided musket manufacturing into separate operations. Then, using metal-working machines and tool guides, he made a different setup for each operation. Gun barrels, for example, were bored on a special boring machine. Whitney adjusted the machine so that all the barrels it produced were exactly alike. It took him two years to set up his machines. But once they were ready, they turned out large quantities of **interchangeable parts**—parts so nearly alike that any one could be changed for any other.

Whitney's "interchangeable system" also made **division of labor** possible within his factory. This meant dividing up the work so that each worker had just one or two simple tasks to do. No single operation required the skill of a trained gunsmith, so Whitney could hire less-skilled workers at lower wages. At the same time, the use of machines increased his workers' productivity. The result was lower manufacturing costs per gun.

These two advantages of the interchangeable system—lower labor costs and higher productivity—led to falling prices for many manufactured goods. There was yet a third advantage to Whitney's system. Products made with interchangeable parts were easy to repair. For example, when one part of a gun broke or wore out, the owner could replace it with a nearly identical part from the factory.

*CT
For discussion: What long-range effects on people's lives did the "interchangeable system" have? (Students should consider, among other factors, the decreasing need for skilled workers and the growing need for factory hands.)

★ ★ ★ ★ ★ ★ ★ **AMERICAN VALUES IN ACTION** ★ ★ ★ ★ ★ ★ ★

REBECCA LUKENS

Rebecca Lukens loved adventure. As a girl, she roamed the Pennsylvania countryside and explored a castle built by her great-grand-father. She read "wild dramatic stories."

Young Rebecca also found adventure in her father's ironworks on Brandywine Creek. There, her father turned iron slabs into nails, blacksmith tools, and barrel hoops. Eagerly, Rebecca listened to her father's tales of the iron trade. And she watched and learned.

When Rebecca married, her new husband leased the Brandywine ironworks. He converted the mill to turn out products for steam-powered transportation. The ironworks now produced iron plates to encase the steam boilers used to power riverboats.

Then, in 1825, Rebecca's husband died, leaving her with children to support and an ironworks burdened with debts. "Necessity is a stern taskmistress," she wrote, "and my

every want gave me courage." Rebecca Lukens resolved to run the mill herself.

Lukens placed a notice in the newspaper. All persons owing money to the mill were asked "to make immediate payment." Those who had claims against the mill were asked to "present them for settlement." Lukens got supplies on credit and found new customers. Her contracts promised boiler plates "rolled in a superior style."

Lukens soon found that transporting the boiler plates to market was a problem. The roads were rough and wagon teams were expensive. Rivers were closed to shipping in the winter and "subject to dangers" from rocks and snags when they opened.

Then competitors built mills upstream from Lukens's ironworks. One sued her for raising the level of Brandywine Creek when she repaired her mill dam. Although her mill depended on the dam for water power, she was forced to lower the creek's level. "You have started out in business taking unfair advantage of your neighbor," she told her competitors, "and you will never prosper."

Lukens, through iron determination, did manage to prosper. When railroads linked Brandywine Valley with Boston and New York, her market expanded. Lukens's boiler plates eventually found their way into steamboats on the Mississippi River.

Lukens found adventure in ironworking. "The manufacture of iron is not a mere local or individual interest," she insisted. She was supplying a "chief element of progress."

TRADE UNIONS

Workshop owners began to copy Whitney's system. Skilled trades were divided into separate operations. As a result, skilled workers, who had spent years as apprentices learning their trade, had to compete for work with half-skilled apprentices or unskilled workers.

Carrying lunch buckets or baskets, hundreds of workers walk from a New England textile mill in this drawing by Winslow Homer. Besides immigrants, the workers include young women and children of elementary school age.

Activity: Students can research and write reports on the beginnings of trade unions and their growth before the Civil War.

To protect their jobs, skilled workers organized "trade associations." These organizations became the nation's first **trade unions.** They wanted to limit the number of apprentices working in each workshop. They also wanted to raise wages and to reduce the working day to 10 hours. By the mid-1830s there were some 200 trade associations with about 200,000 members.

The main weapon of the early unions was the **strike.** In a strike, workers refuse to work until employers agree to their demands. By the 1850s the 10-hour day was standard for skilled trades in the largest cities. But the unions failed more often than they succeeded. Most state courts ruled that strikes were illegal. Striking workers received little public support. The United States was a nation of farmers, who worked from sunrise to sunset. They thought a 10-hour workday was short.

THE "MILL GIRLS"

Factory workers knew better. Unlike farmers, they could not set their own pace. Among the first workers to have their lives ruled by the factory bell were the "mill girls." Francis Lowell could not find enough men to tend his textile machines at Waltham. So he hired young farm women, who would work for one-half the pay of men.

The women worked 12 or 13 hours a day, six days a week. They lived in boarding houses, six to a room. After paying for room and meals, a

Elias Howe put together his first model of a sewing machine in 1846.

Samuel Colt, inventor of the first repeating pistol, set up a factory in Hartford, Connecticut, that produced arms for the Mexican and Civil wars. After his death in 1862, his company turned out the six-shooters so widely used in the West that his name became practically synonymous with *revolver*.

Samuel Colt made this accurate sketch of his new revolver in 1835.

woman might earn two dollars a week. But teaching, sewing, and housework, the only other jobs open to most women, paid even less.

In the early years of the textile industry, "help was too valuable to be mistreated," wrote Harriet Robinson. By the 1830s, however, conditions began to change. New machines increased the pace of work and added to the amount of noise and dust in the mills. Workers had to tend three and even four looms each. The working day grew longer.

In one mill town after another, women walked off the job to protest. After a pay cut in 1836, 1,500 workers marched out for a month. With no wages coming in, the women were finally forced to accept the pay cut and return to work.

By the late 1840s, mill girls were being replaced by immigrants. Most of these newcomers arrived penniless. They were willing to accept low pay and poor working conditions just to have a job.

TOWARD SELF-SUFFICIENCY

As the Industrial Revolution took root in America, the nation became more self-sufficient. The factory system made possible **mass production—** the manufacture of goods in large quantities. Fewer goods had to be imported from Europe.

There seemed to be no end to the new products coming out of American factories and workshops. In 1851 a "Great Industrial Exhibition" was held in London. Fair-goers were fascinated by new products from America—Samuel Colt's revolver, an ice-cream freezer, McCormick's reaper, a hot-air furnace, and machines to sew clothes, bind books, and plane wood. "Every practical success of the season," wrote the London *Times,* "belongs to the Americans."

SECTION REVIEW   Answers will be found on page T 49.

1. Define these words: *Industrial Revolution, factory system, interchangeable parts, division of labor, trade unions, strike, mass production.*

2. Identify: Cyrus McCormick, Eli Whitney, Samuel Slater, Francis Cabot Lowell.

3. How did improved plows and McCormick's mechanical reaper help farm productivity?

4. Why did southerners call cotton the "king" of crops?

5. Why were the first textile mills located in New England?

6. What were three advantages of Whitney's interchangeable system?

7. What were the goals of the early trade unions?

8. Why did Lowell hire women to work in his textile mills?

11-2 TRADE, TRANSPORTATION, AND COMMUNICATION

READ TO FIND OUT

—what the words *investment capital* and *literacy* mean.

—how trade assisted the growth of factories.

—how Americans moved people and goods across the nation.

—what inventions helped Americans to become better informed.

investment capital: money available for investing
literacy: ability to read

The growth of American industry was closely tied to the expansion of trade. Profits from foreign trade gave merchants the **investment capital,** or money available for investing, to build new factories.

PACIFIC TRADE

Independence freed American merchants to seek new trading partners. In 1784 the *Empress of China* sailed from New York to Canton, China, and returned with silks and tea. The China trade followed a three-cornered route. American ships sailed first to the Oregon Country. There they traded manufactured goods with the Indians for otter and beaver furs. In China the furs were sold for tea and luxury goods.

By the 1820s Americans were trading with Californios for tallow and hides. The tallow, or fat from cattle, was sold to candlemakers. The hides were bought by shoemakers and factory owners. Factories needed leather belts to transfer power from waterwheels to machinery.

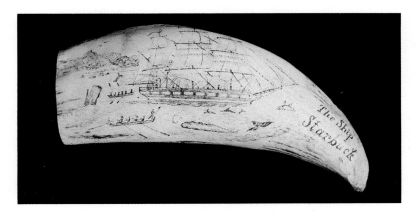

Working during a long voyage, a sailor on a whaling ship carved this whale tooth with a scene of whale hunting. The art of carving scenes on ivory is called scrimshaw.

New England whaling ships chased the valuable "monsters of the deep." Whale oil was burned in lamps and used to lubricate the gears and cogs of the new factory machines. Whalebone was both stiff and flexible enough for buggy whips and corset stays.

Whaling ships often stopped in the Hawaiian Islands for supplies and repairs. By 1850 Honolulu was a major whaling port. "You can walk from one end of Honolulu Harbor to the other, ship to ship," an observer reported, "without getting your feet wet."

New York, Boston, Philadelphia, and Baltimore boomed as trade increased. The docks of these port cities were lined with American-made ships. The large, slow brig was the workhorse of the merchant fleet. The packet was smaller and faster. The fastest ships under sail were the long, sleek clippers. In 1849 the Yankee clipper *Sea Witch* raced from Hong Kong to New York in under 75 days. That journey had taken a brig six months. By the 1850s American clippers had taken over the China trade.

Then demand for the clippers fell off. The future of shipping lay with larger iron ships powered by steam engines. They could carry more freight. Also, they freed shipping from its dependence on the wind. But no one who had seen a clipper under full sail would ever forget "the longest, sharpest, most beautiful ship in the world."

TURNPIKES AND ROADS

Profits from trade helped to build factories, but the success of these businesses depended on improved transportation. The American population was spread out over thousands of miles. Manufacturers needed faster and cheaper ways to carry their goods to customers.

To transport goods, the colonists had depended on rivers that were wide and deep enough for shipping. Boats, however, could not go past the rapids and waterfalls at the Appalachian Fall Line.

As the frontier moved westward, private companies began to build roads called turnpikes. Spiked poles or pikes were placed across the roads at tollbooths. The pike was turned aside to let travelers pass after they had paid their toll, or fee for using the road.

The nation's first turnpike, built from Philadelphia to Lancaster, Pennsylvania, was completed in 1794. The road was paved with stones and then covered with crushed rock to make travel smoother. The Lancaster Turnpike was so profitable that other toll roads were soon built throughout the country.

The National Road was the first highway built with federal funds. It linked Cumberland, Maryland, with the town of Wheeling on the Ohio River in 1818. This main east-west route was an immediate success. By 1852 it had been extended to Vandalia, Illinois.

The most famous of all books concerned with whaling is, of course, *Moby Dick.* You may wish to read passages from this classic American novel to the class.

Roads, Canals, and Waterways 1850

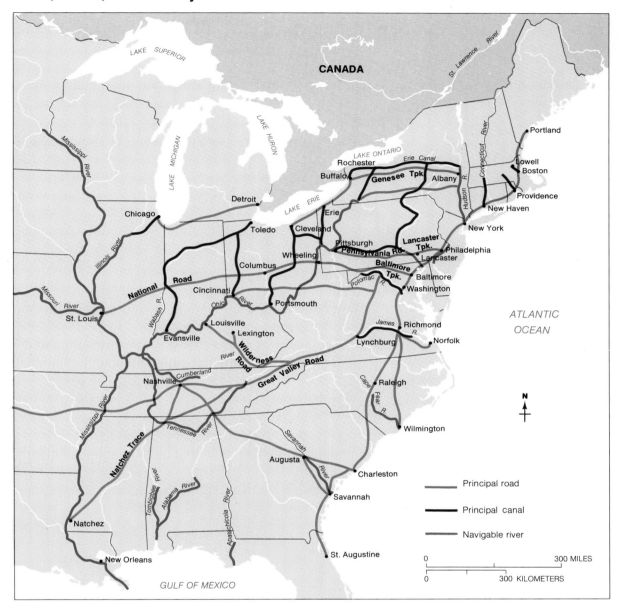

RIVERS AND CANALS

Moving goods by road was very expensive. In 1800 it cost $125 a ton to carry freight by wagon from Philadelphia to Pittsburgh. It was cheaper to send the same goods by ship south along the Atlantic coast, across the Gulf of Mexico, and then back northeast up the Mississippi and Ohio rivers to Pittsburgh.

There were two problems with river travel, however. First, it was difficult to move freight upstream against the current. This problem was

Have students find the Lancaster Turnpike and National Road on the map. Have them determine whether Evansville and Toledo are connected by a road, canal, or river.

USING THE TOOLS OF HISTORY

INTERPRETING ILLUSTRATIONS

*CT

Illustrations are not only interesting to look at, but they also contain information and ideas. Illustrations include drawings, paintings, diagrams, and sketches.

Before studying an illustration, read its title or caption.

1. What information is contained in the caption for the painting on the facing page?

2. Does the title tell you much about what is in this painting? Can you think of a better title?

Some illustrations are very lifelike and record a scene almost exactly as the artist saw it in real life. Other illustrations are clearly imaginary. They show scenes that would probably not be seen in real life.

3. Is this painting lifelike or imaginary? Explain your answer.

Artists often divide their work into parts or sections. The landscape in this painting is divided into foreground and background.

4. What part of the landscape is shown in the foreground, or part closest to the viewer?

5. What part of the landscape makes up the background?

The most interesting illustrations are rich in details. The more you study such pictures, the more you see.

6. What two types of land transportation do you see in this picture?

7. How many types of water transportation do you see? What are they?

8. Which two types of transportation have smokestacks? What does this tell us about how they are powered?

9. What clues has the artist included to tell us what season of the year this painting is set in?

10. Look at the house in the painting. What does its size suggest to you about the people who live there?

The best illustrations do more than give information. They also stir our imaginations.

11. If you could be part of this scene, where would you want to be? What would you choose to be doing?

Answers will be found on page T 49.

Activity: Students can form committees to research and make oral reports on phases of Robert Fulton's career, including his early inventions when still a boy; his concern with canals and canal boats; his invention of a submarine; his experiments with steam.

solved by Robert Fulton. In 1807 he launched the *Clermont,* the nation's first successful steam-powered boat, on the Hudson River.

The first steamboats did not have enough power to battle the mighty Mississippi's current. By 1817, however, steamboats could travel upstream from New Orleans to Louisville, Kentucky, in 25 days. Flatboats took three months to go the same distance. As freight and passenger traffic grew, river towns like Cincinnati, St. Louis, Pittsburgh, and Louisville became bustling port cities.

A second problem was that rivers did not always go where people wanted to take their goods. One solution was to build canals. A horse or mule could pull fifty times as much freight in a canal boat as it could pull in a wagon.

In 1817 New York Governor DeWitt Clinton convinced his state legislature to build a canal from Albany on the Hudson River to Buffalo on

This painting, done about 1850, is titled "Geese in Flight." It is in the National Gallery of Art in Washington, D.C.

Lake Erie. In between were 363 miles (580 kilometers) of wilderness. After eight years of backbreaking work, the Erie Canal was opened in 1825. Now freight could travel by water from the Atlantic to the Great Lakes. The cost of shipping goods from Buffalo to New York City dropped from $100 a ton to $9. The Great Lakes became an important route for shipping farm products to eastern markets.

The success of the Erie Canal set off a wave of canal building across the country. Yet before long, a new form of transportation made canals no longer so important.

RAILROADS

The first railroads in America were coaches pulled along rails by horses or mules. In the 1820s Americans experimented with steam-powered engines imported from England. Then, in 1830, a New York manufacturer named Peter Cooper built a small engine called the *Tom Thumb*. To show off his locomotive, Cooper challenged a horse-drawn railroad car to a race. The *Tom Thumb* sped to an early lead, then broke down. The horse won the contest, but before long, the "iron horse" had defeated its rivals.

Railroads had several advantages over other forms of transportation. Unlike rivers, they could go wherever freight needed to go. Rail lines were cheaper to build than canals and did not freeze in winter. They survived heavy use and bad weather better than roads. And railroads

Activity: In the 1840s, travel by railroad was often quite an adventure. Have students assume they have taken their first ride on a train in 1842 and are writing letters to friends about the experience.

were much faster than horse-drawn wagons or riverboats. By 1840 more than 400 companies were running trains over 3,000 miles (4,800 kilometers) of track.

THE TELEGRAPH AND THE PENNY PRESS

For discussion: How did such developments as canals, railroads, and the telegraph strengthen Americans' awareness that they were citizens of one nation?

Just as the railroad completely changed transportation, the telegraph changed communication. In 1837 Samuel F. B. Morse, a painter, invented a telegraph that used electricity to send signals over wires. Most people made fun of Morse's invention, but in 1844 Congress gave him a chance to demonstrate his "talking wires." In Washington, D.C., the inventor tapped out "What hath God wrought?" in his own Morse code. An instant later, the message was received in Baltimore.

Americans were now convinced that Morse's telegraph worked. New companies such as American Telegraph and Western Union strung wires from town to town. Their first major customers were railroads, which came to depend on the telegraph to follow the movement of trains. By 1860 the nation had been tied together with 50,000 miles (80,465 kilometers) of telegraph wire.

Morse's telegraph was especially useful to newspapers. News could be sent by wire throughout the country in just a few hours. No longer did newspapers have to print stale news.

The number of newspapers in the United States grew rapidly in the first half of the 1800s. But they were too expensive for most people to buy. New inventions, however, helped to bring down the cost of printing a paper. In 1833 the New York *Sun* went on sale at a penny a copy. The "penny press" was born.

Cheap newspapers helped the spread of **literacy,** or the ability to read. Their advertisements told people about the new goods pouring out of factories. And their news stories brought readers closer to the political and economic events that were reshaping America.

SECTION REVIEW   Answers will be found on page T 49.

1. Define these words: *investment capital, literacy.*

2. Identify: Robert Fulton, Erie Canal, *Tom Thumb,* Samuel Morse.

3. After independence, where did America find new trading partners?

4. Of all the goods brought back from the Pacific, which two were most useful to factory owners?

5. How did Americans move goods before the railroads were built?

6. List three advantages of railroads over other forms of transportation.

7. What two inventions helped Americans become better informed about events by the 1850s?

11-3 CITY GROWTH AND IMMIGRATION

READ TO FIND OUT

—what the words *tenements* and *prejudice* mean.

—how improved transportation aided the growth of cities.

—what attracted people to cities.

—what problems cities faced.

—how immigrants contributed to the nation.

tenements: houses divided into many small apartments
prejudice: dislike based on race, religion, or nationality

During the first half of the 1800s, the population of the United States grew at a tremendous rate. The number of Americans increased by roughly one third every ten years. The nation's cities grew even faster than the population. In 1800 only one American in twenty lived in a town of 2,500 or more people. By 1860, one of every five Americans was living in a town or city.

NEW CITIES

West of the Appalachians, cities seemed to spring up almost overnight in the wilderness. Cincinnati, in southwestern Ohio, was a village in 1800. It grew as trade on the Ohio and Mississippi rivers mushroomed.

Steamboats, carts, and wagons carried goods and people to and from the thriving new port city of Cincinnati.

Located at the southern tip of Lake Michigan, Chicago also owed its growth to transportation improvements. Chicago's farm products were shipped to eastern cities by way of the Great Lakes and the Erie Canal. Then, in 1848, a canal linked Lake Michigan to the Mississippi by way of the Illinois River. After that, Chicago could also ship flour and meat south to New Orleans.

During the 1850s, Chicago became the heart of a rail network that reached out into the surrounding prairies. More than a hundred trains arrived daily, bringing in corn, wheat, hogs, and cattle. They left carrying eastern goods and Chicago-made farm machinery to prairie farmers. This trade made Chicago the world's leading grain port by 1860.

THE ATTRACTIONS OF CITY LIFE

The Uncle Sam Range, a wood-burning iron stove, was used for both cooking and heating.

Most of the people who left the countryside to live in cities were drawn by the lure of jobs. But city life offered other attractions as well. There were free libraries, museums, and public lecture halls. For entertainment there were theaters, opera houses, and music halls, and a new pastime—window shopping. In 1845 the world's first department store, with plate glass display windows, opened in New York City.

City shoppers were the first to try out new inventions that made life easier. The new wood-burning iron stove freed city women from the dangers of cooking in a fireplace and kept homes much warmer in the winter. City dwellers tried the sewing machine, invented by Elias Howe in 1846. They were the first to wear raincoats and boots made with vulcanized rubber. The process of vulcanization, invented by Charles Goodyear in 1839, made rubber stronger.

CITY PROBLEMS

*CT
For discussion: What problems of city life in the nineteenth century are still problems today? What can be done to solve these problems?

As cities grew, back yard wells could no longer provide enough safe drinking water. In 1801 Philadelphia began pumping water from the Schuylkill River into the city through wooden pipes. In 1842 New Yorkers constructed a reservoir 40 miles (64 kilometers) away. Its water flowed into the city through an 8-foot (2.5-meter) tunnel.

Even in cities with safe water, sewage still overflowed open gutters along the streets. And garbage collection remained the job of rooting pigs. Such poor sanitation aided the spread of disease. Epidemics of cholera, typhoid fever, smallpox, and yellow fever swept through cities every few years, killing thousands.

City dwellers were also threatened by violent crime and fires. First New York, then other large cities turned to a paid police force to fight crime. Fighting fires, however, remained the task of volunteers. All too often, uncontrolled blazes left entire neighborhoods in ashes.

THE PROBLEM-SOLUTION PATTERN

*CT

Throughout the history of the United States, the American people have been faced with *problems*. Fortunately, most of these problems have a *solution*.

Often history writers will focus on a problem faced by people in the past and how that problem was solved. Sometimes a writer will discuss the cause of the problem as well as its effects. Writers who organize their thoughts in this way are writing in what is known as the problem-solution pattern.

1. In the first paragraph of the subsection titled "City Problems," the problem discussed is the lack of safe drinking water in growing cities. Two solutions to the problem are mentioned. List them on your paper.

2. In the second paragraph, the problem of sewage and garbage is discussed. What was the effect of the problem?

Review the first two sections to complete the following problem-solution patterns.

3. Problem:
Solution: Samuel Slater memorized the details and sailed for New England.

4. Problem:
Solution: Farmers fed corn to hogs.

5. Problem: Skilled workers had to compete with half-skilled or unskilled workers.
Solution:

6. Problem:
Solution: Private companies built roads.

7. Problem:
Solution: Robert Fulton launched a successful steam-powered boat.

8. Problem: Newspapers were too expensive for most people to buy.
Solution:

Answers will be found on page T 49.

IMMIGRATION

Immigrants from Europe played a large part in the growth of cities. Attracted by cheap land and jobs, more than 500,000 newcomers arrived in the United States in the 1830s. During the 1840s, a time of war and starvation in Europe, the number swelled to 1.7 million. It climbed to 2.6 million in the 1850s. The two largest immigrant groups, the Irish and the Germans, made up nearly three fourths of the total. Most of the rest came from the Netherlands, Scandinavia, and England.

After they arrived in eastern ports, many immigrants went west. Because the South used slave labor, few immigrants headed there. The Dutch usually settled in New York or Michigan and Iowa. The Scandinavians farmed or worked as lumberjacks in Wisconsin and Minnesota. Many Germans also farmed the rich soil of the prairies. Skilled workers often went to the growing inland cities of Cincinnati, St. Louis, and Milwaukee.

The Irish remained in the eastern cities. Most were too poor to buy a ticket for a train ride to the West. Even those with money preferred not to farm. In the 1840s a potato blight, or disease, had destroyed the Irish farmers' main crop. Many Irish starved. Those who escaped remembered that farming meant starvation.

Activity: Students can assume they are employers of the 1840s wanting to attract immigrant labor. They can write advertisements, to be posted all over Europe, telling the advantages of living and working in the United States.

"The K N Quickstep" was written for the Know-Nothing party. On this sheet music cover, the Whigs are shown as a dead raccoon and the Democrats as a dead rooster, both tied to the party's banner.

For discussion: For many generations, people have immigrated to the United States because it is the land of opportunity. In what ways is it the land of opportunity today?

The Irish immigrants took any jobs they could find. Women tended machines in factories and worked as household servants. Men paved streets, worked in factories, dug canals, and built railroads. Few could afford decent housing. Landlords turned homes into **tenements,** or houses divided into many small apartments, to rent to immigrants for a quick profit. Together, poverty and greed created slums.

HOSTILITY TO IMMIGRANTS

By the 1840s some native-born Americans began to distrust the immigrants. The Germans spoke a strange language, and the Irish were Catholics in a largely Protestant country. Both groups were accused of taking jobs away from native-born Americans. Occasionally, anger toward immigrants exploded into riots. More often it was expressed in signs and newspaper ads with words like "No Irish need apply."

In the early 1850s the American party was formed. It was founded on **prejudice,** or dislike based on race, religion, or nationality. Because its members claimed, "I know nothing," when questioned, it was called the Know-Nothing party. The American party called for the banning of all foreigners and Catholics from public office. In 1854 and 1855 the party elected state legislators and governors, and it succeeded in gaining some support in Congress.

The Know-Nothings failed to see the contributions that immigrants made to the nation. German immigrants taught American farmers improved farming methods and started new industries in inland cities. Irish workers provided much of the muscle power that built the nation's canals and railroads and kept the factories humming.

Despite hardships and prejudice, many immigrants found living in the United States exciting and rewarding. The United States, a German immigrant declared, was "a new society with almost limitless opportunities open to all."

SECTION REVIEW   Answers will be found on page T 50.

1. Define these words: *tenements, prejudice.*

2. Identify: Elias Howe, Charles Goodyear, Know-Nothings.

3. What improvements in transportation made Chicago the world's leading grain port by 1860?

4. What were some of the attractions of cities?

5. What problems did cities face?

6. Why did most Irish immigrants stay in eastern cities?

7. How did immigrants contribute to the nation?

The first half of the 1800s was a period of rapid growth and change in the United States. Frontier farmers pushed westward across the Mississippi to the edge of the Great Plains. The cotton kingdom spread across the southern Appalachians and onto the Ozark Plateau. In both the North and the South, farmers increased their productivity by using new machines such as Eli Whitney's cotton gin and McCormick's reaper.

During this same period, the Industrial Revolution was beginning in the United States. Two developments changed the way that goods were produced. First, the factory system made possible the mass production of goods such as cloth using water-powered machines. Second, Eli Whitney introduced the interchangeable system and division of labor. The result was lower manufacturing costs and higher productivity.

For women and less skilled workers, these changes in manufacturing brought new job opportunities. For many skilled workers, they meant loss of pay and self-respect. To protect their jobs, skilled workers formed the nation's first trade unions in the 1830s.

Foreign trade provided much of the investment capital that built the new factories. The success of these factories, however, depended on improvements in transportation and communication. Canals were built to link the eastern and western parts of the country. Steamboats made travel up and down major rivers much easier. Railroads expanded rapidly after 1830. The telegraph helped Americans keep in contact with events in every part of their growing nation.

Cities grew at a tremendous rate in the period between 1800 and 1860. As cities grew, city dwellers had to deal with such problems as fires, crime, and poor sanitation.

During the 1830s, the flow of immigrants from Europe became a flood. The largest groups were the Germans and the Irish. The newcomers made important contributions to the growing nation.

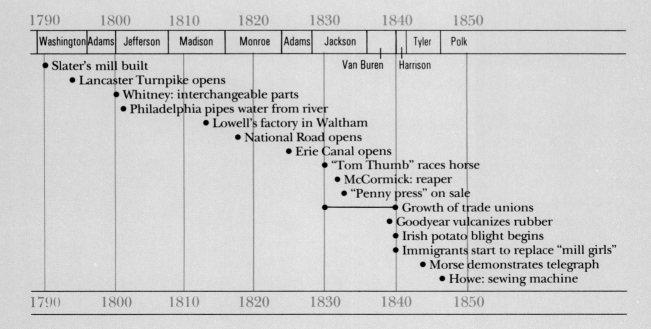

CHAPTER SURVEY

VOCABULARY REVIEW

From this list of vocabulary words, choose the one that best matches the meaning of each word or phrase in heavy type.

(a) division of labor
(b) factory system
(c) Industrial Revolution
(d) interchangeable parts
(e) investment capital
(f) literacy
(g) mass production
(h) prejudice
(i) strike
(j) tenements
(k) trade unions

1. A **major change in how goods were produced** began in the United States after 1800.

2. The **use of factories to produce goods** began first in the textile industry.

3. Eli Whitney made **almost identical parts.**

4. He also experimented with **the separation of work into simple tasks.**

5. Whitney's experiments led to **the manufacture of goods in great quantities.**

6. Business people needed **money available for investing.**

7. Few jobs required **the ability to read.**

8. Craftworkers formed **associations of skilled workers.**

9. Their main weapon was the **refusal to work until their demands were met.**

10. Immigrants working in factories faced **dislike based on their nationality.**

11. Many immigrants lived in **houses that had been broken up into tiny apartments.**

CHAPTER REVIEW

1. What did Cyrus McCormick's horse-drawn reaper, the two-bladed plow, and the interchangeable system have in common?

2. How did the spread of the factory system in the early 1800s help the United States to become more self-sufficient?

3. How was cotton important to (a) the economy of the North? (b) the economy of the South? (c) the nation's foreign trade?

4. (a) How did steamboats affect Pittsburgh, Cincinnati, and St. Louis? (b) How did railroads help Chicago to grow?

5. Why did many mill girls become unhappy with factory work by 1836?

6. By 1850, Americans were using horse power, wind power, water power, steam power, and electric power to do useful work. Which kind of power was used by (a) canal boats? (b) clipper ships? (c) reapers? (d) locomotives? (e) power looms? (f) the telegraph? (g) riverboats? (h) brigs? (i) two-bladed plows? (j) spinning machines?

Eli Whitney's cotton gin changed the economy of the South. In the thirty years after its invention in 1793, cotton production increased fifty fold.

7. (a) What was the goal of the American party (the "Know-Nothings")? (b) What did signs saying "No Irish Need Apply" reveal about the attitude of many Americans toward immigrants?

8. How did the growth of America's foreign trade aid the building of factories?

9. How did improvements in transportation affect shipping costs?

10. (a) What were the two largest groups of immigrants to enter the United States between 1800 and 1850? (b) How did these two groups differ in the places where they settled?

GEOGRAPHY REVIEW

*CT **1.** Look at the map "Agriculture and Industry 1840" on page 273. (a) In what part of the United States was dairy farming most important? (b) How far west had cotton farming spread by 1840? (c) Is rice a coastal or an inland crop? (d) Which major city was the center of the textile industry? (e) Which four industries were found in the Baltimore area? (f) Where was shipbuilding important?

*CT **2.** Refer to the map "Roads, Canals, and Waterways 1850" on page 283. (a) Do most of the roads on this map run generally north-south or east-west? (b) Which section has the most canals, North or South? (c) What ocean and river route could a New England factory owner use to ship products from New York to St. Louis? (d) What river, lake, and canal route could the factory owner use?

USING THE TOOLS OF HISTORY

*CT **Interpreting Illustrations**

Look carefully at the illustration on this page and answer these questions. (a) According to the caption, what is the subject of this illustration? (b) Is this illustration lifelike or clearly imaginary? (c) What two forms of power are shown here? (d) What do the passenger cars have in common?

READING AND THINKING SKILLS

*CT **The Problem-Solution Pattern**
Complete these problem-solution patterns.

1. Problem: Farmers could not harvest as much wheat as they could plant.
Solution: _____

2. Problem: _____
Solution: Canals were built linking rivers and lakes.

3. Problem: _____
Solution: The cotton gin

4. Problem: Factory owners needed to buy miles of leather belts to transfer power to machines.
Solution: _____

In 1830 Peter Cooper's locomotive *Tom Thumb* lost its race with a horse-drawn coach, but soon railroads replaced riverboats and wagons for quick, cheap transport.

CHAPTER 12	1824-1850

EXPANDING DEMOCRACY

THE ELECTIONS OF 1824 AND 1828
ANDREW JACKSON AS PRESIDENT
JACKSON'S SECOND TERM
THE REFORM MOVEMENT

12-1 THE ELECTIONS OF 1824 AND 1828

READ TO FIND OUT

sectionalism: loyalty to one's own section of the country
suffrage: right to vote
illiterate: unable to read

—what the words *sectionalism, suffrage,* and *illiterate* mean.

—why John Q. Adams had troubles as President.

—how the Democrats built a national political party.

—why Andrew Jackson was a hero to the people of the West.

—why the election of 1828 was an important turning point.

By the end of James Monroe's second term as President, there were no national political parties in the United States. The Federalist party had destroyed itself by failing to support the War of 1812. The Republicans then lacked a political enemy to unite against. That party had broken into rival groups.

THE ELECTION OF 1824

In the presidential election of 1824 all the candidates called themselves Republicans, but each looked to his own section of the country for support. Secretary of State John Quincy Adams was the candidate of the

Northeast. Secretary of the Treasury William Crawford of Georgia counted on the voters of the southern states east of the Appalachians. Congressman Henry Clay of Kentucky and Senator Andrew Jackson of Tennessee were rival champions of the West.

When the electoral votes were counted, Jackson led with 99 votes to 84 for Adams. Crawford had 41 votes and Clay only 37. Not one of the candidates had a majority of the votes. According to the Constitution, the House of Representatives now had to choose the next President from the top three candidates.

Henry Clay, who was out of the running, felt that he had more in common with Adams than with Jackson or Crawford. He advised his friends in the House to support Adams. Adams became President. When Adams later chose Clay as his Secretary of State, Jackson charged that the two men had made a "corrupt bargain."

SECTIONALISM MAKES LEADERSHIP DIFFICULT

John Q. Adams was a man of strong principles and deeply felt patriotism, but he was unable to achieve the goals that he set for his administration. One reason for his failure was that he was a nationalist at the

In a holiday mood, people gather on election day outside Philadelphia's Independence Hall. John Lewis Krimmel captured the scene.

Students can review what they learned about Henry Clay and the Missouri Compromise in Chapter 10, page 259.

wrong time. **Sectionalism,** or loyalty to one's own section of the country, was growing rapidly in the 1820s.

Adams believed in a strong national government. He proposed that the federal government pay for internal improvements, like roads and canals. He wanted a national university. He suggested federal aid for science, exploration, industry, agriculture, and the arts.

The southerners in Congress opposed Adams's suggestions. They felt that a strong and active national government was a threat to their section of the country. If Congress was allowed to do all the things Adams proposed, there was no telling what it might decide to do next. It might even pass laws interfering with slavery.

THE PARTY OF THE COMMON PEOPLE

The growth of sectionalism worried Martin Van Buren, a Senator from New York. To keep his country from breaking apart, he decided to build a new, nationwide political party. To please the South's political leaders, the party would favor a weak national government. To win votes in all three sections, it would appeal to the "common" people.

Appealing to the common people was more important than ever before. More and more Americans were gaining **suffrage,** or the right to vote. In the early years of the republic, most states restricted suffrage to men who owned property or paid a certain amount in taxes. Gradually these restrictions were reduced and then removed. At the same time, new western states granted suffrage to all adult white men. Women, Indians, and blacks could not vote. But by 1828 most white men had gained suffrage.

Presidential election rules changed, too. In the past, presidential electors had been chosen by state legislatures. By 1828 voters chose the electors in all but two states.

These changes came about because the nation's faith in democracy was growing stronger. Sensing the mood of the country, Van Buren named the new party the Democratic Republican party. In a few years it would become the Democratic party.

THE PERFECT CANDIDATE

Martin Van Buren's new party needed the right presidential candidate if it expected to win the election of 1828. The candidate would have to stand forth as the champion of the common people. One person met this requirement perfectly.

Andrew Jackson was born in a log cabin on the Carolina frontier. An orphan by the age of fourteen, he became a lawyer, a successful land speculator, and the owner of a Tennessee plantation. To westerners,

The Elections of 1824 and 1828

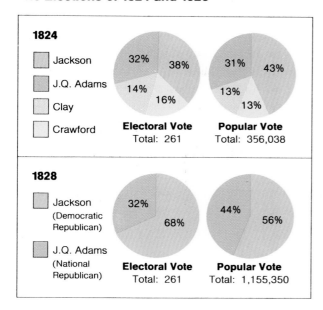

1824

Jackson
J.Q. Adams
Clay
Crawford

Electoral Vote
Total: 261

32% 38%
14% 16%

Popular Vote
Total: 356,038

31% 43%
13% 13%

1828

Jackson
(Democratic Republican)

J.Q. Adams
(National Republican)

Electoral Vote
Total: 261

32% 68%

Popular Vote
Total: 1,155,350

44% 56%

In the election of 1824, Andrew Jackson received more electoral votes than John Quincy Adams. But Henry Clay's support in the House made Adams President.

Jackson was living proof that someone born in a log cabin could become successful. Frontier farmers were grateful to him for leading the Tennessee militia in campaigns against the Indians. All Americans remembered General Jackson as "the Hero of New Orleans."

THE ELECTION OF 1828

Jackson was nicknamed "Old Hickory" by his troops because he was "tough as hickory." When he set a goal, he achieved it. In 1825 he and Van Buren began preparing for the next election.

Many newspapers spread the word that "the Hero" needed the people's help. Most editors in Jackson's time did not feel obliged to present different political points of view. Instead, they proudly supported the opinions of their favorite politician or state political party. While the newspaper editors praised Jackson, local party workers entertained the voters. The Democratic Republican party held rallies, parades, picnics, and barbecues for everyone.

In campaign speeches and newspaper articles, Jackson's supporters seldom discussed the important issues of the day. Instead, they made personal attacks on John Quincy Adams, who was campaigning for a second term. Adams, they claimed, had ridden "like mad" across the New England countryside one Sunday while decent folk were in church. He had bought a billiard table with the taxpayers' money. Above all, he had made a "corrupt bargain" with Henry Clay to gain the presidency. The fact that there was no evidence for these charges did not seem to bother the Democratic Republicans.

*CT

For discussion: Mud-slinging has been a part of many American presidential campaigns. Do students think it is a necessary, or at least an acceptable, part of the political process? Why or why not?

This quilt was made in 1820 in Swansea, Massachusetts. It is a fine example of American folk art.

One witness of the wild scene at Jackson's inauguration remarked, "I never saw such a mixture; the reign of King Mob seemed triumphant." But another defended the people's behavior: "It was a proud day for the people. General Jackson is *their* President."

Adams and his supporters, who now called themselves the National Republican party, were equally skilled in name-calling. Because Jackson was self-educated and read few books, they said he was **illiterate,** or unable to read. They also accused him of being a gambler, a brawler, and, because he had fought a number of duels, a murderer.

The campaigns of the two parties were so successful that more than twice as many Americans voted in 1828 as had voted in 1824. A solid majority chose "Old Hickory" and his vice-presidential running mate, John C. Calhoun of South Carolina. Support for Jackson and Calhoun came mainly from the South, the West, and the key states of New York and Pennsylvania, where the Democratic party was well organized.

THE "PEOPLE'S PRESIDENT" IS INAUGURATED

The crowd that came to watch Andrew Jackson take the oath of office on March 4, 1829, was the largest Washington, D.C., had ever seen. After the ceremony hundreds followed their hero to the White House to celebrate. Furniture was ruined by "men with boots heavy with mud, standing on damask-satin-covered chairs and sofas." Jackson was "nearly pressed to death" and needed his friends' help to escape by a back door. It was, said observer Margaret Bayard Smith, "the People's day and the People's President and the People would rule."

The election of 1828 was a turning point in the nation's history. For the first time, the United States had a President who did not come from "Atlantic America." Jackson's victory was proof that the political power of the West was growing. It also showed the voting strength of the common people. In the future, presidential candidates would depend more and more on well-organized, national parties that could bring out the voters on election day.

SECTION REVIEW   Answers will be found on page T 51.

1. Define these words: *sectionalism, suffrage, illiterate.*

2. Why did Andrew Jackson feel that a "corrupt bargain" had been made in the election of 1824?

3. Why was John Quincy Adams an unsuccessful President?

4. What was Martin Van Buren's strategy for building a national political party?

5. Which group of Americans had been granted suffrage by 1828? To which groups was suffrage denied?

6. Why was Andrew Jackson a hero to the people of the West?

7. In what two ways was the election of 1828 a turning point?

12-2 ANDREW JACKSON AS PRESIDENT

READ TO FIND OUT

—what the words *spoils system, nullify,* and *sovereign* mean.

—how Jackson and Van Buren rewarded party loyalty.

—what the purpose of the Indian Removal Act was.

—what Calhoun proposed in a South Carolina report.

—how Jackson responded to the threat of secession.

spoils system: practice of appointing party members to government posts
nullify: make a law null, or without effect
sovereign: supreme in power

The work of building a national party did not end with Jackson's election. The new President chose cabinet officers from all sections of the country. For advice, however, he relied on a group of friends who often joined him for breakfast. A key member of this "Kitchen Cabinet" was his new Secretary of State, Martin Van Buren.

THE SPOILS SYSTEM

Van Buren believed that local party members must be rewarded for their loyalty and hard work. The best way to reward party workers was to give them government jobs. To Van Buren, elections were battles and government jobs were spoils, or prizes of war. Guided by Van Buren, the President removed a number of Adams's supporters from government posts and replaced them with Jackson's supporters. This practice of appointing party members to government posts came to be called the **spoils system.**

Critics of the spoils system said that party loyalty did not qualify a person to be a postmaster or federal marshal. Government employees, they said, should be chosen for their experience, ability, and honesty.

Jackson insisted that he was making democracy stronger by giving more people a chance to take part in government. Instead of lifetime appointments, he favored "rotation in office." The Presidents who came after Jackson continued to use the spoils system to reward party loyalty.

INDIAN REMOVAL

By the time Jackson became President, the Indians living east of the Mississippi had lost all hope of stopping the onrush of settlers. Northern tribes such as the Sauk and the Fox had been pushed westward by

USING THE TOOLS OF HISTORY

MAKING GENERALIZATIONS

*CT

A generalization is a statement about a number of facts that have something in common. Here are four sentences describing the removal of the Chocktaw, Creek, Cherokee, and Seminole. Read each sentence carefully for facts.

Many of the Choctaw died from the hardships of migration to the Indian Territory.

The Creek were left in Indian Territory without clothing, weapons, and cooking utensils.

More than 4,000 Cherokee lost their lives during removal.

The Seminole lost 40 percent of their people as a result of removal.

1. Which of the following generalizations best fits these facts?

(a) The southern tribes did not resist removal.

(b) The southern tribes lost 40 percent of their people during removal.

(c) The southern tribes suffered terrible hardships as a result of removal.

There are often exceptions to, or facts that do not fit, a generalization.

2. Which of the following facts is an exception to the generalization you chose as the answer to question 1?

(a) The Chickasaw were able to move to Indian Territory without great loss of life.

(b) The Creek lost 45 percent of their people as a result of removal.

3. Choose the generalization below that best fits the information shown on the map on the opposite page.

(a) Indian tribes were moved overland to the Indian Territory.

(b) Many tribes living west of the Mississippi were moved to the Indian Territory.

(c) Many tribes living east of the Mississippi were moved to Iowa Territory.

4. Name the tribes that are exceptions to the generalization you chose in question 3.

Answers will be found on page T 51.

the newcomers. In the South the tribal lands of the Cherokee, Creek, Choctaw, Chickasaw, and Seminole had gradually been surrounded by new settlements.

The settlers believed that the Indians were blocking civilization's westward march. They also believed that large profits could be made from the purchase and sale of Indian land. President Jackson shared these beliefs.

At his urging, Congress passed the Indian Removal Act of 1830. The purpose of the act was to open all lands east of the Mississippi to settlement. The Indian Removal Act allowed the President to make treaties calling for the Indians to give up their tribal lands in exchange for cash payments and land on the Great Plains. Later, in 1834, Congress set up a special Indian territory west of Missouri and Arkansas. Most Americans thought the region was too dry for farming.

Federal agents got tribal leaders to sign removal treaties by confusing or misleading them. Indians were also threatened by armed bands of settlers and speculators.

Remind students that in 1817 Andrew Jackson had commanded an army expedition pursuing Seminole Indians who had been raiding American settlements. Jackson had driven the Seminole into Florida.

Indian Removal 1830-1850

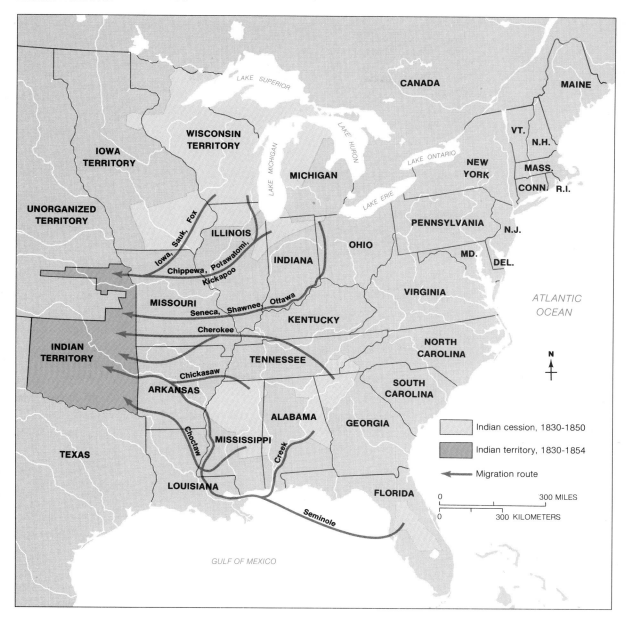

Map labels:

LAKE SUPERIOR · CANADA · MAINE · WISCONSIN TERRITORY · IOWA TERRITORY · LAKE MICHIGAN · LAKE HURON · MICHIGAN · LAKE ONTARIO · VT. · N.H. · NEW YORK · MASS. · CONN. · R.I. · UNORGANIZED TERRITORY · LAKE ERIE · ILLINOIS · PENNSYLVANIA · N.J. · OHIO · MD. · DEL. · Iowa, Sauk, Fox · Chippewa, Potawatomi, Kickapoo · INDIANA · Seneca, Shawnee · Ottawa · MISSOURI · VIRGINIA · ATLANTIC OCEAN · Cherokee · KENTUCKY · NORTH CAROLINA · INDIAN TERRITORY · TENNESSEE · Chickasaw · SOUTH CAROLINA · ARKANSAS · ALABAMA · GEORGIA · Choctaw · MISSISSIPPI · Creek · TEXAS · LOUISIANA · FLORIDA · Seminole · GULF OF MEXICO

N

Legend:
- Indian cession, 1830-1850
- Indian territory, 1830-1854
- Migration route

0 — 300 MILES
0 — 300 KILOMETERS

These methods were used against all the tribal groups. Even those Indians who had tried to protect their lands by changing their way of life were not safe. The Cherokee of Georgia grew cash crops and raised livestock. They built towns with flour mills, blacksmith shops, and schools. They had courts, jury trials, and a written constitution. A member of their tribe, Sequoyah (sih-KWOY-uh), invented a system for writing the Cherokee language. They published books and a newspaper in both Cherokee and English.

Activity: Students can research and make written reports on the life and achievements of Sequoyah, a remarkable American.

In 1838 more than 15,000 Cherokee were forced to move west. Robert Lindeux painted "The Trail of Tears" about a hundred years after the trek began.

*CT
Why might Chief Justice Marshall find that laws allowing others to seize Indian lands are unconstitutional?

Even so, Georgia passed laws giving its citizens the right to seize Cherokee lands. The Supreme Court under Chief Justice John Marshall ruled that these laws were unconstitutional. But President Jackson told Georgians to ignore the ruling.

Most of the Cherokee resisted efforts to push them off their land. Finally, in 1838, they were dragged from their homes and loaded into wagons by the United States Army. During the journey west, more than 4,000 Indians died of hunger and disease. Years later, writers would call the westward migration of the Cherokee "the Trail of Tears." Other tribes also tried to resist removal, with the same result.

CONFLICT OVER THE TARIFF

Some Americans criticized Jackson's treatment of the Indians, but the nation as a whole supported him. On another question, he found the nation badly divided. The North and the South had very different views about the tariff.

The first protective tariff had been passed in 1816. Its purpose was to protect American goods against British competition. Since then, Congress had pushed tariff duties higher. As profits grew, northern manufacturers were able to build more factories. The agricultural South, however, suffered from high tariffs, because southern planters had to pay more for the imported goods they needed.

Higher prices for manufactured goods hit the South at a bad time. During the 1820s, the supply of cotton grew faster than the demand for it. So the price of cotton fell. In South Carolina, worn-out soil made cotton growing expensive. Planters there lost money on every bale they sold. They had to go into debt to buy northern products.

Students should note that this is another instance of the South's resentment of what it considered unequal treatment, a resentment that continued to fester.

THE DOCTRINE OF NULLIFICATION

Then, in 1828, the tariff was raised even higher. In South Carolina rallies were held to protest the "enrichment" of the North at the expense of the South. One speaker asked, "Is it worth our while to continue this Union of states, where the North demands to be our masters?"

John C. Calhoun did not want his home state to secede, or withdraw, from the Union. Instead of secession, he offered the doctrine of nullification. To **nullify** means to make a law null, or without effect. In a written report, Calhoun proposed that a single state could rule an act of Congress to be unconstitutional. The act could then be nullified by a state convention. Nullified laws need not be obeyed.

South Carolina put off nullifying the Tariff of 1828 in the hope that President Jackson would work for lower tariffs. Meanwhile, nullification and states' rights were debated in the Senate.

*CT
For discussion: In what way does the doctrine of nullification work against and contradict the concept of the United States as a unified nation?

THE WEBSTER-HAYNE DEBATE

For nine days in January 1830, Daniel Webster of Massachusetts and Robert Y. Hayne of South Carolina matched wits in a battle of words. "The very life of our system," said Hayne, "is the independence of states." He argued that the states had created the Constitution. Therefore, they were **sovereign,** or possessed supreme power, over the federal government. Hayne said that it was the right of each state to protect the liberty of its citizens when the federal government misused its powers.

Webster attacked Hayne's arguments, insisting that the national government was sovereign. If each state had the right to declare federal

Daniel Webster, standing at right, attacked the doctrine of nullification during the Webster-Hayne debate. At the far left is another fine orator, John C. Calhoun.

laws unconstitutional, he said, the Union would fall apart. Many thought that Hayne won the debate, but Webster's closing words are still remembered. Holding his listeners spellbound, he thundered, "Liberty *and* Union, now and forever, one and inseparable!"

THE PRESIDENT PRESERVES THE UNION

President Jackson strongly opposed nullification, but he did ask Congress to reduce import duties. In 1832 Congress approved a new tariff only slightly lower than the one it replaced.

South Carolina would wait no longer. A state convention nullified the tariffs of 1828 and 1832. Federal officials were banned from collecting customs duties within the state beginning February 1, 1833. South Carolina promised to secede if the federal government used force to collect duties. Funds were voted to build up the state militia.

President Jackson was furious. He had fought to defend the Union before, and he was ready to do so again. The President issued a proclamation to the people of South Carolina, warning that "disunion by armed force is *treason.*" His position was strengthened when the other southern states refused to support nullification. To calm South Carolina, Jackson asked Congress to reduce the tariff further.

John C. Calhoun resigned as Vice-President in order to help represent South Carolina in the Senate. Although he and the President were now political enemies, both hoped to avoid bloodshed. Calhoun urged his fellow South Carolinians not to commit acts of violence. Jackson made no threatening moves with army troops.

Finally, in March 1833, a tariff bill was guided through Congress by Henry Clay. It reduced tariffs gradually over the next ten years. South Carolina declared that its nullification law was no longer in force, and the crisis ended. Showing firmness and patience, the President had preserved the Union. But the issue of secession was far from settled.

You may wish to have students note that once again Henry Clay served as the "Great Pacificator," as he did with the Missouri Compromise.

SECTION REVIEW Answers will be found on page T 51.

1. Define these words: *spoils system, nullify, sovereign.*

2. Identify: Kitchen Cabinet, Sequoyah, Trail of Tears.

3. How did Jackson and Van Buren reward party loyalty?

4. What was the purpose of the Indian Removal Act of 1830?

5. What methods were used to persuade the Indians to sign treaties by which they gave up their tribal lands?

6. What did Calhoun propose in the report issued by South Carolina?

7. How did Jackson respond to South Carolina's threat to secede?

12-3 JACKSON'S SECOND TERM

READ TO FIND OUT

—what the words *nominate, caucuses, specie,* and *depression* mean.

—how the Bank of the United States improved the nation's currency.

—why Jackson was an enemy of the national bank.

—why Jackson issued the Specie Circular.

—why different political groups joined to form the Whig party.

nominate: name someone to run for office
caucuses: private meetings of party officials
specie: gold and silver coins
depression: severe decline in economic activity

In 1832, for the first time, the Democrats and the National Republicans **nominated**, or proposed for office, their presidential candidates at national conventions. In the past, candidates had been chosen by state legislatures or party **caucuses**—private meetings of party leaders. National nominating conventions gave party members a greater voice in choosing candidates. Local party members chose delegates to represent them at the conventions.

The Democrats nominated President Jackson for a second term. Vice-President Calhoun had quarreled with Jackson earlier in the year. The Democrats passed over Calhoun and nominated Martin Van Buren for Vice-President. The National Republicans chose Henry Clay as their presidential candidate.

THE SECOND BANK OF THE UNITED STATES

For the Democrats, the main election issue was the Second Bank of the United States. Congress had chartered this national bank in 1816. It kept the federal government's funds and made payments ordered by the Treasury Department. Like state chartered banks, the Bank of the United States also printed paper dollars. This was necessary because the American economy was growing rapidly. There was not enough **specie** (SPEE-shee), or gold and silver coins, for all the buying and selling that Americans wanted to do.

The banks added paper dollars to the money supply by lending newly printed bank notes to borrowers. Most banks backed their notes with specie. A bank would promise, for example, to exchange one dollar in gold for one of its one-dollar bank notes. As long as people believed this promise, the bank's paper money was "as good as gold." Some specie was kept in reserve in case people brought in their bank notes and demanded coin money.

Thomas Sully drew this charcoal sketch of Andrew Jackson when Jackson was forty-seven. The sketch suggests Jackson's strong will and character.

LITERAL AND INFERENTIAL READING

*CT

In the Approaches to Reading feature in Chapter 1, you learned how to preview a chapter. You discovered that one step in previewing is to study the headings in dark type. Each heading tells the reader the topic of a section or a subsection in the chapter.

Some headings tell the reader directly what the topic is. When this is done, the topic is stated *literally*. Other headings give only hints about the topic. In this case, the topic is stated *inferentially*. Readers must infer, or decide from what they know, what the topic is.

The first heading in Section 3 is "The Second Bank of the United States." The topic is stated literally. The subsection describes how the bank worked, why it made enemies, and who those enemies were.

The second heading reads, " 'The Hero' Battles 'The Monster.' " This heading is less direct. From what you have read, you must make an inference about who "the Hero" is and then find out what "the Monster" is. The word *battles* gives a hint that "the Hero"—who was Jackson—opposed "the Monster." Because this heading provides hints about the topic, it is inferentially stated. After reading this subsection, you will fully understand what the heading means.

There are four remaining headings in this section. Write each of them on a piece of paper. Then write the word *literal* if a heading tells you directly the topic of the subsection. Write the word *inferential* if a heading just provides hints about the topic.

Answers will be found on page T 51.

Activity: Today the Federal Reserve System promotes the stability of banks. Students can report on how the Fed works to keep banks from failing and so defaulting on their obligations.

Nicholas Biddle, the president of the Bank of the United States, insisted on a specie reserve of 50 percent. He kept fifty cents in specie in his vaults for every new paper dollar that he lent. Biddle believed in sound currency, or trustworthy money.

State chartered banks usually kept a reserve of less than 25 percent. In the West many "wildcat banks" kept no reserve at all. Their bank notes were called "rag money." From time to time, Biddle tried to force less cautious banks to print less paper money until they could increase their specie reserves. He did this by refusing to accept their bank notes at branches of the national bank.

"THE HERO" BATTLES "THE MONSTER"

Although most business people approved of Biddle, the Bank of the United States made enemies. State banks in the South and the West did not want the national bank to tell them how much money they could print and lend. Western business people wanted their state banks to lend them as much money as possible. They were eager to buy land and to build canals and railroads.

Some people were suspicious of banks in general. Most Americans made their living by growing crops or making things with their hands. What, they wondered, did bankers make?

This 1836 cartoon shows Andrew Jackson and his supporters fighting "the Monster"—the Bank of the United States. The Bank is shown with many heads. The largest belongs to its president, Nicholas Biddle.

Andrew Jackson shared the West's dislike of the national bank. He called it "the Monster." Jackson believed that the bank's wealthy owners had an unfair advantage over other business people. The bank could lend government funds to increase its profits. It could also lend more to one section of the country than another. In short, the bank had too much economic power.

The bank also made large loans to many of the nation's leading politicians. Jackson decided that the bank had too much political power as well. The President announced that he was against renewing the bank's charter when it ran out in 1836.

Henry Clay, the National Republican candidate for President, supported the bank. He advised Nicholas Biddle to request a new charter during the election year of 1832, instead of waiting until 1836. Clay thought that Jackson would not veto the bank bill for fear he would not be reelected. Biddle followed Clay's advice. Early in 1832 Congress passed a bill to recharter the bank.

Clay misjudged both Jackson and the mood of the people. "The Bank," said Jackson, "is trying to kill me, but I will kill it!" Jackson vetoed the bill to recharter it. He said that the bank was unconstitutional, even though the Supreme Court had ruled that the bank was constitutional in the 1819 case of *McCulloch* v. *Maryland*. National Republicans called Jackson "King Andrew" for trying to overrule the Supreme Court. But the Democrats won the election of 1832 by a landslide.

*CT
For discussion: Considering Jackson's policies and actions, do students think it was fair to call him "King Andrew"? Why or why not?

This five-dollar bank note was issued by the State Bank of Illinois. Each bank created a different design for its currency.

*CT

For discussion: Why is a good reputation important to a bank? What might happen if it loses the trust of its depositors and customers?

To Jackson, his victory was proof that voters wanted him to slay "the Monster." In the fall of 1833, he ordered all payments to the federal government to be deposited in certain state banks. Jackson's critics called them "pet banks." As the government funds remaining in the national bank were spent, it died a slow death.

THE PANIC OF 1837

While Jackson was destroying the national bank, state banks poured out paper money that was not backed by specie. Much of it was lent to speculators. They made quick profits buying and selling land. They also speculated in stock in canal and railroad companies. Land prices rose rapidly. Get-rich-quick fever swept the frontier.

By the summer of 1836, unsound paper money and wild speculation were threatening the country with inflation. Jackson clamped down on reckless bankers and speculators. He ordered the government to accept only specie as payment for public land.

The Specie Circular, as the order was called, slowed land sales. But it also weakened the banking system. If the President did not trust the nation's paper money, Americans reasoned, why should anyone trust it? People brought in their bank notes and demanded hard money.

In 1837 a financial crisis struck Britain. British bankers called for the repayment of specie loans made to American banks. The British also stopped buying American cotton. Cotton prices—and then land prices—tumbled. Cotton dealers and land speculators could not pay back their bank loans. Banks began to collapse. As panic spread, people rushed to withdraw their savings. In May 1837 New York City banks announced that they could no longer pay out gold and silver coins.

The United States slid into a **depression,** or severe decline in economic activity. Business people stopped investing, and foreign trade slowed to a trickle. Factories closed, and workers lost their jobs. Six miserable years passed before the economy recovered.

THE RISE OF THE WHIG PARTY

During Andrew Jackson's war on the bank, a new political party appeared. Former National Republicans Henry Clay and Daniel Webster were joined by Democrats who believed that the country needed a national bank. Because of Jackson's stand against nullification, some states' rights supporters joined the new party.

These different groups were united by a strong dislike of "King Andrew." They all felt that Jackson had misused the powers of the executive branch. They called themselves the Whig party, after a British party that defended Parliament's rights against the king.

In the presidential election of 1836, the Whigs were not strong enough to defeat the Democrats. Martin Van Buren won the election after promising the voters that he would follow in the footsteps of President Jackson. But the Whigs won many seats in the House.

Van Buren's years as President were not happy. Soon after he took office, the Panic of 1837 plunged the nation into depression. To make matters worse, the Whigs were able to vote down the new President's bills in Congress.

Van Buren's only success was the Independent Treasury Act of 1840. The act removed government funds from the "pet banks" and placed them in treasury vaults located in several cities.

THE LOG-CABIN CAMPAIGN

As the election of 1840 approached, the Whigs smelled victory. Van Buren, the Democratic candidate, would certainly be blamed for the depression. If the Whigs could find a candidate who appealed to every section of the country, they were sure to win.

Copying the Democratic campaign of 1828, the Whigs chose a popular general, William Henry Harrison of Ohio. Harrison had defeated Tecumseh's warriors in the Battle of Tippecanoe. To "balance" their party ticket, or list of candidates, the Whigs nominated a southerner, John Tyler of Virginia, for Vice-President.

Instead of taking a stand on issues, each party criticized the other's candidate. If Harrison were given "a barrel of cider," suggested one Democratic editor, he would be happy to "spend his days in a log cabin on the banks of the Ohio."

In truth, Harrison lived in a large house, but the Whigs turned the insult to their own advantage. Harrison became the "log-cabin" candidate. Harrison, the Whigs pointed out, was always ready to welcome visitors to his house. He was, they said, a simple, clean-living farmer, a true representative of the people. By contrast, the Whigs pictured Van Buren as a man who lived expensively. His table, they said, was set with the finest silver.

The Whigs held huge parades and rallies to entertain the voters. They sang songs from the *Log Cabin Songbook* and shouted "Tippecanoe and Tyler Too!" The Democrats were amazed. "We have taught them to conquer us!" moaned one veteran of the 1828 campaign.

In the election of 1840, "Tip and Ty" received four times as many electoral votes as their Democratic rivals. The Whigs also gained control of the House and the Senate. At last Henry Clay could put his "American System" into practice. The Whigs would increase the tariff and vote funds for internal improvements. Above all, they would recharter the Bank of the United States.

Van Buren was overshadowed by his predecessor, and he had a reputation for evasiveness. "Even his best friends," a friend said of him, "were apprehensive that he was overcautious and lacked the . . . courage . . . to meet those exigencies which might require bold and decisive action."

The Whigs intentionally ran Harrison without a party platform. One supporter advised, "Let him not say one single thing about his principles . . . let him say nothing—promise nothing. Let no Committee or Convention . . . ever extract from him a single word about what he thinks now or will do hereafter."

This 1840 election banner, showing William Henry Harrison in uniform, reminded people that he was a military hero. The banner also shows the log cabin where Harrison was supposed to live.

Although historians now have a higher opinion of John Tyler, Theodore Roosevelt expressed the opinion of many when he called Tyler "a politician of monumental littleness."

"HIS ACCIDENCY"

Unfortunately for Clay, the Whig President died one month after his inauguration. Vice-President Tyler became President. John Tyler was a strong believer in states' rights and strict construction. Although he had left the Democratic party because of Jackson's stand on nullification, at heart he was still a Democrat. Tyler vetoed Clay's bank recharter bill. By accident, the Whigs had put an enemy in the White House. Furious at "His Accidency," they expelled the President from the party.

Despite their disappointment with Tyler, the Whigs had accomplished a great deal in the election of 1840. They had become a truly national political party, with support in every section of the country. Americans felt closer to their government than ever before. In the election of 1840, almost four fifths of those who could vote went to the polls. Democracy rooted itself more deeply in American soil.

SECTION REVIEW   Answers will be found on page T 51.

1. Define these words: *nominate, caucuses, specie, depression.*

2. Identify: "wildcat banks," "pet banks," "His Accidency."

3. Why was it necessary for American banks to print paper dollars?

4. Why did Nicholas Biddle keep a specie reserve of 50 percent?

5. Why was Andrew Jackson an enemy of the Bank of the United States?

6. Why did Jackson issue the Specie Circular?

7. How did the Specie Circular weaken the banking system?

8. What united the political groups that formed the Whig party?

12-4 THE REFORM MOVEMENT

READ TO FIND OUT

—what the words *utopias, temperance, abolitionists,* and *emancipation* mean.

—how the revival movement affected Americans.

—what evils were attacked by reformers.

—what the radical abolitionists wanted.

—how the movement for women's rights began.

utopias: perfect communities
temperance: moderation in use of alcohol
abolitionists: people who worked to abolish slavery
emancipation: freeing of someone

During the Jackson era, political parties battled for votes. Meanwhile, many Americans were engaged in personal battles against evil and injustice. They were inspired by a new message of hope coming from the nation's Protestant churches.

A GREAT AWAKENING

The Puritans had believed that only "God's chosen few" could enter heaven. By the 1800s this belief had given way to a new idea. Most ministers now taught that even the worst sinners could uproot the evil in their hearts and become perfect in the sight of God. But it was not enough simply to save oneself. Good Christians also had a duty to battle sin wherever they found it.

Armed with this exciting idea, Protestants launched a powerful revival movement, or campaign to reawaken religious feeling. Traveling preachers spoke to huge crowds at outdoor gatherings called camp meetings. From the West to the East, Americans touched by this movement yearned to make the world perfect.

UTOPIAS

For some, perfection meant building **utopias,** or perfect communities. Small groups of dedicated Christians withdrew from the world around them. They formed religious communities where work and property were shared. Some of the most successful communities were begun by a group called the Shaker Society. Led by Ann Lee Stanley, the Shakers came to America from England in search of religious freedom. Eventually, their communities spread to seven states.

This Shaker basket, made about 1850, is called a "cat's head basket." The Shakers' beautiful and simple designs are still widely admired today.

Shakers first came to America in 1774. Here colonial Shakers gather for worship.

Activity: One notable Utopian community was Brook Farm in Massachusetts, founded by transcendentalists hoping to foster a union between intellectual activity and manual labor. Students can research the Brook Farm experiment or the Oneida community and make oral or written reports about them.

Not all of the utopian communities started during this period were based on religion. Robert Owen, a Welshman, believed that people could overcome their selfishness if farms, factories, and other "means of production" were owned by everyone together, instead of by individuals. This belief became the basis for a community that he started at New Harmony, Indiana, in 1825. But Owen's community failed, like other utopian experiments.

TEMPERANCE

Some Americans tried to reform, or to improve, society instead of withdrawing from it. Large numbers of reformers attacked drunkenness. In Andrew Jackson's time, alcohol was consumed at mealtimes and at most social events. For life's aches and pains, whiskey was the most effective painkiller available. As a result, alcoholism, or addiction to alcohol, was a widespread problem.

At first, reformers urged **temperance,** or moderation in the use of alcohol. Then the revival movement encouraged Americans to make themselves morally perfect. Temperance crusaders began to demand that people stop drinking alcohol completely. In 1836 the first national convention of the American Temperance Union met. By 1855, 13 states had passed laws banning the sale of alcoholic beverages.

CARE FOR THE NEGLECTED

Reformers also worked to make conditions better for people who had been ignored in the past. People such as Margaret Fuller investigated the nation's prisons and tried to improve the care of prisoners. Thomas H. Gallaudet (GAL-uh-DEHT) and Samuel G. Howe established the first schools for the deaf and the blind.

Dorothea Dix, a teacher, visited the mentally ill in jails throughout Massachusetts. In 1843 she told the state legislature that mentally ill people were kept "in cages, closets, cellars, stalls, pens!" They were "beaten with rods, and lashed into obedience!" Then Dix visited other states and found similar conditions. Largely because of her work, hospitals for the mentally ill were built or enlarged in 15 states by 1860.

PUBLIC EDUCATION

Reformers met with the greatest success in their campaign for state-supported public schools. At the beginning of the Jackson era, only private schools for the children of the wealthy provided a good education. Massachusetts had public schools, but they were open for only two or three months a year. School houses had only one room and were dirty and crowded. Teachers were poorly trained.

Dorothea Dix (left) improved care for the mentally ill. She wrote, "They say nothing can be done here. I reply, 'I know no such word.' "

Margaret Fuller said women should be able to follow any career they chose. "Let them be sea captains, if you will," she wrote. "We would have every path laid open to Woman as freely as to Man."

Activity: Students can report on such notable reformers as Dorothea Dix, Horace Mann, Theodore Weld, William Lloyd Garrison, John Greenleaf Whittier, Frederick Douglass, James Forten, and Angelina and Sarah Grimké.

Paul Cuffe, a black merchant, was an early champion of a plan to resettle American blacks in Africa.

James Forten was a leader of the antislavery movement. This picture has been identified as his portrait.

James Forten was a notable abolitionist. He gave financial support to William Lloyd Garrison's newspaper, *The Liberator,* and helped runaway slaves who had fled to the North. He was the grandfather of Charlotte Forten, whom students will encounter in Chapter 15.

In 1837 Horace Mann gave up a successful career in Massachusetts politics to run the state's new board of education. Under his leadership, the school year was lengthened to six months. Colleges were set up to train teachers. More of the state's tax money was spent to build schools and to provide books. Reformers in other states followed Mann's example. By 1860 white children in most northern states could attend free elementary schools.

THE CAMPAIGN AGAINST SLAVERY

No reformers stirred deeper feelings than the **abolitionists.** These men and women worked to abolish, or put an end to, slavery. After the Revolutionary War, a number of antislavery organizations sprang up. They favored gradual **emancipation,** or freeing, of the slaves. Some freed slaves by raising money to buy them from their owners. Some abolitionists also favored sending newly freed blacks out of the country.

In 1817 the American Colonization Society was formed. Its supporters included James Monroe and Henry Clay. The society collected funds to start a colony of American blacks on the west coast of Africa. The colony became the nation of Liberia.

Most free blacks did not join the Colonization Society but worked toward ending slavery. At a protest meeting in Philadelphia, a wealthy sailmaker named James Forten asked his fellow blacks if they wanted to leave America. Their shout of "No!" he wrote, "seemed as if it would bring down the walls of the building." The protesters declared that free blacks would never abandon "the slave population of this country."

RADICAL ABOLITIONISTS

Free blacks in many northern cities continued to protest slavery. In 1829 a Boston clothing dealer named David Walker published his *Appeal to the Colored Citizens of the World.* If the South opposed emancipation, he argued, the slaves should rebel.

Most whites were outraged by Walker's pamphlet. William Lloyd Garrison was one of the few who were not. He opposed violence but respected Walker's courage. In 1831 Garrison published the first issue of the *Liberator,* a radical abolitionist newspaper. He wanted immediate, not gradual, emancipation of the slaves. There would be no compromise with slaveholders. Both Walker's *Appeal* and the *Liberator* were banned in the South.

Garrison, temperance crusader Theodore Dwight Weld, and New York merchants Arthur and Lewis Tappan founded the American Anti-Slavery Society in 1833. In speeches, sermons, newspaper articles, and pamphlets, the society demanded immediate emancipation.

314   CHAPTER 12   1824-1850

Among the society's traveling speakers were former slaves who had escaped and made their way north. Frederick Douglass "stole himself," as he put it, from a slaveholder in Maryland. He began his career as a lecturer in 1841. In an age of great public speakers, Douglass was one of the greatest. He also wrote a popular autobiography and published his own abolitionist newspaper, the *North Star*.

The abolitionists made many enemies. In 1837 Elijah Lovejoy, who printed an antislavery newspaper, was shot to death by a mob in Illinois. But the antislavery movement continued to grow.

Stories of the Underground Railroad inspired many new abolitionists. A secret network of people hid runaway slaves in their homes. They also helped slaves travel north to freedom in Canada. The most famous "conductor" on the railroad was Harriet Tubman. After escaping from slavery herself, she returned to the South many times. Avoiding armed patrols and tracking dogs, she guided more than three hundred people to freedom.

Frederick Douglass, a runaway slave, became a fighter for black freedom.

Harriet Tubman risked her own freedom again and again to lead others to freedom.

THE "GAG RULE"

During the 1830s, abolitionist groups flooded Congress with petitions against slavery. In 1836 southerners in Congress persuaded the other legislators to ban all discussion of antislavery petitions. Abolitionists argued that the "gag rule," as it was called, was a violation of the First Amendment guarantee of the right of petition.

Former President John Quincy Adams, now a Representative from Massachusetts, fought the gag rule in the House for eight years. Finally, in 1844, he gained enough support to defeat it. The conflict over the gag rule increased the bitterness between northerners and southerners. Some northerners accused the slaveholding South of trying to seize control of Congress.

For discussion: Explain why the "gag rule" violates the First Amendment.

★ ★ ★ ★ ★ ★ ★ **AMERICAN VALUES IN ACTION** ★ ★ ★ ★ ★ ★ ★

JANE SWISSHELM

*CT

Slave catchers, wrote Jane Swisshelm, are not fit to "sleep in our barn or take a drink at our pump!" Jane Swisshelm's new newspaper, launched in Pennsylvania in 1847, provoked howls of outrage. A proslavery editor named George Prentiss angrily objected to both the newspaper and its woman editor. "Brother George," a fellow editor warned, "beware of sister Jane."

His warning was apt. With biting wit, Swisshelm attacked her opponents. She had witnessed the "monster fiend" of slavery. She had experienced the bonds of the "woman's sphere." She vowed to fight both.

Readers imagined Swisshelm as "a cross between a woman and a tigress." Those who met her were taken aback to find a small, slender, soft-voiced woman. She had, wrote one person, "a truly enchanting smile."

Swisshelm's newspaper was a popular success but a financial failure. In 1857, tired and penniless, she moved to St. Cloud, Minnesota. She hoped to rest and listen to the "winds, birds, and insects." But she had to earn a living and soon set up another print shop.

"Sister Jane" was back in business. Her newspaper, the *St. Cloud Visitor,* took aim at proslavery targets. One of the biggest was a powerful local politician, Sylvanus Lowry.

One night, Lowry and his friends broke into the *Visitor* office. They destroyed Swisshelm's press and threw away her type. They left a note threatening "a more serious penalty."

Shocked, the townspeople called a meeting. As Swisshelm stood to speak, Lowry's supporters yelled and fired pistols in the air. But the editor, having drawn up her will before the meeting, calmly told her story. The townspeople voted to buy her a new press.

Next, the Lowry group tried to stop her with a libel suit. Unable to afford legal fees, Swisshelm settled out of court. She pledged that the *St. Cloud Visitor* would never again mention Lowry and his friends.

Swisshelm kept her word. She closed down the *Visitor* and started a new paper—the *St. Cloud Democrat*. "We have pledged our honor," she wrote, "that the paper we edit will discuss any subject we have in mind to discuss." The *Democrat* took up the antislavery crusade against the Lowry group. Sister Jane was in business once again.

THE LIBERTY PARTY

While Adams was fighting the gag rule, the antislavery movement split. A group of abolitionists, led by Weld and the Tappans, became dissatisfied with the movement's lack of progress. Abolitionists, they said, must seek political power.

The Democrats and the Whigs refused to oppose slavery. So the Weld-Tappan group organized a third political party—the Liberty party.

Their candidate in the presidential election of 1840 was James G. Birney. He received only 7,000 votes. But the Liberty party helped to spread the idea that Congress would someday have to face the question of slavery.

THE MOVEMENT FOR WOMEN'S RIGHTS

Many abolitionists were women. As they fought against the injustices done to black people, they began to think about their own lack of rights. Women were barred from almost all colleges and denied the chance to become doctors or lawyers. When a woman married, all her earnings and property belonged to her husband. A woman was supposed to live her life inside the circle of the home and family.

Two of the first women to step boldly outside their "sphere," or place, were Sarah and Angelina Grimké (GRIHM-kee). The Grimké sisters grew up on a South Carolina plantation and came to hate slavery. After moving to the North, they joined the abolitionist movement. There was a storm of criticism when the Grimkés spoke in public to mixed gatherings of women and men.

Elizabeth Cady Stanton and Lucretia Mott used their experience as antislavery organizers to start a movement for women's rights. In July 1848 they held the world's first women's rights conference at Seneca Falls, New York. The conference participants issued a Declaration of Sentiments, stating that "all men and women are created equal." The

Women struggled for the right to be as well educated as men. This daguerreotype was taken about 1850 at a Boston school.

Lucretia Mott urged that women be encouraged to develop all their talents so that they "may enter profitably into the active business of life."

Angelina Grimké married another fervent abolitionist, Theodore Weld. Sarah Grimké lived with the Welds until her death at 81.

Susan B. Anthony (left) took as her motto these words: "Men, their rights and nothing more; women, their rights and nothing less."

Elizabeth Cady Stanton championed the right of women to serve on juries and to be legal guardians of their own children.

Activity: Students can research and make written reports about the achievements of feminists such as Lucretia Mott, Elizabeth Cady Stanton, Susan B. Anthony, the Grimkés, Lucy Stone, and Paulina Wright Davis.

women demanded the right to own property and to control their earnings. They wanted equal opportunities in education and employment. They also demanded voting rights for women.

People working for women's rights faced fierce opposition. Newspaper editors and ministers made fun of them, and their meetings were broken up by men shouting insults. A building where Angelina Grimké spoke was burned. But there were signs that the future would be brighter. The first women's college, Mount Holyoke in Massachusetts, was a great success. A few states gave women more legal rights.

Newcomers joined the campaign for women's suffrage. In 1851 Susan B. Anthony began her life-long career as a speaker and organizer. She would guide the women's rights movement into the next century.

SECTION REVIEW   Answers will be found on page T 52.

1. Define these words: *utopias, temperance, abolitionists, emancipation.*

2. Identify: Dorothea Dix, Horace Mann, Frederick Douglass, Harriet Tubman, Sarah and Angelina Grimké.

3. What effect did the traveling preachers of the revival movement have on the American people?

4. What demand did the temperance crusaders make?

5. What was the goal of the radical abolitionists?

6. How did many northerners view the "gag rule"?

7. What rights did women demand in the Declaration of Sentiments?

CHAPTER SUMMARY

Between the elections of 1824 and 1828, the Democratic party was organized. Its leaders hoped to fight sectionalism by gaining supporters in all parts of the country. They pleased the South by favoring a weak national government. At a time when suffrage was expanding, the Democrats won votes by appealing to the common people. Andrew Jackson, defeated in 1824, led the Democrats to victory in the election of 1828.

During his first administration, Jackson strengthened his party, aided the westward movement of settlers, and took a stand against sectionalism. He relied on the spoils system to reward party loyalty. He forced the Indians east of the Mississippi to leave their homelands and to move to the Great Plains. When South Carolina nullified tariff laws passed by Congress, Jackson opposed nullification and warned that secession was treason.

Jackson's war on the national bank united his political enemies. They formed a second national political party, the Whigs. Jackson destroyed the bank at a time when state banks were flooding the nation with unsound paper money. Speculation was widespread. The Panic of 1837 and the depression that followed were blamed on the Democrats. In the election of 1840, the Whigs defeated the Democrats by using their own tactics against them. More and more people took part in politics. In the 1840 election, Americans voted in record numbers.

During the Jackson era, the revival movement inspired many Americans to work for reforms. The reformers preached temperance, improved conditions for the mentally ill, and campaigned for state-supported public schools. Radical abolitionists demanded immediate emancipation of slaves. Gradually they forced Americans to question the morality of slavery. Women in the antislavery movement also led the nation's first campaign for rights of women.

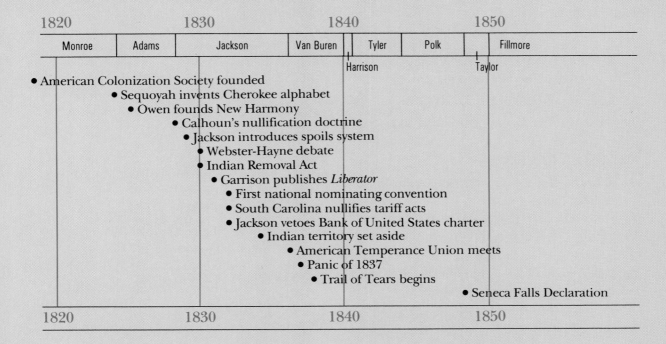

Answers will be found on page T 52.

CHAPTER SURVEY

VOCABULARY REVIEW

From this list of vocabulary words, choose the one that best matches each definition below.

(a) abolitionists   (h) sectionalism
(b) caucuses   (i) sovereign
(c) depression   (j) specie
(d) emancipation   (k) spoils system
(e) illiterate   (l) suffrage
(f) nominate   (m) temperance
(g) nullify   (n) utopia

1. a perfect community

2. giving government jobs to party workers

3. freeing someone from slavery or control

4. loyalty to one section of the country

5. unable to read

6. to name someone to run for office

7. people working to end slavery

8. to make a law null and void

9. the right to vote

10. private meetings of party workers

11. possessing supreme power

12. a severe decline in economic activity

13. little or no drinking of alcoholic beverages

14. money in the form of gold or silver coins

CHAPTER REVIEW

1. (a) In the election of 1824, where did candidates look for support?   (b) Why did southerners in Congress oppose the proposals offered by President John Quincy Adams?

2. (a) How did Martin Van Buren attempt to combat sectionalism?   (b) How did the outcome of the 1828 election show that Van Buren had achieved his goal?   (c) What two parties had become national parties by 1840?

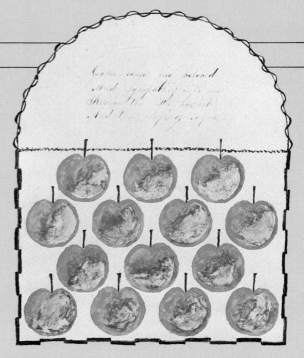

The beautiful simplicity of Shaker art can be seen in Hannah Cohoon's watercolor and ink drawing of a basket of apples.

3. (a) Why did local party workers organize parades, rallies, and barbecues?   (b) How did the Democrats and Whigs reward party loyalty?   (c) Name three ways in which the elections of 1828 and 1840 were similar.

4. Name four ways in which the Cherokee adopted the white settlers' way of life.

5. Why did the North and the South have very different views on the tariff?

6. What was the main argument in the Webster-Hayne debate?

7. (a) Why did many state banks in the West oppose the Bank of the United States? (b) How did Jackson "starve" it?

8. How did the religious revival that began around 1800 help to launch the reform movements of the Jackson era?

9. Why did Theodore Weld and Arthur and Lewis Tappan organize the Liberty party?

10. Name three goals of the early feminists.

*CT GEOGRAPHY REVIEW

Look at the map "Settlement of the United States" in the Resource Center.   (a) Between 1790 and 1820, much new settlement extended along two major rivers. What were they?   (b) Describe three main areas of new settlement between 1820 and 1850. (c) During the colonial period, settlement stopped at the Appalachian Mountains. What natural geographic barrier stopped settlement until after 1850? When was this barrier overcome?

USING THE TOOLS OF HISTORY

*CT Making Generalizations

Which statement makes the generalization that best fits the facts in Section 12–4? Why is that generalization best?
(a) Political parties played an active role in launching the reform movements.
(b) The temperance crusaders and the abolitionists formed their own separate organizations.
(c) Reformers began their campaigns to improve society on their own, without help from political parties or the government.

READING AND THINKING SKILLS

Literal and Inferential Reading

*CT 1. The following are headings from Section 12-4. Which are literal and which are inferential?
(a) A Great Awakening
(b) Utopias
(c) Temperance
(d) Care for the Neglected
(e) Public Education
(f) The Campaign Against Slavery

The Cause-Effect Pattern

*CT 2. On a piece of paper, complete this chain reaction of cause and effect.
(a) In 1837 Britain stopped buying American cotton.
(b) Cotton prices _____
(c) Land _____
(d) Cotton dealers and land speculators were unable to pay their debts.
(e) _____
(f) _____
(g) New York City banks stopped paying out gold and silver.
(h) An economic depression resulted.

Angelina Grimké and her sister Sarah were reformers who wrote in favor of the abolition of slavery and rights for women. They were criticized for stepping out of "woman's proper sphere."

CHAPTER 13	1820-1850

WESTWARD EXPANSION TO THE PACIFIC

INDEPENDENCE FOR TEXAS
TRAILS TO THE FAR WEST
MANIFEST DESTINY

13-1 INDEPENDENCE FOR TEXAS

READ TO FIND OUT

dictator: person with absolute control of a government
garrison: place where soldiers are stationed
armistice: temporary halt in fighting

—what the words *dictator, garrison,* and *armistice* mean.

—what attracted Americans to Texas.

—why Texans became unhappy with Mexico's government.

—how Texans won their independence.

—how Texas became the Lone Star Republic.

Between the Louisiana Territory and the Pacific Ocean lay two huge areas. The Oregon Country was claimed by both Britain and the United States. The other area included New Spain's northern provinces—California, New Mexico, and Texas.

In 1820 Texas was largely an unsettled wilderness. The eastern part of the territory lay on the Gulf Coastal Plain. Here well-watered lowlands offered settlers a long growing season. In the center of Texas lay the Central Plains, a region of woodlands and prairies. Much of western Texas lay on the Great Plains, where the grass grew as tall as a horse. Farther west, the plains became more and more arid. In southwestern Texas, buffalo grass gave way to sagebrush and cactus.

Clement and Sarah Dyer were listed in Stephen F. Austin's ledger as two of the 300 members of Austin's settlement in Texas.

Austin made his first settlements at Washington-on-the-Brazos and Columbus. In 1823 he chose San Felipe de Austin in what is now Austin County as the seat of government.

TEXAS FEVER

In 1820 Moses Austin, a businessman from Missouri, visited Texas and saw that it was a land of opportunity. He asked Spanish officials for permission to start an American colony there. Early in 1821 Austin received a grant of land in eastern Texas, but he died before he could organize his colony.

Moses Austin's son, Stephen F. Austin, carried out his father's plan. When he arrived with the first group of settlers, however, he learned that Texas no longer belonged to Spain. In 1821 Mexico won its independence, set up a republican government, and drew up a constitution. New Spain's northern provinces, including Texas, had become part of Mexico.

Stephen Austin asked the new government to renew the land grant. In 1823 the Mexican government agreed to the settlement of 300 families in Texas. But the government said that the settlers must become Mexican citizens and join the Catholic Church.

In 1824 Texas became part of the new state of Coahuila-Texas (kō-ah-WEE-lah), created by the Mexican government. The state government soon opened Texas to American immigration. "Texas fever" swept through the Mississippi Valley. Advertisements promised cheap, fertile land. Frontier farmers, free blacks, and cotton planters with slaves poured into Texas. The words "Gone to Texas" or simply "GTT" were scrawled on abandoned barns and cabins. By 1830 there were about 20,000 Americans in Texas. The Americans outnumbered the Mexican settlers four to one.

The Texas War for Independence 1835-1836

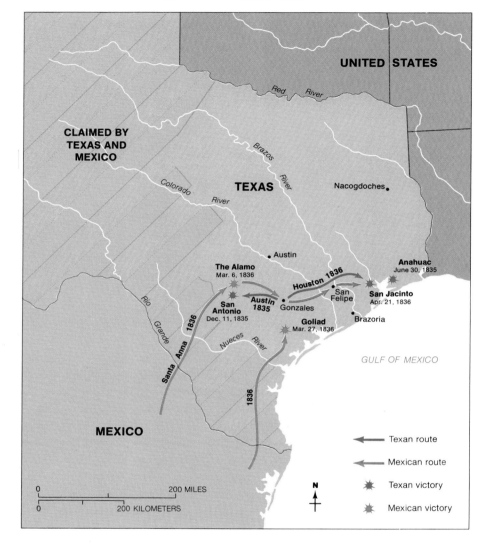

Have students locate the sites of the battles of the Alamo, Goliad, San Antonio, and San Jacinto on the map. Using the map's key, they can determine if these were Texan or Mexican victories.

The Texas War for Independence did not settle the question of Texas's boundary. Mexico said the boundary was the Nueces River. Texas claimed the Rio Grande as its boundary. Even when Texas joined the Union in 1845, the question was still undecided.

CONFLICTS WITH MEXICO

The Mexican government feared that Texas was turning into an American state. Offers from Presidents John Quincy Adams and Andrew Jackson to buy Texas added to Mexican fears. In 1830 Mexico passed a law to stop further American immigration into Texas. Troops were sent north to enforce the law, but American settlers continued to arrive.

As Mexico moved to tighten its control over Texas, tensions between Mexico and the American settlers increased. The Texans did not want to become Catholic. Texas slaveholders were concerned about anti-slavery laws passed by the Mexican government. These conflicts might be settled, Americans believed, if they had more control over their own affairs. They sent Stephen F. Austin to Mexico City to ask that Texas become a separate state within Mexico.

Events in Mexico, however, were not favorable to the Americans. In 1834 General Antonio López de Santa Anna, the president of Mexico, made himself **dictator.** He took absolute control of the government. Santa Anna then moved to tighten Mexico's control over Texas.

THE TEXAS REVOLUTION

In June 1835 a small incident at the port of Anahuac (AN-ah-hwak) began the chain of events that led to the Texas revolution. To protest export taxes, a Texan named Andrew Briscoe filled a box with sawdust and marked it for export. His friends roared with laughter as the customs officer pawed through the sawdust looking for something to tax.

Briscoe was arrested. He was freed by a young lawyer named William Barret Travis. Travis led 25 Texans in an attack on the Anahuac **garrison**—the place where the Mexican soldiers were stationed. The firing of a single cannon ball persuaded the Mexican troops to surrender.

An uneasy peace returned. Then in October 1835, Santa Anna sent Mexican troops to Gonzales to capture the town's lone cannon. Local farmers grabbed their rifles and drove off the soldiers. To Texans, the defense of Gonzales seemed like Lexington and Concord all over again. Even so, Texas leaders were not yet ready to declare independence. They swore loyalty to the government of Mexico but not to Santa Anna.

From Gonzales, Stephen F. Austin led a ragged army to San Antonio, where the main force of Mexican troops was stationed. The Texans surrounded the town and forced the Mexican soldiers to surrender.

With the capture of San Antonio, most Texans thought the war was over. But not Sam Houston. When he took command of the Texas forces, he sent out a call for volunteers. At first, few Texans answered his call. Then, in February 1836, Santa Anna marched more than 5,000 troops toward San Antonio.

Santa Anna's invasion convinced Texans that they could never reach agreement with the dictator. On March 2, representatives meeting in San Felipe declared Texas independent. They drew up a Declaration of Independence and a new constitution. David Burnet, an American, was elected President of the new Republic of Texas. Lorenzo de Zavala, a Mexican, was elected Vice-President.

THE ALAMO AND GOLIAD

Independence had not yet been declared when Santa Anna and his forces reached San Antonio on February 23. There were fewer than 200 Texans in the town. They included William Barret Travis, Texas-born

Santa Anna had many reversals of fortune. After his defeat by the Texans, he was ousted by the Mexicans. But from 1841 to 1844 he once again served as Mexico's president. In 1844, after a revolt, he fled to Jamaica. During the Mexican War, however, he commanded the Mexican army, again suffering military defeat. (See page 339.) In 1853 he became president again but within two years was overthrown and exiled. He returned to Mexico in 1874 and died two years later.

This portrait of Lorenzo de Zavala was copied from one painted on ivory in 1833.

On March 2 Texas celebrates its Independence Day. On April 21 it celebrates San Jacinto Day. (See page 326.)

Captain Juan Seguin, one of the Alamo's defenders, was sent through enemy lines to get reinforcements. Thus he survived to fight at Sam Houston's side at the Battle of San Jacinto.

William Barret Travis was the Alamo's commander. In a plea for help, he declared, "I shall never surrender or retreat. . . . I am determined to . . . die like a soldier who never forgets what is due to his own honor and that of his country."

Susannah Dickerson's husband died at the Alamo. Santa Anna spared her so she could carry the news of the massacre as a warning.

Juan Seguin (say-GEEN), Jim Bowie, and Davy Crockett, a pathfinder and former member of Congress from Tennessee. Sam Houston ordered the Texans to pull out of the town. They refused. There would be no stopping Santa Anna, they said, unless his troops could be delayed in San Antonio. Led by Travis and Bowie, the Texans made their heroic stand in an old mission called the Alamo.

For days Santa Anna's cannon pounded the walls of the Alamo. Travis sent message after message asking for help from Texans and from all Americans. Help could not come in time, however. On March 6 the Mexicans braved the Texans' deadly rifle fire and overran the mission. In the bloody hand-to-hand fighting, Santa Anna took no prisoners. Even men lying in hospital beds, too sick to fight, were killed. But it was a costly victory for Santa Anna, who lost as many as 1,500 soldiers.

The Texans suffered a second defeat a few days later. Near Goliad (GŌ-lee-ad) a force of 400 Texas volunteers was forced to surrender to a second Mexican army. A week later Santa Anna ordered that all prisoners be killed. Only a few Texans, some of them hidden by Mexican women who took pity on them, escaped death.

VICTORY AT SAN JACINTO

Houston wanted to avoid battle until he had a chance of winning. For weeks he retreated, first across the Colorado River and then across the Brazos. While he pulled back, his small army swelled into a force of 800 eager fighters. Many of the volunteers were new arrivals from the United States.

Houston decided to attack when he learned that Santa Anna was camped near the San Jacinto (juh-SIN-tō) River with only 1,250 soldiers. On April 21 Santa Anna's troops were enjoying an afternoon rest. While they slept, the Texans moved silently toward their camp "with the stillness of death."

Suddenly the peace was shattered. The air rang with the roar of cannon and shouts of "Remember the Alamo!" and "Remember Goliad!" When the fighting ended only 18 minutes later, all of Santa Anna's troops were either dead or captured. The next day, Santa Anna himself was taken prisoner.

Despite cries of "Hang him!" from the Texans, Sam Houston protected the defeated Mexican general. Santa Anna signed a treaty agreeing to an **armistice,** or temporary halt in the fighting. The general also ordered all Mexican troops out of Texas and signed a second treaty recognizing Texas independence. The Rio Grande was set as the boundary between Texas and Mexico. The Mexican Congress refused to accept either treaty. To Mexicans, Texas was still part of Mexico. For years, Texas and Mexico would continue to clash over boundaries.

Activity: Students can write biographies of such other notable Texans as Stephen F. Austin, William Barret Travis, David Burnet, and J. Pinckney Henderson (Texas's first state governor).

★ ★ ★ ★ ★ ★ ★ **AMERICAN VALUES IN ACTION** ★ ★ ★ ★ ★ ★ ★ ★

SAM HOUSTON

March 2, 1836, was a historic day for Texas. That day Texans declared their independence from Mexico. It was also Sam Houston's forty-third birthday.

Houston was born in Virginia and had served as governor of Tennessee. But he found his destiny in Texas—"the finest portion of the globe that has ever blessed my vision."

Houston and Texas were well matched: big, bold, the stuff of legends. From his jangling spurs to the feather in his wide-brimmed beaver hat, Houston looked like a frontier hero.

General Sam Houston led the Texan army to victory in the battle for independence. Grateful Texans elected him President of the new Lone Star Republic.

The President's office was a two-room building. Houston worked in one room and slept in the other. The infant republic looked as unpromising as its executive office. Skirmishes between Texans and Mexicans continued, and Indian troubles were brewing. There was a huge war debt and no money to pay it.

Houston strode into action. He smoothed relations with Mexico and the Indians. He raised revenue by taxing imported goods. When money problems continued, he slashed the government payroll and cut his own salary in half. At his second-term inauguration, he wore a homespun shirt and buckskin pants to stress the need for economy.

Houston also worked to get foreign nations to recognize Texas as an independent nation. One day a French diplomat appeared to look over both Texas and Houston. The diplomat's coat was studded with medals. Houston took off his own shirt, displaying his battle scars. "A humble republican soldier, who wears his decorations here, salutes you," Houston declared. In 1839 France recognized the young republic.

Still, the republic's future looked shaky. Like many Texans, Houston felt that its best hope was to become part of the United States. As skillfully as he had managed the war for independence, he steered Texas and the United States together. He insisted that Texas join the Union on terms "beneficial to both countries."

On December 29, 1845, Texas became the twenty-eighth American state. Houston had proudly served Texas as military commander and President. He would serve the new state as a Senator in Washington.

On the day that Texas celebrated its statehood, Houston took no part in the formal ceremonies. He watched, pleased but silent. Then, as the flag of the Republic was lowered for the last time, Sam Houston stepped forward and caught it in his arms.

THE LONE STAR REPUBLIC

In September 1836 Texans approved the constitution that had been drawn up in March. They elected Sam Houston President of the Republic of Texas—the Lone Star Republic.

Texas adopted the lone star flag in 1839. The colors stand for loyalty, strength, and bravery.

Texas's capitol in Austin in the 1840s was a simple wooden building. The present capitol resembles the United States Capitol.

Most Texans did not want to remain independent. They wanted to join the United States. Fearing war with Mexico, President Jackson opposed adding Texas to the Union. Many northerners agreed with Jackson's stand, fearing that the territory of Texas would be divided into several slave states. Thus the balance in the Senate between slave and free states would be upset. For ten years Texas remained an independent republic.

During this time, the Lone Star Republic continued to attract American settlers. Every year Texas planters sent more bales of cotton to the port of Galveston than the year before. And Texas ranchers began rounding up the wild, long-horned cattle first brought to the area by Spanish settlers. They bred these tough range cattle with beefier stock from the United States and created a new cattle industry. Building on the cattle ranching skills of Mexican vaqueros (vah-KEHR-ōs), Texans became America's first cowboys.

For discussion: All Americans take pride in being citizens of particular states. Why are Texans so proud of being Texans?

SECTION REVIEW   Answers will be found on page T 53.

1. Define these words: *dictator, garrison, armistice.*

2. Identify: Stephen F. Austin, Antonio López de Santa Anna, William Barret Travis, Sam Houston, Lone Star Republic.

3. What attracted Americans to Texas?

4. Give three reasons why Texans were unhappy with the government of Mexico.

5. What event led Texans to declare independence?

6. What happened to the defenders of the Alamo?

7. What two concerns kept Texas from becoming part of the United States in 1836?

13-2 TRAILS TO THE FAR WEST

READ TO FIND OUT

—what the word *irrigate* means.

—why traders opened the Santa Fe Trail.

—how mountain men and missionaries encouraged settlement in Oregon.

—why pioneers traveled to California.

—why Mormons settled in the Great Basin.

irrigate: supply with water

For fifty years the American frontier moved steadily westward. Then, in the late 1830s, it stopped at the edge of the Great Plains. Pioneers believed that the grassy plains were too dry for farming. They turned their attention to the lush, green valleys of the Pacific region. Loading their farm tools and household belongings into covered wagons, a few brave families set out for the Far West.

On a map, the Pacific Coast region resembles a giant letter H. The first long line of the H is formed by the Coast Range. This range rises upward from the Pacific shoreline. The second long line is marked by the Cascade Range to the north and the Sierra Nevada to the south. The cross line of the H follows the Klamath Mountains. Inside the arms of the H lie three large fertile valleys—the Willamette (will-LAM-et), the Sacramento, and the San Joaquin (wah-KEEN). To reach these valleys, pioneers followed trails first traveled by trappers and traders.

THE SANTA FE TRAIL

Once Mexico became independent in 1821, frontier traders began making yearly journeys in wagons from Independence, Missouri, to the Mexican outpost of Santa Fe. Their route, the Santa Fe Trail, crossed 800 miles (1,287 kilometers) of flat plains. They traveled the Santa Fe Trail in covered wagons with white canvas tops that looked like sails from a distance. This earned the wagons the name "prairie schooners."

In Santa Fe, traders exchanged their stock of cloth, tools, and firearms for Mexican silver and furs. Soon trade was extended to the Pacific coast. After leaving Santa Fe, the Old Spanish Trail to California made a wide detour northward to avoid the impassable canyons of the Colorado Plateau. It then headed southwest to Los Angeles. The Gila River Trail skirted the southern edge of the plateau to end in San Diego.

James Beckwourth was a trapper, an army scout, and a rancher. He told the story of his life in *Life and Adventures of James Beckwourth.*

Trails to the Far West

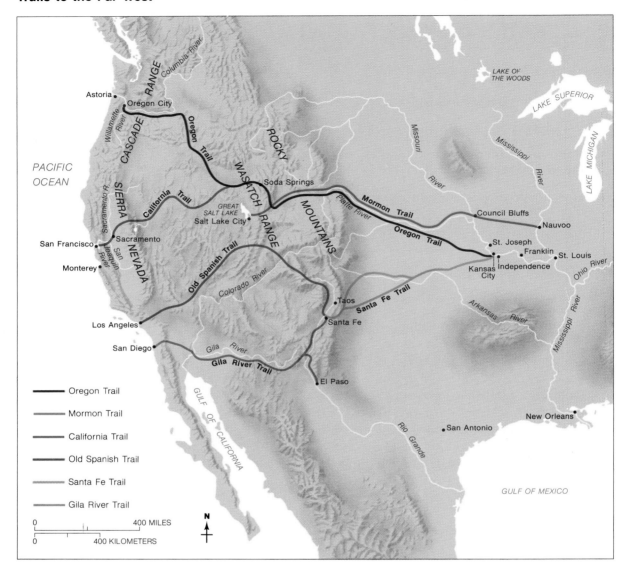

Legend:
- Oregon Trail
- Mormon Trail
- California Trail
- Old Spanish Trail
- Santa Fe Trail
- Gila River Trail

0   400 MILES
0   400 KILOMETERS

N

Spanish missionaries, followed by American fur trappers, blazed the Old Spanish Trail and the Gila River Trail. Later emigrants followed these routes.

THE OREGON TRAIL

The most important route west was first explored by mountain men—trappers and fur traders. In their search for beaver fur, mountain men like Jedediah Smith, Jim Bridger, and James Beckwourth explored the Rocky Mountains and the Sierra Nevada. They discovered hidden mountain valleys, steaming geysers, breathtaking peaks, and a great salty inland sea.

In the 1820s the mountain men crossed the Continental Divide. The divide is the ridge that separates rivers that drain toward the Gulf of Mexico and the Atlantic Ocean from rivers flowing toward the Pacific

F. R. Bennett's painting "Dance on the Sequoia Stump" conveys the size and majesty of the giant sequoias of America's Northwest.

This sketch of Narcissa Whitman was made after her death.

Activity: Students can make oral or written reports on Narcissa Whitman. The reports might include excerpts from her letters.

Ocean. The mountain men found a pass with gentle slopes on either side of the divide. The discovery—South Pass—made wagon travel through the Rockies possible.

By 1830 trappers and traders had explored the Oregon Trail, a route through the Rockies to Oregon's Willamette Valley. The mountain men then guided missionaries who wanted to bring the Christian faith to the Oregon Indians. In 1836 missionaries Marcus and Narcissa Whitman, along with Eliza and Henry Spalding, spent their honeymoon on the Oregon Trail. Narcissa Whitman and Eliza Spalding became the first pioneer women to cross the continent to Oregon.

Traders and missionaries sent home reports of "a pioneer's paradise" in the Willamette Valley. In 1841 the first train of covered wagons to travel the Oregon Trail left Independence, Missouri. Many Oregon Trail pioneers did not survive the six-month journey. Tabitha Brown, who traveled to Oregon at age sixty-six, did more than survive. She started a school for children who had lost their parents on the trip west.

In 1843 the Americans in Oregon formed their own government. They drew up a constitution and a bill of rights. Religious freedom was protected, and slavery outlawed. The settlers also asked Congress to make Oregon a territory of the United States.

UNDERSTANDING GEOGRAPHY

BEYOND THE 100TH MERIDIAN

The 100th meridian, 100° west longitude, slices through the center of the Interior Plains. It cuts through the heart of North Dakota, South Dakota, and Nebraska. Kansas, Oklahoma, and Texas are also split by this line 100° to the west of the prime meridian.

The 100th meridian, however, is much more than a line of longitude. It divides the Interior Plains into two distinct regions. The eastern region, the Central Plains, stretches from the 100th meridian to the Appalachians. The western region, the Great Plains, extends from this line to the Rockies. Each region presented settlers with dramatically different landscapes.

Climate, vegetation, and elevation above sea level are different in the Central Plains and the Great Plains. Of course, climate, vegetation, and elevation do not suddenly change at the 100th meridian. The change is gradual, but it is significant.

The most important difference is in rainfall patterns. The 20-inch (51-centimeter) rainfall line closely follows the 100th meridian. This line divides the plains region into two rainfall areas. East of this rainfall line, most places get more than 20 inches a year. West of the line, most places get less than 20 inches.

The rainfall line also marks changes in vegetation. Trees usually require more than 20 inches of rain a year. Grass can grow with as little as 10 inches. So forested land is found east of the line, and grassland to the west. On the Great Plains, trees are found only along river banks where more water is available or where people have planted and watered them.

Even today, travelers crossing the 100th meridian are struck by the change in landscape. The woodlands of the Central Plains seem closed-in and cozy. On the Great Plains travelers feel as if they can see forever.

Look at the "Physical Map of the United States" in the Resource Center. Find the line where the green and yellow-green areas of the Interior Plains meet. This is a contour line, which connects points that have the same elevation. All the points on this line are at 1,500 feet (500 meters).

The 1,500-foot contour line roughly parallels the 100th meridian. Places east of the line are below 1,500 feet. West of the 1,500-foot contour line, the land gradually rises until it reaches 7,000 feet (2,000 meters) at the base of the Rocky Mountains. Over approximately 400 miles (640 kilometers), the land rises more than a mile in elevation.

People who settled the Interior Plains formed different settlement patterns east and west of the 100th meridian. East of the line there was sufficient rainfall for settlers to grow corn and wheat. But when pioneers first traveled across the 100th meridian, they thought that the land was too dry for farming. Indeed, they called the region the "Great American Desert." Later settlers would learn special farming techniques to grow crops on the arid plains. And they would find that the grassland, where buffalo grazed, was ideal for other grazing animals—cattle.

The 100th meridian is a precise geographic line. It is also a boundary of sorts, which sets off distinctly western and eastern areas of the United States.

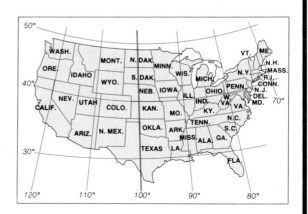

THE CALIFORNIA TRAIL

In 1836 John Marsh, a trader from Independence, Missouri, took the Gila River Trail to California. He settled down to raise cattle in the San Joaquin Valley. Soon Marsh was writing letters home. When Missouri newspapers printed his letters, farmers read his description of "the finest country for wheat I have ever seen." That was enough for a few hardy pioneers. The first wagon train traveling to Oregon in 1841 included a party bound for California.

Led by John Bidwell and John Bartleson, the California pioneers included one woman, eighteen-year-old Nancy Kelsey. She was traveling with her husband and baby daughter. The pioneers left the Oregon Trail at Soda Springs, crossed the Wasatch Range, and dropped down into the Great Basin. There, Bidwell wrote, "We could see nothing before us but extensive arid plains, glimmering with heat and salt." During the desert crossing, the travelers abandoned their heavy wagons. By the time the weary pioneers reached the Sierra Nevada, they had killed their oxen for food.

Crossing the Sierra was an even greater challenge than the dry Basin. It seemed to Bidwell that "only a bird could get through" the maze of forests and canyons. Often the pioneers had to travel on foot. Blisters forced Nancy Kelsey to walk barefoot, carrying her child while leading her horse down rocky hillsides. The ordeal ended when they reached California's Central Valley. The Bidwell-Bartleson party opened the California Trail to American settlers.

Activity: Students can find anthologies containing excerpts from the diaries, letters, and memoirs of pioneer women and read passages to the class.

THE MORMON TRAIL

The first settlers in the Great Basin were Mormons. They were followers of Joseph Smith. Smith had founded the Church of Jesus Christ of Latter-Day Saints in New York. The Mormons left New York in the 1830s because of hostility from their neighbors.

The Mormons settled first in Ohio, then in Missouri, and finally in Nauvoo, Illinois. Each time, non-Mormons forced them to leave. One reason for hostility to the Mormons was their practice of polygamy, or having more than one wife at a time. In 1844 an angry mob in Nauvoo killed Joseph Smith. Brigham Young took over the leadership of the Mormons. He asked them to move once again, to the wilderness near the Great Salt Lake in present-day Utah.

In April 1847 the first wagon train of Mormons set out from Nauvoo. Like settlers bound for Oregon, they followed the Platte River to South Pass. To avoid conflict, however, they made their own trail along the northern bank of the river. From South Pass the Mormons traveled south through the rugged Wasatch Mountains. Coming out of the hills,

Mormons camped on the Missouri River prepare to go still farther west to find a place where they can worship as they choose.

they found "a broad and barren plain hemmed in by mountains, blistering in the burning rays of the midsummer sun."

Under Young's leadership, the Mormons built a thriving farming community in the desert. They dammed mountain streams and dug ditches so that fields could be **irrigated,** or supplied with water. Workshops, mills, and factories were built.

In 1848 the Mormons set up a representative government, with its capital in Salt Lake City. The religious freedom of both Mormons and other Christians was protected. In 1849 the Mormons asked that Congress make the area a state. Instead, in 1850, Congress made it a territory of the United States called the Utah Territory.

On January 4, 1896, Utah was admitted as a state of the Union.

SECTION REVIEW   Answers will be found on page T 53.

1. Define this word: *irrigate.*

2. Identify: mountain men, Continental Divide, South Pass, Narcissa Whitman and Eliza Spalding, Joseph Smith, Brigham Young.

3. What did Missouri traders bring back from Santa Fe?

4. Who first explored the Oregon Trail?

5. Why did pioneers travel to Oregon?

6. Why was the journey of the Bidwell-Bartleson party important?

7. Why did the Mormons leave Illinois?

13–3 MANIFEST DESTINY

READ TO FIND OUT

—what the words *expansionists, manifest destiny, annex,* and *vigilante committees* mean.

—how Texas and Oregon became part of the United States.

—how James K. Polk tried to acquire California without going to war.

—how the Mexican War began.

—who led the Americans to victory.

—what the United States gained in the Treaty of Guadalupe-Hidalgo.

—how the gold rush affected life in California.

—why the United States made the Gadsden Purchase.

expansionists: people who believe a nation should continue to expand its boundaries
manifest destiny: belief that the United States was destined to expand across the continent
annex: add
vigilante committees: groups that took the law into their own hands

The westward movement of pioneers created new interest in the Far West, especially among **expansionists.** Expansionists believed that the United States should continue to expand its boundaries. Newspaper editor John O'Sullivan wrote that it was America's "manifest [clear] destiny to overspread and to possess the whole of the continent."

Mexico and Great Britain claimed the lands to the west. Believers in **manifest destiny,** however, were certain that the nation was destined, or fated, to expand. Americans would spread liberty and democracy across the continent.

THE WEBSTER-ASHBURTON TREATY

President John Tyler was a strong expansionist. In 1842 he ended a dispute with Britain over the boundary between Maine and Canada. Secretary of State Daniel Webster and Britain's Lord Ashburton agreed on a line giving Maine a little more than half of the disputed territory. The Webster-Ashburton Treaty also set a final boundary between the United States and Canada from Lake Superior to Lake of the Woods.

ANNEXATION OF TEXAS

Next Tyler tried to **annex,** or add, Texas to the United States. In April 1844 the President sent an annexation treaty to the Senate. The treaty, however, faced stiff opposition. Some Americans feared war with

Rancher José Antonio Navarro fought for Texas independence. In 1845 he was the only Texas-born delegate to the convention that approved Texas entering the Union.

In 1840 a French visitor to San Antonio, Texas, painted these dancing couples.

Mexico. Free states did not want to admit another slaveholding state to the Union. Tyler's own party, the Whigs, opposed expansion.

The mood of Congress changed when the Democratic candidate, James K. Polk, won the presidential election of 1844. Polk and the Democrats were expansionists, who strongly supported the annexation of Texas. Shortly before Polk took office, in early 1845, both houses of Congress voted to admit Texas to the Union.

THE OREGON TREATY

Polk had campaigned in favor of annexing all of Oregon up to the boundary line of Russian Alaska at 54°40′. Expansionists cheered, shouting "Fifty-four forty or fight!" and "All of Oregon or None!"

Once in office, Polk settled for half of Oregon rather than risk war with Britain. In June 1846 both nations agreed to divide Oregon at the 49th parallel. The 1846 Oregon Treaty extended the Canadian-American boundary set by the Convention of 1818 westward from the Rocky Mountains to the Pacific Ocean.

CALIFORNIA

Polk also hoped to acquire California from Mexico. Otherwise, California might fall into the hands of the British. To prevent a British take-over, Polk reminded Britain of the Monroe Doctrine. He warned that "no future European colony" would be allowed "on any part of the North American continent."

Polk intended to buy California from Mexico. But if the Mexicans refused to sell their province, there might be other ways to acquire it. Polk ordered the navy's Pacific Squadron, under the command of Commodore John O. Sloat, to sail north from Mexico if war broke out between Mexico and the United States. Sloat's mission was to seize San Francisco. The President also sent John C. Frémont, an army surveyor and explorer, to survey a route to the Pacific coast. Early in 1846 Frémont arrived in California with a small force of soldiers.

WAR WITH MEXICO

The annexation of Texas angered Mexico. Mexicans felt that a part of their country had been stolen. Nevertheless, in November 1845, Polk sent Senator John Slidell of Louisiana to Mexico City. He told Slidell to offer the Mexican government $25 million for California and $5 million for New Mexico.

Polk also asked Slidell to settle the boundary between Mexico and Texas. Mexico claimed that the border was the Nueces (noo-AY-sess) River. The United States claimed it was the Rio Grande. The Mexicans refused to see Slidell.

When Slidell reported his difficulties to Polk, the President was furious. He ordered General Zachary Taylor, who commanded a force of American troops at Corpus Christi on the Nueces River, to march to the Rio Grande. On April 24, 1846, Mexican soldiers crossed the Rio Grande and attacked a small group of Taylor's troops.

Polk reacted with a call for war. He declared that Mexican troops had "shed American blood upon American soil." On May 13, 1846, Congress declared war against Mexico. Not all Americans, however, supported "Jimmy Polk's war." Abolitionists saw in it a plot to bring more slave territory into the Union. Whigs, including Abraham Lincoln of Illinois, a

*CT

Activity: Students can hold an informal debate on whether the United States had just cause to declare war on Mexico or whether the stated cause was merely a pretext for expansionism.

In 1842, four years before the Mexican War, an American naval officer invaded Monterey in Mexican California. Henry Myers, an American naval gunner, wrote a letter to a friend telling about and showing the invasion.

The Mexican War 1846-1848

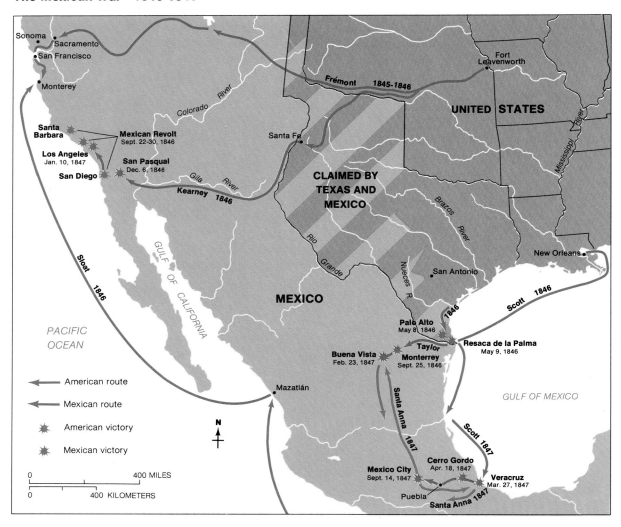

Mexico won no major battles in the Mexican War. But Mexican Californians retook garrisons at Santa Barbara, Los Angeles, and San Diego. It took United States forces three months to regain these garrisons.

member of the House of Representatives, questioned whether American troops had been attacked on American soil. Both Mexico and the United States, Lincoln reminded Congress, claimed this area.

WAR IN NORTHERN MEXICO

Polk planned a three-part strategy for defeating Mexico. An American force would invade northern Mexico from Texas. A second army would head for New Mexico and California. A third force would sail to southern Mexico and march inland to capture Mexico City.

The commander of the northern army was General Zachary Taylor, a veteran of the War of 1812 and Indian wars. Because he often appeared in shirt sleeves, his troops called him "Old Rough and Ready." He lived up to his name by striking against the Mexican forces at once. In battles at Palo Alto and Resaca de la Palma, he drove the Mexican army back across the Rio Grande.

By September 1846 Taylor had reached Monterrey. He took the city in three days. Santa Anna then marched north with fresh troops. The two armies met at Buena Vista in February 1847. The Mexicans out-numbered the Americans three to one, but the Americans had the better position and made deadly use of their artillery. After suffering heavy losses, Santa Anna retreated. The war in the north of Mexico was over.

WAR IN THE FAR WEST

In July 1846 the 1,658 new recruits who made up the American Army of the West began the long march from Kansas to the Pacific. Their leader, Colonel Stephen Watts Kearny, had orders to conquer New Mexico and California. On August 18 the army marched unopposed into Santa Fe and claimed New Mexico as a territory of the United States.

From there, Kearny took the Gila River Trail to California. Along the way he learned that Americans in California had staged a revolt. The rebels had declared California to be an independent republic. Over their capital at Sonoma, they raised a flag decorated with a red star and a grizzly bear.

The Bear Flag Republic lasted only a month. In July 1846 the Pacific Squadron captured Monterey Harbor and San Francisco Bay. Commodore Sloat announced that "henceforth California will be a portion of the United States." The Mexicans in southern California rebelled against American rule. They captured garrisons at Santa Barbara, Los Angeles, and San Diego and set up their own government.

Colonel Kearny arrived in California in early December. His Army of the West had shrunk to 100 half-naked, trail-weary troops. Still they were able to join the Pacific Squadron to defeat the Mexican forces at Los Angeles. This ended the war in the Far West.

The flag with red star and grizzly bear remains as the state flag of California.

THE FALL OF MEXICO CITY

While Kearny was fighting in California, Winfield Scott, the commanding general of the United States Army, was sailing south along the east coast of Mexico. His fleet of 100 ships carried more than 12,000 troops as well as horses and equipment. Scott landed his army near the heavily defended town of Veracruz. He took the city and marched inland toward Cerro Gordo, where Santa Anna was waiting. In April 1847 Santa Anna was forced back to Mexico City.

The American attack on Mexico City lasted a week. Mexican troops fought fiercely in defense of their capital. In the very last battle, at

Winfield Scott, born in Petersburg, Virginia, gave up a law career to join the army in 1808. By 1814 he was a brigadier general and national hero and soon after was promoted to major general. (In 1844 he became lieutenant general.) Scott ran for President in 1852 but was defeated by Franklin Pierce. (See pages 365–366.)

Chapultepec Castle, military cadets as young as twelve years old joined in the fighting. "Los niños" (the boys) knew that the war was lost. In their final stand, however, they chose death over dishonor.

THE TREATY OF GUADALUPE-HIDALGO

Students can write two paragraphs, each expressing a different point of view. The first can express the view of an American expansionist, and the second the view of a Mexican living in a territory now a part of the United States.

A peace treaty was signed on February 2, 1848, at Guadalupe-Hidalgo (GWAH-dah-LOO-pay ee-DAHL-goh), near Mexico City. Mexico recognized Texas as an American state. The Rio Grande was established as the border between the United States and Mexico.

In addition, Mexico ceded, or gave up, one third of its territory to the United States. This included California, Nevada, Utah, and Arizona and parts of Colorado, Wyoming, and New Mexico. For this area, Mexico received $15 million. Mexicans living in these lands were assured that they would have all the rights of American citizens.

American expansionists were delighted at the outcome of the war. But Mexicans living in the new American territories were deeply concerned. The country first settled by their ancestors—Indian and Spanish—had become "a strange land."

CALIFORNIA HERE I COME

This 1851 print shows San Francisco and its bay full of deserted ships. People from many lands flocked to California to seek gold.

"GOLD! GOLD! GOLD IN CALIFORNIA" shouted newspaper headlines in 1848. James Marshall had found gold while building a sawmill for John Augustus Sutter along the American River. As word of Marshall's discovery spread, Californians left their homes and rushed to the Sierra foothills to look for gold.

From all parts of the world—North and South America, Asia, Australia, and Europe—gold seekers poured into San Francisco Bay. Burning with gold fever, sailors jumped ship and took off for the gold fields. By 1850 more than 500 ghost ships were rotting in the bay. The sleepy village of San Francisco became a boom town. Eggs sold for $6 a dozen, and a miner paid $10 a night for a bunk.

Americans who could afford the best sailed to California on a sleek clipper ship. The more direct and cheaper route was overland. In 1849 more than 22,500 gold seekers headed west from Missouri on the Oregon and California trails. These "forty-niners" expected to return home rich in just a year or two.

Finding gold and separating it from worthless rocks and dirt was much harder work than any of them had imagined. Still, fortunes were made digging gold. And even greater fortunes were made mining the miners. Merchants and saloon keepers found that it was more profitable to extract gold from a miner's pocket than from a Sierra hillside. Levi Straus made a fortune by sewing tent canvas into sturdy pants for gold seekers. San Francisco women who called themselves "Clothing Refreshers" charged miners $1.50 to wash and iron a shirt.

LAW AND ORDER

When the gold rush began, California did not have even a territorial government. Life in the gold camps was often dangerous. Robberies and murder were not uncommon. To protect themselves, miners

Activity: Students can research the California gold rush. They can then assume they themselves have come to California seeking gold and write letters back home about their experiences.

Chinese miners were among the thousands who sought wealth in the California gold fields.

USING THE TOOLS OF HISTORY

IDENTIFYING POLITICAL CHANGES ON MAPS

Most physical features of the land do not change much over time. A relief map showing those features a few hundred years ago would look much the same as one made today.

The political features shown on a map, however, may not remain the same. New areas are added to a nation. Territories become states. Boundaries between nations shift.

By comparing political maps made in different years, we can easily see how an area changes politically over time. The maps on pages 261 and 343 illustrate such changes. Notice that the scale and physical features like rivers, lakes, and the coastline are the same on both maps.

One major change is in the boundaries between the United States and its neighbors. Another is the number of states and territories on each map. These changes are reflected in the legends on both maps.

Use both maps to answer the following questions.

1. Are the same symbols used on each map? Do they mean the same things?

2. On the 1822 map, what states and territories lie within the boundaries of the Louisiana Purchase? What new states and territories are in the same area on the 1848 map?

3. Compare the Canadian-American boundary line on the 1822 map with the line on the 1848 map. What changes occurred?

4. Describe the changes that took place along the southern border of the United States between 1822 and 1853.

5. How many new states had been created between 1822 and 1848?

6. How was the Oregon Territory different in 1848 compared to 1822?

Answers will be found on page T 53.

Vigilante is Spanish for "watchman." The vigilante committee was also known as a vigilance committee, suggesting people on the alert for outbreaks of lawless behavior.

For discussion: How might vigilante committees, intended to uphold the law, be themselves a force for lawlessness?

formed **vigilante** (vɪj-ih-LAN-tee) **committees,** groups that took the law into their own hands. People suspected of committing crimes were rounded up and hanged without a legal trial.

In this lawless climate, people often looked at each other with suspicion. New Englanders regarded southerners as quarrelsome, and southerners said that Yankees were cold and stingy. Chinese immigrants were especially unwelcome in the gold camps. Violence against Chinese miners was widespread. Mexicans had brought to California much of the technology used in gold mining. Yet they, too, were treated badly. By the time law and order arrived in the mining camps, there were few Mexicans and Chinese left in the gold fields.

Law and order improved after Californians organized a territorial government in 1849. The first California constitution created a representative government for Californians. Like the Texas constitution, it also preserved several principles of Spanish law.

For women, the most important of these was community property. According to this principle, all property obtained during a marriage is community property, or property held jointly by a husband and wife. Each partner in the marriage has an equal right to that property. In

The United States in 1848

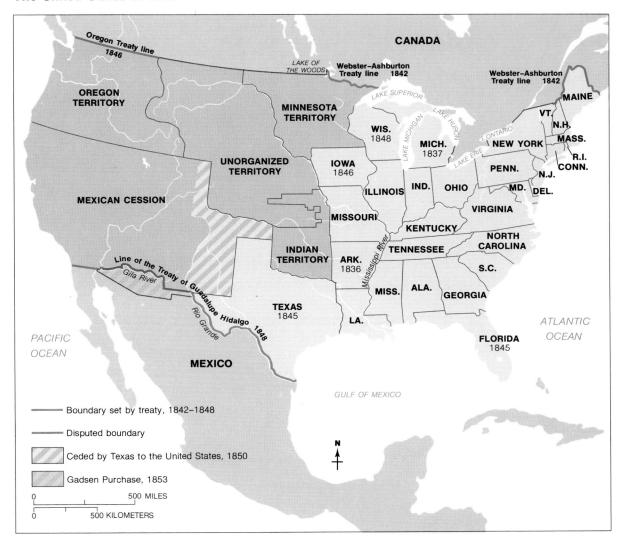

most states in the 1800s, a married woman had no property rights. All property, including money that women earned themselves, belonged entirely to their husbands.

Have students locate the Gadsden Purchase on the map.

THE GADSDEN PURCHASE

With California growing so rapidly, railroad builders began to dream of running tracks across the continent. In 1853 government surveyors discovered that a southern route following the Gila River Trail would take a railroad into Mexican territory.

James Gadsden, the United States minister to Mexico, negotiated a treaty with Santa Anna. The United States bought a 45,000-square-mile

In 1861, Congress asked Emanuel Leutze to paint this mural in the west stairway of the Capitol. Called "Westward the Course of Empire Takes its Way," the painting shows the expansionist feeling of the 1800s.

For discussion: Why might the events related in this chapter encourage Americans' belief in manifest destiny?

(116,550-square-kilometer) strip south of the Gila River for $10 million. The purchase set the southwestern boundary of the United States at the present southern borders of New Mexico and Arizona.

With the Gadsden Purchase, many expansionists believed that the United States had fulfilled its "manifest destiny." The nation reached "from sea to shining sea."

SECTION REVIEW   Answers will be found on page T 54.

1. Define these words: *expansionist, manifest destiny, annex, vigilante committees.*

2. Identify: Webster-Ashburton Treaty, Oregon Treaty, Bear Flag Republic, gold rush, forty-niners, Gadsden Purchase.

3. What event persuaded Congress to annex Texas?

4. Why did Polk send John Slidell to Mexico City?

5. Give two reasons why many Americans opposed the Mexican War.

6. What part did each of these people play in the Mexican War: Zachary Taylor, Stephen Watts Kearny, Winfield Scott?

7. What did the United States gain from Mexico in the Treaty of Guadalupe-Hidalgo?

8. During the gold rush, what happened to law and order in California?

9. Why did law and order improve in 1849?

10. Why did the United States make the Gadsden Purchase?

CHAPTER SUMMARY

In the 1820s American settlers began to emigrate to Texas. In a few years conflicts arose between Americans in Texas and the Mexican government. The issues involved included slavery and future immigration. When Santa Anna became dictator of Mexico, Texans rebelled. By defeating Santa Anna at the Battle of San Jacinto in 1836, Texans won their independence and formed a republic.

By the late 1830s, the farming frontier had stopped at the edge of the Great Plains. Traders and trappers were the first Americans to explore trails across the Great Plains to the Rocky Mountains and beyond. Their glowing reports about the fertile valleys of the Pacific Coast region interested restless pioneers.

Farmers packed their families into covered wagons and headed west on the Oregon and California trails. Mormons traveled west, too, settling in the Great Basin, where they hoped to live in peace.

As Americans moved westward, the belief grew that it was the "manifest destiny" of the United States to spread across the North American continent. In 1845 Texas was annexed to the United States. The following year the southern part of Oregon became American territory. President Polk also hoped to buy California from Mexico.

In 1846 a border clash near the Rio Grande led to war between the United States and Mexico. The conflict ended when the American army under Winfield Scott captured Mexico City. Mexico agreed to cede California and New Mexico to the United States for $15 million in 1848.

That same year gold was discovered in California. The gold rush brought thousands of Americans to the Sierra foothills and made San Francisco a boom town. Interest in building a railroad to California led to the purchase from Mexico of a strip of desert along the Gila River. With the Gadsden Purchase, America seemed to have fulfilled its "manifest destiny." The nation stretched from coast to coast, or "from sea to shining sea."

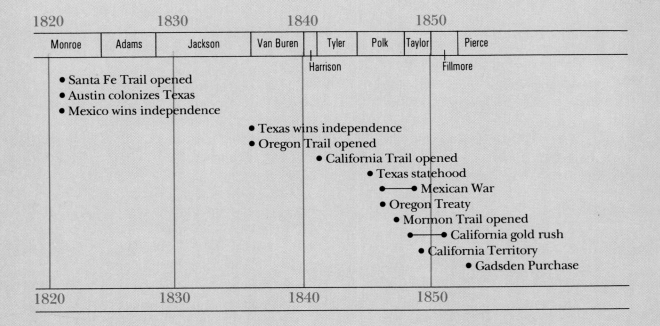

CHAPTER SURVEY

VOCABULARY REVIEW

From this list of vocabulary words, choose the one that best matches the meaning of each word or phrase in heavy type.

(a) annex   (e) garrison
(b) armistice   (f) irrigate
(c) dictator   (g) manifest destiny
(d) expansionists   (h) vigilante committees

1. Santa Anna wanted to become the **complete and absolute ruler** of Mexico.

2. William Barret Travis captured the **place where Mexican soldiers were stationed** in Anahuac.

3. After San Jacinto there was a **truce** between the Texas Republic and Mexico.

4. After the election of Polk, Congress voted to **attach** Texas to the United States.

5. In Utah the Mormons dammed mountain streams and dug ditches to **bring water to farm fields.**

6. The election of 1844 showed that many Americans were **people who believed that the nation should continue to gain land.**

7. In California's boom towns and mining camps there were **groups that took the law into their own hands.**

8. Expansionists based their actions on **a belief that the United States was fated to expand across the continent.**

CHAPTER REVIEW

1. (a) Why did the Mexican Congress ban American immigration into Texas in 1830? (b) Why did American settlers in Texas send Stephen F. Austin to Mexico City? (c) Did Austin succeed or fail in his mission?

2. (a) When Santa Anna led a large force of soldiers across the Rio Grande, how did the Texans defending San Antonio respond? (b) What agreements did Santa Anna and Sam Houston make about Texas? (c) Why did the Lone Star Republic come to an end in 1845?

3. Why did the farming frontier fail to move slowly westward across the Great Plains until it reached the Pacific coast?

4. Historians have made the generalization that settlement follows trade. (a) Does this generalization fit the facts about American settlement of the Pacific Coast region? Why or why not? (b) Does this generalization fit the facts about the settlement of Utah? Why or why not?

5. (a) What did expansionists see as the "manifest destiny" of the United States? (b) What expansionist goal was fulfilled by President Tyler?

6. (a) What did expansionists mean by the slogan "All of Oregon or None!"? (b) What did President Polk settle for in his negotiations with Great Britain?

7. (a) What fear led President Polk to restate "Mr. Monroe's Doctrine" in 1845? (b) How did Polk hope to acquire California from Mexico? (c) In what way did American settlers in California follow the example of Texas in 1846?

8. In May 1846 Polk declared that Mexican troops had "shed American blood on American soil." (a) What part of this statement did the Whigs accept as true? (b) What part of this statement did the Whigs deny, and why did they deny it?

9. What was the American strategy for winning the war with Mexico? Who commanded the northern army?

10. Between 1842 and 1853, four treaties established the boundaries of the region Americans would later call "the forty-eight states." Name these treaties.

GEOGRAPHY REVIEW

Look at the map "Trails to the Far West" on page 330.   (a) What three mountain ranges did the Oregon Trail cross?   (b) What two rivers did it follow?   (c) Where did the California Trail separate from the Oregon Trail?   (d) What two rivers did the Old Spanish Trail cross on the way to California?

USING THE TOOLS OF HISTORY

Identifying Political Changes on Maps

*CT **1.** Use the map "The Texas War for Independence 1835–1836" on page 324 and the map "The Mexican War 1846–1848" on page 338 to answer these questions.   (a) Are the same symbols used on each map? Do they mean the same things?   (b) Where did fighting take place in 1835–1836? In 1846–1848?   (c) What is the difference in the number of battles shown on the two maps? What is the difference in the number of Mexican victories shown?

Analyzing Change and Continuity

*CT **2.** In 1845 the Republic of Texas became the 28th state of the United States. Which of the following items must have undergone change then? Which ones probably remained about the same?

(a) the Texas constitution
(b) the cattle industry
(c) the use of slaves on cotton plantations
(d) visits by foreign diplomats to Texas
(e) Texas laws taxing imported goods
(f) the sale of Texas cotton
(g) the Mexican belief that Texas had been stolen by the United States
(h) relations between Texans and the Plains Indians

READING AND THINKING SKILLS

Main Ideas and Topic Sentences

*CT **1.** Reread the paragraph just above the heading "Law and Order" on page 341. Which sentence in that paragraph best states its main idea?

Details

*CT **2.** Continue rereading to the end of the section. Then answer the four "W" questions about vigilante committees and about the Gadsden Purchase.

James Walker painted "Charros at the Roundup," showing life on a California cattle ranch in the 1800s. Charros, or vaqueros, were the first cowboys. Many of the vaqueros' Spanish words, like *lariat* and *rodeo*, came into use in English.

Answers will be found on page T 55.

UNIT SURVEY

UNIT REVIEW

1. (a) What effect did Eli Whitney's "interchangeable system" have on the lives of farm women in New England?   (b) What effect did Whitney's cotton gin have on farming?   (c) Whitney's developments were part of a great change in the way goods were produced. What is that change called?

2. (a) What two transportation problems were solved by steamboats and by canals? (b) What effect did steamboats and canals have on trade?   (c) What effect did steamboats and canals have on cities?

3. How were cities in the 1850s different from cities in colonial days in   (a) location, (b) population, and   (c) news about current events?

4. (a) How were restrictions on voting the same in the new western states such as Illinois and Indiana as in the colonies? (b) How were the voting restrictions different? (c) How did politicians react to the changes in voting restrictions?

5. (a) Why did the South oppose protective tariffs?   (b) What did South Carolina do about the tariffs of 1828 and 1832?   (c) What did South Carolina threaten to do to back up its actions on the tariffs?   (d) What did President Jackson do to avoid bloodshed on the issue of tariffs?

6. (a) Why did Alexander Hamilton want to set up the original Bank of the United States? (b) Why did Andrew Jackson want to destroy the Second Bank of the United States? (c) What happened to the supply of money after Jackson moved to destroy the bank?

7. (a) In the 1830s, what group tried to make slavery an issue in Congress?   (b) Who wanted to avoid all discussion by Congress of

In Terence Kennedy's 1840 painting "Political Banner," the American eagle surveys advances in farming, transportation, and industry. Proud Americans in the 1800s believed of their achievements, "The sky's the limit."

the end of slavery?   (c) What was the "gag rule"?   (d) What happened to this rule?

8. (a) Why were there few settlements in Texas when the land was under Spanish rule? (b) After Mexico became independent in 1821, what did it do to encourage settlement in Texas?   (c) What fear caused Mexico to change that policy in 1830?   (d) What was the political result of new settlements in Texas?

9. (a) Why were the Great Plains a barrier to frontier farming?   (b) In colonial days, what was the main physical barrier to westward movement?   (c) In what ways were these two barriers alike? In what ways were they different?

10. (a) Why did Meriwether Lewis and William Clark travel to Oregon?   (b) Why did the mountain men travel into the Rocky Mountains?   (c) Why did Marcus and Narcissa Whitman and Eliza and Henry Spalding travel to Oregon?   (d) Why did people travel to Oregon in the 1840s?

LINKING THE PAST AND THE PRESENT

*CT 1. Canal routes helped some towns flourish. Other towns, not on the new shipping routes, declined. List the different transportation routes that connect your town or city to others. Try to discover how changes in these routes have affected local businesses.

*CT 2. Look for pictures, descriptions, or examples of coins and paper money that circulated in the United States between 1820 and 1850. Find out how the coins and paper money then compare with money today.

3. Compare an up-to-date road atlas with the map "Roads, Canals, and Waterways 1850" on page 283 or the map "Trails to the Far West" on page 330. Choose any two places shown on one of the maps. Find the shortest highway route between those places today.

MEETING THE BUILDERS OF AMERICA

*CT 1. Review the descriptions of Rebecca Lukens (page 278), Jane Swisshelm (page 316), and Sam Houston (page 327). In what ways did they contribute to America?

*CT 2. Prepare a report about the contribution to American life of some other person or group mentioned in Unit 4. For example, look for information about Eli Whitney, Samuel F. B. Morse, Sequoyah, Dorothea Dix, Frederick Douglass, or Sarah and Angelina Grimké. You may be able to use one of the following books as a source of information.

Campbell, C. W. *Sequoyah.* Minneapolis: Dillon Press, 1973.

Levison, Nancy Smiler. *The First Women Who Spoke Out.* Minneapolis: Dillon Press, 1983.

Quarles, Benjamin, ed. *Narrative of the Life of Frederick Douglass, an American Slave.* Cambridge, MA: Harvard, 1971.

Remini, Robert V. *The Revolutionary Age of Andrew Jackson.* New York: Harper & Row, 1976.

SUGGESTIONS FOR FURTHER READING

Blos, Joan W. *A Gathering of Days: A New England Girl's Journal, 1830–1832.* New York: Scribner's, 1979.

Boardman, Fon W., Jr. *America and the Jacksonian Era.* New York: Walck, 1975.

Collier, Peter. *When Shall They Rest? The Cherokee's Long Struggle with America.* New York: Holt, Rinehart, and Winston, 1973.

Lawson, Don. *The United States in the Mexican War.* New York: Abelard-Schuman, 1976.

Tunis, Edwin. *Frontier Living.* Cleveland: World, 1961.

American painter Eastman Johnson's rural scenes are among his best works. "In the Fields" bathes the landscape in a golden glow.

Detail from *Prisoners from the Front* by Winslow Homer, 1866.

YEARS OF DIVISION

THE NATION DIVIDES
THE CIVIL WAR
RESTORING THE UNION

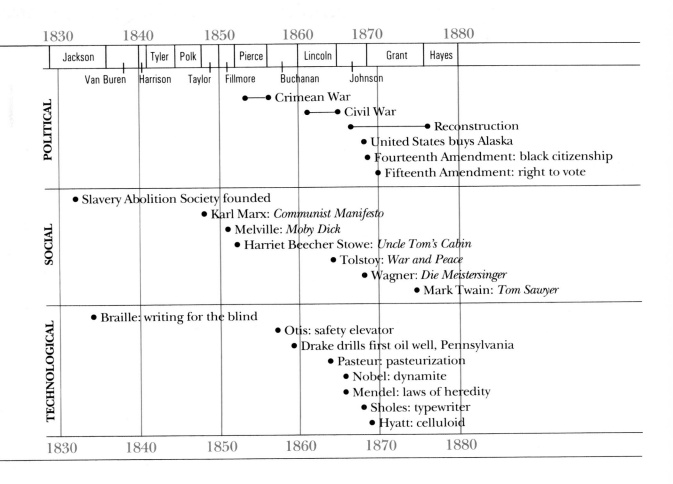

1830	1840	1850	1860	1870	1880

POLITICAL

- Crimean War
- Civil War
- Reconstruction
- United States buys Alaska
- Fourteenth Amendment: black citizenship
- Fifteenth Amendment: right to vote

SOCIAL

- Slavery Abolition Society founded
- Karl Marx: *Communist Manifesto*
- Melville: *Moby Dick*
- Harriet Beecher Stowe: *Uncle Tom's Cabin*
- Tolstoy: *War and Peace*
- Wagner: *Die Meistersinger*
- Mark Twain: *Tom Sawyer*

TECHNOLOGICAL

- Braille: writing for the blind
- Otis: safety elevator
- Drake drills first oil well, Pennsylvania
- Pasteur: pasteurization
- Nobel: dynamite
- Mendel: laws of heredity
- Sholes: typewriter
- Hyatt: celluloid

Presidents: Jackson, Van Buren, Harrison, Tyler, Polk, Taylor, Fillmore, Pierce, Buchanan, Lincoln, Johnson, Grant, Hayes

Introducing: Ask students what they know about slavery (including what they learned from reading, watching TV, and studying American history.) Tell the class they will now study the institution of slavery.

CHAPTER 14 1850-1861

THE NATION DIVIDES

LIFE UNDER SLAVERY
THE ECONOMIES OF THE SOUTH AND THE NORTH
WESTERN LANDS—SLAVE OR FREE
GROWING CONFLICT OVER SLAVERY
SECESSION AND WAR

14-1 LIFE UNDER SLAVERY

slave codes: collections of laws to strengthen control of slave owners
racism: belief that one race is inferior to another

READ TO FIND OUT

—what the words *slave codes* and *racism* mean.

—why living conditions of slaves improved during the 1800s.

—why southern states passed "slave codes."

—how slaves resisted the master's control.

—what family life was like for slaves.

In 1860 there were about four and one-quarter million black people living in the South. Out of this number almost four million were slaves. The great majority of the slaves were field hands. On plantations and in southern cities, many worked as house servants.

Slaves, however, also worked in sawmills, tobacco factories, textile mills, ironworks, tanneries, shipyards, and laundries. Some became skilled workers—carpenters, blacksmiths, mechanics. On the frontier in southwestern Texas, many of the early cowboys were slaves.

Sunday was the only day most slaves had free for amusement. They made musical instruments from logs, bones, gourds, or whatever they could find to use.

THE WORKING DAY

About half of the slaves lived on plantations having twenty slaves or more. Most slaves did field work. On large plantations, field hands were directed by an overseer hired by the plantation owner.

Field hands worked six days a week. The length of the working day depended on the master, the season, and the crop grown. On a cotton plantation in summer, slaves labored about fourteen hours—from sunrise to sunset. They were usually given two hours off during the hottest part of the day.

Field work was only part of a slave's workday. Slaves had to walk to and from the fields. And there were extra tasks to do after sundown. Men fed livestock and gathered firewood for the "big house," where the master and his family lived. Women had sewing and cooking to do for the big house and also for their own families.

THE NECESSITIES OF LIFE

During the 1800s living conditions gradually improved for slaves. One reason for this change was that the price of slaves went up after Congress forbade the import of slaves in 1808. With slaves more expensive to replace, masters tried harder to keep them healthy. Another reason was that slaveholders wanted to show people that slavery was not as bad as the abolitionists said it was. Southern political leaders urged slaveholders to provide slaves with the basic necessities—food, clothing, shelter, and medical care.

You may wish to read to the class passages from books by ex-slaves describing their former life. One good source is Frederick Douglass's autobiography.

Some slaves who had vegetable gardens also raised a little cotton or tobacco for sale. The money they earned was spent to buy utensils, toys for children, or clothing. Some were even able to buy their freedom.

For food, masters provided pork, cornmeal, and molasses. Slaves improved their diets with vegetables when they were allowed to have gardens. In summer they received two or three changes of clothing made from coarse cotton cloth. Winter clothing was usually made from thin woolen cloth. By 1850 most slave cabins had wood floors and small windows that were not covered by glass.

Conditions varied from master to master. Some saw their slaves as part of their plantation family, both white and black. Others showed no concern for their slaves' well-being. Although most slaves probably lived better than very poor people in the city slums of the North, they lacked what even the poorest northerners had—freedom.

THE PROBLEM OF CONTROL

Masters hoped that improving living conditions would make their slaves more content and willing to obey them. Slaves, however, continued to dream of freedom. Some Virginia planters warned that slaves who were allowed to have "the hope of freedom" could become "almost wholly unmanageable." By 1860 all the southern states had passed laws making it nearly impossible for a slave to gain freedom.

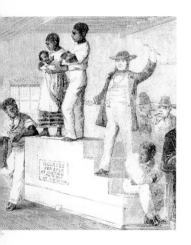

Sometimes slave families were kept together when sold at auction. But more often the sale of slaves meant the breakup of a family.

Southern states also passed **slave codes,** which were collections of laws designed to strengthen slaveholders' control. Slaves could not leave their plantations without permission or meet in large groups without a white person present. It was illegal to teach a slave to read. A slave could not testify against a white person in court.

Slave codes alone could not solve the problem of control. Masters also relied on the whip. Although most masters beat slaves only as a last resort, they did not think whipping was wrong. Rebellious slaves were beaten severely.

Racism, the belief that one race is inferior to another, helped the masters justify slavery. Masters often called the management of slaves a "duty" or a "burden," and thought of slaves as children who needed to be controlled and cared for. As long as they believed that black people could not run their own lives successfully, slaveholders could argue that slavery was morally right. They refused to accept evidence that blacks could care for themselves. If that were true, then slavery would be wrong, just as the abolitionists said.

RESISTANCE AND REBELLION

Racism, slave codes, and the whip could not crush the slaves' yearning for freedom and self-respect. Slaves found ways to resist the master's control. They stopped work when the overseer looked away, broke tools,

Runaway slaves were less likely to be caught if they traveled in darkness through dense forests and swamps. At night they could "follow the drinking gourd," the Big Dipper, which points toward the North Star.

and put rocks in their cotton sacks before weighing. They also pretended not to understand orders.

There were more dangerous forms of resistance. Some slaves refused to accept punishment. Masters feared such people and sometimes left them alone. More often, they sold them or simply had them killed.

Running away was a more common form of resistance than refusing punishment, but it was almost as dangerous. The odds against a successful escape were very high. Slaves living on plantations seldom had the opportunity to learn about the world outside. Most simply tried to "follow the North Star" to freedom. Pursued by trained bloodhounds and professional slave-catchers, they were usually caught. Then they were severely punished.

There were also slave rebellions. In 1822 a free black named Denmark Vesey organized a rebellion among slave craftworkers and house servants in Charleston, South Carolina. He planned to arm the slaves on nearby plantations and seize the city. When an informer revealed the plot, Vesey and 36 others were hanged.

Nine years later, Nat Turner, a slave preacher in Virginia, led a group of about 70 men from plantation to plantation murdering white families. Before the revolt was crushed, 57 whites had lost their lives. Whites

*CT
For discussion: How does the comparison of slaves to children (see page 354) make it easier for people to accept slavery? Would slave resistance make it easier or harder to believe the comparison is valid? Explain.

Activity: Students can research and write reports on the lives of Denmark Vesey and Nat Turner.

Nat Turner was captured after leading the most famous slave revolt in United States history. Born on a Virginia plantation, Turner was encouraged by his parents and grandmother to educate himself and to fight slavery.

responded by killing about 100 blacks, most of whom had had nothing to do with the rebellion. Turner was tried and executed. Because state militias were well organized and the white population was armed, slave rebellions in the South had no chance of succeeding.

SLAVE FAMILIES

Acts of resistance were not the only way slaves kept their self-respect. They also cared for each other and worked together to overcome hardships. In their close family life, they disproved the masters' claim that they could not take care of themselves. Family life also provided precious moments when the master was not in control.

Slave families lived with uncertainty. Southern law defined slaves as property. Husbands and wives or parents and children could be sold away from each other at any time. Masters usually tried to avoid breaking up families, but it did happen. When families were broken up, slaves rebuilt them as best they could. Children who had lost their parents were cared for by other adults, whom they called "Uncle" or "Aunt."

SECTION REVIEW   Answers will be found on page T 56.

1. Define these words: *slave codes, racism.*

2. Identify: Denmark Vesey, Nat Turner.

3. Why did the slaves' living conditions improve during the 1800s?

4. What was the purpose of the slave codes?

5. List three different ways slaves resisted the master's control.

6. What was the uncertainty that haunted slave families?

14-2 THE ECONOMIES OF THE SOUTH AND THE NORTH

READ TO FIND OUT

—what the word *corporation* means.

—why southern farmers looked to the planters for leadership.

—how the northern and the southern economies differed.

—why the South feared the growing power of the North.

corporation: company owned by stockholders

Abolitionists pictured the South as a land of wealthy planters and huge plantations. Parts of the South fit that picture. Thousand-acre plantations were common in the rice lands along the coast of South Carolina and Georgia. The same was true in the band of fertile soil known as the Black Belt of Alabama. The Mississippi bottom lands were famous for large plantations.

Wealthy planters and their families gathered at places like the Oakland House Race Course for the popular sport of horse racing. Robert Brammer and Augustus A. Von Smith painted Oakland House in Louisville, Kentucky, in 1840.

Southern White Families Owning Slaves   1850

				3.2% owned 20-99

69.2% of southern white families owned no slaves	6% owned 1	9.4% owned 2-4	12% owned 5-19	

0.15% owned 100 or more

FARMERS AND PLANTERS

Yet in 1850 there were only 8,000 planters in the entire South who owned fifty slaves or more. More than three fifths of the South's slaveholders owned fewer than ten slaves. Seven white families out of ten owned no slaves at all.

Most southern whites were farmers who worked small landholdings. Some owned slaves, some did not. Many grew cotton, tobacco, and other cash crops for the world market, just as the planters did. They also produced corn, wheat, and livestock.

Like the planters, most farmers supported slavery. Farmers accepted wealthy planters as their leaders. They depended on the planters for services such as cotton ginning. Many farmers hoped to buy slaves and become planters themselves. The strongest tie between farmers and planters was the idea that freedom for blacks would be a disaster for the South. Farmers and planters alike believed that whites and blacks could never live together as equals.

In the 1850s, the Industrial Revolution continued to change the North. While northern factories manufactured more and more goods, the South still depended mainly on agriculture. Southern factories, which produced cotton textiles, flour, and tobacco products, made up only 15 percent of the nation's industry.

Planters saw no reason to build factories. Cotton prices were rising, and plantation agriculture was still profitable. Mills in the North and in Britain could use as much cotton as the South could grow.

Planters' attitudes toward trade and industry also differed from those of northern manufacturers. Just as some Europeans thought money earned from land was "better" than money earned in trade, planters thought manufacturing was not a proper occupation. Instead of simply making money, planters were expected to do their civic duty by holding public office.

It was also a gentleman's duty to take care of his workers, planters believed. Southerners took pride in their ability to protect their plantation families. Northern factory owners, who used Irish and German immigrants as laborers, seemed to care little for the well-being of their workers. In northern factories, men, women, and children worked 12-hour days for very low wages. At least, the planters argued, slaves were fed and clothed and given housing.

You may wish to read to the class passages from Margaret Mitchell's *Gone With the Wind* that depict the world of the southern planter.

Agriculture in the South 1860

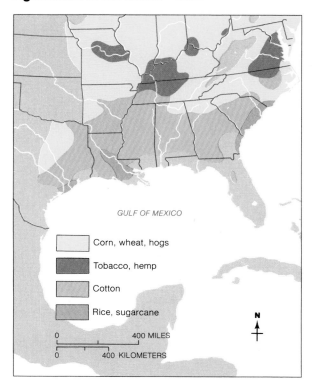

GULF OF MEXICO

- Corn, wheat, hogs
- Tobacco, hemp
- Cotton
- Rice, sugarcane

0 — 400 MILES
0 — 400 KILOMETERS

N

Cotton Production 1800–1860

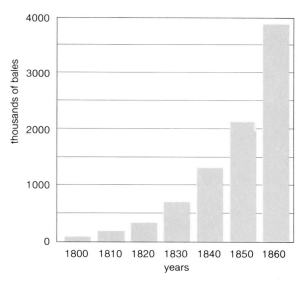

thousands of bales

years

Between 1800 and 1860, the production of cotton almost doubled each decade.

By 1860 cotton was grown across the South wherever the climate and soil were suitable.

CORPORATIONS

Southern planters disapproved of one northern business method in particular. People in the North were forming **corporations,** or companies owned by stockholders. If a corporation went out of business while owing money, the stockholders were not liable, or legally responsible, for its debts. The amount that stockholders could lose was limited to the money they had invested. This feature of a corporation, called limited liability, seemed dishonorable to planters. They believed that they were honor-bound to pay their debts.

Corporations fueled the Industrial Revolution in the North. Limited liability made investors less fearful about buying stock in new companies. Large amounts of investment capital were raised by corporations to be invested in canals and railroads.

THE INDUSTRIAL NORTH GAINS POWER

The planters were proud of their way of life. But they feared the growing economic power of the North. In 1860, while the entire South produced $245,000,000 worth of manufactured goods, the Northeast alone produced $1,213,900,000 worth. Most of the nation's canals and railroads, like its factories, were in the North.

For discussion: Other than limited liability, why might southern planters (who were reluctant to see themselves primarily as businesspeople) find the idea of a corporation particularly distasteful?

You may wish to have students review differences between the North and the South. Divide the chalkboard into two columns, "North" and "South." Under "South" write "slave labor" and under "North" "free labor." Ask students to add contrasting items to the list.

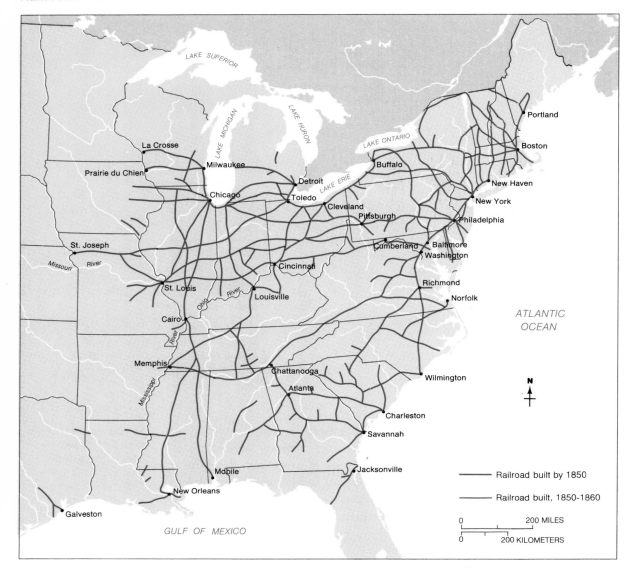

Using the map, have students locate the routes of several railroads built by 1850 and several built between 1850 and 1860.

After 1850, railroads linked the Northeast with the Northwest. In the past, northwestern farmers had shipped most of their grain and pork to market on the Mississippi River. River trade declined when Chicago became a railroad center. Northwestern farmers shipped their crops east by train through Chicago.

The North's political power was also growing. By the late 1840s, immigrants were pouring into the northern states. As its population grew, the North gained more seats in the House of Representatives. These gains strengthened the North's control of the House. In the Senate, power was equally divided between slave and free states. But northern farmers were moving west, and new free states would soon appear.

THE COMPARISON-CONTRAST PATTERN

You have already seen how writers use different patterns to organize information. Historians sometimes organize their facts into a chronological pattern, a cause-effect pattern, or a problem-solution pattern to explain events. You have also seen how different signal words are used in different patterns.

In this chapter the *comparison-contrast pattern* is used. Comparing means showing how groups of people or events are similar or what they have in common. Contrasting means showing how they are different from each other. Here are some of the signal words that may alert you to this pattern.

> like, unlike, alike, same, different,
> in contrast, similarly, as well as,
> on the other hand, however, just as, but,
> but also, although, yet

Reread the paragraph that follows the heading "The Economies of the South and the North." It pictures the South as seen by abolitionists. Now continue to the subsection titled "Farmers and Planters," and answer these questions on a piece of paper.

*CT

1. Which signal word begins the first paragraph of that subsection?

2. Is the purpose of the first paragraph to show how the South compared to or was like the abolitionists' picture? Or does it show how the South contrasted with or was not like their image of that region? What facts in that paragraph support your answer?

3. What signal words can you find in the second paragraph of that subsection?

4. Do these signal words suggest a similarity between farmers and planters or a difference between them?

5. How were the groups discussed in the next-to-last paragraph similar or different?

6. Judging from the signal words and what you read, would you say this subsection is about comparisons or about contrasts?

Answers will be found on page T 56.

Southerners feared that a Senate controlled by the North might vote funds for such improvements as railroads for the West. They might also vote for a high tariff on imported goods. Southerners would gain nothing except higher prices for nearly all the products they had to buy.

Worse yet, a Congress controlled by northerners could pass laws that interfered with slavery. The planters felt that their best hope for protecting their way of life was to create new slave states in the West.

SECTION REVIEW Answers will be found on page T 56.

1. Define this word: *corporation.*

2. How did limited liability protect a corporation's stockholders?

3. How did the economies of the South and the North differ?

4. How did the growth of railroads in the Northwest affect trade along the Mississippi?

5. Why did southerners fear the growing political power of the North?

14-3 WESTERN LANDS—SLAVE OR FREE

READ TO FIND OUT

—what the words *popular sovereignty* and *transcontinental* mean.

—what the Free-Soilers wanted.

—what the Compromise of 1850 accomplished.

—why northerners opposed the Kansas-Nebraska Act.

popular sovereignty: idea that the people living in a territory should decide whether or not it should be open to slavery

transcontinental: across the continent

In August 1846 David Wilmot of Pennsylvania asked that a proviso (pruh-VĪ-zō), or amendment, be added to a bill in the House of Representatives. The Wilmot Proviso banned slavery from all lands that might be acquired from Mexico as a result of the Mexican War. After passing the House, the proviso was rejected by the Senate. But it set off a fierce debate over the expansion of slavery.

CONFLICT OVER THE WILMOT PROVISO

In the North, every state legislature but one passed resolutions supporting the Wilmot Proviso. There was growing opposition to slavery among northerners, who were beginning to view it as morally wrong. There was also the fear that if slavery were allowed in the West, wealthy planters would end up with the best land. Ordinary farmers would have no chance. Furthermore, white laborers would be competing with slaves and would have to accept lower pay.

Many northerners also believed, like Wilmot, that the western lands should be a place for whites only. In the Northwest a number of states banned not only slavery but free blacks as well.

Northern support for the Wilmot Proviso angered southerners. Speaking for the South, John C. Calhoun reminded northerners that slaves were property. Slaveholders, he said, had the same property rights as other Americans. If they chose to settle in the western territories, they had the right to take their property with them.

Between Wilmot and Calhoun was a third point of view. Its main supporters were Senator Lewis Cass of Michigan and Senator Stephen A. Douglas of Illinois. Cass and Douglas proposed that the people living in a territory should decide whether it would be open to slavery. This idea became known as **popular sovereignty.**

*CT Activity: Students can assume that they are Mariano Vallejo or one of his associates and write papers arguing (with good supporting reasons) that California's future lies with the United States.

★ ★ ★ ★ ★ ★ ★ **AMERICAN VALUES IN ACTION** ★ ★ ★ ★ ★ ★ ★ ★

MARIANO GUADALUPE VALLEJO

Mariano Vallejo (vah-YEH-hō) of California seemed to have everything. He was a handsome man, with thick black hair and lush sideburns. He had a beautiful wife and fine children. He was a respected leader in Mexican California. He owned vast lands and thousands of cattle and horses.

Yet Vallejo was not satisfied. As a child, he had seen French pirates attack his homeland. California was at that time a colony of faraway Spain, which provided little defense for the Californios.

When California became a Mexican colony, it fared no better. Californios who supported Mexican rule clashed with those who wanted local government. Californios and Indians fought. And by the 1840s, American settlers were streaming into California without permission from Mexico.

Vallejo yearned to bring order to his homeland. In 1833 he had been appointed military commander of northern California. Some people complained of his lordly ways and iron rule. Yet the haughty commander could unbend, embracing strangers with true warmth. He once invited Americans to celebrate the Fourth of July at a huge festival on his estate.

Vallejo warned the government of Mexico that California was slipping away from its control. But Mexico did nothing. Finally, Vallejo met with other leaders in California.

It was California's destiny, he argued, to become part of the United States. "We shall have a stable government and just laws," he said. "California will grow strong and flourish. Its people will be prosperous, happy, and free."

Vallejo's dream came true when the United States won California in the Mexican War. In 1849 he attended California's constitutional convention. Vallejo and other delegates decided that California should be a free state.

Vallejo welcomed statehood. At last his beloved homeland would be secure.

THE ELECTION OF 1848

As the election of 1848 approached, the Democrats chose Senator Cass, a veteran of the War of 1812, as their candidate. He supported popular sovereignty. Northern Democrats who supported the Wilmot Proviso were angered by Cass's nomination. A group led by Martin Van Buren left the party.

The Whigs chose General Zachary Taylor of Louisiana as their candidate. He was a slaveholder, a nationalist, and a hero of the war with Mexico. To Whig leaders he was the perfect candidate because his views on the Wilmot Proviso were unknown. But northern Whigs who opposed slavery refused to support Taylor. They took the name Conscience Whigs.

Conscience Whigs, Wilmot Democrats, and the antislavery Liberty party held a convention of their own. They wanted the federal government to exclude slavery from the territories and to provide free homesteads to settlers. Their slogan was "Free Soil, Free Speech, Free Labor, and Free Men." The Free-Soil party chose former President Martin Van Buren to run against Cass and Taylor.

In the election, Van Buren did not win a single state. But in New York, the Free-Soil party took enough votes from Cass to help Taylor become President.

THE COMPROMISE OF 1850

When Congress met in December 1849, it had to face the issues raised by the Wilmot Proviso. Californians had drawn up a constitution and were asking to join the Union as a free state. New Mexico too was drawing up a free-state constitution. But most southerners in Congress would not even consider California's request. Another free state would give the North control of the Senate.

Instead, southerners called for a strong fugitive, or runaway, slave law. They wanted federal law officers to help slave-catchers who came north in pursuit of runaways. Southerners also supported Texas's claim that the Rio Grande was its western boundary. If Texas kept the eastern half of New Mexico, all that land would be part of a slave state. Northerners responded by demanding that Congress support the Wilmot Proviso and outlaw slavery in the District of Columbia.

By January 1850 Congress was deadlocked. Talk of secession grew louder. Then Henry Clay offered the last of his famous compromises. His proposals started one of the greatest debates in American history. John C. Calhoun defended southern rights. Daniel Webster supported Clay and warned that secession meant civil war, or a war between different groups in the same country. Webster gave a powerful speech for "the preservation of the Union."

In midsummer, President Taylor became ill and died. He was succeeded by Vice-President Millard Fillmore, who supported Clay's plan. Finally, after almost nine months of bitter argument, Congress accepted the Compromise of 1850.

Under the compromise, California was admitted to the Union as a free state. Utah and New Mexico were organized as territories in which the people would decide whether or not to allow slavery. Texas was paid $10 million to surrender its claims to the eastern half of New Mexico. The slave trade, but not slavery, was outlawed in the District of Columbia. And a strong fugitive slave law was passed by Congress.

The compromise pleased most Americans. In Washington, D.C., crowds surged through the streets shouting, "The Union is saved!"

You may wish to have students review what they have learned about Henry Clay as the "Great Pacificator" and about John C. Calhoun as a spokesman for the South.

Fillmore disapproved of slavery but opposed its abolition. He said, "God knows that I detest slavery, but it is an existing evil . . . and we must endure it . . . till we can get rid of it without destroying the last hope of free government in the world."

The Compromise of 1850

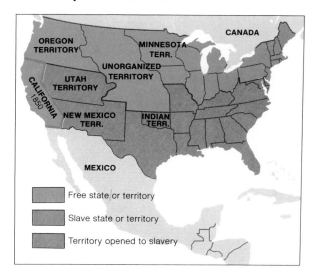

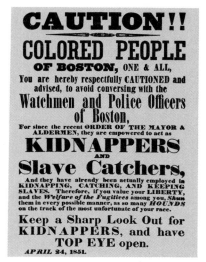

GROWING OPPOSITION TO SLAVERY

Despite widespread support for the Compromise of 1850, the new Fugitive Slave Act caused trouble in the North. In public meetings across the North, speakers called for its repeal. Many northern states also passed "personal liberty" laws. These laws said that state officials could not help anyone who was trying to enforce the Fugitive Slave Law.

The book *Uncle Tom's Cabin*, published in 1852, made the Fugitive Slave Act even more difficult to enforce. Written by Harriet Beecher Stowe, *Uncle Tom's Cabin* was an emotional look at slavery. Northerners were moved by the hardships faced by the slaves who were the main characters. Southerners, however, angrily declared that the picture of slavery in *Uncle Tom's Cabin* was unreal and designed to stir up antislavery feelings. The book was a great success, outselling any other book up to that time except the Bible.

Southerners felt betrayed. Northerners had agreed to the Fugitive Act as part of the Compromise of 1850. Yet they failed to enforce it. Southerners were also worried about the powerful effect of *Uncle Tom's Cabin*. How long would it be, they wondered, before abolitionists gained control of the national government?

THE ELECTION OF 1852

In the election of 1852, the Democrats tried to reassure the South. They promised to uphold the Compromise of 1850. They also stated that their party would oppose any effort to bring up the question of slavery in Congress. Their candidate for President was Franklin Pierce of New Hampshire. He was known to be sympathetic to the South.

Posters warned blacks in Boston to avoid police enforcing the Fugitive Slave Act. Opposition to the act increased after Harriet Beecher Stowe (below) published *Uncle Tom's Cabin* in 1852.

You may wish to read to the class passages from *Uncle Tom's Cabin,* especially those depicting an abolitionist's view of the cruelties of slavery.

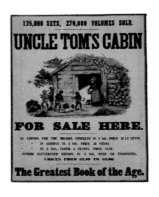

Uncle Tom's Cabin was an immediate best-seller, and a play based on the story was soon touring the country. Mary E. Webb, a free black woman from Philadelphia, gave readings from the book.

Some contemporaries called Pierce a "doughface," a north-erner with southern principles.

The Whigs also supported the Compromise of 1850. But a group of northern Whigs, led by William H. Seward of New York, refused to accept the Fugitive Slave Act. Many southern Whigs would not support the party's candidate for President, General Winfield Scott. They feared that he was an ally of Seward.

The Free-Soilers were the only party to oppose the Compromise of 1850. By doing so, they lost many votes. Pierce and the Democrats, the strongest backers of the compromise, won an overwhelming victory.

THE KANSAS-NEBRASKA ACT

During the Pierce administration, the spirit of compromise received a death blow. It came in the form of a bill introduced in Congress by Senator Stephen Douglas.

You may wish to tell students that they will learn more about Stephen A. Douglas when they study the Lincoln-Douglas debates (pages 371–372).

In 1854 plans for the nation's first **transcontinental** railroad, a rail line across the continent, were being discussed in Congress. Senator Douglas wanted the railroad to go from Chicago through the unorganized portion of the Louisiana Purchase. This vast area was still Indian country. To encourage settlement, Douglas proposed that the region be organized into two territories, Kansas and Nebraska.

The Missouri Compromise had closed the Louisiana Purchase north of 36°30′ to slavery. To gain southern support, Douglas suggested that the compromise be repealed. He also proposed popular sovereignty for the new territories. Southerners in Congress voted for the Kansas-Nebraska bill. They thought slaveholders from Missouri would move west and make Kansas a slave state.

The Kansas-Nebraska Act 1854

The Kansas-Nebraska Act erased the Missouri Compromise line of 1820. The free Northeast was separated from the free West by a vast slave territory.

Northerners were outraged by the repeal of the Missouri Compromise. They accused Douglas of joining a "slaveholders' conspiracy," or plot, against the North. Despite strong opposition, Congress passed the Kansas-Nebraska bill. President Pierce signed it into law.

The struggle over the Kansas-Nebraska Act caused major changes in the nation's politics. The Whig party split into northern and southern groups. Many southern Whigs became Democrats. Northern Whigs joined anti-Nebraska Democrats and Free-Soilers in a new party—the Republican party. The Republicans were a sectional party, with support only in the North.

With the breakup of the Whigs, the Democrats became the last national party. The bond between northern and southern Democrats was a tie that helped hold the nation together. But as the Democratic party was pulled southward, that tie began to weaken.

Leaders of the new party adopted the name "Republican" to show their ties to the party of Thomas Jefferson. Because of Jefferson's influence, the Northwest Ordinance of 1787 banned slavery in the lands north of the Ohio River.

SECTION REVIEW   Answers will be found on page T 57.

1. Define these words: *popular sovereignty, transcontinental.*

2. Identify: Wilmot Proviso, Millard Fillmore, Harriet Beecher Stowe, Franklin Pierce, Stephen A. Douglas.

3. What did the Free-Soil party stand for?

4. What did the Compromise of 1850 accomplish?

5. Which part of the Compromise of 1850 caused trouble in the North?

6. Why were northerners opposed to the Kansas-Nebraska Act?

7. How did the Kansas-Nebraska Act affect the nation's politics?

14-4 GROWING CONFLICT OVER SLAVERY

READ TO FIND OUT

party platform: list of campaign statements
plank: statement

—what the words *party platform* and *plank* mean.

—how popular sovereignty led to violence in Kansas.

—what the election of 1856 showed about political parties.

—how the Dred Scott decision affected the spread of slavery.

The battle over slavery in the territories divided northerners and southerners. Southerners thought northern talk about "free soil" was the first step in a campaign to destroy slavery. Northerners thought the South was trying to choke off the westward movement of free farmers in order to weaken the North. Then came "bleeding Kansas."

BLOODSHED IN KANSAS

The Kansas-Nebraska Act started a race between northerners and southerners for control of the Kansas Territory. Proslavery settlers from Missouri were the first to arrive. They were soon outnumbered, how-

This 1856 election cartoon shows slavery as a monster. While Democrats try to drag the monster into Kansas, Republican candidate Frémont orders it back. The third candidate, Fillmore, sits uncommitted on the fence.

THE PRESIDENTIAL CAMPAIGN OF '56.

ever, by free-soil farmers. Some of the free-soilers were sent to Kansas by New England antislavery groups.

Elections were held to set up a territorial legislature. Armed bands of proslavery Missourians crossed into Kansas to vote and then went home. As a result, the proslavery side won the election. The new legislature began passing laws to protect slavery. The antislavery settlers then set up a government of their own. They declared that Kansas was a free territory. Then fighting broke out, and by the end of 1856, almost 200 people had been killed. Northern newspapers blamed the South for the ugly conflict in "bleeding Kansas." Southerners blamed the North.

Violence also erupted in the Senate. In the spring of 1856, Senator Charles Sumner of Massachusetts gave an angry speech on "the crime against Kansas." He blamed a number of southern leaders, including a Senator from South Carolina. A few days later, a South Carolina Congressman walked into the Senate and beat Sumner senseless with a cane. Southern newspapers applauded the act. In the North, protest meetings were held everywhere.

THE ELECTION OF 1856

The election of 1856 was held during the uproar over "bleeding Kansas and bleeding Sumner." The Democratic **party platform,** or list of campaign statements, included a **plank,** or statement, defending the Kansas-Nebraska Act. The Democratic leaders knew it would cost the party votes in the North. To limit these losses, they chose James Buchanan of Pennsylvania as their candidate for President. His views on Kansas-Nebraska were not well known.

The Republicans nominated the explorer John C. Frémont of California. Their platform stressed the right of Congress to ban slavery from the territories. The party's campaign slogan was "Free Soil, Free Speech, Free Men, and Frémont." The third contender in 1856 was former President Millard Fillmore, now a candidate for the anti-immigrant American or Know-Nothing party.

In the election, Fillmore won in Maryland. Buchanan carried the rest of the South and enough northern states to defeat Frémont. A few hundred more Republican votes in Pennsylvania and Illinois would have swung the election the other way.

The election of 1856 showed that sectionalism was the strongest force in American politics. The Democrats had won every southern state but one. Their support in the North was weakening. The Republicans, with no help from the South, had almost won the election. On the main political issue of the time—the question of slavery in the territories—the Democrats had spoken for the South, and the Republicans had represented northern opinion.

In 1856 the new Republican party came within a few votes of putting John C. Frémont in the White House. Jessie Benton Frémont was a well-known writer.

Dred Scott was freed two months later by his new owner. But the Supreme Court decision enraged many northerners.

Dred Scott v. *Sanford* was the first case since *Marbury* v. *Madison* in which the Supreme Court declared an act of Congress unconstitutional.

THE DRED SCOTT DECISION

President Buchanan believed that the best way to preserve the Union was to protect the rights of slaveholders. He was deeply disturbed by the conflict over slavery.

On March 6, 1857, two days after Buchanan took office, the Supreme Court handed down its decision in the case of *Dred Scott* v. *Sanford*. Scott, a slave, was owned by a Missouri army surgeon. His owner took Scott to Illinois and then to Wisconsin Territory, where slavery was prohibited. He then returned with his owner to Missouri. Aided by abolitionists, Scott sued for his freedom. His lawyers claimed that his stay in a free state and in a free territory had made him a free man.

The Court rejected Scott's claim. It ruled that black people were not citizens of the United States. Since Scott was not a citizen, he had no right to sue in any federal court. Scott was subject to the laws of the state in which he now lived—Missouri.

The Court also declared the Missouri Compromise unconstitutional because it had placed a ban on slavery in a federal territory. Slaves, said the Court, were property. The Fifth Amendment to the Constitution says that Congress cannot take away people's property without proper legal or court action. Therefore, it was unconstitutional for Congress to outlaw slavery in the territories.

Northerners were thunderstruck. The platform of the Republican party was now outside the law. The Republicans, however, did not abandon their campaign against slavery in the territories. Instead, they blamed the Supreme Court. They charged that the Court, along with the President and the Democratic party, had joined the "slaveholders' conspiracy." The Dred Scott decision, then, served to widen the gap between the North and the South.

SECTION REVIEW   Answers will be found on page T 57.

1. Define these words: *party platform, plank.*

2. Identify: James Buchanan.

3. What effect did "bleeding Kansas and bleeding Sumner" have on public opinion in the North?

4. Which political party supported the Kansas-Nebraska Act in the election of 1856?

5. (a) Which party became more a party of the South in the election of 1856? (b) Which party represented only the North?

6. What were the main rulings in the Dred Scott decision?

7. How did Republicans react to the Dred Scott decision?

14-5 SECESSION AND WAR

READ TO FIND OUT

—what issues were debated by Lincoln and Douglas.

—how John Brown's raid at Harpers Ferry affected the South.

—why the election of 1860 brought about secession.

By 1858 the slavery question had divided northern Democrats into two groups. One group was led by President Buchanan, who supported the South's claim that slavery could not be banned in the territories. The other group was led by Senator Stephen A. Douglas of Illinois. Douglas was the hero of the northwestern Democrats and the nation's leading defender of popular sovereignty.

THE LINCOLN-DOUGLAS DEBATES

Douglas ran for reelection to the Senate from Illinois in 1858. His Republican opponent was Abraham Lincoln. Lincoln was an Illinois lawyer with little political experience. He had served only a single term as a Whig Congressman. He was not well known nationally. In his home

Large crowds turned out for the Lincoln-Douglas debates. Students at Knox College in Galesburg, Illinois, decorated the college with banners for the fifth debate on October 7, 1858.

state, however, Lincoln was widely respected for his honesty, sense of humor, and ability to think clearly. Both men opposed the expansion of slavery and wanted to preserve the Union.

The two candidates met in a series of spirited debates that attracted national attention. Lincoln insisted that blacks should have "all the natural rights listed in the Declaration of Independence, the right of life, liberty, and the pursuit of happiness." To most white Americans in 1858, this was a radical statement.

The two candidates also disagreed about how important the problem of slavery was. Douglas did not think it was a moral issue. He thought the best way to preserve the Union was to allow each state to make its own decision about slavery. The nation, Douglas insisted, could "exist forever divided into free and slave states."

Lincoln said that slavery was morally wrong. He believed, however, that radical abolitionists went too far in their attacks on slavery. They were, he felt, spoiling any chance for compromise by making southerners fear the North. Slavery, Lincoln said, would die out naturally.

In a debate at Freeport, Illinois, Lincoln asked Douglas how he could support the Dred Scott decision and popular sovereignty. According to the Dred Scott ruling, a territorial government could not ban slavery. Yet popular sovereignty gave the people in a territory the right to accept or reject slavery.

Douglas answered that despite the Dred Scott decision, people in a territory could refuse to pass slave codes. Then slaveholders would be afraid to bring their slaves into the territory. This argument became known as the Freeport Doctrine.

Douglas's defense of popular sovereignty helped him defeat Lincoln in Illinois. But the Freeport Doctrine turned southern Democrats against him. The debates made Lincoln famous across the country.

JOHN BROWN'S RAID

John Brown's deep hatred of slavery seems to burn in his eyes. To philosopher Ralph Waldo Emerson, he was "a new saint." To the South, he was a demon.

In the fall of 1859, an abolitionist named John Brown spread terror throughout the South. Brown plotted a slave rebellion. He bought weapons with funds provided by radical abolitionists. Then he and 18 followers, including five blacks, seized the federal arsenal at Harpers Ferry, Virginia.

Brown's band took a few local citizens as prisoners and barricaded themselves inside the arsenal. They waited for the rebellion to begin, but no slaves came to their aid. Instead they were surrounded by militia troops. Brown and six of his band were captured and hanged.

Most northerners condemned the attack. But southerners charged that the "invasion" was condemned "only because it failed." Southern Democrats claimed that Republican leaders had encouraged Brown.

Meanwhile, among abolitionists, John Brown became a martyr, or a person who suffers or dies for moral principles. The author Louisa May Alcott called him "St. John the Just."

John Brown's raid on Harpers Ferry had extremely serious results. Southerners believed that the abolitionists had begun a campaign to stir up slave rebellions across the South. As a result, those who favored secession gained widespread support.

THE ELECTION OF 1860

By the election of 1860, the Democrats were no longer able to hold their party together. Southern Democrats demanded that the party platform include a plank calling for a federal slave code. They insisted that slavery be not only permitted in the territories, but protected there. The Douglas Democrats insisted on popular sovereignty. The result was a split between northern and southern Democrats. The northern Democrats nominated Douglas. The southern Democrats chose John C. Breckinridge of Kentucky as their candidate for President.

The Republicans nominated Abraham Lincoln. Their party platform proposed that there be no attempt to end slavery in the South. But it strongly supported a ban on slavery in the territories. To please the Northeast, the Republicans called for a protective tariff. To win votes in the Northwest, they supported the building of a cross-country railroad. They also supported a law that would give western lands to settlers. Finally, they called for the admission of Kansas to the Union as a free state.

Some former Whigs and American party members formed the Constitutional Union party. It tried to appeal to all sections of the nation. It promised to uphold "the Constitution of the country, the Union of the states and the enforcement of the laws." The candidate of the Constitutional Union party was John Bell of Tennessee.

Lincoln won the election, with more electoral votes than all his opponents combined. But he received only 40 percent of the popular vote. Lincoln won in every northern state but New Jersey, which he split with Douglas. He did not receive a single electoral vote from the South. The election of 1860 showed how deeply divided the nation had become over the question of slavery.

THE CONFEDERATE STATES OF AMERICA

Before the election, Lincoln tried to convince the South that he did not want to end slavery. Southerners did not believe him. Lincoln as President, the Charleston *Mercury* warned, meant "the loss of liberty, property, home, country." With Lincoln in the White House, secession seemed to be the only way for southerners to protect their way of life.

Louisa May Alcott is best remembered for her books *Little Women* and *Little Men.*

Republicans held their convention in Chicago in 1860. While women participated, they were not yet allowed to vote as delegates.

The Election of 1860

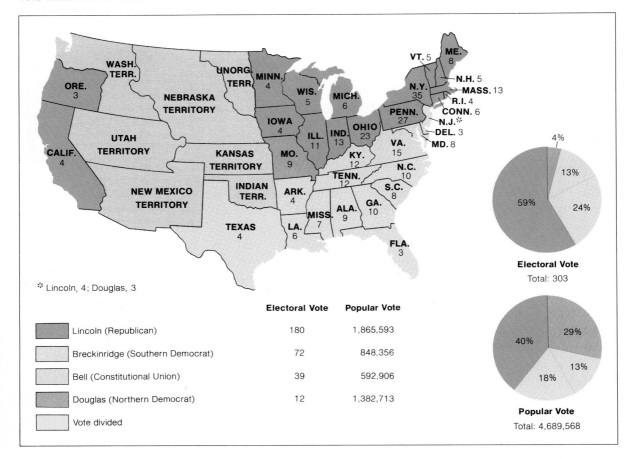

WASH. TERR.

ORE. 3

UNORG. TERR

MINN. 4

WIS. 5

MICH. 6

VT. 5

ME. 8

N.H. 5

N.Y. 35

MASS. 13

R.I. 4

CONN. 6

NEBRASKA TERRITORY

IOWA 4

ILL. 11

IND. 13

OHIO 23

PENN. 27

N.J.※

DEL. 3

MD. 8

UTAH TERRITORY

CALIF. 4

KANSAS TERRITORY

MO. 9

KY. 12

VA. 15

N.C. 10

INDIAN TERR.

ARK. 4

TENN. 12

S.C. 8

NEW MEXICO TERRITORY

TEXAS 4

MISS. 7

LA. 6

ALA. 9

GA. 10

FLA. 3

※ Lincoln, 4; Douglas, 3

Electoral Vote — Total: 303
- 59%
- 24%
- 13%
- 4%

Popular Vote — Total: 4,689,568
- 40%
- 29%
- 18%
- 13%

	Electoral Vote	Popular Vote
Lincoln (Republican)	180	1,865,593
Breckinridge (Southern Democrat)	72	848,356
Bell (Constitutional Union)	39	592,906
Douglas (Northern Democrat)	12	1,382,713
Vote divided		

Although Sam Houston opposed secession, Texas joined the Confederacy in March 1861. Houston refused to swear allegiance to the Confederacy and resigned as governor.

Jefferson Davis distinguished himself in the Mexican War. He served as Congressman, Senator, and Pierce's Secretary of War. After the Civil War, he retired to Mississippi and wrote The Rise and Fall of the Confederate Government (1881).

Still, a number of southern leaders tried to hold the nation together. Governor Sam Houston of Texas opposed calls for secession. Congressman Alexander Stephens told his fellow Georgians that Lincoln was "powerless" to do the South "any great mischief." The Republicans, he pointed out, had not gained control of Congress. But the efforts of Stephens, Houston, and other southern moderates were not successful.

On December 20, 1860, South Carolina seceded from the Union. Within two months, six more states in the lower South had seceded. In 1861 delegates from six of the seven states that had seceded met in Montgomery, Alabama. They formed a new union called the Confederate States of America. They also selected a flag with three stripes and seven stars on a blue field and wrote a constitution for a new nation.

The Confederate constitution was similar to the Constitution of the United States, but there were important differences. Each Confederate state was "sovereign and independent." Also, the new constitution protected slavery. The delegates chose Jefferson Davis of Mississippi as their President. For Vice-President, they chose Alexander Stephens.

USING MAPS AND GRAPHS TO INTERPRET DATA

Many maps combine physical information, such as the routes of rivers, with political information, such as the boundaries of nations. The map on page 374 is strictly a political map. It deals only with the election of 1860. No physical features are shown because they do not relate to the subject of the election. All the map space is used to provide election information for each state.

Look at the legend and the map. Color is used to show the candidate who won in each state. The two circle graphs use the same colors to show how the electoral vote and the popular vote were divided. Use all this information to answer the following questions.

1. How many states gave all their electoral votes to Lincoln?

2. What state gave some of its electoral votes to Lincoln?

3. How many electoral votes did Lincoln receive? What percentage of the total electoral vote was this? What percentage of the popular vote did he receive?

4. Which candidate received the second largest percentage of the popular vote? How many states did he carry? What percentage of the electoral vote did he receive?

5. Where did Stephen Douglas get his 12 electoral votes?

6. To win the presidency, a candidate must win a majority of the electoral votes. In 1860 how many votes were needed for a majority?

7. If one of the states that voted for Lincoln had voted for another candidate, no single candidate would have received a majority of the votes. The House of Representatives would have had to decide the election. Which state could have made this difference?

*CT

Answers will be found on page T 57.

FORT SUMTER

On March 4, 1861, Abraham Lincoln gave his inaugural address to the nation. Once again he pledged not to interfere with slavery "in the states where it exists." But he also warned the South that no state "can lawfully get out of the Union." Lincoln now had to decide whether to back his words with force.

By the time Lincoln took office, most of the federal arsenals, naval yards, and forts in the seceded states had been seized by the Confederacy. One of the few forts remaining in federal control was Fort Sumter. Fort Sumter was located on an island in Charleston Harbor. Lincoln had received word from Major Robert J. Anderson, the fort's commander, that his soldiers were running out of supplies. Sending a supply ship, the President knew, would probably be seen as an act of war by the Confederate government.

The choice facing Lincoln was both clear and terrible. He could allow the Union to split in two. Or he could plunge the country into civil war. Most members of his Cabinet advised him to avoid conflict at all costs. After delaying for a month, Lincoln made his decision. He sent ships to resupply Fort Sumter.

Lincoln told the South, "In your hands . . . and not in mine, is the momentous issue of civil war. The government will not assail you. You have no conflict without being yourselves the aggressors."

After the surrender of Fort Sumter, the flag of the Confederate States of America flew over the fort. The seven stars on the flag stand for the seven states that had seceded by April 1861.

As the ships drew near the harbor, Confederate General P. G. T. Beauregard demanded that Major Anderson give up the fort at once. Anderson refused to surrender until his supplies ran out. At 4:30 A.M. on April 12, 1861, Beauregard ordered his artillery to open fire. The Confederate guns fired all day and into the night.

The ships sent by Lincoln had to remain outside the harbor. The battle continued until Anderson's ammunition ran out. Then he surrendered. Anderson and his troops were allowed to leave the fort and board the Union supply ships.

The Union and the Confederacy were at war.

SECTION REVIEW   Answers will be found on page T 57.

1. Identify: Freeport Doctrine, Jefferson Davis, Alexander Stephens.

2. What was Lincoln's opinion about slavery and its future?

3. How did John Brown's raid at Harpers Ferry affect the South?

4. What happened to the Democratic party as it prepared for the election of 1860? Why?

5. What caused the states of the lower South to secede?

6. What happened when Fort Sumter was fired upon?

CHAPTER SUMMARY

Slavery was essential to the economy of the South. Masters usually tried to provide slaves with the basic necessities. But they had the legal right to use whatever force was needed to control their property. Slaves were part of the master's plantation "family," but they did not lose the hope of freedom. They kept their self-respect as best they could by resisting the master's control and by caring for each other.

Most white southerners were independent farmers. Yet it was the slave-owning planters who led the South. They saw no reason to exchange agriculture for factories. Meanwhile, the North was transformed by the Industrial Revolution, city growth, and immigration. The planters were proud of their way of life, but they feared the growing economic and political power of the North.

The issue that put the North and South on a collision course was the expansion of slavery. Henry Clay's last compromise eased tensions for a while, but the Fugitive Slave Act and *Uncle Tom's Cabin* helped turn northern public opinion against slavery. Then the Kansas-Nebraska Act destroyed the spirit of compromise and gave birth to a strong sectional party that supported free soil.

Bitterness between northerners and southerners increased when the conflict over Kansas became violent. The Dred Scott decision widened the gap between the North and the South still further.

The final break came after Lincoln was elected President in 1860. Southerners decided that their way of life could not be protected if they remained in the Union. They reached this conclusion after the raid on Harpers Ferry and the election of a Republican President. Seven states left the Union and established a new nation, the Confederate States of America. When the Confederacy fired on Fort Sumter, the Civil War began.

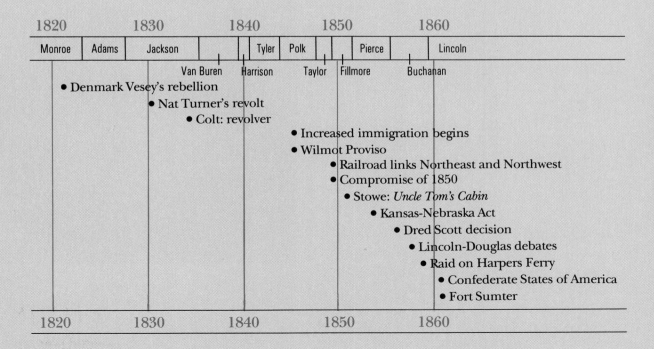

Answers will be found on page T 58.

CHAPTER SURVEY

VOCABULARY REVIEW

For each numbered word or phrase below, choose the best synonym—the word or phrase closest in meaning to the numbered word.

1. racism
   (a) prejudice against a religious group
   (b) hatred of others   (c) belief that one race is inferior to another

2. corporation
   (a) company owned by stockholders
   (b) company that has 500 workers
   (c) company that manufactures textiles

3. party platform
   (a) list of campaign statements   (b) moral principles   (c) political foundation

4. transcontinental
   (a) throughout a continent   (b) across a continent   (c) outside a continent

5. platform plank
   (a) piece of wood   (b) political belief
   (c) statement in a party platform

6. slave codes
   (a) laws lessening control of slaveholders
   (b) laws strengthening control of slaveholders   (c) laws regarding importation of slaves

7. popular sovereignty
   (a) government decides whether slavery is allowed in a territory   (b) church allows slavery in a territory   (c) people vote whether slavery is allowed in a territory

CHAPTER REVIEW

1. (a) Why did slaveholders think of caring for slaves as "a duty and a burden"?   (b) What was the strongest tie between southern farmers and wealthy planters?

2. (a) Did improving living conditions make it easier for masters to control their slaves? (b) What did slaves do to try to maintain their self-respect?

3. Were southern whites right in fearing slave rebellions?

4. (a) In what ways was the North ahead of the South by 1860?   (b) Why did most people in the South prefer to invest in land and slaves rather than railroads and factories?

5. (a) What question did the Wilmot Proviso bring before Congress?   (b) Explain how the doctrine of popular sovereignty was supposed to answer that question.   (c) The Dred Scott decision provided another answer to that question. What was it?

6. (a) Which part of the Compromise of 1850 was hardest for southerners to accept?

Winslow Homer painted "The Cotton Pickers" in 1876, after the slaves had been freed. This painting, one of a series about the experiences of blacks, shows the simple dignity of the workers.

(b) Which part was hardest for northerners to accept? (c) How did northern states work against this part of the compromise?

7. (a) Why was the Kansas-Nebraska Act so difficult for northerners to accept? (b) Did the doctrine of popular sovereignty work well in Kansas? Explain your answer.

8. What happened to the nation's two national parties between 1850 and 1860?

9. (a) What did John Brown hope to start with his raid on the Harpers Ferry arsenal? (b) How did anti-slavery northerners like Louisa May Alcott view Brown? (c) How did Brown's raid help radicals who favored secession in the South?

10. Explain this statement: When Lincoln sent ships to resupply Fort Sumter, he fired the first shot in the Civil War.

GEOGRAPHY REVIEW

1. Look at the map "The Kansas-Nebraska Act 1854" on page 367. (a) What territories were opened to slavery by the Compromise of 1850? (b) What territories were opened to slavery by the Kansas-Nebraska Act? (c) What territories remained free after 1854?

*CT **2.** Look at the map "Agriculture in the South 1860" on page 359. (a) What crops were grown mainly along the coast or coastal waterways? (b) What crops were seldom grown any farther north than North Carolina? (c) Which of the crops shown was most important in Florida?

*CT **3.** Look at the map "Railroads 1860" on page 360. (a) Do most of the rail lines connect the North with the South or the East with the West? (b) By what date was there rail service between Atlanta and Chattanooga? Between Chattanooga and Memphis?

Americans often used patriotic symbols as decoration. Two blocks of this wedding quilt, made in 1850, show the monument to Washington in Baltimore, Maryland, and a pumper wagon.

USING THE TOOLS OF HISTORY

Using Maps and Graphs to Interpret Data

*CT Look at the map "The Election of 1860" on page 374. (a) Which candidate won the same percentage of popular votes and electoral votes? (b) Which candidate received more than 1 out of every 4 popular votes but only 1 out of every 25 electoral votes? (c) In what sense was Lincoln a minority President? (d) In what sense was he a sectional President?

READING AND THINKING SKILLS

The Comparison-Contrast Pattern

*CT Reread the subsection under the heading "The Industrial North Gains Power" on page 359. (a) List all the signal words in the first paragraph for the comparison-contrast pattern. (b) Judging from the signal words, do you think the paragraph is more about comparisons or contrasts? (c) The first two paragraphs show the economic power of the North. What comparison and what contrast are made in the third paragraph? (d) In the paragraph beginning "Southerners feared," a contrast between the South and the North is implied rather than stated with a signal word. What is the contrast between the regions' attitudes toward tariffs?

CHAPTER 15	1861-1865

THE CIVIL WAR

PREPARING FOR WAR
THE WAR IN 1861-1862
THE WAR EFFORT AT HOME
THE WAR IN 1863
THE FINAL CAMPAIGNS

15-1 PREPARING FOR WAR

READ TO FIND OUT

habeas corpus: right of a person to appear in front of a judge before being put in prison
martial law: rule by the military

—what the words *habeas corpus* and *martial law* mean.

—what southerners and northerners were fighting for in 1861.

—what advantages each side had as the war began.

—what happened to the border states.

When cannon shells burst on Fort Sumter, the confusion of the past months cleared away. New England poet Ralph Waldo Emerson wrote, "Sometimes gunpowder smells good." Four years later, after bitter warfare and 600,000 deaths, the gunpowder no longer smelled good. But in the spring of 1861 no one expected a long war. Southerners felt sure they would defeat the North in a few short battles. Most northerners agreed with Philadelphia lawyer Sidney George Fisher when he said, "I cannot imagine that the South has resources for a long war or even a short one."

While shells rained on Fort Sumter in the center of the harbor, the people of Charleston watched from rooftops. Some cheered. Others wept at the event that meant warfare could no longer be avoided.

ADVANTAGES OF THE NORTH

Northerners were confident that their great economic advantages would bring victory. Three fourths of the nation's wealth was in the North. The North had four fifths of the nation's factories, which would soon be producing guns and uniforms. The North grew more food than the South.

The North also controlled two thirds of the nation's railroad lines. These would be essential for moving troops and supplies. The North had a large number of merchant and navy ships, while the South had only a few merchant ships and no navy. Finally, the North's population was three times as large as the white population in the South.

ADVANTAGES OF THE SOUTH

The South's main economic resource was cotton. Southerners knew that cotton was very important to European textile mills. They believed that Great Britain and France would support the Confederacy in order to obtain cotton for their textile industries.

After students learn about the advantages of both sides, you may wish to have students cite such advantages and to list them on the chalkboard in two columns, one for the North and the other for the South.

Union and Confederacy 1861

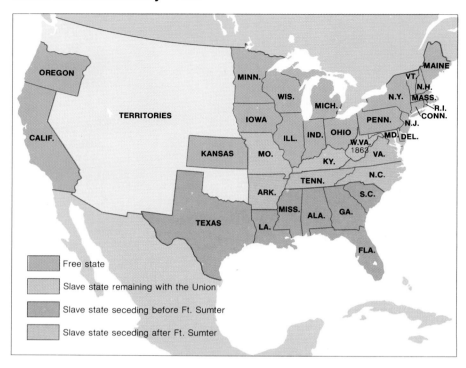

The southerners had the advantage of fighting a defensive war. To win, they needed only to push back invading Union forces. This would take fewer troops than the North would need to conquer the Confederacy. Also, southerners were fighting to protect their homes and their way of life. Because of this, the Confederate army could count on large numbers of volunteers. For these reasons, the difference in population did not seem important at first.

The Confederate army also had many of the nation's best military officers. One of them was Robert E. Lee of Virginia. During the war with Mexico, Lee had been described by General Winfield Scott as "the very best soldier that I ever saw in the field."

Lee had opposed secession. But when Virginia joined the Confederacy, he was forced to choose between his state and his nation. With a heavy heart, he decided to "return to my native state and share the miseries of my people." Looking back on his decision, he later wrote, "I did only what my duty demanded. I could have taken no other course without dishonor."

THE BORDER STATES

"There can be no neutrals in this war," Stephen Douglas said after the attack on Fort Sumter, "only patriots—or traitors." Most northerners were ready to fight for the Union and their flag.

In a letter to his son, Robert E. Lee wrote, "I can anticipate no greater calamity than a dissolution of the Union. . . . I hope . . . that all constitutional means will be exhausted before there is a resort to force. Secession is nothing but revolution. . . . Still, a Union that can only be maintained by swords and bayonets . . . has no charm for me."

Choosing sides was harder for the eight slave states between the Confederacy and the free states. By May 1861, four of these "border states"—Virginia, Arkansas, Tennessee, and North Carolina—had seceded. The western counties of Virginia, however, were loyal to the Union. They formed the new state of West Virginia. It joined the Union in 1863.

Delaware also rejected secession, but Maryland was deeply divided. In April 1861 a Massachusetts regiment passing through Baltimore was attacked by a pro-secession mob. Acting quickly, Lincoln set aside the right of **habeas corpus.** Habeas corpus is the right of a person to appear in front of a judge before being put in prison. The Constitution allows a President to suspend this right in a national emergency. Lincoln had several Maryland secessionists jailed without trial. After that, there was less talk of secession in Maryland.

Kentucky tried to remain neutral. But when Union and Confederate forces began fighting inside its borders, Kentucky sided with the Union. In Missouri, conflict between unionists and secessionists led to violence. Lincoln put the state under **martial law,** or rule by the military. Missouri did not secede, but 30,000 Missourians fought for the South.

In Virginia and states to the south, young men were quick to wear Confederate gray and take up arms against Union soldiers.

AMERICAN AGAINST AMERICAN

As Americans chose sides, they began to see why a civil war is the most painful kind of war. The conflict divided states, towns, and even families. Relatives of Varina Howell Davis, First Lady of the Confederacy, joined the Union army. Union First Lady Mary Todd Lincoln had three brothers in the Confederate army.

Meanwhile, both sides got ready for war. In the Confederate capital of Richmond, one woman watched "troops by the trains from all parts of the southern country coming to the rescue of old Virginia." Writing to her mother in New York, she warned, "Little do you dream at the North of what stuff they are made."

SECTION REVIEW   Answers will be found on page T 59.

1. Define these words: *habeas corpus, martial law.*

2. Identify: Robert E. Lee.

3. What were southerners fighting for in 1861?

4. What were northerners fighting for in 1861?

5. List at least three advantages the North had over the South.

6. List at least three advantages the South had over the North.

7. (a) How did Lincoln defeat Maryland's secessionists? (b) How did he stop violence between secessionists and unionists in Missouri?

Julia Ward Howe wrote "The Battle Hymn of the Republic," a popular marching song among the soldiers who chose to fight for the Union.

15-2 THE WAR IN 1861-1862

READ TO FIND OUT

unconditional surrender: total surrender without any advance agreement on terms

—what the term *unconditional surrender* means.

—how the Union planned to defeat the Confederacy.

—why Union forces were unable to capture the Confederate capital.

—what new developments in shipbuilding changed naval warfare.

—why the victories of Grant and Farragut were important.

—why Lincoln issued the Emancipation Proclamation in 1862.

In this patriotic Union poster, "country" meant all 34 states—including the states that had seceded—as shown by the 34 stars on the flag.

Union forces usually named battles after geographic features, Confederates after the nearest settlement. Thus many battles are known by two names.

In the spring of 1861, Lincoln and General Winfield Scott planned Union strategy. Scott wanted to set up a naval blockade along the Atlantic and Gulf coasts to prevent the South from trading cotton for supplies from Europe. Next, Union forces in the West would divide the Confederacy by taking control of the Mississippi, weakening the enemy. Union troops in the East would capture the Confederate capital, Richmond.

Scott's strategy was called the "anaconda plan." Like the anaconda snake, it would slowly, steadily crush the enemy. Most northerners, however, wanted a quick victory. Many believed that the war could be won with a single, all-out attack on Richmond.

THE FIRST BATTLE OF BULL RUN

By the early summer of 1861, 30,000 troops of the Union's newly formed Army of the Potomac were camped near Washington. In July the order to attack the Confederate capital came. General Irvin McDowell led the army out of Washington. The soldiers shared the road with sightseers who were eager to watch the war's first major battle.

Near Manassas Junction, the Union army met a large Confederate force at a stream called Bull Run. When the Union cannons boomed, one woman exclaimed, "Is that not first rate? I guess we will be in Richmond this time tomorrow." But Confederate General Thomas J. Jackson and his regiment stood their ground "like a stone wall." In the late afternoon "Stonewall" Jackson and the Confederates attacked Union lines. The Union troops fled in a panic back to Washington.

In the South news of the Battle of Manassas, as it was called, made people confident of winning the war. Northern dreams of quick victory, wrote poet Walt Whitman, had been "smashed like a china plate."

Displaying the flag of the Confederacy, the large, ironclad ship *Virginia,* earlier known as the *Merrimac,* engaged the Union ironclad *Monitor* in a long battle in 1862.

THE NAVAL WAR

For the next year the Army of the Potomac remained in Washington, gathering and training troops. Meanwhile, the anaconda plan was put into effect. Union warships began a blockade of southern ports.

When the war began, the Confederacy had no warships. But its able Secretary of the Navy, Stephen Mallory, acted quickly. He raised a warship that had been sunk when Union forces abandoned a Virginia naval yard. This ship, the *Merrimac,* was a large, steam-powered wooden vessel. Mallory had it covered with thick iron plates.

On March 8, 1862, the *Merrimac,* renamed the *Virginia,* chugged into Chesapeake Bay. The iron monster destroyed two wooden ships of the Union navy and threatened the entire blockading fleet. But the Union had built its own armored "cheesebox on a raft," the *Monitor.* The new ship arrived the next day to take on the Confederate "ironclad."

The two ships pounded each other for five hours. Then the *Virginia* headed back toward safer waters. The battle, one witness wrote, proved that "wooden vessels cannot contend with iron-clad ones." After that battle, more ironclads were added to both navies, but the South was never able to break the Union blockade.

Activity: Students can assume they are newspaper reporters during the Civil War and write eyewitness accounts for their papers of the battle between the *Monitor* and the *Virginia.*

THE WAR IN THE WEST

In 1862 Union forces also moved to gain control of the Mississippi River. In April David G. Farragut led a Union force of 46 vessels, the largest American fleet ever assembled, up the Mississippi. By April 26 Farragut forced New Orleans to surrender. Union troops occupied, or maintained control over, the city. By early May, Farragut's gunboats had captured Baton Rouge as well.

Farther north, Union forces under Ulysses S. Grant were also advancing toward the Mississippi. On February 6, 1862, Fort Henry on the Tennessee River fell to Grant. He then began a siege of Fort Donelson on the Cumberland River. The defenders of the fort asked for an armistice. Grant would accept nothing but an **unconditional surrender,** or a total surrender without any advance agreement on terms. After that, U. S. Grant was known as "Unconditional Surrender" Grant.

With the fall of Fort Donelson, Confederate troops under General Albert Sidney Johnston retreated south to Corinth, Mississippi. Grant followed. On April 6 he was surprised by Johnston as his army camped near Shiloh Church. By evening the Confederates had the better position. Most generals would have retreated, but not Grant.

The next day Grant ignored a bone-chilling rain and led a counterattack, or an attack against the attackers. By the end of the day, he had pushed the Confederates back to Corinth. The Battle of Shiloh left the Union in control of Kentucky and much of Tennessee.

From there the Union forces advanced to Memphis, Tennessee, and captured the city. The Union now controlled much of the Mississippi. Only Vicksburg and Port Hudson were still in Confederate hands.

THE WAR IN THE EAST

While Grant was fighting his way to the Mississippi, the Army of the Potomac under General George B. McClellan marched and drilled. In the White House, Lincoln grew more and more impatient.

By spring McClellan was ready to move. He sent 100,000 troops by ship to take Richmond, the Confederate capital. McClellan landed his forces south of Richmond on the Virginia peninsula. On June 1, 1862, southern troops under General Joseph D. Johnston stopped the Union advance in the Battle of Seven Pines. Johnston was badly wounded. The command of the Confederate forces passed to General Robert E. Lee.

General Lee launched a series of counterattacks called the Seven Days' Battles. McClellan retreated and then evacuated, or removed, his troops by sea. He planned to join General John Pope and his forces in northern Virginia. The combined forces would then march on Richmond.

Lee hurried north to attack Pope's forces before McClellan could join them. Lee and Stonewall Jackson defeated a Union force under Pope at the second Battle of Bull Run. As Pope's troops retreated, Lee did the unexpected. He crossed the Potomac River into Maryland. Lee hoped this action would persuade Maryland to join the Confederacy. He also wanted to capture Harrisburg, Pennsylvania, an important railroad center, to cut off Washington, D.C., from the rest of the Union.

Grant was known for his steadfastness and unwillingness to retreat. After the Battle of Shiloh, many northerners called for Grant's removal because of the large number of Union casualties. Lincoln replied, "I can't spare this man—he fights!"

Lincoln became so impatient with McClellan that he sent the general a note saying, "My dear McClellan: If you don't want to use the army, I should like to borrow it for a while. Yours respectfully. A. Lincoln."

The Civil War 1861–1862

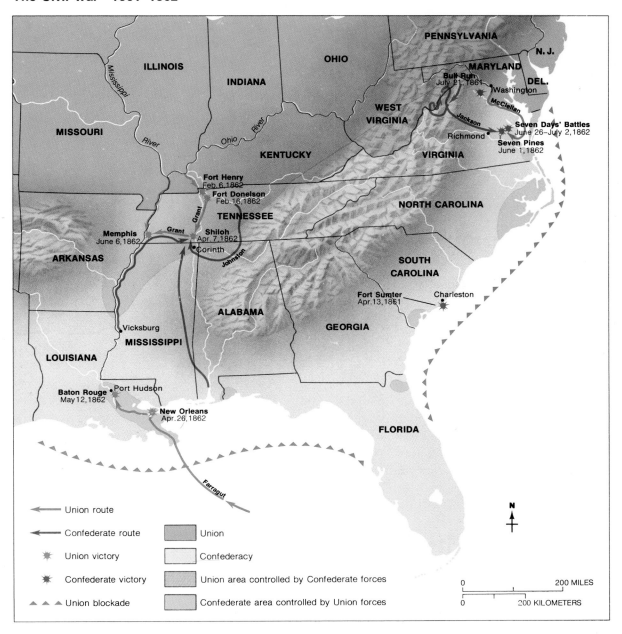

Map legend:
- ← Union route
- ← Confederate route
- ✳ Union victory
- ✳ Confederate victory
- ▲ ▲ ▲ Union blockade
- Union
- Confederacy
- Union area controlled by Confederate forces
- Confederate area controlled by Union forces

0   200 MILES
0   200 KILOMETERS

ANTIETAM

At Sharpsburg, Lee divided his army. Jackson led his troops to Harpers Ferry, where they captured the federal arsenal. Lee waited at Antietam Creek to meet McClellan once again. On September 17, 1862, the two armies clashed. Again and again the Union army hit Lee's badly outnumbered forces, but the Confederate line held. Before the Battle of

You may wish to remind students of John Brown's raid on the arsenal at Harpers Ferry in 1859.

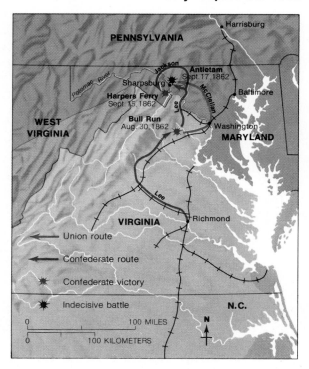

King Abraham before and after issuing
the Emancipation Proclamation.

The Union claimed a victory in the Battle of Antietam, fought on September 17, 1862. On September 22 Abraham Lincoln announced freedom for slaves in the South, effective January 1. A newspaper published the cartoon of Lincoln, titled "Masks and Faces."

Antietam ended, 5,000 soldiers lay dead and 18,000 more were wounded. It was the bloodiest day of the war. As Lee retreated across the Potomac, McClellan claimed victory. Many soldiers who fought at Antietam saw the slaughter as "a defeat for both armies."

The Battle of Antietam did, however, have important effects on the war. It broke the Confederate offensive in the East. And it was enough of a Union victory to enable Lincoln to take steps to end slavery.

THE EMANCIPATION PROCLAMATION

A week after Antietam, Lincoln issued the Emancipation Proclamation. He announced that on January 1, 1863, all slaves in Confederate territory were to be emancipated, or set free. Since the start of the war, Lincoln had resisted pleas from abolitionists to end slavery. The purpose of the war, he insisted, was to preserve the Union. Freeing the slaves might drive the loyal border states into the Confederacy.

By the fall of 1862, Lincoln was worried that Britain and France might recognize the Confederacy as an independent nation. A statement about emancipation, he hoped, would bring public opinion in those countries to the Union side. He waited to make his announcement until after a Union victory. He did not want the proclamation to seem like an act of desperation.

The Emancipation Proclamation took effect on New Year's Day. It did not free any slaves at once. Slaves in states loyal to the Union were not affected. And Lincoln had no real power to free slaves in the Confederate states. But the proclamation kept European nations from aiding the Confederacy.

The Emancipation Proclamation also turned the war into a struggle for freedom. "The time came," Lincoln said, "when I felt that slavery must die that the nation might live."

In the Emancipation Proclamation, Lincoln urged "the people so declared to be free to abstain from all violence unless in necessary self-defense; and I recommend to them that, in all cases when allowed, they labor faithfully for reasonable wages."

SECTION REVIEW Answers will be found on page T 59.

1. Define this term: *unconditional surrender.*

2. Identify: *Virginia* and *Monitor*, Thomas J. "Stonewall" Jackson, David Farragut, Ulysses S. Grant, Emancipation Proclamation.

3. Explain the anaconda plan.

4. What did the battle between the *Virginia* and the *Monitor* prove?

5. By mid-1862, the Union had fought four major battles in an effort to take Richmond. Tell what the outcome of each battle was.

6. Why did Lincoln issue the Emancipation Proclamation in 1862?

15-3 THE WAR EFFORT AT HOME

READ TO FIND OUT

income tax: a tax on the money people receive for work or investments
conscription: draft

—what the words *income tax* and *conscription* mean.

—what problems Lincoln and Davis faced as wartime Presidents.

—how black soldiers overcame prejudice against them.

—how women contributed to the war effort.

Abraham Lincoln

President Lincoln and President Davis faced difficult problems at home. Both leaders had cabinets made up of strong-willed people who had their own ideas about running a wartime government. Davis also had to deal with state governors who strongly supported states' rights. Such leaders did not like taking orders from the Confederate President.

Both Presidents also faced opposition to the war itself. In the South, some people openly backed the Union and opposed secession. In the North a group of Democrats demanded an end to the war and a negotiated peace. Republicans called them "Copperheads," after the poisonous copperhead snake. Both Davis and Lincoln suspended the right of habeas corpus in order to put down opposition. People suspected of being disloyal were jailed without trial.

MONEY AND SUPPLIES

As hopes for a quick victory faded, both sides faced problems raising revenue to pay for the war. The Confederate Congress was not willing to impose high taxes. When the Confederacy could not borrow enough money to pay its bills, it turned to the printing press. Paper dollars flooded the South, and the Confederacy was soon faced with runaway inflation—rapidly rising prices.

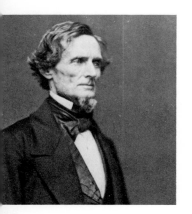

Jefferson Davis

The worst blow to the southern economy was the success of the Union naval blockade. The Confederacy asked the British to help southern ships break through the blockade, but Britain refused. Without help from the British navy, the South could not ship its cotton to foreign markets. Nor could it import needed supplies.

Southern farmers planted their fields with food crops to feed both soldiers and civilians, or people not in the military. Yet the South was often short of food. Invading Union armies destroyed crops and cut railroad lines, interfering with the shipment of food to southern cities and army camps. Factory products were also in short supply.

You may wish to read to the class passages from *Mary Chesnut's Civil War*, edited by C. Vann Woodward.

Mary Boykin Chesnut kept a diary of the war. She met and wrote about Jefferson Davis and other southern leaders.

Money for the war effort was raised at bazaars and fairs. This magazine cover showed the Metropolitan Fair of 1864.

The Confederate army faced growing shortages of food, uniforms, boots, and horses as the war went on. Mary Boykin Chesnut, whose husband was a military aide to President Davis, noted such changes in her diary. In the early years of the war, she had written of well-dressed troops. By 1863 she wrote of soldiers dressed in "rags and tags."

The North raised taxes and sold bonds to pay for the war. In 1861 Congress passed the nation's first **income tax.** Northerners were required to pay taxes on the money they received for work or investments. When taxes and bond sales did not raise enough money, the government printed money. The new federal bank notes were called "greenbacks" because of their color. Since they were not backed by silver or gold, they lost about half their value during the war. Still, inflation was not as bad in the North as in the South.

Nor did northern soldiers suffer from shortages. Aided by labor-saving inventions such as the reaper, Union farmers produced large crops of wheat and corn. The sewing machine and the Gordon McKay shoe machine sped up the production of uniforms and boots. Shortages of cotton were met by increased production of wool.

Inflation in the South reduced the value of this $500 bill to about $10 in gold or silver.

In the South as well as the North, those drafted could buy substitutes to soldier for them. In July 1863 Confederate General Braxton Bragg and fellow officers protested "that unfortunate provision of the exemption bill . . . unprincipled substitutes . . . desert at the first favorable moment."

FILLING THE RANKS

After the first rush of volunteers, both sides had trouble finding enough troops. In April 1862 the Confederate Congress passed a **conscription,** or draft, law forcing any man between 18 and 35 to serve in the army. Slaveholders who owned at least 20 slaves were excused from the draft.

As a result, southerners protested that it was "a rich man's war but a poor man's fight." By 1865 slaveholders were no longer excused, and the draft was extended to men between 17 and 55.

In 1863 the Union also turned to a draft. Many people resented the fact that a person could be excused from the draft by paying $300. Riots protesting the draft broke out in several states. The worst fighting occurred in New York City in July.

The Union army was aided by the stream of immigrants pouring into the North. Eventually, immigrants made up one fifth of the Union forces. In one division, orders were given in four languages.

BLACK SOLDIERS

Blacks, both slave and free, also aided the Union and Confederate war effort. The Confederacy used slaves in mines, in factories, and on railroads. But service as a soldier, in combat, was not allowed until near the end of the war. In March 1865 the Confederate Congress called for the enlistment of 300,000 slaves as soldiers. A few black units were organized, but none ever went into action.

After the Emancipation Proclamation was issued, the Union finally allowed blacks to serve as soldiers. Massachusetts was one of the first states to organize black regiments. When the black soldiers of the 54th Massachusetts Infantry learned that they were being paid less than white soldiers, they refused to accept any pay at all. To have accepted their pay would have meant accepting unequal treatment. In 1864, at Lincoln's urging, Congress finally granted black soldiers equal pay, including all back pay.

Regiments of black soldiers were also organized in Union-occupied territory in the South. As Union troops advanced into the Confederacy, thousands of slaves fled to Union lines. Many worked for wages for the Union as carpenters, cooks, nurses, and scouts. In time, many also joined the Union army.

Some whites doubted that ex-slaves could be made into soldiers. But the leaders of black units learned to respect their troops. "You have no idea how my prejudices with regard to Negro troops have been dispelled by the battle the other day," wrote one white officer. "The brigade of Negroes fought splendidly; could not have done better. They are superior in discipline to the white troops and just as brave."

WOMEN AND THE WAR

For women on both sides, the war brought new burdens and new opportunities. On farms and plantations women replaced men behind the plow. Women moved into factory jobs that had been closed to them

Sojourner Truth spoke out for equal treatment of blacks as soldiers as well as citizens.

CHAPTER 15   1861-1865

You may wish to inform students that Charlotte Forten was the granddaughter of James Forten, whom they studied in Chapter 12 (page 314).

★ ★ ★ ★ ★ ★ ★ **AMERICAN VALUES IN ACTION** ★ ★ ★ ★ ★ ★ ★ ★

CHARLOTTE FORTEN

In October 1862 the steamer *United States* left New York Harbor. On board was twenty-seven-year-old Charlotte Forten, setting out on the adventure of her life.

Forten's destination was the Sea Islands off South Carolina. Island plantation owners, fleeing Union forces, had left behind thousands of slaves. To northern reformers, this was a golden opportunity. They would educate the ex-slaves and prove that they could function as free citizens.

Charlotte Forten, a free black northerner, rushed to volunteer. Forten had been nourished on talk of equal rights around the family dinner table. She was educated, a teacher, but she had known prejudice.

When Forten arrived on St. Helena, one of the islands, she found it like "a strange wild dream." She stared at huge oaks bearded with lacy moss. She saw oranges ripening in the dead of winter.

No less unusual were the ex-slaves. They had come directly from Africa and been isolated for generations on the islands. It was a challenge, Forten discovered, to learn their customs and "decipher" their speech.

Teaching, too, was a challenge. Forten had to be ready to teach anybody. "Part of my scholars are very tiny—babies, I call them," she wrote. "I never before saw children so eager to learn." Black soldiers also came to the schoolhouse to hear Forten's lessons.

At times, she nearly dropped from the long hours and the steaming heat. But "let me not forget," she told herself, "that I came here to work." She did not forget. She had come to help break down the barriers of racism and slavery. To Forten, education was the key.

---

in the past. In Washington, D.C., women were hired to work in the Treasury Department for the first time. They were paid $600 a year, an almost unheard-of salary for a woman at that time. Soon other government agencies were hiring women.

Women served both armies as soldiers and spies. Harriet Tubman and Sojourner Truth were scouts for the Union army. Tubman guided the black 2nd South Carolina Volunteers in their raids along the Combahee River. They returned from one expedition with 727 slaves they had freed. Confederate spy Rose O'Neal Greenhow was accused of passing General McClellan's plans to the enemy, forcing him "four times to change them."

Women made their greatest contribution as nurses. Dorothea Dix, Superintendent of Nurses for the Union, knew that many men thought women did not belong in camp hospitals. Women were slowly accepted as nurses, however. Their training was directed by Dr. Elizabeth Blackwell, the first American woman to graduate from a medical college.

Women nurses soon understood why soldiers tried hard to stay out of camp hospitals. Kate Cummings, a Confederate nurse, wrote, "Nothing that I had ever heard or read had given me the faintest notion of the horrors witnessed here." Hospitals lacked ways of treating water and sewage to prevent the spread of disease. Scientists had not yet discov-

Charlotte Forten

Activity: Students can research and report on the remarkable life and career of Dr. Elizabeth Blackwell.

In a workshop in Massachusetts, women prepared cartridges for Union guns. The gunpowder on hand made the work dangerous.

Caught smuggling some medicine to the South, a woman faced arrest and jail. Other southern women succeeded in smuggling war goods.

Later, Clara Barton served as a battlefront nurse in the Franco-Prussian War and observed the work of the International Red Cross. Returning home, she worked to convince Americans that they had need of such an organization. After the American Red Cross was founded, she served as its first president from 1882 to 1904.

ered the importance of antiseptics in preventing infection. Thousands of soldiers died from wounds and disease.

Women were not allowed at the front lines. But Clara Barton ignored the ban. She risked her life to carry food and medical supplies to the wounded in battle areas. By the end of the war she was known as the "Angel of the Battlefield." Barton built on her wartime experience when she founded the American Red Cross in 1881.

The contributions made by women did not escape the attention of President Lincoln. "If all that has been said by orators and poets since the creation of the world in praise of women was applied to the women of America," he said, "it would not do them justice for their conduct during the war."

SECTION REVIEW Answers will be found on page T 59.

1. Define these words: *income tax, conscription.*

2. Identify: Copperheads, Elizabeth Blackwell, Clara Barton.

3. (a) What problems did Lincoln face in uniting northerners behind the war effort? (b) What problems did Davis face?

4. (a) How did the South pay for the war? (b) How did the North?

5. How did the Union blockade hurt the South?

6. When they ran out of volunteers, how did both the North and the South meet their need for soldiers?

7. What did the black 54th Massachusetts Infantry do to protest unequal pay?

8. List at least four jobs done by women during the war.

15-4 THE WAR IN 1863

READ TO FIND OUT

—why Lee invaded the North in 1863.

—how Lee's offensive ended at Gettysburg.

—how Grant divided the Confederacy.

For the Confederacy, 1863 marked the turning point in the war. The seemingly unbeatable Confederate force led by Robert E. Lee finally suffered a crushing defeat. For Abraham Lincoln, 1863 was a year spent searching for a general who could lead the Union to victory.

FREDERICKSBURG AND CHANCELLORSVILLE

After the Battle of Antietam, Lincoln urged General McClellan to attack Lee's retreating army. But the cautious general refused. Lincoln replaced him with Ambrose E. Burnside. The new general confessed to his officers that he was "not fit for so big a command."

Arrayed at the Battle of Fredericksburg, Union troops behind the lines could see wounded soldiers as well as the smoke of distant fighting. This painting is by John Richards.

Gettysburg

McClellan's reluctance to engage the enemy (page 395) was one of Lincoln's greatest problems. A story has it that a northerner asked Lincoln for a pass to Richmond. Lincoln replied, "My dear sir, if I should give you one, it would do you no good. . . . I have given McClellan and more than 200,000 others passes to Richmond, and not one of them has gotten there!"

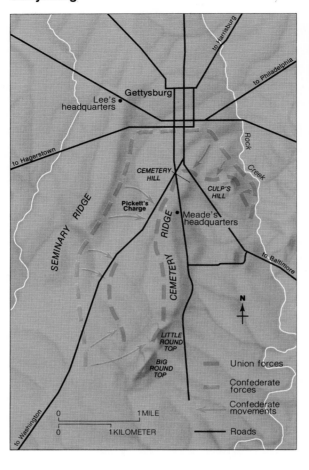

Confederates carried this flag into battle. Its design became part of a larger flag chosen as the banner of the South in 1863.

Like a crooked spine at the center of the battlefield, Cemetery Ridge gave a strong defensive position to Union riflemen.

A month after Antietam, Burnside marched 113,000 troops toward Richmond. By early December 1862, they had taken the Virginia town of Fredericksburg. But Lee was waiting on Marye's Heights above the town. Burnside ordered his troops to attack. As they charged up the hill, "sheet after sheet of flame shot forth from the heights." By the time Burnside gave up the assault, he had lost 12,700 troops. Lee had lost 5,300. "The army of the Potomac is thoroughly demoralized," wrote Charles Francis Adams, Jr., as the Union forces staggered back to Washington. "Desertion is the order of the day."

Next Lincoln turned the Army of the Potomac over to Joseph Hooker. "Fighting Joe" rebuilt the army until it was, in his eyes, "the finest on the planet." In the first days of May 1863, however, his 130,000 troops were defeated by Lee's 60,000 seasoned soldiers near Chancellorsville, Virginia. Hooker ordered another Union retreat.

Again Lee had proved himself the superior general. His joy at this major victory, however, was clouded by the death of Stonewall Jackson, the man who had served him as "my right arm."

Using the map, students can show where Pickett's forces encountered the enemy and (as the text indicates) where Lee "tried to punch through the Union line on both ends."

UNDERSTANDING GEOGRAPHY

THE GEOGRAPHY OF A BATTLE

One of the bloodiest battles of the Civil War was fought during the first three days of July 1863. The battle site was near the town of Gettysburg, Pennsylvania. Neither side, however, had planned to fight there.

General Lee was moving his Confederate army of 75,000 soldiers into Pennsylvania. Some 90,000 Union troops, under General George Meade, were tracking Lee's army. On July 1 advance troops from both sides accidentally came upon one another in Gettysburg. Shots were exchanged. Confederate and Union troops hurried toward Gettysburg. By the end of the day, battle lines were drawn in the countryside outside the town.

The countryside is hilly, rising to steep ridges and dropping to wheat fields. West of town is a Lutheran seminary. From there, Seminary Ridge stretches north and south. About 1 mile (1.6 kilometers) to the east, roughly paralleling Seminary Ridge, is Cemetery Ridge. Slightly to the northeast of Cemetery Ridge is Cemetery Hill and Culp's Hill. About 2 miles south of Cemetery Ridge rise two other hills: Little Round Top and Big Round Top.

The Union troops took up positions along Cemetery Ridge and on the two sets of hills. Their battle line resembled an upside-down fishhook, with the hook curving to the northeast around Cemetery and Culp's hills. The Confederate troops lined up opposite the Union line, along Seminary Ridge.

On July 2 Lee's army tried to punch through the Union line on both ends. The Confederates gained the fields at the foot of the two Round Tops and a foothold on Culp's Hill. But they did not dislodge the Union fishhook.

On the night of July 2, General Meade met with his officers. They guessed that Lee would next attack the center of the Union line, having failed to break through the flanks.

The Union had an excellent defensive position, although it had developed more by accident than by planning. Cemetery Ridge was topped by stone walls, behind which Union soldiers could kneel to fire. From the ridge they had a clear view of the fields below. Troops and cannons could be moved quickly from the left or right to reinforce the center.

Lee wished to avoid a direct charge against Union lines. But geography left him no choice. He ordered an attack on the center of the Union line, hoping to split it in two.

On July 3 some 15,000 Confederate soldiers charged forward. Many were mowed down as they crossed the open fields. The survivors vainly tried to scramble up Cemetery Ridge in the face of withering cannon and rifle fire. Finally, the remaining soldiers staggered back to Seminary Ridge.

The next day—the Fourth of July—the two armies stood facing one another. One soldier wrote that they were "like spent lions nursing their wounds." Meade did not counterattack, and Lee began leading his broken army back to Virginia. The Battle of Gettysburg was over.

GETTYSBURG

After Chancellorsville, Lee felt confident enough to risk another invasion of the North. He wanted to slice into Pennsylvania, cutting off the Northeast from the Northwest. Such a move might convince Britain and France to recognize the Confederacy as an independent nation. Lee also hoped that the invasion would cause northerners to lose faith in their leaders and demand peace.

As Lee marched north, Lincoln again changed generals. George C. Meade was given command of the Army of the Potomac. Two days later he faced Lee at Gettysburg, Pennsylvania. On July 1, 1863, Union forces lined up on a ridge near Gettysburg known as Cemetery Ridge. A mile to the west, the Confederate army gathered behind Seminary Ridge.

On July 2 the Confederates poured around the edges of Cemetery Ridge, looking for weak spots in the Union line. But the Union ranks held firm. The next day Lee ordered an all-out attack against the center of the Union position. As cannons filled the air with smoke and thunder, General George Pickett led 15,000 Confederate troops toward Cemetery Ridge. Pickett's charge was a disaster. The attackers were forced to retreat in a "storm of lead and iron." The Confederates did not attack again. On July 4 Lee led his remaining troops back to Virginia.

While Lee retreated, the Union army buried the 7,000 soldiers who died at Gettysburg. Four months later Lincoln dedicated a national cemetery on the field of battle. In his Gettysburg Address, the President reminded Americans that they were fighting for a nation that had been born in liberty and was committed to the idea that all people are created equal. While honoring the dead, he said, it was up to the living to see that "this nation, under God, shall have a new birth of freedom: and that government of the people, by the people, for the people, shall not perish from the earth."

You may wish to read (or have a student read) to the class the whole of Lincoln's Gettysburg Address, a classic of American literature.

VICKSBURG AND PORT HUDSON

While Lee's and Meade's forces fought at Gettysburg, Grant was marching to victory in the West. Since the middle of 1862, he had tried to capture Vicksburg and Port Hudson. Together, they guarded a 400-mile (644-kilometer) stretch of the Mississippi River.

The capture of Vicksburg seemed impossible. The city sat on a bluff above a hairpin bend in the river. It had been heavily fortified, or strengthened. But after several fierce battles, Union troops surrounded the town. For six weeks Vicksburg lay under siege. Civilians dug caves into the cliffs to escape Union cannon fire. The defenders survived by eating mules, horses, and rats.

Vicksburg finally surrendered on July 4, 1863. Five days later Port Hudson surrendered to Union troops. The Mississippi was in Union hands. The Confederacy had been divided.

CHATTANOOGA AND CHICKAMAUGA

While Grant was advancing toward Vicksburg, General William Rosecrans marched the Union's Army of the Cumberland toward Tennessee. His target was Chattanooga, an important Confederate railroad center

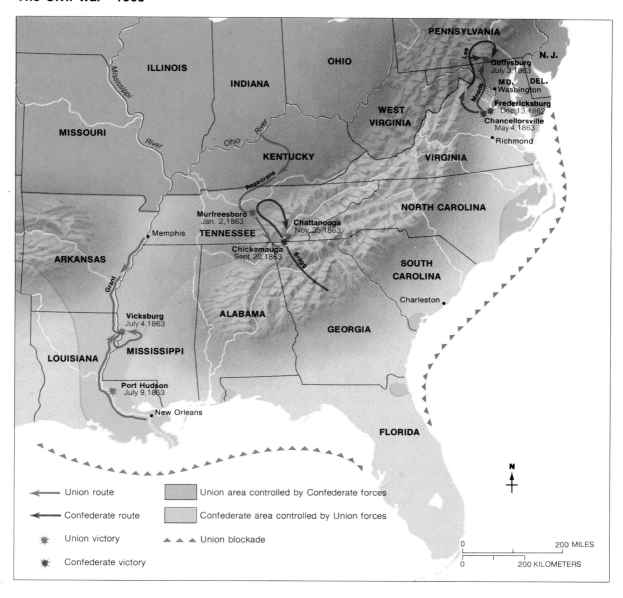

on the Tennessee River. On January 2, 1863, he met a large Confederate force led by General Braxton Bragg at Murfreesboro. The bloody clash of armies ended with Bragg in retreat. Combined casualties totaled more than 24,000.

Rosecrans left Murfreesboro in June. By September he faced Bragg once more along a creek called Chickamauga, an Indian word meaning "river of death." In two days of combat, the creek earned its name. As the rest of the Union line crumbled, General George Thomas stood his ground. Only the courage of "the rock of Chickamauga" and his troops kept the battle from ending in complete disaster for the Union.

Have students locate the sites of the Battles of Vicksburg, Chancellorsville, Gettysburg, Fredericksburg, and Chickamauga on the map.

Among the Union troops sent to Tennessee were the black soldiers of this artillery unit, one of twelve such units in the northern army. Pioneer photographer Mathew Brady took this photograph.

For discussion: Do students agree that 1863 was the turning point of the war? Why or why not?

The Army of the Cumberland was able to retreat to Chattanooga. But as Bragg's forces surrounded the city, Rosecrans found that his target had become a trap. The Confederate artillery, posted on the heights south of the city, controlled Union supply routes. Rosecrans's army was soon dangerously short of supplies.

The Confederate siege was ended when fresh troops under Grant reached Chattanooga by rail. After three days of fighting, Bragg's army left Tennessee on November 15, 1863. Dismayed, President Jefferson Davis replaced Bragg with General Joseph Johnston.

The heroes of the Battle of Chattanooga were the soldiers of IV Corps. They had driven the Confederates off Missionary Ridge near the town. Carl Schurz wrote that "without orders,—it may almost be said against orders,—they rushed forward like wildcats." When the Union troops had appeared on the top of the ridge, the Confederates "fled in wild confusion." In Schurz's eyes, "It was a soldier's triumph, one of the most brilliant in history."

SECTION REVIEW Answers will be found on page T 60.

1. Identify: George C. Meade, George Pickett, George Thomas, Gettysburg Address.

2. What were Lee's two goals in invading the North?

3. Why were Grant's victories at Vicksburg and Port Hudson important to the Union?

4. Why was the capture of Chattanooga important to the Union?

15-5 THE FINAL CAMPAIGNS

READ TO FIND OUT

—what the term *total war* means.

—what Grant's strategy was for winning the war.

—how Union victories influenced the election of 1864.

—what events led to Lee's surrender at Appomattox.

total war: war on the enemy's will to fight and ability to support an army

After Chattanooga, Lincoln decided that General Grant was the person who could bring the war to an end. Early in 1864 Grant arrived in Washington to take charge of the Union forces. Writer Richard Henry Dana was surprised by his "slightly seedy look, as if he was out of office and on half pay, nothing to do but hang around."

TOTAL WAR

There was nothing grand about Grant. He looked at the war in a common-sense way. "The art of war is simple enough," he wrote. "Find out where your enemy is. Get at him as soon as you can. Strike at him as hard as you can and as often as you can, and keep moving on." Grant believed in **total war**—war on the enemy's will to fight and ability to support an army. In total war, civilians are in as much danger as soldiers.

First Grant put General William Tecumseh Sherman in charge of all western armies. Sherman was ordered to march into Georgia and destroy the Confederate army under General Joe Johnston. Meanwhile, Grant would lead the Army of the Potomac against Lee's army and capture Richmond.

"ON TO RICHMOND"

On May 4, 1864, Grant moved into Virginia with 100,000 troops. They met Lee's army of 60,000 soldiers in the Wilderness, a dense forest. After a two-day nightmare of bloody fighting, Grant had lost 18,000 troops. Instead of turning back to Washington, he pressed on.

The two armies next met at Spotsylvania Court House. Again Grant suffered heavy losses, but he would not retreat. "I propose to fight it out along this line," he said, "if it takes all summer." He followed Lee to Cold Harbor, where he lost 7,000 soldiers in just fifteen minutes of desperate fighting.

The Civil War   1864–1865

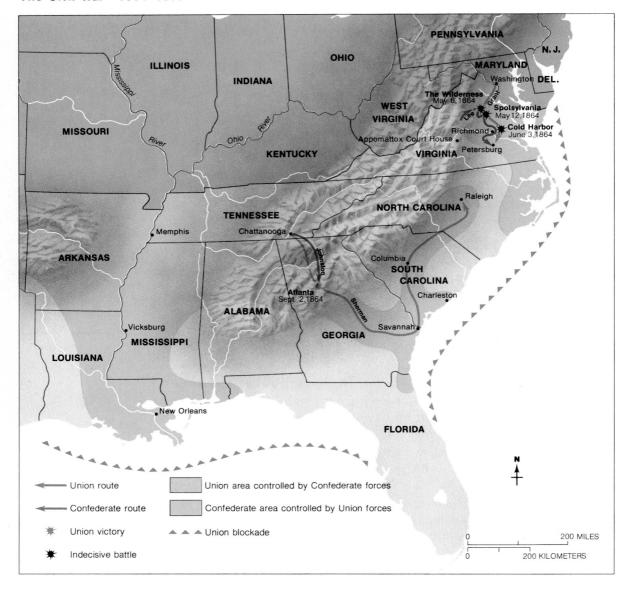

Using the map, students can identify states (or parts of states) controlled by the Confederacy and the sites of indecisive battles.

Lee moved on to defend Petersburg. This important railroad center was 20 miles (32 kilometers) south of Richmond. Grant followed, placing Petersburg under siege. His casualties by that time had almost equaled Lee's entire army. But he was able to reinforce the army with fresh troops.

Lee was not so fortunate. There were no more men to replace his losses. His only hope was to hang on a little longer. Antiwar feeling was growing in the North with each new report of Grant's losses. Perhaps the election of 1864 would produce a new President who would seek peace with the Confederacy on acceptable terms.

The morale, or sense of purpose, of the North received a serious blow when Confederate General Jubal A. Early almost captured Washington in July 1864. Grant sent General Philip H. Sheridan to destroy Early's force and its base in the Shenandoah Valley. "Leave nothing to invite the enemy to return," Grant ordered. "Let that valley be so left that crows flying over it will have to carry their rations along with them." Houses, barns, and fields were destroyed as Sheridan waged total war.

MARCHING THROUGH GEORGIA

In May 1864 Sherman left Chattanooga with 100,000 troops. Besides chasing Johnston, his orders were to move into enemy country and inflict "all the damage you can against their war resources." By September, Sherman's army had reached Atlanta, a major manufacturing and railroad center. They set the city ablaze. "We have utterly destroyed Atlanta," wrote a Union private.

News of Sheridan's victory in the Shenandoah Valley and the fall of Atlanta boosted Lincoln's reelection campaign. Lincoln and his running mate, Andrew Johnson of Tennessee, had been expected to lose to Democratic candidate General George McClellan. But when the votes were totaled, Lincoln had overwhelmed McClellan.

While the North celebrated Lincoln's reelection, gloom spread across the South. From Atlanta, Sherman marched eastward toward Savannah, promising to "make Georgia howl." His troops left behind a path of destruction 60 miles (97 kilometers) wide. Railroads were torn up, farms burned, and houses looted. After taking Savannah in December, Sherman marched north through the Carolinas. By March Sherman was camped near Raleigh, North Carolina. There he waited for Grant's final attack on Richmond.

1864 election poster

Union wagons like these at Petersburg, Virginia, kept Grant's army well supplied in the final months of the war, a time when the South had few military goods and no way to replace them.

The Final Days

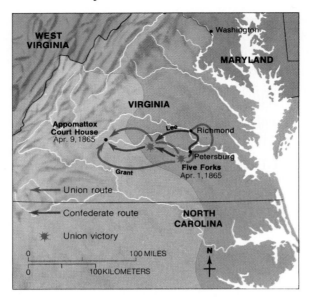

At the Battle of Five Forks, Lee made his last attack of the war. It failed, and southern troops left both Petersburg and Richmond.

APPOMATTOX

On April 1, 1865, Union forces broke through Lee's defenses at the Battle of Five Forks. Within a few days Grant took both Petersburg and Richmond. The two armies met for the last time at the village of Appomattox Court House on April 9. When Lee saw that he was surrounded, he told his officers, "There is nothing left for me to do but to go and see General Grant, and I would rather die a thousand deaths."

Grant and Lee met at a house in the village to discuss the terms of surrender. The Confederate troops were free to go home if they promised to fight no longer. Lee asked that his soldiers be allowed to take their horses and mules to help with spring plowing. Grant agreed. The Union leader also sent food to the half-starved Confederate army.

As Lee returned to his headquarters, Union troops began to cheer wildly and fire their cannons. Grant told them to end the celebration. "The war is over," he said, "the rebels are our countrymen again."

SECTION REVIEW Answers will be found on page T 60.

1. Define this term: *total war.*

2. Identify: William Tecumseh Sherman, Andrew Johnson, Appomattox Court House.

3. What two Union victories helped Lincoln to win reelection?

4. What Union advantage helped Grant to defeat Lee in 1865?

5. What were the terms of the Confederate surrender?

In his farewell message to the Army of Northern Virginia, Lee wrote that he had "been compelled to yield to overwhelming numbers and resources. I need not tell the survivors of so many hard-fought battles . . . that I have consented to this result from no distrust of them; but feeling that valor and devotion could accomplish nothing that would compensate for the loss that must have attended the continuance of the conflict, I determined to avoid the useless sacrifice."

When the Civil War began, both sides expected a short war. The North had an advantage over the South in economic strength and population. But the South had better military leaders and could fight a defensive war. After Fort Sumter, four border states chose secession while four remained in the Union.

During the first two years of the war, the Union navy set up a blockade of the Confederacy and captured New Orleans. In the West, Union forces led by Grant began to gain control of the Mississippi. In the East, Lee proved himself to be a brilliant commander. Again and again, he beat back attacks on the Confederate capital of Richmond. He then invaded Maryland, only to be driven back at Antietam. After that battle, Lincoln announced his Emancipation Proclamation, promising an end to slavery in the Confederacy.

As the war dragged on, Lincoln and Davis faced similar problems in raising money and finding soldiers for their armies. Both sides turned to conscription to fill the ranks. The need for troops led the Union to organize black regiments in the North and in Union-occupied territory in the South. On both sides women moved into jobs once held mainly by men and helped the war effort.

The year 1863 marked a turning point in the war. Lee's second invasion of the North was turned back at Gettysburg. Union forces gained control of the entire Mississippi River and the Confederate railroad center of Chattanooga. In Grant, Lincoln found a general who could lead Union forces to victory.

The last two years of the war brought suffering and destruction to large parts of the South. In Virginia, Georgia, and the Carolinas, Union forces led by Sheridan and Sherman waged total war. Grant finally succeeded in capturing Richmond and forcing Lee to surrender. The war that cost the nation some 600,000 lives ended at Appomattox Court House on April 9, 1865.

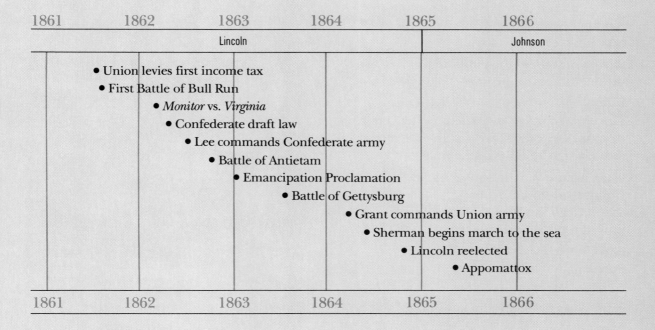

1861	1862	1863	1864	1865	1866
		Lincoln			Johnson

- Union levies first income tax
- First Battle of Bull Run
- *Monitor* vs. *Virginia*
- Confederate draft law
- Lee commands Confederate army
- Battle of Antietam
- Emancipation Proclamation
- Battle of Gettysburg
- Grant commands Union army
- Sherman begins march to the sea
- Lincoln reelected
- Appomattox

CHAPTER SURVEY

VOCABULARY REVIEW

From this list of vocabulary words, choose the one that best completes each sentence below.

(a) conscription (d) martial law
(b) habeas corpus (e) total war
(c) income tax   (f) unconditional
         surrender

1. Grant demanded the ____ of enemy forces.

2. ____ results in the drafting of civilians into the military.

3. ____ is war against civilians as well as against the enemy army.

4. Rule by the military is ____.

5. Once Lincoln suspended ____, Copperheads could be jailed without first being brought before a judge.

6. ____ is a payment made to the government on money received from work or investments.

CHAPTER REVIEW

1. How did the North and the South differ in economic strength and population at the beginning of the Civil War?

2. What effect did these differences have on the later stages of the war?

3. (a) Which border states seceded despite Lincoln's efforts to keep them in the Union? (b) What emergency powers did Lincoln use to keep Maryland from seceding?

4. (a) What two main strategies did the Union try during the war? (b) How did they differ? (c) Which strategy finally proved more successful?

5. (a) In what way was the Emancipation Proclamation a failure? (b) In what ways was it a success?

6. (a) What problems did both Lincoln and Davis face in organizing the war effort? (b) What special problems did Davis have?

7. What new opportunities for women occurred during the war?

8. The year 1863 has been called the turning point in the Civil War. (a) Name the major Union victories in that year. (b) What did the Confederacy lose in these battles, besides land? (c) What did the Union gain?

9. (a) What resistance did Grant meet when he marched into Virginia in 1864? (b) How were his casualties then like the casualties of other Union generals who had invaded Virginia? (c) What made Grant's campaign different from those of others?

10. (a) What were Grant's orders to Sherman

The aristocratic Robert E. Lee was very different from the rough and uncultured Ulysses S. Grant. Both generals, however, were superb military leaders.

Frank Bellew drew this cartoon in late 1864. The paper in Lincoln's hand says, ''Congratulations. Re-elected four years.''

"a little longer"? (c) How had voters made Lincoln's presidency "a little longer"? (d) Is this cartoon meant to be humorous or political or both?

Identifying Changes on Maps

*CT **2.** Look at the maps "The Civil War 1861–1862" on page 387, "The Civil War 1863" on page 399, and "The Civil War 1864–1865" on page 402. (a) What Union area was controlled by Confederate forces in 1861–1862? (b) What had happened to this area by 1863? (c) What had happened to this area by 1864–1865? (d) How was the Confederacy split into two parts and then again into three, as shown on these maps? (e) Compare the legend on the map of 1863 with the legend on the map of 1864–1865. How are the two legends different?

in Georgia? (b) How did Sherman's troops carry out his orders? (c) What did the orders mean for the people who were in the path of Sherman's army?

GEOGRAPHY REVIEW

Look at the map "Union and Confederacy 1861" on page 382. (a) How many states joined the Confederacy? (b) How many slave states were part of the Union? (c) What two Union states were separated from the rest of the Union?

USING THE TOOLS OF HISTORY

Interpreting Political Cartoons

*CT **1.** The cartoon above appeared in *Harper's Weekly* just after the 1864 presidential election. It was titled "Long Abraham Lincoln a Little Longer." (a) In what way was Lincoln "long"? (b) In what way did the cartoonist make him

READING AND THINKING SKILLS

*CT **Literal and Inferential Reading**

Some of the quotations in this chapter are literal statements. They state a meaning directly. Others are inferential. They give hints about what the speaker meant. For example, when Grant told Sheridan to leave the Shenandoah Valley "so that crows flying over it will have to carry their rations along with them," he meant that Sheridan should destroy all farms and food crops in the valley.

Decide which of the following quotations are inferential and which are literal, and tell what the inferential ones mean.

(a) "Sometimes gunpowder smells good."
(b) "I never before saw children so eager to learn."
(c) The *Monitor* was a "cheesebox on a raft."
(d) "The rebels are our countrymen again."

CHAPTER 16   1865-1877

RESTORING THE UNION

THE NATION AT WAR'S END
PRESIDENTIAL RECONSTRUCTION
CONGRESSIONAL RECONSTRUCTION
THE SOUTH UNDER RECONSTRUCTION

16-1 THE NATION AT WAR'S END

READ TO FIND OUT

assassinate: murder

—what the word *assassinate* means.

—why the Thirteenth Amendment was added to the Constitution.

—how war had affected the economies of the North and the South.

—what problems former slaves faced at the end of the war.

On March 4, 1865, Abraham Lincoln was inaugurated President for the second time. Lincoln had proved to be a great leader. He dealt with quarrelsome cabinet officers and difficult generals. He suffered as casualties grew. Still, he worked to preserve the Union.

As he began his second term, Lincoln felt hopeful. The Confederate armies were retreating. Congress had recently passed the Thirteenth Amendment to the Constitution. This amendment abolished slavery in every state, including the slave states that had remained in the Union. In his second inaugural address, Lincoln spoke of "a just and lasting peace." He asked Americans to look past the bitterness of war. "With malice toward none; with charity for all," he said, "let us strive to finish the work we are in; to bind up the nation's wounds."

You may wish to read to the class the whole of Lincoln's second inaugural address.

These rifles were stacked in Petersburg, Virginia, in the first few days of April 1865. Within a week the war was over, and within two weeks Abraham Lincoln was dead.

THE ASSASSINATION OF LINCOLN

Five weeks later the President was **assassinated,** or murdered. On April 14, 1865, he was shot while watching a play at Ford's Theater. The assassin, an actor named John Wilkes Booth, escaped.

The nation was stunned. An Illinois soldier said, "We have lost the best, the fairest, the truest man in America. Take him altogether, he was the best man this country ever produced." Most northerners felt that they had lost a dear friend.

Booth was shot ten days later. He died believing he had struck down "a tyrant." But Jefferson Davis feared that Booth had killed "our best friend in the court of the enemy." The task of reuniting the North and South now fell to Lincoln's Vice-President, Andrew Johnson.

THE POSTWAR SOUTH

The North and South stood in sharp contrast at the end of the war. In the North, the war had encouraged farmers to increase their output. Business people had built many new factories. The signs of prosperity, or economic well-being, were everywhere.

The South lay in ruins. Many of its cities had been burned. Its economy was bankrupt, or financially ruined. Confederate currency and bonds once worth billions of dollars were worthless. Investments in

You may wish to have students review General Sherman's and General Sheridan's destructive campaigns (page 403), major causes of the South's destitution.

USING THE TOOLS OF HISTORY

ANALYZING PRIMARY SOURCES

*CT

When writers of history try to decide what happened in the past, they make use of *primary sources.* A primary source is an account of an event written or recorded by a person involved in it. A *secondary source,* such as this textbook, is written later and is often based on primary sources.

The account below is a primary source. It was written by Ward Hill Lamon, Abraham Lincoln's longtime law partner and trusted friend. Lamon went to Washington with Lincoln and served as his close adviser.

> The most startling incident in the life of Mr. Lincoln was a dream that he had only a few days before his assassination. . . . I give it as nearly in his own words as I can, from notes which I made immediately after its recital [telling]. There were only two or three persons present. . . .
>
> "About ten days ago," said he, "I retired very late. . . . I soon began to dream. . . . I heard subdued sobs, as if a number of people were weeping. I thought I left my bed and wandered downstairs. There the silence was broken by the same pitiful sobbing, but the mourners were invisible. I went from room to room . . . until I arrived at the East Room, which I entered. There I met with a sickening surprise. Before me was a catafalque [platform], on which rested a corpse. . . . Around it were stationed soldiers who were acting as guards; and there was a throng of people, some gazing mournfully upon the corpse, whose face was covered, others weeping pitifully. 'Who is dead in the White House?' I demanded of one of the soldiers. 'The President,' was his answer; 'he was killed by an assassin!' Then came a loud burst of grief from the crowd, which woke me from my dream."

A historian might ask these questions before accepting such a story as true. Answer them with the information you have.

1. Was the person who wrote this an eyewitness to what was described?

2. Did this person write the account while his or her memory of it was still fresh?

3. Is this witness trustworthy? Why or why not?

4. Were there other witnesses to this event who might have left accounts to check against this source?

Answers will be found on page T 61.

---

slaves were simply wiped out. The South's human losses were enormous. A sixth of its able-bodied men had been lost in the war. Many of those who survived were sick or wounded.

The only source of wealth left was the land. But making the land produce crops was difficult. Farm tools and seed were in short supply. Perhaps a third of the South's horses and mules had disappeared. In many places, if there was still a plow to use, men and women had to drag it through the fields themselves.

With the defeat of the Confederacy, many southerners could see nothing beyond "poverty, with no future and no hope." When Jefferson Davis was imprisoned in Fortress Monroe, Virginia, their concern grew. Despite a guard of seventy soldiers, heavy iron weights were fastened to his legs. If Davis could be treated so harshly, southern whites wondered, what would the northerners do to them?

Like other cities of the South, Richmond lay in ruins after the war. Farms, crops, and rail lines were ruined, too.

THE FREEDMEN'S BUREAU

For the South's four million slaves, the end of the war brought sudden freedom. But just what freedom meant was not clear. Some freed slaves stayed with their former masters and worked for them. Others took to the road in search of lost family members. For most, freedom brought the right to choose a last name, learn to read and write, be legally married, and travel freely.

To assist the freed slaves, Congress established the Freedmen's Bureau in March 1865. The bureau set up schools for former slaves, helped them find work at fair wages, and provided food to the unemployed. Despite these efforts, many of the freed slaves found they had traded slavery for poverty, hunger, and uncertainty.

For discussion: What might be some of the problems newly-freed slaves would have to face? (In answering, students should consider all the choices free people make every day. Slaves' masters would have made many of these choices for them.)

SECTION REVIEW Answers will be found on page T 61.

1. Define this word: *assassinate.*

2. Identify: Thirteenth Amendment, John Wilkes Booth, Freedmen's Bureau.

3. What effect did the war have on the economy of the North?

4. What kinds of losses did the South suffer in the war?

5. What were some of the problems facing freed slaves?

16-2 PRESIDENTIAL RECONSTRUCTION

READ TO FIND OUT

—what the words *Reconstruction, amnesty, black codes, franchise,* and *segregation* mean.

—how Reconstruction began under Lincoln.

—how Johnson organized Reconstruction.

—why southern legislatures enacted black codes.

—why Republicans opposed Lincoln's and Johnson's plans for Reconstruction.

Reconstruction: reorganization of Confederate states to bring them back into the Union
amnesty: general pardon
black codes: laws to define the legal rights of freed slaves
franchise: right to vote
segregation: separation on basis of race

In the spring of 1865, a newspaper reporter toured the South and found white southerners "prepared for the worst." Yet only a few former Confederates were arrested. The Freedmen's Bureau was soon providing more food to poor whites than to blacks in several states. And the nation's leaders were talking about **Reconstruction,** the reorganization of the Confederate states in order to bring them back into the Union.

LINCOLN'S TEN PERCENT PLAN

During the war, Lincoln had presented a plan for Reconstruction. He had asked the citizens of the Confederate states to take an oath of loyalty to the Constitution and the Union. In each state, a new government could be organized when 10 percent of the citizens who had voted in the 1860 presidential election took the oath. In 1864 Arkansas and Louisiana were reorganized under Lincoln's "ten percent plan."

Republicans in Congress opposed Lincoln's plan. They believed that Congress, not the President, should control Reconstruction. Some Republicans also thought that Lincoln's plan was too generous. They became known as the Radical Republicans.

In July 1864 the Radicals passed the Wade-Davis Reconstruction bill. It said that a state could not be reorganized until a majority of those who had voted in 1860 had taken a loyalty oath. No southerners who had supported the Confederacy could vote or hold office. Lincoln thought the Wade-Davis bill was too harsh and vetoed it. Congress responded by refusing to admit into Congress Representatives and Senators from the states reorganized under Lincoln's plan.

In his last public address, Lincoln stated that Reconstruction "is fraught with great difficulty. . . . We simply must begin with and mold from discordant elements. Nor is it a small additional embarrassment that we, the loyal people, differ among ourselves as to the mode . . . of Reconstruction."

JOHNSON'S RECONSTRUCTION PLAN

Andrew Johnson, a former Democratic Senator from Tennessee, had remained loyal to the Union even when his state seceded. The Republicans had nominated him for Vice-President in 1864. They hoped that he would bring support to the party in the South after the war.

As President, Johnson continued Lincoln's Reconstruction plan. In May 1865 he declared that Louisiana, Tennessee, Arkansas, and Virginia had been reconstructed. Johnson offered **amnesty,** or a general pardon, to all southerners who took a loyalty oath except former high-ranking Confederate officers and officials. He set up temporary governments in the remaining seven former Confederate states.

These states held constitutional conventions in 1865 to reorganize their governments. Once the new governments had repealed their secession laws, ratified the Thirteenth Amendment, and canceled their war debts, they could rejoin the Union.

THE BLACK CODES

One of the first actions taken by southern legislatures was to replace their slave codes with a new collection of laws called **black codes.** The first purpose of the codes was to define the legal rights of freed slaves. In most southern states, blacks could sue or be sued, own property, testify in court, and be married legally. Other rights, such as serving on juries and owning weapons, were denied them. No southern state granted blacks the **franchise,** or the right to vote.

Andrew Johnson was proud of his humble origins. Apprenticed to a tailor when he was ten, he continued making his own clothes until he became a Congressman. When governor of Tennessee, he made a suit for the governor of Kentucky. (His fellow governor, a former blacksmith, presented Johnson with a shovel and tongs he had made.)

After the war, blacks formed groups to buy farm equipment or to set up cotton gins like this one.

The Freedmen's Bureau provided schooling for students of all ages. The teacher had traveled from New England to Mississippi to conduct classes.

THE PERSUASIVE PATTERN

Writers or speakers who use the cause-effect pattern or the comparison-contrast pattern hope to inform their readers or listeners. People who use the *persuasive pattern* have a different purpose. They hope to persuade others to act or to accept some belief.

People using this pattern usually begin by making an assertion, a forceful statement of an opinion. Radical Republican Thaddeus Stevens, for example, made this assertion after the Civil War: Congress should divide up southern plantations in order to give every freedman "forty acres of land and a hut."

An assertion is then supported with facts and opinions so that people will accept it as true. Here is what Stevens said to Congress in 1865 to support his assertion.

We have turned loose four million slaves without a hut to shelter them or a cent in their pockets. The infernal laws of slavery have prevented them from acquiring an education, understanding the commonest laws of contract, or managing the ordinary business of life. This Congress is bound to provide for them until they can take care of themselves. If we do not furnish them with homesteads and hedge them about with protective laws; if we leave them to the legislation of their late masters, we had better have left them in bondage.

1. What two generalizations did Stevens use to support his assertion?

2. What two opinions did he state in support of his assertion?

Writers and speakers using the persuasive pattern have an expected outcome in mind. They may want others to agree with them or do something. The desired outcome can be stated clearly or can be implied—left unstated.

3. What outcome did Stevens want?

4. Is this outcome clearly stated or implied?

Answers will be found on page T 61.

The Mississippi code provided that any person convicted of the attempt to "persuade, entice, or cause any . . . Negro . . . to desert from any legal employment . . . shall be fined not less than $50 and not more than $500 . . . and, if said fine shall not be immediately paid, the court shall sentence said convict to not exceeding six months' imprisonment in the county jail."

A second purpose of the new black codes was to help bring about an improvement in economic conditions. To rebuild their ruined plantations, the planters needed a dependable work force. The black codes helped planters by requiring freed slaves to work. Blacks without jobs could be arrested and then hired out to planters. The codes gave the planters many of the benefits of slavery without the responsibilities.

The black codes also limited most freed slaves to farm work or to work as servants. Blacks could not enter many trades and could not start businesses. In most states they were not allowed to rent land or own farms. Finally, the black codes called for **segregation,** or separation on the basis of race, in a number of public places. Ex-slaves, for example, were not allowed to attend schools with whites.

THE REPUBLICAN REACTION

In December 1865 President Johnson announced that Reconstruction was over. The Radical Republicans, however, believed it had hardly begun. From the South came reports that blacks were being driven "back to plantations by force." To the Radicals, the black codes were proof that southern whites were trying to treat blacks as slaves again. As a result, Congress refused to admit the Senators and Representatives elected by the former Confederate states.

The Republicans opposed Johnson's Reconstruction plan for two reasons. First, the Radical Republicans believed that simple justice demanded punishment for the disloyal "rebels." Justice also demanded that the ex-slaves, many of whom had fought for the Union, be treated fairly. Most Republicans felt that the President's plan for Reconstruction meant "the pardon of every rebel for the crime of rebellion." At the same time, it did nothing to help former slaves.

Second, the Republicans worried that the return of the former Confederate states would end their control of Congress. During the war the Republicans in Congress had passed laws to encourage industry and trade. They had raised tariffs to protect American manufacturers. The Treasury was given permission to issue federal paper money, the "greenbacks" that gave the nation a single national currency. Republicans provided federal aid for the building of the nation's first transcontinental railroad. They also encouraged settlement of the West. In 1862 Congress had passed the Homestead Act. It promised 160 acres (65 hectares) to any settler who would farm the land for five years.

To insure the future economic growth of the nation, the Republicans felt they had to continue to control Congress. But the return of southern Representatives threatened their majority.

Before the Civil War, each slave had been counted as three fifths of a person in deciding how many Representatives each state should have. With slavery ended, southern blacks were to be counted the same as whites. The result would be 15 more southerners in the House of Representatives than there had been before the war. The Republicans felt that letting southern Democrats back into Congress would be "nothing less than political suicide."

*CT
Activity: Students can consult their notebooks for a definition of *Reconstruction.* (See page 412.) They can then write two further definitions of the word: as Andrew Johnson would define it and as a Radical Republican would define it. The class can compare and analyze definitions.

Prairie homesteaders made their own farm tools. This wooden barley fork (left) and hay fork were made in the mid-1800s.

SECTION REVIEW   Answers will be found on page T 61.

1. Define these words: *Reconstruction, amnesty, black codes, franchise, segregation.*

2. Identify: ten percent plan, Radical Republicans, Wade-Davis bill, Homestead Act.

3. Why did Lincoln veto the Wade-Davis bill?

4. What three things did Johnson ask of the former Confederate states before readmitting them to the Union?

5. List three purposes of the black codes.

6. Why did Republicans oppose Johnson's Reconstruction plan?

16–3 CONGRESSIONAL RECONSTRUCTION

READ TO FIND OUT

—what the words *civil rights, due process of law,* and *disfranchise* mean.

—how the Civil Rights Act was passed.

—what was included in the Fourteenth Amendment.

—how the Radical Republicans took control of Reconstruction.

—why Andrew Johnson was impeached.

civil rights: rights guaranteed to all individuals by the Constitution
due process of law: following the legal steps established to protect the rights and liberties of individuals
disfranchise: deny the right to vote

Activity: Students can research and make oral or written reports on Charles Sumner and Thaddeus Stevens.

During 1866 and 1867, President Johnson and the Radical Republicans in Congress battled over Reconstruction. The Republicans were led by two strong-willed lawmakers—Thaddeus Stevens of Pennsylvania and Charles Sumner of Massachusetts.

Stevens was a member of the House of Representatives who believed that "the safety of this great nation" depended on his party remaining in power. Senator Sumner had long supported equal rights for blacks. When others argued that the Constitution left most questions about the rights of blacks up to the states, Sumner answered, "There can be no state rights against human rights."

THE CIVIL RIGHTS BILL OF 1866

Early in 1866, Congress passed two bills to protect the freed slaves. The first extended the life of the Freedmen's Bureau and gave it more power. Johnson called the bill unconstitutional and vetoed it. He reasoned that the people of the 11 former Confederate states were not yet represented in Congress. To make laws that applied to people who were without representation was unconstitutional. Also, he said, the Constitution did not allow a federal agency for the needy.

The second bill was designed to protect the **civil rights** of blacks. Civil rights are the rights guaranteed to individuals by the Constitution. This second bill gave citizenship to blacks and stated that they should have the same legal and property rights as other citizens. Again President Johnson responded with a veto. He argued that the Constitution gave the states, not Congress, the power to decide such issues. An angry Congress voted to override Johnson's vetoes of the Civil Rights bill and the Freedmen's Bureau bill.

Protected by a federal official, blacks in Virginia were able to register to vote for the first time. Voting rights for blacks were backed by the Fourteenth Amendment, ratified by the states in 1868.

THE FOURTEENTH AMENDMENT

Republicans worried that the Supreme Court might declare the Civil Rights Act unconstitutional. They remembered the ruling in the Dred Scott case that no blacks, slave or free, were citizens of the United States. Another amendment to the Constitution was needed, the Radicals argued, to protect the rights of black people.

The Fourteenth Amendment was written in five sections. The first section states that any person born in the United States is a citizen. No state can deny a citizen equal treatment under the law. Nor can a state take away a citizen's "life, liberty, or property, without due process of law." **Due process of law** means following the legal steps established to protect the rights and liberties of individuals.

The second section encourages states to give all male citizens the right to vote. It says that any state denying the vote to some citizens cannot count those citizens for purposes of representation in the House of Representatives. If blacks, for example, are denied the vote, they cannot be included when a state's population is counted to decide how many seats it should have in the House. This section, then, was aimed at southern states that did not give blacks the vote. Such states faced the loss of seats in the House of Representatives.

The third section took away the right to hold public office from anyone who had taken an oath of loyalty to the Constitution before the war and then had broken that oath. The fourth section banned states from

You may wish to have students read to the class the five sections of the Fourteenth Amendment (pages 547–548).

Many women strongly supported the Fourteenth and Fifteenth Amendments. After black men were given the vote, women asked for it too. In this print, Victoria Claflin Woodhull argues in the Judiciary Committee of the House of Representatives.

repaying Confederate war debts and claims by slave owners for the loss of slaves. The last section of the Fourteenth Amendment gave Congress the power to enforce the amendment.

While Congress was debating the Fourteenth Amendment, rioting between blacks and whites broke out in Memphis and New Orleans. Many blacks were killed or wounded. The riots made many northerners feel that the rights of blacks should be protected in the Constitution. Johnson disagreed. He advised states not to ratify the Fourteenth Amendment. Tennessee did approve the amendment, and Congress voted to admit its Senators and Representatives. The other ten Confederate states, however, rejected it.

THE ELECTION OF 1866

The Fourteenth Amendment and the fate of blacks in the South became major issues in the fall congressional elections of 1866. President Johnson toured the nation, speaking in support of his Reconstruction policies. Once, when hecklers began to shout at him, Johnson shouted back. He called Radical Republicans "traitors at the North." General Grant, who was along on the tour, said that Johnson was like "a man making speeches at his own funeral."

The Radical Republicans argued that the outcome of the war was at stake in the election. If Republicans did not win, they said, the sacrifices of Union soldiers would have been in vain. The Republicans won huge victories in the election, and the Radicals gained control of Congress. With two thirds of the seats in both houses, the Radicals now had enough votes to override any presidential veto.

*CT

Activity: Students can write newspaper editorials supporting either Johnson's or Congress's stand on the Fourteenth Amendment. The class can decide whether they rely primarily on logical arguments or appeals to emotion.

RADICAL RECONSTRUCTION

The Radicals pushed their own Reconstruction plan through Congress. Over Johnson's veto, they enacted the Reconstruction Acts of 1867. The South was divided into five military districts, each governed by a general who was backed by federal troops. The existing state governments were declared illegal. New governments were to be formed by state constitutional conventions. Only blacks and loyal whites could vote for convention delegates. Southerners who had supported the Confederacy were **disfranchised,** or denied the right to vote.

Once a state convention had written a new constitution that gave black men the right to vote, the state could hold elections. The newly elected state legislature had to approve the Fourteenth Amendment. Only then could the state apply for readmission to the Union.

THE IMPEACHMENT OF JOHNSON

To make sure that Johnson could not interfere with their plan, the Republicans passed two bills that limited his authority. The Command of the Army Act reduced the President's power as Commander in Chief of the armed forces. The President would have to give all military orders through the General of the Army, Ulysses S. Grant. The Tenure of Office Act said that the President could not remove from office anyone that he had appointed and that the Senate had approved, unless the Senate agreed to the removal. Johnson believed both bills were unconstitutional and vetoed them. Congress overrode both vetoes.

In February 1868 Johnson tested the Tenure of Office Act by firing Secretary of War Edwin Stanton. The Radicals in the House voted to impeach, or bring charges against, the President. Johnson was accused of breaking a federal law by firing Stanton and of making speeches harming the reputation of Congress.

From March to May 1868, the President was on trial in the Senate. His lawyers met the first charge by pointing out that Abraham Lincoln, not Johnson, had appointed Stanton. Therefore, the Tenure of Office Act did not apply. The lawyers argued that, even if the act did apply, the Supreme Court should decide whether or not it was constitutional before the President was accused of breaking the law.

When Johnson learned of his impeachment by Congress, he exclaimed, "Impeach me for violating the Constitution! . . . Haven't I been struggling ever since I have been in this chair to uphold the Constitution they trample under foot!"

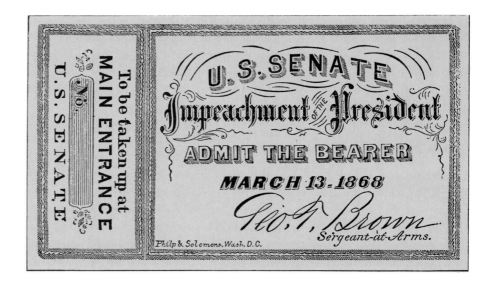

U.S. SENATE
Impeachment of the President
ADMIT THE BEARER
MARCH 13-1868
Geo. T. Brown
Sergeant-at-Arms.

U.S. SENATE
To be taken up at MAIN ENTRANCE
No.
U.S. SENATE
Philp & Solomons. Wash. D.C.

Impeached by the House of Representatives, Andrew Johnson was tried by the Senate in a proceeding that drew huge crowds of spectators.

In 1875 Andrew Johnson returned to Washington as a Senator from Tennessee, an office he had held before becoming Vice-President. When he entered the Senate chamber, there was at first an embarrassed silence. Then other Senators came up to shake his hand, and a Senate page presented him with flowers.

As to the second charge, the lawyers argued that according to the Constitution, a President could be impeached only for "high crimes and misdemeanors." A President should not be removed from office simply because he disagreed with Congress. If that happened, "No future President will be safe who happens to differ with a majority of the House and Senate."

Two thirds of the Senate had to find Johnson guilty to remove him from office. Against very heavy pressure, seven Republican Senators joined the twelve Democratic Senators in voting "not guilty." Johnson escaped removal by just one vote. The President finished his term in office, but his power was broken.

SECTION REVIEW Answers will be found on page T 62.

1. Define these words: *civil rights, due process of law, disfranchise.*

2. Identify: Thaddeus Stevens, Charles Sumner, Civil Rights Bill of 1866, Fourteenth Amendment, Reconstruction Acts of 1867.

3. What did the first two sections of the Fourteenth Amendment try to do for blacks?

4. What were the results of the congressional election in 1866?

5. Under the Reconstruction Acts of 1867, what steps did a state have to go through before applying to become part of the Union again?

6. What were the main charges brought against President Johnson when he was impeached by the House?

7. What was the outcome of Johnson's impeachment trial in the Senate?

16-4 THE SOUTH UNDER RECONSTRUCTION

READ TO FIND OUT

—what the words *sharecropping* and *racial discrimination* mean.

—who gained political power in the South under congressional Reconstruction.

—how the sharecropping system came about.

—why the Fifteenth Amendment was added to the Constitution.

—how southern Democrats regained control of state governments.

—how the Compromise of 1877 brought Reconstruction to an end.

sharecropping: system in which a landowner lends land, tools, and seed in return for a share of the profits from the harvest

racial discrimination: unfair difference in treatment based on race

Following the Reconstruction Acts of 1867, the Union army once again took control of the Confederate states. The army's first task was to register the voters who would elect delegates to state constitutional conventions. By the fall of 1867 more than 700,000 blacks and 666,000 whites had registered. Political power passed from the planters to new groups.

CARPETBAGGERS AND SCALAWAGS

Many of the whites who registered were northerners who had moved to the South after the war. Some came to help blacks register to vote or to teach in black schools. Others wanted to buy farms or start businesses. Often, like other travelers of the time, they carried small suitcases called carpetbags. Southern whites called these people "carpetbaggers." The name suggested that the northerners had come to grab what they could in a short time and then go home.

The rest of the whites who registered were southerners who had remained loyal to the Union during the war. Many were poor whites who were taking part in political affairs for the first time. To former Confederates, such people were worthless "scalawags."

THE BLACK AND TAN CONVENTIONS

The convention delegates elected by the new voters were viewed with suspicion. Because some of the delegates were black, the state constitutional conventions were called the "black and tan conventions."

A real carpetbag was made of two squares of carpet sewn together. The cartoon carpetbag represents the burden of the South under Reconstruction. U. S. Grant rides in the carpetbag. He is surrounded by bayonets that are symbols of the military rule of the South.

You may wish to have students consult "The Nation Reunites" (page 423) to learn the order and years in which the Confederate states were readmitted to the Union.

This description was meant to be scornful. Among the blacks elected as delegates, however, were many exceptionally able leaders, such as Beverly Nash, Francis Cardozo, Robert Smalls, and J. W. Hood. Together the black and white delegates wrote new constitutions guaranteeing equal rights to all citizens.

The state governments organized under the new constitutions carried out important reforms. For the first time southern states set up public school systems and gave aid to the sick and needy. Tax laws and penal codes, or laws dealing with various crimes and their punishments, were made fairer. The new state governments also voted for internal improvements such as railroads.

By the end of 1868, eight states had written acceptable constitutions, elected new governments, ratified the Fourteenth Amendment, and been readmitted to the Union. By 1870 the last three states—Virginia, Mississippi, and Texas—were also readmitted.

THE SHARECROPPING SYSTEM

Although the new constitutions protected the rights of ex-slaves, they did little to solve the economic problems faced by southerners. Most slaves, when given freedom, owned little more than the clothes on their backs. The economic position of most whites was not much better. Even the once wealthy planters faced hardships. The planters needed workers but had no money to pay them. Blacks, on the other hand, were eager to have their own land to farm, but had no money to buy it. Out of the needs of both groups came the system called **sharecropping.**

The Nation Reunites

	Readmitted to the Union	Reconstruction government ended
Tennessee	1866	1869
Alabama	1868	1874
Arkansas	1868	1874
Florida	1868	1877
Louisiana	1868	1877
North Carolina	1868	1870
South Carolina	1868	1877
Georgia	1870	1871
Mississippi	1870	1875
Texas	1870	1873
Virginia	1870	1870

Sharecropping is a system in which a landowner lends out land in return for a share of the profits made by the renter. Planters divided their land into small plots and provided tools and seed. The farmers who worked these plots—the sharecroppers—split the profits of their harvest with the landowner.

For sharecroppers, black or white, this system usually meant a life of debt. To survive until harvest time, sharecroppers had to buy food and supplies on credit from a local storekeeper. Often they ended up "sharing" as much as 80 percent of their harvest with landowners and storekeepers. Few sharecroppers ever made enough money to pay off their debts, much less buy land of their own.

THE ELECTION OF 1868

In the election of 1868, new black voters in the South helped to make the Republicans into a national party. The Republican candidate was General U. S. Grant. The Democrats nominated New York Governor Horatio Seymour, who attacked Republican Reconstruction policies. Republicans won northern votes by "waving the bloody shirt," or keeping the memory of the war alive. In Philadelphia a Republican parade featured wagonloads of wounded Union soldiers.

You may wish to tell students that Grant accepted the presidential nomination saying, "Let us have peace." Nevertheless, not peace but war was the keynote of those campaigning for him.

Grant won the election, but he received only 306,000 more popular votes than his rival. More than 500,000 blacks voted, most of them for Grant. Without the black vote, the election would have gone to Seymour.

THE FIFTEENTH AMENDMENT

To make sure that blacks did not lose their franchise, Congress, with Grant's support, approved another amendment to the Constitution. The Fifteenth Amendment said that a citizen's right to vote "shall not be denied . . . by the United States or any state on account of race, color, or previous condition of servitude [slavery]."

Seven blacks from southern states were elected to Congress in 1870. They included Hiram Revels, Senator from Mississippi, left, and six Representatives.

You may wish to have students read both sections of the Fifteenth Amendment (pages 548–549).

Opponents of the amendment argued that deciding who should vote was the right of each state. They also pointed out that few northern states allowed blacks to vote. Despite these arguments, Congress approved the amendment and, in 1870, it was ratified.

With the passage of the Fourteenth and Fifteenth Amendments, many northerners assumed that the problems of southern blacks had been solved. They pointed to the number of blacks elected to state offices throughout the South in 1870. That year Hiram Revels became the first black Senator in the nation's history. He was joined in Washington by black Congressmen Joseph Rainey, Robert Elliot, James Rapier, John Roy Lynch, Alonzo Ransier, and Richard Cain.

THE WHITE REACTION

The appearance of blacks in positions of power did not, however, mean the end of racial problems in the South. Most whites were not ready to accept blacks as equals. Throughout the South, blacks faced **racial discrimination,** or an unfair difference in treatment based on race.

When Representative James Rapier took the train from his home in Alabama to Washington, D.C., he was forced to ride "in a dirty rough box with the drunkards, apple-sellers, railroad hands." He spent his nights in railway stations after finding that "there is not an inn between Washington and Montgomery, a distance of more than a thousand miles, that will accommodate me to a bed or meal."

Blacks who fought back against discrimination risked a midnight visit from the Knights of the White Camellia or the Ku Klux Klan. These secret societies wanted to put blacks in "their place" and return the South

★ ★ ★ ★ ★ ★ ★ **AMERICAN VALUES IN ACTION** ★ ★ ★ ★ ★ ★ ★

HIRAM REVELS

In February 1870 a tall, portly man entered the chamber of the United States Senate. With quiet dignity, he took a seat. Senators swarmed around to shake his hand.

The newcomer was Hiram Revels, Senator-elect from Mississippi. Mississippi had not had a Senator since Jefferson Davis resigned in 1861 to lead the Confederacy. Now the state had sent Revels, a black, to Washington. It was, a newspaper headlined, a "NOVEL SCENE IN THE SENATE CHAMBER."

All Washington buzzed with talk about Revels. He received more attention than a visiting British prince. Newspapers reported his every move and dug into his background.

Revels, a minister and teacher, had worked to achieve equal rights for black Americans. In Missouri he was imprisoned for preaching to blacks. "I refrained from doing anything that would incite slaves to run away," Revels wrote. "But when in free states, I always assisted the fugitive slave to make his escape."

Now, one reporter asked, would he represent white as well as black Mississippians? Revels answered that he was a "representative of the state, irrespective of color."

Revels could not represent anybody until the Senate officially admitted him. That touched off three days of angry debate. One Senator claimed that under the Dred Scott ruling, Revels was not an American citizen. Another Senator responded that the Fourteenth Amendment had repealed that ruling.

As words of abuse and praise swirled around him, Revels listened in silence. Finally, Senator Charles Sumner concluded the debate. "Today, we make the Declaration a reality," he said. "The Declaration was only half established by independence. In assuring the equal rights of all we complete the work."

Forty-eight Senators agreed and voted to admit Revels. Only eight voted against him. On February 24, 1870, the nation's first black Senator took the oath of office.

Revels spoke out, as promised, for all Mississippians. He asked that former Confederates who now showed loyalty to the Union be given back their citizenship rights. He demanded that blacks be treated as full citizens.

The Senator spoke bluntly about segregation. Go to the railroad depot, he told his fellow Senators, "and what will you see?"

Revels told them. "A well-dressed colored lady, with her little children by her side, comes to the cars, and where is she shown to?" She would not be allowed in the first-class car. She would be put "into the smoking car, where men are cursing, swearing, spitting on the floor. . . ." It was the duty of the government, said Revels, to outlaw segregation.

It took nearly a century for the government to respond. For blacks, it was a century of struggle to gain—and hold on to—their rights. But Revels and the many black leaders of Reconstruction helped light the way.

At a Boston meeting celebrating the Fifteenth Amendment, an old abolitionist looked at Revels in wonder. "Here," he whispered, "is the Fifteenth Amendment in flesh and blood!"

to "white man's government." The Ku Klux Klan called on whites "to oppose Negro equality, both social and political." An Alabama newspaper stated their goal in these words: "We must kill or drive away leading Negroes and only let the humble and submissive remain."

These groups turned to threats and violence. Wearing peaked hoods and long ghostly robes, Klan "nightriders" burned crosses to warn black and white Republicans that it was dangerous to vote. Warnings were followed by beatings, murders, and the burning of black people's homes, schools, and churches. The number of blacks killed by terrorists during Reconstruction ran into the thousands.

In 1870 and 1871, Congress passed the Force Acts. These acts were designed to protect voters from terrorism. Anyone who interfered with another person's voting rights could be arrested or fined. In spite of these laws, terrorism continued. Whites organized rifle clubs with harmless sounding names like "Mother's Little Helpers" or the "Allendale Mounted Baseball Club." Members of these clubs attended political meetings in order to frighten blacks.

President Grant sent federal troops back into South Carolina, Louisiana, and Arkansas to protect Republican voters. But after he was elected to a second term in 1872, Grant found little support in Congress for using troops to enforce the Fourteenth and Fifteenth Amendments or the Force Acts. The Radical Republicans had either died or turned their attention to new issues.

THE DEMOCRATS TAKE CONTROL

In 1872 Congress passed the Amnesty Act, which allowed most former Confederates to vote and hold office once again. Southern Democrats began to attack the state governments, which were controlled by Republicans. They accused Republicans of bribery and dishonesty in office and of spending too much tax money.

These charges were widely believed. There were instances of corruption, and taxes and state spending had gone up. But many black leaders, such as Congressman Alonzo Ransier, were working hard to remove dishonest politicians from office. Higher taxes had been necessary to build public schools, hospitals, and homes for orphans. Black politician Francis Cardozo studied state spending in South Carolina. He found that tax money spent per free citizen had actually dropped from $2.05 before the war to $1.67 afterward. But newspapers ignored his report.

In state after state, Democrats regained control of southern governments. As terrorism against black voters increased, the number casting ballots fell rapidly. Those blacks who courageously continued to vote often found that "a hole gets in the bottom of the [ballot] boxes some way and lets out our votes."

The Election of 1876

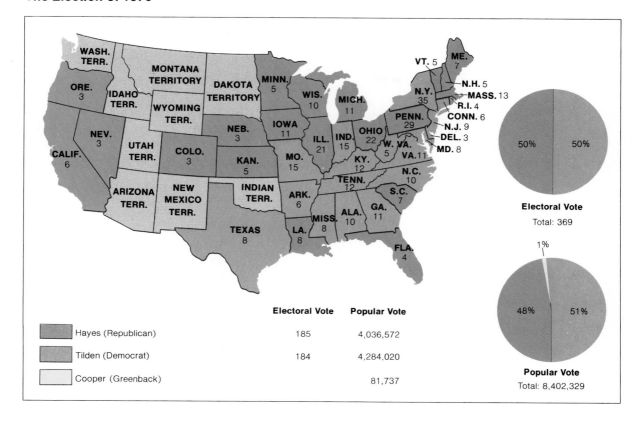

	Electoral Vote	Popular Vote
Hayes (Republican)	185	4,036,572
Tilden (Democrat)	184	4,284,020
Cooper (Greenback)		81,737

Electoral Vote
Total: 369

Popular Vote
Total: 8,402,329

THE END OF RECONSTRUCTION

By the election year of 1876, most Americans had lost interest in Reconstruction. The Democratic candidate for President, New York Governor Samuel J. Tilden, won 184 electoral votes. This was just one short of a majority. The Republican candidate, Ohio Governor Rutherford B. Hayes, claimed 165 electoral votes. The election was disputed in Florida, South Carolina, and Louisiana. Each party in these states claimed victory and accused the other of election fraud, or cheating.

The deadlock was broken by an electoral committee chosen by Congress. In an agreement known as the Compromise of 1877, Democrats agreed to accept Hayes as President. In return, the Republicans promised to remove the remaining federal troops from the South. Within a year, all southern governments had been returned to "white man's rule" under the Democratic party.

Reconstruction ended just as the nation finished celebrating its first centennial. One hundred years earlier, in 1776, thirteen independent states had joined to create a union. Surprising the world, that union survived. Now, after being torn apart by a civil war, it was stitched back together. The stitching left scars. Still, the nation survived. There would

Because of accusations of cheating, some Americans referred to Hayes as "Rutherfraud B. Hayes," "His Fraudulency," and "the Usurper."

In 1876 the attention of many Americans turned to celebrations of their nation's 100th birthday. People put on their finest clothes and went out to hear speeches about the importance of the Fourth of July.

be time to heal, freedom to build dreams into reality. Surprising the world, Americans began their second century as they began their first—confident as a nation.

SECTION REVIEW Answers will be found on page T 62.

1. Define these words: *penal codes, racial discrimination.*

2. Identify: carpetbaggers, scalawags, Fifteenth Amendment, Hiram Revels, Rutherford B. Hayes.

3. What groups gained political power in the South as congressional Reconstruction began?

4. Why were sharecroppers unable to save enough money to buy land of their own?

5. (a) What was the purpose of groups like the Ku Klux Klan? (b) How did they achieve their goals?

6. How did southern Democrats regain control of state governments?

7. How did the Compromise of 1877 bring about an end to Reconstruction?

CHAPTER SUMMARY

As the Civil War drew to a close, the nation's best hope for a "just and lasting peace" was murdered by John Wilkes Booth. The task of reuniting the nation fell to Andrew Johnson.

The North and the South stood in sharp contrast at the end of the war. In the North the Industrial Revolution was surging ahead. Signs of prosperity were everywhere. The South was a scene of poverty and destruction.

President Johnson followed Lincoln's plan to reunite the nation as quickly as possible. Radical Republicans, however, could not accept Johnson's approach to Reconstruction. It seemed to treat the former Confederates too generously. It offered no protection to the freed slaves. And it threatened the Republican majority in Congress.

During 1866 the Radical Republicans and President Johnson battled for control of Reconstruction. Congress passed the Fourteenth Amendment extending citizenship to blacks, despite Johnson's opposition. The election of 1866 gave the Radicals complete control in Congress. When Johnson tested the Tenure of Office Act, he was impeached by the House. He escaped being removed from office by just one vote in the Senate.

In 1867 Congress sent troops back into the South to reconstruct the former Confederate states. Only blacks, and whites who had not rebelled, could vote and hold office. New state constitutions were written that gave blacks the franchise. For the first time, southern state governments supported public schools.

Many southern whites were unable to accept blacks as equals. Groups like the Ku Klux Klan were formed to put blacks in "their place" and return the South to white rule. To achieve these goals they used terrorism. By the mid-1870s, the North was losing interest in Reconstruction. In the Compromise of 1877, Rutherford B. Hayes was elected President in exchange for his promise to bring Reconstruction to an end.

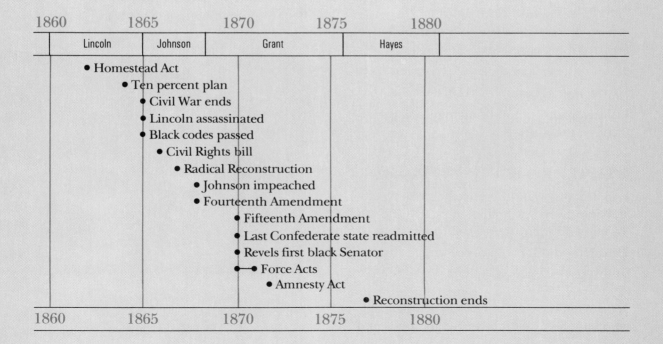

CHAPTER SURVEY

VOCABULARY REVIEW

From this list of vocabulary words, choose the one that best matches each definition below.

(a) amnesty

(b) assassinate

(c) black codes

(d) civil rights

(e) disfranchise

(f) due process of law

(g) franchise

(h) racial discrimination

(i) Reconstruction

(j) segregation

(k) sharecropping

1. a general pardon of a group of people

2. a collection of laws defining the rights of freed slaves

3. to kill by surprise

4. the right to vote

5. to take away a citizen's right to vote

6. the process of reorganizing the former Confederate states after the Civil War

7. the separation of one group from another on some basis such as race, sex, or age

8. a system in which land is lent in exchange for part of the crop raised on it

9. unfair treatment of people based on race

10. the rights shared by all citizens

11. the process of following regular legal steps through the courts

CHAPTER REVIEW

1. (a) What major difference between North and South disappeared as a result of the war? (b) What differences grew sharper?

2. (a) How did Lincoln plan to reconstruct the Confederate states? (b) Why did Congress oppose his plan?

3. (a) What did defeat mean to southerners who had their wealth invested in bonds and slaves? (b) What did planters need to produce crops? (c) How did sharecropping help to meet that need?

4. (a) What did sharecropping offer former slaves? (b) Did sharecropping bring prosperity to blacks? Why or why not?

5. (a) Why did the Radicals view Johnson's Reconstruction plan as unjust? (b) How did it threaten Republican control of Congress?

6. (a) How did the Fourteenth Amendment answer the Dred Scott decision? (b) What does the amendment say about "life, liberty, and property"? (c) What treatment does this amendment guarantee to each citizen?

7. (a) Which new groups gained political power in the South under congressional Reconstruction? (b) What kinds of organizations were formed to drive these groups out of power? (c) How did these organizations achieve their goal?

8. (a) What right was guaranteed by the Fifteenth Amendment? (b) Since southern

This rug was hooked to honor Abraham Lincoln's memory. His initials, birthdate, and presidential dates are in the lower left corner.

states already gave the right to vote to blacks, which states were most affected by this amendment?

9. (a) What did the Amnesty Act of 1872 do? (b) Which party was helped most by this act? (c) What did the passage of this act reveal about the power of the Radicals in Congress?

10. (a) What did the Democrats give up in the Compromise of 1877?   (b) What did they gain?   (c) What did the Republicans gain? (d) What did black voters in the South lose?

Frances Benjamin Johnston photographed mathematics students at Hampton Institute in Virginia. Hampton was founded in 1868 to educate black students. The Freedmen's Bureau helped to fund the school.

GEOGRAPHY REVIEW

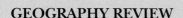 Look at the map "The Election of 1876" on page 427.   (a) How many states west of the Mississippi voted for Tilden?   (b) How many New England states voted for Hayes? (c) How many New England states are there? (d) In 1876, three states still had Reconstruction governments. These three were South Carolina, Florida, and Louisiana. How is this fact reflected in the map?

USING THE TOOLS OF HISTORY

*CT Analyzing Primary Sources

This primary source is a letter written by a southerner just before the 1868 election.

> This morning I discharged 3 of my hands. . . . I gave them from last Monday until Saturday night to decide as to whether or not they would vote. They being unwilling to give me a positive answer, I thereupon told them I would dispense with their services. . . . I retain two who promised me last week without any parley [talking] that they would stay at the mill & attend to their work [on election day].

(a) Was the writer probably black or white? Male or female?   (b) Were the "hands" probably black or white? Male or female? (c) What power did the writer have over the workers?   (d) How did the writer use that power?   (e) How did the five workers respond to this use of power?   (f) What does this letter show about economic power and voting rights?

READING AND THINKING SKILLS

*CT The Persuasive Pattern

Reread the paragraphs under the heading "The Election of 1868" on page 423. (a) When the Republicans were campaigning before the election, what was the outcome they expected? (b) What did the Republicans do to win northern votes? (c) Which of these forceful statements of opinion would have best suited the Republican campaign?   (1) "Our party stands for justice."   (2) "We carry on in the name of those who died so the Union might live." (3) "We alone want freedom for all." (d) What action by the Republicans supported their main point in the campaign?

Answers will be found on page T 63.

UNIT SURVEY

UNIT REVIEW

1. (a) In what way was the location of the slave population in 1860 the same as in 1660? (b) In what way was the location of the slave population different?

2. (a) Why did life in the North seem neither dignified nor honorable to many slave owners in 1860? (b) What part of the northern economic system was not common in the South?

3. (a) What two territories were opened to slavery by the Compromise of 1850? (b) What two territories were opened to the possibility of slavery by the Kansas-Nebraska Act of 1854? (c) What territories were opened to slavery by the Dred Scott decision of 1857?

4. (a) A slave owner in 1860 needed to worry about the ideas of people in the North, but a slave owner in 1660 did not. Why not? (b) How did Harriet Beecher Stowe influence ideas in the North? (c) How did northerners react to the Kansas-Nebraska Act and the Dred Scott decision?

5. (a) What event triggered the secession of states in the lower South? (b) What event marked the start of the Civil War? (c) At that time, what kind of war did most northerners expect? (d) How long did the war last?

6. (a) What was Lincoln's stand on abolition after his election in 1860? (b) What was his stand on abolition early in 1863? (c) How was his stand in 1863 important to the Union?

7. (a) What did total war mean for the Shenandoah Valley of Virginia and for much of Georgia? (b) What did the surrender of Richmond and Petersburg, Virginia, mean for Lee's army? (b) Was the agreement at Appomattox Court House an unconditional surrender? Why or why not?

8. (a) Which group of states—New England, Middle, or Southern—contained sites of major battles during the Revolutionary War? (b) Which of these three groups of states contained sites of major battles during the Civil War? (c) What Civil War battle site was farthest north? (d) What did the location of battles in the Civil War mean to the South?

9. (a) What was the purpose of Reconstruction? (b) How did Lincoln plan to achieve Reconstruction? (c) What group in Congress prevented President Johnson from ending Reconstruction quickly? (d) About how long did Reconstruction last?

10. (a) When slavery ended in the South, what system of farm work took its place? (b) After blacks gained voting rights during Reconstruction, what kept large numbers of them from voting? (c) How did the election of 1876 lead to the withdrawal of all Federal troops from the South?

Civil War photographer Mathew Brady caught a peaceful moment in the camp of the 31st Pennsylvania Regiment. Whole families went to war.

LINKING THE PAST AND THE PRESENT

*CT **1.** In the years after 1850, many newspapers and magazines published political cartoons. These cartoons attacked or supported slavery, the North, the South, elected officials, the process of Reconstruction, and so on. Find examples of political cartoons in publications today. Study each one to see what it is for or against.

2. Look for ways in which the Civil War is memorialized now. For example, find out whether schools or streets or parks in your area are named for people prominent in the war. If you live in a place involved in the war, find out whether local museums, monuments, or cemeteries reflect events of the war years.

The regulation Confederate uniform included a sun-guard on the cap, but most soldiers wore a soft slouch hat instead. It made a good pillow.

MEETING THE BUILDERS OF AMERICA

*CT **1.** Review the descriptions of Mariano Vallejo (page 363), Charlotte Forten (page 393), and Hiram Revels (page 425). In what ways did they contribute to America?

*CT **2.** Prepare a report about the contribution to American life of some other person or group mentioned in Unit 5. For example, look for information about Harriet Beecher Stowe, Robert E. Lee, Stonewall Jackson, Elizabeth Blackwell, Louisa May Alcott, or Clara Barton. You may be able to use one of the following books as a source of information.

Fritz, Jean. *Stonewall.* New York: Putnam, 1979.
Heidish, Marcy. *A Woman Called Moses.* Boston: Houghton Mifflin, 1976.
Mitgang, Herbert. *Fiery Trial: A Life of Lincoln.* New York: Viking, 1974.
Scott, John Anthony. *Woman Against Slavery: The Story of Harriet Beecher Stowe.* New York: Crowell, 1978.

SUGGESTIONS FOR FURTHER READING

Bacon, Margaret Hope. *Rebellion at Christiana.* New York: Crown, 1975.
Davis, Burke. *Mr. Lincoln's Whiskers.* New York: Coward, McCann & Geoghegan, 1978.
Goldston, Robert. *The Coming of the Civil War.* New York: Macmillan, 1972.
Hoobler, Dorothy and Thomas. *Photographing History; the Career of Mathew Brady.* New York: Putnam's, 1977.
Lawson, Don. *The United States in the Civil War.* New York: Abelard-Schuman, 1977.
Trelease, Allen W. *Reconstruction: The Great Experiment.* New York: Harper & Row, 1971.

AMERICAN VOICES

In the readings that follow, men and women who have made American history speak for themselves. The passages from their books, speeches, articles, letters, and diaries are a valuable source of information about the past. Americans young and old, rich and poor, in peace and in war tell their experiences in their own voices.

In some of the readings, the original wording and punctuation have been adapted, or changed, for clarity. Words in brackets ([ ]) have been added to some selections as a help in understanding. Some of the passages appear in their entirety. Others have been shortened for the sake of space. Ellipses (. . .) indicate omissions from the original material.

UNIT 1 Prehistory–1718

DISCOVERING THE AMERICAS

CHAPTER 1

THE FIRST AMERICANS

THE LAW OF THE GREAT PEACE

In the 1500s, five northeastern Indian tribes banded together to form the League of the Iroquois. These tribes—the Onondaga, Seneca, Cayuga, Oneida, and Mohawk—drew up a constitution, the Law of the Great Peace. Here is a part of their constitution.

The constitution mentions Atotarho, leader of the Onondaga. Other leaders are Hononwirehton and Skanawate.

With the statesmen of the League of Five Nations, I plant the Tree of the Great Peace.

I plant it in your territory, Atotarho, and the Onondaga Nation. . . .

I name the tree *Tsioneratasekowa,* the Great White Pine. . . .

Roots have spread out from the Tree of the Great Peace. One root is to the north, one to the east, one to the south, and one to the west. These are the Great White Roots, and their nature is Peace and Strength. If any people of the Five Nations shall obey the laws of the Great Peace, they may trace back the roots to the Tree. If they promise to obey the Council, they shall be welcomed to take shelter beneath the Great Evergreen Tree.

We place at the top of the Tree of Great Peace an eagle, who is able to see afar. If he sees any danger threatening, he will at once warn the people of the League.

When there is any business to do, a messenger shall be sent to Atotarho or Hononwirehton or Skanawate. Then Atotarho shall call his cousin chiefs together. They shall decide whether the business is important enough to call to the attention of the Council of the League. If so, Atotarho shall send messengers to all the chiefs of the League.

When the statesmen are assembled, the Council Fire shall be lit. Atotarho shall open the Council. Then shall Atotarho and his cousin statesmen announce the subject for discussion.

The smoke of the Council Fire of the League shall ever rise and pierce the sky. Then the other nations who may be allies can see the Council Fire of the Great Peace.

Reprinted by permission of White Roots of Peace from *The Law of the Great Peace,* published by White Roots of Peace, Mohawk Nation via Rooseveltown, NY 13683.

1. Why is the tree planted? For what does it stand? For what do the roots stand? The eagle?

2. How are the chiefs of the tribes assembled?

3. Why is the Council Fire lit?

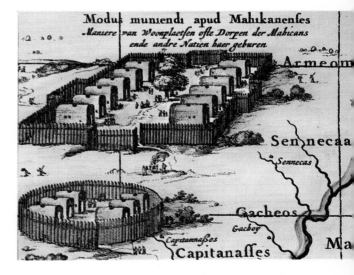

Nicholas Visscher's map of New Belgium, printed in 1651, shows a Minisink village. The Minisink were an Iroquois tribe. The village looks much like Pomeiooc, near Roanoke colony (see page 66).

CHAPTER 1   AMERICAN VOICES **435**

A PAPAGO RAIN SONG

Indians created many songs and poems that were meant to be sung and chanted. The songs and poems were part of a tribe's traditions. They were not written but handed down orally from adults to children.

Only in the last hundred years have these poems been written down on paper and so preserved. Here is one of them, a Papago (PAH-puh-GŌ) rain song. The Papago are a southwestern tribe.

Close to the west the great ocean is singing.
The waves are rolling toward me, covered with
 many clouds.
Even here I can catch the sound.
The earth is shaking beneath me and I hear the
 deep rumbling.

From *Literature of the American Indian* by Thomas E. Sanders and Walter W. Peek (Copyright © 1973 by Benziger Bruce & Glencoe, Inc.) Reprinted by permission of Macmillan Publishing Company.

1. This song has word pictures that appeal to the senses. What word picture appeals to the eye? To the ear? To the sense of touch?

2. What does this song show about the Papago's closeness to nature?

WE MUST PART

People in all times and all cultures have written poems about love. Here is a young woman's love poem traditional to the Oglala Sioux, a plains tribe.

Many are the youths indeed.
But you alone are pleasing to me.
You, O chief, I love.
But we must part
And long will be the time!

From *Indians' Book: Songs and Legends of the American Indians,* revised edition by Natalie Curtis. © 1968 Dover Publications, Inc.

1. Would you call this a happy poem or a sad one? Why do you think so?

2. The poem does not say why the woman must part from her beloved. What might be the reason?

ZUÑI CORN-GRINDING SONG

People who do the same tasks over and over again often sing as they work. The song provides a rhythm for the work. Indian women made up songs to accompany their grinding of corn. Zuñi women in the pueblos of the Southwest sang this song.

O, my lovely mountain,
 To' yallanne!
O, my lovely mountain,
 To' yallanne!
 To' yallanne!
High up in the sky,
Rain Makers
See Rain Makers seated,
Hither come the rain-clouds now.
 He-ya, ha-ya, he-ya!
Behold, yonder
All will soon be abloom
Where the flowers spring—
Tall shall grow the
 youthful corn-plants.

From *Indians' Book: Songs and Legends of the American Indians,* revised edition by Natalie Curtis. © 1968 Dover Publications, Inc.

1. Women made corn meal from dried corn with *metates* (meh-TAH-tehz), or stone grinders. Would you expect the rhythm of their song to be fast or slow? Why?

2. What is the song about? What does it have to do with the work?

Some people still use grinding stones, called metates, to make corn meal and flour. This is a copy of one made by the Hohokam, an ancient people of Arizona. The Papago may be their descendants.

Ancestors of the Wasco tribe probably made this grinding dish between A.D. 1000 and 1200. It combines human, owl, and serpent heads.

A WASCO LEGEND

Like other peoples, the Indians created many tales and legends. Many of the tales explain happenings in nature. Here is a legend from the Wasco, an Oregon Indian tribe.

During a hard winter among the people at Dog River, a great snowstorm set in. It snowed for seven months without stopping. The snow buried even the tallest trees out of sight. The people lived under the snow.

At the Cascades [mountains] people were catching salmon. There was no snow there. It snowed in just one place. The people under the snow did not know that it was summer everywhere else. The way they found it out was this:

A little bird came with a strawberry in its bill to an airhole they had made up out of the snow. They asked the bird what it was that had brought such a storm to Dog River only. The bird told them that one of the girls in the village had struck a bird. It was proved against the girl, and they offered her parents a great price for her. The parents would not sell her for a long time.

At last the people bought her. They put her on the ice as it floated down the river, and pushed the ice into the middle of the stream. In that way they got rid of the snow. A few days later a wind came, bringing heat. The snow melted away at once, and things began to grow.

The girl floated on, day and night, down the river. Five years she floated. At the end of that time she came back up to the place where she had been put on the ice. When she returned, there was only a small piece of ice under her. It was just enough to hold her bones up. For she was almost gone. Only skin and bones remained.

They took the girl into the village. She died. She was no longer accustomed to the smell of people, and died from the odor of them. After a while she came to life again, but it was a year before she could eat much.

Adapted from Jarold Ramsey, comp. and ed., *Coyote Was Going There: Indian Literature of the Oregon Country* (Seattle: University of Washington Press, 1977), pp. 72–73.

1. What was unusual about the snowstorm at Dog River?

2. What caused the storm? How did the people learn this? What did they do about it?

3. What happened to the girl?

4. How do you know this is a legend and not a real-life story?

CHAPTER 2

THE ARRIVAL OF THE EUROPEANS

BJARNI HERJULFSON SEARCHES FOR GREENLAND

Bjarni Herjulfson (BYAR-nee her-YŌL-sun), a Norse trader, sailed for Greenland in 985 to join his father. He told his crew, ''I want to sail my ship to Greenland, if you are willing to come with me.'' Here is his story, as told in ''Saga of the Greenlanders.''

They all answered that they would do what he thought best. Then Bjarni said, "This voyage of ours will be thought foolhardy. Not one of us has ever sailed the Greenland Sea."

Still, they put to sea as soon as they were ready. They sailed for three days until land was lost to sight below the horizon. Then fog set in. For many days they had no idea what their course was. After that they saw the sun again and were able to get their bearings. They hoisted sail again. After a day's sailing they saw land.

A manuscript from the 1100s shows three Vikings at sea. Most Viking ships used a single square sail.

They discussed among themselves what country this might be. Bjarni said he thought it could not be Greenland. The crew asked if Bjarni wanted to land there or not. He answered, "I think we should sail in close."

They did so. Soon they could see that the country was not mountainous. It was well wooded with low hills. So they put to sea again. After sailing northeast for two days, they sighted land again.

Bjarni's men asked him if he thought this was Greenland yet. He said he did not think this was Greenland any more than the last one. "For there are said to be huge glaciers in Greenland."

They quickly got close to the land and saw it was flat and wooded. Then the wind failed. The crew all said they thought it best to land there. But Bjarni refused. They said they needed both firewood and water. But Bjarni said, "You have no shortage of either."

He ordered them to hoist sail, and they did so. They headed out to sea. They sailed before a southwest wind for three days before they saw a third land. This one was high and mountainous and topped by a glacier. Again they asked Bjarni if he wished to land there. He answered, "No, for this country seems to be worthless."

They followed the coastline and saw it was an island. They sailed northeast now for four days, until they saw a fourth land.

The men asked Bjarni if he thought this was Greenland or not.

"This agrees most closely with what I have been told about Greenland," he answered. "And here we shall go in to land."

They did so and landed as dusk was falling at a place where they saw a boat. This was where Bjarni's father, Herjolf, lived. It has been called Herjolfsness for that reason ever since.

Adapted and abridged from *Grœnlandinga Saga:* "Saga of the Greenlanders."

1. How does Bjarni know the second land they see is not Greenland?

2. Why does he decide not to stop at the third land they see?

3. Why does he decide that the fourth land is Greenland?

QUEEN ISABELLA AND KING FERDINAND MAKE AN AGREEMENT WITH COLUMBUS

In 1492 Christopher Columbus set out to find a new route to Asia. Before he sailed, he bargained with Queen Isabella and King Ferdinand of Spain, who were paying for the voyage. He was taking great risks and wished to be justly rewarded.

Finally, two agreements were signed by Isabella and Ferdinand. The agreements say what rewards Columbus should have. Here is a part of the first agreement.

Agreement of April 17, 1492

The things asked for and which your Highnesses give to Christopher Columbus are as follows:

First, that your Highnesses make from this time the said Don Christopher Columbus your Admiral in all those islands and mainlands which by his hand shall be discovered.

Likewise, that your Highnesses make the said Don Christopher Columbus your Governor General in all the said islands and mainlands. . . .

Also, that all merchandise, whether it be pearls, precious stones, gold, silver, spices, or other things, your Highnesses grant to the said Don Christopher. He may take the tenth part for himself, the other nine parts remaining for your Highnesses. . . .

These are executed with the responses of your Highnesses in the town of Santa Fe de la Vega de Granada, on the seventeenth of April. . . .

By order of the King and of the Queen.

Adapted from Charles Gibson, ed., *The Spanish Tradition in America* (New York: Harper & Row, 1968), pp. 27–29.

1. What honors and positions did Isabella and Ferdinand give Columbus?

2. What material wealth was Columbus to have as his reward?

A woodcut in Sebastian Munster's *Cosmographia*, published in 1550, shows the sea monsters thought to live in northern lands.

JACQUES CARTIER CLAIMS GASPÉ BAY FOR FRANCE

In the spring of 1534, the French sailor Jacques Cartier set sail from St. Malo, France, to North America. He was in command of two ships. Crossing the North Atlantic, the ships made their way to the east coast of Newfoundland and then to the Gulf of St. Lawrence. By mid-July, Cartier's two ships were in Gaspé Bay.

We lay at the entrance [of Gaspé Bay] until the 16th [of July]. That day the wind increased so much that one of our ships lost an anchor. We had to enter seven or eight leagues farther up this stream to a good and safe harbor. We were in this harbor and stream until the 25th day of the month, unable to go out in the bad weather.

During this time we saw a great number of Indians. They had come into the stream to fish for mackerel. There were men, women, and children, more than two hundred persons. They came freely with their boats close alongside our ships. We gave them knives, combs, and other articles of little worth, for which they made many signs of joy.

We went with our boats to the place where they were on shore of the stream. They showed great joy, and all the men began to sing and dance in two or three bands. We found a great quantity of mackerel that they had caught with the nets which they have for fishing. . . .

An unknown artist painted a Hudson Bay Eskimo fishing with a handmade spear.

The 24th day of the month we had a cross made thirty feet in height. The cross had an inscription carved in large letters: "VIVE LE ROY DE FRANCE" ["Long live the king of France"]. And this cross we planted at the entrance of the harbor before the Indians. After it was made, we all fell on our knees, with hands joined, while adoring it in front of them. They showed much admiration, turning and gazing at the cross.

Adapted from Paul M. Angle, *The American Reader: From Columbus to Today* (Skokie, IL: Rand McNally & Company, 1958), pp. 13–15.

1. Why, on July 16, did Cartier have his ships move farther inland?

2. How did the Indians react to the coming of Cartier and his sailors?

3. By what ceremony did Cartier claim Gaspé Bay for France?

THE DREAM

Sister Juana Inés de la Cruz lived in a convent in Mexico City in the 1600s. The nuns woke every day at sunrise to pray in the chapel. This poem describes daybreak. It is written in the style of poetry in Europe at the time.

The sun draws up just below the horizon,
Spilling over the rim in rays of pure light.
Thousands of rays like darts of golden metal
Shoot into the sky of sapphires gleaming bright.
Now things on earth are glowing with
    brilliant colors.
It is the ending of night and the day's break.
The whole hemisphere is sparkling with radiance.
The world is full of sunlight! Now I am awake!

Verse believed to be taken from *Primero sueño:* "First Dream" (1692?).

1. What word pictures does Sister Juana use to describe the sunrise?

2. Do you think Sister Juana was happy to be awake so early? What words in the poem are clues to her feelings?

HERNANDO DE SOTO DISCOVERS THE MISSISSIPPI RIVER

Hernando de Soto was a Spaniard who was appointed governor of Florida. Searching for gold, he explored Florida, Georgia, and Alabama. In April 1541 he and his troops came upon a great river later known as the Mississippi. A member of de Soto's party wrote about the expedition's travels. Here he reports the discovery of the Mississippi.

The report mentions a unit of distance called a league. It is about 3 miles (5 kilometers) long. The report also tells that some of de Soto's soldiers were armed with crossbows. The crossbow was a common weapon of the times. An arrow shot from a crossbow could have almost the force of a bullet.

A book published in Venice in 1556 showed Europeans a surprising plant from the New World—an ear of corn.

Three days went by since the search for maize [Indian corn] had begun. Little had been found. The Governor [de Soto] had to move at once. He set out for Quizquiz [an area in what is now western Tennessee]. He marched seven days through a wilderness. He arrived at a town in Quizquiz without being seen and seized the people before they could come out of their houses. . . .

There was little maize in the place. The Governor moved to another town half a league from the great river [the Mississippi]. He went to look at the river. He saw that near it was much timber from which canoes might be made. It was a good place to set up camp.

He moved there, built houses, and settled on a plain not far from the water. The Indians soon came up and told the Governor they served a great chief named Aquixo. They told him Aquixo would come the next day with all his people.

The next day the chief arrived with two hundred canoes filled with armed men. The barge in which the chief came had an awning. The chief said to the Governor that he had come to visit, serve, and obey him. He had heard that he was the greatest of lords, the most powerful on earth.

The Governor expressed his pleasure and asked him to land. But the chief did not answer. He ordered three barges to draw near, on which there was a great quantity of fish and loaves. Receiving them, de Soto gave him thanks and asked him once again to land.

Presenting the gift had been a pretense to see if any harm could be done [to the Spaniards]. But the Governor and his people were on their guard. Seeing this, the chief began to draw away from the shore. The [Spanish] crossbowmen with loud cries shot at the Indians. They struck down five or six of them.

The Indians retreated. Afterwards they came many times and landed. When approached, they would go back to their barges. These were fine-looking people, very large and well-formed. . . .

[During the next 30 days de Soto had four canoes built to carry soldiers to the opposite shore of the Mississippi. They were to seize and hold that land.] When the sun was up two hours high, the people had all got over. The distance was nearly half a league. If a man were standing on the shore, it could not be told from the other side if he were a man or something else.

The stream was swift and very deep. There were many fish of various sorts, most of them different from the fresh-water fish of Spain.

Adapted from Paul M. Angle, *The American Reader: From Columbus to Today* (Skokie, IL: Rand McNally & Company, 1958), pp. 9–11.

1. Where was Quizquiz? Why did de Soto move his soldiers there?

2. Do you think de Soto was right to distrust the Indians? Why or why not?

3. De Soto was looking for gold. He did not seem to think the discovery of the Mississippi was very important so the report does not stress it. Find sentences in the report that deal with the discovery.

CHAPTER 3

THE FRENCH, ENGLISH, AND DUTCH PLANT COLONIES

QUEEN ELIZABETH I ADDRESSES HER SAILORS

In 1588 King Philip II of Spain launched the Invincible Armada, a great fleet of warships, to invade England. After a ten-day battle, the English defeated this far superior force, destroying many of the Armada's ships. England was now safe from invasion.

Before the English went out to face the power of Spain, their queen, Elizabeth I, spoke to them.

My Loving People:

Under God, I have placed my chief strength in the loyal hearts and good will of my subjects. Therefore, I am come among you at this time, not for my recreation. I am resolved in the midst and heat of battle to live or die among you all, to lay down for my people my honor and my blood, even in the dust. . . .

I think foul scorn that Spain or any prince of Europe should dare to invade the borders of my realm. Rather than cause dishonor I will take up arms. I will be your general, judge, and rewarder of every one of your virtues in the field. . . .

We shall shortly have a famous victory over those enemies of my God, of my kingdom, and of my people.

Adapted from Judith Mara Gutman, *The Colonial Venture* (New York: Basic Books, Inc., 1966), p. 36. Reprinted by permission of the publisher.

1. What sentences show Elizabeth's bravery?

2. Do you think Elizabeth's speech helped her sailors fight bravely? Explain.

EXPLORING WITH LA SALLE

Robert Cavelier, Sieur de La Salle, was a French explorer and fur trapper. He explored much of the land along the Mississippi River and claimed it for France. One member of his party was a priest, Father Zenobe Membré. Here, in a letter, Father Membré tells of meeting a band of Indians of the Arkansas tribe.

The whole village came down to the shore to meet us. I cannot tell you the kindness we received. The Indians brought us poles to make huts, gave us firewood, and took turns in feasting us.

But this gives no idea of the good qualities of the Indians, who are civil and free-hearted. The young men are so modest that none of them would take the liberty to enter our hut, but all stood quietly at our door. They are so well formed that we are in admiration of their beauty. We did not lose the value of a pin while we were among them.

Adapted from a letter by Father Zenobe Membré as it appears in *La Salle and the Discovery of the Great West*, by Francis Parkman (Boston, 1907).

1. What impresses Father Membré about the Indians' appearance?

2. What impresses him about their behavior?

3. Explain the last sentence of the letter.

A 1698 French engraving shows La Salle landing on the coast of the Gulf of Mexico 13 years before.

JOHN SMITH TELLS OF HIS RESCUE BY POCAHONTAS

Pocahontas's rescue of John Smith is a famous incident in American history. John Smith was one of the settlers of Jamestown. Pocahontas was an Indian princess, daughter of the great chief Powhatan.

Smith tells the story himself in his book *The General History of Virginia, New England, and the Summer Isles.* As Smith reports it, he and a group of men set out to explore the Chickahominy River. They were attacked by Indians. He was taken prisoner. At length, the Indians brought Smith to Chief Powhatan.

In the book, Smith tells his story in third, not first, person. He refers to himself as *he*, not *I*.

At last they brought Captain Smith to Meronoco-moco, where was Powhatan, their emperor. Here more than two hundred of those grim people stood wondering at him, as if he had been a monster.

Before a fire upon a seat like a bedstead sat Powhatan. He was covered with a great robe made of raccoon skins with all the tails hanging on it. On either hand did sit a young girl of sixteen or eighteen years.

On each side of the house sat two rows of men, and behind them as many women, with all their heads and shoulders painted red. Many of their heads were decorated with white feathers. They wore great chains of white beads about their necks.

At his entrance before the king, all the people gave a great shout. The queen brought him water to wash his hands. Someone else brought him a bunch of feathers instead of a towel to dry them.

Having feasted him in their best manner, they held a long consultation. The conclusion was that two great stones were brought before Powhatan. Then as many as could laid hands upon Captain Smith. They dragged him to the stones and laid his head on them. They were ready with their clubs to beat out his brains.

Pocahontas, the king's dearest daughter, begged them to stop. When they would not, she got his head in her arms and laid her own upon his to save him from death.

At this point Powhatan granted that he should live. He would have to make hatchets for the emperor and bells, beads, and copper for his daughter. They thought him as much a master of all occupations as themselves. For the king himself will make his own robes, shoes, bows, arrows, and pots. He will plant, hunt, or do anything as well as the rest.

From *The Annals of America,* Vol. 1, *1493–1754: Discovering a New World* (Chicago: Encyclopedia Britannica, Inc., 1969), pp. 25–26.

1. What details in the second and third paragraphs give an idea of Powhatan's great position among the Indians?

2. What do the Indians decide to do to Smith? How does Pocahontas rescue him?

3. What sort of work does Powhatan then assign Smith? What does this tell you about these Indians, even Powhatan?

Governor John White of the Roanoke colony drew and painted in watercolors many of the people he found in America. This man wearing body paint posed for his portrait in Carolina in 1585.

LADY MARGARET WYATT CROSSES THE ATLANTIC

Crossing the Atlantic in a crowded wooden ship could be a miserable experience. In 1623 Lady Margaret Wyatt wrote a letter about her trip to her sister in England. Her husband, Sir Francis Wyatt, was the governor of Virginia. Despite her troubles, Lady Wyatt kept her sense of humor.

Dear Sister,

Before this you should have heard from me, if sickness had not till now prevented me. For our ship was so crowded with people and goods that we were full of infection. After a while we saw little but throwing folks overboard. It pleased God to send me my health until I came to shore. Three days after, I fell sick, but I thank God I am well recovered. Few else are left alive that came in that ship. Many have died—husbands, wives, children, and servants.

They told me they sent the ship less crowded for me, but no ship ever came so full to Virginia as ours. I had not so much as my cabin free to myself. Our captain seemed to be troubled at it, and to make the people amends, died himself.

This was our fortune at sea, and on land it was little better. Our people as well as our cattle have died, so that we are all undone, especially we that are newcomers. Unless our friends help us it will go hard with us next winter. Who besides yourself to send to for help, I know not.

Because my mother was so far off that she could give me none when I left, your help did me a great pleasure. So did my other sisters' help. If she [my mother] talks of sending me some butter and bacon, ask that it may be butter and cheese instead. Since the Indians and we fell out, we dare not send men a-hunting.

Adapted from Bernard A. Weisberger, *The American Heritage History of the American People* (New York: American Heritage Publishing Co., 1971), Vol. 1, p. 55.

1. How does Lady Wyatt say the captain made amends for overcrowding?

2. Why do the Virginians need help from their friends and relatives in England?

A COLONIST CRITICIZES PETER STUYVESANT

Peter Stuyvesant was governor of New Netherland, the Dutch colony set up in North America by the West India Company. (It later became New York.)

Stuyvesant was stubborn. He refused to listen to advice or protests. By 1650 many settlers were unhappy with him. A group of settlers led by Adriaen van der Donck complained to the West India Company. Here is a part of their complaint.

Mr. Stuyvesant has most all the time been busy building, making, breaking, repairing, and the like, but with little profit to it. At the first, he repaired the church and shortly afterward made a wooden wharf. Yet after this time we do not know that anything has been done that is entitled to the name of a public work. . . .

Thus, in a short time, very great discontent has sprung up. Protests were made on account of the cost resulting from unnecessary council members, officers, and servants. But it was all in vain. There was very little or no reform. For Stuyvesant's pride has ruled instead of justice. It was as if it were disgraceful to follow advice, and as if everything should come from one head.

Great distrust has also been created on account of Mr. Stuyvesant being so ready to seize ships in the name of the government. No one who has any property considers it to be at all safe.

Besides this, the country is so taxed that the inhabitants are not able to undertake any enterprise. It seems that all the inhabitants of New Netherland agree that the managers of the colony have scarce any regard for New Netherland, except when there is something to receive.

Adapted from *The Annals of America,* Vol. 1, *1493–1754: Discovering a New World* (Chicago: Encyclopedia Britannica, Inc., 1969), p. 208.

1. What sentences in the complaint refer to Stuyvesant's spending too much money?

2. What sentences refer to his stubbornness and refusal to listen to advice?

3. What complaint does van der Donck make about taxes?

UNIT 2   1620–1783

FROM COLONIES TO INDEPENDENT STATES

CHAPTER 4

THE THIRTEEN ENGLISH COLONIES

MARGARET WINTHROP TO HER HUSBAND

Margaret Winthrop's husband, John, was a founder of Massachusetts Bay Colony. He was also the colony's first governor. Margaret and John's many letters to each other show they were a devoted couple. Following is a letter from Margaret written two years before John arrived in North America.

My most sweet husband,

How dearly welcome thy kind letter was to me. The sweetness of it did much refresh me. I blush to hear myself praised, knowing my own faults. But it is your love that understands the best, and makes all things seem better than they are.

I wish that I may be always pleasing to thee. May those comforts we have in each other be daily increased, as far as they be pleasing to God. I cannot do enough for thee, but thou art contented to accept my wishes as if they were deeds.

I have many reasons to make me love thee, of which I will name two. First because thou lovest God. And second, because thou lovest me.

But I must leave this talk and go about my household affairs. I should not be so long from them, but I must borrow a little time to talk with thee, my sweet heart.

I hope thy business draws to an end. It will be but two or three weeks before I see thee, though they be long ones. God will bring us together in His good time, for which time I shall pray.

I thank the Lord, we are all in health. The Lord make us thankful for all His mercies to us and ours. And thus, with my mother's and my own best love

to yourself, I shall leave scribbling. The weather, being cold, makes me make haste. Farewell my good husband, the Lord keep thee.

Your obedient wife,
Margaret Winthrop

Adapted from John C. Miller, ed., *The Colonial Image: Origins of American Culture* (New York: George Braziller, 1962), p. 77–78.

1. What two reasons does Margaret Winthrop give for loving her husband?

2. What reasons does she give for ending the letter?

3. For Puritans such as the Winthrops, God was a strong force in their daily lives. What sentences in the letter show the presence of this force?

This kitchen is part of a restored house in Malden, Massachusetts, built in the 1600s. The large fireplace was used for both cooking and heating. Although colonists brought some furniture with them, they built most of it themselves.

WILLIAM PENN REPORTS ON PENNSYLVANIA

William Penn acquired Pennsylvania as a haven for his fellow Quakers. But the colony was not exclusively reserved for Quakers. As Penn intended, people of various nations and faiths settled there. In 1685 Penn published a book about his colony, called *A Further Account of the Province of Pennsylvania.* Here is a part of his *Account.*

The people are a collection of different nations in Europe, such as French, Dutch, Germans, Swedes, Danes, Finns, Scots, Irish, and English. But as they are of one kind and in one place and under one allegiance, so they live like people of one country. . . .

Philadelphia is two miles long and a mile broad, and at each end it lies a mile upon a navigable river. Besides the High Street that runs in the middle, it has eight streets more that run the same course. And besides Broad Street, which crosses the town in the middle, there are twenty streets more that run the same course. . . .

During the first ten months since our arrival we had got up 80 houses at our town, and some villages were settled about it. During the next year the town advanced to 357 houses. Many of them were large and well-built, with good cellars and three stories. Some had balconies.

There is also a fair wharf of about three hundred square feet. . . .

There lived most sorts of useful tradespeople such as carpenters, bricklayers, masons, plasterers, plumbers, smiths, glaziers, tailors, shoemakers, butchers, bakers, tanners, shipwrights. . . .

The hours for work and meals to laborers are fixed and known by ring of bell. . . .

Some vessels have been built here and many boats, which are useful for passage of people and goods. . . .

With the natives we live in great friendship. I have made seven purchases. And in pay and presents they have received at least twelve hundred pounds [English units of money] of me.

They generally leave their guns at home when they come to our settlement. They offer us no insult, not so much as to one of our dogs. If any of them break our laws, they submit to be punished by them.

SOME
ACCOUNT
OF THE
PROVINCE
OF
PENNSILVANIA
IN
AMERICA;
Lately Granted under the Great Seal
OF
ENGLAND
TO
William Penn, &c.

Together with Priviledges and Powers necef-
fary to the well-governing thereof.

Made publick for the Information of fuch as are or may be
difpofed to Tranfport themfelves or Servants
into thofe Parts.

LONDON: Printed, and Sold by *Benjamin Clark*
Bookfeller in *George-Yard Lombard-ftreet,* 1681.

A book published in 1681 promised readers information about the new colony of Pennsylvania. It was meant to encourage immigration to America.

We leave not the least wrong done to them unsatisfied. Justice gains and awes them. They have some great people among them, I mean for wisdom, truth, and justice.

Adapted from William Penn, *A Further Account of the Province of Pennsylvania* (London?, 1865), pp. 2–6, 17–18, 20.

1. What, according to Penn, causes the people of different nations to live together "like people of one country"?

2. What details does Penn give to show how Pennsylvania has grown and prospered?

3. Part of Penn's account is about the colony's dealings with the Indians. Do you think the Indians were treated fairly? Why or why not?

AULKEY HUBERTSE BECOMES AN INDENTURED SERVANT

During colonial times, many poor people chose to become indentured servants. Some bound themselves for several years to a master in return for passage to the colonies. Sometimes orphans became indentured servants because they had no one to look after them.

Like slaves, indentured servants had to do whatever their masters wanted. The masters had to provide food, housing, and clothing. Unlike slaves, however, indentured servants knew they would be free at the end of their service. And no one could force them to become indentured servants. Aulkey Hubertse was quite young when she signed this agreement in New York in 1710.

This indenture witnesses that Aulkey Hubertse of Rensselaerwyck, daughter of the [dead] John Hubertse, has bound herself as a house servant. She has of her own free will bound herself as a house servant to John Delemont, a weaver of the City of Albany. The deacons of the Reformed Dutch Church have given their consent. She will serve from the date of these present indentures [1710] until she shall come of age.

During this term the servant shall serve her master faithfully. She shall keep his secrets and gladly obey his lawful commands. She shall do no damage to her master nor see it done by others without telling her master. She shall not waste her master's goods, nor lend them unlawfully to anyone.

At cards, dice, or any other game she shall not play. She shall not buy or sell her own goods or the goods of others during the term. She shall not be absent day or night from her master's service without his permission. She shall not go to ale-houses, taverns, or playhouses. In all things she shall behave as a faithful servant.

And the master, during the term, shall provide enough meat and drink, washing, lodging, and clothing. He shall also provide all other necessities fit for such a servant.

It is further agreed between the master and servant that in case Aulkey Hubertse should marry before she shall come of age, then the servant is free from her service.

At the end of her service, John Delemont shall deliver to the servant clothes fit for wearing on the Lord's Day as well as on working days. This includes both linen and woolen stockings and shoes and other necessities. For the true performance of all and every part of this agreement, the two parties bind themselves to each other.

From Alice Morse Earle, *Colonial Days in Old New York* (New York: Charles Scribner's Sons, 1896), pp. 84–86, adapted.

1. Name three things Aulkey Hubertse is forbidden to do by this contract.

2. What does John Delemont promise to provide for Aulkey Hubertse?

3. How can Aulkey Hubertse end her service before she comes of age?

ELIZA LUCAS PINCKNEY, PLANTER

Eliza Lucas Pinckney's father was a planter in South Carolina. When he was away, she was put in charge of running his three plantations. It was a great responsibility for a teenager. Here, in a letter, she tells of her life and responsibilities.

In the letter she refers to the nearby city Charles Town. Later its name was changed. Today it is Charleston, South Carolina.

I like this part of the world. I prefer England to it, 'tis true, but think Carolina greatly preferable to the West Indies. Were my Papa here, I should be very happy.

We know many people from whom we have received much friendship. Charles Town, the main one in this province, is a polite, agreeable place. The country is in general fertile and abounds with venison and wild fowl. The venison is much higher flavored than in England, but 'tis seldom fat.

My Papa and Mama leave it to me to choose our place of residence, either in town or country. I think it best for my Mama and self to be in the country during my father's absence.

We are seventeen miles by land and six by water from Charles Town. We have about six agreeable families around us with whom we live in great harmony. I have a little library in which I spend part

Mulberry Castle, a plantation in South Carolina, had rows of slave cabins behind the great house. Thomas Coram painted it in oils on paper about 1800.

of my time. My music and the garden, which I am very fond of, take up the rest that is not employed in business. Of that my father has left me a pretty good share, and indeed 'twas unavoidable. . . .

I have the business of three plantations to transact. This requires much writing and more business than you can imagine. But do not imagine it too heavy a burden to a girl at my early time of life. Let me assure you I think myself happy that I can be useful to so good a father. By rising very early, I find I can go through with much business.

Do not think I shall be quite depressed with this way of life. I can inform you there are two worthy ladies in Charles Town who like me enough to wish to have me stay with them. I am sometimes with the one or the other for three weeks or a month at a time. Then I enjoy all the pleasures Charles Town affords.

Taken in modified form from Mary R. Beard, Editor, *America Through Women's Eyes,* The Macmillan Co., 1933, pp. 33–34.

1. Eliza Lucas Pinckney writes, "I like this part of the world" (the Carolinas). What does she tell about "this part of the world" to explain her liking for it?

2. Eliza Lucas Pinckney led a busy life. What kept her busy? What did she do for pleasure?

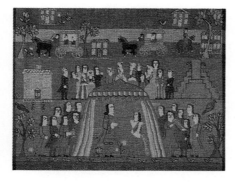

In addition to their regular work, women in colonial days were expected to become expert needleworkers. Mary Williams created this needlepoint picture in about 1744. It is called "The Queen of Sheba."

CHAPTER 5

LIFE IN THE COLONIES

A NEW ENGLAND ALPHABET

Many colonial children learned how to read from the *New England Primer.* First published in 1683, this book went through a number of printings in the eighteenth century.

In *A*dam's fall
We sinned all.

Thy life to mend
This *B*ook attend.

The *C*at doth play
And after slay.

A *D*og will bite
A thief at night.

An *E*agle's flight
Is out of sight.

The idle *F*ool
Is whipt at school.

As runs the *G*lass [hourglass]
Man's life doth pass.

My book and *H*eart
Shall never part.

*J*ob feels the rod,
Yet blesses God.

*K*ings should be good;
Not men of blood

The *L*ion bold
The *L*amb doth hold.

From *The Annals of America,* Vol. 1, *1493–1754: Discovering a New World* (Chicago, Encyclopedia Britannica, Inc., 1969), p. 276.

1. What words introduce children to the following letters: *A, G, J, L?*

2. What verse shows the importance of hard work to the Puritans? What verses show the importance of religion to them?

A SLAVE'S EPITAPH

A slave in Concord, Massachusetts, had the following epitaph carved on his gravestone. An *epitaph* is a short statement in memory of a dead person.

> GOD
> Wills us free.
> Man
> Wills us slaves.
>
> I will as God wills,
> God's will be done.
>
> Here lies the body of *JOHN JACK,*
> A native of Africa, who died March, 1773,
> Aged about *sixty years.*
>
> Tho' *born* in a land of *slavery,*
> He was born *free.*
> Tho' he lived in a land of *liberty,*
> He lived a *slave.* . . .
>
> Death, the grand Tyrant,
> Gave him his final emancipation [freedom]
> And set him on a footing with kings. . . .

From *Eyewitness: The Negro in American History* by William Loren Katz. Copyright © 1974 by David S. Lake Publishers, Belmont, CA.

1. What contrast between God and humanity is made at the beginning? What contrast is made in the sentences that begin, "Tho' *born* in a land . . ."?

2. What did "Death" do for the slave? Why is he now "on a footing with kings"?

Colonial sculptors put their imaginations to work carving tombstones for New England families. They chose subjects to remind passersby of the shortness of life so that they would lead godly lives.

ANNE BRADSTREET TO HER HUSBAND

Anne Bradstreet was one of the first American poets. Her first collection of poems was published in 1650. In 1678, six years after her death, a larger, revised collection appeared. Many of the poems are about her life with her husband and children. The following poem is named "To My Dear and Loving Husband."

> If ever two were one, then surely we.
> If ever man were loved by wife, then thee.
> If ever wife was happy in a man,
> Compare with me ye women if you can.
> I prize thy love more than whole mines of gold,
> Or all the riches that the East doth hold.
> My love is such that rivers cannot quench,
> Nor ought [anything] but love from thee, give
>   recompense [reward].
> Thy love is such I can no way repay,
> The heavens reward thee manifold [in many ways]
>   I pray.
> Then while we live, in love let's so persevere
>   [continue],
> That when we live no more, we may live ever.

From *The Annals of America,* Vol. 1, *1493–1754: Discovering a New World* (Chicago: Encyclopedia Britannica, Inc., 1969), p. 198.

1. Explain the poem's first line.

2. How may the poet and her husband live forever (line 12)? How does this line reflect the Puritans' religious beliefs?

CANASSATEEGO'S SPEECH

Canassateego was a chief of the Six Nations of the League of the Iroquois. Originally the league was made up of five tribes: Mohawk, Oneida, Onondaga, Cayuga, and Seneca. In 1722 the Tuscarora (TUS-kuh-ROR-uh) became part of the league.

In 1742 chiefs of the league met with officials of Pennsylvania Colony. Much of the talk was about land rights. The league was concerned that some English settlers were living on Indian land. Chief Canassateego made the following speech to the Pennsylvania officials on July 7, 1742.

Brethren, governor and council, and all present.

According to our promise, we now propose to return you an answer to the several things mentioned to us yesterday. You put us in mind of William Penn's constant care to seek friendship with all the Indians and of a treaty we held with one of his sons, about ten years ago. . . .

We are all very aware of the kind regard that good man William Penn had for all the Indians. We cannot be but pleased to find that his children have the same. . . .

Brethren, we received from the proprietors yesterday some goods for our release of the lands on the west side of the Susquehanna River. If the goods were only to be divided among the Indians present, a single person would have but a small portion. But if you consider what numbers are left behind, there will be extremely little. We therefore desire you will give a little more to us.

We know our lands are now become more valuable. The white people think we do not know their value. But we are sensible that the land is ever-lasting, and the few goods we receive for it are soon worn out and gone. In future, we will sell no land without knowing beforehand the quantity of goods we will receive.

Besides, we are not well used with respect to the lands still unsold by us. Your people daily settle on these lands and spoil our hunting. We must insist on your removing them. You know they have no right to settle north of Kittochtinny Hills. . . .

It is a custom with us to make a present of skins whenever we renew our treaties. We are ashamed to offer our brethren so few. But your horses and cows have eaten the grass our deer used to feed on. This has made them scarce. If we could have spared more, we would have given you more. But we are really poor. We desire you will not consider the quantity, but, few as they are, accept them as proof of our regard.

Adapted from *Makers of America*, Vol. 1, *The Firstcomers: 1536–1800* (Chicago: Encyclopedia Britannica Educational Corporation, 1971), pp. 193–194.

1. Why does Canassateego call William Penn a "good man"? In your opinion, does the chief think the present officials are as good? Explain.

2. Why does Canassateego think the Indians are entitled to more payment for land already sold? What is his concern about the land not sold?

3. Canassateego says the Indians "are really poor." What has caused their poverty?

"WHAT THEN IS THE AMERICAN?"

Michel Guillaume Jean de Crèvecoeur (KREV-KOOR) was a Frenchman who went to Canada. Later he settled on a farm in the colony of New York, becoming a New York citizen in 1765. Under a pen name, he published *Letters from an American Farmer,* a book famous for a question. "What then is the American, this new man?" asked Crèvecoeur. His book was an answer to this question.

Crèvecoeur saw that in America "individuals of all nations are melted into a new race, whose labors will one day cause great changes in the world." In the following passage from *Letters,* Crèvecoeur compares Europeans and Americans.

A traveler to America is arrived on a new continent. A modern society offers itself, different from what he had previously seen. It is not composed, as in Europe, of great lords who possess everything, and of a herd of people who have nothing. Here are no noble families, no kings. The rich and the poor are not so far removed from each other as they are in Europe.

Some few towns excepted, we are all tillers of the earth. We are a people of farmers, scattered over a huge territory, united by a mild government. We all respect the laws, without dreading their power, because they are fair. We are all moved with the spirit of hard work because we work for ourselves.

If the visitor travels through our rural districts, he views not the hostile castle contrasted with the clay-built hut. The meanest of our log-houses is dry and comfortable. Lawyer or merchant are the most noble titles our towns offer. Farmer is the only title of the rural inhabitants of our country.

There, on a Sunday, he sees at church respectable farmers and their wives, all clad in neat homespun [cloth made of yarn spun at home]. We have no princes for whom we toil, starve, and bleed. We are the most perfect society now existing in the world. Here people are free as they ought to be.

Adapted from Thomas A. Bailey, ed., *The American Spirit: United States History As Seen by Contemporaries* (Boston: D. C. Heath and Company, 1963), pp. 81–82. Reprinted by permission of the publisher.

1. In Europe, says Crèvecoeur, there is a huge gap between the rich and the poor. Does one exist in America?

2. Why, according to Crèvecoeur, do Americans work hard?

3. What might foreign travelers see in America's "rural districts"? What might they see in a church there that would point out the difference between Europe and America?

An English engraver in 1768 showed the beginning of an American settlement on the left of this picture and the completion of it on the right.

CHAPTER 6

THE COLONIES MOVE TOWARD INDEPENDENCE

PONTIAC CALLS FOR WAR

Chief Pontiac of the Ottawa was an enemy of the British and an ally of the French. On May 5, 1763, he spoke to a group of Ottawa, Pottawatomie, and Huron, urging them to attack the British. The resulting war is known as Pontiac's Rebellion. Here is a part of Pontiac's speech.

It is important for us, my brothers, that we exterminate [wipe out] from our lands this nation that seeks only to destroy us. The English sell us goods twice as dear as the French do, and their goods do not last. Scarcely have we bought a blanket before we must think of getting another. And when we wish to set out for our winter camp they do not want to give us any credit as our brothers, the French, do.

When I go to see the English commander and say to him that some of our comrades are dead, instead of bewailing their death, as our French brothers do, he laughs at me and at you. If I ask for anything for our sick, he refuses with the reply that he has no use for us. From all this you can well see that they are seeking our ruin. Therefore, my brothers, we must all swear their destruction and wait no longer. Nothing prevents us. They are few in numbers, and we can accomplish it.

All the nations who are our brothers attack them—why should we not strike too? Are we not men like them? Our great father [King Louis XV] tells us to strike them. What do we fear? It is time.

Adapted from Annette Rosenstiel, *Red & White: Indian Views of the White Man 1492–1982* (New York: Universe Books, 1983), p. 90.

1. What reasons does Pontiac give for taking up arms against the British?

2. A war speech cannot simply give reasons. It must rouse people to action. Point out sentences you think roused the Indians against the British.

THE STAMP ACT: BENJAMIN FRANKLIN TESTIFIES

In 1765 the English Parliament passed the Stamp Act. This act required that every legal document and newspaper in Britain's American colonies be printed on special stamped paper or have a special stamp.

The colonists objected to the Stamp Act because they thought it was "taxation without representation." American colonists could not elect members to Parliament. So they had no voice in whether the Stamp Act should have been passed or not. There was a storm of protest against the act.

In 1766 Benjamin Franklin was in London, acting as a colonial agent. Here is part of his testimony before a committee of Parliament.

Q. What is your name, and place of abode?

A. Franklin, of Philadelphia.

Q. Do the Americans pay any heavy taxes among themselves?

A. Certainly many, and very heavy taxes.

Q. Are not all the people very able to pay?

A. No. The frontier counties are very poor. They are able to pay very little tax. . . .

Q. Are not the colonies very able to pay the stamp duty?

A. In my opinion there is not gold and silver enough in the colonies to pay the stamp duty for one year. . . .

Q. Do you think it right that America should be protected by this country and yet pay no part of the cost?

A. That is not the case. The colonies raised, clothed, and paid, during the last war, near·25,000 men, and spent many millions. . . .

Q. Do not you think the people of America would pay the stamp duty if it was lessened?

A. No, never, unless forced by arms.

Q. What was the temper of America towards Great Britain before the year 1763?

A. The best in the world. They submitted willingly to the government of the Crown.

Q. What is your opinion of a future tax like the Stamp Act? How would the Americans receive it?

A. Just as they do this. They would not pay it.

Q. Can anything less than a military force put the Stamp Act into effect?

A. I do not see how a military force can be applied to that purpose.

Q. Why may it not?

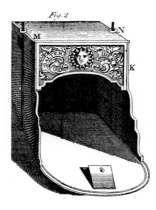

Benjamin Franklin designed his famous stove just before he began his experiments with electricity. The flue acted as a radiator to warm the air in the room.

A. Suppose a military force is sent into America. They cannot force anyone to take stamps who chooses to do without them. They will not find a rebellion. They may indeed make one.

Q. If the act is not repealed, what do you think will be the results?

A. A total loss of the respect and affection the people of America bear to this country.

Q. How can trade be affected?

A. You will find that, if the act is not repealed, they will take very little of your manufactures in a short time.

Q. Is it in their power to do without them?

A. I think they may very well do without them.

Q. If the Stamp Act were repealed, would the assemblies of America repeal their resolutions against the Stamp Act?

A. No, never.

Q. Is there no way to force them to repeal those resolutions?

A. None that I know of. They will never do it, unless forced by arms.

Q. Is there a power on earth that can force them to repeal them?

A. No power, how great soever, can force people to change their opinions. . . .

Q. What used to be the pride of the Americans?

A. To buy the fashions and manufactures of Great Britain.

Q. What is now their pride?

A. To wear their old clothes over again, till they can make new ones.

Adapted from Thomas A. Bailey, ed. *The American Spirit: United States History As Seen by Contemporaries* (Boston: D. C. Heath and Company, 1963), pp. 86–89. Reprinted by permission of the publisher.

1. How, according to Franklin, has the attitude of the American colonists toward England changed? How will trade be affected?

2. What does Franklin say will happen if a military force is sent to America?

3. Explain the last sentence of Franklin's testimony to the committee.

THE DAUGHTERS OF LIBERTY ORGANIZE BOYCOTTS

In the 1770s American colonists were outraged at British attempts to tax them. In protest, they refused to buy English products. They hoped their boycott would hurt trade. Then Parliament might listen to the complaints of the colonists.

Women organized Daughters of Liberty groups. They encouraged boycotts in letters like these printed in colonial newspapers. The first letter is an agreement by three hundred women in Boston. The second was signed by "a Planter's Wife" in Virginia.

This is a time when our rights are attacked in an illegal and most alarming manner. We are being criticized for not resisting. Therefore, we agree with the true Friends of Liberty in all the measures they have taken to save this country from ruin and slavery.

Particularly we join with the merchants and other inhabitants of this town in their resolution to do completely without the use of TEA. The greatest part of the revenue raised by the latest acts from England comes from the duty paid on tea. Therefore we do strictly agree that we will *totally* do without the use of tea (sickness excepted) in our families. We will also absolutely refuse it, if it should be offered to us on any occasion whatsoever.

Boston Evening Post, February 12, 1770

To the Ladies of South Carolina
My Sisters and Countrywomen,

One of our sister colonies [Massachusetts] is suffering under the iron hand of power [British control] in the cause of American liberty. Surely, my sisters, we cannot just watch when so much remains for us to do. We may reasonably be expected to help.

By continuing to use East India Tea, we have helped the enemies of America to enslave ourselves and future Americans. Let us now prove to the world that we have some regard for our country. Let us now join cheerfully in a promise to give up the use of all foreign tea and also every kind of East India goods. On Heaven alone, and our general agreement, the saving of America depends.

The Virginia Gazette, September 15, 1774

Boston Evening Post, February 12, 1770. American Museum, August, 1787, p. 165. *The Virginia Gazette,* September 15, 1774.

1. What do the Boston women agree to do?

2. In the letter from the planter's wife, who are the "enemies of America" who would "enslave ourselves and future Americans"?

3. What do these letters show about the way colonists felt?

An English cartoon made fun of fifty-one women in Edenton, North Carolina, who met October 25, 1774, to boycott English tea. The women are shown ignoring a baby and flirting as they gather to sign their resolution.

* **CT** Discussion: Contrast Andrew's eyewitness testimony about the Boston Massacre with accounts in Boston newspapers (page 146). Why were there such differences?

THE BOSTON MASSACRE: ANDREW'S TESTIMONY

On March 5, 1770, British soldiers fired on a group of Bostonians who were jeering at them and throwing things. Five Bostonians were killed. One of them was a sailor named Crispus Attucks. A slave named Andrew testified at the trial of the British soldiers. (Andrew refers to Crispus Attucks as "a stout man.")

On the evening of the 5th of March, I was at home. I heard the bells ring, and went to the gate. I saw one of my acquaintances, and we ran down to the end of the lane. We saw another acquaintance coming up, holding his arm. I asked him, "What's the matter?"

He said the soldiers were fighting. They had got cutlasses [swords] and were killing everybody. One of them had struck him on the arm and almost cut it off. He told me I had best not go down. I said a good club was better than a cutlass. . . .

I went to the Town House and saw the sentinels placed at the main guard. Numbers of boys across the street were throwing snowballs at them. The sentinels were enraged.

I turned about and saw the officer standing before the men. One or two persons were engaged in talk with him. A number were jumping on the backs of those who were talking with the officer, to get as near as they could. I went as close to the officer as I could. One of the persons who was talking with the officer turned about quick to the people. He said, "He is going to fire."

Upon that they gave a shout and cried out, "Fire. Who cares for you? You dare not fire." They began to throw snowballs and other things, which then flew very thick.

Q. Did they hit any of them?

A. Yes. I saw two or three of them hit. One struck a soldier on the hat. The people had sticks. And as the soldiers were pushing with their guns, they struck their guns. One hit a soldier on the fingers. A number of people were crying, "They dare not fire. We are not afraid of them."

One of these people, a stout man with a long cordwood stick, threw himself in, and made a blow at the officer. I saw the officer try to ward off the stroke. The stout man then turned round and struck the soldier's gun. He knocked his gun away and struck him over the head.

This stout man cried, "Kill the dogs. Knock them over." This was the general cry. The people then crowded in. . . .

I was between the officer and the soldier. I turned to go, when I heard the word "fire." At the word "fire," I thought I heard the report of a gun. I then saw the soldier swing his gun and fire it.

Q. Do you know who this stout man was?

A. I thought and still think it was Crispus Attucks who was shot.

Q. Do you know the soldier who fired?

A. I then thought it was Killroy. I now think it was he, but I can't positively swear to it.

From *Eyewitness: The Negro in American History* by William Loren Katz. Copyright © 1974 by David S. Lake Publishers, Belmont, CA.

A regiment of black Patriots from Boston served bravely in the War for Independence. For their loyal military service, John Hancock presented them with a special flag decorated with a stag and a tree.

1. What did the Bostonians do to anger the soldiers? What did the soldiers do to enrage the Bostonians?

2. What part did the "stout man" play in attacking the soldiers?

3. It is not entirely clear how Attucks was killed. Judging from what Andrew tells, what seems to have happened?

CHAPTER 7

THE WAR FOR INDEPENDENCE

LETTER TO A BRITISH ARMY OFFICER

The following letter was written by a Philadelphia woman to a British army officer in Boston. The letter's exact date is not known.

I will tell you what I have done. My only brother I have sent to the camp with my prayers and my blessings. I hope he will not disgrace me. I am confident he will behave with honor. Had I twenty sons and brothers they should go.

I have cut back every unnecessary expense in my family. Tea I have not drunk since last Christmas. Nor have I bought a new cap or gown. Although I have never done it before, I have learned to knit. I am now making stockings of American wool. This way I do my bit for the public good.

I know this—that as free I can die but once. But as a slave I shall not be worthy of life.

I have the pleasure to assure you that these are the feelings of all my sister Americans. Our husbands, brothers, and sons are as with one heart determined to die or be free. It is not a trifle that we are fighting for. It is this plain truth—that no one has a right to take their money without their consent.

You say you are no politician. Oh, sir, it requires no scheming head to discover this tyranny and oppression. It is written with a sunbeam. Everyone shall see and know it. And we shall be unworthy of the blessings of Heaven if we ever submit to it.

Taken in modified form from Mary R. Beard, Editor, *America Through Women's Eyes,* The Macmillan Co., 1933, p. 81.

1. What sentences in the letter express the woman's patriotism?

2. What "plain truth" does the letter state? To what British actions does the truth refer?

These small articles were carried by American soldiers during the Revolutionary War. They include a tin lantern, a mirror, clay pipes, and eating utensils.

DEBORAH CHAMPION'S DARING RIDE

Deborah Champion, the twenty-two-year-old daughter of an American general, rode through enemy lines to carry a message to General Washington. Afterward she described her daring ride in a letter to a friend.

My Dear Patience:

I would have answered your last letter long before now, but I have been away from home. I know that you will hardly believe that such a stay-at-home as I should go and all alone too, to where do you think? To Boston! I will tell you all about it.

I had settled myself to spend a long day with my spinning. Just as I was busily engaged, I noticed a horseman enter the yard. Knocking on the door with the handle of his whip, he asked for General Champion. After a brief talk, he entered the house with father.

When I returned [from doing errands], the visitor was gone. My father was walking up and down the long hall with hasty steps and a worried look. He would not have thought it proper for a child of his to question him, so I passed on to find mother. "My father is troubled, Mother, is anything amiss?" "I cannot say, Deborah. You know he has many cares, and the public business presses heavily at times. It may be he will tell us."

Just then my father stood in the doorway. "Wife, I would speak with you." Mother hastily joined him in the keeping room. They seemed to have a long and anxious talk. Finally, to my astonishment, I was called. Father laid his hand on my shoulder and said solemnly: "Deborah, I have need of thee. Hast thou the heart and the courage to go out in the night and ride as fast as may be until thou comest to Boston town?" "Surely, my father, if it is thy wish."

"I do not believe, Deborah, that there will be actual danger, or I would not ask thee. But the way is long and the business urgent. The horseman that was here awhile back brought messages that General Washington must receive as soon as possible. I cannot go. The wants of the army call me at once to Hartford, and I have no one to send but my daughter. Dare you go?"

"Dare! father, and I your daughter—and the chance to do my country and General Washington a service. I am glad to go."

So, dear Patience, it was finally settled that I should start in the early morning. Before it was fairly light, mother called me, though I had seemed to have hardly slept at all. I found a nice hot breakfast ready, and a pair of saddle-bags packed with such things as mother thought might be needed. Father told me again of the haste with which I must ride and the care to use for the safety of the messages.

The British were at Providence, in Rhode Island, so it was thought best I should ride due north to the Massachusetts line, and then east to Boston. The weather was perfect, but the roads none too good as there had been recent rains. We met few people on the road. Almost all the men were with the army, and only the very old men and the women were at work in the villages and farms. War is a cruel thing! But I was so glad that I could do even so little to help!

I heard that it would be almost impossible to avoid the British unless I went far out of the way. But too much time would be lost, so I plucked up what courage I could. Hiding my papers in a small pocket in the saddle-bags under all the eatables mother had filled them with, I rode on. I was determined to ride all night. It was very early in the morning that I heard the call of the sentry. Now, if at all, the danger point was reached.

Pulling my bonnet still farther over my face, I went on. Suddenly, I was ordered to halt. I did so. A soldier in a red coat proceeded to take me to headquarters. I told him it was too early to wake the captain, and to please let me pass. I said I had been sent in haste to see a friend in need. That was true, if misleading. To my joy, he let me go. Evidently he was as glad to get rid of me as I of him.

That is the only bit of adventure that befell me in the whole long ride. When I arrived in Boston, I was so very fortunate as to find friends who took me at once to General Washington. I gave him the papers, which proved to be of great importance.

He complimented me most highly on the courage I had displayed and my patriotism. Oh, Patience, what a man he is, so grand, so kind, so noble. I am sure we will not look to him in vain to save our fair country for us.

Taken in modified form from Mary R. Beard, Editor, *America Through Women's Eyes,* The Macmillan Co., 1933, pp. 73–75.

1. Where does Deborah Champion say the British were camped? Where was General Washington?

2. How did Deborah Champion avoid capture by the British army?

3. What was Deborah Champion's opinion of General Washington?

GOD BLESS OUR ARMES

C. Randle painted this watercolor of the American fleet in 1776. The little navy was a collection of mismatched vessels, but it fought well against the British on Lake Champlain.

"AND ALL THE PEOPLE SHALL SAY AMEN"

In June 1776 the Second Continental Congress appointed a committee to draw up a declaration of the colonies' independence from Great Britain. The Congress chose five delegates: Benjamin Franklin, Robert Livingston, Roger Sherman, John Adams, and Thomas Jefferson. Jefferson was to do the actual writing.

On July 4, 1776, Congress adopted the Declaration of Independence. Seventeen days later it was read aloud in Boston, Massachusetts. Here, Abigail Adams writes her husband, John, about the reaction in Massachusetts. Similar celebrations took place throughout the colonies.

Boston, 21 July, 1776.

Last Thursday I heard a very good sermon. Afterward, I went with the crowd into King Street to hear the Proclamation for Independence read and proclaimed. Some cannons were brought there. The troops appeared under arms, and all the inhabitants assembled there. Smallpox prevented many thousands from coming from the country.

Colonel Crafts read the proclamation from the balcony of the State House. Great attention was given to every word. As soon as he ended, the cry from the balcony was, "God save our American States." Then three cheers tore through the air.

The bells rang, the ships and the forts fired their guns, and the cannon were discharged. Every face appeared joyful. Mr. Bowdoin then gave a sentiment, "May American independence last forever."

After dinner, the King's Arms were taken down from the State House. Every trace of him was taken from every place in which it appeared, and burnt in King Street. Thus ends royal authority in this state. And all the people shall say Amen.

Adapted from Paul M. Angle, *The American Reader: From Columbus to Today* (New York: Rand McNally & Company, 1958), pp. 102–103.

1. What details does Abigail Adams include in her letter that show the importance of this occasion?

2. Abigail Adams writes, "Thus ends royal authority in this state." What was done to show it had ended?

"Warmed by one heart, united by one band," the 13 American colonies are shown as 13 hands grasping a single chain. An unknown artist made this engraving in honor of the Declaration of Independence in 1776.

FROM THE DIARY OF MARGARET HILL MORRIS

Margaret Hill Morris, a widow, lived in Burlington, New Jersey, near Trenton. During the early years of the Revolutionary War, she kept a diary. In it she recorded the news of battles and her contacts with American and enemy soldiers.

Early in 1777, the news reached her of General Washington's victories at Trenton and Princeton, New Jersey. Here she tells what it was like to live in the middle of a war.

January 1, 1777: This New Year's day has not been ushered in with the usual ceremonies and rejoicing. Indeed, I believe it will be the beginning of a sorrowful year to very many people. Yet hope bids me look forward with confidence and trust in Him who can bring order out of this great confusion. . . .

Jan. 3: This morning between 8 and 9 o'clock we heard very distinctly a heavy firing of cannon. The sound came from towards Trenton. About noon a number of [American] soldiers, upwards of 1,000, came into town in great confusion. From these soldiers we learn there was a smart engagement [battle] yesterday at Trenton, but were not able to say which side was victorious. They were again quartered on the inhabitants. We did not have any lodged with us.

Several of those who lodged in Col. Cox's house last week returned tonight. They asked for the key, which I gave them. At about bedtime I went into the next house to see if the fires were safe. My heart was melted with compassion to see such a number of my fellow creatures lying like swine on the floor, fast asleep, and many of them without even a blanket to cover them. . . .

Jan. 4: The accounts hourly coming in are so contradictory and various that we know not which to give credit to. We have heard our people have gained another victory [Battle of Princeton], that the English are fleeing before them, some at Brunswick, some at Princeton. A number of sick and wounded were brought into town—calls upon us to extend a hand of charity towards them. . . .

Jan. 6: We are told today that 2,000 New England men fell in the late engagement.

Jan. 8: All the soldiers are gone from the next house. Only one of the number stopped to bid me farewell. But I did not resent it.

I went into the house after they had left it, and was grieved to see such loads of provisions [supplies] wastefully lying on the floor. I sent my son to desire an officer in town to order it away. He desired me "to keep it from spoiling." That was, to make use of it. As it was not his to give, and I had no stomach to keep it from spoiling, I sent it to another person, who had it taken to the sick soldiers.

Abridged from Elizabeth Evans, *Weathering the Storm: Women of the American Revolution* (agent: Dorothy Pitman, 1975), pp. 93–95.

1. When is Margaret Hill Morris first aware of the Battle of Trenton? How?

2. What does she learn about the Battles of Trenton and Princeton?

3. What details in the diary reveal her sympathy for others? Her unselfishness?

Our Country, a book published in 1876 for the Centennial, showed the hardships at Valley Forge.

VALLEY FORGE: FIRE CAKES AND WATER

Late in 1777, George Washington set up camp in Valley Forge, Pennsylvania. There, short of food and clothing, the Continental Army spent a miserable winter. Soldiers died by the hundreds.

Albigence Waldo was a surgeon who kept a diary of his time with the army. Here he tells of the early painful days of that winter. (The diary refers to "fire cakes." These are small loaves of bread baked over an open fire.)

December 21, 1777. Preparations made for huts. Provisions scarce. Heartily wish myself at home. My skin and eyes are almost spoiled with continual smoke. A general cry through the camp this evening among the soldiers: "No meat! No meat!"

"What have you for your dinners, boys?"

"Nothing but fire cakes and water, sir."

At night: "Gentlemen, the supper is ready."

"What is your supper, lads?"

"Fire cakes and water, sir." . . .

December 22. Lay excessive cold and uncomfortable last night. My eyes are started out from their orbits, like a rabbit's eyes, because of the great cold and smoke.

"What have you got for breakfast, lads?"

"Fire cakes and water, sir."

December 24. Huts go on being built slowly. Cold and smoke make us fret. . . .

December 25, Christmas. We are still in tents when we ought to be in huts. The poor sick suffer much in tents in this cold weather. . . .

December 28. Building our huts.

December 29. Continued the work. Snowed all day pretty briskly. The party of the 22d returned. It had lost 18 men, who were taken prisoner. . . .

December 31. We finished the year with thankful hearts in our new hut, which stands on a high point that overlooks the brigade. It is in sight of the front line. . . .

January 6, 1778. We have got our huts to be very comfortable and feel ourselves happy in them. I only want my family, and I should be as happy here as anywhere, except for food, which is sometimes pretty scanty.

Adapted from Paul M. Angle, *The American Reader: From Columbus To Today* (New York: Rand McNally & Company, 1958), pp. 111–112.

1. What do the soldiers eat for dinner (the midday meal), supper, and breakfast? What does this tell you about the hardships they endured?

2. About what other hardships does Albigence Waldo tell? What finally makes his life in the camp more comfortable?

The General Assembly of Virginia freed volunteer James Armistead Lafayette, a slave, in return for his outstanding Revolutionary War service. John B. Martin painted his portrait in 1824.

THE BRAVE VOLUNTEERS

Many songs came out of the Revolutionary War. The following song hails the volunteers who fought the British. It was probably written by Henry Archer, a Scotsman. He came to America in 1778 and enlisted in the Continental Army.

Here's to the squire [gentleman] who goes
    to parade,
Here's to the citizen soldier;
Here's to the merchant who fights for his trade,
Whom danger increasing makes bolder.
Let mirth appear,
Union is here,
The toast that I give is the brave volunteer.

Here's to the lawyer, who leaving the bar,
Hastens where honor doth lead, sir,
Changing the gown [of a lawyer] for the ensigns
    [banners] of war,
The cause of his country to plead, sir.
Freedom appears,
Every heart cheers,
And calls for the health of the law volunteers.

Here's to the soldier, though battered in wars,
And safe to his farm-house retired.
When called by his country, he never thinks of
    his scars,
With ardor [zeal] to join us inspired.
Bright fame appears,
Trophies uprear [rise up],
To veteran chiefs who became volunteers.

Abridged from "The Volunteer Boys" in Frank Moore, ed., *Songs and Ballads of the American Revolution.* New York, 1856, p. 285.

1. What specific lines of work does this patriotic song mention?

2. It is a lawyer's usual job to plead a case in court. How may the lawyer-soldier plead the "cause of his country"?

3. The song's last stanza is about a veteran soldier. He has retired to his farm. But when "called by his country," he volunteers again. How might such a veteran win "bright fame"?

UNIT 3 · 1777–1824

BUILDING A NEW NATION

CHAPTER 8

FORMING A UNION

SAUL'S PETITION

During the Revolutionary War, freedom was offered to slaves who would desert their masters and fight on the British side. Saul, a Virginia slave owned by George Kelly, did not desert his master. Instead he fought, both as a soldier and a spy, for the Americans.

In 1792 Saul asked the Virginia General Assembly for his freedom as a reward for his loyal military service. Saul's petition was granted.

About 1790, a Swedish immigrant to America named J. A. Brunstrom made this pewter tankard. It shows the graceful but sturdy lines typical of the best American metalsmiths' work. Pewter was a metal made by combining tin and copper. Many pewter designs copy those of expensive silver.

To the Honorable Speaker and Members of the General Assembly:

In the beginning of the recent war that gave America independence, your petitioner shouldered his musket [gun] under the American flag. British proclamations invited slaves to free themselves by killing their masters. Your petitioner avoided that rock, which too many of his race were shipwrecked on. He was taught to know that war was waged on America, not to free blacks, but to enslave whites. He thought the number of slaves should not be increased.

With this understanding, your petitioner actually served in both armies. He served in the American army as a soldier. He served in the British army as an American spy.

In this double profession, your petitioner thinks he performed essential services for his country. He would have performed many more had he not been betrayed in the campaign of 1781.

He was betrayed by a Negro whom the British had employed in the same business [as a spy] in General Muhlenberg's camp. Your petitioner was then in Portsmouth, a British garrison, collecting information for Colonel Josiah Parker. His heels saved his neck. He fled to the advance post commanded by Colonel Parker.

Your petitioner will trouble this honorable body no further by listing his different kinds of services. He hopes the legislature of a republic will not allow him to remain a transferrable property.

Adapted from the General Assembly, Petitions, Norfolk, August–October, 1792, Virginia State Library, Richmond, Virginia.

1. What two kinds of services did Saul perform for America?

2. How was Saul nearly caught? What does he mean when he said, "His heels saved his neck"?

Activity: Abigail Adams is one of the great letter writers of all time. Her letters provide vivid pictures of American life from the Revolution through the Federalist years. Students can research and write reports on her life.

Elizabeth Freeman, painted on ivory by Susan Sedgwick, defended the Sedgwick house during Shays' Rebellion. She won freedom for slaves in Massachusetts in a famous lawsuit based on the new state's Bill of Rights.

ABIGAIL ADAMS ON SHAYS' REBELLION

In 1787 Daniel Shays led 1,200 men in a raid on a federal arsenal in Springfield, Massachusetts. What had roused Shays and his followers was high taxes. State troops put down Shays' Rebellion quickly enough. Still, many Americans were alarmed by this armed defiance of the government.

Abigail Adams was in Britain when Shays' Rebellion broke out, but she was concerned about this threat to law and order. Here she writes to Thomas Jefferson, then the United States minister to France, about the rebellion.

You ask about the revolt in my native state. I wish I could say the report was exaggerated. It is too true, sir, that the revolt was so extreme that it stopped the courts of justice in several counties.

Outlaws have persuaded a mob to follow their flag. They have complaints that exist only in their minds. Some of them cry out for a paper currency. Others demand that property be divided equally among all. Some are for wiping out all debts. Others claim that the Senate is a useless branch of government. They say that the Court of Common Pleas was unnecessary. . . .

This list will show you the kind of people making up this rebellion. It also shows why the strong-est measures are needed to put it down. These rebels want to destroy the government all at once.

But these people make up only a small part of the nation, when compared to the more sensible. They create much trouble and uneasiness. Even so, I cannot help thinking that they will be good for the nation. They will lead to an investigation of the causes which have produced such a rebellion.

Luxury and spending too freely have become common to all our countrymen and women. Such wasteful spending has been sapping the independence of every class of citizens. It has caused them to pile up debts that they were unable to pay. Vanity was becoming more powerful than patriotism.

The lower classes of the community found it difficult to pay their taxes. Although they owned property, they were unable to answer the demand for taxes. Those who possessed money were afraid to lend it.

By the papers I send you, you will see the good effects that have already been produced. An act of the legislature sets a tax of 15 percent on many articles of British manufacture. It totally prohibits other imports.

A number of volunteers—lawyers, physicians, and merchants from Boston—have made up a group of cavalry. Lieutenant Colonel Jackson went out in pursuit of the rebels. He captured three of the main leaders: Shattucks, Parker, and Page. Shattucks defended himself and was wounded in the knee with a sword. He is in jail in Boston. No doubt, he will be made an example of.

Julian P. Boyd, *The Papers of Thomas Jefferson,* Vol. II: *January 1787 to August 1787.* Copyright 1955, © renewed 1983 by Princeton University Press. Excerpt pp. 86–87 adapted with permission of Princeton University Press.

1. What, according to Abigail Adams, do Daniel Shays and the other rebels want? Why does she have a low opinion of the rebels?

2. Abigail Adams reports to Jefferson about the causes that have produced the rebellion. What causes does she report?

3. Why does Abigail Adams think that Shays' Rebellion may have been a good thing in the long run? What good effect has it already had?

DELEGATES TO THE CONSTITUTIONAL CONVENTION

Major William Pierce was a delegate from Georgia to the Constitutional Convention. A shrewd observer of people, he took notes on his fellow delegates. Here he tells about three delegates: Benjamin Franklin, George Washington, and James Madison.

Doctor Franklin is well known to be the greatest philosopher of the present age. All the operations of nature he seems to understand. The very heavens obey him. The clouds yield up their lightning to be imprisoned in his lightning rod. But what claim he has to be a politician, the future must determine. It is certain that he does not shine much in public council. He is no public speaker. Nor does he seem to let politics engage his attention.

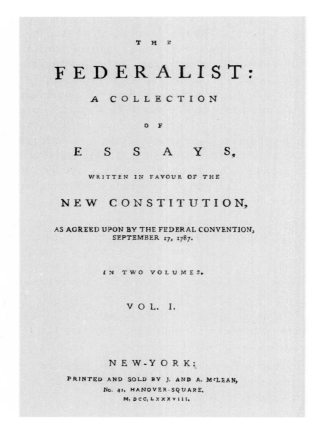

THE

FEDERALIST:

A COLLECTION

OF

E S S A Y S,

WRITTEN IN FAVOUR OF THE

NEW CONSTITUTION,

AS AGREED UPON BY THE FEDERAL CONVENTION,
SEPTEMBER 17, 1787.

IN TWO VOLUMES.

VOL. I.

NEW-YORK:

PRINTED AND SOLD BY J. AND A. M‘LEAN,
No. 41, HANOVER-SQUARE.
M, DCC, LXXXVIII.

The Federalist Papers, essays by Alexander Hamilton, John Jay, and James Madison, convinced many Americans to support the new Constitution.

He is, however, a very unusual man. He tells a story in a style more charming than anything I have ever heard. He is eighty-two years old and his active mind is equal to that of a youth of twenty-five years of age. . . .

General Washington is well known as the commander in chief of the late American army. Having brought these states to independence and peace, he now comes to assist in framing a government. Like Cincinnatus [a Roman general], he returned to his farm perfectly contented with being only a plain citizen. After enjoying the highest honor of the confederation, now he only seeks the approval of his countrymen by being virtuous and useful.

The general was conducted to the chair as President of the Convention by the unanimous voice of its members. He is now in the fifty-second year of his age. . . .

Mr. Madison has long been in public life. What is very remarkable, every person seems to admit his greatness. He blends together the politician and the scholar. In the management of every great question, he evidently took the lead in the Convention.

Though he cannot be called an orator, he is a most agreeable and convincing speaker. He possesses a spirit of hard work and deep study. He always comes forward the best-informed person of any point in a debate. The affairs of the United States, he perhaps has the most correct knowledge of, of anyone in the Union. He has twice been a member of Congress and was always thought one of its ablest members. Mr. Madison is about thirty-seven years of age. He is easy and unreserved among people he knows and has a most agreeable style of conversation.

Adapted from *Documents Illustrative of the Formation of the Union of the United States,* edited by C. C. Tansill (Washington, D.C., 1927).

1. One of Benjamin Franklin's inventions was the lightning rod. In what sense do "the very heavens obey him"?

2. What shortcoming in Franklin does Major Pierce see?

3. What does William Pierce admire about George Washington? James Madison?

ON A SLAVE SHIP

Olaudah Equiano was born in Benin, in West Africa. When he was eleven years old, he was captured by slavers and taken to the African coast. There he was put aboard a slave ship bound for Virginia. Years later he told his life story in *The Interesting Narrative.* The book became a best seller. Here, in a passage from his *Narrative,* he tells about his life on the slave ship.

The first object I saw when I arrived on the coast was the sea and a slave ship. The ship was riding at anchor and waiting for its cargo. These filled me with astonishment, which soon changed to terror. When I was carried on board I was handled by some of the crew to see if I were healthy. I now believed that I had got into a world of bad spirits. They were going to kill me.

I was not long allowed my grief. I was soon put down under the decks. There I received such an odor in my nostrils as I had never experienced before. So that with the disgusting smell and the crying I became so sick and low that I was not able to eat. When I refused food, I was beaten.

In a little time, amongst the poor chained men, I found some of my own nation. I asked them what was to be done with us. They told me we were to be carried to these white people's country to work for them. I was a little relieved. I thought, if it were no worse than working, my situation was not so desperate. But still I feared I should be put to death because the white people looked and acted in so savage a manner. I had never seen among any people such brutal cruelty. . . .

The smell of the hold was so foul that it was dangerous to remain there for any time. The closeness of the place and the heat almost suffocated us. The ship was so crowded that we scarcely had room to turn. . . .

The groans of the dying made the whole a scene of horror almost not to be imagined. Because I was so young I was not put in chains. . . .

One day two of my countrymen, preferring death to such a life of misery, jumped into the sea. Immediately another followed their example. I believe many more would have done the same if they had not been prevented by the ship's crew.

The crew went after the escapees in a boat. Two of them were drowned. But they got the other and flogged him without mercy for preferring death to slavery. In this manner we continued to undergo more hardships than I can now relate.

From *Eyewitness: The Negro in American History* by William Loren Katz. Copyright © 1974 by David S. Lake Publishers, Belmont, CA.

1. What did Olaudah Equiano fear most when he was put on the slave ship? What does he mean by the following sentence? "I thought if it were no worse than working, my situation was not so desperate."

2. What happened to the three slaves who tried to escape?

3. What details does Equiano give to show the horror of life on the ship?

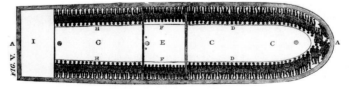

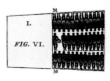
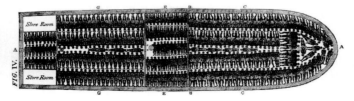

"Description of a Slave Ship" was published in 1789, the same year as Equiano's autobiography. It shows how carefully slavers calculated the number of captives they could pack into a ship.

CHAPTER 9

THE FEDERALISTS LAUNCH THE REPUBLIC

THE LIFE OF A *LLAVERA*

In the early 1800s, women saw to the day-to-day running of Spanish missions in the Southwest. These women were called *llaveras* (yah-VEH-rahs). *Llavera* means "keeper of the keys." Eulalia Perez worked as a keeper of the keys. Here she tells about her life at the San Gabriel Mission in California.

The priests brought me the mission keys. This was in 1821, if I remember rightly. My daughter Maria Rosario was seven years old. I was at that time the *llavera.*

The *llavera* had many duties. In the first place she passed out daily rations. She saw to the supplies for the Indian people and for the priests' kitchen. She held the key to the clothes storeroom. This contained the cotton goods for clothing for women and for children. She also saw to the cutting of clothes for men. . . .

Everything concerned with the making of clothes was done under my direction. I would cut and fit while my five daughters sewed the pieces. In addition, I took care of the huge laundry and the wine presses. I myself worked the crushing ma-

chines which pressed the oil from olives. I gave out all the items for the making of saddles. Also I managed supplies for the belt and shoe-making shop.

Every eight days, I delivered rations for the troops and the servants of the upper classes. These rations included beans, maize, garbanzos [chick peas], candles, and soap. To help me, I had been given an Indian servant, Lucio.

In the San Gabriel Mission there were many Indians who had accepted the Catholic religion. The married ones lived on their ranches while their children were young. There were two divisions for unmarried persons. One, for the women, was called the nunnery. The other was for the men.

Little girls of seven, eight, and nine years were brought to the nunnery. They were raised there until they left to marry. They were cared for by an Indian nun. Every evening they were locked in.

In the morning the girls were taken out. First they went to the Mass with Father Zalvidea, for he spoke Indian. Afterwards they went to the kitchen to have breakfast.

After breakfast, each girl went to a task. Her job might be at the loom, or in the sewing room, or unloading—whatever needed to be done. All work stopped at eleven. Everyone came to the dining room to eat at twelve. At one they returned to their jobs. The workday ended at sundown. Everyone returned to the dining room for supper.

It was I, with my daughters, who made the chocolate, the oil, the candy, the lemonade. I made

San Gabriel mission was built in 1771. This photograph was taken in the late 1800s or early 1900s.

so much lemonade that some of it was even bottled and sent to Spain.

Adapted from Eulalia Perez, "Keeper of the Keys." From "Una vieja y sus recuerdos dictados" by Eulalia Perez, translated by Erlinda Gonzales-Berry. Original in the Bancroft Library, University of California, Berkeley.

1. What were Eulalia Perez's duties as a *llavera*?

2. Many young Indian girls came to the mission to live. How did they spend a typical day there?

THE LOG CABIN

F. A. Michaux (mee-SHŌ) was a French botanist who traveled in the United States in the 1780s and 1790s. His book *Travels to the West of the Allegheny* tells what he saw. Here he describes the pioneer's typical home, the log cabin.

In the United States they give often the name of town to a group of seven or eight houses. The way of building them is not the same everywhere. At Philadelphia the houses are built with brick. In the other towns and country places that surround them, most are built with wood.

In places west of the Allegheny Mountains, one third of the inhabitants live in log houses. These dwellings are made with the trunks of trees. The logs are from twenty to thirty feet in length, about five inches in diameter. The trunks are placed upon one another and kept up by notches cut at their ends.

The roof is formed with pieces of similar length but not quite so thick. They are gradually sloped on each side. Two doors are made by sawing away a part of the trunks that form the body of the home. Often there are no windows.

The chimney is likewise made with the trunks of trees. The back of the chimney is made of clay, about six inches thick, which separates the fire from the wooden walls. . . .

The space between these trunks of trees is filled up with clay but very carelessly. As a result, these huts are very cold in winter, despite the amazing quantity of wood that is burned.

Four or five days are enough for two men to finish one of these houses. Not a nail is used. The floor is raised one or two feet above the surface of the ground and boarded. They generally make use of feather beds or feathers alone and not mattresses. The clothes belonging to the family are hung up round the room or suspended on a long pole.

Adapted from Paul M. Angle, *The American Reader: From Columbus to Today* (New York: Rand McNally & Company, 1958), pp. 156–157.

1. According to Michaux, how are the sides of the cabins built? The roof?

2. Why are the cabins very cold in winter?

3. Why is clay used for the inside of the chimney?

4. What material is used for the beds?

THE WHISKEY REBELLION

In 1794 farmers in southwestern Pennsylvania refused to pay a tax on whiskey. The tax was Alexander Hamilton's idea. As Secretary of the Treasury, he had urged Congress to impose it.

When the farmers acted against the government, President Washington called out 13,000 troops to put down the "Whiskey Rebellion." Using a pen name, Hamilton wrote the following newspaper article criticizing the farmers.

Let us then see what is this question. It is plainly this: Shall the majority govern or be governed? Shall the nation rule or be ruled? Shall the general will prevail, or the will of a faction? Shall there be government or no government? It is impossible to deny that this is the true and the whole question. No false argument can cover it up.

The Constitution contains this clause: "The government shall have power to lay and collect taxes and excises [taxes on goods]." You have, then, decided that your representatives in Congress shall have the power to lay excises. You have done nothing since to change that decision.

Your representatives in Congress have laid an excise. At three succeeding sessions they have revised that act. It has gone into general operation. And *you* have actually paid more than a million dollars on account of it.

But the four western counties of Pennsylvania try to change your decision. You have said, "The

Congress shall have power to lay excises." They say, "The Congress shall not have this power." Your representatives have said, "An excise on distilled spirits shall be collected." They say, "It shall not be collected. We will punish the officers who shall attempt the collection. The control of government shall not reside with you but with us."

Adapted from Thomas A. Bailey, ed., *The American Spirit: United States History As Seen by Contemporaries* (Boston: D. C. Heath and Company, 1963), pp. 152–153. Reprinted by permission of the publisher.

1. What, according to Hamilton, is the important question about the Whiskey Rebellion?

2. How does Hamilton try to show that the rebellion is a serious challenge to the government? Point out sentences suggesting that these farmers want to overthrow the government.

THE LIFE OF A YOUNG SOUTHERN WOMAN

Lucinda Lee was a member of one of Virginia's best-known families. The diary she kept provides a record of how some wealthy Virginians lived. In the diary she tells of a visit to close relatives.

September 19, 1782. Today we dine at old Mrs. Gordon's. I flatter myself I shall spend this day agreeably. This evening Colonel Ball insisted on our drinking tea with him. We did, and I was much pleased with my visit. . . .

I don't think I ever met with kinder, better people in my life. They do everything in their power to make you happy. I have almost made up my mind not to go to the horse races this fall. Everyone appears to be astonished at me, but I am sure there is no solid happiness to be found in such amusements.

I have no notion of sacrificing my own happiness to the opinion of the world in these matters. They say that other girls will be enjoying races and balls. I will not go unless I feel like it. I would not have you think from this that I pay no regard to the opinion of the world. Far from it. Next to that of a good conscience, the opinion of the world is to be regarded. Always pay due regard to that.

September 22. We had a very pleasant walk. The gentlemen dined today at Mr. Masenbird's. Mrs. Gordon and sister are come. They have proposed cards, and I am called to join them.

October 3. Cousin Nancy and myself have just returned from taking an outing in the carriage. We went to Stratford [a nearby estate]. We walked in the garden, sat about two hours under a beautiful shade tree, and ate as many figs as we could. . . .

October 5. Mr. Pinkard and Mr. Lee came here today from the Fredericksburg races. How sorry I was to hear Republican [a horse] was beaten. I was really interested in that race. It is a delightful evening. Nancy and myself are going to take a ride out in the carriage. Nancy calls me.

Adapted from Albert Bushnell Hart, ed., *American History told by Contemporaries,* Vol. III, *National Expansion 1783–1845* (New York: Macmillan Company, 1928), pp. 27–29.

1. How does Lucinda Lee pass the time during her visit? What do you learn from the diary about Virginia social life?

2. In the diary entry for September 19, Lucinda Lee writes that she does not intend to go to the races. Judging by the entry for October 5, do you think she keeps this resolution? Why or why not?

Wealthy young southern women were expected to learn to play musical instruments and to draw. Thomas Sully painted one woman playing her harp.

The Reverend Absalom Jones of Philadelphia, painted by Raphaelle Peale, preached a famous sermon January 1, 1808. He called for a day of thanksgiving for the end of the slave trade to America.

MARGARET BAYARD SMITH AT JEFFERSON'S INAUGURATION

Margaret Bayard Smith wrote many letters that are a valuable record of Washington life in the early 1800s. She was a keen observer of events.

Her husband, Samuel Harrison Smith, was one of Thomas Jefferson's strongest supporters. He published Washington's leading newspaper. In the paper, Samuel Smith spoke out for the ideals of the new Republican party.

Margaret Smith knew most of the important people in Washington in her day. Here she describes Jefferson's inauguration in a letter to her sister Susan.

March 4, 1808

Let me write to you, my dear Susan, before my glow of enthusiasm has fled. Let me congratulate you and all my fellow citizens on an event that will be so good for their political welfare.

I have this morning witnessed one of the most interesting scenes a free people can ever witness. In every age and government, the changes of administration generally have been times of confusion, villainy, and bloodshed. But in this, our happy country, they take place without any kind of disorder.

This day, one of the most worthy of men has taken that seat to which he was called by the voice of his country. I cannot describe the concern I felt when I looked around at the crowd. But I listened to a speech containing the best of sentiments spoken in the most elegant language. Its manner was as mild as it was firm.

If doubts of Mr. Jefferson's honesty and talents ever existed in anyone's mind, this speech must forever erase them.

The Senate chamber was so crowded that I believe not another creature could enter. On one side of the house the Senate sat. The other was given up by the Representatives to the ladies. Every inch of ground was occupied. Several people have estimated that there were near a thousand persons within the walls. The speech was delivered in so low a tone that few heard it.

Mr. Jefferson had given your brother [Samuel Smith] a copy early in the morning. As soon as we came out of the house, the newspaper was handed out. Since then there has been a constant stream of persons coming for the papers.

I have been stopped several times in this letter by the gentlemen of Congress. They have been to bid us their goodbyes. Since three o'clock, they have come in a steady stream. Mr. Claiborn, a most agreeable man, called the moment before he left. There is no one whose society I shall more regret the loss of. Gouverneur Morris, Mr. Dayton, and Bayard drank tea here. They have just gone after sitting nearly two hours.

Adapted from Margaret Bayard Smith, *Forty Years of Washington Society* (New York: Charles Scribner's Sons, 1906), pp. 25–26.

1. Margaret Bayard Smith writes about "changes of administration," or changes of governments. How does she contrast other such changes with the present inauguration of Jefferson?

2. What details does she give to show how crowded the Senate chamber was?

CHAPTER 10

THE REPUBLICANS IN CHARGE

WITH LEWIS AND CLARK

In 1804 President Thomas Jefferson appointed Meriwether Lewis and William Clark to lead an expedition. They were to explore the rivers of the West and find a route to the Pacific.

Lewis and Clark set out from the mouth of the Wood River, near St. Louis, and traveled west on the Missouri River. They spent the winter in what is now South Dakota. In the spring of 1805, they began their voyage again.

Here Meriwether Lewis tells about six men on the expedition who had a narrow escape.

Tuesday, May 14, 1805

Some fog on the river this morning. Saw huge herds of buffalo today, also elk, deer, wolves, and antelopes. Passed three large creeks, none of which had any running water. Captain Clark killed a very fine buffalo cow.

I felt like eating some veal. I walked on shore and killed a very fine buffalo calf and a large wolf, much the whitest I had seen. It was quite as white

A book telling of Lewis and Clark's expedition made Americans aware of the vast new lands gained by the Louisiana Purchase.

as the wool of the common sheep. One of the party wounded a brown bear very badly. Being alone, he did not think it proper to pursue him.

In the evening, the men in two of the rear canoes discovered a large brown bear. He was lying on the open ground. Six of them went out to attack him. They were all good hunters. They got within forty paces of him without being seen.

Two of them saved their fire as had been planned. The four others fired nearly at the same time and each put his bullet through him. Two of the balls passed through his lungs.

In an instant, this monster ran at them with open mouth. The two who had saved their fires now fired. Both of them struck him, one only slightly. The other fortunately broke his shoulder, but this only slowed his motion for a moment.

The men, unable to reload their guns, took to flight. The bear pursued and had very nearly overtaken them before they reached the river. Two of the party went to a canoe. The others separated and hid among the willows.

They reloaded their pieces. Each fired at him as they had an opportunity. They struck him several times, but the guns served only to direct the bear to them. In this manner, he pursued two of them separately. He was so close that they had to throw away their guns and dive into the river.

So enraged was this animal that he plunged into the river only a few feet behind the second man. One of those who still remained on shore shot him through the head and finally killed him.

They then took him on shore and butchered him. They found that eight balls had passed through him in different directions. The bear being old, the flesh was not very good. They therefore took only the skin and fleece. The latter made us several gallons of oil.

Adapted from Paul M. Angle, *The American Reader: From Columbus to Today* (Boston: Rand McNally & Company, 1958), pp. 161–162.

1. What plan did the six men make to fire at the bear? What was the result?

2. What did the fleeing men do? How was the bear finally stopped?

3. What use was made of the dead bear?

THE BRITISH INVADE WASHINGTON

When the British invaded Washington, D.C., in 1814, Dolley Madison was forced to flee the White House. Here, on August 24, 1814, she writes to her sister about this time of crisis. During the day, she added to the letter several times.

Dolley Madison did manage to escape safely to Virginia. Two days later, President James Madison, her husband, joined her.

Wednesday morning, twelve o'clock

Dear sister,

Since sunrise, I have been turning my spyglass [small telescope] in every direction. I have been hoping to discover the approach of my dear husband and his friends. I can make out only groups of military wandering in all directions. . . .

Three o'clock. Will you believe it, my sister? We have had a battle, or skirmish, near Bladensburg. I am still here within sound of the cannon! Two messengers, covered with dust, come to bid me flee. But I wait for him. . . .

At this late hour a wagon has been obtained. I have had it filled with the dishes of silver and gold and the most valuable articles in the house that can be easily carried. Whether the wagon will reach its destination or fall into the hands of British soldiers, events must determine.

Our kind friend, Mr. Carroll, has come to hurry my departure. He is in a very bad humor with me. I insist on waiting until the large picture of George Washington is safe. It must be unscrewed from the wall. This process took too long for these perilous moments. I have ordered the frame to be broken and the canvas taken out. It is done.

And now, my dear sister, I must leave this house. The retreating army will soon fill up the road I must take. When I shall again write to you or where I shall be tomorrow, I cannot tell!

Adapted and abridged from the Dolley Madison Papers, the Library of Congress.

1. Why does Dolley Madison put off making her escape from the White House?

2. What does she take with her? What does she have done at almost the last moment?

August 24, there was a severe action at Bladensbur[g] as acquired immortal honor by the brave resistance the bold volunteers." The same day " in solid col [th]e CITY OF WASHINGTON. Their number supp[osed] [i]s 3 or 4,000. The British destroyed considerable pr[ivate] public property, at the City—Navy-Yard, Georgetow[n]

Nathaniel Coverly, Jr., of Boston, printed this picture of the British army burning the city of Washington, D.C., in 1814.

MARGARET BAYARD SMITH: "THE POOR CAPITOL!"

Margaret Bayard Smith (see page 467) fled Washington when the British invaded and burned it in 1814. Here, in a letter, she tells what she found when she returned.

We found our house just as we had left it. There was no trace of the enemy. . . .

The poor capitol! Nothing but its blackened walls remained. Four or five houses in the neighborhood were also in ruins.

We afterwards looked at the other public buildings. None were so thoroughly destroyed as the House of Representatives and the President's House [White House]. Those beautiful pillars in that Representatives Hall were cracked and broken. The roof, that noble dome, lay in ashes.

In the President's House, not an inch but its cracked and blackened walls remained. That scene, when I last visited it, was so splendid! It was crowded with the great, the ambitious, and patriotic heroes. Now it was nothing but ashes.

Was it these ashes, now crushed underfoot, which once had the power to inflate pride? Alas, yes, and this is human grandeur! How fragile! Who would have thought that this mass, so magnificent, should in the space of a few hours be thus destroyed? Oh, vanity of human hopes!

Adapted from Margaret Bayard Smith, *Forty Years of Washington Society* (New York: Charles Scribners Sons, 1906), pp. 109–110.

1. Which two buildings does Margaret Bayard Smith find have been damaged most by the British? What damages does she report?

2. What does she mean when she writes, "Oh, vanity of human hopes"?

JEFFERSON'S EPITAPH

Thomas Jefferson achieved many great things. But at his direction, only three of his achievements are recorded on his gravestone. Here he tells what he wanted there.

Jefferson mentions an obelisk (AHB-uh-lisk). An obelisk is a four-sided pillar of stone. The top of the pillar is shaped like a pyramid.

The following epitaph would be the most pleasing to my spirit.

On the grave a plain die, or cube, of three feet. It should be surmounted by an obelisk of six feet height. Each should be made of a single stone. On the faces of the obelisk should be the following inscription and not a word more:

Here was buried
Thomas Jefferson
author of the Declaration of American
Independence
of the Statute of Virginia for religious freedom
and father of the University of Virginia.

By these, as testimonials that I have lived, I wish to be most remembered.

Adapted from Thomas A. Bailey, *The American Spirit: United States History As Seen by Contemporaries* (Boston: D. C. Heath and Company, 1963), p. 192. Reprinted by permission of the publisher.

1. What three achievements were most important to Jefferson?

2. About what other achievements do you know? Why do you think he wanted these three to be remembered more than the others?

Caleb Boyle painted Thomas Jefferson in front of the Natural Bridge, which Jefferson described as "the most sublime of nature's works." The rock formation is on part of the property Jefferson bought in 1773.

UNIT 4   1820–1850

LOOKING WEST

CHAPTER 11

INVENTIONS AND IMPROVEMENTS

LIFE ON A GEORGIA PLANTATION

Rebecca Latimer Felton grew up to be the first woman to serve as a United States Senator. Here she tells what it was like to live on a Georgia plantation before the Civil War.

In 1832, *The Penny Magazine* explained how to grow and process cotton, the base of the South's economy. The picture unrealistically shows a cotton boll bursting open and a flower blooming at the same time.

It was my Georgia grandmother, Mrs. Lucy Talbot Swift, around whom my early memories cluster. I was often at her home. I was a close observer of her housekeeping methods and of her great hospitality. She was the mother of eleven children. Her industry, her management, and her executive ability in carrying on her household affairs are still wonderful memories.

Grandfather had a plantation, a grain mill, and a sawmill, which kept him busy with his own duties. It was grandmother's skill as a homemaker that impressed me most in that early time of my life. Then, I trotted around after her as she went from the dwelling to the garden and to the milk dairy, to the poultry house, to the loom house, to the big meat house, and to the flour house. . . .

She had fowls of all domestic kinds to look after, and there were fattening pigs in the pen also. She had geese to raise feathers for the family beds. Quilt making was never stopped, winter or summer. Quilts made by hand were the bedcoverings in well-to-do Georgia homes. My own mother made and quilted fifty quilts in the first ten years of her married life. . . .

When my grandmother, Lucy Swift, began housekeeping, wool and flax were depended on for clothing. The use of cotton was difficult. Before there were any cotton gins, the cotton lint was picked from the seed by human fingers. The lint was then carded by hand, spun on homemade wheels, then reeled into what were called "hanks" by use of homemade reels. Then the warp was prepared for the homemade loom by a variety of processes, all slow.

In this way all the clothing of the masses was made. Well-to-do men generally managed to get a broadcloth coat, maybe once in a lifetime. The rest had coats of plain jeans. Silk dresses were scarce. Women wore them only for weddings and special occasions.

The shoe problem was huge. The hides were generally tanned, stretched out, dressed, and dried at home. The traveling shoemaker made periodic visits. One pair of shoes per year was considered generous for grown-ups. The children as a rule all went barefooted summer and winter.

I recall the first time the family shoemaker measured my feet for a pair of shoes. He brought along a piece of white pine board. I stood flat-footed on the board, while he marked a line in front of my toes with his big coarse horn-handled knife. Then he marked another line behind my heel. I felt quite a somebody when the new shoes came home. . . .

My grandmother made all the starch she used, sometimes from whole wheat, oftener from wheat bran. Her seven girls, big and little, delighted in dainty white muslin frocks. . . .

Laundry work for thirteen in family was always going on. She was a rare soapmaker, and every pound was prepared at home with care. The meat scraps and bones were used and cooked with lye, drained in ash hoppers. It made perfect soap for domestic uses. For wounds and baby usage there could be bought Castile soap. Except salt, iron, sugar, and coffee, everything was raised by those early Georgia planters necessary for human comfort and sustenance.

Adapted from *Country Life in Georgia in the Days of my Youth,* by Rebecca Latimer Felton (Atlanta, Georgia, 1919).

1. Rebecca Latimer Felton writes that on a Georgia plantation, nearly everything "necessary for human comfort and sustenance" was raised or made there. What food was raised? What things were made?

2. Felton admires her grandmother's "industry, her management, and her executive ability." What details show her grandmother's abilities?

A MILL WOMAN'S THOUGHTS

The women mill workers of Lowell, Massachusetts, were encouraged to submit stories and essays to the *Lowell Offering,* a magazine. Here, from the *Offering,* is Elizabeth E. Turner's essay, a "Factory Girl's Reverie." (A reverie is a daydream.)

This colored engraving of a "mill girl" was printed in 1841.

Evening is the time for thought and reflection. All is lovely outside, and why am I not happy? I cannot be, for a feeling of sadness comes stealing over me. I am far, far from that loved spot, where I spent the evenings of childhood's years. I am here, among strangers—a factory girl—yes, *factory girl;* a name that is thought so degrading by many. . . .

But here I am. I toil day after day in the noisy mill. When the bell calls I must go. Must I always stay here, and spend my days within these walls, with this constant noise my only music?

I am sometimes asked, "When are you going home?" *Home,* that name ever dear to me. But they would not often ask me, if they only knew what sadness it creates to say, "*I have no home.*" . . .

I will once more visit the home of my childhood. I will cast one long lingering look at the grave of my parents and brothers, and bid farewell to the spot. I have many friends who would not see me in want. I have uncles, aunts, and cousins, who have kindly urged me to share their homes. But I have a little pride yet. I will not be dependent upon friends while I have health and ability to earn bread for myself.

I will no more allow this sadness. I will wear a cheerful face, and make myself happy by contentment. I will earn all I can, and lay by something against a stormy day. I will do all the good I can, and make those around me happy as far as lies in my power. I see many whose brows are marked with sorrow and gloom. With them I will sympathize, and dispel their gloom if I can.

I will spend my leisure hours in reading good books, and trying to acquire what useful knowledge I can. I will ever strive to be contented, and not make myself unhappy by complaining. I will try to live in reference to judgment day, and ever hope to meet my parents in a land of bliss.

Adapted and abridged from Benita Eisler, ed., *The Lowell Offering: Writings by New England Mill Women (1840–1845)* (New York: Harper & Row, Publishers, Inc., 1977), pp. 136–137.

1. What does Elizabeth Turner mean when she says, "*I have no home*"?

2. What about her life in the mill makes her sad?

3. Despite her sadness, what does she resolve to do?

AMERICAN TRADERS VISIT THE CALIFORNIOS

In 1840 an American trading ship sailed along the California coast. The Americans visited Prudencia Higuera's (ee-GEH-rah) family. Many years later, she told of the visit.

In the autumn of 1840 my father lived near what is now called Pinole Point, in Contra Costa County, California. I was then about twelve years old. I remember the time because it was then that we saw the first American vessel that traded along the shores of San Pablo Bay. One afternoon a horseman came to our ranch. He told my father that a great ship was about to sail from Yerba Buena to buy hides and tallow.

The next morning my father gave orders. My brothers, with the workers, went on horseback into the mountains and smaller valleys to round up all the best cattle. They drove them to the beach, killed them there, and salted the hides. They melted out the tallow in iron kettles.

As we did not have any barrels, we followed the common plan in those days. We cast the tallow in round pits. Before the melted tallow was poured into the pit, an oaken staff was thrust down in the center. By the two ends of it the heavy cake could be carried more easily. By working very hard, we had a large number of hides and many pounds of tallow ready on the beach when the ship appeared.

The captain soon came to our landing with a small boat and two sailors. One of them was a Frenchman who knew Spanish very well. He acted as interpreter. The captain looked over the hides, and then asked my father to get into the boat and go to the vessel. Mother was much afraid to let him go. We feared they would carry my father off and keep him a prisoner. . . .

The captain told her: "If you are afraid, I will have the sailors take him to the vessel. I will stay here until he comes back. He ought to see all the goods I have, or he will not know what to buy." After a bit my mother let him go with the captain.

He came back the next day, bringing four boatloads of cloth, axes, shoes, fish-lines, and many new things. There were two grindstones, and some cheap jewelry. My brother had traded some deerskins for a gun and four toothbrushes, the first ones I had ever seen.

A lithograph made in 1839 showed Californios roping cattle near San Francisco. This engraving was made from it a few years later.

After the captain had carried all the hides and tallow to his ship he came back, very much pleased with his bargain. He gave my father, as a present, a little keg of what he called Boston rum. We put it away for sick people.

After the ship sailed, my mother and sisters began to cut out new dresses, which the Indian women sewed. On one of mine mother put some big brass buttons about an inch across, with eagles on them. How proud I was! I used to rub them hard every day to make them shine, using the toothbrush and eggshell powder.

Adapted from John and Laree Caughey, *California Heritage: An Anthology of History and Literature* (Los Angeles: Ward Ritchie Press, 1962), pp. 126–128.

1. How does the family first learn the ship is coming? What does its captain seek?

2. Tallow is an animal fat used in candles and soap. How do the Higueras make tallow? What do they receive for their hides and tallow?

3. Why does the captain invite Prudencia Higuera's father on board ship? Why is the family afraid for him? What does this incident show about the Californios' opinion of Americans?

ELLEN BIGELOW SAILS ON THE *ILLINOIS*

In the 1830s many people traveling west preferred to make the trip on a Great Lakes ship rather than go overland. In 1835 Ellen Bigelow, who was nineteen years old, traveled from Massachusetts to join her parents in Peoria, Illinois. Part of her trip was made on the *Illinois,* a ship sailing from Buffalo to Chicago. Here, in a letter to her aunt, she tells of the voyage.

The *Illinois* is the largest ship on the lake. It was packed with as much freight as it could carry. The deck was crowded with bags, boxes, and barrels of every description. No rest could be found even for the sole of a foot. The cabin, if possible, was more unpleasant still. Persons applied for passage until the cabins were completely filled. . . .

We stayed on deck until it began to storm violently. Then we retreated to our berths. Dr. H. had as much as he could do to go from one patient to another, giving out medicines for seasickness. Towards night, the wind lulled a little. We were all hoping for rest.

Travel by coach in the 1830s was rough, even on private roads like the Maysville Turnpike. Most people still preferred to travel by water.

Then about 10 o'clock, to our great horror, the ship struck a rock. There was great alarm. But the waves were running high and soon took us off. We all went back to our beds and, except for myself, were soon soundly sleeping. A fit of foreboding [fear of something bad about to happen] would not let me close my eyes.

My fears were soon realized. About 12 o'clock all were awakened by a loud shout from the cook. We were going to the bottom. Sure enough, there was little doubt of it. In fact, we were convinced that we were already there. The ship had grounded on a rocky shoal. Every wave made her quiver and shake. We remained there about an hour. An hour of greater fright I never passed.

We sat in fear and trembling till the deck load was thrown overboard. Then the cheerful voice of an old Irish sailor told us that the ship was off. If it had been an old one, it must have received much injury from the strain. But being entirely new, its damage was only a splintering of the keel beneath her bows. . . .

We reached Detroit Monday. It is bigger than I expected. We were forced to anchor twenty miles from Detroit. The only channel through which the ship could pass was so narrow it had to be pointed out by stakes. As its location varies, the stakes have to be moved often. This duty, it seems, had been neglected. By following the channel of a former season, we were soon brought hard aground. . . .

Much labor was required to heave the vessel off. It was at last accomplished. . . .

We went speedily through the Straits of Mackinaw and down Lake Michigan. We anchored at Chicago Friday forenoon. It was just fourteen days from the time we left Buffalo. Considering the various perils we encountered, it may be set down as a very good trip.

Adapted from Paul Angle, *The American Reader: From Columbus to Today* (New York: Rand McNally & Company, 1958), pp. 196–199.

1. Ellen Bigelow writes of the perils the ship encountered. Tell about two of them.

2. What, other than these perils, made the trip uncomfortable? Do you think traveling is as uncomfortable today as it was then?

Folk artist Mary Keys painted ''Lockport on Erie Canal'' in 1832. She drew its five double locks as a geometric pattern rising up the steep hill that made the locks necessary. The bridge at the top is painted much larger than it really is.

A SONG OF THE ERIE CANAL

This song, about a barge worker, gives an idea of what life along the Erie Canal in the 1800s was like. The song is popular even today.

1. I've got a mule, her name is Sal,
   Fifteen miles on the Erie Canal.
   She's a good old worker and a good old pal,
   Fifteen miles on the Erie Canal.
   We've haul'd some barges in our day,
   Fill'd with lumber, coal and hay.
   And we know ev'ry inch of the way
   From Albany to Buffalo.
   Refrain:
   　Low bridge, ev'rybody down!
   　Low bridge, for we're going through a town.
   　And you'll always know your neighbor,
   　You'll always know your pal,
   　If you ever navigated on the Erie Canal.
2. We better get along on our way, old gal
   Fifteen miles on the Erie Canal.
   Cause you bet your life I'd never part with Sal,
   Fifteen miles on the Erie Canal.

Git up there, mule, here comes a lock,
We'll make Rome [New York] 'bout six o'clock.
One more trip and back we'll go
Right back home to Buffalo.
Refrain:
　Low bridge, ev'rybody down!
　Low bridge, for we're going through a town.
　And you'll always know your neighbor,
　You'll always know your pal,
　If you ever navigated on the Erie Canal.

From "Low Bridge, Everybody Down" or "Fifteen Years on the Erie Canal."

1. According to the song, at what cities along the canal did the barges stop?

2. The song calls Sal "a good old worker and a good old pal." Sal, the mule, did not ride in the barge. She walked along the bank. What job did Sal do?

3. The refrain's first line is "Low bridge, ev'rybody down!" Explain.

CHAPTER 12

EXPANDING DEMOCRACY

MARGARET BAYARD SMITH: ANDREW JACKSON'S INAUGURATION

Margaret Bayard Smith was a leading Washington hostess. In her book, *Forty Years of Washington Society,* she wrote about Andrew Jackson's inauguration. Here is part of her report.

Someone came and informed us the crowd before the President's house was so far lessened that they thought we might enter. But what a scene did we witness! The majesty of the people had disappeared into a mob of boys, women, children, scrambling, fighting, romping. What a pity! . . .

We came too late. The President had retreated. He had been nearly pressed to death and almost torn to pieces by the people in their eagerness to shake hands with Old Hickory. Cut glass and china to the amount of several thousand dollars had been broken. Ladies fainted. Men were seen with bloody noses. Such a scene of confusion took place as is impossible to describe. Those who got in could not get out by the door but had to scramble out of windows.

At one time the President could only be made safe by a number of gentlemen making a kind of barrier of their own bodies. Colonel Bomford said that at one time he was afraid they should have been pushed down on the President. . . .

Ladies and gentlemen only had been expected at this reception, not the people in a mass. But it was the people's day, and the people's President, and the people would rule.

Adapted from Margaret Bayard Smith, *The First Forty Years of Washington Society* (New York, 1906).

1. Margaret Bayard Smith also wrote about Thomas Jefferson's inauguration. Review her letter on page 467. Then point out an important difference between Jefferson's and Jackson's inauguration ceremonies.

2. In what way did Jackson's inauguration show that a new era in American government was beginning? (In answering, think about Smith's statement about "the people's day.")

HARRIET MARTINEAU IN WASHINGTON

Harriet Martineau (MAR-tih-nō) was a wealthy young Englishwoman who traveled through America in the 1830s. When she returned to England, she wrote two books about her travels. Here, this rather snobbish woman writes about her stay in Washington, D.C.

We arrived at Washington on the 13th of January, 1835. . . .

It is in Washington that varieties of manners are easy to see. There the southerners appear to the most advantage and the New Englanders to the least. The ease and frank courtesy of the South contrasts favorably with the cautious and too respectful air of the North.

The odd mortals that wander in from the western border cannot be described as a class. Nobody is like anybody else. One has a neck like a crane, making a space of several inches between tie and chin. Another wears no tie, apparently because there is no room for one. A third has lank black hair parted accurately down the middle and arranged in bands in front. . . .

Our pleasantest evenings were spent at home. Ladies would spend an hour with us on their way from a dinner or to a ball. Members of Congress would rest themselves by our fireside. Mr. [Henry] Clay, sitting upright on the sofa, would speak for many an hour in his even, soft tone. He amazed us with his moderate speech, for he has a quick temper. Mr. [Daniel] Webster, leaning back at his ease, telling stories, cracking jokes, or smoothly speaking, would brighten an evening now and then.

Mr. [John C.] Calhoun would come in sometimes. He meets men and scolds them by the fireside as in the Senate. He is made like a piece of machinery. He either passes by what you say or twists it to be suitable with what is in his head and begins to lecture again.

Thus, he is more complained of than blamed by his enemies. His moments of softness in his family are hailed as a relief equally to himself and others. Those moments are as touching as tears on the face of an old soldier.

Adapted from Clement Eaton, ed., *The Leaven of Democracy: The Growth of the Democratic Spirit in the Time of Jackson* (New York: George Braziller, 1963), pp. 77–79.

1. What does Harriet Martineau think of the southerners she sees in Washington? The New Englanders? The westerners? Why might this wealthy woman from England look down on some of the Americans?

2. What does Martineau think of Henry Clay? Daniel Webster?

3. Martineau compares John C. Calhoun to "a piece of machinery." What does the comparison imply about his style of conversation? When, according to Martineau, does he drop this manner of talking?

FREDERICK DOUGLASS LEARNS ABOUT ABOLITION

Frederick Douglass spent miserable years as a slave before managing to escape. He became a leading figure in the movement to end slavery. After the Civil War, he was a symbol of what a person who had been born a slave could achieve. Here he writes about his time as a slave and how he first heard about abolition and abolitionists.

I found myself regretting my own existence. I wished myself dead. While in this state of mind, I was eager to hear any one speak of slavery. I was a ready listener.

Every little while, I could hear something about the abolitionists. It was some time before I found what the word meant. It was always used in such connections as to make it an interesting word to me. If a slave ran away, or did anything very wrong in the mind of a slaveholder, it was spoken of as the fruit of *abolition.* I set about learning what it meant. The dictionary gave me little or no help. I found it was "the act of abolishing." But I did not know what was to be abolished.

I did not dare to ask anyone about the word's meaning. I believed they did not want me to know.

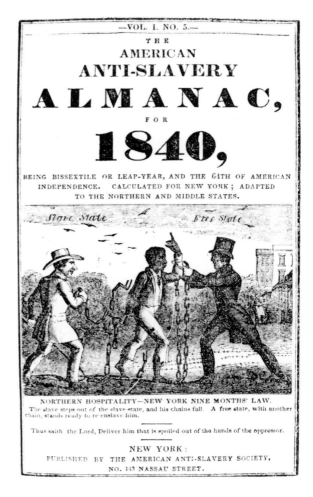

Abolitionist feelings ran high in the years between 1830 and 1860. The American Anti-Slavery Society published a yearly almanac that called for freeing the slaves in the South and criticized northerners for allowing slavery to continue.

After a patient waiting, I got one of our city papers. It contained an account of a number of petitions from the North. They asked for the abolition of slavery in the District of Columbia and of the slave trade between the states. From this time I understood the words *abolition* and *abolitionist.* I always drew near when that word was spoken, expecting to hear something important to me and fellow slaves.

I went one day down to the wharf. Seeing two Irishmen unload stones, I went unasked and helped them. One of them asked if I were a slave. I told him I was. He said to the other that it was a pity so fine a little fellow as myself should be a slave for life. They both advised me to run away to the North. I pretended not to be interested in what they said. Nevertheless, I remembered their advice. From that time I resolved to run away.

Adapted from Philip Butcher, ed., *The Minority Presence in American Literature, 1600–1900* Volume I (Washington, D.C.: Howard University Press, 1977), pp. 332–333.

1. How does Frederick Douglass learn the meanings of *abolition* and *abolitionist?*

2. What makes him resolve to run away?

American abolitionists wore medallions like this silk one, made in England about 1830, to show their antislavery sentiments.

FANNIE JACKSON COPPIN GOES TO COLLEGE

Fannie Jackson Coppin was born a slave. When she was a child, her aunt bought her freedom. Living in Massachusetts, she managed to get an elementary school education.

The African Methodist Episcopal Church helped her go to college in 1860, and afterwards she taught school. Eventually she became the head of the Female Department of the Institute for Colored Youth in Philadelphia.

In 1913 Fannie Jackson Coppin wrote *Reminiscences of School Life.* Here, in a passage from her book, she tells of her education at Oberlin College in Ohio.

My aunt in Washington still helped me. I was able to pay my way to Oberlin. Oberlin was then the only college in the United States where colored students were permitted to study. The faculty did not forbid a woman to take the men's course. But they did not advise it. There was plenty of Latin and Greek in it. There was as much mathematics as one could shoulder.

It was the custom in Oberlin that forty students from the junior and senior classes should teach the preparatory classes. The faculty told me that they intended to give me a class. I was to understand that if the pupils rebelled against my teaching, the faculty did not intend to force it.

There was a little surprise on the faces of some when they came into class and saw the teacher. But fortunately for my own dear love of teaching, there were no signs of rebellion. The class went on increasing in numbers until it had to be divided. I was given both divisions. . . .

When I was within a year of graduation, an application came from a Quaker school in Philadelphia. They wanted a colored woman who could teach Greek, Latin, and higher mathematics. The answer they got was: "We have the woman. But you must wait a year for her."

Whenever I rose to recite in my classes at Oberlin, I felt that I had the honor of the whole African race on my shoulders. If I failed, it would be thought I failed because I was colored.

Fannie Jackson Coppin, *Reminiscences of School Life* (Philadelphia: African Methodist Episcopal Book Concern, 1913), pp. 12, 15.

1. What did Fannie Jackson Coppin fear when she was given a preparatory class to teach? Why might she have this fear? What happened?

2. How did Fannie Jackson Coppin feel about reciting while at Oberlin? What does this fact suggest about her sense of the importance of her going to college?

Activity: Students can research and make oral reports on the lives of Angelina and Sarah Grimké or Emily Dickinson.

ANGELINA GRIMKÉ ON WOMEN'S RIGHTS

Angelina and Sarah Grimké were born in Charleston, South Carolina. Growing up on a plantation, they saw how cruel slavery could be. When they moved north, they became abolitionists.

The Grimké sisters also fought for women's rights. Here Angelina Grimké writes to fellow abolitionists Theodore Weld and John Greenleaf Whittier. She points out how strange it is for abolitionists to wish to free the slaves and confine women at the same time.

Emily Dickinson is considered one of America's major poets. This daguerreotype was probably made in December 1847, when she was seventeen.

Can you not see that woman *could* do a hundred times more for the slave if she were not confined? We are told that we are out of our sphere even when we hand out petitions. We are out of our "appropriate sphere" when we speak to women only. We are out of it when we sing in churches. Silence is *our* province, submission *our* duty. . . .

If we are to do any good in the antislavery cause, our *right* to labor in it *must* be firmly established. *We* cannot push Abolitionism forward with all our might *until* we take up the stumbling block out of the road. How can we hold meetings much longer when people are taught to despise us for stepping out of the sphere of woman!

Adapted from Clement Eaton, ed., *The Leaven of Democracy: The Growth of the Democratic Spirit in the Time of Jackson* (New York: George Braziller, 1963), pp. 358–359.

1. Angelina Grimké writes of taking "the stumbling block out of the road." What does she mean by the "stumbling block"? What does it block?

2. Why is it inconsistent for abolitionists to wish to keep women in their "sphere"?

A FEMALE SEMINARY

Female seminaries were schools for young women of upper-class and middle-class families. In 1847 Emily Dickinson attended Mount Holyoke Female Seminary. (Later it became Mount Holyoke College.) Here, in a letter, she writes of her life there.

The school is very large. Perhaps you know that Miss Lyon is raising her standard of study a good deal. She makes the tests more difficult than usual.

I will tell you my order of time for the day. At 6 o'clock we all rise. We breakfast at 7. Our study hours begin at 8. At 9 we all meet in Seminary Hall for prayers. At 10:30 I recite a review of ancient history from our reading. At 11 I recite a lesson in Pope's "Essay on Man" [a long poem]. At 12 I practice calisthenics. At 12:15 I read until dinner, which is at 12:30.

After dinner, from 1:30 until 2 I sing in Seminary Hall. From 2:45 until 3:45 I go to Section, where we give in all our accounts for the day. This includes absence, tardiness, breaking silent study hours, receiving company in our rooms, and ten thousand other things. At 4:30 we go into Seminary Hall and receive advice from Miss Lyon.

We have supper at 6 and silent study hours from then until the retiring bell. This rings at 8:15. One thing is certain. Miss Lyon and all the teachers seem to consult our comfort and happiness in everything they do. You know that is pleasant.

Adapted from a letter by Emily Dickinson, dated November 6, 1847, to Abiah P. Root, in Mount Holyoke College Library.

1. At what time does Emily Dickinson study ancient history? At what time does she practice calisthenics? What happens at 4:30?

2. What is "Section"?

3. Do you think young women today would like to attend a seminary like the one Emily Dickinson describes? Explain.

CHAPTER 13

WESTWARD EXPANSION TO THE PACIFIC

THE ALAMO

The Alamo is an old Spanish mission in San Antonio, Texas. There, in 1836, a small band of Texans held out for 11 days against a much greater Mexican force. Finally, on March 6, the Alamo fell. Here, William Barret Travis, commander of the Alamo, appeals to Texans and "all Americans" for help.

An engraving made in 1859 shows the ruins of the Alamo. The cannons of the Mexican army pounded away at the old mission for 11 days in 1836. Inside, the Texans vowed never to surrender.

February 24, 1836

To the People in Texas and
All Americans in the World

Fellow Citizens and Compatriots:

I am besieged by a thousand or more of the Mexicans under Santa Anna. I have sustained a continual bombardment and cannonade for twenty-four hours and have not lost a man. The enemy have demanded a surrender. Otherwise the garrison is to be put to the sword if the fort is taken. I have answered the summons with a cannon shot. Our flag still waves proudly from our walls. *I shall never surrender or retreat.*

I call on you, in the name of Liberty, of Patriotism, and of everything dear to the American character, to come to our aid. The enemy are receiving reinforcements daily. I am determined to sustain myself as long as possible and die like a soldier who never forgets what is due to his own honor and that of his country. *Victory* or *death!*

W. Barret Travis
Lieutenant Colonel, Commanding

Adapted and abridged from Paul M. Angle, *The American Reader: From Columbus to Today* (Skokie, IL: Rand McNally & Company, 1958), pp. 235–236.

1. What does William Barret Travis know will happen if the Alamo does not surrender?

2. What keeps him from surrendering to Santa Anna's superior force?

SAM HOUSTON AT THE BATTLE OF SAN JACINTO

In 1836 the Texan army, led by General Sam Houston, crushed the Mexican army and gained independence for Texas. For weeks, Houston had retreated from the Mexicans, who were led by General Santa Anna. Then, when Santa Anna's troops were camped near the San Jacinto River, Houston attacked. Here, in a letter to Texas President David Burnet, Houston tells of the victory.

About nine o'clock on the morning of April 21, the enemy were reinforced by five hundred choice troops under the command of General Cós. This increased their force to upward of fifteen hundred men. Our force for the field numbered seven hundred and eighty-three.

At half past three o'clock in the evening, I ordered the officers of the Texan army to parade their respective commands. Meanwhile, I ordered the bridge on the road to the Brazos to be destroyed. This cut off all possibility of escape. Our troops paraded with spirit and were eager for the contest. The difference in numbers seemed only to increase their enthusiasm and confidence.

Our cavalry was sent to the front of the enemy's left to attract notice. The rest of our forces gathered in the trees. They advanced quickly through an open prairie, without any protection whatever for our men.

Colonel Sherman, with his regiment, began the action upon our left wing. The whole line, advancing in double-quick time, rang the war cry, "Remember the Alamo!" They received the enemy's fire and advanced within point-blank shot before our lines fired a single shot.

The conflict lasted about eighteen minutes from the time of close action until we were in possession of the enemy's camp. We took one piece of cannon (loaded), all their camp equipment, their food and supplies, and baggage.

Our cavalry pursued the fleeing enemy to the bridge. Captain Karnes, always the foremost in danger, commanded the pursuers. Many of the troops fought hand to hand. Not having any bayonets, our riflemen used their guns as war clubs.

The rout began at half past four. The pursuit by the main body continued until twilight. In the battle, our loss was two killed and twenty-three wounded, six of them mortally. The enemy's loss was six hundred and thirty killed; wounded, two hundred and eight; prisoners, seven hundred and thirty.

Adapted from "Official Report of General Sam Houston," in *History of Texas,* by Henderson Youkum (New York, 1856).

1. By about how many soldiers did the Mexicans outnumber the Texans?

2. In the hand-to-hand fighting, how did the Texans make up for their lack of bayonets?

3. What details does Houston give to show the greatness of his victory?

The sloop of war "Austin," named after Stephen F. Austin, was the flagship of the Texas navy.

Activity: Students can consult Beckwourth's autobiography, *The Life and Adventures of James P. Beckwourth,* or biographies of Beckwourth or Whitman and write reports on Beckwourth's or Whitman's life.

JAMES BECKWOURTH DISCOVERS BECKWOURTH'S PASS

James Pierson Beckwourth was born a slave in 1798, but he lived most of his life a free man. He was a trader, fur trapper, explorer, and army scout. For 11 years he lived with the Crow Indians and was made a chief. Here he tells how he discovered the pass that bears his name.

While on this trip [for gold] I discovered what is now known as "Beckwourth's Pass" in the Sierra Nevada. I spotted a place far away to the south that seemed lower than any other. I made no mention of it to my companion. I thought that at some future time I would look into it further. . . .

I stayed a short time in the American Valley. Then I again started out with a prospecting party of twelve men. We went in an easterly direction. All busied themselves in searching for gold. But my errand was of a different kind. I had come to discover what I suspected to be a pass.

It was near the end of April when we entered a large valley. It was at the northwest end of the Sierra range. There were no traces of humans. Our steps were probably the first to mark the spot. We struck across this beautiful valley to the waters of the Yuba. From there we went to the waters of the Truckee. These flowed in an easterly direction, telling us we were on the eastern slope of the mountain range. This slope, I at once saw, would furnish the best wagon road into the American Valley.

On my return to the American Valley, I made known my discovery to a Mr. Turner. He agreed enthusiastically with my views. If I could turn travel into that road, he thought my fortune would be made for life. He drew up a subscription list [to build the road]. He headed the subscription with two hundred dollars.

Adapted from *The Life and Adventures of James P. Beckwourth,* written from his own dictation, by T. D. Bonner (New York: Harper and Brothers, 1856), pp. 515–516.

1. How does James Beckwourth spot what would come to be known as Beckwourth's Pass?

2. How is the project to build a road there begun?

NARCISSA PRENTISS WHITMAN TRAVELS WEST

Narcissa Prentiss grew up in Amity, New York. In 1836 she married Marcus Whitman, a missionary and doctor. The couple traveled by wagon to set up a mission in Oregon. Here, in a letter back home, she writes about the trip west.

June 4, 1836

We have two wagons in our company. Henry and Eliza Spalding and my husband and I ride in one. Mr. Gray and the baggage are in the other. Our Indians drive the cows. . . .

Our manner of living is far preferable to any in the States [back East]. I never was so contented and happy before. Neither have I enjoyed such health for years. As soon as day breaks, the first we hear is the word, "Arise! Arise!" Then the mules set up such noise as you never heard. This puts the whole camp in motion.

We camp in a large ring. The baggage, men, tents, and wagons are on the outside. All the animals except the cows are fastened to stakes within the circle. This makes watching easier for the guards. They stand watch regularly every night and day to protect our animals. . . .

While the horses are feeding, we get our breakfast in a hurry and eat it. We are ready to start usually at six. We travel till eleven. Then we make camp, rest, and feed. We start again about two and travel until six. . . .

Since we have been in the prairie, we have done all our cooking. When we left, we expected to take bread to last us part of the way. But we could not get enough to carry us any distance. We found it awkward work at first to bake out of doors. Now we do it very easily.

We have tea and plenty of milk. That is a luxury in this country. I never saw anything like buffalo meat to satisfy hunger. We do not need anything else with it. I have now eaten three meals of it, and it tastes good. Supper and breakfast we eat in our tent. We do not pitch it at noon. We have prayers right after supper and breakfast.

T. C. Elliot, compiler, *The Coming of the White Women, 1836, as told in Letters and Journals of Narcissa Prentiss Whitman* (Portland, Oregon: Oregon Historical Society, 1937), p. 46.

1. How are the wagons and animals arranged at night? Why?

2. What skill does Narcissa Whitman have to master on the trip?

3. The travelers rise at daybreak. After that, what kind of schedule do they keep?

SAN FRANCISCO DURING THE GOLD RUSH

Vicente Pérez Rosales was a Chilean who came to California during the gold rush. He, his half brothers, and a cousin arrived in San Francisco. Then they set out for the gold fields.

They set up camp on the American River, not far from Sutter's Fort. When it was necessary to return to San Francisco for supplies, it was decided that Pérez Rosales would go. Here he tells how San Francisco has changed since his first arrival.

How different San Francisco was from what it had been. Instead of a village with foundations marked off on which buildings were to rise, now the buildings were finished. Others were under rapid construction. The tents, huts, and windbreaks of old were now lined up beside streets in the suburbs. By the look of things, all these suburbs too would soon be built over. Building lots were already being laid out. Prices had gone out of sight!

The bay was full of ships, all of them abandoned. Their passengers and crews had swelled the town's population to thirty thousand. . . .

Business was at the mercy of the shifting tides in that city. Sometimes the high water invaded everything, reducing the value of the highest quality merchandise. At other times it left everything high and dry. The most careful merchant was not safe from the ruin an unexpected high or low tide might produce. One man might get rich with no idea how it happened. Another would be ruined despite great care. . . .

Nobody, however, was discouraged. Even the lowest-priced items could be made valuable by arranging for convenient fires. We saw such fires break out all over town day after day. There was great danger that the fires would spread.

In this theater, no actor played the role assigned him in his native country. Masters were transformed into servants. A lawyer might be a freight agent; a doctor, a stevedore. Sailors found themselves digging excavations. . . .

The most showy signs had been hung up everywhere. A wooden barracks bore the name "Hotel Frémont." One man had a sign that said "So-and-so, Physician and Surgeon" painted on the flap of his tent, though he had never been more than a gravedigger. An insurance salesman from Valparaíso had a hut that bore two signs: "So-and-so, Attorney at Law," and "So-and-so and Company, General Insurance Brokers." An arbor made of poles called itself "French Hotel."

Adapted from Edwin A. Beilharz and Carlos U. Lopez, transl. and eds., *We Were 49ers! Chilean Accounts of the California Gold Rush* (Pasadena, Cal.: Ward Ritchie Press, 1976), pp. 65–67.

An unknown artist made this wash drawing of Chinese emigrants panning gold in California in the mid-1800s.

1. What change in San Francisco does Vicente Pérez Rosales first notice upon his return? What has happened to this once-quiet village?

2. Why is business in the city "at the mercy of the shifting tides"?

3. Pérez Rosales writes that no person in San Francisco "played the role" played in his native land. What examples does he give?

4. Based on what Pérez Rosales writes, do you think you would have liked living in San Francisco during the gold rush? Explain.

THE LIFE OF A CALIFORNIA WOMAN

Mary Jane Megquier and her husband, a doctor, moved from Maine to San Francisco. There they opened a hotel. It was soon flourishing. Here, Megquier writes to her daughter in Maine about her life in California.

San Francisco, June 30, 1850

Dear Daughter,

I should like to give you an account of my work if I could do it justice. In the morning, the boy gets up and makes a fire. By seven o'clock I get up and make the coffee. Then I make the biscuit. Then I fry the potatoes, then broil three pounds of steak and as much liver. Meanwhile the woman is sweeping and setting the table. At eight the bell rings, and they are eating until nine. I do not sit until they are nearly all done. . . .

After breakfast, I bake six loaves of bread, then four pies or a pudding. Then we have lamb, beef, and pork, baked turnips, beets, potatoes, radishes, salad, and that everlasting soup every day. We dine at two. For tea we have hash, cold meat, bread, and some kind of cake. I have cooked every mouthful that has been eaten. I make six beds every day and do the washing and ironing.

You must think I am very busy. When I dance all night, I am obliged to trot all day. Had I not the constitution of six horses, I should have been dead long ago. But I am going to give up in the fall as I am sick and tired of work.

From the book *Apron Full of Gold: Letters from San Francisco* edited by Robert G. Cleland (1949). Used by permission of the Huntington Library.

1. What jobs does Mary Jane Megquier do at the hotel? Why does she need the "constitution of six horses"? Why is she about to "give up"?

2. If you were to describe Mary Jane Megquier's life with one word, what word would it be?

Independence, Missouri, was the starting place for many pioneer wagon trains to the West. In 1853 *United States Illustrated* published Hermann J. Meyer's picture of the town.

UNIT 5	1850–1877

YEARS OF DIVISION

CHAPTER 14

THE NATION DIVIDES

A MODEL PLANTATION

Thomas Dabney moved from Virginia to Hinds County, Mississippi. There he bought a plantation and raised cotton. Dabney was known for his success as a planter and for his kind treatment of his slaves. Here, Susan Dabney Smedes writes about the system of work on her father's plantation.

His plantation was considered a model one. It was visited by planters anxious to learn his methods. He was asked how he made his Negroes do good work. His answer was that a laborer could do more work and better work in five and a half days than in six. He used to give the half of Saturdays to his Negroes, unless there was a great press of work.

But a system of rewards was more effective than any other method. He distributed prizes of money among his cotton-pickers every week during the season. One dollar was the first prize. The master gave money to all who worked well for the prizes, whether they won them or not. When one person picked six hundred pounds in a day, a five-dollar gold-piece was the reward. . . .

The Negroes were helped in every way to gather the cotton. Some of the men were detailed to carry the cotton-hampers to the wagons so that the pickers might lift no weights. Water-carriers went up and down the rows handing water to the pickers. Some pickers would get so excited over the work that they had to be made to leave the fields at night. . . . The cotton was weighed three times a day, and the number of pounds picked by each Negro was put opposite his or her name on a slate.

In addition to the cotton crop, corn was raised. A lock on a corn-crib was not known. After the mules and horses were fed in the evening, the Negroes carried home all that they cared to have. They raised chickens by the hundred. . . .

Every other year the master distributed blankets on the plantation, giving one blanket apiece to each individual. . . .

In addition to the blankets, comforts were quilted for every woman who had a young baby. The every-day clothes of all the Negroes were cut out and made in the house. For Sundays, a bright calico dress was given to each woman. The thrifty ones had more than they needed. The clothes were in their chests a year before they were put on. . . .

All the Negroes were encouraged to come freely to the house to see the master and mistress. They were fond of making visits there. They came even when there was nothing more important to say than to ask after the young masters off at college.

The master and mistress taught the Negroes truthfulness and honesty, as they taught their own children, by not tempting them, and by trusting them. The master believed that it made a child honest and truthful to believe its word.

Adapted from *Land That Our Fathers Plowed: The Settlement of Our Country as Told by the Pioneers Themselves and Their Contemporaries,* Compiled and Edited by David B. Greenberg. Copyright 1969 by the University of Oklahoma Press.

1. Point out details showing Dabney's kind treatment of his slaves.

2. Dabney's plantation was very productive. How did he get his slaves to work so hard?

3. Point out sentences showing that Dabney did not regard his slaves as equals. To whom are the slaves compared?

4. Considering the kind treatment, would you like to have lived as a slave on Thomas Dabney's plantation? Why or why not?

THE LIFE OF A SLAVE

Solomon Northup was a free black who was kidnapped and made a slave. It took him 12 years to win his freedom again. He wrote about his experiences in his book, *Twelve Years a Slave*. Here he writes about life on a cotton plantation.

When a new hand is sent for the first time into the field, he is whipped up smartly and made for that day to pick as fast as he possibly can. At night his sack is weighed, so that his capability in cotton picking is known. He must bring in the same weight each night following. If it falls short, a greater or less number of lashes is the penalty.

An ordinary day's work is two hundred pounds. A slave who is accustomed to picking is punished, if he or she brings in less than that. . . .

The hands are required to be in the cotton field as soon as it is light in the morning. They are not permitted to be a moment idle until it is too dark to see. When the moon is full, they often labor till the middle of the night. They do not dare to stop, even at dinner time, until the order to halt is given.

The day's work over in the field, the baskets are "toted," or in other words, carried to the gin-house. There the cotton is weighed. This done, the labor of the day is not yet ended, by any means. Each one must then attend to his respective chores. One feeds the mules, another the swine, another cuts the wood, and so forth. Besides, the packing is all done by candlelight.

Finally, at a late hour, they reach the quarters, sleepy and overcome with the long day's toil. Then a fire must be kindled in the cabin, the corn

Henry Brown, a slave, escaped to Philadelphia in a crate. Frederick Douglass is second from left.

ground in the small hand-mill, and supper, and dinner for the next day in the field, prepared.

All that is allowed them is corn and bacon, which is given out every Sunday morning. Each one receives, as his weekly allowance, three and a half pounds of bacon, and corn enough to make a peck of meal. That is all—no tea, coffee, sugar. Except for a very scanty sprinkling now and then, they have no salt.

From *Eyewitness: The Negro in American History* by William Loren Katz. Copyright © 1974 by David S. Lake Publishers, Belmont, CA.

1. How were new field slaves treated? Why?

2. What details show the hardness of the slaves' lives as cotton pickers? What else must they do?

3. Reread Susan Dabney Smedes' account of a model plantation. (See page 485.) Contrast details in this and in Solomon Northup's account that provide far different pictures of slavery.

JOHN C. CALHOUN'S LAST SPEECH

John C. Calhoun wrote his last speech for the Senate debate over the Compromise of 1850. (See page 364.) Calhoun was too sick to deliver the speech himself. So, on March 4, 1850, a fellow Senator—James A. Mason of Virginia—delivered it. On March 31, 1850, Calhoun died.

One issue under debate was the admission of California to the Union as a free state. Southerners feared the creation of new free states out of the western lands acquired from Mexico. The balance between slave states and free states would be broken. The slave states would be outnumbered in the Senate.

In his speech, Calhoun discusses this and other issues. Here is part of Calhoun's speech.

How can the Union be saved? There is but one way. That is by a full and final settlement of all the questions at issue between the two sections [North and South]. The South asks for justice, simple justice. She has no compromise to offer but the Constitution. She has no concession or surrender to make. She has already surrendered so much that she has little left to surrender.

Such a settlement would go to the root of the evil. It would remove all cause of discontent. It would satisfy the South that she could remain honorably and safely in the Union. Nothing else can save the Union.

But can this be done? Yes, easily, but not by the weaker party. The North has only to will it to accomplish it. The North can do justice by conceding to the South an equal right in the acquired territory. She can do her duty by causing the laws relative to fugitive slaves to be faithfully fulfilled. . . .

But will the North agree to do this? It is for her to answer this question. At all events, the responsibility of saving the Union rests on the North and not on the South.

Adapted from *The Annals of America*, Vol. 8, *1850–1857: A House Dividing* (Chicago: Encyclopedia Britannica, Inc., 1969), pp. 23–24.

1. Find sentences in the speech that deal with the balance between slave states and free states.

2. Why, according to Calhoun, can only the North save the Union?

A colored engraving shows Henry Clay offering his historic compromise to the Senate February 5, 1850.

HARRIET BEECHER STOWE: THE FREED SLAVE

In 1852 the novel *Uncle Tom's Cabin* was published. It was written by Harriet Beecher Stowe, a minister's daughter. In its first year alone, the novel sold more than 300,000 copies.

Uncle Tom's Cabin is about slaves and their masters. The picture it paints of slavery roused many northerners against the South. Southerners, however, said that Stowe's picture of slavery was not accurate.

In the last chapter of the novel, Stowe speaks directly to the reader. She argues that slavery is a sin and must be abolished. What then might happen to the freed slaves? Could they support themselves? Here, at the end of her novel, Harriet Beecher Stowe answers these questions.

The author gives the following statements of facts with regard to emancipated slaves now living in Cincinnati. They are given to show the capability of the race, even without any particular help and encouragement. . . .

B-----. Furniture maker. Twenty years in the city. Worth ten thousand dollars, all the result of his own earnings. . . .

C-----. Stolen from Africa. Sold in New Orleans. Been free fifteen years. Paid for himself six hundred dollars. A farmer, owns several farms in Indiana. Probably worth fifteen or twenty thousand dollars, all earned by himself.

K-----. Dealer in real estate. Worth thirty thousand dollars. About forty years old. Free six years. Paid eighteen hundred dollars for his family. Received a legacy from his master, which he has taken good care of and increased.

G-----. Coal dealer. About thirty years old. Worth eighteen thousand dollars. Made all his money by his own efforts—much of it while a slave, hiring his time from his master and doing business for himself. A fine, gentlemanly fellow.

W-----. Barber and waiter, from Kentucky. Nineteen years free. Paid for self and family over three thousand dollars. Worth twenty thousand dollars, all his own earnings. . . .

The writer well remembers an aged colored woman. She was employed as a washerwoman in her father's family. The daughter of this woman married a slave. She was a remarkably active and capable young woman.

By her industry and thrift and self-denial, she raised nine hundred dollars for her husband's freedom. She paid, as she raised it, into the hands of

Eyre Crowe sketched the "Slave Market in Richmond, Virginia" in 1853. He then painted the scene in oils in his studio. He commented on the neat gray dresses and white aprons of the women patiently waiting with their children to be sold at auction.

his master. She yet lacked a hundred dollars of the full price for her husband when he died. She never recovered any of the money.

These are but a few facts to show the self-denial, energy, patience, and honesty that the slave has exhibited in a state of freedom.

Adapted and abridged from Harriet Beecher Stowe, *Uncle Tom's Cabin; or, Life Among the Lowly* (1852).

1. What examples does Harriet Beecher Stowe give of slaves who have prospered as free persons?

2. Stowe tells about the daughter of her family's washerwoman. What qualities of the daughter does this story show?

FROM CHARLOTTE FORTEN'S JOURNAL

In September 1854 Charlotte Forten was seventeen years old. She was a member of a well-to-do black family living in the North. But she could not help thinking about the lot of other, less fortunate blacks. Here, in an entry from her journal, she dreams of the day when "slavery and prejudice shall vanish."

September 2, 1854

I wonder that every colored person is not a misanthrope [hater of people]. Surely we have everything to make us hate mankind. I have met girls in the schoolroom. They have been thoroughly kind and cordial to me. Perhaps the next day I have met them in the street. They feared to recognize me. These I can but regard now with scorn and contempt. Once I liked them, believing them incapable of such meanness.

These are but trifles to the great public wrongs that we as a people must endure. But to those who experience them, these trifles are discouraging.

O! it is hard to go through life meeting contempt with contempt, hatred with hatred. . . .

In the bitter feelings of my soul, there rise the questions: "When, oh! when, shall this injustice cease? How long, oh! how long, must we continue to suffer, to endure?"

Conscience answers it is wrong to despair. Let us labor to acquire knowledge, to break down the barriers of prejudice and oppression. Let us take courage. Let us never cease to work. Let us hope and believe that, if not for us, for another generation there is a better, brighter day in store. Then slavery and prejudice shall vanish before the glorious light of liberty and truth.

Adapted from a selection from the "Journal of Charlotte L. Forten" as it appears in *The Annals of America,* Vol. 8 (Chicago, 1969).

1. What experiences make Charlotte Forten bitter? To what does she compare these "trifles"?

2. What keeps her from despairing?

CHAPTER 15

THE CIVIL WAR

The "Bonnie Blue Flag" of the Confederacy decorated the cover of the sheet music for the song.

TWO CIVIL WAR SONGS

Many rousing songs came out of the Civil War. Following are passages from two of the most popular. "The Battle Cry of Freedom" was written by George Frederick Root. He wrote it just a few hours after President Lincoln's call for troops. "The Bonnie Blue Flag" was written by Harry McCarty. The song celebrates an early Confederate flag on which a single white star appears on a blue field.

From "The Battle Cry of Freedom"

We are springing to the call of our brothers
gone before,
    Shouting the battle cry of freedom.
And we'll fill the vacant ranks with a million
freemen more,
    Shouting the battle cry of freedom.

We will welcome to our numbers, the loyal,
true, and brave,
    Shouting the battle cry of freedom.
And although they may be poor, not a man
shall be a slave,
    Shouting the battle cry of freedom.

So we're springing to the call from the East
and from the West,
    Shouting the battle cry of freedom.
And we'll hurl the rebel crew from the land
we love the best,
    Shouting the battle cry of freedom.

From "The Bonnie Blue Flag"

First gallant South Carolina
    Nobly made the stand.
Then came Alabama,
    Who took her by the hand.
Next quickly Mississippi,
    Georgia, and Florida.
All raised on high the Bonnie Blue Flag
    That bears the single star.

And here's to old Virginia—
    The Old Dominion State—
With the young Confed'racy
    At length has linked her fate.
Impelled by her example,
    Now other states prepare
To hoist on high the Bonnie Blue Flag
    That bears the single star.

Then here's to our Confed'racy.
    Strong are we and brave.
Like patriots of old we'll fight
    Our heritage to save.
And rather than submit to shame,
    To die we would prefer.
So cheer for the Bonnie Blue Flag
    That bears the single star.

Abridged from *The Annals of America*, Vol. 9, *1858–1865: The Crisis of the Union* (Chicago: Encyclopedia Britannica, Inc., 1969), pp. 304–305.

1. Both songs are rallying songs. What sentences in each song might lead people to join the Union or the Confederate army?

2. "The Battle Cry" uses the word *freedom* many times. What does this word imply about the northern cause?

3. "The Bonnie Blue Flag" mentions the South's "heritage" and submitting to "shame." What do these words imply about the Confederate cause?

ELIZABETH KECKLEY AND THE CONTRABAND RELIEF ASSOCIATION

Elizabeth Keckley was born a slave. As a free woman, she founded the Contraband Relief Association to help escaped slaves. (During the Civil War, slaves who fled behind Union lines were known as contraband.) Here she tells how she started the association.

In the summer of 1862, freedmen began to flock into Washington from Maryland and Virginia. They came with great hope in their hearts. They had all their worldly goods on their backs. Fresh from the bonds of slavery, they came to the capital looking for liberty. Many of them did not know it when they found it. The North is not warm and impulsive. For one kind word spoken, two harsh ones were uttered. The bright joyous dreams of freedom to the slave faded.

One summer evening I was walking down a street of Washington with a friend. A band of music was heard in the distance. We quickened our steps and discovered that it came from the house of Mrs. Farnham. Ladies and gentlemen were moving about. The band was playing some of its prettiest tunes. We approached the sentinel on duty at the gate. We asked what was going on. He told us it was a festival for the benefit of the sick and wounded soldiers.

This suggested an idea to me. White people can give festivals to raise funds for the relief of suffering soldiers. Why should not the well-to-do colored people join in doing something for the benefit of suffering blacks?

The next Sunday I suggested in the colored church that a society of colored people labor for the benefit of unfortunate freedmen. The idea proved to be a popular one. In two weeks the Contraband Relief Association was organized, with forty working members.

Elizabeth Keckley, *Behind the Scenes or Thirty Years a Slave and Four Years in the White House* (New York: G. W. Carleton & Co., 1868), pp. 111–114.

1. Why did the "bright joyous dreams of freedom" of the ex-slaves fade?

2. How did Elizabeth Keckley get her idea? What did she do about it?

As an artist for *Harper's* magazine, Winslow Homer sketched many scenes during the Civil War. Here, a woman writes a letter for a wounded soldier in a hospital.

VICTORY AT GETTYSBURG

Captain William Lusk was a Yale graduate. When war broke out, he was studying medicine in Europe. He returned to the United States and enlisted in the 79th New York Regiment. Here he writes a cousin about the reaction in Wilmington, Delaware, to the Union victory at Gettysburg.

Wilmington, Delaware
July 7, 1863

Dear, dear Cousin Lou:

We have had the dark hour. The dawn has broken. The collapsed Confederacy has no place where it can hide its head. Bells are ringing wildly all over the city. Citizens grin at one another with fairly idiotic delight. One is on top of his house, frantically swinging a dinner bell. Bully for him!

How I envy the heroes of Meade's army. It would be worthwhile to die, in order that one's friends might say, "He died at Gettysburg." I can laugh. I can cry with joy. All hysterical nonsense is pardonable now. Slavery has fallen. I believe Heaven as well as earth rejoices.

These enthusiastic citizens of Wilmington have taken to firing cannons. The boys are discharging pistols into empty barrels. My letter must be short and jubilant. I cannot do anything long today.

Adapted and abridged from *War Letters of William Thompson Lusk* (1911).

1. Before the Battle of Gettysburg, the Union army suffered several defeats. What sentences in Captain William Lusk's letter show he thinks Gettysburg is a turning point?

2. What details in the letter show Wilmington's great joy at the victory?

SOJOURNER TRUTH MEETS PRESIDENT LINCOLN

Former slave Sojourner Truth was an abolitionist and a champion of women's rights. In 1864 she and her friend Lucy N. Colman visited Abraham Lincoln. In a letter to a friend, she tells of the meeting.

In her letter, Sojourner Truth refers to Daniel in the lion's den. Daniel was a prophet in the Bible's Old Testament. The Book of Daniel tells about many events in his life. At one point, Daniel was thrown into a den of lions, where he remained for hours. Miraculously, he was not attacked.

He was seated at his desk. Mrs. Colman said to him, "This is Sojourner Truth. She has come all the way from Michigan to see you."

He then arose. He gave me his hand and said, "I am glad to see you."

I said to him, "Mr. President, when you first took your seat, I feared you would be torn to pieces. I compared you unto Daniel, who was thrown into the lion's den." I then said, "I appreciate you. You are the best President who has ever taken the seat."

He replied, "I expect you have reference to my having emancipated the slaves." He mentioned the names of several of his predecessors, particularly Washington. "They were just as good and would have done just as I have, if the time had come." He pointed across the Potomac. "And if the people over the river had behaved themselves, I could not have done what I have."

Newspapers during the Civil War asked their readers to write letters to soldiers at the front. Here, a "true friend to our brave soldiers" writes to a "noble volunteer." Both the North and the South felt they were fighting to preserve the ideals of the American Revolution.

I replied, "I thank God you were the instrument selected by Him and the people to do these things."

Adapted from Dorothy Sterling, ed., *We Are Your Sisters: Black Women in the Nineteenth Century* (New York: W. W. Norton & Company, 1984), p. 252.

1. Sojourner Truth compares Lincoln to the prophet Daniel. In what sense may Lincoln have been "thrown into the lion's den"?

2. What words reveal Lincoln's modesty?

Discussion: Women such as Catherine Deveraux Edmonston ran plantations while their husbands were away at war. What problems might they have had to face?

Loyal southerners bought Confederate bonds to pay for the war. This one, paying 8 percent interest, was worthless long before it was due to be repaid in 1868.

THE VIEW FROM LOOKING GLASS PLANTATION

Catherine Deveraux Edmonston was the mistress of Looking Glass Plantation, in Halifax County, North Carolina. The diary she kept shows how one southern woman lived during the Civil War. Following are two entries from her diary. The first was written just before the war. The second was written at the war's end.

March 4, 1861. Today was inaugurated that wretch, Abraham Lincoln, President of the U.S. We are told not to speak evil of dignities [important people]. But it is hard to realize that he is a dignity. Ah, would that Jefferson Davis were our President. He is a man to whom a gentleman could look as chief of the nation. Well—we have a rail splitter and a tall man at the head of our affairs!

April 16, 1865. How can I write it! How to find words to tell what has befallen us at last. *General Lee has surrendered.* . . .

That Lee should be a prisoner seems too dreadful to be realized. Noble old man, we almost forget our own loss in sympathy with you! He has not been outmaneuvered but crushed, crushed by mere brute force. . . .

Since we heard of the disaster, I seem as though in a dream. I sleep—sleep—sleep endlessly. If I sit in my chair ten minutes, I doze. I sit benumbed. In the vain attempt to grasp it, I fall asleep. I am not dejected, not cast down. Seemingly the loss of New Orleans and of Vicksburg affected me much more. What is it that sustains me? Not faith in the army. That is gone. The land of heroes has melted away. *I believe it is faith in the country.*

From *True Tales of the South at War: How Soldiers Fought and Families Lived 1861–1865* by Clarence Poe. Copyright the University of North Carolina Press 1961. Used with permission of the publisher.

1. Contrast Catherine Deveraux Edmonston's opinions of Abraham Lincoln and Robert E. Lee. Point out sentences showing the contrast.

2. Why has Edmonston lost faith in the Confederate army? What might the last sentence of the second diary entry mean?

CHAPTER 16

RESTORING THE UNION

THE DEATH OF LINCOLN

Charles W. Eliot, who was to become president of Harvard University, was in Rome when he learned of Lincoln's death. Here he writes his mother about this tragic event. He describes the feelings of the North toward the South, and then he gives his view of Lincoln's work and reputation as President.

Dear Mother,

Thursday, April 27, in the morning, we got the news of the assassination at Washington. What a horrible shock it was. The loss of great battles would have been as nothing. The horrible crime of assassination for political reasons has stained the history of the republic.

This is the horror of it to my mind—that an American President has been assassinated by an American. This is the crowning fruit of slavery. First, civil war, and now, political assassination. . . .

In our admiration of Lee and his army, we felt like embracing our enemies and welcoming them back to Peace and Country. But here is the most awful crime thrown all at once across the path of conciliation. . . .

I am no worshipper of men. Even now, I don't like to hear Lincoln's name put too near Washington's. But his character seems to me a rough and ungraceful but truly noble growth of republican institutions. He grew to his work. You can count on your fingers the names of those leaders that History will rank with his.

If the assassins thought that the government would be thrown into confusion by their work, they will be disappointed. Lincoln's death will make holy his policy. People will be found to carry it out. He did not lead the people. He rather followed the wisest and best thought of the people. His successors will do likewise.

Adapted and abridged from *Life and Letters of Charles W. Eliot,* by Henry James, Houghton Mifflin Company, Boston, Mass.

1. What, to Charles Eliot, is especially horrible about Lincoln's death? What does he think it will do to relations between the North and South?
2. What is Eliot's opinion of Lincoln? Why does he think Lincoln's policies will be carried out?

THOMAS DABNEY AFTER THE CIVIL WAR

Before the Civil War, Thomas Dabney's Mississippi plantation was famous for its productivity. (See page 485.) But the war ruined Dabney. He lost much of his property and went deeply into debt. Here Susan Dabney Smedes tells how her father and his family managed to survive.

He had come home to a house stripped of every article of furniture. The plantation was stripped of the means of cultivating any but a small portion of it. A few mules and one cow made up the stock. . . .

He owned nothing that could be turned into money without great sacrifice but five bales of cotton. The household was put on an economical footing. The plantation Negroes were hired to work in the fields. . . .

In the Civil War, much of the South was destroyed. Theodore Davis sketched a family living in the ruins of Columbia, South Carolina, in 1866.

He determined to spare his daughters all such labor as he could perform. General Sherman had said that he would like to bring every southern woman to the washtub. "He will never bring my daughters to the washtub," Thomas Dabney said. "I will do the washing myself." And he did it for two years. He was in his seventieth year when he began to do it. . . .

During a period of eighteen months, no light in summer and none but a fire in winter was seen in the house. He was fourteen years in paying debts that fell on him in his sixty-ninth year. He lived but three years after the last dollar was paid.

When he was seventy years of age, he decided to learn to cultivate a garden. He had never performed manual labor. Now he applied himself to learn to hoe. He made his garden, as he did everything, in the most careful manner. The beds and rows and walks were models of exactness and neatness. The garden supplied the daily food of his family nearly all the year round. . . .

Oftentimes he was so exhausted when he came in to dinner that he could not eat for a while. He had his old bright way of making everyone take an interest in his activities. He showed with pride what he had done in gardening and in washing. He placed the clothes on the line as carefully as if they were meant to hang there always. He said, and truly, that he had never seen snowier ones.

Adapted from Susan Dabney Smedes, *Memorials of a Southern Planter* (Baltimore, 1887).

1. What details show how Thomas Dabney managed to survive the difficulties that confronted him after the war?

2. What details reveal Dabney's pride?

3. Do you think Dabney's actions after the war should be admired? Explain.

CONGRESSMAN RICHARD CAIN SPEAKS

Richard Harvey Cain, a black minister, served two terms as a representative from South Carolina. When a white congressman said that blacks in the South enjoyed the same rights as whites, Cain answered him. Here is part of Cain's speech to the House.

Sir, a gentleman states that in the state of North Carolina the colored people enjoy all their rights as far as the highways are concerned. He says that in the various public places of resort, they have all the rights given to any other class of citizens in the United States.

It may not have come under his observation, but it has under mine, that such is not really the case. The reason why I know and feel it more than he does is because my face is painted black and his is painted white. We who have the color know and feel all this.

A few days ago, I entered a public place where hungry men are fed. I did not dare—I could not without trouble—sit down to the table. My colleague [a black Congressman] a few months ago entered a restaurant and sat down to be served. A gentleman stepped up to him and said, "You cannot eat here." All the other men were eating there. He showed fight, however, and got his dinner. . . .

Mr. Speaker, the colored people of the South do not want the adoption of any force measure. No, they do not want anything by force. All they ask is that you will give them by law the right to enjoy precisely the same privileges given to every other class of citizens.

Adapted from Annjennette Sophie McFarlin, *Black Congressional Reconstruction Orators And Their Orations 1869–1879* (Metuchen, N.J.: Scarecrow Press, Inc. 1976), pp. 36–37.

1. What, according to Richard Harvey Cain, do blacks of the South want?

2. What examples does he give to show unequal treatment of blacks?

SARAH ALLEN TESTIFIES BEFORE CONGRESS

After the Civil War, northerners volunteered to educate the newly-freed slaves. One such teacher was Sarah A. Allen. In 1871 she testified before a congressional committee about her experiences as a northern teacher in the South.

Q. Please state your place of residence and occupation to the committee.

A. Geneseo, Henry County, Illinois. I have no occupation at home. I am teaching here.

Q. Were you teaching a white or colored school?

A. A colored school.

Q. You may state to the committee whether you were interrupted by any persons in your business.

A. I taught six weeks, until I think the 18th of March, when I was told to leave. I was warned to leave between one and two o'clock at night by about fifty men, I think. They were disguised. There were but two that came into my room.

Q. Do you say they came into your room?

A. Between one and two o'clock I was wakened by a great noise outside. They told me to get up. I went to the window and asked them what they wanted. They said they wanted to talk to me. I said, "Very well." I admitted them.

Q. What did they say to you?

A. They asked me my name and occupation and where I came from and what I was doing. We talked about an hour on politics, mostly against Colonel Huggins and his whipping. He had been whipped about one week before that. They asked me if I had heard of it and what I thought of it. They also asked me if I had heard that other teachers had been sent away and what I intended to do. I told them it was very short notice, and I did not know. They said they never gave a person more than one warning. . . .

Q. Was there any threat made of what would be the consequence of your continuing to teach in that school?

A. No, sir.

Q. Further than the remark that they never gave a second notice?

A. Yes, sir. That was all.

Q. What did you infer from that?

A. Well, I supposed that they would, if I should stay and continue, take harsher means.

Q. Did you discontinue your school in consequence of this warning?

A. Yes, I did.

Ex-slaves could attend the Freedmen's Union Industrial School in Richmond, Virginia, in 1866.

Q. After you had been teaching colored people about six weeks?

A. I taught just six weeks. . . .

Q. Did they say what their motive was for breaking up the school?

A. Yes. They did not want radicals there in the South. They did not want northern people teaching there. They thought the colored people could educate themselves if there was any need for them to have an education. . . .

Q. The men were all disguised that you saw?

A. Yes, sir.

Q. Can you give the committee a description of the disguises they wore?

A. They wore long white robes. A loose mask covered the face, trimmed with scarlet stripes.

Q. Did you recognize any of the number?

A. I did not. . . .

Q. They did not threaten you, I understand?

A. They yelled like Comanche Indians.

Q. When they went away?

A. Yes, sir. . . .

Q. Did they advise you to leave because you would not be paid?

A. No. They advised me to leave because I was a white person teaching in a colored school.

U.S. Congress, Joint Select Committee to Inquire into the Condition of Affairs in the Late Insurrectionary States, 2 Vols. (Washington, D.C.: U.S. Govt. Printing Office, 1872), "Mississippi, II: 777–779."

1. Who visited Sarah Allen late one night in March 1871? How were the visitors dressed?

2. Why did they tell Sarah Allen about Colonel Huggins's beating?

3. What did the visitors say about their motives? Why did they want Allen to leave?

"WE ARE A PEOPLE WORTHY TO BE FREE"

Even though the slaves had been freed, many people, in the North as well as the South, believed that blacks were inferior to whites. In 1865 a black with pride in his race wrote the following to the *National Freedman*.

It is not enough to tell us that we will be respected according as we show ourselves worthy of

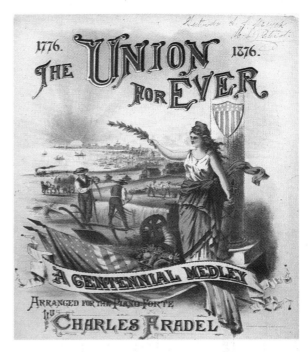

A number of patriotic songs were written in honor of the United States' hundredth birthday—the Centennial—in 1876. This one shows progress in farming and trade under the olive branch of peace.

it. When we have rights that others respect, self-respect will greatly increase.

I do not think that to have these rights would rob white people of their glory. We do not flatter ourselves with the idea that we are yet fitted to fill high stations. Yet we do think that often white people are put in positions over us that might be better filled by a person of our own race.

Surely the heroic deeds of colored men on the battlefield will remove our difficulties and enable us to show the world that we are a people worthy to be free, worthy to be respected.

Adapted and abridged from *The National Freedman*, April 1, 1865.

1. What does the writer think will lead to an increase in black self-respect?

2. What does he think blacks have done to earn different treatment by whites?

High atop the dome of the Capitol Building in Washington, D.C., stands the Statue of Freedom. Designed by Thomas Crawford, the bronze female figure is over 19 feet tall and weighs 14,985 pounds. The figure representing Freedom wears a headdress circled with stars and topped with an eagle's head and feathers. She was placed on the Capitol when the dome was added during the Civil War. The Statue of Freedom continues to symbolize the ideals of a nation dedicated to ''liberty and justice for all.''

REFERENCE SECTION

RESOURCE CENTER

Settlement of the United States

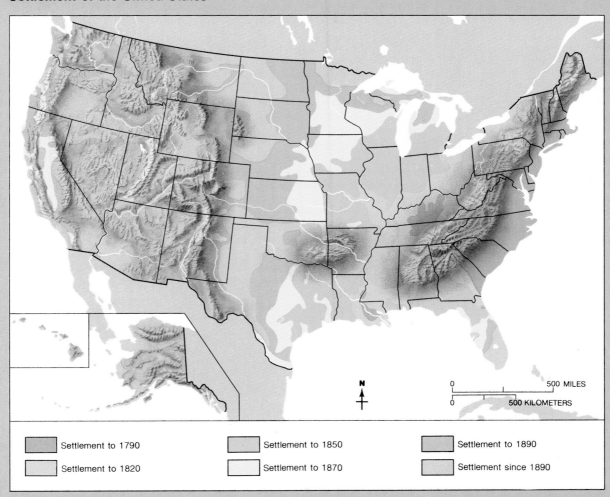

Settlement to 1790	Settlement to 1850	Settlement to 1890
Settlement to 1820	Settlement to 1870	Settlement since 1890

Territorial Growth of the United States

The Original United States	1783	Treaty with Great Britain	845,882 sq mi	(2,190,834 sq km)
Louisiana Purchase	1803	Purchased from France	831,321	(2,153,121)
Red River Basin	1818	Ceded by Great Britain	46,253	(119,795)
Florida	1819	Ceded by Spain	69,866	(180,953)
Texas	1845	Annexed	384,958	(997,041)
Oregon Country	1846	Compromise with Great Britain	283,439	(734,107)
Mexican Cession	1848	Ceded by Mexico	530,706	(1,374,529)
Gadsden Purchase	1853	Purchased from Mexico	29,640	(76,768)
Alaska	1867	Purchased from Russia	591,004	(1,530,700)
Hawaii	1898	Annexed	6,471	(16,760)

Physical Map of the United States

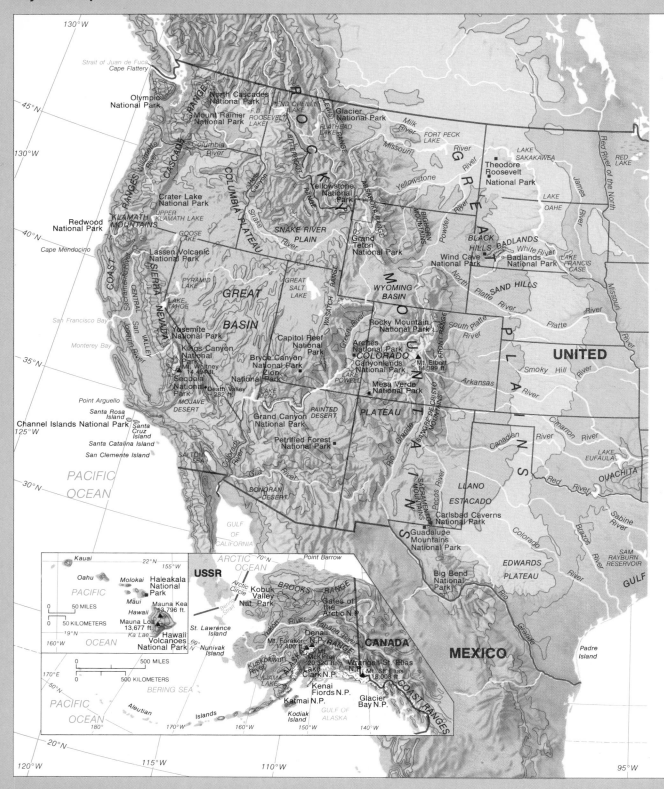

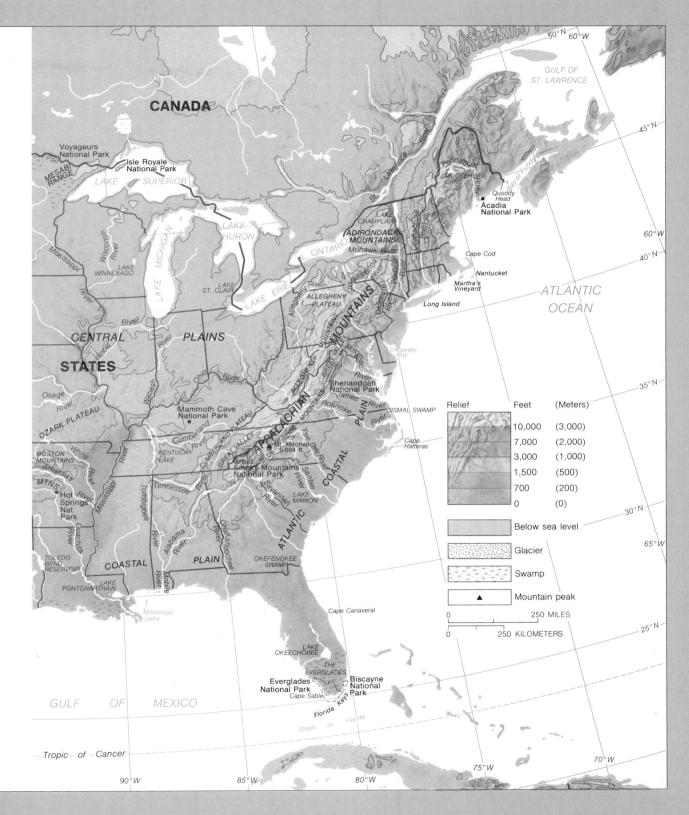

CANADA

Voyageurs
National Park

MESABI
RANGE

Isle Royale
National Park

LAKE   SUPERIOR

Wisconsin
River

LAKE
MICHIGAN

LAKE
HURON

Mississippi

LAKE
WINNEBAGO

LAKE
ST. CLAIR

LAKE ERIE

Allegheny River

River

CENTRAL   PLAINS

STATES

Illinois   River

Wabash

Ohio   River

River

Osage
River

OZARK PLATEAU

Mammoth Cave
National Park

Cumberland

KENTUCKY
LAKE

River

BOSTON
MOUNTAINS

White

Arkansas

MTNS.

Hot
Springs
Nat.
Park

Ouachita
River

Tennessee

Great
Smoky Mountains
National Park

TOLEDO
BEND
RESERVOIR

LAKE
PONTCHARTRAIN

COASTAL   PLAIN

Tombigbee

River

Alabama   River

Chattahoochee   River

Mobile   River

Mississippi
Delta

GULF   OF   MEXICO

Tropic of Cancer

90°W   85°W   80°W

St. Lawrence River

Penobscot
River

MOOSEHEAD
LAKE

Bay of Fundy

Quoddy
Head
Acadia
National Park

L. ONTARIO

LAKE
CHAMPLAIN

ADIRONDACK
MOUNTAINS

Mohawk River

Connecticut River

Susquehanna River

ALLEGHENY
PLATEAU

MOUNTAINS

Hudson River

Cape Cod

Nantucket

Martha's
Vineyard

Long Island

Delaware River

Potomac River

Delaware
Bay

GREAT VALLEY

Shenandoah
National Park

James   River

Roanoke   River

DISMAL SWAMP

Cape
Hatteras

APPALACHIAN

ALLEGHENY MOUNTAINS

BLUE RIDGE MOUNTAINS

Mt. Mitchell
6,684 ft.

CUMBERLAND PLATEAU

GREAT VALLEY

Santee   River

Pee Dee River

LAKE
MARION

Savannah   River

ATLANTIC

COASTAL

PLAIN

OKEFENOKEE
SWAMP

Cape Canaveral

LAKE
OKEECHOBEE

THE
EVERGLADES

Everglades
National Park

Biscayne
National
Park

Cape Sable

Florida Keys

Straits   of   Florida

75°W   70°W

GULF OF
ST. LAWRENCE

ATLANTIC
OCEAN

50°N 60°W

45°N

60°W

40°N

35°N

30°N

65°W

25°N

Relief   Feet   (Meters)

10,000   (3,000)
7,000   (2,000)
3,000   (1,000)
1,500   (500)
700   (200)
0   (0)

Below sea level

Glacier

Swamp

▲   Mountain peak

0   250 MILES

0   250 KILOMETERS

Political Map of the United States

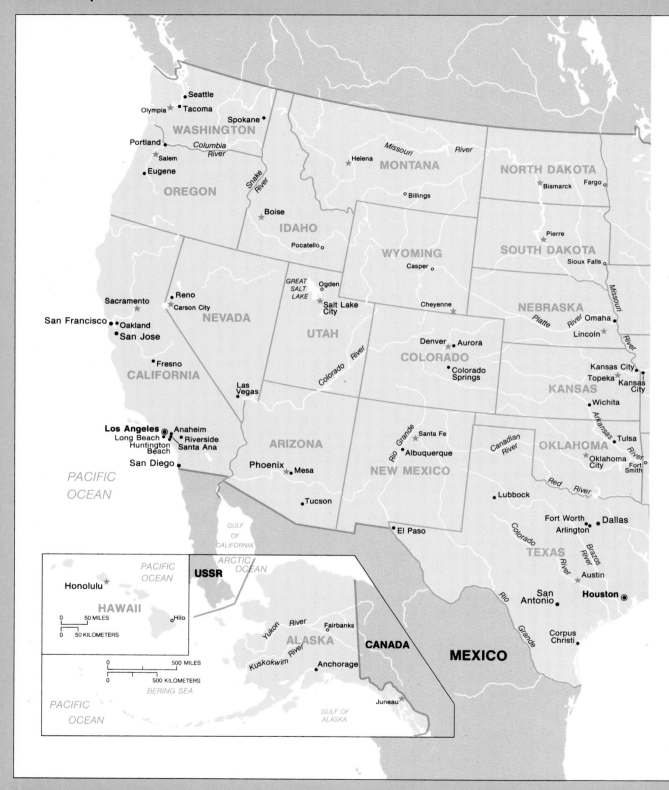

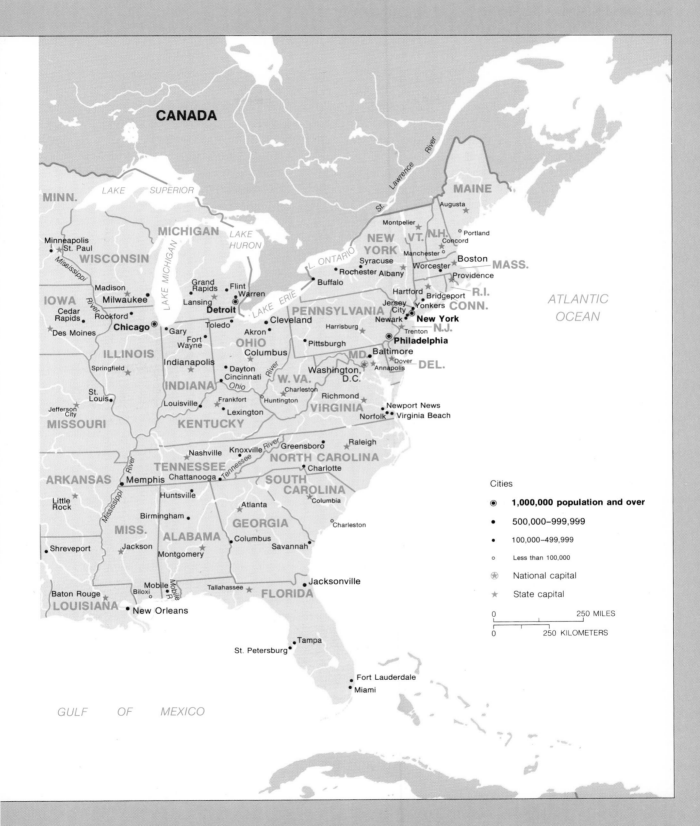

CANADA

MINN.

LAKE SUPERIOR

MICHIGAN

LAKE HURON

Minneapolis
★St. Paul

WISCONSIN

LAKE MICHIGAN

Madison
Milwaukee

IOWA

Cedar
Rapids
Rockford

Des Moines

Chicago ◉

ILLINOIS

Springfield ★

St.
Louis.

Jefferson
City

MISSOURI

Grand
Rapids   Flint
        •Warren
Lansing★
      Detroit

•Gary
  Fort
  Wayne

Indianapolis
    ★

INDIANA

Louisville
    ★Frankfort
      •Lexington

KENTUCKY

Toledo

OHIO
Columbus

•Dayton
Cincinnati

Ohio River

Charleston
•Huntington

Cleveland•

Akron
•

L. ONTARIO

Buffalo•

LAKE ERIE

PENNSYLVANIA

Harrisburg★

Pittsburgh

MAINE

Augusta★

Montpelier★   ○Portland
      VT. N.H. Concord
NEW   Manchester○
YORK   Albany   Boston★
Syracuse•   Worcester•   MASS.
Rochester• Albany★ •Providence
            Hartford R.I.
            ★ •Bridgeport CONN.
        Jersey•Yonkers
        City
    Newark•★New York
         Trenton N.J.
        ◉Philadelphia

MD. •Baltimore
Washington, •Dover
D.C.   Annapolis★ DEL.

ATLANTIC
OCEAN

W. VA.

VIRGINIA

Richmond★
        •Newport News
Norfolk•Virginia Beach

ARKANSAS

Little
Rock

Shreveport•

Memphis•

TENNESSEE

Nashville★
Chattanooga•
Huntsville•

Birmingham•

MISS.   ALABAMA
Jackson★
  Montgomery★

Knoxville•

Tennessee River

Greensboro•   Raleigh★

NORTH CAROLINA

•Charlotte

SOUTH
CAROLINA
      •Columbia

GEORGIA

Atlanta★

Columbus•
    Savannah•

○Charleston

Mississippi River

Baton Rouge★
Biloxi•   Tallahassee★
LOUISIANA •New Orleans
Mobile• Mobile R.

FLORIDA

•Jacksonville

GULF   OF   MEXICO

•Tampa
St. Petersburg•

Fort Lauderdale•
•Miami

Cities

◉ **1,000,000 population and over**

• 500,000–999,999

• 100,000–499,999

○ Less than 100,000

✪ National capital

★ State capital

0 ———————— 250 MILES
0 ———————— 250 KILOMETERS

The United States in the World

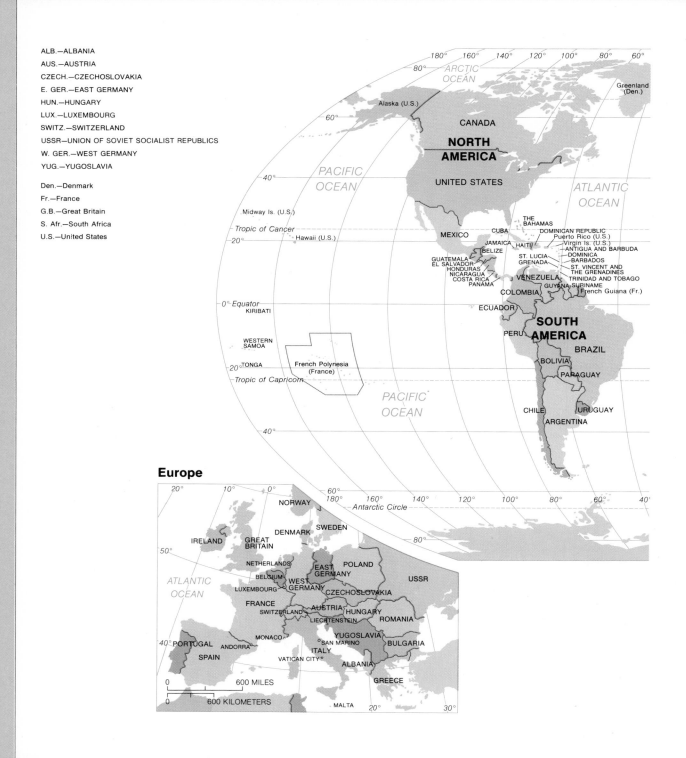

ALB.—ALBANIA
AUS.—AUSTRIA
CZECH.—CZECHOSLOVAKIA
E. GER.—EAST GERMANY
HUN.—HUNGARY
LUX.—LUXEMBOURG
SWITZ.—SWITZERLAND
USSR—UNION OF SOVIET SOCIALIST REPUBLICS
W. GER.—WEST GERMANY
YUG.—YUGOSLAVIA

Den.—Denmark
Fr.—France
G.B.—Great Britain
S. Afr.—South Africa
U.S.—United States

Europe

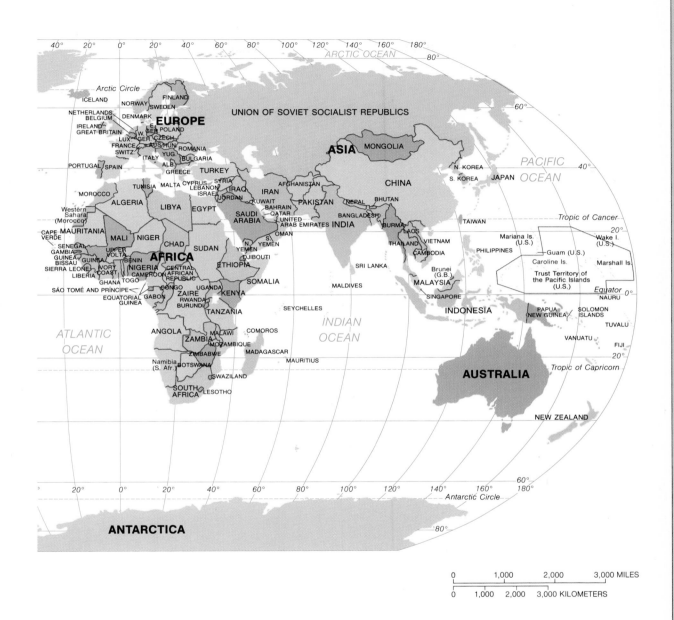

Arctic Circle

ARCTIC OCEAN

80°

ICELAND
NORWAY
FINLAND
SWEDEN
60°

NETHERLANDS
BELGIUM
DENMARK
IRELAND
GREAT BRITAIN
LUX.
FRANCE
SWITZ.
PORTUGAL
SPAIN
ITALY
ALB.
GREECE

EUROPE

E.
GER.
W.
GER.
POLAND
CZECH.
AUS. HUN.
YUG.
ROMANIA
BULGARIA

UNION OF SOVIET SOCIALIST REPUBLICS

ASIA

MONGOLIA

N. KOREA
S. KOREA
JAPAN

40°

PACIFIC
OCEAN

TURKEY
CYPRUS
MALTA
TUNISIA
SYRIA
LEBANON
ISRAEL
JORDAN
IRAQ
IRAN
AFGHANISTAN
CHINA

MOROCCO
ALGERIA
LIBYA
EGYPT
KUWAIT
BAHRAIN
QATAR
UNITED
ARAB EMIRATES
SAUDI
ARABIA
PAKISTAN
NEPAL
BHUTAN

Tropic of Cancer

20°

Western
Sahara
(Morocco)
CAPE
VERDE
MAURITANIA
MALI
NIGER
CHAD
SUDAN
N.
YEMEN
S.
YEMEN
OMAN
BANGLADESH
INDIA
BURMA

TAIWAN

Mariana Is.
(U.S.)

Wake I.
(U.S.)

AFRICA

SENEGAL
GAMBIA
GUINEA-
BISSAU
GUINEA
SIERRA LEONE
LIBERIA
IVORY
COAST
GHANA
TOGO
BENIN
NIGERIA
CAMEROON
CENTRAL
AFRICAN
REPUBLIC
DJIBOUTI
ETHIOPIA
LAOS
THAILAND
VIETNAM
CAMBODIA
PHILIPPINES

Guam (U.S.)
Caroline Is.

Marshall Is.

SÁO TOMÉ AND PRÍNCIPE
EQUATORIAL
GUINEA
GABON
CONGO
ZAIRE
RWANDA
BURUNDI
UGANDA
KENYA
SOMALIA

SRI LANKA

MALDIVES

Brunei
(G.B.)
MALAYSIA
SINGAPORE

Trust Territory of
the Pacific Islands
(U.S.)

Equator
NAURU

0°

ATLANTIC
OCEAN

ANGOLA
TANZANIA
ZAMBIA
MALAWI
COMOROS
MOZAMBIQUE
MADAGASCAR

SEYCHELLES

INDIAN
OCEAN

INDONESIA

PAPUA
NEW GUINEA

SOLOMON
ISLANDS

TUVALU

Namibia
(S. Afr.)
ZIMBABWE
BOTSWANA
MAURITIUS

VANUATU

FIJI

20°

SWAZILAND
SOUTH
AFRICA
LESOTHO

Tropic of Capricorn

AUSTRALIA

NEW ZEALAND

60°

Antarctic Circle

20°
0°
20°
40°
60°
80°
100°
120°
140°
160°
180°

80°

ANTARCTICA

| 0 | 1,000 | 2,000 | 3,000 MILES |

| 0 | 1,000 | 2,000 | 3,000 KILOMETERS |

Population Growth 1790–1980

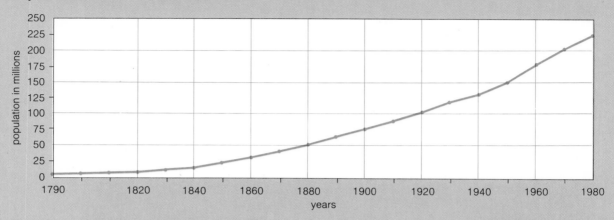

Immigration 1820–1980

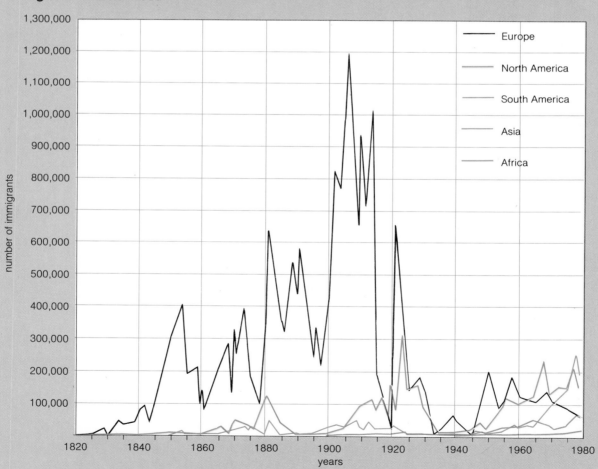

Total Immigration from Leading Countries of Origin   1820–1979

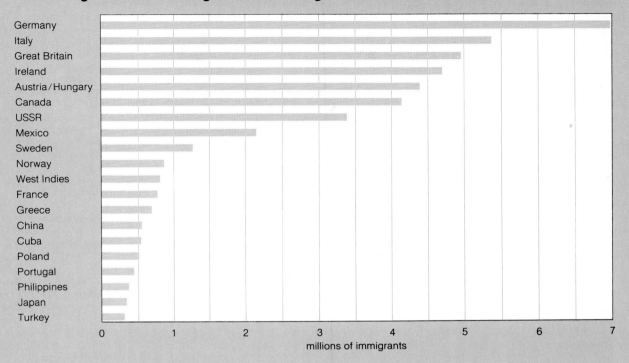

millions of immigrants

Racial Origins of Americans   1980

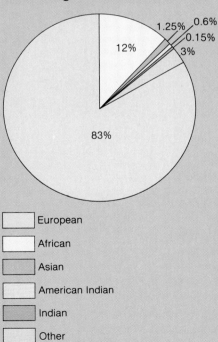

12%

1.25% 0.6%
0.15%
3%

83%

☐ European
☐ African
☐ Asian
☐ American Indian
☐ Indian
☐ Other

Americans of Hispanic Origin   1980

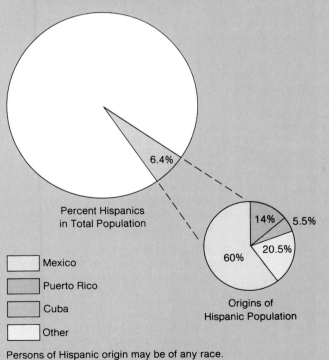

6.4%

Percent Hispanics
in Total Population

14%   5.5%
60%   20.5%

Origins of
Hispanic Population

☐ Mexico
☐ Puerto Rico
☐ Cuba
☐ Other

Persons of Hispanic origin may be of any race.

Population Distribution by Region   1790–1980

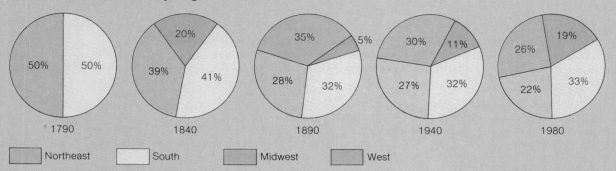

1790 — Northeast 50%, South 50%

1840 — Midwest 20%, Northeast 39%, South 41%

1890 — Midwest 35%, West 5%, Northeast 28%, South 32%

1940 — Midwest 30%, West 11%, Northeast 27%, South 32%

1980 — Northeast 26%, West 19%, Midwest 22%, South 33%

Northeast · South · Midwest · West

Rural and Urban Populations   1790–1980

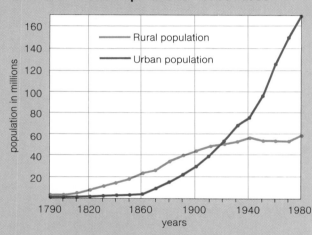

— Rural population
— Urban population

population in millions

years

Population Distribution in Urban Areas 1950–1980

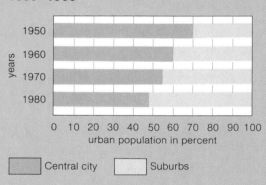

years

1950
1960
1970
1980

urban population in percent

Central city · Suburbs

Number of Farms and Average Farm Size   1850–1980

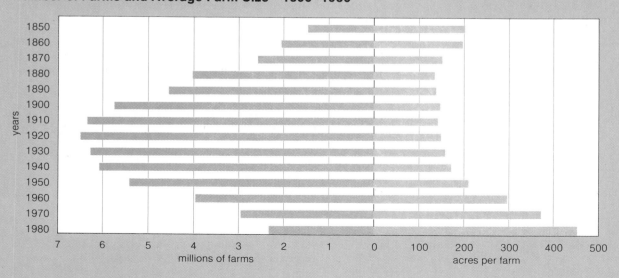

years

1850
1860
1870
1880
1890
1900
1910
1920
1930
1940
1950
1960
1970
1980

millions of farms   acres per farm

Population Density in the United States 1980

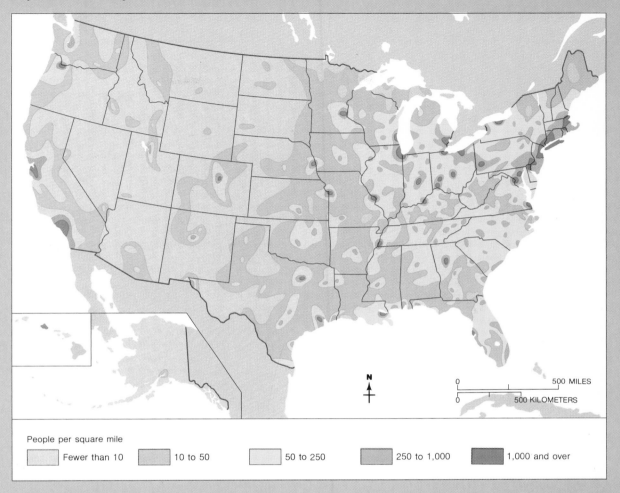

People per square mile

Fewer than 10	10 to 50	50 to 250	250 to 1,000	1,000 and over

Population per Square Mile   1790–1980

1790

1840

1890

1940

1980

☽ equals 5 persons

Life Expectancy at Birth 1900–1980

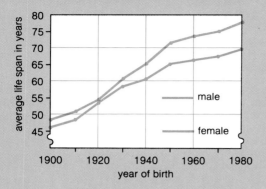

Average Size of Households 1790–1980

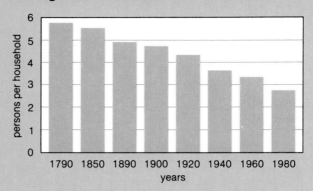

School Enrollment 1870–1980

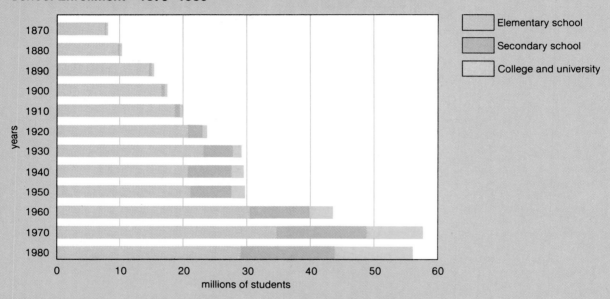

Elementary school

Secondary school

College and university

Distribution of Population by Age 1890–1980

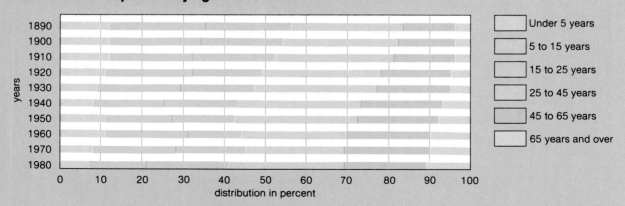

Under 5 years

5 to 15 years

15 to 25 years

25 to 45 years

45 to 65 years

65 years and over

Climates of the United States

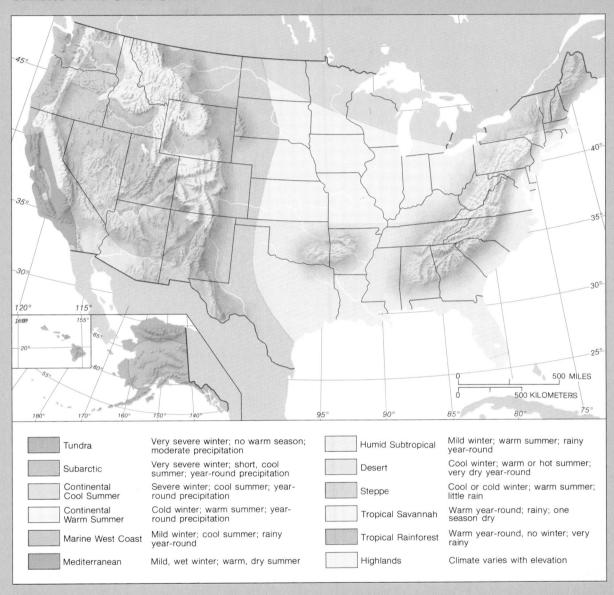

Tundra	Very severe winter; no warm season; moderate precipitation		Humid Subtropical	Mild winter; warm summer; rainy year-round
Subarctic	Very severe winter; short, cool summer; year-round precipitation		Desert	Cool winter; warm or hot summer; very dry year-round
Continental Cool Summer	Severe winter; cool summer; year-round precipitation		Steppe	Cool or cold winter; warm summer; little rain
Continental Warm Summer	Cold winter; warm summer; year-round precipitation		Tropical Savannah	Warm year-round; rainy; one season dry
Marine West Coast	Mild winter; cool summer; rainy year-round		Tropical Rainforest	Warm year-round, no winter; very rainy
Mediterranean	Mild, wet winter; warm, dry summer		Highlands	Climate varies with elevation

The Nation's Crops Ranked by Percent of Farm Sales   1981

Cattle	20.2%	Hogs	6.8%	Eggs	2.5%
Feed crops	12.7%	Vegetables	5.9%	Tobacco	2.3%
Dairy products	12.6%	Fruits, nuts	4.6%	Sheep	.3%
Oilbearing crops	9.8%	Poultry	4.4%	Wool	.1%
Food grains	8.6%	Cotton	3.2%	Others	6.0%

Mineral Resources of the United States

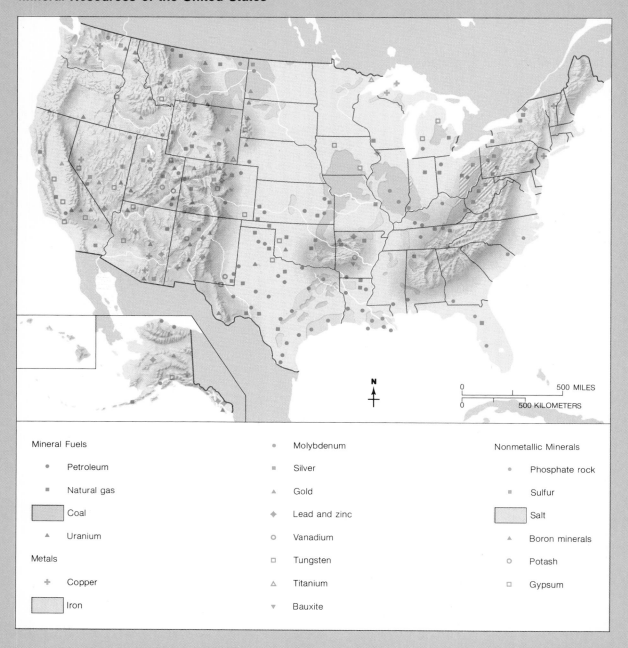

Mineral Fuels

- Petroleum
- Natural gas
- Coal
- Uranium

Metals

- Copper
- Iron

- Molybdenum
- Silver
- Gold
- Lead and zinc
- Vanadium
- Tungsten
- Titanium
- Bauxite

Nonmetallic Minerals

- Phosphate rock
- Sulfur
- Salt
- Boron minerals
- Potash
- Gypsum

Principal Minerals Ranked by Value of Production   1980

Petroleum	$66,670,000,000	Sand and gravel	$2,638,000,000	Salt	$656,200,000
Natural gas	32,670,000,000	Molybdenum	1,344,200,000	Silver	646,600,000
Coal	20,510,000,000	Phosphate rock	1,256,900,000	Gold	582,800,000
Cement	3,801,000,000	Uranium	1,228,000,000	Lead	514,400,000
Stone	3,393,500,000	Clays	898,900,000	Boron minerals	366,800,000
Copper	2,638,000,000	Lime	842,900,000	Potash	353,900,000
Iron ore	2,547,500,000	Sulfur	720,500,000	Zinc	276,300,000

Energy Sources   1980

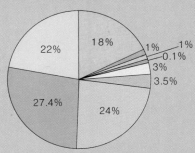

Domestic Production

- Crude oil
- Natural gas
- Coal
- Water power
- Nuclear power
- Geothermal and other sources

Imports

- Crude oil and refined petroleum
- Natural gas
- Others

Energy Use   1980

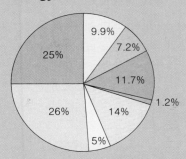

Direct Use

- Transportation
- Industry
- Export
- Home and business

Generation of Electricity

- Home use
- Business use
- Industrial use
- Other

Iron Ore Consumption   1860–1980

- Imports
- Domestic production

millions of long tons

years

Petroleum Consumption   1860–1980

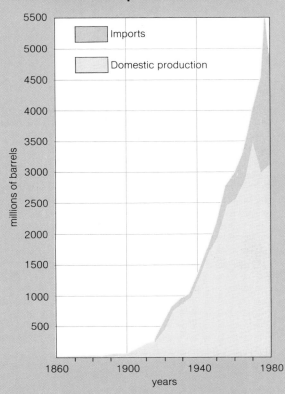

- Imports
- Domestic production

millions of barrels

years

Bituminous Coal Consumption   1860–1980

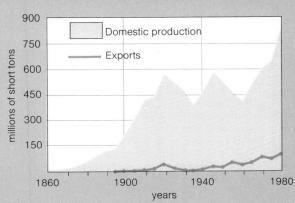

- Domestic production
- Exports

millions of short tons

years

Civilian Labor Force   1890–1980

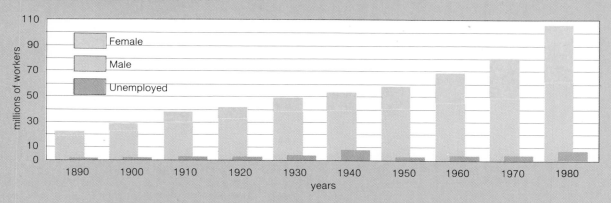

millions of workers

Female
Male
Unemployed

1890 1900 1910 1920 1930 1940 1950 1960 1970 1980

years

Union Membership   1900–1980

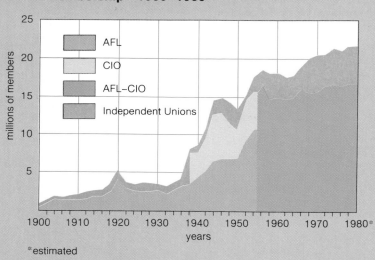

millions of members

AFL
CIO
AFL–CIO
Independent Unions

1900 1910 1920 1930 1940 1950 1960 1970 1980*

years

*estimated

The American Economy
1790–1980

"The American Economy" describes the nation's economic activity, or business cycle. This graph illustrates periods of recession, depression, recovery, and prosperity. The graph was computed from several sources such as indexes of business activity and production, and information about commodity prices, imports and exports, government income and expenditures, banking activities, and stock prices.

Periods of Seaborne Commerce Prosperity   Postwar Prosperity   Era of Good Feelings   Bank Credit Land Boom

War: France and England   Half War   Embargo Depression   War of 1812   Panic of 1819   Panic of 1837

1790 1795 1800 1805 1810 1815 1820 1825 1830 1835

Occupational Groups   1900–1980

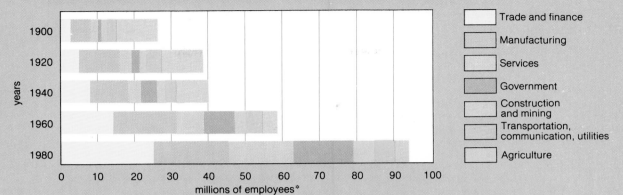

years

millions of employees*

Legend:
- Trade and finance
- Manufacturing
- Services
- Government
- Construction and mining
- Transportation, communication, utilities
- Agriculture

*excludes the self-employed and members of the Armed Forces

Consumer Prices and Purchasing Power   1929–1981

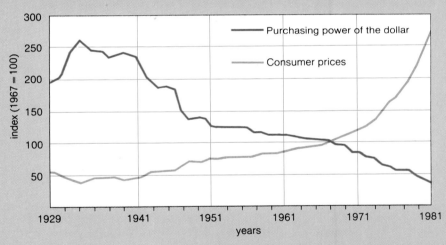

index (1967 = 100)

- Purchasing power of the dollar
- Consumer prices

years

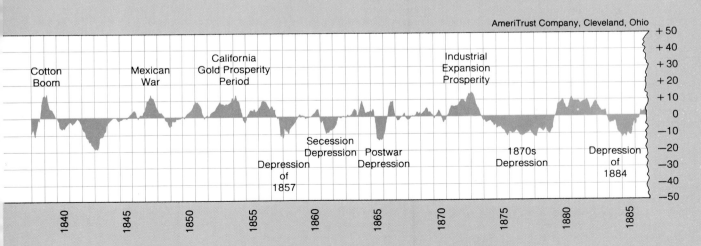

Cotton Boom

Mexican War

California Gold Prosperity Period

Depression of 1857

Secession Depression

Postwar Depression

Industrial Expansion Prosperity

1870s Depression

Depression of 1884

AMERICA AT WORK   RESOURCE CENTER

Major Industries: Value of Products, Number of Employees 1980

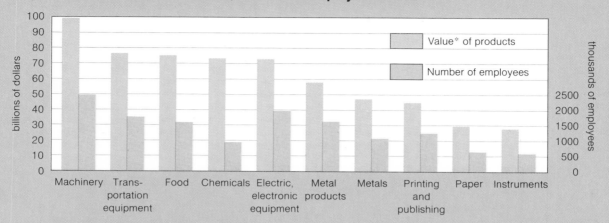

*Value refers to the difference between the cost of production and the selling price.

Gross National Product 1929–1981

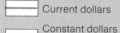

Gross National Product per Person 1929–1981

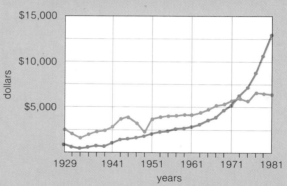

Current dollars — Expressed in terms of the current value of the dollar in each year; the rising values reflect inflation.

Constant dollars (1972 = 100) — Expressed in terms of a constant value of the dollar (what a dollar could purchase in 1972) to measure economic growth undistorted by the effects of inflation.

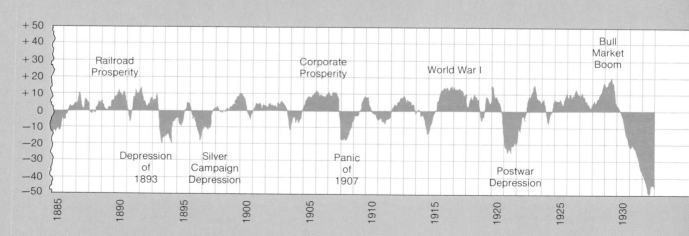

Imports   1830–1980

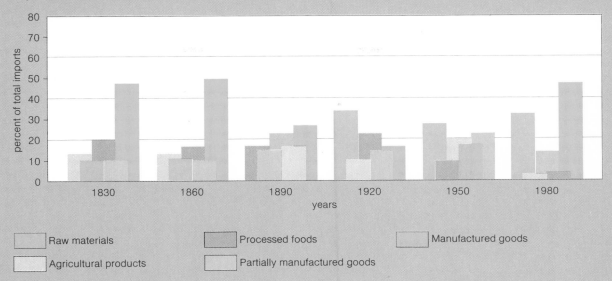

percent of total imports

years

| Raw materials | Processed foods | Manufactured goods |
| Agricultural products | Partially manufactured goods | |

Exports   1830–1980

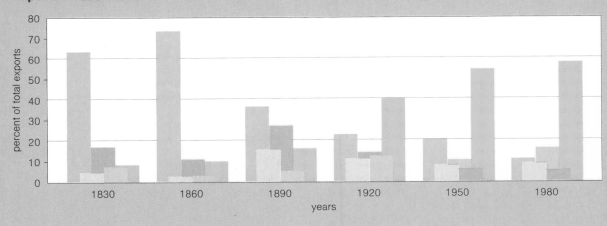

percent of total exports

years

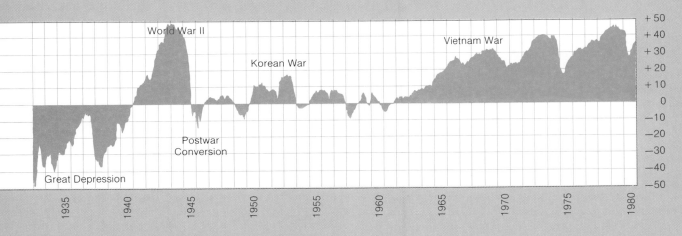

World War II

Vietnam War

Korean War

Postwar
Conversion

Great Depression

+50
+40
+30
+20
+10
0
−10
−20
−30
−40
−50

1935 1940 1945 1950 1955 1960 1965 1970 1975 1980

Populations of the States of the United States   1840, 1890, 1980

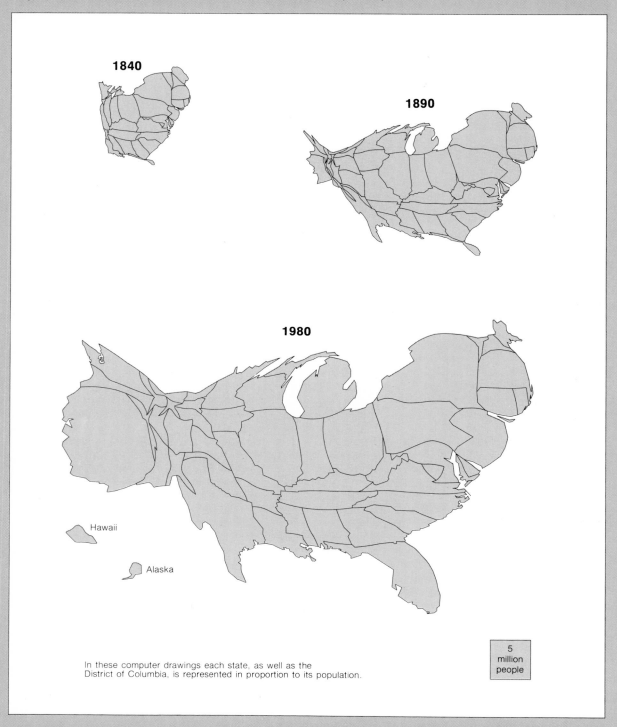

1840

1890

1980

Hawaii

Alaska

In these computer drawings each state, as well as the
District of Columbia, is represented in proportion to its population.

5
million
people

Facts About the States

State	Capital	Date of Entry to Union	Order of Entry	Area in Square Miles (Square Kilometers)		Population in 1980	People per Square Mile*	Percent Urban Population
Alabama	Montgomery	1819	22	51,705	(133,915)	3,890,000	77	60
Alaska	Juneau	1959	49	591,004	(1,530,700)	400,000	1	65
Arizona	Phoenix	1912	48	114,000	(295,260)	2,718,000	24	84
Arkansas	Little Rock	1836	25	53,187	(137,754)	2,286,000	44	52
California	Sacramento	1850	31	158,706	(411,049)	23,669,000	151	91
Colorado	Denver	1876	38	104,091	(269,595)	2,889,000	28	81
Connecticut	Hartford	1788	5	5,018	(12,997)	3,108,000	638	79
Delaware	Dover	1787	1	2,044	(5,295)	595,000	308	71
Florida	Tallahassee	1845	27	58,664	(151,939)	9,740,000	180	84
Georgia	Atlanta	1788	4	58,910	(152,576)	5,464,000	94	62
Hawaii	Honolulu	1959	50	6,471	(16,759)	965,000	150	87
Idaho	Boise	1890	43	83,564	(216,432)	944,000	12	54
Illinois	Springfield	1818	21	56,345	(145,934)	11,418,000	205	83
Indiana	Indianapolis	1816	19	36,185	(93,720)	5,490,000	153	64
Iowa	Des Moines	1846	29	56,275	(145,753)	2,913,000	52	59
Kansas	Topeka	1861	34	82,277	(213,098)	2,363,000	29	67
Kentucky	Frankfort	1792	15	40,409	(104,660)	3,661,000	92	51
Louisiana	Baton Rouge	1812	18	47,752	(123,677)	4,204,000	94	69
Maine	Augusta	1820	23	33,265	(86,156)	1,125,000	36	48
Maryland	Annapolis	1788	7	10,460	(27,092)	4,216,000	429	80
Massachusetts	Boston	1788	6	8,284	(21,456)	5,737,000	733	84
Michigan	Lansing	1837	26	58,527	(151,586)	9,258,000	163	71
Minnesota	St. Paul	1858	32	84,402	(218,601)	4,077,000	51	67
Mississippi	Jackson	1817	20	47,689	(123,515)	2,521,000	53	47
Missouri	Jefferson City	1821	24	69,697	(180,516)	4,917,000	71	68
Montana	Helena	1889	41	147,046	(380,848)	787,000	5	53
Nebraska	Lincoln	1867	37	77,355	(200,350)	1,570,000	21	63
Nevada	Carson City	1864	36	110,561	(286,352)	799,000	7	85
New Hampshire	Concord	1788	9	9,279	(24,032)	921,000	102	52
New Jersey	Trenton	1787	3	7,787	(20,169)	7,364,000	986	89
New Mexico	Santa Fe	1912	47	121,593	(314,925)	1,300,000	11	72
New York	Albany	1788	11	49,108	(127,189)	17,557,000	371	85
North Carolina	Raleigh	1789	12	52,669	(136,413)	5,874,000	120	48
North Dakota	Bismarck	1889	39	70,702	(183,119)	653,000	9	49
Ohio	Columbus	1803	17	41,330	(107,044)	10,797,000	263	73
Oklahoma	Oklahoma City	1907	46	69,956	(181,186)	3,025,000	44	67
Oregon	Salem	1859	33	97,073	(251,419)	2,633,000	27	68
Pennsylvania	Harrisburg	1787	2	45,308	(117,348)	11,867,000	264	69
Rhode Island	Providence	1790	13	1,212	(3,140)	947,000	898	87
South Carolina	Columbia	1788	8	31,113	(80,582)	3,119,000	103	54
South Dakota	Pierre	1889	40	77,116	(199,730)	690,000	9	46
Tennessee	Nashville	1796	16	42,144	(109,152)	4,591,000	112	60
Texas	Austin	1845	28	266,807	(691,030)	14,228,000	54	80
Utah	Salt Lake City	1896	45	84,899	(219,889)	1,461,000	18	84
Vermont	Montpelier	1791	14	9,614	(24,900)	511,000	55	34
Virginia	Richmond	1788	10	40,767	(105,586)	5,346,000	135	66
Washington	Olympia	1889	42	68,139	(176,479)	4,130,000	62	74
West Virginia	Charleston	1863	35	24,231	(62,759)	1,950,000	81	36
Wisconsin	Madison	1848	30	56,153	(145,436)	4,705,000	86	64
Wyoming	Cheyenne	1890	44	97,809	(253,326)	471,000	5	63
District of Columbia				69	(178)	638,000	10,127	100
Puerto Rico	San Juan			3,515	(9,103)	3,188,000	922	67

*Based on land area rather than total area per state

The Federal Budget   1940–1982

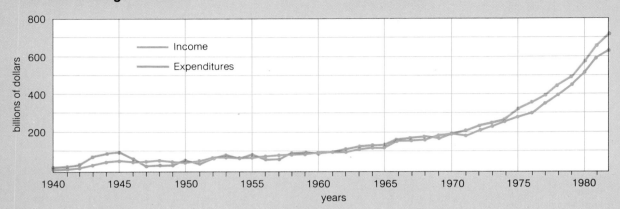

billions of dollars

Income
Expenditures

years

The Federal Budget: Sources of Income   1940–1980

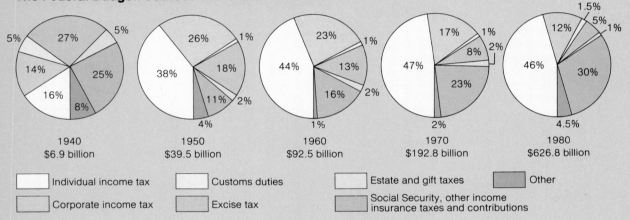

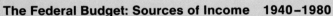

1940	1950	1960	1970	1980
$6.9 billion	$39.5 billion	$92.5 billion	$192.8 billion	$626.8 billion

- Individual income tax
- Corporate income tax
- Customs duties
- Excise tax
- Estate and gift taxes
- Social Security, other income insurance taxes and contributions
- Other

The Federal Budget: Expenditures   1940–1980

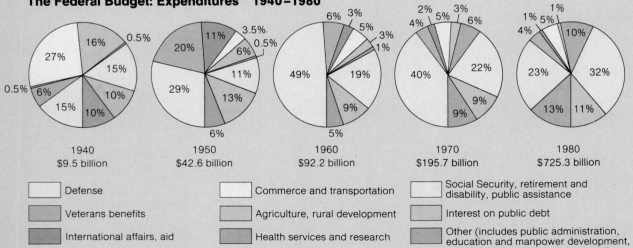

1940	1950	1960	1970	1980
$9.5 billion	$42.6 billion	$92.2 billion	$195.7 billion	$725.3 billion

- Defense
- Veterans benefits
- International affairs, aid
- Commerce and transportation
- Agriculture, rural development
- Health services and research
- Social Security, retirement and disability, public assistance
- Interest on public debt
- Other (includes public administration, education and manpower development, space, resources and environment)

Presidents and Vice-Presidents of the United States

President	Term of Office	Political Party	Born	Died	State Birth—Residence	Occupation other than Politics	Vice-President
1. George Washington	1789–1797	None	1732	1799	Virginia	Planter, soldier	John Adams
2. John Adams	1797–1801	Federalist	1735	1826	Massachusetts	Lawyer	Thomas Jefferson
3. Thomas Jefferson	1801–1809	Republican	1743	1826	Virginia	Lawyer	Aaron Burr George Clinton
4. James Madison	1809–1817	Republican	1751	1836	Virginia	Lawyer	George Clinton Elbridge Gerry
5. James Monroe	1817–1825	Republican	1758	1831	Virginia	Lawyer	Daniel D. Tompkins
6. John Quincy Adams	1825–1829	Nat. Rep.	1767	1848	Massachusetts	Lawyer	John C. Calhoun
7. Andrew Jackson	1829–1837	Democratic	1767	1845	S.C.—Tenn.	Lawyer, soldier	John C. Calhoun Martin Van Buren
8. Martin Van Buren	1837–1841	Democratic	1782	1862	New York	Lawyer	Richard M. Johnson
9. William Henry Harrison	1841	Whig	1773	1841	Va.—Ohio	Soldier	John Tyler
10. John Tyler	1841–1845	Whig	1790	1862	Virginia	Lawyer	
11. James K. Polk	1845–1849	Democratic	1795	1849	N.C.—Tenn.	Lawyer	George M. Dallas
12. Zachary Taylor	1849–1850	Whig	1784	1850	Va.—La.	Soldier	Millard Fillmore
13. Millard Fillmore	1850–1853	Whig	1800	1874	New York	Lawyer	
14. Franklin Pierce	1853–1857	Democratic	1804	1869	New Hampshire	Lawyer	William R.D. King
15. James Buchanan	1857–1861	Democratic	1791	1868	Pennsylvania	Lawyer	John C. Breckinridge
16. Abraham Lincoln	1861–1865	Republican	1809	1865	Ky.—Ill.	Lawyer	Hannibal Hamlin Andrew Johnson
17. Andrew Johnson	1865–1869	Republican	1808	1875	N.C.—Tenn.	Tailor	
18. Ulysses S. Grant	1869–1877	Republican	1822	1885	Ohio—Ill.	Soldier	Schuyler Colfax Henry Wilson
19. Rutherford B. Hayes	1877–1881	Republican	1822	1893	Ohio	Lawyer	William A. Wheeler
20. James A. Garfield	1881	Republican	1831	1881	Ohio	Teacher, lawyer	Chester A. Arthur
21. Chester A. Arthur	1881–1885	Republican	1829	1886	Vt.—N.Y.	Lawyer	
22. Grover Cleveland	1885–1889	Democratic	1837	1908	N.J.—N.Y.	Lawyer	Thomas A. Hendricks
23. Benjamin Harrison	1889–1893	Republican	1833	1901	Ohio—Ind.	Lawyer	Levi P. Morton
24. Grover Cleveland	1893–1897	Democratic	1837	1908	N.J.—N.Y.	Lawyer	Adlai E. Stevenson
25. William McKinley	1897–1901	Republican	1843	1901	Ohio	Lawyer	Garret A. Hobart Theodore Roosevelt
26. Theodore Roosevelt	1901–1909	Republican	1858	1919	New York	Rancher, writer	Charles W. Fairbanks
27. William Howard Taft	1909–1913	Republican	1857	1930	Ohio	Lawyer	James S. Sherman
28. Woodrow Wilson	1913–1921	Democratic	1856	1924	Va.—N.J.	Lawyer, teacher	Thomas R. Marshall
29. Warren G. Harding	1921–1923	Republican	1865	1923	Ohio	Journalist	Calvin Coolidge
30. Calvin Coolidge	1923–1929	Republican	1872	1933	Vt.—Mass.	Lawyer	Charles G. Dawes
31. Herbert C. Hoover	1929–1933	Republican	1874	1964	Iowa—Cal.	Engineer	Charles Curtis
32. Franklin D. Roosevelt	1933–1945	Democratic	1882	1945	New York	Lawyer	John N. Garner Henry A. Wallace Harry S. Truman
33. Harry S. Truman	1945–1953	Democratic	1884	1972	Missouri	Merchant	Alben W. Barkley
34. Dwight D. Eisenhower	1953–1961	Republican	1890	1969	Tex.—N.Y., Pa.	Soldier	Richard M. Nixon
35. John F. Kennedy	1961–1963	Democratic	1917	1963	Massachusetts	Writer	Lyndon B. Johnson
36. Lyndon B. Johnson	1963–1969	Democratic	1908	1973	Texas	Teacher, rancher	Hubert H. Humphrey
37. Richard M. Nixon	1969–1974	Republican	1913		Cal.—N.Y., Cal.	Lawyer	Spiro T. Agnew Gerald R. Ford
38. Gerald R. Ford	1974–1977	Republican	1913		Neb.—Mich.	Lawyer	Nelson A. Rockefeller
39. Jimmy (James Earl) Carter	1977–1981	Democratic	1924		Georgia	Farmer	Walter F. Mondale
40. Ronald Reagan	1981–	Republican	1911		Ill.—Cal.	Actor	George Bush

HISTORIC DOCUMENTS

On arriving at Plymouth, the Pilgrims signed an agreement called the Mayflower Compact. It was the first document in the English colonies to describe the type of government that would be observed there. The Mayflower Compact was based on English laws and the consent of those to be governed.

THE MAYFLOWER COMPACT

This day, before we came to harbor, observing some not well affected to unity and concord, but gave some appearance of faction [disagreement], it was thought good there should be an association and agreement that we should combine together in one body, and to submit to such government and governors as we should by common consent agree to make and choose, and set our hands to this that follows word for word.

In the name of God, Amen. We whose names are underwritten, the loyal subjects of our dread sovereign lord, King James, by the grace of God, of Great Britain, France, and Ireland, King, Defender of the Faith, etc.

Having undertaken for the glory of God, and advancement of the Christian faith, and honor of our king and country, a voyage to plant the first colony in the northern parts of Virginia, do by these present, solemnly and mutually, in the presence of God and one another, covenant [agree] and combine ourselves together into a civil body politic, for our better ordering and preservation and furtherance of the ends aforesaid, and by virtue hereof to enact, constitute, and frame such just and equal laws, ordinances, acts, constitutions, and offices from time to time as shall be thought most meet [good] and convenient for the general good of the colony; unto which we promise all due submission and obedience. In witness whereof we have hereunder subscribed our names, Cape Cod, 11th of November, in the year of the reign of our sovereign lord, King James, of England, France, and Ireland 18, and of Scotland 54. Anno Domini 1620.

On October 14, 1774, the Continental Congress wrote a declaration of rights for the colonies. The ideas and problems mentioned in this document can be seen in the Declaration of Independence, signed two years later, and the Constitution. The colonists rejected British rule, but not traditions of English law and ideas about government. Part of the document is printed here.

DECLARATION AND RESOLVES OF THE CONTINENTAL CONGRESS

The good people of the colonies, justly alarmed at the arbitrary proceedings of Parliament and administration, have [chosen] deputies to meet in the city of Philadelphia in order that their religion, laws, and liberties may not be subverted:

The deputies so appointed being now assembled, in a full and free representation of these colonies, do, as Englishmen, their ancestors, in like cases have usually done, declare,

That the inhabitants of the English colonies in North America, by the immutable [changeless] laws of nature, and the principles of the English constitution, have the following rights:

1. That they are entitled to life, liberty, and property, and they have never ceded to any sovereign power whatever a right to dispose of either without their consent.

2. That our ancestors, who first settled these colonies, were at the time of their emigration from the mother country entitled to all the rights, liberties, and immunities of free and natural-born subjects within the Realm of England.

3. That by such emigration they by no means surrendered or lost any of those rights, but that they were, and their descendants now are, entitled to the exercise and enjoyment of all that their circumstances enable them to enjoy.

4. That the foundation of English liberty, and of all free government, is a right of the people to participate in their legislative council. As the English colonists are not represented, and from their circumstances cannot properly be represented in the British Parliament, they are entitled to a free and exclusive power of legislation in their provincial legislatures in all cases of taxation and internal polity [government] subject only to the negative [veto] of their sovereign. We cheerfully consent to such acts of the British Parliament as are restrained to the regulation of our external commerce, for the purpose of securing the commercial advantages of the whole empire to the mother country, and the commercial benefits of its respective members; excluding every idea of taxation, internal or external, for raising revenue on the subjects in America without their consent.

5. That the colonies are entitled to the common law of England, and more especially to the great privilege of being tried by their peers according to the course of that law.

6. That they are entitled to the benefit of such English statutes [laws] as existed at the time of their colonization.

7. That these, His Majesty's colonies, are likewise entitled to all the immunities and privileges granted to them by royal charters, or secured by their codes of provincial laws.

8. That they have a right peaceably to assemble, consider their grievances, and petition the King.

9. That the keeping of a standing army in these colonies, in times of peace, without the consent of the legislature of that colony in which such army is kept is against law.

10. It is necessary to good government, and rendered essential by the English constitution, that the branches of the legislature be independent of each other; that therefore, the exercise of legislative power in several colonies, by a council appointed by the Crown, is unconstitutional, dangerous, and destructive to the freedom of American legislation.

Resolved that the following acts of Parliament are infringements [trespasses] and violations of the rights of colonists; and that the repeal of them is necessary in order to restore harmony between Great Britain and the American colonies:

The acts that impose duties for the purpose of raising revenue in America, deprive the American subject of trial by jury, require oppressive security from a claimant of ships and goods seized before he shall be allowed to defend his property, and are subversive of American rights.

Also the three acts passed in Parliament for stopping the port and blocking up the harbor of Boston, and for altering the charter and government of Massachusetts Bay.

To these grievous acts and measures Americans cannot submit, but in hopes that their fellow subjects in Great Britain will, on a revision of them, restore us to that state in which both countries found prosperity, we have for the present only resolved to pursue peaceable measures.

THE DECLARATION OF INDEPENDENCE

When, in the course of human events, it becomes necessary for one people to dissolve the political bands which have connected them with another, and to assume, among the powers of the earth, the separate and equal station to which the laws of nature and of nature's God entitle them, a decent respect to the opinions of mankind requires that they should declare the causes which impel them to the separation.

When a group of people find it necessary to dissolve their government, they should explain their reasons for doing so.

We hold these truths to be self-evident, that all men are created equal, that they are endowed by their Creator with certain unalienable rights, that among these are life, liberty, and the pursuit of happiness. That, to secure these rights, governments are instituted among men, deriving their just powers from the consent of the governed. That, whenever any form of government becomes destructive of these ends, it is the right of the people to alter or to abolish it, and to institute new government, laying its foundation on such principles, and organizing its powers in such form, as to them shall seem most likely to effect their safety and happiness.

All humans are born with certain rights they cannot give away ("unalienable"). No one has the right to take away from another person life, liberty, or the opportunity to seek happiness. In the 1700s, these rights were understood to include the right to own property as well.

Humans create governments to protect their rights. The power of the government comes from the consent of the people. If a government abuses their rights, people are justified in changing it. The new government should be planned in the form that seems most likely to provide safety and happiness to the people it governs.

Prudence, indeed, will dictate that governments long established should not be changed for light and transient causes; and, accordingly, all experience has shown that mankind are more disposed to suffer, while evils are sufferable, than to right themselves by abolishing the forms to which they are accustomed.

A government should be abolished only for very good reasons. Most people will suffer as long as they can before they take drastic measures against their government.

But when a long train of abuses and usurpations, pursuing invariably the same object, evinces a design to reduce them under absolute despotism, it is their right, it is their duty, to throw off such government, and to provide new guards for their future security. Such has been the patient sufferance of these colonies; and such is now the necessity which constrains them to alter their former systems of government. The history of the present King of Great Britain is a history of repeated injuries and usurpations, all having in direct object the establishment of an absolute

When a government deprives its people of their natural rights, the people have a duty to break away from it. The American colonists had reached the end of their patience. In the following paragraphs, they accuse King George III of tyranny and list specific examples of his abuses.

tyranny over these states. To prove this, let facts be submitted to a candid world.

He has refused his assent to laws the most wholesome and necessary for the public good.

He has forbidden his governors to pass laws of immediate and pressing importance, unless suspended in their operation till his assent should be obtained; and when so suspended, he has utterly neglected to attend to them.

He has refused to pass other laws for the accommodation of large districts of people, unless those people would relinquish the right of representation in the legislature; a right inestimable to them and formidable to tyrants only.

He has called together legislative bodies at places unusual, uncomfortable, and distant from the depository of their public records, for the sole purpose of fatiguing them into compliance with his measures.

He has dissolved representative houses repeatedly, for opposing with manly firmness his invasions on the rights of the people.

He has refused for a long time, after such dissolutions, to cause others to be elected; whereby the legislative powers, incapable of annihilation, have returned to the people at large for their exercise; the state remaining in the meantime exposed to all the dangers of invasion from without, and convulsions within.

He has endeavored to prevent the population of these states; for that purpose obstructing the laws for naturalization of foreigners; refusing to pass others to encourage their migrations hither, and raising the conditions of new appropriations of lands.

He has obstructed the administration of justice, by refusing his assent to laws for establishing judiciary powers.

He has made judges dependent on his will alone, for the tenure of their offices, and the amount and payment of their salaries.

He has erected a multitude of new offices, and sent hither swarms of officers to harass our people, and eat out their substance.

The king had refused to agree to laws that the colonial legislatures proposed for the welfare of the colonists. He felt that some of the laws would be harmful to Britain.

Partly because of poor communications, it sometimes took months or even years for laws proposed in the colonies to be approved by the king. In the meantime, the royal governors could not enforce the laws.

People in newly settled areas might have to wait for years before they were given representation in the legislatures.

To discourage participation in government, the royal governors sometimes had the legislatures meet in inconvenient places.

The king or royal governors often dismissed the legislatures when the colonists proposed laws the monarch did not like.

After dismissing the legislatures, the royal governors sometimes waited a long time before calling new elections.

The colonists wanted to encourage new settlement, especially in the West. In 1763 King George claimed all the western lands. In 1774 he raised the price for buying land, thus discouraging settlement. In 1773 the king said foreign immigrants could not become colonial citizens.

Britain had objected to North Carolina's proposed court system. As a result, the colony had no courts for several years.

The king appointed judges and controlled their salaries. Judges were therefore under pressure to do what the king wanted.

The colonists were taxed to support officials sent by the king. The Americans especially resented the royal tax agents.

He has kept among us, in times of peace, standing armies, without the consent of our legislatures.

He has affected to render the military independent of and superior to the civil power.

He has combined with others to subject us to a jurisdiction foreign to our constitution, and unacknowledged by our laws; giving his assent to their acts of pretended legislation:

For quartering large bodies of armed troops among us;

For protecting them, by a mock trial, from punishment for any murders which they should commit on the inhabitants of these states;

For cutting off our trade with all parts of the world;

For imposing taxes on us without our consent;

For depriving us, in many cases, of the benefits of trial by jury;

For transporting us beyond seas to be tried for pretended offenses;

For abolishing the free system of English laws in a neighboring province, establishing therein an arbitrary government, and enlarging its boundaries, so as to render it at once an example and fit instrument for introducing the same absolute rule into these colonies;

For taking away our charters, abolishing our most valuable laws, and altering fundamentally the forms of our governments;

For suspending our own legislatures, and declaring themselves invested with power to legislate for us in all cases whatsoever.

He has abdicated government here, by declaring us out of his protection, and waging war against us.

He has plundered our seas, ravaged our coasts, burnt our towns, and destroyed the lives of our people.

He is at this time transporting large armies of foreign mercenaries to complete the works of death, desolation, and tyranny already begun with circumstances of cruelty and perfidy scarcely paralleled in the most barbarous ages, and totally unworthy the head of a civilized nation.

He has constrained our fellow citizens, taken captive on the high seas, to bear arms against their country, to become the executioners of their

The colonists wanted King George to send home the troops who had come to America during the French and Indian War.

In Massachusetts, the head of the British army in America was appointed governor.

Parliament had claimed the authority to make laws for the colonies. The colonists had never consented to this power, but the king had approved it.

The colonists resented having to provide lodging for British troops.

British soldiers accused of crimes in the colonies could be tried in England, where they were likely to escape punishment.

Parliament claimed the right to control trade in the colonies.

Colonists opposed all taxes since the Sugar Act of 1764 as "taxation without representation."

Colonists accused of smuggling could be tried in admiralty courts, which had no juries.

Colonists accused of treason could be taken to Britain for trial.

The Quebec Act of 1774 set up a royal government in Canada much like the former French government there. It also extended the border of Canada to the Ohio River.

In 1774 the king claimed the power to appoint the councilors of Massachusetts. He also appointed judges there.

In 1767 Parliament had suspended the New York Assembly. Parliament then made laws for New York.

After Lexington and Concord, King George had declared the colonies to be in revolt. The colonists claimed that he had given up his legal authority in America by ordering the British army and navy to attack them.

The British army used large bodies of German mercenaries to fight in the colonies. These mercenaries were called Hessians.

The colonists were outraged by impressment of American sailors into the British navy.

THE DECLARATION OF INDEPENDENCE

friends and brethren, or to fall themselves by their hands.

He has excited domestic insurrections among us, and has endeavored to bring on the inhabitants of our frontiers, the merciless Indian savages, whose known rule of warfare is an undistinguished destruction of all ages, sexes, and conditions.

In every stage of these oppressions, we have petitioned for redress in the most humble terms. Our repeated petitions have been answered only by repeated injury. A prince, whose character is thus marked by every act which may define a tyrant, is unfit to be the ruler of a free people.

Nor have we been wanting in attentions to our British brethren. We have warned them from time to time of attempts by their legislature to extend an unwarrantable jurisdiction over us. We have reminded them of the circumstances of our emigration and settlement here. We have appealed to their native justice and magnanimity, and we have conjured them by the ties of our common kindred to disavow these usurpations, which would inevitably interrupt our connections and correspondence. They too have been deaf to the voice of justice and of consanguinity. We must, therefore, acquiesce in the necessity, which denounces our separation, and hold them, as we hold the rest of mankind, enemies in war, in peace, friends.

We, therefore, the representatives of the United States of America, in General Congress assembled, appealing to the Supreme Judge of the world for the rectitude of our intentions, do, in the name and by authority of the good people of these colonies, solemnly publish and declare, that these united colonies are and of right ought to be free and independent states; that they are absolved from all allegiance to the British Crown, and that all political connection between them and the state of Great Britain is and ought to be totally dissolved; and that, as free and independent states, they have full power to levy war, conclude peace, contract alliances, establish commerce, and to do all other acts and things which independent states may of right do. And for the support of this declaration, with a firm reliance on the protection of Divine Providence, we mutually pledge to each other our lives, our fortunes, and our sacred honor.

The British offered freedom to colonial slaves who would join their army. Britain also encouraged the Indians to attack American settlers.

The king had met requests for better treatment with further abuses. A monarch who does not respond to his or her subjects is not fit to rule.

Colonial requests to Parliament had also been spurned. Appeals to the British people brought no relief from the royal abuses. The British people did not appear to feel a sense of kinship with the colonists. Nor did they see the justice of the Americans' complaints. Therefore the colonists would consider them enemies during wartime.

The colonists declare their good intentions and the justice of their arguments. They state their total independence of Great Britain. As a free nation, they can wage war, make peace treaties, and deal with other nations. Finally, the colonists promise to support one another completely.

THE DECLARATION OF INDEPENDENCE

THE CONSTITUTION OF THE UNITED STATES

The text of the Constitution appears to the left below. In this version, spelling, capitalization, and punctuation have been modernized. Brackets in the text mark passages that have been changed or voided by amendments. The words to the right below are comments on the meaning and history of the Constitution.

PREAMBLE

We the people of the United States, in order to form a more perfect Union, establish justice, insure domestic tranquility, provide for the common defense, promote the general welfare, and secure the blessings of liberty to ourselves and our posterity, do ordain and establish this Constitution for the United States of America.

ARTICLE 1

Section 1

All legislative powers herein granted shall be vested in a Congress of the United States, which shall consist of a Senate and House of Representatives.

Section 2

Clause 1. The House of Representatives shall be composed of members chosen every second year by the people of the several states, and the electors in each state shall have the qualifications requisite for electors of the most numerous branch of the state legislature.

Clause 2. No person shall be a representative who shall not have attained to the age of twenty-five years, and been seven years a citizen of the United States, and who shall not, when elected, be an inhabitant of that state in which he shall be chosen.

Clause 3. Representatives and direct taxes shall be apportioned among the several states which may be included within this Union, according to their respective numbers, [which shall be determined by adding to the whole number of free persons, including those bound to service for a term of years, and excluding Indians not taxed, three fifths of all other persons]. The actual enumeration shall be made within three years after the first meeting of the Congress of the United States, and within every subsequent term of ten years, in such manner as they shall by law direct. The number of representatives shall not exceed one for every thirty

PREAMBLE

The Preamble lists the purposes of the new government, based on the will of the people. Following the Preamble are the first three articles of the Constitution. They divide the powers of government among three distinct branches. They create a system of checks and balances as shown in the chart on page 206.

ARTICLE 1. The Legislative Branch

Section 1. A Two-Part Congress

The legislative branch is empowered to make laws. Its powers are given to both the Senate and the House of Representatives.

Section 2. The House of Representatives

Clause 1. Elections and Voters. All the members of the House are elected every two years. Voters for House members must be qualified to vote in certain state elections.

Clause 2. Qualifications of Representatives

Clause 3. Apportionment of Representatives. The number of Representatives from each state is based on the state's population. Originally, indentured servants ("those bound to service") were counted as if they were free. But slaves ("all other persons") were counted as three fifths of a person. Thus it took 500 slaves to equal 300 free persons in deciding numbers of Representatives. When slavery was ended by the Thirteenth Amendment in 1865, the three-fifths rule became meaningless.

The "actual enumeration," or census, was first made in 1790. It has been repeated every ten years since. Today there is no worry that the number of Representatives might exceed one for every thirty

thousand, but each state shall have at least one representative; [and until such enumeration shall be made, the state of New Hampshire shall be entitled to choose three, Massachusetts eight, Rhode Island and Providence Plantations one, Connecticut five, New York six, New Jersey four, Pennsylvania eight, Delaware one, Maryland six, Virginia ten, North Carolina five, South Carolina five, and Georgia three].

Clause 4. When vacancies happen in the representation from any state, the executive authority thereof shall issue writs of election to fill such vacancies.

Clause 5. The House of Representatives shall choose their speaker and other officers, and shall have the sole power of impeachment.

Section 3

Clause 1. The Senate of the United States shall be composed of two senators from each state, [chosen by the legislature thereof,] for six years; and each senator shall have one vote.

Clause 2. Immediately after they shall be assembled in consequence of the first election, they shall be divided as equally as may be into three classes. The seats of the senators of the first class shall be vacated at the expiration of the second year, of the second class at the expiration of the fourth year, and of the third class at the expiration of the sixth year, so that one third may be chosen every second year; [and if vacancies happen by resignation, or otherwise, during the recess of the legislature of any state, the executive thereof may make temporary appointments until the next meeting of the legislature, which shall then fill such vacancies].

Clause 3. No person shall be a senator who shall not have attained to the age of thirty years, and been nine years a citizen of the United States, and who shall not, when elected, be an inhabitant of that state for which he shall be chosen.

Clause 4. The Vice-President of the United States shall be president of the Senate, but shall have no vote, unless they be equally divided. •

Clause 5. The Senate shall choose their other officers and also a president pro tempore, in the absence of the Vice-President, or when he shall exercise the office of President of the United States.

thousand persons. A typical House member now represents about five hundred thousand persons.

Clause 4. Filling Vacancies. The "executive authority" refers to a state governor. If a House seat becomes vacant between regular elections, the governor is empowered to call a special election to fill the seat.

Clause 5. Officers; Power of Impeachment. The Speaker of the House is the leading officer of the House. Only the House can bring impeachment charges. (See Section 3, Clauses 6 and 7, below.)

Section 3. The Senate

Clause 1. Elections. Senators were elected by state legislatures until the Seventeenth Amendment, ratified in 1913. Since then, Senators have been chosen directly by the voters of each state.

Clause 2. Overlapping Terms of Office; Filling Vacancies. By dividing Senators into three classes, or groups, the Constitution set up a system of overlapping terms in office. Every two years, one third of the Senators must leave office or stand for reelection. Thus the Senate changes somewhat every two years, even though Senators are elected to six-year terms.

The method of filling vacancies in the Senate was changed by the Seventeenth Amendment. It gave the power of choosing replacements to the voters of each state.

Clause 3. Qualifications of Senators

Clause 4. President of the Senate. The Vice-President serves as president of the Senate, but votes only in case of a tie.

Clause 5. Election of Senate Officers. The Senate elects officers, including a temporary president of the Senate. The president pro tempore, or pro tem, leads meetings when the Vice-President is absent.

Clause 6. The Senate shall have the sole power to try all impeachments. When sitting for that purpose, they shall be on oath or affirmation. When the President of the United States is tried, the Chief Justice shall preside. And no person shall be convicted without the concurrence of two thirds of the members present.

Clause 7. Judgment in cases of impeachment shall not extend further than to removal from office, and disqualification to hold and enjoy any office of honor, trust, or profit under the United States; but the party convicted shall nevertheless be liable and subject to indictment, trial, judgment, and punishment, according to law.

Section 4

Clause 1. The times, places, and manner of holding elections for senators and representatives shall be prescribed in each state by the legislature thereof; but the Congress may at any time by law make or alter such regulations, [except as to the places of choosing senators].

Clause 2. The Congress shall assemble at least once in every year, [and such meeting shall be on the first Monday in December,] unless they shall by law appoint a different day.

Section 5

Clause 1. Each house shall be the judge of the elections, returns, and qualifications of its own members, and a majority of each shall constitute a quorum to do business; but a smaller number may adjourn from day to day, and may be authorized to compel the attendance of absent members, in such manner and under such penalties as each house may provide.

Clause 2. Each house may determine the rules of its proceedings, punish its members for disorderly behavior, and, with the concurrence of two thirds, expel a member.

Clause 3. Each house shall keep a journal of its proceedings and from time to time publish the same, excepting such parts as may in their judgment require secrecy; and the yeas and nays of the members of either house on any question shall, at

Clause 6. Impeachment Trials. The Senate serves as a jury in impeachment cases. A conviction requires a two-thirds vote of the members present. In 1868 the House impeached President Andrew Johnson, but the Senate acquitted him. In 1974 the House considered impeaching President Richard M. Nixon. Nixon resigned before the House made a final decision about impeachment.

Clause 7. Penalty for Conviction. If an impeached person is convicted, the person will be removed from office (see Article 2, Section 4) and barred from other federal office. The Senate cannot impose further punishment, but the convicted person can then be tried in a regular court. The Senate has convicted only four persons, all judges. They were removed from office but not tried in regular courts.

Section 4. Times of Elections and Meetings

Clause 1. Elections. Each state regulates its own congressional elections, but Congress can change the regulations. In 1872 Congress required that every state hold congressional elections on the same day.

Clause 2. Meetings. Congress must meet once a year. The Twentieth Amendment, ratified in 1933, changed the first day of the meeting to January 3, unless Congress specifies a different day.

Section 5. Basics of Organization

Clause 1. Members; Attendance. Each house can judge whether new members have been elected fairly and are qualified to serve. A quorum is the minimum number of members who can act for all. Discussion and debate can go on without a quorum. A quorum is required for voting by either house, however.

Clause 2. Determining Procedures. Each house can set up its own rules of conducting business.

Clause 3. Written Records. Since 1873 the journals of the House and Senate have been published together in the *Congressional Record*. It appears each day when Congress is meeting. A member of either house may insert a speech in the published

the desire of one fifth of those present, be entered on the journal.

Clause 4. Neither house, during the session of Congress, shall, without the consent of the other, adjourn for more than three days, nor to any other place than that in which the two houses shall be sitting.

Section 6

Clause 1. The senators and representatives shall receive a compensation for their services, to be ascertained by law, and paid out of the Treasury of the United States. They shall in all cases, except treason, felony, and breach of the peace, be privileged from arrest during their attendance at the session of their respective houses, and in going to and returning from the same; and for any speech or debate in either house, they shall not be questioned in any other place.

Clause 2. No senator or representative shall, during the time for which he was elected, be appointed to any civil office under the authority of the United States which shall have been created, or the emoluments whereof shall have been increased, during such time; and no person holding any office under the United States shall be a member of either house during his continuance in office.

Section 7

Clause 1. All bills for raising revenue shall originate in the House of Representatives; but the Senate may propose or concur with amendments as on other bills.

Clause 2. Every bill which shall have passed the House of Representatives and the Senate shall, before it becomes a law, be presented to the President of the United States. If he approve he shall sign it, but if not, he shall return it, with his objections, to that house in which it shall have originated, who shall enter the objections at large on their journal and proceed to reconsider it. If, after such reconsideration, two thirds of that house shall agree to pass the bill, it shall be sent, together with the objections, to the other house, by which it shall likewise be reconsidered, and, if approved by

Record even though the speech was not actually delivered on the floor of the House or Senate.

Clause 4. Adjournment. Both houses must agree to any adjournment longer than three days.

Section 6. Special Rights and Restrictions

Clause 1. Salaries and Privileges. The members of Congress can by law set their own salaries. When Congress is in session, members cannot be arrested except on certain criminal charges. Thus the work of Congress cannot be disrupted by lawsuits against Senators and Representatives. In particular, the members of Congress cannot be sued for "any speech or debate in either house." While taking part in the work of Congress, members can write or say anything about anyone without fear of being sued for libel or slander.

Clause 2. Employment Restrictions. Members of Congress cannot create new federal jobs or increase the "emoluments," or payments, for old ones and then leave Congress to take those jobs. Nor can anyone holding a federal job outside Congress serve at the same time as a member of Congress. This restriction prevents the members of Congress from simultaneously working for other branches of the federal government.

Section 7. Procedures for Making Laws

Clause 1. Tax Bills. All tax bills must begin in the House. The Senate, however, can thoroughly revise such bills.

Clause 2. Submitting Bills to the President. After Congress passes a bill, it goes to the President. The bill can then become a law in one of three ways. First, the President may approve the bill and sign it. Second, the President may veto the bill and return it to Congress with objections. If Congress is able to override the President's veto by a two-thirds vote of both houses, the bill becomes law. Third, the President may do nothing. In that case the bill becomes law after 10 days (not counting Sundays), provided Congress is in session at that time.

The bill can fail to become law in two ways. First, the President may veto it. If Congress is unable to

two thirds of that house, it shall become a law. But in all such cases the votes of both houses shall be determined by yeas and nays, and the names of the persons voting for and against the bill shall be entered on the journal of each house respectively. If any bill shall not be returned by the President within ten days (Sundays excepted) after it shall have been presented to him, the same shall be a law, in like manner as if he had signed it, unless the Congress by their adjournment prevent its return, in which case it shall not be a law.

Clause 3. Every order, resolution, or vote to which the concurrence of the Senate and House of Representatives may be necessary (except on a question of adjournment) shall be presented to the President of the United States; and before the same shall take effect, shall be approved by him, or being disapproved by him, shall be repassed by two thirds of the Senate and House of Representatives, according to the rules and limitations prescribed in the case of a bill.

override the veto, the bill dies. Second, the President may do nothing. If Congress adjourns within 10 days, the bill dies. This method is called a pocket veto. A President may use it to avoid an open veto of a controversial bill.

Clause 3. Submitting Other Measures to the President. If other measures require agreement by both houses and are in effect bills, they must go to the President. Thus Congress cannot avoid submitting bills to the President by calling them orders or resolutions. When such measures reach the President, they are treated as bills.

Section 8

The Congress shall have power:

Clause 1. To lay and collect taxes, duties, imposts, and excises, to pay the debts and provide for the common defense and general welfare of the United States; but all duties, imposts, and excises shall be uniform throughout the United States;

Clause 2. To borrow money on the credit of the United States;

Clause 3. To regulate commerce with foreign nations, and among the several states, and with the Indian tribes;

Clause 4. To establish a uniform rule of naturalization and uniform laws on the subject of bankruptcies throughout the United States;

Clause 5. To coin money, regulate the value thereof, and of foreign coin, and fix the standard of weights and measures;

Clause 6. To provide for the punishment of counterfeiting the securities and current coin of the United States;

Clause 7. To establish post offices and post roads;

Section 8. Powers Granted to Congress

Clause 1. Taxation. Congress can impose "duties," taxes on imported goods. But Congress cannot tax exports. (See Section 9, Clause 5, below.) "Excises" are taxes on making, selling, or using items such as cigarettes within the nation. "Imposts" are taxes of any sort.

Clause 2. Borrowing

Clause 3. Regulating Interstate Trade. This is the "interstate commerce clause," the basis of many federal regulations.

Clause 4. Naturalization; Bankruptcy

Clause 5. Coining Money. The federal government's power to print paper money derives from this clause.

Clause 6. Punishment of Counterfeiting. The "securities" referred to are government bonds.

Clause 7. Providing Postal Service

Clause 8. To promote the progress of science and useful arts, by securing for limited times to authors and inventors the exclusive right to their respective writings and discoveries;

Clause 9. To constitute tribunals inferior to the Supreme Court;

Clause 10. To define and punish piracies and felonies committed on the high seas and offenses against the law of nations;

Clause 11. To declare war, grant letters of marque and reprisal, and make rules concerning captures on land and water;

Clause 12. To raise and support armies, but no appropriation of money to that use shall be for a longer term than two years;

Clause 13. To provide and maintain a navy;

Clause 14. To make rules for the government and regulation of the land and naval forces;

Clause 15. To provide for calling forth the militia to execute the laws of the Union, suppress insurrections, and repel invasions;

Clause 16. To provide for organizing, arming, and disciplining the militia, and for governing such part of them as may be employed in the service of the United States, reserving to the states respectively the appointment of the officers and the authority of training the militia according to the discipline prescribed by Congress;

Clause 17. To exercise exclusive legislation in all cases whatsoever over such district (not exceeding ten miles square) as may, by cession of particular states and the acceptance of Congress, become the seat of the government of the United States, and to exercise like authority over all places purchased by the consent of the legislature of the state in which the same shall be for the erection of forts, magazines, arsenals, dockyards, and other needful buildings; and

Clause 18. To make all laws which shall be necessary and proper for carrying into execution the foregoing powers and all other powers vested by this Constitution in the government of the United States, or in any department or officer thereof.

Clause 8. Encouraging Authors and Inventors. Through this clause authors receive copyrights and inventors receive patents.

Clause 9. Establishing Lower Courts. Federal courts "inferior to the Supreme Court" include district courts and the United States Court of Appeals.

Clause 10. Punishment of Crimes at Sea

Clause 11. Declaring War. "Letters of marque and reprisal" authorize private ships to attack and seize enemy ships.

Clause 12. Raising Armies

Clause 13. Maintaining a Navy

Clause 14. Regulating the Armed Forces

Clause 15. Calling Out the Militia. Congress can empower the President to call out state militia units, now known as the National Guard.

Clause 16. Maintaining the Militia. The federal government and each state government share in providing funds for the National Guard.

Clause 17. Control of Federal Property. Congress makes laws for the District of Columbia and for federal land on which forts, naval bases, and other federal structures stand.

Clause 18. Carrying Out Granted Powers. This clause, known as the "necessary and proper" clause, gives Congress a basis for dealing with matters not specifically named in the Constitution. The clause is also known as the "elastic clause."

Section 9

Clause 1. The migration or importation of such persons as any of the states now existing shall think proper to admit shall not be prohibited by Congress prior to the year 1808, but a tax or duty may be imposed on such importation, not exceeding ten dollars for each person.

Clause 2. The privilege of the writ of habeas corpus shall not be suspended, unless, when in cases of rebellion or invasion, the public safety may require it.

Clause 3. No bill of attainder or ex post facto law shall be passed.

Clause 4. No capitation [or other direct] tax shall be laid, unless in proportion to the census or enumeration hereinbefore directed to be taken.

Clause 5. No tax or duty shall be laid on articles exported from any state.

Clause 6. No preference shall be given by any regulation of commerce or revenue to the ports of one state over those of another; nor shall vessels bound to or from one state be obliged to enter, clear, or pay duties in another.

Clause 7. No money shall be drawn from the Treasury but in consequence of appropriations made by law; and a regular statement and account of the receipts and expenditures of all public money shall be published from time to time.

Clause 8. No title of nobility shall be granted by the United States. And no person holding any office of profit or trust under them shall, without the consent of the Congress, accept of any present, emolument, office, or title of any kind whatever from any king, prince, or foreign state.

Section 9. Powers Denied to Congress

Clause 1. Ending the Slave Trade. Congress was forbidden to end the importing of slaves before 1808. In that year, Congress declared that further importing of slaves was illegal.

Clause 2. Suspending the Writ of Habeas Corpus. A writ of habeas corpus is a legal order saying that a person who is held in custody must be brought into court so that a judge can decide whether the person is being held illegally. During the Civil War (a case of "rebellion or invasion"), President Abraham Lincoln suspended the right to habeas corpus in some areas.

Clause 3. Imposing Certain Penalties. A "bill of attainder" allows a person to be punished without a jury trial. An "ex post facto law" allows a person to be punished for an act that was not illegal when it was committed.

Clause 4. Taxing Individuals Unfairly. A "capitation tax," also known as a "head tax," is paid by individuals directly to the government. This clause requires that any such tax be divided fairly among the states according to their population. The Sixteenth Amendment, ratified in 1913, prevents this clause from being applied to income taxes.

Clause 5. Taxing Exports. Here "exported" means sent out of a state, whether to another state or to another country.

Clause 6. Taxing Trade Unfairly; Allowing Ships to Be Taxed in Trade Between States

Clause 7. Unlawful Spending. The federal government can spend money only when Congress authorizes the spending. Federal spending and receipts must be recorded and published.

Clause 8. Creating Titles of Nobility; Allowing Gifts from Foreign Countries Without Permission. Congress cannot give anyone a title such as duchess or count. Congress has passed laws letting federal officials accept small gifts from foreign countries. Larger gifts become the property of the United States government.

Section 10

Clause 1. No state shall enter into any treaty, alliance, or confederation; grant letters of marque and reprisal; coin money; emit bills of credit; make anything but gold and silver coin a tender in payment of debts; pass any bill of attainder, ex post facto law, or law impairing the obligation of contracts, or grant any title of nobility.

Clause 2. No state shall, without the consent of the Congress, lay any imposts or duties on imports or exports, except what may be absolutely necessary for executing its inspection laws; and the net produce of all duties and imposts laid by any state on imports or exports shall be for the use of the Treasury of the United States; and all such laws shall be subject to the revision and control of the Congress.

Clause 3. No state shall, without the consent of Congress, lay any duty of tonnage; keep troops or ships of war in time of peace; enter into any agreement or compact with another state or with a foreign power; or engage in war, unless actually invaded, or in such imminent danger as will not admit of delay.

ARTICLE 2

Section 1

Clause 1. The executive power shall be vested in a President of the United States of America. He shall hold his office during the term of four years, and, together with the Vice-President, chosen for the same term, be elected as follows:

Clause 2. Each state shall appoint, in such manner as the legislature thereof may direct, a number of electors, equal to the whole number of senators and representatives to which the state may be entitled in the Congress; but no senator or representative, or person holding an office of trust or profit under the United States, shall be appointed an elector.

Clause 3. [The electors shall meet in their respective states and vote by ballot for two persons, or whom one at least shall not be an inhabitant of

Section 10. Powers Denied to the States

Clause 1. Certain Foreign, Financial, and Legal Dealings. Some of these powers are given exclusively to the federal government. Others are denied to any government, state or federal.

Clause 2. Taxing Imports or Exports Without Permission. Except with the consent of Congress, a state cannot tax any goods entering or leaving the state. The state can charge a small fee, however, to pay for inspection of the goods.

Clause 3. Taxing Ships or Making Military or Diplomatic Arrangements Without Permission. "Tonnage" is the number of tons of cargo a ship can carry. States cannot tax ships that use their ports without the agreement of Congress.

Except with the consent of Congress, a state cannot prepare for war or wage war unless there is a military emergency.

ARTICLE 2. The Executive Branch

Section 1. The Offices of President and Vice-President

Clause 1. The President as Executive; Term of Office. As chief executive, the President is responsible for executing, or carrying out, the laws passed by Congress.

Clause 2. Choosing Electors. This clause set up the electoral college, the group of people who elect the President and Vice-President. At first the electors were chosen mainly by state legislatures. After 1800 the electors were chosen increasingly by popular vote. Today all electors are chosen in this way.

Clause 3. Voting by Electors. Originally each elector voted for two candidates. Either might become President. As a result, the Republican candidate for

the same state with themselves. And they shall make a list of all the persons voted for and of the number of votes for each; which list they shall sign and certify, and transmit sealed to the seat of the government of the United States, directed to the president of the Senate. The president of the Senate shall, in the presence of the Senate and House of Representatives, open all the certificates, and the votes shall then be counted. The person having the greatest number of votes shall be the President, if such number be a majority of the whole number of electors appointed; and if there be more than one who have such majority, and have an equal number of votes, then the House of Representatives shall immediately choose by ballot one of them for President; and if no person have a majority, then from the five highest on the list the said house shall in like manner choose the President. But in choosing the President, the votes shall be taken by states, the representation from each state having one vote; a quorum for this purpose shall consist of a member or members from two thirds of the states, and a majority of all the states shall be necessary to a choice. In every case, after the choice of the President, the person having the greatest number of votes of the electors shall be the Vice-President. But if there should remain two or more who have equal votes, the Senate shall choose from them by ballot the Vice-President.]

Clause 4. The Congress may determine the time of choosing the electors and the day on which they shall give their votes, which day shall be the same throughout the United States.

Clause 5. No person except a natural-born citizen, or a citizen of the United States at the time of the adoption of this Constitution, shall be eligible to the office of President; neither shall any person be eligible to that office who shall not have attained to the age of thirty-five years and been fourteen years a resident within the United States.

Clause 6. In case of the removal of the President from office, or of his death, resignation, or inability to discharge the powers and duties of the said office, the same shall devolve on the Vice-President, and the Congress may by law provide for the case of removal, death, resignation, or in-

President in 1800, Thomas Jefferson, received the same number of electoral votes as the Republican candidate for Vice-President, Aaron Burr. The choice was then left to the House of Representatives, which finally chose Jefferson.

To prevent similar ties between candidates for President and Vice-President, Congress passed the Twelfth Amendment in 1803. The amendment was ratified in June 1804, before the next presidential election. It required electors to cast one ballot for President and a separate ballot for Vice-President.

Clause 4. Time of Elections. Congress has decided that presidential elections are to be held every four years. The people vote on the Tuesday following the first Monday of November. Electoral votes are cast on the Monday after the second Wednesday in December.

Clause 5. Qualifications of the President

Clause 6. Presidential Succession. In 1886 Congress specified that the line of succession would go from the Vice-President to members of the cabinet. In 1947 Congress changed the line of succession to go from the Vice-President to the speaker of the House, then to the president pro tempore of the

ability, both of the President and Vice-President, declaring what officer shall then act as President, and such officer shall act accordingly until the disability be removed or a President shall be elected.

Clause 7. The President shall, at stated times, receive for his services a compensation, which shall neither be increased nor diminished during the period for which he shall have been elected, and he shall not receive within that period any other emolument from the United States or any of them.

Clause 8. Before he enter on the execution of his office, he shall take the following oath or affirmation: "I do solemnly swear (or affirm) that I will faithfully execute the office of President of the United States, and will, to the best of my ability, preserve, protect, and defend the Constitution of the United States."

Senate, and then to the cabinet. The Twenty-fifth Amendment, ratified in 1967, prevents a long vacancy in the office of Vice-President. The amendment also establishes procedures in case the President is disabled.

Clause 7. Presidential Salary

Clause 8. The Oath of Office. The Constitution does not say who will administer the oath. Ordinarily it is the Chief Justice of the Supreme Court. Federal Judge Sarah Hughes administered the oath of office to Lyndon Johnson after President John F. Kennedy's assassination in 1963.

Section 2

Clause 1. The President shall be commander in chief of the army and navy of the United States, and of the militia of the several states when called into actual service of the United States. He may require the opinion, in writing, of the principal officer in each of the executive departments upon any subject relating to the duties of their respective offices. And he shall have power to grant reprieves and pardons for offenses against the United States, except in cases of impeachment.

Clause 2. He shall have power, by and with the advice and consent of the Senate, to make treaties, provided two thirds of the senators present concur; and he shall nominate, and by and with the advice and consent of the Senate, shall appoint ambassadors, other public ministers and consuls, judges of the Supreme Court, and all other officers of the United States whose appointments are not herein otherwise provided for, and which shall be established by law; but the Congress may by law vest the appointment of such inferior officers as they think proper in the President alone, in the courts of law, or in the heads of departments.

Clause 3. The President shall have power to fill up all vacancies that may happen during the recess of the Senate, by granting commissions which shall expire at the end of their next session.

Section 2. Powers Granted to the President

Clause 1. Military Powers; Executive Powers; Reprieves and Pardons. Together, the military powers of the President and of Congress assure civilian control of the armed forces.

The President may grant a reprieve to stop punishment after a trial or a pardon to prevent a trial. In 1974 President Gerald R. Ford issued a pardon to Richard M. Nixon. Nixon then could not be tried on federal charges related to the Watergate scandal.

Clause 2. Treaties and Appointments. The President may make treaties and appointments. This power can be checked by the power of the Senate to reject them.

Clause 3. Temporary Appointments. When the Senate is not in session and cannot confirm appointments, the President may fill vacancies on a temporary basis.

Section 3

He shall from time to time give to the Congress information of the state of the Union, and recommend to their consideration such measures as he shall judge necessary and expedient; he may, on extraordinary occasions, convene both houses, or either of them, and in case of disagreement between them with respect to the time of adjournment, he may adjourn them to such time as he shall think proper; he shall receive ambassadors and other public ministers; he shall take care that the laws be faithfully executed, and shall commission all the officers of the United States.

Section 4

The President, Vice-President, and all civil officers of the United States shall be removed from office on impeachment for, and conviction of, treason, bribery, or other high crimes and misdemeanors.

ARTICLE 3

Section 1

The judicial power of the United States shall be vested in one Supreme Court, and in such inferior courts as the Congress may from time to time ordain and establish. The judges, both of the Supreme and inferior courts, shall hold their offices during good behavior, and shall, at stated times, receive for their services a compensation which shall not be diminished during their continuance in office.

Section 2

Clause 1. The judicial power shall extend to all cases, in law and equity, arising under this Constitution, the laws of the United States, and treaties made, or which shall be made, under their authority; to all cases affecting ambassadors, other public ministers and consuls; to all cases of admiralty and maritime jurisdiction; to controversies to which the United States shall be a party; to controversies between two or more states; [between a state and citizens of another state;] between citizens of different states; between citizens of the same state claiming lands under grants of different states; and between a state, or the citizens thereof, and foreign states, [citizens, or subjects].

Section 3. Duties of the President

The President delivers a State of the Union message to Congress each January. On many occasions, especially in the 1800s, the President has called Congress into special session. No President has needed to adjourn Congress.

The duty of receiving ambassadors fits the President's power to make treaties. The duty to "take care that the laws be faithfully executed" places the President in charge of federal law enforcement.

Section 4. Impeachment

Among the "civil officers" who can be impeached are cabinet members and federal judges.

ARTICLE 3. The Judicial Branch

Section 1. Federal Courts

Congress has established district courts and appeals courts under the Supreme Court.

Congress also has decided from time to time how many justices serve on the Supreme Court. But Congress can neither abolish the Supreme Court nor remove any federal judges unless they are impeached and convicted. Nor can Congress put pressure on judges by lowering their "compensation," or salaries.

Section 2. Jurisdiction of Federal Courts

Clause 1. Types of Cases. This clause names the types of cases that federal courts can rule on. These include "all cases . . . arising under this Constitution." Therefore the Supreme Court can exercise the right of judicial review, as asserted by Chief Justice John Marshall in the case of *Marbury* v. *Madison*. Thus the court can declare a law unconstitutional. First, though, the law must be involved in a lawsuit. The court cannot review a law unless it is presented to the court as part of a case.

Clause 2. In all cases affecting ambassadors, other public ministers and consuls, and those in which a state shall be party, the Supreme Court shall have original jurisdiction. In all the other cases beforementioned, the Supreme Court shall have appellate jurisdiction, both as to law and fact, with such exceptions and under such regulations as the Congress shall make.

Clause 3. The trial of all crimes, except in cases of impeachment, shall be by jury; and such trial shall be held in the state where the said crimes shall have been committed; but when not committed within any state, the trial shall be at such place or places as the Congress may by law have directed.

Section 3

Clause 1. Treason against the United States shall consist only in levying war against them or in adhering to their enemies, giving them aid and comfort. No person shall be convicted of treason unless on the testimony of two witnesses to the same overt act, or on confession in open court.

Clause 2. The Congress shall have power to declare the punishment of treason, but no attainder of treason shall work corruption of blood or forfeiture except during the life of the person attainted.

Clause 2. Original Cases and Appeals Cases. Cases of "original jurisdiction" go directly to the Supreme Court. Cases of "appellate jurisdiction" go first to lower courts. Then, if the lower court proceedings are appealed, the cases go to the Supreme Court. Congress sets the rules for appeal. Nearly all cases heard by the Supreme Court begin in the lower courts.

Clause 3. Cases Requiring Trials by Jury. This clause covers trials involving federal crimes. The clause does not require juries in civil cases, which involve individual rights, or in criminal cases under state laws.

Section 3. Treason

Clause 1. Limits of the Crime. To be convicted of treason against the United States, a person must commit an overt act, one that can be seen. Merely talking or thinking about treason is not a crime.

Clause 2. Limits of the Punishment. "Attainder of treason" and "corruption of blood" refer to punishing the family of a traitor. Such punishment is banned by this clause.

ARTICLE 4

Section 1

Full faith and credit shall be given in each state to the public acts, records, and judicial proceedings of every other state. And the Congress may by general laws prescribe the manner in which such acts, records, and proceedings shall be proved, and the effect thereof.

Section 2

Clause 1. The citizens of each state shall be entitled to all privileges and immunities of citizens in the several states.

Clause 2. A person charged in any state with treason, felony or other crime, who shall flee from jus-

ARTICLE 4. Relations Among the States, the Territories, and the United States

Section 1. Official Acts of the States

Every state must recognize and honor the official acts of other states. Congress can decide what official proofs (for example, marriage certificates) must be accepted from state to state.

Section 2. Privileges and Liabilities of Citizens

Clause 1. Privileges. No state can discriminate against a citizen of another state except in special cases, such as residence requirements for voting or entrance requirements for state colleges.

Clause 2. Liabilities of Fugitive Criminals. If a person commits a crime in one state and then flees to

tice and be found in another state, shall, on demand of the executive authority of the state from which he fled, be delivered up to be removed to the state having jurisdiction of the crime.

Clause 3. [No person held to service or labor in one state under the laws thereof, escaping into another, shall, in consequence of any law or regulation therein, be discharged from such service or labor, but shall be delivered up on claim of the party to whom such service or labor may be due.]

Section 3

Clause 1. New states may be admitted by the Congress into this Union; but no new state shall be formed or erected within the jurisdiction of any other state; nor any state be formed by the junction of two or more states, or parts of states, without the consent of the legislatures of the states concerned as well as of the Congress.

Clause 2. The Congress shall have power to dispose of and make all needful rules and regulations respecting the territory or other property belonging to the United States; and nothing in this Constitution shall be so construed as to prejudice any claims of the United States, or of any particular state.

Section 4

The United States shall guarantee to every state in this Union a republican form of government, and shall protect each of them against invasion, and, on application of the legislature or of the executive (when the legislature cannot be convened), against domestic violence.

ARTICLE 5

The Congress, whenever two thirds of both houses shall deem it necessary, shall propose amendments to this Constitution or, on the application of the legislatures of two thirds of the several states, shall call a convention for proposing amendments, which, in either case, shall be valid, to all intents and purposes, as part of this Constitution when ratified by the legislatures of three

another state and is caught, the governor of the state where the crime took place can demand the person's return.

Clause 3. Liabilities of Fugitive Slaves or Servants. The phrase "held to service or labor" refers to slavery or to service as an indentured servant. The Thirteenth Amendment nullified this clause.

Section 3. Admitting New States and Regulating Territories

Clause 1. New States. Congress can add new states to the Union. New states cannot be formed by dividing existing states (as when Maine separated from Massachusetts in 1820) or by combining parts of existing states unless both Congress and the states involved consent to the changes.

Clause 2. Territories. Besides having power over federal property of various kinds, Congress has the power to govern federal land. This land includes territory not organized into states and also federal land within states.

Section 4. Protection of the States

The federal government promises that each state will have some form of representative government. The federal government also promises to protect each state from invasion. It will send help, when requested, to stop rioting within a state.

ARTICLE 5. Methods of Amending the Constitution

There are two ways to propose amendments to the Constitution. One is by a two-thirds vote of both the House and the Senate. The other way—which has not yet been used—is by a special convention demanded by two thirds of the states.

Once an amendment is proposed, there are two ways to ratify it. First, three fourths of the state legislatures may vote to approve it. Second, special

fourths of the several states, or by conventions in three fourths thereof, as the one or the other mode of ratification may be proposed by the Congress; provided [that no amendment which may be made prior to the year 1808 shall in any manner affect the first and fourth clauses in the ninth section of the first article; and] that no state, without its consent, shall be deprived of its equal suffrage in the Senate.

conventions in three fourths of the states may approve the amendment. This way has been used only once, to ratify the Twenty-first Amendment. Congress decides which method of ratification to use.

The three-fourths requirement for ratification means that 38 states must now approve a proposed amendment before it becomes law.

ARTICLE 6

Clause 1. All debts contracted and engagements entered into before the adoption of this Constitution shall be as valid against the United States under this Constitution as under the Confederation.

Clause 2. This Constitution and the laws of the United States which shall be made in pursuance thereof, and all treaties made, or which shall be made, under the authority of the United States, shall be the supreme law of the land; and the judges in every state shall be bound thereby, anything in the constitution or laws of any state to the contrary notwithstanding.

Clause 3. The senators and representatives beforementioned, and the members of the several state legislatures, and all executive and judicial officers, both of the United States and of the several states, shall be bound by oath or affirmation to support this Constitution; but no religious test shall ever be required as a qualification to any office or public trust under the United States.

ARTICLE 6. Federal Debts and the Supremacy of Federal Laws

Clause 1. Federal Debts. This clause promises that all debts incurred by Congress under the Articles of Confederation will be honored by the United States under the Constitution.

Clause 2. Supremacy of the Constitution and of Federal Laws. The Constitution and federal laws or treaties made under it are the highest laws of the nation. When federal laws are in conflict with state laws or constitutions, state judges must follow the federal laws.

Clause 3. Oaths to Support the Constitution. All federal and all state officials must promise to support the Constitution. But federal officials must not be required to meet any religious standards in order to hold office.

State officials may be required to meet religious standards, but since the 1840s no state has set such requirements for its officials.

ARTICLE 7

The ratification of the conventions of nine states shall be sufficient for the establishment of this Constitution between the states so ratifying the same.

Done in convention by the unanimous consent of the states present the seventeenth day of September in the year of our Lord one thousand seven hundred and eighty-seven, and of the inde-

ARTICLE 7. Ratification of the Constitution

"Conventions" refers to special conventions held in the states to approve or disapprove the Constitution. Nine state conventions voted their approval by June 21, 1788. The Constitution was signed on September 17, 1787, in the 12th year of the country's independence. George Washington signed first as the president of the Philadelphia

pendence of the United States of America the twelfth. In witness whereof we have hereunto subscribed our names,

convention. He was not elected President of the United States until 1789. Of the 55 delegates to the Philadelphia convention, 39 signed the Constitution and 16 did not.

George Washington,
President and deputy from Virginia

New Hampshire
John Langdon
Nicholas Gilman

Massachusetts
Nathaniel Gorham
Rufus King

Connecticut
William Samuel Johnson
Roger Sherman

New York
Alexander Hamilton

New Jersey
William Livingston
David Brearley
William Paterson
Jonathan Dayton

Pennsylvania
Benjamin Franklin
Thomas Mifflin
Robert Morris
George Clymer
Thomas FitzSimons
Jared Ingersoll
James Wilson
Gouverneur Morris

Delaware
George Read
Gunning Bedford, Jr.
John Dickinson
Richard Bassett
Jacob Broom

Maryland
James McHenry
Dan of St. Thomas Jenifer
Daniel Carroll

Virginia
John Blair
James Madison, Jr.

North Carolina
William Blount
Richard Dobbs Spaight
Hugh Williamson

South Carolina
John Rutledge
Charles Cotesworth Pinckney
Charles Pinckney
Pierce Butler

Georgia
William Few
Abraham Baldwin

AMENDMENTS TO THE CONSTITUTION

The first ten amendments, called the Bill of Rights, were proposed as a group in 1789 and ratified in 1791. Other amendments were proposed and ratified one at a time. The dates in parentheses below are the years of ratification.

AMENDMENT 1

Congress shall make no law respecting an establishment of religion or prohibiting the free exercise thereof, or abridging the freedom of speech or of the press, or the right of the people peaceably to assemble and to petition the government for a redress of grievances.

AMENDMENT 1 (1791). Religious and Political Freedoms

Congress cannot establish an official religion or interfere with freedom of worship. It cannot prohibit free speech or other political freedoms.

These freedoms are not absolute, though. They are limited by the rights of others. For example, the right of free speech does not include slander—the spreading of false stories to damage another person's reputation. Nor does the right of free speech include words that present what the Supreme Court has termed a "clear and present danger," such as screaming "fire" in a crowded theater.

AMENDMENT 2

A well-regulated militia being necessary to the security of a free state, the right of the people to keep and bear arms shall not be infringed.

AMENDMENT 2 (1791). The Right to Bear Arms

For the purpose of maintaining a state militia, citizens may keep and bear arms. Congress has prohibited the possession of certain firearms, however, such as sawed-off shotguns and machine guns.

AMENDMENT 3

No soldier shall, in time of peace, be quartered in any house without the consent of the owner, nor in time of war but in a manner to be prescribed by law.

AMENDMENT 3 (1791). The Quartering of Soldiers

In peacetime, soldiers cannot be quartered, or given lodging, in any private home unless the owner consents. In wartime, soldiers can be quartered in private homes, but only as directed by law.

AMENDMENT 4

The right of the people to be secure in their persons, houses, papers, and effects against unreasonable searches and seizures shall not be violated, and no warrants shall issue, but upon probable cause, supported by oath or affirmation, and

AMENDMENT 4 (1791). Freedom from Unreasonable Searches and Seizures

People and their homes and belongings are protected against unreasonable searches and seizures. As a rule, authorities must go before a court and obtain a search warrant before seizing evidence. They must get an arrest warrant before

particularly describing the place to be searched and the persons or things to be seized.

arresting someone. To obtain a legal warrant, the authorities must explain why it is needed, where the search will take place, and who or what will be seized.

AMENDMENT 5

No person shall be held to answer for a capital or otherwise infamous crime unless on a present-ment or indictment of a grand jury, except in cases arising in the land or naval forces, or in the militia, when in actual service in time of war or public danger; nor shall any person be subject for the same offense to be twice put in jeopardy of life or limb; nor shall be compelled in any criminal case to be a witness against himself, nor be deprived of life, liberty, or property without due process of law; nor shall private property be taken for public use without just compensation.

AMENDMENT 5 (1791). Rights Regarding Life, Liberty, and Property

A person cannot be placed on trial in a federal court for a crime punishable by death or for any other major crime without a formal written accusa-tion by a grand jury. This rule does not apply if the person is a member of the armed services during war or a time of public danger.

A grand jury can decide that there is not enough evidence to accuse a person of a crime. Or the jury can make a formal accusation. The charge can be based on evidence the jury gains on its own (a pre-sentment) or on evidence presented by a prose-cutor (an indictment). The accused person can then be held for trial before a trial jury.

If a person is found not guilty of a certain crime, the person cannot be tried again for the same of-fense (double jeopardy) in a federal court. This rule does not prevent the person from being tried for the same offense in a state court, however.

A person accused of a federal crime cannot be forced to give evidence against himself or herself. Nor can a person lose his or her life, liberty, or property in federal proceedings except as specified by law. When the government takes private prop-erty for public use (through the right of eminent do-main), the government must pay a fair price.

AMENDMENT 6

In all criminal prosecutions, the accused shall en-joy the right to a speedy and public trial by an im-partial jury of the state and district wherein the crime shall have been committed, which district shall have been previously ascertained by law, and to be informed of the nature and cause of the ac-cusation; to be confronted with the witnesses against him; to have compulsory process for ob-taining witnesses in his favor, and to have the as-sistance of counsel for his defense.

AMENDMENT 6 (1791). The Right to a Trial by Jury in Criminal Cases

A person accused of a crime has the right to a prompt, public trial. The case will be heard by a jury selected from the district in which the crime was committed. That district must be one that already has been described by law, such as an established city or county.

Accused persons must be informed of the exact charges against them. They must be allowed to face and question witnesses. Any accused person has the power to force witnesses to appear in court and has the right to a defense lawyer.

AMENDMENT 7

In suits at common law, where the value in controversy shall exceed twenty dollars, the right of trial by jury shall be preserved, and no fact tried by a jury shall be otherwise reexamined in any court of the United States than according to the rules of the common law.

AMENDMENT 8

Excessive bail shall not be required, nor excessive fines imposed, nor cruel and unusual punishments inflicted.

AMENDMENT 9

The enumeration in the Constitution of certain rights shall not be construed to deny or disparage others retained by the people.

AMENDMENT 10

The powers not delegated to the United States by the Constitution, nor prohibited by it to the states, are reserved to the states respectively, or to the people.

AMENDMENT 11

The judicial power of the United States shall not be construed to extend to any suit in law or equity

AMENDMENT 7 (1791). The Right to a Trial by Jury in Civil Cases

Common law is based on customs and on decisions made by judges in previous cases. (Statute law, in contrast, is established by legislatures.)

Suits at common law usually involve disputes between private parties or corporations. They usually are tried in state courts. When such suits involve more than $20 and are tried in federal courts, either side can insist on a jury trial. If both sides agree, they can choose not to have a jury.

Once a jury reaches a decision, that decision cannot be overturned merely because a judge disagrees with the jury's findings.

AMENDMENT 8 (1791). Bail, Fines, and Punishments

Bail is money or property that an accused person gives temporarily to a court as a guarantee that he or she will appear for trial. The amount of bail varies. The more serious the crime, usually the higher the bail. The amount also depends on the reputation and circumstances of the accused person. Unreasonably high bail is forbidden. So are unreasonably high fines and cruel and unusual punishments.

AMENDMENT 9 (1791). Further Rights of the People

The naming of certain rights in the Constitution does not mean that people are limited to those rights only. People may claim other rights as well.

AMENDMENT 10 (1791). Powers Reserved to the States and to the People

The federal government is granted certain powers under the Constitution. All other powers, except those denied to the states, belong to the states or to the people.

AMENDMENT 11 (1795). Lawsuits Against the States

This amendment came about because the states feared a loss of authority if they could be sued in

commenced or prosecuted against one of the United States by citizens of another state, or by citizens or subjects of any foreign state.

federal courts by foreigners or by citizens of other states. The amendment prevents such lawsuits from taking place in federal courts.

AMENDMENT 12

The electors shall meet in their respective states and vote by ballot for President and Vice-President, one of whom at least shall not be an inhabitant of the same state with themselves; they shall name in their ballots the person voted for as President, and in distinct ballots the person voted for as Vice-President, and they shall make distinct lists of all persons voted for as President and of all persons voted for as Vice-President and of the number of votes for each, which lists they shall sign and certify and transmit sealed to the seat of government of the United States, directed to the president of the Senate. The president of the Senate shall, in the presence of the Senate and House of Representatives, open all the certificates and the votes shall then be counted. The person having the greatest number of votes for President shall be the President, if such number be a majority of the whole number of electors appointed; and if no person have such majority, then from the persons having the highest numbers not exceeding three on the list of those voted for as President, the House of Representatives shall choose immediately, by ballot, the President. But in choosing the President the votes shall be taken by states, the representation from each state having one vote; a quorum for this purpose shall consist of a member or members from two thirds of the states, and a majority of all the states shall be necessary to a choice. And if the House of Representatives shall not choose a President whenever the right of choice shall devolve upon them, [before the fourth day of March next following,] then the Vice-President shall act as President, as in the case of the death or other constitutional disability of the President. The person having the greatest number of votes as Vice-President shall be the Vice-President, if such number be a majority of the whole number of electors appointed, and if no person have a majority, then from the two highest numbers on the list the Senate shall choose the Vice-President; a quorum for the purpose shall consist of two

AMENDMENT 12 (1804). Separate Voting for President and Vice-President

In each presidential election before 1800, the two leading candidates received differing numbers of electoral votes. The candidate with the higher number became President. The second-place candidate became Vice-President.

In 1800, electors voted along party lines. The Republican candidates for President and Vice-President received equal numbers of electoral votes. To prevent similar ties in later elections, this amendment requires separate electoral voting for President and Vice-President.

If no single candidate for President has a majority of the electoral votes for President, the House of Representatives must choose, by ballot, from the three leading candidates. In the balloting, each state may cast only one vote, no matter how many Representatives it has. If no single candidate for Vice-President has a majority of the electoral votes for Vice-President, the Senate must choose between the two leading candidates.

thirds of the whole number of senators, and a majority of the whole number shall be necessary to a choice. But no person constitutionally ineligible to the office of President shall be eligible to that of Vice-President of the United States.

AMENDMENT 13

Section 1

Neither slavery nor involuntary servitude, except as a punishment for crime whereof the party shall have been duly convicted, shall exist within the United States or any place subject to their jurisdiction.

Section 2

Congress shall have power to enforce this article by appropriate legislation.

AMENDMENT 14

Section 1

All persons born or naturalized in the United States and subject to the jurisdiction thereof are citizens of the United States and of the state wherein they reside. No state shall make or enforce any law which shall abridge the privileges or immunities of citizens of the United States; nor shall any state deprive any person of life, liberty, or property without due process of law; nor deny to any person within its jurisdiction the equal protection of the laws.

Section 2

Representatives shall be apportioned among the several states according to their respective numbers, counting the whole number of persons in each state, [excluding Indians not taxed]. But when the right to vote at any election for the choice of electors for President and Vice-President of the United States, representatives in Congress, the executive and judicial officers of a state, or the members of the legislature thereof is denied to any of the male inhabitants of such state, being twenty-one years of age and citizens of the United States, or in any way abridged, except for

AMENDMENT 13 (1865). Abolition of Slavery

Section 1. Abolition

The Emancipation Proclamation, which took effect in 1863, applied only to the area then controlled by the Confederacy. This amendment bans slavery throughout the United States. The amendment also bans forced labor—"involuntary servitude"—except as legal punishment for crimes.

Section 2. Power of Enforcement

Congress has the power to pass laws to enforce this amendment.

AMENDMENT 14 (1868). Citizenship and Civil Rights

Section 1. Citizenship

This section defines state citizenship. It prevents states from setting up their own definitions of citizenship in order to exclude blacks or other groups.

The section also applies the due-process clause of the Fifth Amendment to actions by state governments. Since all citizens have "equal protection of the laws," states may not pass laws to discriminate unreasonably against any group.

Section 2. Representation and Voting Rights

Before 1865, each slave was counted as three fifths of a free person in determining the number of Representatives a state could send to Congress. This section does away with the three-fifths rule and sets up a different rule. If a state denies the right to vote to male citizens age 21 or over—excepting those who have taken part in a rebellion or other crimes—that state will lose a proportional number of Representatives in Congress.

The rule was meant to force former slave states to allow black men to vote. It has never been enforced. Instead, the Fifteenth Amendment, ratified

participation in rebellion or other crime, the basis of representation therein shall be reduced in the proportion which the number of such male citizens shall bear to the whole number of male citizens twenty-one years of age in such state.

Section 3

No person shall be a senator or representative in Congress, or elector of President and Vice-President, or hold any office, civil or military, under the United States, or under any state, who, having previously taken an oath as a member of Congress or as an officer of the United States or as a member of any state legislature or as an executive or judicial officer of any state to support the Constitution of the United States, shall have engaged in insurrection or rebellion against the same, or given aid or comfort to the enemies thereof. But Congress may by a vote of two thirds of each house remove such disability.

Section 4

The validity of the public debt of the United States, authorized by law, including debts incurred for payment of pensions and bounties for services in suppressing insurrection or rebellion, shall not be questioned. But neither the United States nor any state shall assume or pay any debt or obligation incurred in aid of insurrection or rebellion against the United States or any claim for the loss or emancipation of any slave; but all such debts, obligations, and claims shall be held illegal and void.

Section 5

The Congress shall have power to enforce, by appropriate legislation, the provisions of this article.

AMENDMENT 15

Section 1

The right of citizens of the United States to vote shall not be denied or abridged by the United States or by any state on account of race, color, or previous condition of servitude.

in 1870, has been used in lawsuits concerning voting rights for blacks.

Section 3. Disqualification of Former Confederate Leaders

Former state and federal officials who had served in the Confederacy were disqualified from holding state or federal office again, unless Congress voted otherwise. Congress did not completely remove this disqualification until 1898.

Section 4. Legal and Illegal Debts

The payment of the federal debt cannot be questioned, according to this section. This referred to debts that the Union incurred during the Civil War. Payment of the Confederate debt by any state or by the United States is illegal. Former slave owners have no legal claim to payment of any kind for their loss of slaves.

Former Confederate states were not allowed back into the Union until their legislatures ratified the Thirteenth and Fourteenth Amendments.

Section 5. Power of Enforcement

Congress has the power to pass laws to enforce this amendment.

AMENDMENT 15 (1870). Suffrage for Blacks

Section 1. The Right to Vote

Race, color, or "previous condition of servitude"—status as an ex-slave—cannot be used by any state or by the United States to deny a person's right to vote. For a long time, states were able to use literacy tests and other devices to prevent many blacks from voting, despite this amendment.

Section 2

The Congress shall have power to enforce this article by appropriate legislation.

AMENDMENT 16

The Congress shall have power to lay and collect taxes on incomes, from whatever source derived, without apportionment among the several states, and without regard to any census or enumeration.

AMENDMENT 17

Section 1

The Senate of the United States shall be composed of two senators from each state, elected by the people thereof for six years; and each senator shall have one vote. The electors in each state shall have the qualifications requisite for electors of the most numerous branch of the state legislatures.

Section 2

When vacancies happen in the representation of any state in the Senate, the executive authority of such state shall issue writs of election to fill such vacancies, provided that the legislature of any state may empower the executive thereof to make temporary appointments until the people fill the vacancies by election as the legislature may direct.

Section 3

This amendment shall not be so construed as to affect the election or term of any senator chosen before it becomes valid as part of the Constitution.

AMENDMENT 18

Section 1

After one year from the ratification of this article the manufacture, sale, or transportation of intoxicating liquors within, the importation thereof into, or the exportation thereof from the United

Section 2. Power of Enforcement

Congress has the power to pass laws to enforce this amendment.

AMENDMENT 16 (1913). Income Taxes

Before this amendment, Congress could not levy an income tax. Article 1 of the Constitution (Section 2, Clause 3, and Section 9, Clause 4) says that federal taxes collected, state by state, must be in proportion to the states' population. This amendment allows an income tax to be levied on individuals and corporations without regard to the populations of the states.

AMENDMENT 17 (1913). Direct Elections of Senators

Section 1. Regular Elections

Article 1 of the Constitution (Section 3, Clause 1) says that Senators are to be elected by state legislatures. This amendment gives the power to elect Senators to the voters of each state.

Section 2. Special Elections

Any vacancy in the Senate must be filled through a special election called by the state governor. The state legislature may let the governor appoint someone to fill the vacancy temporarily, until an election can be held.

Section 3. Time of Effect

This amendment takes effect only when it is ratified as part of the Constitution, and not before.

AMENDMENT 18 (1919). National Prohibition

Section 1. The Ban on Alcoholic Beverages

Manufacturing, selling, and transporting alcoholic beverages are to be illegal in the United States and its territories. The ban takes effect one year after the ratification of this amendment. Exporting and

States and all territory subject to the jurisdiction thereof for beverage purposes is hereby prohibited.

Section 2

The Congress and the several states shall have concurrent power to enforce this article by appropriate legislation.

Section 3

This article shall be inoperative unless it shall have been ratified as an amendment to the Constitution by the legislatures of the several states, as provided in the Constitution, within seven years from the date of the submission hereof to the states by the Congress.

importing alcoholic beverages are to be illegal at the same time. This amendment was repealed in 1933 by the Twenty-first Amendment.

Section 2. Power of Enforcement

Both Congress and the states have the power to pass laws to enforce this amendment.

Section 3. Time Limit for Ratification

This amendment is not to take effect unless it is ratified by state legislatures within seven years.

AMENDMENT 19

Section 1

The right of citizens of the United States to vote shall not be denied or abridged by the United States or by any state on account of sex.

Section 2

Congress shall have power to enforce this article by appropriate legislation.

AMENDMENT 19 (1920). Suffrage for Women

Section 1. The Right to Vote

Women and men have an equal right to vote in the elections of the United States and of all the states.

Section 2. Power of Enforcement

Congress has the power to pass laws to enforce this amendment.

AMENDMENT 20

Section 1

The terms of the President and Vice-President shall end at noon on the 20th day of January, and the terms of senators and representatives at noon on the 3rd day of January, of the years in which such terms would have ended if this article had not been ratified; and the terms of their successors shall then begin.

Section 2

The Congress shall assemble at least once in every year, and such meeting shall begin at noon on the 3rd day of January, unless they shall by law appoint a different day.

AMENDMENT 20 (1933). Terms of the President, Vice-President, and Congress

Section 1. Ending Dates of Terms

The terms of the President and Vice-President end on January 20 in their final year. The terms of Senators and Representatives end on January 3.

Before this amendment, the terms of the President, Vice-President, and Congress ended on March 3. Defeated officeholders had to serve until March as "lame ducks," with little political power. This amendment, known as the "lame duck amendment," greatly reduces the time during which defeated officeholders remain in office.

Section 2. Meetings of Congress

Congress must meet at least once a year, beginning on January 3. Congress, however, can choose a different day.

Section 3

If, at the time fixed for the beginning of the term of the President, the President-elect shall have died, the Vice-President-elect shall become President. If a President shall not have been chosen before the time fixed for the beginning of his term, or if the President-elect shall have failed to qualify, then the Vice-President-elect shall act as President until a President shall have qualified; and the Congress may by law provide for the case wherein neither a President-elect nor a Vice-President-elect shall have qualified, declaring who shall then act as President, or the manner in which one who is to act shall be selected, and such person shall act accordingly until a President or Vice-President shall have qualified.

Section 4

The Congress may by law provide for the case of the death of any of the persons from whom the House of Representatives may choose a President whenever the right of choice shall have devolved upon them, and for the case of the death of any of the persons from whom the Senate may choose a Vice-President whenever the right of choice shall have devolved upon them.

Section 5

Sections 1 and 2 shall take effect on the 15th day of October following the ratification of this article.

Section 6

This article shall be inoperative unless it shall have been ratified as an amendment to the Constitution by the legislatures of three fourths of the several states within seven years from the date of its submission.

AMENDMENT 21

Section 1

The eighteenth article of amendment to the Constitution of the United States is hereby repealed.

Section 3. Death or Lack of Qualification of a President-elect

If a President-elect dies before taking office, the Vice-President-elect will become President. If there is a deadlocked election and no President-elect has been qualified to take office, the Vice-President-elect will become President temporarily. If neither a President-elect nor a Vice-President-elect has been qualified to take office by the start of the term, Congress will decide on a temporary President.

Section 4. Death of a Likely President-elect or a Likely Vice-President-elect

If no candidate for President receives a majority of the electoral votes, then, under the Twelfth Amendment, the House of Representatives must choose a President from among the three leading candidates. If one of those three dies before the House makes its choice, Congress can decide how to proceed, under this section.

Similarly, Congress can decide how to proceed in case a vice-presidential election goes to the Senate and one of the two leading candidates dies before the Senate makes its choice between them.

Section 5. Time of Effect

The first two sections of this amendment take effect on October 15 after the amendment is ratified.

Section 6. Time Limit for Ratification

This amendment is not to take effect unless it is ratified by state legislatures within seven years.

AMENDMENT 21 (1933). Repeal of Prohibition

Section 1. Repeal

National prohibition is no longer required by law.

Section 2

The transportation or importation into any state, territory, or possession of the United States for delivery or use therein of intoxicating liquors, in violation of the laws thereof, is hereby prohibited.

Section 3

This article shall be inoperative unless it shall have been ratified as an amendment to the Constitution by conventions in the several states, as provided in the Constitution, within seven years from the date of submission hereof to the states by the Congress.

Section 2. Carrying Alcohol into "Dry" States

If a state is "dry"—if it prohibits alcoholic beverages—then carrying alcoholic beverages into that state is a federal crime.

Section 3. Method and Time Limit for Ratification

This amendment must be ratified by special state conventions. The amendment is not to take effect unless it is ratified by the state conventions within seven years.

AMENDMENT 22

Section 1

No person shall be elected to the office of the President more than twice, and no person who has held the office of President or acted as President for more than two years of a term to which some other person was elected President shall be elected to the office of the President more than once. But this article shall not apply to any person holding the office of President when this article was proposed by the Congress, and shall not prevent any person who may be holding the office of President or acting as President during the term within which this article becomes operative from holding the office of President or acting as President during the remainder of such term.

Section 2

This article shall be inoperative unless it shall have been ratified as an amendment to the Constitution by the legislatures of three fourths of the several states within seven years from the day of its submission to the states by the Congress.

AMENDMENT 22 (1951). The Ban on Third Terms for Presidents

Section 1. Limit on Presidential Terms

No person can be elected President more than twice. If a Vice-President or someone else succeeds to the presidency and serves for more than two years, that person cannot then be elected President more than once. This ban does not apply to the person who is President at the time of proposal of this amendment.

Harry S. Truman was President in 1947, when this amendment was proposed.

Section 2. Time Limit for Ratification

This amendment is not to take effect unless it is ratified by state legislatures within seven years.

AMENDMENT 23

Section 1

The district constituting the seat of government of the United States shall appoint in such manner as the Congress may direct: A number of electors of

AMENDMENT 23 (1961). Electoral Votes for the District of Columbia

Section 1. The Number of Electors

The District of Columbia can have the same number of electors it would be entitled to if it were a state. But that number cannot be greater than the number

President and Vice-President equal to the whole number of senators and representatives in Congress to which the district would be entitled if it were a state, but in no event more than the least populous state; they shall be in addition to those appointed by the states, but they shall be considered, for the purposes of the election of President and Vice-President, to be electors appointed by a state; and they shall meet in the district and perform such duties as provided by the twelfth article of amendment.

Section 2

The Congress shall have power to enforce this article by appropriate legislation.

of electors from the state with the smallest population. Since each state has at least one Representative and two Senators, the smallest number of electors possible is three. The District of Columbia may therefore have three electors.

The effect of this amendment is to let residents of Washington, D.C., vote in presidential elections.

Section 2. Power of Enforcement

Congress has the power to pass laws to enforce this amendment.

AMENDMENT 24

Section 1

The right of citizens of the United States to vote in any primary or other election for President or Vice-President, for electors for President or Vice-President, or for senator or representative in Congress, shall not be denied or abridged by the United States or any state by reason of failure to pay any poll tax or other law.

Section 2

The Congress shall have power to enforce this article by appropriate legislation.

AMENDMENT 24 (1964). Abolition of Poll Taxes

Section 1. Abolition

Neither the United States nor any state can require a citizen to pay a poll tax—a tax per head, or individual—in order to vote in a presidential or congressional election. The effect of this amendment is to prevent states from using poll taxes to keep poor people, especially blacks, from voting.

Section 2. Power of Enforcement

Congress has the power to pass laws to enforce this amendment.

AMENDMENT 25

Section 1

In case of the removal of the President from office or of his death or resignation, the Vice-President shall become President.

Section 2

Whenever there is a vacancy in the office of the Vice-President, the President shall nominate a Vice-President who shall take office upon confirmation by a majority vote of both houses of Congress.

AMENDMENT 25 (1967). Presidential Disability and Succession

Section 1. Replacement of the President

If the President is removed from office or dies or resigns, the Vice-President becomes President.

Section 2. Replacement of the Vice-President

When the vice-presidency becomes vacant, the President will choose a Vice-President. The choice must be confirmed by both houses of Congress.

Section 3

Whenever the President transmits to the president pro tempore of the Senate and the speaker of the House of Representatives his written declaration that he is unable to discharge the powers and duties of his office, and until he transmits to them a written declaration to the contrary, such powers and duties shall be discharged by the Vice-President as Acting President.

Section 4

Whenever the Vice-President and a majority of either the principal officers of the executive departments or of such other body as Congress may by law provide, transmit to the president pro tempore of the Senate and the speaker of the House of Representatives their written declaration that the President is unable to discharge the powers and duties of his office, the Vice-President shall immediately assume the powers and duties of the office as Acting President.

Thereafter, when the President transmits to the president pro tempore of the Senate and the speaker of the House of Representatives his written declaration that no inability exists, he shall resume the powers and duties of his office unless the Vice-President and a majority of either the principal officers of the executive department or of such other body as Congress may by law provide, transmit within four days to the president pro tempore of the Senate and the speaker of the House of Representatives their written declaration that the President is unable to discharge the powers and duties of his office. Thereupon Congress shall decide the issue, assembling within forty-eight hours for that purpose if not in session. If the Congress, within twenty-one days after receipt of the latter written declaration, or, if Congress is not in session, within twenty-one days after Congress is required to assemble, determines by two-thirds vote of both houses that the President is unable to discharge the powers and duties of his office, the Vice-President shall continue to discharge the same as Acting President; otherwise, the President shall resume the powers and duties of his office.

Section 3. Temporary Replacement of the President with the President's Consent

If the President sends Congress notice in writing that he or she is disabled from performing official duties, the Vice-President becomes Acting President. The President may resume office when he or she sends Congress written notice of renewed ability to serve.

Section 4. Temporary Replacement of the President Without the President's Consent

If a President is disabled and cannot or will not send written notice to Congress, the Vice-President and a majority of the cabinet (or some other group named by Congress) can send such notice. The Vice-President will then become Acting President.

The Vice-President will step down when the President sends Congress written notice of renewed ability to serve, unless the Vice-President and others disagree. If they disagree, they must send written notice to Congress within four days.

Congress then must meet within 48 hours to decide whether the President is still disabled. Within 21 days they must vote. If two thirds or more of both houses vote that the President is disabled, the Vice-President remains in office as Acting President. If they do not, the President resumes official duties.

AMENDMENT 26

Section 1

The right of citizens of the United States, who are eighteen years of age or older, to vote shall not be denied or abridged by the United States or by any state on account of age.

Section 2

The Congress shall have power to enforce this article by appropriate legislation.

AMENDMENT 26 (1971). Suffrage at Age Eighteen

Section 1. The Right to Vote

Neither the United States nor any state can deny the vote to citizens of age 18 or older because of their age. The effect of this amendment is to lower the voting age from 21, the former minimum in federal and most state elections, to 18.

Section 2. Power of Enforcement

Congress has the power to pass laws to enforce this amendment.

GLOSSARY

Certain words in the Glossary and in the text have been respelled as an aid to pronunciation. A key to pronouncing the respelled words appears below.

The words in the Glossary are defined to clarify their meaning in the text. The page numbers given after the definition refer to the places in the text where the words first appear. The words selected for definition in the Glossary are important in United States history.

PRONUNCIATION KEY

Like certain other words in this book, the word *Appalachian* has been respelled to indicate its pronunciation: AP-uh-LAY-chun. The small capital letters mean that the first syllable should be spoken with a minor stress. The large capital letters mean that the third syllable should be spoken with a major stress. The vowel sounds shown by the letters *uh, ay,* and *un* in the respelling correspond to the vowel sounds in the key below.

Pronounce	a	as in	hat
	ah		father
	ar		tar
	ay		say
	ayr		air
	e, eh		hen
	ee		bee
	eer		deer
	er		her
	ew		new
	g		go
	i, ih		him
	ī		kite
	j		jet
	ng		ring
	o		frog
	ō		no
	oo		soon
	or		for
	ow		plow
	oy		boy
	sh		she
	th		thick
	u, uh		sun
	z		zebra
	zh		measure

abolitionist: a person who worked to abolish, or put an end to, slavery (page 314)

alien: a foreigner (page 232)

alliance: an agreement between two or more nations to aid each other (page 169)

ally: a person or a group who agrees to help another in time of trouble (page 60)

amend: to change (page 208)

amnesty: general pardon (page 413)

annex: to add (page 335)

apprentice: person who agrees to work for a skilled worker for some period in order to learn a trade (page 113)

aristocrat: a person who has risen above the rest of the community in wealth, power, or social standing (page 125)

armistice: temporary halt in fighting (page 326)

assassinate: to murder (page 409)

balance of trade: the difference between the value of goods a nation sells abroad and the value of goods bought from other nations (page 53)

bicameral: having two chambers, or houses (page 196)

black codes: collection of laws to define the legal rights of freed slaves (page 413)

blockade: the forced closure of an area to keep people and supplies from going in or out (page 245)

boycott: to refuse to buy or to use (page 143)

bribe: money given to persuade someone to do something wrong or illegal (page 231)

campaign: a planned series of connected military actions (page 168)

candidate: a person running for office (page 126)

cash crop: a crop that could be sold for profit (page 99)

caucus: a private meeting of political party leaders (page 305)

cede: to transfer (page 189)

census: population count (page 221)

charter: a written document from a government giving a person or a group permission to do something (page 67)

checks and balances: a system that gives each branch of government a way to check, or limit, the powers of the other two (page 206)

civil rights: the rights guaranteed to individuals by the Constitution (page 416)

colony: a settlement made by a group of people in a faraway region that is under the control of their home country (page 33)

commerce: business (page 258)

communication: the exchange of information and ideas (page 24)

compact: a written agreement (page 86)

compromise: an agreement in which each side gives up part of what it wants (page 198)

conquistador: (kohn-KEES-tah-DOR): a Spanish conqueror (page 40)

conscription: draft (page 391)

constitutional: allowed by the Constitution (page 205)

corporation: a company owned by stockholders (page 359)

credit: ability to borrow money (page 222)

crop rotation: the practice of growing different crops on the same land in different years in order to preserve the soil's fertility (page 113)

culture: a people's way of life, including their customs, skills, tools, and ideas (page 10)

currency: money (page 188)

customs duties: charges paid on goods imported into a country (page 139)

czar: a monarch (page 262)

delegate: a person chosen to speak and act for others (page 132)

democracy: government by the people (page 125)

depression: severe decline in economic activity (page 308)

dictator: a person with absolute control of a government (page 325)

diplomacy: the art of conducting negotiations between nations (page 229)

disarm: to remove weapons from (page 260)

disfranchise: to deny the right to vote (page 419)

division of labor: the dividing up of work so that each worker does only one or two simple tasks (page 277)

due process of law: the process of following the legal steps established to protect the rights and liberties of individuals (page 417)

economy: the way a nation produces, uses, and divides up goods, services, and money (page 257)

elite: a powerful group of wealthy aristocrats (page 238)

emancipation: the freeing of someone (page 314)

embargo: a government order to end trade with another country (page 247)

emigration: the act of leaving one country to settle in another (page 104)

equator: an imaginary line that circles the earth halfway between the North Pole and the South Pole (page 32)

executive branch: branch of government that carries out laws (page 195)

expansionist: a person who believes that his or her nation should continue to expand its boundaries (page 335)

export: a product sent to another country to sell (page 118)

factory system: the use of factories for making goods (page 276)

federalism: division of power between the states and the national government (page 207)

federation: a union formed by an agreement among states, nations, or groups (page 188)

feudalism: system of land ownership based on military and other kinds of service (page 24)

forager: a person who travels from place to place, searching for wild plants and small game (page 6)

franchise: the right to vote (page 413)

frontier: the edge of a settled area, where the wilderness begins (page 47)

garrison: a place where soldiers are stationed (page 325)

geography: an area's lands, climate, plants, animals, and people (page 26)

glacier: thick sheet of ice (page 2)

guerrilla: a soldier who sets up a base in a remote area and launches hit-and-run attacks on the enemy (page 175)

habeas corpus: the right of a person to appear in front of a judge before being put in prison (page 383)

illiterate: unable to read (page 298)

immigrant: a foreigner entering a country to settle there (page 232)

impeach: to bring charges against an official (page 207)

import: a product brought in from another country to sell (page 120)

impress: to force to serve in the British navy (page 228)

inaugurate: to bring into office formally (page 219)

income tax: a tax on money received for work or investments (page 391)

indentured (in-DEN-churd) **servant:** a person who signs a contract to work for four to seven years for the colonist who paid for his or her passage to America (page 71)

Industrial Revolution: the shift of manufacturing from homes and workshops into factories with machines (page 273)

inflation: a general increase in the level of prices (page 171)

interchangeable parts: parts so nearly alike that any one could be changed for any other (page 277)

interest: a payment for the use of borrowed money (page 222)

interstate: from one state to another (page 257)

invest: to use money to make a profit (page 67)

investment capital: money available for investing (page 281)

irrigate: to supply with water (page 334)

joint-stock company: a business organization that raises money by selling shares of stock to investors (page 67)

judicial branch: branch of government that judges the meaning of laws (page 195)

judicial review: the power to decide whether a law is constitutional (page 205)

latitude: on a map, distance in degrees north or south of the equator (page 119)

legislative branch: branch of government that makes laws (page 195)

legislature: group of people responsible for making laws (page 71)

liberator: a person who sets people free (page 250)

literacy: the ability to read (page 286)

longitude: on a map, distance in degrees east or west of the prime meridian (page 119)

Loyalist: a colonist who remained loyal to Britain (page 151)

manifest destiny: belief that the United States was fated to expand across the continent (page 335)

manufactured goods: products made by people working with tools or machines (page 119)

martial law: rule by the military (page 383)

mass production: the manufacture of goods in large quantities (page 280)

massacre: the random killing of many people (page 146)

mercantilism (MUR-kuhn-tih-LIHZ-uhm): the theory that a nation can increase its wealth and power by controlling trade with other nations (page 53)

mercenary: a hired soldier (page 164)

mesa: a small plateau with steep sides (page 15)

migration: movement of people from one land to another (page 34)

militia (muh-LISH-uh): a group of citizens who are trained to fight in an emergency (page 132)

minority group: a group of people who differ in language, race, religion, or some other way from most of the population (page 75)

mission: a settlement where missionaries teach about their religion and ways of life to people of other faiths (page 43)

missionary: a person who goes to another country to preach and to spread the teachings of a religion (page 43)

moderate: a person who prefers gradual change (page 158)

monopoly: complete control by a person or a group of the sale of a product, especially the price (page 59)

nationalism: a feeling of loyalty to one's nation (page 255)

navigation: the science of finding a ship's location and direction at sea (page 29)

negotiate: to hold discussions in order to reach an agreement (page 223)

neutral: to be unwilling to take sides in a conflict (page 228)

nomadic: wandering (page 13)

nominate: to propose someone to run for office (page 305)

nullify: to make a law null, or without effect (page 303)

ocean current: a flow of water in a definite direction within the larger body of water (page 32)

offensive: advance into enemy territory (page 252)

ordinance: law (page 189)

Parliament: the English legislature (page 121)

party platform: list of campaign statements of a political party (page 369)

Patriot: a colonist who supported the Continental Congress (page 151)

peninsula: a piece of land that is connected to the mainland but is mostly surrounded by water (page 41)

petition: to make a formal request to the government (page 122)

Piedmont (PEED-mahnt): rolling, upland plateau between the Fall Line and the Appalachians (page 98)

Pilgrim: a person who made the journey to America for religious reasons (page 86)

pioneer: first settler of a new region (page 214)

plank: a campaign statement (page 369)

plantation: a large farm that includes housing for the farm's workers (page 104)

plateau: land that is raised and level (page 15)

popular sovereignty: idea that the people living in a territory should decide whether or not it would be open to slavery (page 362)

precedent: example to be followed in the future (page 219)

prejudice: dislike based on race, religion, or nationality (page 290)

prevailing winds: winds caused by the circulation, or movement, of air around the earth (page 32)

privateer: a privately owned warship sailing with government permission (page 54)

proclamation: official announcement (page 137)

proprietary colony: a colony in which the proprietor, or owner, chose the governor (page 91)

Puritan: a Protestant who wanted simpler, "purer" forms of worship in the Church of England (page 85)

racial discrimination: an unfair difference in treatment based on race (page 424)

racism: the belief that one race is inferior to another (page 354)

radical: a person who favors extreme change (page 158)

ratify: to approve (page 201)

raw material: product still in its natural state (page 119)

Reconstruction: the reorganization of the Confederate states in order to bring them back into the Union (page 412)

refuge: a safe place (page 54)

region: an area, of any size, in which the shape of the land, the climate, and the plants are similar (page 4)

repeal: to do away with (page 140)

representative: a person with the power to speak and act for others (page 71)

republic: a government based on the will of the people, in which elected representatives act for the people (page 186)

revenue: income to meet the expenses of government (page 138)

royal colony: a colony controlled by a monarch, who chooses the governor and the council of advisers (page 71)

rural: in the country (page 108)

scale: a series of marks along a line to show what distance on the earth is represented by a given measurement on a map (page 166)

secession: withdrawal from the Union (page 253)

sectionalism: loyalty to one's own section of the country (page 296)

sedition: speech or action that stirs up people against their government (page 232)

segregation: separation on the basis of race (page 414)

self-governing colony: a colony in which the governor, the council, and the assembly are chosen by voters (page 90)

self-sufficient: able to take care of one's own needs (page 112)

separation of powers: division of powers among separate branches of government (page 205)

sharecropping: a system in which a landowner lends land, tools, and seed in return for a share of the profits from the harvest (page 423)

slave codes: collections of laws designed to strengthen the control of slaveholders (page 354)

sound: a long, broad inlet from the sea (page 102)

sovereign: supreme in power (page 303)

specie (SPEE-shee): gold and silver coins (page 305)

speculator: a person who seeks large profits from a risky investment (page 132)

spoils system: practice of appointing party members to government posts (page 299)

states' rights: doctrine that the powers not given to the national government in the Constitution remain with the states, including at times the idea that the individual states have the right to refuse to enforce any unconstitutional acts of Congress (page 233)

strategy: overall plan (page 134)

strike: a refusal by workers to work until employers agree to their demands (page 279)

suffrage: the right to vote (page 296)

tariff: a tax on imports (page 222)

technology: the application of knowledge to practical problems (page 29)

temperance: moderation in the use of alcohol (page 312)

tenement: a house divided into many small apartments (page 290)

toleration: freedom for people of different beliefs (page 90)

topography: landscape, including lakes, rivers, and elevation (page 241)

total war: war on the enemy's will to fight and ability to support an army (page 401)

trade union: an organization of skilled workers formed to improve work conditions (page 279)

transcontinental: across the continent (page 366)

treason: actions taken to overthrow the government (page 95)

treaty: a written agreement between nations (page 34)

triangular trade: colonial pattern of trade between North America, the West Indies, and Africa (page 119)

tribute: money paid by a weak nation to a strong one as the price for peace or protection (page 231)

tundra: vast, treeless plains (page 18)

tyranny: cruel and unjust use of power (page 163)

unconditional surrender: a total surrender without any advance agreement on terms (page 386)

unicameral: having one chamber, or house (page 196)

utopia: perfect community (page 311)

veteran: a former soldier (page 173)

veto: to refuse to approve (page 122)

vigilante (vij-ih-LAN-tee) **committee:** group that took the law into its own hands (page 342)

INDEX

The numbers in heavy type indicate pages on which glossary terms first appear. The *F* before numbers indicates material in features.

St. Lawrence River, 38, 59, 60, 61, 64
St. Leger, Barry, 168, 169
St. Louis, 88, 242, 284, 289
St. Marks, FL, 261
Salomon, Haym, 171
Salt Lake City, UT, 334
Sampson, Deborah, F172
San Antonio, TX, 64, 336
San Diego, CA, 216, 339
San Francisco, CA, 340, 341, 483
San Francisco Bay, 216, 262, 339
San Jacinto, Battle of, 326, 480–481
San Joaquin Valley, 329, 333
San Lorenzo, Treaty of, 230
San Salvador, 31
Santa Anna, Antonio López de, 325–326, 339, 343
Santa Fe, NM, 47, 243, 329, 339
Santa Fe Trail, 329
Santo Domingo, 33
Saratoga, Battle of, 169
Sauk tribe, 299
Saul (slave), 460
Savage, Edward, 162
Savannah, GA, 103, 175, 403
Scalawags, 421
Schools: colonial, 115; reform in, 313–314; women in, 317, 318, 478, 479
Schurz, Carl, 400
Schuylkill River, 97, 288
Scotch-Irish pioneers, 107
Scott, Dred, 370
Scott, Winfield, 339, 366, 382, 384
Sea Witch, 282
Search warrant, 209
Secession, **253**, 373–374
Sectionalism, **296**, 369
Sedgwick, Susan, 461
Sedition Act, **232**–233, 234, 239
Segregation, **414**
Seguin, Juan, 326
Self-governing colonies, **90**, 121
Seminole tribe, 10, 261, 300
Senate, 198, 205, 206, 207. *See also* Congress

Senators, term of, 206
Seneca Falls Conference, 317–318
Seneca tribe, F11, 435, 450
Separation of powers, **205**
Separatists, 85, 86
Sequencing events, F56
Sequoyah, 301
Serapis, 174, 175
Serra, Junipero, 215–216
Servants, indentured, **71**, 99, 446–447
Seven Cities of Cíbola, 44, 45, 46
Seven Pines, Battle of, 386
Seward, William H., 366
Sewing machine, 280, 288, 391
Seymour, Horatio, 423
Shaker Society, 311, 312
Sharecropping, **422**–423
Shawnee tribe, 248–249
Shays, Daniel, 192, 461
Shays' Rebellion, 192–193, 194, 461
Sheridan, Philip H., 403
Sherman, Roger, 162, 198
Sherman, William Tecumseh, 401, 403
Shiloh, Battle of, 386
Shoshone tribe, 16
Sierra Nevada, 333
Singletary, Amos, 202
Sioux Indians, 13, 436
Slater, Samuel, 276, 277
Slave codes, **354**
Slave families, 354, 356
Slave revolts, 355–356
Slave trade, 28, 99, 104, 118–119, F197, 364, 463
Slavery: beginnings of, 43, 99; Constitution on, 198; end of, 193, 388–389, 477–478; life under, 352–356, 449, 485, 486, 494–496; in new states, 258–259, 362–367, 486–487; in Northwest Territory, 190; opposition to, 314–315, 316, 354–356, 365, 368–370, 372, 477–478, 487–488, 490; in

South, 259, 352–356, 358, 365, 485–486, 494–496
Slidell, John, 337
Sloat, John O., 337
Smalls, Robert, 422
Smede, Susan Dabney, 485, 493–494
Smith, Jedediah, 330
Smith, John, 68–69, 443
Smith, Jonathan, 202
Smith, Joseph, 333
Smith, Margaret Bayard, 298, 467, 469–470, 476
Smith, Samuel Harrison, 467
Smith, Sarah, 172
Society of Friends. *See* Quakers
Sons of Liberty, 143, 145
Sources, primary, F410
South: advantages of, 381–382; in Civil War, 380, 381–382, 384–404; economy of, 357–358, 359, 361; post-Civil War, 409–410; under Reconstruction, 421–428; secession of, 374; slavery in, 259, 352–356, 358, 365, 485–486, 494–496
South America, 33, 41–43, 262–264
South Carolina, F101, 102–103, 121, 175–176, 202, 304, 357, 369, 374, 426, 427
South Dakota, 332
South Pass, 333
Southern Colonies, 98–103, 124
Spain: American empire of, 39–48, 52–54, 177, 192, 214–216, 260–262; Armada of, 56–57, 442; exploration by, 31, 33, 34, 39–41, 44–46, 439, 441; treaties with, 230, 261
Spalding, Eliza, 331
Spalding, Henry, 331
Spanish Armada, 56–57, 442
Specie, **305**
Specie Circular, 308
Speculators, **132**, 308
Speech, freedom of, 209
Spinning machines, 276–277
Spoils system, **299**

ILLUSTRATION CREDITS

Cover: (center) Old Sturbridge Village; photo © Henry E. Peach. (right) © William S. Nawrocki/Nawrocki Stock Photo. (bottom left) Smithsonian Institution No. 82-2953. (bottom right) Ligature, Inc.

Title Page: Index of American Design, National Gallery of Art, Washington, D.C.

Unit 1: Map of the world by Juan Vespucci, Seujlla, 1526 (K4z). Hispanic Society of America.

Chapter 1: 3 Photo Archives, Denver Museum of Natural History. **5** (left) © M. Timothy O'Keefe/Tom Stack and Associates. **5** (right) © Caron Pepper/Tom Stack and Associates. **7** © Image Finders; by permission of National Museum of Anthropology, Mexico. **8** St. Louis Art Museum, gift of Morton D. May. **9** © Image Finders. **10** Ohio Historical Society. **11** New York State Museum. **13** Museum of the American Indian, Heye Foundation, N.Y. **15** Museum of the American Indian, Heye Foundation, N.Y. **16** Nevada State Museum. **17** Roloc Color Slides. **18** (left) Hudsons Bay Company. **18** (right) Hudsons Bay Company. **20** American Museum of Natural History. **21** © Robert Frerck/Odyssey Productions, Chicago.

Chapter 2: 23 The Granger Collection. **24** The Granger Collection. **25** The Bettmann Archive. **26** The Granger Collection. **30** The New York Public Library, Rare Books and Manuscripts Division, Astor, Lenox and Tilden Foundations. **31** The Granger Collection. **32** Bibliothèque Nationale, Paris. **34** Ianthe Ruthven*/The British Museum. **35** National Maritime Museum, London. **37** The New-York Historical Society. **39** (left) Bibliothèque Nationale, Paris. **39** (right) © Robert Frerck/Odyssey Productions, Chicago. **42** The Granger Collection. **44** Historical Pictures Service, Chicago; by permission of the John M. Carroll Collection. **46** Elihu Blotnick*. **47** © Ernst Haas. **48** Peabody Museum, Harvard University. **50** The Granger Collection. **51** Scala/Art Resource, N.Y.

Chapter 3: 53 (left) *Elizabeth I* by M. Gheeraerts the Younger. National Portrait Gallery, London. **53** (right) The Granger Collection. **55** The Granger Collection. **57** The Granger Collection. **58** No. HM 29. Huntington Library, San Marino, California. **59** The New York Public Library, Rare Books and Manuscripts Division, Astor, Lenox and Tilden Foundations. **59** The New York Public Library, Rare Book Division, Astor, Lenox and Tilden Foundations. **60** Historical Pictures Service, Chicago. **61** Historical Pictures Service, Chicago. **64** Scala/Art Resource N.Y. **66** The British Museum; Photo © Michael Holford. **67** The Granger Collection. **68** Roloc Color Slides. **69** The Granger Collection. **70** (top) The Bettmann Archive. **70** (bottom) Historical Pictures Service, Chicago. **71** © Image Finders. **72** The Bettmann Archive. **73** National Maritime Museum, London; photo © Michael Holford. **74** The Granger Collection. **75** (left) The New-York Historical Society. **75** (right) The Bettmann Archive. **78** The Granger Collection. **79** The New York Public Library, Rare Books and Manuscripts Division, Astor, Lenox and Tilden Foundations. **81** Musée des Tissus, Lyon; photo © Gamet/Rapho.

Unit 2: 82 Detail from *The Plantation* by an unknown artist, oil on wood, circa 1825. The Metropolitan Museum of Art, gift of Edgar William and Bernice Chrysler Garbisch, 1963, Accession No. 63.201.3.

Chapter 4: 85 (left) *The Mason Children, David, Joanna and Abigail* by an unknown American artist, 1670. The Fine Arts Museum of San Francisco, gift of Mr. & Mrs. John D. Rockefeller 3rd. **85** (right) The Bayou Bend Collection, gift of Miss Ima Hogg. **86** Folger Shakespeare Library, Washington, D.C. **87** Culver Pictures. **88** The New York Public Library, Astor, Lenox and Tilden Foundations. **89** Pilgrim Society. **90** Culver Pictures. **91** (top) The Granger Collection. **91** (bottom) The Granger Collection. **92** (top) The New York Public Library, Rare Book Division, Astor, Lenox and Tilden Foundations. **92** (bottom) © Larry Stevens/Nawrocki Stock Photo. **93** Culver Pictures. **95** *Pennsylvania Farmstead with Many Fences* by an anonymous American. Museum of Fine Arts, Boston, M. & M. Karolik Collection. **96** *Spring Blessing* by an anonymous American. Museum of Fine Arts, Boston, M. & M. Karolik Collection. **97** *Bowles' Moral Pictures* by Bowles & Carver. Yale University Art Gallery, the Mabel Brady Garvan Collection. **98** No. 8631 Vol. 7. Huntington Library, San Marino, California. **100** Maryland Historical Society, Baltimore. **101** Map Collection of the Charleston Library Society. **110** No. 270004 Vol. 1. Huntington Library, San Marino, California. **111** Georgia Department of Archives and History.

Chapter 5: 113 The Bettmann Archive. **115** (left) Massachusetts Historical Society. **115** (right) The Granger Collection. **117** The Granger Collection. **120** The Bettmann Archive. **122** Culver Pictures. **124** Historical Pictures Service, Chicago. **125** The Granger Collection. **126** *McCormick Family* by Joshua Johnston. Maryland Historical Society, Baltimore. **129** Detail from *Fishing Lady*, embroidery, ca. 1750. Museum of Fine Arts, Boston, Seth Kettell Sweetser Fund.

Chapter 6: 131 The Granger Collection. **133** Historical Pictures Service, Chicago. **135** Royal Ontario Museum, Toronto, Canada. **137** Historical Pictures Service, Chicago. **138** The Granger Collection. **139** (left) *Mrs. Ruben Humphreys* by Richard Brunton. Connecticut Historical Society. **139** (right) © William S. Nawrocki/Nawrocki Stock Photo. **141** Roloc Color Slides. **142** American Antiquarian Society. **143** Culver Pictures. **144** Library of Congress. **145** L. L. Bean, Trenton, New Jersey. **146** Study for portrait of John Adams by John Singleton Copley. The Metropolitan Museum of Art, Harris Brisbane Dick Fund, 1960. (60.44.8 obverse). **147** The Granger Collection. **148** (right) *Mrs. James Warren (Mercy Otis)* by John Singleton Copley. Museum of Fine Arts, Boston, bequest of Winslow Warren. **150** Library of Congress. **152** *Sons of Liberty Bowl* by Paul Revere II, 1768. Museum of Fine Arts, Boston, gift by subscription and Francis Bartlett Fund. **154** Massachusetts Historical Society. **155** Daughters of the American Revolution Museum, gift of Mrs. Franklin E. Campell.

Chapter 7: 157 Concord Antiquarian Museum, Concord, Massachusetts. **159** Massachusetts Historical Society. **160** The New-York Historical Society. **162** Historical Society of Pennsylvania. **165** The Mariners Museum. **168** *Battle of Princeton* by William Mercer. Historical Society of Pennsylvania. **169** Guilford Courthouse. National Military Park. **170** Valley Forge Historical Society. **171** The Granger Collection. **172** Sophia Smith Collection, Smith College. **173** AP/Wide World. **175** Library of Congress. **180** American Philosophical Society. **181** Massachusetts Historical Society. **182** Colonial Williamsburg photograph. **183** Library of Congress.

Unit 3: 184 E. P. Dutton.

Chapter 8: 187 (left) The Bettmann Archive. **187** (right) Roloc Color Slides. **190** © William S. Nawrocki/Nawrocki Stock Photo. **192** Culver Pictures. **193** Museum of Art, Rhode Island School of Design, gift of Lucy T. Aldrich. **195** Independence National Historical Park. **196** (left) Independence National Historical Park. **196** (right) © Image Finders. **197** The New-York Historical Society. **198** The Granger Collection. **199** *Tontine Coffee House* by Francis Guy. The New-York Historical Society. **200** Independence National Historical Park. **201** (top) Detail from *Alexander Hamilton* by John Trumbull. National Gallery of Art, Washington, D.C., gift of the Avalon Foundation. **201** (center) The Bettmann Archive. **201** (bottom) The Granger Collection. **203** The New-York Historical Society. **204** © William S. Nawrocki/Nawrocki Stock Photo. **205** Gabor Demjen/Stock, Boston. **210** Historical Pictures Service, Chicago. **212** The New-York Historical Society. **213** Rhode Island Historical Society.

Chapter 9: 215 *Costumes de Guerre* by Choris. Bancroft Library, University of California. **216** Culver Pictures. **217** Culver Pictures. **218** *Flax Scutching Bee* by Linton Park. National Gallery of Art, Washington, D.C., gift of Edgar William and Bernice Chrysler Garbisch. **220** Detail from *Salute to General Washington in New York Harbor* by L. M. Cooke. National Gallery of Art, Washington, D.C., gift of Edgar William and Bernice Chrysler Garbisch. **223** (right) Maryland Historical Society, Baltimore. **224** The Granger Collection. **225** The New-York Historical Society. **227** The Granger Collection. **228** Detail from *Treaty of Greenville* by an unknown artist 1914.1. Chicago Historical Society. **230** Mount Vernon Ladies' Association. **232** Franklin D. Roosevelt Library. **236** Library of Congress. **237** National Maritime Museum, London.

Chapter 10: 239 Grand Lodge A. F. & A. M. of Massachusetts, Boston. **241** Library of Congress. **242** © John G. Zimmerman. **243** *A View of New Orleans Taken from the Plantation of Marigny* by Boqueto de Woiserie 1932.18. Chicago Historical Society. **244** The Mariners Museum. **245** The New-York Historical Society. **246** Thomas Jefferson Memorial Foundation. **247** Culver Pictures. **248** Historical Pictures Service, Chicago. **252** The Granger Collection. **253** Maryland Historical Society, Baltimore. **256** The Bettmann Archive. **257** *Progress of Cotton (# 9: Reeding or Drawing In)* by Barfoot for Darton. Yale University Art Gallery, the Mabel Brady Garvan Collection. **259** *Head of a Negro* by John Singleton Copley, American, 1738-1815, oil on canvas, 21 x 16¼", Accession No. 52.118. Detroit Institute of Arts, Founders Society Purchase, Gibbs-Williams Fund. **262** Historical Pictures Service, Chicago. **264** Historical Pictures Service, Chicago. **266** *The Red Mill near Yellow Springs, Ohio* by an unknown artist. The Edison Institute, Henry Ford Museum and Greenfield Village. **267** The New-York Historical Society. **268** The Bettmann Archive. **269** Library Company of Philadelphia.

Unit 4: 270 Detail from *Prairie Scene: Mirage* by A. J. Miller, 1858-1860. Walters Art Gallery.

Chapter 11: 274 Chicago Historical Society. **275** (left) Library of Congress. **275** (right) Library of Congress. **276** Smithsonian Institution No. P64260. **278** Lukens, Inc. **279** Library of Congress. **280** (top) The

Granger Collection. **280** (bottom) Culver Pictures. **281** © William S. Nawrocki/Nawrocki Stock Photo. **285** *Geese in Flight* by Leila T. Bauman. National Gallery of Art, Washington, D.C., gift of Edgar William and Bernice Chrysler Garbisch, 1958. **287** Cincinnati Historical Society. **288** Historical Pictures Service, Chicago. **290** Culver Pictures. **292** National Archives. **293** Library of Congress.

Chapter 12: 295 Historical Society of Pennsylvania. **298** Old Sturbridge Village; photo © Henry E. Peach. **302** Woolaroc Museum, Bartlesville, Oklahoma. **303** Culver Pictures. **305** Detail from *Portrait of Andrew Jackson, after the Battle of New Orleans* by Thomas Sully, American, 1783–1872, charcoal on grayish blue paper, 14⅝ x 11½″, Accession No. 50.53. Detroit Institute of Arts, gift of Mrs. Walter O. Briggs. **307** The New-York Historical Society. **308** © William S. Nawrocki/Nawrocki Stock Photo. **310** Western Reserve Historical Society. **312** (left) Hancock Shaker Village, Inc. **312** (right) Hancock Shaker Village, Inc. **313** (right) The Metropolitan Museum of Art, gift of I. N. Phelps Stokes, Edward S. Hawes, Alice Mary Hawes, Marion Augusta Hawes, 1937. (37.14.10). **314** (top) Historical Pictures Service, Chicago. **314** (bottom) Historical Society of Pennsylvania. **315** (left) National Archives Exhibit No. 55. **315** (right) The Granger Collection. **316** Minnesota Historical Society. **317** (left) The Metropolitan Museum of Art, gift of I. N. Phelps Stokes, Edward S. Hawes, Alice Mary Hawes, Marion Augusta Hawes, 1937. (37.14.22). **317** (right) ICHI-11897 Chicago Historical Society. **318** (left) The Bettmann Archive. **318** (right) Sophia Smith Collection, Smith College. **320** Hancock Shaker Village, Pittsfield, Massachusetts. **321** The Granger Collection.

Chapter 13: 323 (left) The University of Texas at Austin. **323** (top right) Fort Bend County Museum Association. **323** (bottom right) Fort Bend County Museum Association. **325** The University of Texas Institute of Texan Cultures at San Antonio. **326** (top) Archives Division, Texas State Library. **326** (bottom) Texas State Library. **327** Texas State Library. **328** (left) Star of the Republic Museum; photo © H.K. Barnett. **328** (right) The University of Texas at Austin. **329** Colorado Historical Society. **331** (top) *Dance on the Sequoia Stump* by F. R. Bennett. New York State Historical Association, Cooperstown. **331** (bottom) Oregon Historical Society. **334** *Winter Quarters* by C. C. A. Christensen. Collection of Brigham Young University, gift of the Christensen Family. **335** Texas State Library. **336** *Fandango* by Theodore Gentilz. Library of the Daughters of the Republic of Texas at the Alamo. **337** *Taking of Monterey* by W. H. Meyers. Bancroft Library, University of California. **340** The New York Public Library, Print Collection, Astor, Lenox and Tilden Foundations. **341** California Historical Society. **344** Architect of the Capitol. **347** The Kennedy Galleries, N.Y. **348** New York State Historical Association, Cooperstown. **349** Detail from *In the Fields* by Eastman Johnson, American, 1824–1906, oil on board, 17¾ x 27½″, Accession No. 38.1. Detroit Institute of Arts, Founders Society Purchase, Dexter M. Ferry Fund.

Unit 5: 350 Detail from *Prisoners from the Front* by Winslow Homer, 1866. The Metropolitan Museum of Art, gift of Mrs. Frank B. Porter.

Chapter 14: 353 Abby Aldrich Rockefeller Folk Art Center, Williamsburg, Virginia. **354** Historical Pictures Service, Chicago. **355** *Slaves Escaping Through the Swamp* by Thomas Moran. Philbrook Art Center, Laura A. Clubb Collection. **356** Library of Congress. **357** *Oakland House and Race Course, Louisville, 1840* by Robert Brammer and Augustus A. Von Smith Sr. From the collection of the J. B. Speed Art Museum, Louisville, Kentucky. **363** California Department of Parks and Recreation. **365** (top) Library of Congress. **365** (bottom) Schlesinger Library, Radcliffe College. **366** (left) The Granger Collection. **366** (right) The Granger Collection. **368** The New-York Historical Society. **369** Culver Pictures. **370** Missouri Historical Society, No. 001-004394, POR S-10. **371** The Bettmann Archive. **372** The George Lill Collection; photo © Nawrocki Stock Photo. **373** (top) Concord Free Public Library. **373** (bottom) The Granger Collection. **376** National Archives No. 121-BA-914A. **378** Detail from *The Cotton Pickers* by Winslow Homer, United States, 1836–1918. Los Angeles County Museum of Art: Acquisition made possible through Museum Trustees: Robert O. Anderson, R.

Stanton Avery, B. Gerald Cantor, Edward W. Carter, Justin Dart, Charles E. Ducommun, Mrs. Daniel Frost, Julian Ganz, Jr., Dr. Armand Hammer, Harry Lenart, Dr. Franklin D. Murphy, Mrs. Joan Palevsky, Richard E. Sherwood, Maynard J. Toll and Hal B. Wallis. **379** America-Hurrah Antiques, N.Y.C.

Chapter 15: 381 Library of Congress. **383** (top) Cook Collection, Valentine Museum. **383** (bottom) Library of Congress. **384** Collection of Mrs. Katharine McCook Knox. **385** Collection of Oliver Jensen. **388** The Virginia Historical Society. **390** (top) Library of Congress. **390** (bottom) National Archives No. 111-B-4146. **391** (top left) The Bettmann Archive. **391** (top right) National Portrait Gallery, Smithsonian Institution, on loan from Serena Williams Miles Van Rensselaer. **391** (bottom) © William S. Nawrocki/Nawrocki Stock Photo. **392** Sophia Smith Collection, Smith College. **393** Moorland-Spingharn Collection, Howard University. **394** (left) The Bettmann Archive. **394** (right) Culver Pictures. **395** Rockefeller Collection. **396** Washington and Lee University, Lexington, VA. **400** Library of Congress. **403** (left) Library of Congress. **403** (right) The New-York Historical Society. **406** (left) Cook Collection, Valentine Museum. **406** (right) Library of Congress. **407** © William S. Nawrocki/Nawrocki Stock Photo.

Chapter 16: 409 Library of Congress. **411** Library of Congress. **413** (left) National Archives Exhibit No. 116. **413** (right) Historical Pictures Service, Chicago. **415** The Granger Collection. **417** Historical Pictures Service, Chicago. **418** The Granger Collection. **420** Historical Pictures Service, Chicago. **422** (left) Smithsonian Institution, Division of Political History No. 72-8046. **422** (right) The New York Public Library, Print Collection, Astor, Lenox and Tilden Foundations. **424** The Granger Collection. **425** Culver Pictures. **428** The Kennedy Galleries, N.Y. **430** Edison Institute, Henry Ford Museum and Greenfield Village. **431** Library of Congress. **432** Library of Congress. **433** The Museum of the Confederacy.

Readings: 434 *The Muse*, Susan Walker Morse by Samuel F. B. Morse, 1835. The Metropolitan Museum of Art. **435** The Granger Collection. **436** Field Museum of Natural History, Chicago. **437** Museum of the American Indian, Heye Foundation, N.Y. **438** Bodleian Library, Oxford. **439** The Granger Collection. **440** The British Museum. **441** © Image Finders. **442** The Granger Collection. **443** The Granger Collection. **445** The Granger Collection. **446** The Bettmann Archive. **447** Collection of Carolina Art Association, Gibbes Art Gallery. **448** The Granger Collection. **449** American Antiquarian Society. **451** The Granger Collection. **452** The Granger Collection. **453** The Granger Collection. **454** Massachusetts Historical Society. **455** The Granger Collection. **456** Fort Ticonderoga Museum. **457** Massachusetts Historical Society. **458** © William S. Nawrocki/Nawrocki Stock Photo. **459** The Valentine Museum. **460** The Granger Collection. **461** Massachusetts Historical Society. **462** The Granger Collection. **463** Peabody Museum of Salem. **464** Culver Pictures. **466** Historical Pictures Service, Chicago. **467** Delaware Art Museum. **468** The Bettmann Archive. **469** Massachusetts Historical Society. **470** Lafayette College, Alan P. Kirby Collection. **471** Historical Pictures Service, Chicago. **472** The Granger Collection. **473** The Granger Collection. **474** Culver Pictures. **475** Munson Williams Proctor Institute, Utica, N.Y. **478** Daughters of the American Revolution Museum. **479** The Granger Collection. **480** Historical Pictures Service, Chicago. **481** Texas State Archives, Texas State Library. **483** The Bettmann Archive. **484** *Independence Missouri*, engraving after Hermann J. Meyer, illustration from C. A. Dana, 1853. The Metropolitan Museum of Art. **486** The Granger Collection. **487** The Granger Collection. **488** The Bettmann Archive. **489** The Lester L. Levy Collection, Special Collections Division, The Milton S. Eisenhower Library, The Johns Hopkins University. **490** The Bettmann Archive. **491** © William S. Nawrocki/Nawrocki Stock Photo. **492** © William S. Nawrocki/Nawrocki Stock Photo. **493** Historical Pictures Service, Chicago. **495** The Granger Collection. **496** Culver Pictures. **497** © Robert Llewellyn.

* Photographs provided expressly for the publisher.